The Psychology of Environmental Problems

3rd Edition

The Psychology of Environmental Problems

PSYCHOLOGY FOR SUSTAINABILITY

3rd Edition

Susan M. Koger and
Deborah Du Nann Winter

Psychology Press
Taylor & Francis Group

New York   London

This book is printed on recycled paper.

Psychology Press
Taylor & Francis Group
711 Third Avenue, 8th Floor,
New York, NY 10017

Psychology Press
Taylor & Francis Group
27 Church Road
Hove, East Sussex BN3 2FA

© 2010 by Taylor and Francis Group, LLC
Psychology Press is an imprint of Taylor & Francis Group, an Informa business

Printed in the United States of America on acid-free paper
10 9 8 7 6 5 4

International Standard Book Number: 978-1-84872-807-3 (Hardback) 978-1-84872-809-7 (Paperback)

Library of Congress Cataloging-in-Publication Data

Koger, Susan M.
    The psychology of environmental problems : psychology for sustainability /
Susan M. Koger, Deborah Du Nann Winter. -- 3rd ed.
    p. cm.
    In the 2nd ed. Deborah Du Nann Winter's name came first.
    Includes bibliographical references and index.
    ISBN 978-1-84872-807-3 (hardcover : alk. paper) -- ISBN 978-1-84872-809-7
(pbk. : alk. paper)
    1. Environmental responsibility. 2. Environmental psychology. 3.
Environmental psychology--History. I. Winter, Deborah Du Nann. II. Winter,
Deborah Du Nann. Psychology of environmental problems. III. Title.

GE195.7.W46 2010
333.72--dc22
                                                2009044528

Visit the Taylor & Francis Web site at
http://www.taylorandfrancis.com

and the Psychology Press Web site at
http://www.psypress.com

Mom, this one's for you. I miss you. SMK

To all the children on this beautiful planet—
because your lives will undoubtedly be shaped
by its environmental limits. DDW

CONTENTS

FOREWORD

In 1950 the planet Earth carried 2.5 billion people and 50 million cars. Today it has nearly 7 billion people and 600 million cars, and we increasingly burn coal and oil to electrify, heat, and cool our buildings and dwellings. Moreover, in populous developing countries, such as China and India, consumption is soaring.

The resulting greenhouse gases threaten our, and especially our grandchildren's, long-term future. "The Earth's climate is now clearly out of balance and is warming," noted the American Geophysical Union (2007). Glaciers and polar ice caps are melting. Sea levels are rising. Altered rainfall distributions have created increased flooding and droughts, contributing to conflict. (The Darfur carnage has roots in rainfall decline, ecological economist Jeffrey Sachs (2006) has observed.) If we don't soon get on a different path, "We're toast," surmises NASA climate scientist James Hansen (quoted by the Associated Press, 2008).

New York Times essayist Nicholas Kristof (2007) invites us to consider:

> If we learned that Al Qaeda was secretly developing a new terrorist technique that could disrupt water supplies around the globe, force tens of millions from their homes and potentially endanger our entire planet, we would be aroused into a frenzy and deploy every possible asset to neutralize the threat. Yet that is precisely the threat that we're creating ourselves, with our greenhouse gases.

As Sue Koger and Deborah Winter explain in this important and well-argued book, many pundits can be categorized as either doomsters or boomsters. Pessimistic doomsters wring their hands. It's hopeless. Today's fertility combined with tomorrow's prosperity equals future calamity. But "if we do not believe in the future, we will become more apathetic, indifferent and scared," respond Winter and Koger.

Optimistic boomsters are much less worried. The free market that has solved so many problems—witness our increasing life expectancy, agricultural productivity, and technological efficiency—will surely enable the earth's growing population to happily inhabit the ecosphere.

Koger and Winter reside between the fatalism of doomsters and the denialism of boomsters. They remind us that action requires a blend of enough pessimism to spark concern with enough optimism to sustain hope. Recognizing that energy policies and lifestyles reflect human attitudes and behaviors, they are not doomsters. Rather, they outline psychology's contribution to a redefined quality of life. This text reveals how insights from many subdisciplines of psychology can aid in understanding and reversing dangerous contemporary trends.

In the end, they offer guidance toward what Yale University Environmental Science Dean, James Gustave Speth (2008, p. 199) calls "new consciousness"—a new worldview in which people see humanity as part of nature, see nature as having value that we must steward, value future generations as well as our own, appreciate humanity's global interdependence, and define quality of life not just materialistically but also relationally and spiritually.

Without claiming all the answers, Koger and Winter raise the right questions. They also inform our dialogue with pertinent information and personal examples, provoking us with their passion for creating a healthier planet on which our descendants may flourish. As one who writes from a place called Hope, I salute their effort.

David G. Myers
Hope College
Holland, Michigan

PREFACE: THE WHY, THE WHAT, AND THE HOW OF THIS BOOK

This book represents the third edition of Deborah Winter's text, *Ecological Psychology: Healing the Split Between Planet and Self* (1996; we changed the name to *The Psychology of Environmental Problems* for the second edition). In this introduction we will explain why we wrote and revised this book and then briefly describe the content of the text.*

Deborah was moved to do the first edition after being profoundly affected by an experience while living in Europe. Although it would be simplistic to claim just one event could change her life, there really was one that seems to have changed her life path. Deborah was on a sabbatical from her teaching position at Whitman College, Washington, living in Copenhagen in the winter of 1988, when she visited a friend in Hamburg, Germany. They walked along the shore of the Elbe River one dreary November afternoon, past some beautiful Victorian homes. Deborah tried to visualize how pleasant these houses would be in the summer sun, facing the water. She pictured well-dressed little children in white lace, frolicking along the water's edge, with their nannies looking

---

* You may notice the occasional blank page in the book between some of the chapters. Chapters and articles in scholarly books and journals are often typeset to begin on a right-hand page, which means the preceding left-hand page may be blank if the text from the previous chapter does not flow onto it. As authors, we were concerned about the wasted space on these blank pages and requested that the publisher eliminate them before the book was printed. However, printers print books like this in large sheets containing multiples of 8, 16, or 32 pages. The elimination of the blank pages would actually not have reduced the overall total of large sheets necessary for the printing of this book, so we were satisfied to leave the blanks where they stood.

on. As they continued on, her friend asked what she would like to eat for dinner that evening. Deborah suggested fish, since they were at the waterfront. Her friend answered that fish was very difficult to get and not very good. But why, she asked, when the city is on a river? Her friend responded, "The water is dead here. It's been dead for years. Nothing grows in it." "Oh, ok," Deborah said and suggested pasta instead.

As they continued on, Deborah's thoughts returned to the phrase "dead water." Suddenly, she stepped into a new world: A world where the industrial pollutants of a city could actually kill water. Not just water in an isolated lake but water in a big river. She looked at that water then, and saw it was black and ominous. It looked like liquid death. Deborah had never thought of water as alive or dead before. It was just the backdrop for the more interesting and tasty beings who inhabited it. But at that moment, she saw the graveyard of an entire ecosystem in which not one living organism existed. No seaweed, no fish, no amoebae, nothing but blackness, lapping up against the landscaped grounds of the beautiful estates.

What she experienced in those next steps was an important shift in her worldview. As a psychologist, Deborah had always thought of the physical world as the mere background against which more fascinating animals called human beings loved, fought, conquered, created, suffered, and enjoyed pleasures, such as those on the lovely estates. Walking along the shore path in Hamburg, she saw that the physical world made human civilization possible: The Victorian estates rested on the industrial wealth from manufacturing and shipping. But human civilization was destroying the physical world in return. Those beautiful estates, financed by the wealth of Hamburg's industries, now face the deathly result of that civilization, the black liquid that laps up against their shores.

As a person from the United States living in Europe, Deborah immensely enjoyed many pinnacles of human civilization so salient there: the music, art, ballet, cathedrals, cuisine, and the ambiance of urban sophistication. But as glorious and magnificent as human civilization is (and in Europe that glory and magnificence is absolutely stunning), *Western civilization is not sustainable*. In Germany and northern Europe, it is easier to see the ugly ramifications of too many people and too much pollution, where trees in the Black Forest are dying because of automobile pollution from the autobahn, no wilderness exists anymore, and an entire river can die. In the United States, unsustainable patterns are less obvious because there is more space per person. But we are not far behind our European friends. The realization that we are all living in an unsustainable world has stayed with Deborah ever since.

Sue Koger can also trace much of her concern about environmental issues to one event. While at a party for graduate students at the University of New Hampshire (UNH) in 1989, she offered to get a friend a piece of cake. He declined because it was being served on styrofoam. Sue put two pieces on a napkin, sat down, and realized that everything we do has an impact. Thus, we can make choices that reduce the adverse consequences of our actions. Over the next several years, Sue became more and more conscious of her everyday behaviors, and to this day she strives to live as lightly on the planet as possible.

As psychologists, Sue and Deborah continually ask themselves "What does psychology have to say about the fact that humans and other animals will likely perish unless people change a lot of what they're doing? Given that our culture is unsustainable, why are we* even teaching psychology?" Students at Willamette University, Salem, Oregon and Whitman College, Walla Walla, Washington keep these questions alive with their fundamental concerns about their futures, choice of livelihoods, and the reasons, if any, as to why anyone should bother studying psychology. We have found that many of our students feel uncertain and unhopeful about the future. Although they plan and hope to "get a good job," few think their lives will be as comfortable as their parents. In fact, there is a foreboding among most of our students, a collective feeling that the world is quickly approaching the limits of industrial growth, and that their generation will have to pay the costs of the unsustainable practices instituted by our generation. Most of the time, this gloomy vision is buried beneath the demands of academic classes, social lives, and personal development, which are so crucial in the undergraduate years. But behind the layers of busy activity, pessimism prevails.

Yet our students are also idealistic, and it is their idealism for which we are most grateful, and to which we wish to speak. In our many years of college teaching, we have seen that most of our students truly want to help the world; they seek careers not only for good money but for good meaning; their hearts are still as open as their minds; and they ask really good questions about values, choices, and purpose. While most of their parents' generation are locked into mortgages, family responsibilities, and firmly set identities, our students have less certainty, as

---

* Although we want to keep our personal experiences salient in this book, we've struggled with how to refer to ourselves in the clearest way. The first person "I", "we," and "our" is most direct, but not always accurate when we are referring to one of us. So when we speak of both Deborah and Sue together, we will use the first person "we"; but when we refer to one of us, we'll use her specific name. We hope this switching between first and third person will be clear to you, our reader.

well as less confidence, about their own lives. Consequently, they have more motivation and more authenticity in their struggle to make good choices.

In his classic book *Varieties of Religious Experience* (1929), William James argued that conversion experiences are real, but only if supported by many other congruent events. Deborah's walk in Hamburg and Sue's lesson in styrofoam were pivotal only because many other experiences came both before and after them. In addition to continual work with students, Deborah married a geologist who has taken her to extraordinarily beautiful wilderness areas and taught her that rocks and dirt are crucial features of ecosystems. Before Deborah married John, she was a typical social scientist who thought of rocks and dirt as a stable (and boring) setting, on which the interesting stuff like plants and animals (especially people) grew. But John helped her recognize that the biological world is possible because of the nonbiological (inorganic) world; in fact, there is no easy figure–ground separation like she had assumed. The inorganic world is just as dynamic, fluid, and dramatic, although it takes a different sense of time to perceive its impressive changes through melts, flows, and tectonic dances.

After Sue's epiphany, she joined environmental groups and became an activist. During a sabbatical from teaching at Willamette University, she decided to integrate two of her passions: her environmental concerns and academic psychology. When Sue discovered Deborah's book, she wrote to inquire about collaborating on a second edition. Each of us felt like we had found a soul sister, especially upon discovering we had both graduated from the same doctoral program at the University of New Hampshire (albeit 20 years apart). Happily, the second, and now, third editions are the outcome.

We have many things in common: We share a common worldview because of forces that at first seem tangential; both of us were born during the Baby Boom years and are White, middle-aged, professional females who enjoy the fruits of industrialized civilization while struggling to reconcile what we know about the ecological world with how we live. As privileged people, we are economically secure enough to have the luxury of considering larger questions of survival than just our own. And as neither of us have children, we may be more concerned about the future of the planet than some of our friends, whose parenting responsibilities understandably require more immediate focus on much smaller numbers of people.

Our situated identities lead to biases. Many statements about overconsumption will seem irrelevant or self-indulgent to those who are struggling to support a family, stay employed in an extractive industry, or just survive in an economically and socially insecure world. Environmental devastation is largely caused by overconsumption by the world's rich and desperation of the world's poor, but we focus more on the former because we fall into that category, and we expect that most of you, our readers, do as well. We will say more about U.S. residents and people in other industrialized countries because we believe that relatively wealthy people such as ourselves have the most opportunity, and thus responsibility, to design crucial changes. We hope this book will help you, our readers, in your roles as decision makers and active citizens in the design of a more sustainable world.

We tell you these things about ourselves and why we wrote this book because authors are always alive and potent in any intellectual work, no matter how stringent their attempts to be objective. Knowledge is always shaped by values, assumptions, cognitive styles, and the peculiar and arbitrary conjunction of sociological factors over which one has no control but from which a sense of meaning is derived.

Having disclosed our idiosyncrasies to you, we also call on Erik Erikson to help illuminate the path toward wisdom. Erikson proposed that wisdom comes from what he called *ego integrity,* by which he meant living with the paradox of being able to see the arbitrary, accidental basis for one's deepest beliefs, and at the same time employing the courage to stand by them with utter conviction. Recognizing the personal and sociological reasons for our views, we offer them to you with the hope that they are clear and vivid enough to illuminate the ones you share, as well as the ones you must rework to support your own ego integrity.

THE ORGANIZATION OF THIS BOOK

This text applies psychological theory and research to "environmental problems." We think this endeavor is important because there *really are no environmental problems per se*. Rather, environmental degradation has been caused by human behavior, reflecting a mismatch between how humans meet their needs and wants, and the natural ecological order. Chapter 1 (What on Earth Are We Doing?) begins this project by outlining looming environmental crises. Here we argue that because environmental destruction is caused by human behaviors, beliefs, decisions, and values, psychology is crucial for finding solutions. Chapter 2 is a revision of the Nature of Western Thought chapter that appeared in Deborah's first edition but was cut for the second edition to the dismay of many readers. Here, we highlight features of the Western worldview that supports exploitation and destruction of the natural world. Chapters 3 through 10 each examine a particular subfield or perspective in psychology, as they illuminate environmental issues. Note that this (third) edition includes a new chapter (9) Developmental Psychology: Growing Healthy Children in Nature. Also, we split a chapter from the second edition (Physiological and Health Psychology) into two chapters for this third edition: Chapter 6 (Neuropsychology of Toxic Exposures) and Chapter 8 (Health and the Psychology of Environmental Stress), because of the volume of new literature available on these topics. Likewise, due to an explosion of recent work, Chapter 4: Social Psychology is extensively revised (essentially new) in this edition. The last chapter summarizes insights from the previous chapters, and offers six operating principles for how to approach solutions. While we retained the basic organization from the first and second editions, we updated the literature wherever possible and many sections were significantly revised. We wrote for both novice and upper level psychology and environmental studies students, as well as the layperson who may wonder if psychology has anything useful to say about mounting ecological difficulties.

This book not only talks *about* ecological thinking, it also illustrates it. As ecophilosopher Warwick Fox (1990) once wrote:

> I do not see how anyone can write about ideas and not develop at least some degree of ecological consciousness. Such writing inevitably leads one to realize just how much one's 'own' ideas are a complex interactive function of the ideas that one has absorbed from others—others whose 'own' ideas are in turn, a complex interaction of the ideas they have absorbed, and so on. (p. xiii)

Deborah's husband John recently noted that nobody in their right mind would agree to write (or revise) a book if they realized how much work it would turn out to be. At the end of this year-long project, we smile in acknowledgment of his observation, but we also are grateful for the chance to work together again, learn from each other, and create our own little intellectual ecosystem contained herein.

ACKNOWLEDGMENTS

We are grateful to the countless people who inspired and supported us through our efforts in developing, writing, and revising this text. We particularly appreciate the faith of Paul Dukes at Taylor & Francis who signed this edition, and his assistant, Lee Transue, for his administrative support. Sue acknowledges Willamette University and the Center for Sustainable Communities for sabbatical time and funding. We thank Acacia McGuire at Willamette University for her research and section drafts for the Developmental and Health Chapters. We also thank Gary Klein and Honey Wilson at Willamette University, and Lee Keene, Cally Schneider, and William Maier at Whitman College for their assistance and persistence tracking down citations; Chris Gramlich and Darick Dang of Willamette Integrated Technology Services for their assistance with graphics; and several colleagues/friends for their very helpful comments on early drafts: Wendy Boring, Monique Bourke, Karin Cooke, Tim Kasser, Renee Lertzman, Kari Norgaard, Jeremy Miller, Carolyn Mondress, Britain Scott, and Janice Wizinowich. We are also grateful to the following reviewers for their time, expertise, encouragement, and commentary: Susan Bodnar, Amara Brooke, John Davis, Thomas Doherty, Sorah Dubitsky, Joseph Mishan, Gene Myers, Rosemary Randall, Carol Saunders, Wes Schultz, John Scull, Steve Shapiro, Tod Sloan, Joseph Smith, Don Snow, Fred Toates, and Charles Vlek. And we thank Elizabeth Guillette, Arthur Johnson, David Myers, Carmine Pariante, Ted Schettler, Viviane Simon-Brown, Paul Slovic, Bernie Weiss, the Environmental Working Group, and the Woods Hole

Research Center for their generous permission to use their art and graphics.

It is difficult to overstate our appreciation and admiration for David Myers, who wrote the Foreword for this edition. For decades we have marveled at and been inspired by his textbooks, and hope we have approached the clarity, accuracy, and personal voice in this volume that he achieves so continuously in his. We particularly esteem his willingness to speak loudly about things that matter, especially sustainability, but also gay rights and world peace.

Sue expresses much appreciation to her partner, Kris Rieck, for the back rubs, pep talks, and continually enthusiastic support (and editing!); and her puppy, Phoebe, for always being there with a wag and a walk. Mostly, Sue is exceptionally thankful to Deborah for putting her retirement on hold in order to realize this revision. "I couldn't have done it without you!"

Deborah thanks Sue for her leadership on this third edition. She certainly wouldn't have done it without Sue, but she's glad they have! And now Deborah is looking forward to living, rather than just writing about, sustainability.

1

WHAT ON EARTH ARE WE DOING?

> The environmental crisis is an outward manifestation of a crisis
> of mind and spirit. There could be no greater misconception of
> its meaning than to believe it is concerned only with endangered
> wildlife, human-made ugliness, and pollution. These are part of
> it, but more importantly, the crisis is concerned with the kind of
> creatures we are and what we must become in order to survive.
> (Lynton K. Caldwell, quoted by Miller, 2002, p. 1)

What will your future be like? If you are like most people, you have
hopes of a happy life with your family and friends. You desire secure,
meaningful work, good physical health, rewarding interests, and
enough leisure time to enjoy them. Yet you might also have a notion,
ranging from an inkling to a grave fear, that the future will not be as
pleasant or comfortable as your present life. National and world events
compound the realization that current ways of operating cannot be
sustained. Human beings are running out of available resources,
changing the climate, polluting air and water, and reproducing too
quickly.

Yet most people proceed as though their normal lives will continue. A vague sense of pessimism about the future coexists with a
"business as usual" attitude, and most people worry more than they
take action. While 67% of North Americans agree that environmental conditions are worsening (Saad, 2007), only 28% say they have
made major lifestyle changes to protect the environment, and only
55% made some minor changes (J. M. Jones, 2008). While ecological systems deteriorate, individuals continue to go to school and
work, do the shopping and laundry, visit friends, take vacations,

1

and try not to think about the fact that the planet cannot possibly sustain current lifestyles for much longer. Perhaps people hope that the doomsday scientists will find they had it wrong or come up with some good technological fixes. By just waiting it out, people may think that all will be well, after all. But that seems doubtful, and many North Americans acknowledge that "immediate drastic action" is required (Saad, 2007), particularly in regards to climate change. More than 90% of U.S. residents surveyed indicated that the United States "should act to reduce global warming even if it has economic costs" (Leiserowitz, Maibach, & Roser-Renouf, 2009a, p. 5). The disparity between people's acknowledgement of the urgent need for change while largely continuing to live the status quo forms a psychological question and the basis of this book.

Many people hope that the experts will save us, but the reality is that while looking to scientists and other specialists might feel more comfortable, it is unlikely they can offer salvation. While their expertise will certainly be needed to reverse ecological degradation, just as scientific knowledge was needed to produce it, the physical problems that threaten the survival of life on this planet are too huge, too complicated, and too serious to be solved by a small group of physical scientists (Smith, Shearman, & Positano, 2007). Although human beings have always altered their physical environment in order to survive, the pace and scale of current environmental changes knows no precedent. And the longer people wait, the worse the problems become, making solutions seem even more difficult. In short, betting on the smaller and smaller odds of technological solutions is likely to become more and more irrational.

More important, entrusting the future to physical scientists and their technicians misses the primary cause of the current predicament and a crucial strategy for lasting solutions: changing human behavior. It is critical to examine the psychological dimensions of planetary difficulties because "environmental problems" are really *behavioral* problems: They are caused by the thoughts, beliefs, values, and worldviews upon which human beings act (Smith et al., 2007; Winter, 1996). Human behavior is ultimately responsible for rapidly deteriorating natural systems on which the survival of all species (including human) depends. Greenhouse gases are literally threatening life on Earth because billions of people drive gasoline-powered cars, fly in planes, heat their homes, raise cattle, and ship food and other products all over the globe. Human behavior is accompanied by beliefs and attitudes that make business as usual seem sensible, even though business as usual is jeopardizing all life. Thus, solutions to environmental problems will require more than just technological answers. Individuals will also have to make psychological changes, for example, in the ways they behave, how they see themselves, how they experience their relationship to nature, and even, perhaps, the way they understand the meaning of their lives. As Einstein's well-known dictum puts it, problems can't be solved from the same mind-set that created them.

PSYCHOLOGY AS AN ENVIRONMENTAL SCIENCE

Psychology is defined as the study of behavior and mental life, and recently celebrated its first century of existence as an independent discipline. Although psychology has had myriad impacts on modern culture in the United States, it is not typically seen as an environmental science (Koger & Scott, 2007); as having something relevant to say about how human cultures have created such a mess and how to clean it up. Instead, psychology seems to have three very different manifestations. In the college classroom, it is taught as a science: Empirical studies including statistical analyses are used to illuminate basic behavioral and mental processes like learning, perception, motivation, and thinking. In the shopping mall, however, psychology looks very different. Much to the academics' consternation, the trade bookstore places psychology books alongside self-help books and books on the occult; there, psychology looks like a do-it-yourself method for managing a divorce or experiencing past lives. Neither the academic nor the marketplace version of psychology is completely correct or completely wrong, nor does either represent the biggest constituency. The majority (over 60%) (Weiten, 2011) are applied psychologists; that is, trained professionals who apply psychological principles to problems of mental health, personnel management, and consumer marketing, to name a few.

Using psychology to examine environmental degradation offers an important opportunity to integrate the scientific and applied facets of the discipline. As you will see in the chapters to follow, psychology offers an extensive array of empirical data, theoretical insights, and useful strategies for building a more sustainable world: One that balances current human activities and needs with those of other species and future generations, taking into account ecological as well as social and economic factors (Schmuck & Schultz, 2002; see also United Nations, n.d.). Interest in the psychology of environmental problems has been growing quickly over the last decade, with psychologists joining discussions on listservs, attending conferences, publishing books and journal articles, and designing college courses. A recent issue of the journal, *Conservation Biology*, highlighted some of the contributions psychology can make toward ensuring "a decent future for humanity" (Kaplan & Kaplan, 2008, p. 826; see also Mayer & Frantz, 2008; Orr, 2008). The label **Conservation Psychology** has emerged, defined as the "scientific study of the reciprocal relationships between humans and the rest of nature, with a particular focus on how to encourage conservation of the natural world" (Saunders, 2003, p. 138; see also Clayton & Myers, 2009*). Hopefully, our discussion of this quickly expanding work will inspire you to join the cause!

Most people are at least somewhat familiar with the sobering facts of current environmental conditions, and certainly you have already heard at least some of what is to follow. Thus, we invite you to think about ecological problems as a psychologist. You will learn more if you consider your own behavior, thoughts, and emotions as you read the rest of this chapter and this book. *Keep track of your own reactions*, which constitute the raw data of psychology. These observations will enable you to judge the adequacy and relevance of the psychological perspectives discussed in subsequent chapters. Psychological responses are what this book is about, so treat yours with respect: They will enhance your understanding of the material, your world, and yourself.

THE NATURE OF THE PROBLEM

Since the publication of Rachel Carson's widely read book, *Silent Spring* (1962), scientists have documented worsening threats to the survival of the entire **biosphere** (the global ecosystem and all inhabitants): pollution, overpopulation, climate change, species extinctions, deforestation, ozone depletion, topsoil loss, and coral reef destruction, to name a few. In 1992, 1670 prestigious scientists, including over 100 Nobel Laureates, signed a "World Scientists' Warning to Humanity," urging public attention to the "human activities which inflict harsh and often irreversible damage on the environment and on critical resources" (Union of Concerned Scientists, 1992); yet nearly 20 years later, the news continues to get worse.

Not surprisingly, most people cannot stay tuned for very long—to do so is too depressing, perhaps too terrifying. So, they turn their attention

---

* See also http://www.conservationpsychology.org

to present concerns such as family obligations, work or school, paying bills, enjoying friends. Such a response is understandable and consistent with an evolutionary perspective. Human perceptual systems evolved in an environment where any threats to safety were sudden and dramatic, and earlier beings had no need to track gradually worsening problems or assaults that took many years to manifest (Ornstein & Ehrlich, 2000). As a result, the human species is shortsighted and has difficulty responding to potentially catastrophic, but slowly developing, harmful conditions. Rather than working to prevent crises, people have a strong tendency to delay action until problems are large scale and readily apparent, at which time they attempt to respond. Unfortunately, by then it may be too late.

Despite such "hardwiring," the human species is also capable of dramatic and rapid cultural evolution, as the pace of the agricultural,

industrial, and technological revolutions reveals (Ehrlich & Ehrlich, 2008; Ornstein & Ehrlich, 2000). For example, as undergraduates, we used typewriters for writing papers after engaging in grueling research with massive publication indexes. Now, the idea of using anything other than high-speed word processing programs and sending and editing drafts via email feels horribly impractical and inefficient. The Internet has made research fast and convenient, and computerized networking between libraries enables access to collections far more extensive than any single library's holdings. While it is easy to blame technology for the current predicament, the human capacity for rapid behavioral change could quickly reverse current ecological trends given sufficient attention and public will (Smith, Positano, Stocks, & Shearman, 2009).

Unfortunately, "the U.S. Government has frequently played an obstructive role" in cultural progress toward sustainability (Oskamp, 2000, p. 502; see also Kennedy, 2004). However, the global predicament cannot be blamed on any particular governmental body or presidential administration. Contemporary environmental crises have taken centuries to develop, and rest largely on a western world-view and accompanying beliefs that encourage the use and abuse of nature (a topic that is explored further in the next chapter, The Nature of Western Thought). The march toward ecological catastrophe can best be understood by considering the planet's carrying capacity.

Biology's Bottom Line: Carrying Capacity

While an array of interconnected problems created the current situation, the bottom line that causes so many to worry is that the earth has limits. Carrying capacity is a concept developed by biologists to describe the maximum number of any species a habitat can support. If the territory is isolated and the population cannot migrate to a new one, the inhabitants must find a balance with its resource base. Alternatively, if the population grows too quickly so that it depletes its resources suddenly, the population will crash.

Such crashes have happened in both nonhuman and human populations. Islands, which segregate ecosystems and prevent migration, provide the clearest examples. For instance, in 1944 the U.S. Coast Guard imported 29 yearling reindeer to the isolated St. Matthew Island in the Bering Sea (between Alaska and Russia). The island was ideal for the propagation of reindeer, so by 1963, the population had grown from 29 to over 6000. However, the terrain became badly overgrazed, food supplies dwindled, and the population crashed in the winter of 1964. The island could have sustainably supported about 2,300 reindeer, but after the crash only 3% of that figure survived (Catton, 1993).

Population crashes also happen to humans. Archaeological evidence from Easter Island, off the coast of Chile, shows that a very complex but unsustainable human population grew there for sixteen centuries. To support themselves, the islanders cut more and more of the surrounding forests so that eventually soil, water, and cultivated food supplies were depleted. The population crashed in the seventeenth century, falling from 12,000 in 1680 to less than 4000 by 1722. In 1877, only 111 people still survived (Catton, 1993).

When carrying capacity is exceeded in mainland civilizations, the picture is more complicated, because declining wealth makes the civilization more vulnerable to outside attack. However, the Sumerians of Mesopotamia and the Maya of the Yucatan region provide two clear examples of exceeded carrying capacity. The Sumerians were the first literate society in the world, leaving detailed administrative records of their civilization and its decline between 3000 and 2000 BC The complicated agricultural system that supported their population also depleted their soil through salinization and siltation. Crop yields fell 42% between 2400 and 2100 BC and 65% by 1700 BC In the words of environmental historian Clive Ponting (1991):

> The artificial agricultural system that was the foundation of Sumerian civilization was very fragile and in the end brought about its downfall. The later history of the region reinforces the point that all human interventions tend to degrade ecosystems and shows how easy it is to tip the balance towards destruction when the agricultural system is highly artificial, natural conditions are very difficult, and the pressures for increased output are relentless. It also suggests that it is very difficult to redress the balance or reverse the process once it has started. (p. 72)

Similarly, the Maya, who developed what are now parts of Mexico, Guatemala, Belize, and Honduras, built a complex civilization on the fragile soil of tropical forests. Clearing and planting supported a population from 2000 BC to 800 AD As the population grew, land that needed to recover between plantings was overused. In about 800 AD the population crashed; within a few decades cities were abandoned, and only a small number of peasants continued to survive in the area. The remains of their civilization, buried under the tropical jungle, were not discovered until the nineteenth century. Skeletal samples show widespread malnutrition killed massive numbers of people.

In the past, population crashes have occurred in one part of the world without seriously affecting those in another. Today, however, global conditions are in crisis and are threatening to collapse (Beddoe et al., 2009; Diamond, 2005), as humans continue to degrade "the great life-supporting systems of the planet's biosphere" (Speth, 1993, p. 27). Thus, because of the array of interconnected global problems described below, the threat of an ecological catastrophe on a *planetary level* is looming (Diamond, 2005; Kuntsler, 2005; Smith et al., 2007). The earth is, essentially, a large island, with no way to borrow resources or dump pollution elsewhere. Particularly in First World countries, people are using resources unsustainably while simultaneously polluting the environment, thereby weakening its ability to restore and supply basic physical requirements to sustain life. Unfortunately, both human population growth and resource depletion are accelerating at exponential rates, which is what makes the problem so pressing, yet so difficult to directly perceive.

Exponential growth is deceptive because it starts off slowly but accelerates quickly. It occurs when a quantity increases by a fixed percentage of the whole, which means that it will double after a certain interval, rather than grow incrementally (which is linear growth; see Figure 1.1). The concept of exponential growth is so important to understanding the current predicament that it's worth spending a moment with a conceptual example. Imagine that you have a bottle with one bacterium in it, which will double every minute. Assume that it is now 11:00 p.m. and the bottle will be completely full by midnight. When will the bottle be half full? If you suggest 11:30, you are thinking in terms of linear growth, rather than exponential growth. Actually, the bottle would be half full at 11:59 because the bacteria double every minute. Next question (and this involves a little more imagination): When do you think the bacteria might start to notice that things are getting a little crowded? Probably not even at 11:55, because at this point the bottle is still only 3% full. Remember, exponential growth begins slowly but accelerates quickly. Final question: Suppose the Royal Bacteria Society sponsored Sir Francis Bacterium to leave the bottle and go exploring for new space, and suppose Sir Francis got really lucky and found three new bottles, quadrupling the space for the society. How much time

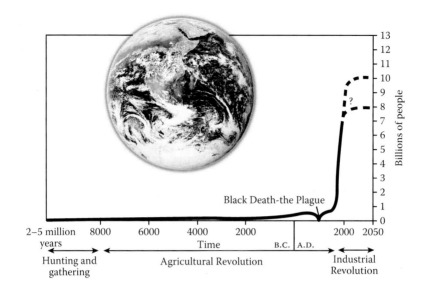

Figure 1.1 The J-shaped curve of past exponential world population growth, with projections to 2050 (this figure is not to scale). Notice that exponential growth starts off slowly, but as time passes the curve becomes increasingly steep. Unless death rates rise, the current world population of 6.6 billion people is projected to reach 8–10 billion people sometime this century. Data from World Bank and United Nations; photo courtesy of NASA. (Adapted from Miller, G.T., *Living in the Environment,* 15E., p. 6, © Brooks/Cole, a part of Cengage Learning, Inc., 2007. With permission.)

did he buy? Although it may seem at first that their problems are solved, it would actually only give them two more minutes until all four bottles were completely full.*

Unfortunately the human population picture is even worse than this example, because exponential growth rates have themselves increased, meaning that the doubling time has grown shorter and shorter. In 1650 it would have taken 250 years to double the human population, but at present the population is expected to *triple* in the 48 least developed countries, and to double in many more nations by 2050 (Engelman, Halweil, & Nierenberg, 2002). With this super-exponential growth, the world population will increase from 6.7 billion people in 2008 to 9.2 billion in 2050 (United Nations, 2007b). Like the bacterium example, finding new supplies of food or energy (e.g., oil) or even a new planet or two would only very temporarily solve the problems.

---

* Special thanks to John Du Nann Winter for this teaching example.

Although industrialized countries have managed to bring birthrates down, population continues to explode in the world's less developed countries, which are home to four fifths of the planet's human beings. Improved medical care has lowered the death rates in these countries, without a corresponding decrease in birth rates. Campaigns to curb birthrates have failed largely because families who live at subsistence levels must have as many children as possible to help provide the family food supply, and insure parents some measure of protection during old age. Since infant mortality rates are high, more children must be born than can be expected to survive. Gender bias contributes as well, as families keep on producing children until enough boys are born to afford economic security or social status in the community. Thus, poverty and sexism together drive population growth.

Some experts argue that until the world's distribution of wealth is altered, population will not be controlled. For example, Piel (1994) proposed that population control closely follows economic development, which enables people to escape from the poverty cycle. In other words, as poverty lessens, birthrates also decrease because women have better educational and professional opportunities and access to birth control (see also Engelman et al., 2002; Penn, 2003). Lowered infant mortality accompanies economic development, and improved nutrition and medical care also helps to reduce birthrates. Although leaders of 189 nations met in 2000 to articulate a commitment to reduce world poverty, hunger, and disease; to improve maternal and infant survival prospects; to provide better education for children; to provide equal opportunities for women; and to create a healthier environment by 2015 (United Nations Millennium Declaration, 2000), global poverty has worsened. As of 2007, 20% of the world's population, or 1.3 billion people, live in extreme poverty without basic resources such as clean water, adequate food, or shelter (United Nations, 2007a). Nearly half of the world's population (2.6 billion) subsists on $2 per day or less and one billion people on $1 per day or less (World Resources Institute, 2008). Even in developed countries such as the United States, 37.3 million people (12.5%) fell below the official poverty line in 2007 (United States Census Bureau, 2008).

Paradoxically, at the same time that poverty has increased, so has consumption of the global resource base, but at an even greater rate. Energy is the most basic resource; its consumption is measured in terms of the daily number of kilocalories (1000 calories) that people use for food, shelter, clothing, and other human creations including cities, cars, movies, and cell phones. One million years ago, about a million people engaged in hunting–gathering subsistence, and each consumed a daily average of about 2000 kilocalories for all their activities. By the early agricultural stage about 12,000 years ago, energy consumption had jumped to 15,000 kilocalories per person, as cities were built and wealth was accumulated. Now, the lifestyles of citizens in contemporary industrialized nations demand over 600,000 kilocalories per person each day (Miller, 2007).

Some of this utilized energy is renewable, but as of 2007, only 7% was generated from renewable sources (e.g., sun, food, wind, and hydropower) in the United States (Energy Information Administration, 2006). Although new technologies, enhanced efficiency, and lower costs could eventually enable the replacement of carbon-based fuels with renewable energy sources (Flavin, 2008), to this point progress has been slow. Reliance on nonrenewable energy sources (e.g., oil, coal, gas, and uranium) is unsustainable, and access to remaining supplies will become increasingly expensive. Some deposits of nonrenewable energy are identifiable and extractable now, although with associated environmental costs; some are identifiable but too expensive or difficult to extract; and some remain unidentified. However, at present rates of consumption, sources of nonrenewable energy cannot last very long. For example, as Hubbert predicted in 1956, oil production in the United States peaked in 1970 (Duncan & Youngquist, 1999) and is expected to peak globally within the next 10 to 20 years (Flavin, 2008); already, demand is severely exceeding supply (McPherson & Weltzin, 2008). Even if population and consumption rates stabilized, contemporary culture would use up known gas and oil reserves in less than one lifetime. Due to exponential growth, even doubling the national supply of oil (from, say, getting really lucky in Alaska) would extend consumption only by 20 or 30 years at the most.

During the energy crisis of the 1970s, sudden price escalations and shortages of gasoline helped people understand the nation's dependency on petroleum products, and conservation efforts increased. However, the crisis ended and old habits returned. Yet if U.S. citizens had continued conservation measures employed from 1976 to 1985 or bought cars with slightly higher fuel efficiency (5 mpg), Middle Eastern oil imports would have been unnecessary after 1985 (Lovins & Lovins, 2001). Such efforts might have prevented the Persian Gulf War in the early 1990s, the Iraq War in 2003, and at the same time provided insulation from price shocks in the international oil market, and the wildly unstable global market conditions of late 2008 (for a thorough and sobering discussion of the international *geopolitical* issues surrounding **peak oil**, see Kunstler, 2005).

Ironically, worsening economic conditions may be forcing an overdue change. The U.S. Congress is working to significantly increase fuel efficiency (Ramstack, 2008), and escalating gas prices are causing consumers to purchase smaller and more efficient cars. In 2008, sales of subcompact cars increased by 33%; large SUV sales declined 29% (Durbin, 2008). But because 85% of U.S. energy currently comes from burning fossil fuels that change the climate (Energy Information Administration, 2006), catastrophic consequences seem imminent.

Climate Change

Since Al Gore's widely distributed film, *An Inconvenient Truth* (David et al., 2006), most people know something about the serious threat of climate change. Gases such as carbon dioxide, methane, nitrous oxide, and water vapor trap heat in the atmosphere. The resulting **greenhouse effect** is necessary to stabilize atmospheric temperatures and maintain a climate suitable for life on the planet. Gas levels vary naturally to some extent, but industrialization has created an unprecedented and dangerous increase in levels of greenhouse gases since 1750. For example, carbon dioxide in the earth's atmosphere is at its "highest level in 650,000 years" (Gardner & Prugh, 2008, p. 3) and is clearly correlated with planetary warming patterns (see Figure 1.2).

The scientific debate regarding the reality and human causes of climate change effectively ended in 1995 with the first report from the Intergovernmental Panel on Climate Change (IPCC), an international

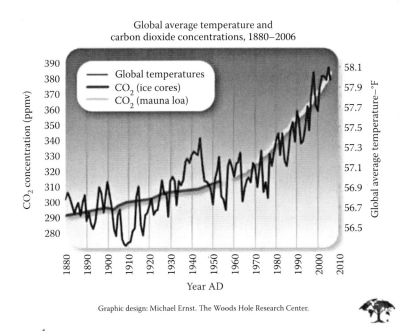

Graphic design: Michael Ernst. The Woods Hole Research Center.

Figure 1.2 Global temperature and CO_2 concentrations since 1880. (Reprinted from Woods Hole Research Center. Available at: http://www.whrc.org/resources/online_publications/warming_earth/scientific_evidence.htm. With permission.)

coalition of 2000 eminent climatologists and other scientists. In its most recent report, the IPCC (2007) predicted that the earth could warm as much as 11°F by 2100. To put that number in perspective, the world was only 9°F cooler during the last ice age than it is today. Thus, there is a very real possibility of planetary temperature changes of ice age magnitudes within this century. Already, warming trends are evident, based on increased average ocean and air temperatures, widespread melting of ice and snow, and rising global sea level (IPCC, 2007). For example, the years between 1995 and 2006 were 11 of the 12 warmest years since 1850 when recording of global temperatures began.

Climate change will impact ecosystems both directly and indirectly, via flooding, drought, wildfires, insect proliferation, changes in land use, and fragmentation of natural systems. As a result, 20–30% of known plant and animal species are estimated to be at an increased risk of extinction (IPCC, 2007); and "all currently fished marine species

Reprinted from Toles, © 2004. *The Washington Post.* With permission from Universal Press Syndicate. All rights reserved.

could collapse by 2050" (Gardner & Prugh, 2008, p. 3). Weather events such as typhoons and hurricanes are likely to become more intense, and while it is impossible to directly associate any particular storm with climate change, the devastation wrought by Hurricane Katrina in 2005 exemplifies what is expected. Coastal regions are at particular risk due to rising sea levels, erosion, and flooding. Densely populated areas, islands, and poor communities are especially vulnerable (IPCC, 2007), and such regions constitute home to nearly half of the planet's population (Gelbspan, 2001). Climate change also carries significant public health costs. Millions of people are likely to suffer or die from associated malnutrition, starvation, disease (including diarrheal, cardiorespiratory, and infectious), and injury due to extreme weather (IPCC, 2007; see Figure 1.3).

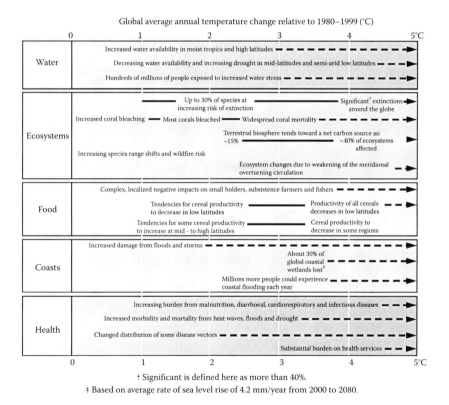

Figure 1.3 Examples of impacts associated with global average temperature change. Impacts will vary by extent of adaptation, rate of temperature change, and socioeconomic paths. From the Intergovernmental Panel on Climate Change (2007). Climate Change 2007: Synthesis Report, p. 51. Available at http://www.ipcc.ch/pdf/assessment-report/ar4/syr/ar4_syr.pdf

Climate change will damage or bankrupt already weakened economies via property damage, insurance claims, loss of crops, and other costs (Gelbspan, 2001, 2004). A recent study by the former chief economist of the World Bank concluded that unmitigated climate change could decrease global economic production by 5–20% (Stern, 2007). Although the industries based on fossil fuels have warned of economic collapse if emissions are reduced as quickly as advised by climate scientists, new energy options and technological innovation suggest the opposite conclusion (Flavin, 2008). Even though the costs of stabilizing the climate are significant, they are manageable; alternatively, "delay would be dangerous and much more costly" (Stern, 2007, p. xvi). Climate change also poses a significant threat to national and international security (Climate change poses serious threat, 2007); a risk even greater than terrorism (Steffen, 2006).

Other Resource Issues

The bad news about climate change should not occlude other resource issues that are simultaneously threatening survival of all life, and that will be exacerbated by climate change.

Arable Land: While population doubled over the last 40 years, land area available for food production shrunk because of farmland conversion to residential use. The Green Revolution, which used chemical fertilizers, pesticides, and genetic engineering, substituted for less land availability to triple crop production since 1950 (Miller, 2007). However, per capita grain production is now falling because of shrinking land base, continued population growth, and because inorganic chemical fertilizers quickly damage land by acidifying and compacting soil (Halweil, 2002). Populations of bees, bats, and other pollinating species are dwindling, endangering agriculture and biodiversity (Gardner & Prugh, 2008; Novacek, 2008). Topsoil is also being lost at an astonishing rate: each decade, about 7% is eroded or blown into streams, lakes, and oceans. Currently, only 6–8 inches of topsoil "is all that stands between much of the world and mass starvation" (Miller, 2007, p. 278). Due to the effects of climate change on farmlands, agriculture will move toward the poles, causing disruptions in food supplies, requiring new dams and irrigation, and migration of human populations. Tropical climates will replace temperate ones, speeding the decay of organic matter in the soil and releasing more greenhouse gases.

Water Shortages: Fresh water supplies are seriously threatened by overpopulation and urbanization. Agricultural, industrial, and domestic uses of toxic chemicals pollute groundwater, lakes, rivers, and oceans. The portion of the hydrological cycle that provides fresh water to wells and springs is being interrupted. Rainwater can no longer replenish aquifers because deforestation, urbanization, and overgrazing make it more likely that water will run off, rather than seep into the ground and replace what is used. The Green Revolution required extensive irrigation, which not only water-logged and salinized soils, but also quickly depleted aquifers. At current rates of population and economic growth, two thirds of the world's population will face water stress by 2025 (Gardner, 2002). Already more than one billion people on the planet do not have safe drinking water, and half of the population in developing nations lacks access to basic sanitation. Even in the United States, at least one quarter of the groundwater that is withdrawn is not replenished, and many regions are experiencing severe water shortages as a result of droughts.

Climate change is anticipated to intensify these pressures by reducing snow cover, melting glaciers, altering patterns of precipitation, and increasing droughts. Consequent impacts include reduced water supplies, diminished hydropower energy production, and public health costs (IPCC, 2007), along with international conflict over resources including water (Patel, 2007).

Reprinted from Kirk Anderson © [www.kirktoons.com]. With permission.

Forests: Wood extraction, deforestation, and urbanization are shrinking forests. Forests act like the lungs of the earth, converting carbon dioxide to oxygen. Thus, the planet's available oxygen supply is dwindling, and forest loss increases erosion, desertification, and siltation of waterways, as well as accumulation of carbon dioxide contributing to climate change. Deforestation has devastated communities and cost many lives. For example, hundreds of people are killed annually during landslides and flooding in Indonesia, where frequent rain combines with years of deforestation and poor urban planning to destabilize soil (Deutsch, 2007). Less than half of the world's original forest cover still remains, but the rate of cutting continues to accelerate. Some areas are replanted, but replacement crops are much more homogeneous genetically, and thus vulnerable to disease. In addition, as the climate warms and droughts become more common, insect infestations and diseases worsen (Lee, 2008). Thus, in an unfortunate feedback loop, climate change kills trees causing an exacerbation of climate change.

Biodiversity: Tropical forests, home to most of the planet's astoundingly varied life-forms, are disappearing at record rates. Countless life-forms are going extinct faster than when dinosaurs became extinct about 65 million years ago. One third of species in the United States are classified as vulnerable or endangered (Wilson, 2007). Loss of nonhuman species is problematic for humans for at least three reasons:

1. Biodiversity confers enormous economic benefits in the form of foods, medicines, and industrial products.
2. Species are the working parts of natural ecosystems that provide the essential services necessary to sustain life.
3. As Earth's dominant species, [humans] have an ethical and moral responsibility to protect diverse life (Novacek, 2008, p. 11574).

Wilson (1993) argued that loss of biodiversity is the most harmful aspect of environmental degradation:

The variety of organisms ... once lost, cannot be regained. If diversity is sustained in wild ecosystems, the biosphere can be recovered and used by future generations to any degree desired and with benefits literally beyond measure. To the extent it is diminished, humanity will be poorer for all generations to come. (p. 35)

Pollution: If loss of natural resources weren't threatening enough, their use and misuse introduces another array of problems—pollution of air, water, food, and bodies. Toxic chemicals endanger health directly and indirectly, as we will show in Chapters 6 (Neuropsychology) and 8 (Health Psychology). In addition, burning tropical forests releases huge amounts of carbon dioxide, which join emissions from automobiles and other fossil fuel-driven technologies, to dramatically increase atmospheric levels of greenhouse gases that cause climate change.

Scientists and skeptics continue to argue about some of the specific numbers and rates of resource depletion, pollution, and climate change. Nonetheless, it is commonly understood that the planet is losing its ability to protect life, regenerate resources, disperse pollution, and provide food for the quickly escalating number of human inhabitants, let alone for other species of life. On the current course, humans are quickly approaching Earth's carrying capacity, if it hasn't already been surpassed.

PSYCHOLOGICAL REACTIONS TO ENVIRONMENTAL THREATS

Most people are familiar with the outlines of these problems, but reactions to them are a psychological issue that is rarely addressed. As you were reading the above material, did you feel despair? Anxiety? Irritation? Did you scan the material, thinking to yourself that you already knew it? Did you find yourself growing overwhelmed or angry? Or did you wonder what any of this has to do with you? These responses are important because they mediate how the problems are understood and what people are willing to do about them.

Reprinted from MUTTS © Patrick McDonnell. King Features Syndicate. With permission.

One way reactions differ is basic optimism versus pessimism. Some people might read the above material and feel growing hopelessness, while others might be thinking that while the picture seems gloomy, surely the creative spirit of human beings will enable inventions and solutions. These two views have been called the **Doomster** and **Boomster** responses, respectively (Bailey, 1993). The Boomster view (also called the cornucopian view) was exemplified by economist Julian Simon (1981; Simon & Kahn, 1984), who argued that population growth is good because people eventually produce more than they consume. Human beings are not limited by the carrying capacity of an ecosystem, he argued, because, unlike other animals, humans have the intelligence to redesign their habitat by inventing technology. Therefore, human ingenuity is likely to produce technological solutions that will solve problems in ways unimaginable at present. As resources are depleted, their market costs will begin to rise, slowing use, and encouraging development of alternative technologies. Human beings are (as in the title of Simon's book) "the ultimate resource." The free market will allow inventiveness to flourish, and therefore, products, economies, and well-being will continue to boom (see also Bailey, 2002; Gordon, 2006). Indeed, many people, "particularly in the West, are inclined to interpret all difficulties and impediments as merely problems that by definition are solvable with enough money, research, and technology" (Orr, 2008, p. 819).

While the Boomster view remains in the minority, it is worth taking seriously because of its psychological implications. Boomsters argue that a headline-hungry media, needing to create bad news in order to assure public attention for sufficient Nielsen ratings and healthy advertising budgets, has exaggerated the environmental problems discussed above. For example, in spite of graphic television pictures of the Exxon Valdez oil spill in 1989 showing oil-drenched wildlife and blackened beaches, Boomster Ronald Bailey (1993, 2002) argued that U.S. surface water quality *improved* since 1960. Bailey cited examples, such as Lake Erie along with other waterways that were cleaned up because of pollution control measures. Similarly, U.S. air quality has improved since 1970, as has air in cities around the world where the average per capita income surpasses $4–$5000. Boomsters believe that as capital wealth accumulates, countries can afford better pollution control measures. Further, as humans deplete resources, they develop alternative technologies, such as the use of iron to replace bronze in 700 BC, and optic fibers to replace copper in the 1980s.

In his book *The Skeptical Environmentalist*, Lomborg (2001) also argued that things are getting better, not worsening. Life expectancy has increased, infant mortality is declining, and human prosperity has improved overall. Lomborg agreed that starvation, poverty, and pollution represent real challenges, but argued that while

> Being overly optimistic is not without costs . . . *being too pessimistic also carries a hefty price tag* [italics in original]. If we do not believe in the future, we will become more apathetic, indifferent and scared—hiding within ourselves. And even if we choose to fight for the planet, it will very probably be as part of a project that is born not of reasonable analysis but of increasing fear. (p. 351)

Lomborg believes that scientists and environmental groups have exaggerated or even falsified information about global environmental problems; yet falsification is exactly what many scientists and review committees accused Lomborg of doing (Revkin, 2003; Union of Concerned Scientists, 2002).

Contemporary Boomsters are also known as environmental skeptics, who dispute the authenticity and severity of various environmental problems (e.g., climate change), and reject the available scientific literature as politically motivated and corrupt. This minority faction is dominated by conservative think tanks (Jacques, Dunlap, & Freeman, 2008; Mooney, 2007). In light of public anxiety about environmental issues, one would expect the Boomster view to become quite popular, because it would relieve discomfort about an uncertain future. It certainly was an effective tactic during the George W. Bush presidency (2001–2008), and contributed to the weakening of the U.S. Government's environmental regulations, as well as a reduction of public concern about environmental issues (Jacques et al., 2008).

Yet the alternative Doomster vision remains popular, particularly among younger and better educated individuals (see further discussion in Chapter 4). Boomsters attribute the popularity of Doomsters' views to irresponsible muckraking by the media, as well as deep psychological, even religious, needs (Bailey, 1993, 2002). From a Boomster perspective, Doomsters are the modern day versions of the fire and brimstone preachers of previous centuries. Describing the coming environmental hell in graphic detail, they scare their audience with dreadful prophecies, then promise salvation through conversion to a new ecological worldview. Boomsters also see environmentalists' concerns about social justice and inequities in distribution of wealth as merely the most current version of the Marxist vision of a world collapsing because of evil capitalism. A secular society that has lost the psychological services of the church still has deep-seated needs to be saved by somebody, and the environmentalists dish out a very successful version of apocalyptic visions with moral imperatives. In contrast, Boomsters suffer the problem of having only the status quo to offer.

As psychologists, we find this debate illuminating because it demonstrates that perceptions of and responses to information about the environment depend on psychological needs. Boomsters and Doomsters argue their cases with numbers and data, but obviously their conclusions are based on more than facts; they are also based on assumptions and values. The invocation of religious needs to explain environmental attitudes explains the counterintuitive reality that most people are willing to take a more pessimistic viewpoint, even though a more optimistic one would make them feel better. This explanation also implicates the role of the press in affecting beliefs, forcing a consideration of how information is presented, what assumptions people hold, and how they construct conclusions. Whatever else the Boomster position does, it makes a good case for the importance of *psychology as an environmental science.* We respect and discuss both informational and spiritual dimensions of environmental concern in the following chapters as we examine the psychological aspects of environmental problems.

As the majority, Doomsters show variations on their basic theme of pessimism and do not always agree with each other, especially with respect to solutions. Some suggest that the problems can only be solved by massive governmental regulations, while others argue that only transformation of people's deepest spiritual values will provide deliverance. Disagreement over solutions is inevitable, but giving up altogether is a big risk of the Doomster position. Lomborg had a good point: The complete "gloom and doom" picture can lead to the conclusion that there is no hope for warding off environmental catastrophes. The problems can seem too huge, too complex, and too expensive for human beings to manage, and government control seems as unlikely as spiritual transformation. In light of inevitable collapse, the best way of coping might be to try to ignore these issues, because their damaging effects will occur regardless of understanding or efforts to delay them. Thus, many people assume that the only thing they can do is to live the best they can in the present and try not to worry about a dismal future.

Whether one takes a Boomster or a Doomster viewpoint depends upon one's assumptions about the future, and the future, of course, has not yet happened. Therefore, no one can say that one is more correct; instead both are guesses. Arguments about specific data on particular environmental threats usually evolve to the conclusion that the past is not a sure guide for the future. For example, Doomsters would say that even though technology has bailed us out so far, it may not always do so. Boomsters would say that just because some resources are running out and pollution is accumulating, an as-yet unimagined human ingenuity will surely solve these problems.

These predictions about the future are contradictory and both cannot be totally true at the same time. It is likely that something in each view is partially correct. That is, although environmental difficulties are grave, some aspects can be and have been addressed by human effort. In any case, while pessimism may be understandable and may even be inevitable, *it is also unaffordable if it leads people to ignore ecological threats.* Allowing the luxury of slipping into despair is to bet against future generations and perhaps against all the life systems on the planet. "Hope is simply a necessity if we as a species, now conscious of the improbable and extraordinary journey taken by life in the universe, are to survive" (Kates, 1994, p. 122).

The Psychology of Overconsumption

An equally passive response to these issues would be to conclude "they are not my problems because I am not personally causing them." Since most readers have two or less children, you might assume that you are not contributing directly to population growth. Similarly, most of you are not directly working on Third World development and are not personally adding to the exponential growth rates of energy consumption and pollution there, nor are you logging forests or dumping wastes in the air and ocean. What, then, are *we as a society* doing to deplete the capacity of the planet to sustain life? The most obvious answer lies in the extravagant use and misuse of the world's natural resources, especially energy and land.

Those who live in the United States have the largest **ecological footprints, consuming more resources and generating more waste than any other people on the planet.*** "If everyone in the world had an ecological footprint equivalent to that of the typical North American or Western European, global society would overshoot the planet's biocapacity three to five fold" (Kitzes et al., 2008, p. 468). Globally, human demand is exceeding the regenerative capacity of the planet by about one quarter; that is, humans are using the equivalent of one and one-quarter planet Earths (Kitzes et al., 2008). This is a striking increase in less than 50 years, as humans were utilizing about one half of the planet's capacity in 1961.

---

* You can calculate your own footprint, as well as learn ways to reduce your impact, at http://www.myfootprint.org/

As we discussed earlier, energy represents one of the most overconsumed resources and is one of the major contributors to climate change. People living in the United States are by far the biggest users and wasters of the world's commercial energy. Constituting less than 5% of the planet's population, U.S. citizens live in a region that possesses only about 3% of the planet's oil supply (Kunstler, 2005), yet uses 25% of the total commercial supply (Energy Information Administration, 2007), 20,802,160 barrels of oil *per day*. (The next largest consumer is China at 6,720,000 barrels per day.*) The "addiction to oil" in the United States is fostering a dangerously unstable international climate because over half of the planet's oil is located in nations of the Middle East (Kunstler, 2005), stimulating military-based foreign policies that emphasize control and access (e.g., Klare, 2001; Winter & Cava, 2006). Wars over resources including oil will likely become more common.

Amazingly, about 84% of the planet's expended energy is wasted. Some waste is inevitable: As energy is converted to various forms of food, fuel, shelter, and consumer products, waste heat is always lost. However human beings waste energy through remarkably inefficient behaviors, and North Americans waste over 43% through completely avoidable actions—by selecting energy inefficient automobiles, home heating systems, and appliances, when more efficient choices are available (Miller, 2007). Energy expert Amory Lovins (2002) claimed that it is possible to *quadruple* the energy efficiency of the United States with current technology and without lifestyle changes or new power plants, simply by using superefficient motors, lighting, appliances, and building components. In Lovins's words, "If the United States wants to save a lot of oil and money and increase national security, there are two simple ways to do it: Stop driving Petropigs and stop living in energy sieves" (quoted in Miller, 2007, p. 385).

Many people literally throw wealth out the window by heating rooms with poor insulation. Most houses have enough energy leaks to equal a large window-sized hole in the wall. Although people may even realize that they are misusing their share of energy, they often continue to do so. Deborah provided a good, although troubling example. When she wrote the first edition of this text, she observed that a tremendous amount of heat was escaping through the beautiful windows in her home office in Washington state. It was March and the electric heater had been on for several hours warming her workspace. She and her husband talked about converting over to gas heat (which is much more efficient) but

---

* http://www.eia.doe.gov/iea/wec.html Table 1.2: 1.2 World Petroleum Consumption (Thousand Barrels per Day), 1980–2005.

they did not have gas lines available. They also talked about retrofitting their house with windows that would be more efficient than insulated walls. However, retrofitting is expensive and laborious, and the couple would have needed to throw out the very expensive double pane windows they chose 15 years earlier. Yet retrofitting would have paid for itself in saved energy within five years. Deborah still cannot think of a good reason for not having undertaken this action. Is it because electricity is so cheap they don't notice the waste? Is it because they don't give a hoot about the world's carrying capacity, but only their own comforts? Or is it because they believe their own waste doesn't really make that much of a difference? These are psychological questions, requiring psychological inquiry. Finding answers is crucial to solving global problems, for unless individuals better understand their own behavior and how to change it, sophisticated technological solutions will not be adopted, even when available.

Of course, Deborah and her husband aren't alone in their unfortunate environmental choices. Everyday behaviors of millions of people in industrialized countries result in astonishing inefficiencies and incredible amounts of solid waste. North Americans generate more than 4.5 pounds of garbage per person per day (Miller, 2007), about 10 times their body weight every year. Approximately 2.5 million nonreturnable plastic bottles are thrown away *every hour* (Harper, 2008) and about *25 billion* styrofoam coffee cups are tossed in the garbage each year (Dineen, 2005). Electronic, or "e-waste," is growing exponentially. Each year, U.S. residents discard more than *300 million* cell phones, computers, televisions, and other electronics; 80% ends up in landfills (Block, 2008). But even careful household recycling will not change the biggest solid waste problem: Commercial and industrial activities generate 98.5% of the world's waste. The average citizen sponsors this enormous waste by buying products inefficiently manufactured, packaged, and distributed through commercial operations. In fact, *overconsumption is the biggest drain on the earth's carrying capacity.**

Many people suffer from "affluenza," an unsustainable addiction to consumption and materialism (de Graaf, Wann, & Naylor, 2005).† The average North American uses more than 30 times the amount of gasoline, and consumes more than four times the amount of meat as

---

* For a fascinating series of graphic depictions of the astonishing quantities of consumer goods used in the United States, see Chris Jordan's (2008) Web site, Running the Numbers, at http://www.chrisjordan.com/current_set2.php?id=7. For example, he illustrates 15 million sheets of office paper, representing 5 minutes of paper use; 106,000 aluminum cans for 30 seconds of can consumption, and so on.
† A recent video on this topic is available at http://www.pbs.org/kcts/affluenza/

the average person in a developing country (World Resources Institute, 2001). North Americans use 19 times more paper than those in developing countries, and most ends up in the trash (Gardner, 2002); less than half of the paper used in the United States gets recycled (Miller, 2007). Perhaps most disconcerting is U.S. citizens' penchant for soft and fluffy toilet paper. Resistance to recycled toilet paper alone results in the harvest of millions of trees, including from old-growth forests (Kaufman, 2009).

Virtually all of the things people buy (the fast food burger and soda, jacket, cell phone, and compact disc) are produced from materials that leave a long trail of pollution in many Third World countries that is invisible to the U.S. consumer. A pair of pants made of polyester and sold in a U.S. department store may be sewn in a sweatshop in Indonesia, from synthetic material manufactured in Singapore, which originated in oil collected in the Middle East and refined in Mexico.* United States consumer culture is spreading quickly, so that people in developing countries are aiming for the good life, hurrying to develop the same extravagant lifestyles modeled through movies, television, advertising, and tourism. Opening up trade barriers via efforts like the North American Free Trade Agreement and the World Trade Organization has only exacerbated that trend.

Yet, there is good reason to believe that overconsumption is not delivering the "goods." Empirical studies of people's happiness shows that it is not how much stuff people own, but the quality of their social relations, fulfillment from meaningful work, and enough leisure time, which determines how much happiness people experience (e.g., Durning, 1992). In fact, the race to pay for material possessions is more likely to detract from these primary predictors of happiness. This conclusion is addressed in more detail in Chapter 4. The main point now is that overconsumption does not lead to happiness, and attempting to meet psychological needs through materialistic pursuits jeopardizes not only physical habitat, but also human psyches (Kasser, 2002). You have all heard of the three Rs: Reduce, Reuse, Recycle. But effective solutions to environmental problems must start with *Refusing* to buy things that aren't really necessary. (See Figure 1.4. For more ideas about how you can walk more lightly on the earth, please see the Appendix.)

---

* An excellent review of production and consumption costs is available at http://www.storyofstuff.com/

The UnShopping Card

Do I __really__ need this?

Is it made of recycled or renewable materials?

Is it recyclable or biodegradable?

Could I borrow, rent or buy it used?

Is it worth the time I worked to pay for it?

Oregon State UNIVERSITY OSU Extension Service

viviane.simon-brown@oregonstate.edu

The UnShopping Card

Do I __really__ need this?

Is it overpackaged?

How long will it last?

If it breaks, can it be fixed?

How will I dispose of it?

What is its environmental cost?

Is it a fair trade product?

Oregon State UNIVERSITY OSU Extension Service

541-737-3197

Figure 1.4 Reprinted from the Oregon State University Extension Service, Sustainable Living Project [http://www.cof.orst.edu/cof/extended/sustain/]. With permission.

Cultural Versus Biological Carrying Capacity

The issue of overconsumption brings us back to the problem of carrying capacity, the maximum number an ecosystem can support. This means that the maximum number would be living at the lowest possible standard. Some biologists estimated that the earth could support 50 billion people, but of course that would mean they would exist at a very meager standard of living. Supporting more people would require giving up luxuries, including lighting, recreation, cars, fine arts, and (horror of all horrors!) higher education. Most readers would probably prefer to see fewer people living at a higher standard, but which cultural amenities should be selected? And who should decide? From a biological point of view, carrying capacity can be estimated numerically, but when it comes to human populations, **cultural carrying capacity** is always much less than the maximum number, because human beings use more resources than necessary. Determining what needs are basic requires a debate of values (Hardin, 2002). Undoubtedly, many people in developing countries would have different and more conservative answers about minimum luxuries than people in industrialized countries.

A more formal way of conceptualizing cultural carrying capacity is to consider the formula for environmental impact given by population scientists (Ehrlich & Ehrlich, 1991; Ehrlich & Holdren, 1971).

$I = P \times A \times T$
where I is the impact of any group or nation
P is the population size
A is the per-capita affluence, as measured by consumption
T refers to the technologies employed in supplying that consumption.

With this formula, one can see that doubling a population will double its environmental impact if affluence and technology remain constant. Of course, impact is not as simple as this, since these terms are not completely independent. For example, as population and affluence grows, so does technological impact because it becomes more difficult to extract resources the more they are used (mines must be dug deeper, forests will be harvested earlier).

What this formula illustrates, however, is that the United States is the world's most overpopulated nation. To see population as only a Third World problem is a fallacy that many people, including a lot of environmentalists, still hold. Population in the United States and in other industrialized countries must continue to decrease if current levels of resource use are to be sustained. Or if population does not decrease, affluence will fall, either systematically with planning or suddenly through ecological collapse.

Giving up comforts and conveniences may be unfathomable, and reverting to preindustrial culture is irrelevant. Even if it was possible to scale down consumption to preindustrial levels, most people wouldn't want to. However, many preindustrial cultures have persisted for centuries, demonstrating that sustainable culture is achievable. While copying preindustrial cultures may not be feasible, selecting certain features might be useful. At the same time, sustainable cultures may offer some benefits to human psychological needs that are not well provided for by industrialized cultures. The modern western tradition of emphasizing the individual has produced both unsustainable technologies and increased social alienation. Using a modern western worldview, people try to use the former to mitigate the latter.

Yet it may not be necessary to give anything up in order to accomplish a reduction or reversal of environmental degradation. Improving efficiency or productivity is typically more effective than significantly reducing overall use and much relevant technology is already available. For instance, it would probably be far easier to find an automobile with twice the fuel efficiency of your present car than to cut your driving miles in half, and buying an efficient water heater is a lot easier than reducing use of hot water (Gardner & Stern, 2008; Stern, 2000).

CONCLUSIONS

It would be naïve to suggest that any one academic discipline will provide the solution to such a complex interplay of issues as those underlying current ecological conditions, and it is clear that interdisciplinary collaborations are urgently needed (Smith et al., 2009). However, psychology has a lot to offer for understanding how environmental degradation developed and the psychological forces maintaining it. As a science, psychology can illuminate the empirical dimensions of behaviors that contribute to and result from environmental threats. Bringing psychology to speak to the unspoken pessimism about the future on an overcrowded and overburdened planet will make psychological theory personally and intellectually meaningful, and provide insight into how to design a sustainable future. Before examining the specific contributions of psychology, however, we step back to study the cultural context in which both psychology and industrialization developed in Chapter 2.

2

THE NATURE OF WESTERN THOUGHT

Please indicate, by circling the appropriate response, how much you agree or disagree with each of the following statements.

1. We are approaching the limit of the number of people the earth can support.
Strongly Agree
Mildly Agree
Mildly Disagree
Strongly Disagree

2. The so-called ecological crisis facing humankind has been greatly exaggerated.
Strongly Agree
Mildly Agree
Mildly Disagree
Strongly Disagree

3. If things continue on their present course, we will soon experience a major ecological catastrophe.
Strongly Agree
Mildly Agree
Mildly Disagree
Strongly Disagree

4. Humans were meant to rule over the rest of nature.
Strongly Agree
Mildly Agree
Mildly Disagree
Strongly Disagree

These statements are illustrative examples taken from the New Ecological Paradigm scale, one way researchers measure environmental beliefs (Dunlap, Van Liere, Mertig, & Jones, 2000). If you agree with the second and fourth statements more than you agree with the first and third, you probably hold a **Dominant Social Paradigm** (DSP; Pirages & Ehrlich, 1974). The DSP reflects a belief in "abundance and progress, growth and prosperity, faith in science and technology, and commitment to a laissez-faire economy, limited governmental planning and private property rights" (Dunlap & Van Liere, 1978, p. 10). If you agree with the first and third statements more than the second and fourth, you probably hold what is called a **New Environmental Paradigm** (NEP), which reflects opinions that ecological issues are quite pressing and humans need to address them seriously now.

Up until recently, most people living in the United States would have agreed with the DSP statements. These views were considered dominant because they illustrated the Western worldview that most people held for many generations (Pirages & Ehrlich, 1974). Those who embrace these assumptions believe land that is not used for economic gain is wasted; that individuals have the freedom and right to develop property for economic profit;, and that human beings should convert however much of the natural world they can procure to support their private well-being. Faith in science usually mitigates concern about approaching ecological limits or destruction of the ecosphere. This viewpoint continues to be held by many people in the present (we referred to them as Boomsters in Chapter 1). It was vividly expressed in the campaign speeches of Republican Vice Presidential Candidate Sarah Palin, who repeated the anthem, "Drill, baby, drill," signifying her probusiness, antienvironmental record as a small town mayor and state Governor of Alaska (Apuzzo, 2008; Cart, 2008).

Belief in the DSP also includes

- Support for the status quo ("We should know if something new will work before taking a chance on it")
- Distrust of government ("Regulation of business by government usually does more harm than good")
- Support for private property rights ("Property owners have an inherent right to use their land as they see fit")
- Faith in science and technology ("Most problems can be solved by applying more and better technology")
- Support for economic growth ("The positive benefits of economic growth far outweigh any negative consequences").

People who have high DSP scores show less concern about environmental problems (Dunlap & Van Liere, 1984; Kilbourne & Polonsky, 2005; Pierce, Dalton, & Zaitsev, 1999; Widegren, 1998), and report fewer environmentally friendly behaviors (Pahl, Harris, Todd, & Rutter, 2005). Evidence for the link between environmental views and economic and political beliefs has been documented across many cultures (Heath & Gifford, 2006; Hodgkinson & Innes, 2000; Kilbourne, Beckmann, & Thelen, 2002). Other research has shown greater endorsement of the NEP in countries where more collectivist (as opposed to individualist) values prevail (Schultz, Unipan, & Gamba, 2000; Vikan, Camino, Biaggio, & Nordvik, 2007).

Globally, concern about the environment is growing (see Table 2.1). And in the United States at least, environmental issues are polarizing. A recent study of those who identify themselves as Democrats versus Republicans reveal widening gaps on opinions about climate change and whether it poses a serious threat (Dunlap & McCright, 2008a; see Figure 2.1).

Table 2.1 Growing Concern Over Environmental Problems

	Named as Top Global Threat		
	2002 %	2007 %	Change
United States	23	37	+14
Argentina	28	53	+25
Brazil	20	49	+29
Britain	30	46	+16
France	29	52	+23
Bulgaria	28	45	+17
Poland	20	33	+13
India	32	49	+17
Japan	55	70	+15
Ghana	11	22	+11
Uganda	8	22	+14

Note: Adapted from The Pew Global Attitudes Project; Pew Research Center, June 27, 2007. Retrieved March 9, 2009 from http://pewglobal.org/reports/display.php?ReportID=256

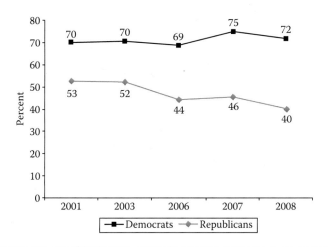

Figure 2.1 Opinion polls measuring agreement with the statement, "the seriousness of global warming is generally exaggerated in the news" demonstrate that concern about climate change is growing more divergent across political parties. (Reprinted from Dunlap, R.E., & McCright, A.M., (2008). A widening gap: Views on climate change. *Environment: Science and Policy for Sustainable Development, 50*(5), 26–35, p. 29. With permission.)

THE INTELLECTUAL ROOTS OF THE DSP AND PSYCHOLOGY

Belief in the Dominant Social Paradigm is a product of a centuries-long trail of Western intellectual and cultural history. This history forms the foundation for both the predominant view of nature in the Western world, as well as the science of psychology—and science in general. Psychology emerged as its own discipline in the late 19th century, in the quickly industrializing cities of Europe and the United States. In this new modern culture, belief that people are individuals, separate from each other and separate from nature, quickly spread and set the stage for both psychology and a quickly accelerated pace of ecological destruction from industrialization. The fact that both psychology and industrialization rest on the assumption of individualism has been used to explain why psychologists have been slow to confront environmental issues (Kidner, 2001).

Too often, psychology is approached outside of its historical context, without enough attention to the wider set of ideas that informs it. So we begin our discussion of the psychology of environmental problems by describing this cultural backdrop, and the ideas that saturated the cultural transition to industrialization. In this chapter, we will outline the philosophical contributions of a few key thinkers in Europe and the United States that remain powerful contributors to the DSP, and explain how their thinking helped shape contemporary assumptions about the natural environment.

The value placed on individualism, on resource extraction, and on human use of nature is a modern worldview, but it seeped into the Western mindset over the course of centuries. Contemporary beliefs about nature derive from many sources; among the most important are the Greek philosophers, the Judeo-Christian tradition, the Enlightenment thinkers and the Scientific Revolution, European colonialism, and the Industrial Revolution. Concern about the depletion of nature is not new. In the first century BC, Lucretius pointed out that the fertility of the soil was declining, and many civilizations have failed because of resource depletion, as we discussed in Chapter 1.

But in terms of human history, both the extravagant use of nature and views encouraging that use are relatively recent events. The brain structure of modern humans (Homo Sapiens), with its enlarged frontal lobes and language abilities, has existed for roughly 150,000 years; the modern worldview and its accompanying profligate resource use has been in place for no more than 300 years.

To get a sense of how recent modern beliefs are, imagine the (conservatively estimated) 150,000 year human history reduced to 12 months. If human beings came into existence on January 1, most of their year was spent in small bands of hunting–gathering tribes. Agriculture and the formation of the first cities in the Near East did not begin until December 6 (about 10,000 years ago). The Greeks, to whom the contemporary DSP owes much of its heritage, did not create their celebrated civilization until December 15. The Scientific Revolution, responsible for a massive change in the way Europeans viewed nature, happened on the morning of December 31, at the same time European civilization began to spread to the rest of the world through colonialization. And the Industrial Revolution (nineteenth century) did not occur until around noon on the last day of the year, just about when psychology as an academic discipline was getting started. We will examine how each of these events helped shape the modern worldview, but the point right now is that *even the most ancient roots of our Western worldview occurred very recently in human history.*

People usually take their worldview as given and accept its assumptions as obvious and commonsensical. Unless one participates in an intellectual community where debates are frequent and vigorous, worldviews are rarely contended. Rather worldviews provide a conceptual framework from which people interpret their experience,

© Marian Henley. Reprinted with permission.

create meaning, and make decisions. Each culture develops methods for knowing the world based on assumptions that are consistent with prevailing views about reality. But every worldview, including the DSP and NEP, is arbitrary, distinct, and limited. From the perspective of a different worldview, Western thought looks distorted and irrational. For example, to a Choctaw Indian, White people elicit "a strange kind of pity . . . These hopeless . . . creatures . . . possesses no magic at all, no union with Earth or sky, only the ability to hurt and kill. . . They are sad and dangerous like a broken rattlesnake" (quoted by Haslam, 1983). In Hawai'i, White people are often called "haolie," meaning without spirit, without breath.

It may seem logical to view nature as a set of resources awaiting human use, and all societies (as well as all species) do transform some part of the natural world for their subsistence. However, modern industrialized society is converting ecosystems at unprecedented rates. The central premise of this chapter is that *humans are approaching planetary limits in carrying capacity at least in part because the modern worldview (DSP) provides a set of beliefs that encourages people to use and abuse natural resources*. Examining the intellectual history that shaped the DSP provides an opportunity to become more conscious about its operation in human decisions about the environment.

But before proceeding, let us offer a few caveats.

First, although we argue that human assumptions are potent determinants of environmentally relevant behavior, we also recognize that the assumptions that become popular, and therefore deeply embedded in any cultural tradition are in turn shaped by the institutions and cultural events during which they are created. In other words, human ideas and institutions are dialectically related to each other: Ideas shape history, and history affects which ideas become powerful. Material events affect philosophy, just as ideas affect material events. Case in point: We doubt we would be questioning the DSP if we didn't notice some of the disturbing environmental problems described in Chapter 1. But like all worldviews, the DSP wouldn't have become dominant if it wasn't useful. The Western worldview delivers a "set of attitudes and ideas, originating with the ancients and extended and modified over time, [which] became privileged and eventually grew to be hegemonic by virtue of their functional successes—in politics, economics, and even religion" (D.R. Snow, personal communication, February 24, 2009). Thus, none of the thinkers whose work we will discuss could have become so important without their historically relevant context, including their philosophical predecessors, their immediate colleagues offering counterarguments, and the events that made their ideas seem sensible.

Second, to argue that some understanding of Western intellectual history is crucial for illuminating the psychology of environmental problems is not to claim that all environmental problems stem from that history. Clearly environmental damage has occurred throughout human history, not just in the recently industrialized West (Diamond, 1988, 1992; Redman, 1999). Humans have caused massive extinctions and resource declines all over the world during every century. Nor are we saying that people merely have to change their ideas in order to solve environmental problems. Indeed it may be that the very process of *having* ideas of *any* sort—that is, conceptualizing and creating meaning from words—separates people from their direct experience of the natural world and sets the stage for abuse of it (Manes, 1996). The under-recognized role of literacy can help explain why nations across the planet, including those outside the West, also have dismal environmental records. Language interrupts direct experience with the natural world, and this is as true in the East as it is in the West. We will have much more to say about the importance of nonverbal (direct) experience in Chapter 10. For now, our point is that worldview assumptions are a potent, but not a sufficient, cause of environmental problems.

Third, while articulating some key components of the DSP, we acknowledge that there are many versions and variations of the Western Worldview. Debates and disagreements about their particulars are alive in academia, and we are simplifying Western intellectual history here in order to contribute a basic understanding of the philosophical and cultural backdrop surrounding the rise of environmental problems in the West. All history is told with some purpose, which sculpts what part of the story is articulated, and what other parts are ignored.

Finally, confronting the problem of the planet's limited carrying capacity means examining suppositions that have been operating for centuries. If debates about the environment get heated and angry, it is often because precious assumptions, those most deeply embedded in the Western worldview, are being challenged. Core identities are at stake, with emotional responses easily triggered (Clayton & Opotow, 2003). People who hold DSP beliefs aren't necessarily stubborn individualists (although they may be that as well). Whatever their emotional reactions, they are expressing their cultural heritage, their earnest faith in the Western worldview, a worldview that has historically worked for at least some significant part of the population. There are many positive and valuable outcomes from the Western worldview: a successful science and technology that has solved many practical, medical, and industrial problems; a sense of freedom and opportunity that is unknown in most parts of the world; a creative and hardworking populace whose output is tied to economic reward; and a lively, forward looking, quickly evolving society that enjoys unparalleled material abundance. Yet as seemingly sensible and valuable as the Western worldview is, like all worldviews, it is subjectively constructed.

THE WESTERN VIEW OF NATURE

All worldviews provide a particular definition of nature and the human relationship to it. The Western worldview, defined here as the DSP, embraces the ideas that

1. Nature is composed of inert, physical elements
2. Which can and should be controlled
3. By individual human beings seeking private economic gain
4. Whose work results in progress (mostly economic development).

In a relatively short amount of time, human beings changed from living in small tribes of hunter–gatherers where nature was often imbued with a living and sacred quality (Sabloff, 2001), to living in technologically based cities, where nature became a set of resources awaiting human use. The immensity, rapidity, and potency of this change cannot be underestimated, and we will examine how it came about by addressing each of the four assumptions.

Assumption 1: Nature is Composed of Inert, Physical Elements

In most preindustrial cultures, nature is seen as a living, organic unity intimately tied to the activities of human beings (Merchant, 1980; Sabloff, 2001). Even most of Western history shows allegiance to the idea that the natural world is divinely ordered and alive. Plato in his *Timeas* proposed that the world was united by a *spiritus mundi* (soul of the world), which was the source of all movement and activity in the universe. Likewise, the Stoics of third century BC Athens and first century AD Rome saw the world as an intelligent organism. Matter was alive with expansion and contraction, which gave life to all objects in the universe. Similarly, for most people in most ages, daily, immediate interaction with the natural world accompanied a belief that nature is not only alive, but also imbued with the same qualities as human beings (Manes, 1996). In most societies, rituals recreate and honor the link between the living human and nonhuman worlds. Such animistic and anthropomorphic beliefs underlie prayers, ceremonies, and sacrifices, linking the individual to the natural and supernatural realms.

Clearly, modern life in the Western world shows a very different orientation. Housed in cities and buildings that remove the natural world from daily experience, people experience nature as separate from humans. Natural phenomena such as weather, earthquakes, and volcanoes are the result of inherently inert matter that responds to physical, rather than spiritual, forces. Weather is caused by shifts of wind and temperature, not the work of angry gods and goddesses. Up until the recent recognition of human impacts on climate, people in industrialized countries assumed they had no effect on these events. For instance, hurricanes do not happen because of human errors or angry gods; they believed such events happen because of physical phenomena outside human control and often outside understanding as well. Nature works like a machine: orderly, if not always predictable.

Deborah was recently reminded about this assumption when reading newspaper accounts of an active volcano on the Big Island of Hawaii, where she now lives. Kilauea Volcano has been erupting for years and has emitted noxious gases called vog almost daily throughout 2008 and 2009, leading to frequent news articles stressing health risks. But interestingly, even mainstream media mention Pele, the ancient goddess of fire, in their headlines. For example a major Honolulu newspaper ran the story, "Pele Turns Up the Heat" (Thompson, 2008) and even the United

(a)   (b)

Figure 2.2 (a) Halema'uma'u crater of Kilauea emitting sulfide gasses. (Courtesy of United States Geological Survey.) (b) Painting of Pele, Goddess of Fire, hanging in the Volcano National Park. (Reproduced with kind permission from the artist, Arthur Johnson.)

States Geological Survey wrote "Pele's Cooking More than Vog: Precious Jewels Also Stewing in her Cauldron" (U.S.G.S., 2008; see Figure 2.2) Most scientists and mainland citizens would see these references to Pele as a quaint form of anthropomorphism, a cultural anachronism because scientists have evolved past such mythical explanations to believe that mechanical forces, rather than spirits, control natural events.

Where did the mechanical view of nature come from? Although the separation between the human and physical worlds had many contributors throughout Western history, the most important transition from a spiritual to a mechanical universe took place during the Enlightenment period. In Europe between 1500 and 1700, thanks to the work of Copernicus (1473–1543), the geocentric model of the universe was replaced by the heliocentric model. In the heliocentric model, the earth moves around the sun, instead of heavenly bodies around the earth. This new perspective

struck at the core of Aristotelian and Christian belief [because it] removed the earth from the centre of the universe and so from the focus of God's purpose. In the new scheme man [sic]* was no

---

* Throughout this book we denote use of the word "man" instead of "human" with [sic] because of the gender bias that so-called generic masculine language promotes (Winter, 2002; Gastil, 1990; Wilson & Ng, 1988). Such language is no longer acceptable in publications, as illustrated by the American Psychological Association's guidelines on use of discriminatory language (see *APA Publication Manual*, 2010, 6th ed., pp. 71–77). We point out sexist language, even in historical documents (and even though we realize it was considered appropriate in its day), because doing so illuminates how its use helped keep women out of the mental picture created by public discourse.

longer the creature for whose use and elucidation the cosmos had been created. (Burke, 1985, p. 135)

Moreover, during this period, the natural world came to be understood as a machine, made up of small, separate units (which are now called atoms) operating according to mechanical laws.

There were many contributors to the mechanical worldview, none more important and influential than the French philosopher Rene Descartes (1596–1650). Descartes asserted that God had made the world, and that the world's complete orderliness was proof of God's all-knowing intelligence. Since God was all-powerful, God created a world with unchanging laws of physical reality. Thus, once created, the world operated with clockwork-like precision without God's intervention. In Descartes view, everything in the universe was mechanical, save one thing: the human mind. "The soul" argued Descartes, "is entirely distinct from the body . . . and would not itself cease to be all that it is, even should the body cease to exist" (1627/1958, p. 119). This mind–body dualism is one of Descartes' most lasting contributions, and provides a basis for the *split between human consciousness and the rest of nature*. The human mind, imbued with soul, was under the jurisdiction of the church; the rest of nature, including bodies, "lower" animals, and all other objects were material, and operated strictly according to mechanical laws. These laws could be known through logic and rationality (just as the Greeks had argued several centuries earlier). The emotions, belonging to the body, were not to contaminate the pure rationality of the mind. We'll return to the implications of Descartes's severing the mind from its emotional context in Chapter 10. The point now is that for Descartes, humans did not anger the gods who then produced natural events at whim; instead the natural world operated according to strict mechanical principles.

This transformation of nature—from a dynamic, alive, and spiritual entity to an orderly, mechanical, and clockwork machine has been called "the death of nature" by historian Carolyn Merchant:

In 1500 the parts of the cosmos were bound together as a living organism; by 1700 the dominant metaphor had become a machine. . . . The rise of mechanism laid the foundation for a new synthesis of the cosmos, society, and the human being, construed as ordered systems of mechanical parts subject to governance by law and to predictability through deductive reasoning. A new concept of the self as a rational master of the passions housed in a machinelike body began to replace the concept of the self as an integral part of a close-knit harmony of organic parts united to the cosmos and society. Mechanisms rendered nature effectively dead, inert, and manipulable from without. (Merchant, 1980, pp. 214–215).

Seeing the world as a mechanical system had three important ramifications. First, it freed humans from the worry of placating certain gods. Second, it lifted what now seem like irrational superstitions that underlay some nefarious rituals, such as human sacrifices. Third, it liberated human energy to adjust the machine. Thus, a mechanical and spiritless natural world allows for the possibility (and eventually, as we shall see, the moral mandate) of human control over natural phenomena. To see the world as a machine is to see it made up of discrete parts that operate according to regular laws; a machine can be studied in a limited, specifically defined domain; it can be manipulated, and most importantly, it can be controlled by human intervention.

By the middle of the seventeenth century, Descartes's ideas were widely discussed and increasingly substantiated. Sir Isaac Newton (1642–1727), whose *Principia* (1687) spelled out the mechanical principles of force and motion in the physical world, validated Descartes's view of a mechanical universe by providing mathematically verifiable predictions about the movement of stars and objects. Newton's work still supplies the basis of the modern worldview today: Matter is inherently inert; it is made up of objects that move only because outside forces move them, like billiard balls whose direction and motion can be successfully predicted. Although Newton agreed with Descartes that only God could have created such an exquisitely ordered universe, Newton helped pave the way for the modern secular worldview by demonstrating how orderly and precisely predictable is the movement of objects (objects above the level of the molecule, that is; modern physics of the twentieth century, which focused on the movement of atoms and their parts, gives a very different view of nature).

Assumption 2: Nature Can and Should be Controlled

To see nature as inert matter without spirit is to invite human control and use of it. After all, those with consciousness should use anything that lacks consciousness for their own higher spiritual ends. Therefore, along with the mechanization of nature during the Enlightenment period came calls for the control of nature; this view also served as the foundation for the Scientific Revolution of the sixteenth and seventeenth centuries.

An important voice in the plea for human control of nature was Francis Bacon (1561–1626), named by Alfred North Whitehead "one of the great builders who constructed the mind of the modern world" (quoted by Dick, 1955, p. ix). Bacon's views of science were tremendously persuasive and helped escort the secular worldview to primacy over the medieval Christian worldview. Before the Scientific Revolution, knowledge was delivered through the church, according to key texts and religious insights produced by contemplation of divine principles. Since the Scientific Revolution, knowledge about the world comes from observation of it, best done through controlled experiments. Bacon was an important architect of the Scientific Revolution by virtue of his forceful writing on the conduct and goals of science. As a successful member of the British Parliament and holder of highest appointed offices under King James I, his passionate criticisms of the ineffectual, contemplative knowledge of his day had great impact. Bacon argued that philosophy had been unproductive because it was based on speculation, rather than on fact. Vowing to free knowledge from the strangle hold of the cloistered institutions of church and university, Bacon argued that society must abandon "the little cells of human wit" for the "reverence of the greater world" (Bacon, 1620/1955, p. 437) and bring nature to light through observation rather than by "triumphs of confutation, or pleadings of antiquity, or assumption of authority, or even by the veil of obscurity" (p. 435). Moreover, Bacon argued that one must study nature (which he saw as female) by controlling "her." In his view, science should observe

> not only nature free and at large (when *she* is left to *her* own course and does *her* work *her* own way),—such as that of the heavenly bodies, meteors, earth and sea, minerals, plants, animals,—but much more of nature under constraint and vexed; that is to say, when by art and the hand of man *she* is forced out of her natural state and *squeezed and moulded* . . . seeing that the nature of things betrays itself more readily under the vexations of art than in its natural freedom. (italics added; p. 447)

Thus, only by constraining nature and subduing "her" could "man" understand her secrets, and thereby gain mastery over the world. In Chapter 4, we will look more closely at the problematic psychological impact of conceptualizing nature as female, to be "squeezed and molded" by inquiring man. For now, let's examine Bacon's view that controlling the natural world was a moral imperative. Bacon used the Biblical story of creation to argue this point. To Bacon, science was the way back to paradise. When humans were expelled from the Garden of Eden, they lost their dominion over the earth and its creatures, and were subjected to the earth's nefarious processes, such as droughts and floods. Bacon believed that God, "who gavest the visible light as the first fruits of creation, and didst breathe into the face of man [sic] the intellectual light as the crown and consummation thereof," would bless scientific understanding as "coming from Thy goodness [and] return to Thy glory" (1620/1939, p. 23). Thus, humans can regain their blessed place in creation by exerting their power over nature through scientific understanding; science thereby offers human salvation. By learning about nature through scientific inquiry, humans can return to their original state of dominion over the natural world. Science, in other words, will give them control over the rest of creation, which will return them to God's favor.

As much as the Enlightenment philosophers of the seventeenth century were setting a new direction away from the church, most of them still relied on the fundamental belief in a Judeo-Christian God and "His" creation of the universe. Bacon's use of the creation story shows how important this tradition is in shaping the modern view of nature. All societies have creation stories—explanations for how the world was made—which deliver understandings about human beings and their relationship to the rest of the world. Unsurprisingly, the Genesis story from the Old Testament reveals the Western assumptions about nature and use of it:

> And God said, Let us make man [sic] in our image, after our likeness: and let them have *dominion* over the fish of the sea, and over the fowl of the air, and over the cattle, and over all the earth, and over every creeping thing that creepeth upon the earth. So God created man in his own image, in the image of God created he him; male and female created he them. And God blessed them and said unto them, Be fruitful and multiply, and replenish the earth, and *subdue* it: and have *dominion* over the fish of the sea, and over the fowl of the air, and over every living thing that moveth upon the Earth. (Genesis, Chapter 1, verses 26–28, italics added)

It is especially the words "dominion" and "subdue" that have been blamed for human beings' arrogant attitudes about, and abuses of, the natural world. For example, in an influential essay called "The Historical Roots of our Ecologic Crisis," historian Lynn White argued that "Christianity, in absolute contrast to ancient paganism and Asia's religions . . . not only established a dualism of man and nature but also insisted that it is God's will that man exploit nature for his proper ends" (White, 1967, p. 405).

Unfortunately, the Biblical story has been used by antienvironmentalists as a justification for human control of nature, and the Christian community has often been either indifferent or even antagonistic toward environmental concerns. For example, Pat Buchanan's quarterly newsletter *From the Right* published an antienvironmentalist manifesto by Llewellyn Rockwell that concluded:

> In holy scripture, God told us to "fill the Earth and subdue it, and rule over the fishes of the sea, and the fowls of the air, and all living creatures that move upon the Earth," for they are ours "to feed upon." We are created in "His own image." And with the Incarnation, the Creator of the universe became a child. Thus any philosophy that equates man [*sic*] with animals or plants, or subordinates him to nature, is a heresy of astounding proportions. (Rockwell, 1990, p. 9)

Blaming the ecological crisis on Christianity alone would be an oversimplification, perhaps even an unfair distortion of the original meaning in the Biblical text. Christians concerned with ecological problems, most notably former U.S. Vice President Albert Gore (1992), have argued that the word *dominion* has been mistranslated to mean domination. Instead *dominion* should imply responsibility for stewardship. And while a growing segment of the Christian community is addressing the responsibilities of Christians to nurture and protect the natural environment* (Bratton, 1984; Catholic Coalition on Climate Change, 2008; Haegele, 2008; McDaniel, 1994; Ruether, 1992; U.S. Conference of Catholic Bishops, 2001), environmental problems generally receive much less pulpit-time than other issues, such as marriage, abortion, and prayer in schools. Recent controversy within the National Association of Evangelicals (NAE) erupted in 2007 over the question of whether climate change is an appropriate topic for Christian concern when James Dobson and other national leaders called for the silencing of an NAE officer who spoke too often on the topic (Cooperman, 2007). This debate seems ironic since almost half of U.S. citizens say that "protecting God's creation" is a major reason why they are concerned about climate change (Leiserowitz, Maibach, & Roser-Renouf, 2009a).

So even if you agree with Gore that dominion *should* be understood as responsible stewardship, in large part it has not been. Attendance and membership in Christian churches generally predicts

---

* See http://creationcare.org/

antienvironmental attitudes (Gardner & Stern, 2002; Schultz, Zelezny, & Dalrymple, 2000), though the size of that relationship shrinks when controlling for age, gender, education, political affiliation, and other factors (Gardner & Stern, 2002; Shekat & Ellison, 2007; we will discuss these demographic variables in more detail in Chapter 4).

The view that nature should be controlled is not limited to conservative Christians. This view is very deeply embedded in the entire Western tradition, as illustrated by the following. While Deborah was writing this chapter for the first edition of this book, she had a friend over to dinner who, as she was cooking, asked her how the book was going and what she was working on. Deborah described some of the thinking in this chapter, particularly the idea that people see humans as superior to the rest of nature, which is subject to their control. As she was describing this idea, a carpenter ant crawled across the counter and Deborah automatically smashed it. "Is that a problem?" her friend asked. "Yes," Deborah answered, still thinking about the view of nature, "because it allows people to unconsciously manipulate or harm anything in the name of human convenience." "No" her friend said, "I mean is *that* a problem?" pointing to the smashed ant. "Yes, those damn things are destroying our house." "But isn't that *the* problem?" persevered the friend. Deborah looked up in puzzlement and then realized what she had done. Even though she had spent all day writing about the unconscious assumption that people have the duty and right to control nature, she hadn't even realized she was using that very assumption when she automatically smashed the ant. Her worldview is so deeply ingrained that even as she wrote and thought about it, she still unconsciously used it. The point of this example is not necessarily that she was wrong to kill the ant (in fact, she still smashes them), but that she is unconscious about her relationship to other species. Deborah is still struggling with these kinds of issues, since she believes that all species must impact others in order to survive, yet humans have abused neighboring species. At this point, she tries to live with this problem by becoming more aware of her own decisions. Now when she kills an ant, she tries to remember to apologize to it for taking its life so that she can be comfortable. She hopes that by developing an apologetic attitude, she might be less likely to abuse other species for inconsequential reasons.

As Christian and scientific heritages laid a framework for human control over nature, important political institutions followed that further convinced Western people of the human right to control the natural world. Locke (1632–1704), a British philosopher and political theorist, worked out the philosophical foundation of democracy by stressing the importance of land ownership. According to Locke, owning and cultivating land entitled the owner to vote; managing one's land for production showed merit, since "God and his reason commanded him [*sic*] to subdue the earth, i.e., improve it for the benefit of life, and therein lay out something upon it that was his own, his labor. . ." (Locke, 1690/1939, p. 415). In this way, Locke attempted to put some constraints on private ownership by suggesting that men should own only as much land as they could successfully cultivate.

Note that it was *men* (not women, slaves, the uneducated, or anyone else who supposedly couldn't reason abstractly) who should own land and thereby participate in democracy through voting. Locke rarely mentioned the role of women, except in his lengthy discussion of the importance of both the mother and the father in teaching the child an early obedience to patriarchy (Locke, 1690/1939, Chapter VII). However, a quick passing comment about the reasoning power of women demonstrates his lack of confidence in them: "Tis well if men of [wage-earner] rank (to say nothing of the other sex) can comprehend plain propositions, and a short reasoning about things familiar to their minds, and nearly allied to their daily experience. Go beyond this, and you amaze the greatest part of mankind" (as quoted by MacPherson, 1962, pp. 224–225). Thus for Locke, most *men* can't reason properly, never mind women. The sexism promoted by male land ownership is still apparent. The United Nations estimates that women produce between 60% to 80% of the world's food supply (Food and Agriculture Organization, 2009), but globally they own less than 2% of arable land (Mehra & Rojas, 2008).

Thus, by proposing that private ownership is a gendered and God-given right and that land use is a God-given responsibility, Locke helped tie democratic institutions to the private ownership of common resources, a theme that becomes important in the export of the modern worldview through Third World development. Moreover, Locke's emphasis on land use as a starting point for democracy helped promote the notion that unused land is wasted land, and that private property owners have the right to do whatever they want to their land, including destroy other species.

Assumption 3: Individual Human Beings Seek Private Economic Gain

One of the best ways to examine a worldview is to consider what it says about "human nature." A frequent claim in the West is that humans are motivated primarily by material gain, that "It's the buck that counts," or in political campaigns, "It's the economy, stupid." The assumption is that nothing is more important in human affairs than material rewards.

Reprinted from © Chris Madden. With permission.

Where did the attribution of a core economic motivation come from? Materialistic goals superseded spiritual goals when the mechanical worldview displaced the primacy of the church. Again, Locke helped out. Locke provided a positive spin on economically driven land use, first by arguing that God intended humans to own land, and by so doing, humans obeyed God's orders. Secondly, Locke provided a convenient justification for material wealth by arguing that "the chief end of trade is Riches & Power" (quoted by MacPherson, 1962, p. 263), which are essential for the defense of the nation. Locke's viewpoint provided a basis for early trickle down economics, since he assumed that private ownership by the wealthy class enables the poorer class to sell their labor and thus gain livelihood. In this way, the problem of limited land for the vast majority was deftly avoided, since poorer people could work for the rich. Locke also noted that "The New World" furnished unlimited land, so that ownership was determined by a person's will rather than circumstance. No better proof of the value of labor is the pathetically clad natives who were land rich and labor poor:

> Full as the world seems ... let him plant in some inland vacant places of America... . The extent of the ground is of such little value ... there is land enough in the world to suffice double the inhabitants... . For it is labor indeed that puts the difference of value on everything... . There cannot be a clearer demonstration of anything than several nations of the Americans are of this, who are rich in land and poor in all the comforts of life; whom nature, having furnished as liberally as any other people with the materials of plenty—i.e. a fruitful soil, apt to produce in abundance what might serve for food, raiment, and delight; yet, for want of improving it by labor, have not one hundredth part of the conveniences we enjoy, and a king of a large and fruitful territory there feeds, lodges, and is clad worse than a day laborer in England. (Locke, 1690/1936, Chapter V, Sections 36, 41)

In proposing the use of the New World, Locke conveniently "ignored any inconvenience to either emigrants or Indians" (Clark, 1989, p. 263). Instead he pitied the poor Native Americans who were poorly dressed by European standards, simply because they did not work their land. In Locke's vision, landowners should provide the poor a means of livelihood, and the laboring class could in turn provide a commodity by which national wealth could be derived. By this symbiotic relationship between the wealthy and the poor, wealth could be accumulated by the rich. With this formula, the basic features of colonial expansion were put in philosophical order, and the British Empire proceeded to grow through land grabs of large portions of Asia, Australia, Africa, and America since wealthy landowners were simply providing "enhanced opportunities" to the native populations they plundered. The only constraint on land use that Locke proposed was that nobody should own land that wasn't cultivated; on the other hand, money could be accumulated, especially if it was subsequently reinvested into the public good. As a result, capital investment in the support of colonization was a good way to gain God's favor.

While it is difficult to underestimate the potency of Locke's legacy on the DSP, it is worth noting that Locke (and his colleagues in this his-story) wasn't working from nefarious motives. In fact, his hope (and accomplishment) was to set the philosophical foundation of democracy and, by doing so, bring some peace to the bloody power struggles going on at the time in Europe. He worked from an ethical perspective and tried to set some ethical parameters on land use.

But the ethical dimensions of accumulating capital were soon to dwindle. Locke's writing was preceded by that of Thomas Hobbes (1588–1679) whose less attractive arguments did not initially have as much impact as Locke's; eventually, however, Hobbes's views superseded Locke's by bypassing the moral constraints that Locke proposed. Locke, along with Descartes and Newton, had seen an important role for God in both creating the universe and setting moral limits for human conduct. But Hobbes carried the mechanistic view of the universe to ultimate lengths by positing that everything—including people, minds, brains, and ideas—is nothing but material and material events. In proposing this irreducible materialism, Hobbes argued that human beings are locked in a continual state of competition with each other for material goods and for power. For Hobbes (like Freud, whom we will meet soon in Chapter 3), nature is chaotic and dangerous, and humans must fight for their own survival against nature and against each other. Hobbes's view of human nature was not a pretty one.

> The life of man [sic] [is] solitary, poor, nasty, brutish, and short . . .
> the condition of man . . . is a condition of war of everyone against
> everyone; in which case everyone is governed by his own reason,
> and there is nothing he can make use of that may not help until him
> in preserving his life against his enemies. (1651/1962, pp. 100, 103)

Thus Hobbes believed the basis of human nature is competitive self-interest; because people are inherently in competition against each other, they must enter into market contracts to create some semblance of social order. And those market contracts define each person since "the value or worth of a man [sic], is as of all other things, his price" (1651/1962, p. 73). In other words, people owe society nothing, but instead are driven by selfish concerns. Without a spiritual foundation or creator, worthiness as human beings can be calculated entirely by material holdings.

As negative as Hobbes's vision of human nature was, it was made progressively more palatable by several important thinkers who followed: Adam Smith, the Scottish economist–philosopher (1723–1790) argued that the state should leave individuals alone to amass their material wealth because what is good for the individual is eventually good for the state. The utilitarian British philosopher Jeremy Bentham (1748–1832) proposed that human nature always attempts to maximize pleasure and minimize pain, so morality could be defined by the greatest happiness for the greatest number (rather than by duty or obligation). While Bentham defined happiness, other utilitarians set about to measure it. "And so, if it wasn't already, material wealth became equated with that which all persons, by their nature, most desire" (Clark, 1989, p. 267).

Add to this material basis of motivation the work of the liberal democrats, such as Thomas Paine (1737–1809), who successfully argued that governments should not interfere with "natural rights, . . . those which appertain to man[*sic*] in right of his existence" (1791–1792/1953, p. 84). As you know, the United States Declaration of Independence argued the same point: "All men [*sic*] are endowed by their Creator with certain unalienable Rights that among these are Life, Liberty, and the pursuit of Happiness." This primacy of the individual over the state became a hallmark feature of the new democratic government. And thus the modern worldview was written into a federal constitution and into a national psyche: No longer do people have essential moral or psychological responsibilities to their clan or community. Instead, individuals are responsible for their own well-being. No longer is the most important purpose of life to ensure passage to heaven or honor for one's ancestors; no longer is fundamental identity based on family or kin relationship. Instead, lives are lived as individuals, competitive and separate, pursuing personal material wealth through the God-given rights of freedom and noninterference from the state. This is the great achievement of the modern age.

Finally, we cannot leave the discussion of materialistic individualism without mentioning the contribution of the Protestant reformers. They upgraded the Hobbesian view of human purpose as material accumulation by reinstating a moral and religious meaning. To the Calvinists who helped settle the United States and promulgate the Industrial Revolution in England, work was a divine calling; material rewards were signs of God's blessings for labor well done. Concomitantly, poor people deserve their punishment because of their lack of effort; rich people simply reflect God's approval. In Protestant modernism, work and wealth are good; leisure and poverty are sin. Furthermore, as Max Weber (1864–1920) argued (1904/1930), Protestant beliefs encouraged industrial development by

> sharply limiting the uses that could be made of [earned] wealth. In reaction against the softness and luxury of Rome, Protestantism was ascetic and forbade expenditures on pleasures of the flesh. One of the few things one could do in good conscience with savings was to "plow them back into the firm." (Brown, 1965, p. 451)

In other words, invest. In this way Calvinism encouraged the perfect combination of hard work and ascetic self-denial that enabled capital to be reinvested, and thus, capitalism to flourish.

While Weber argued that Protestantism established the impetus for the rise of capitalism, his interpretation was really an extension and critique of Karl Marx's theory (1818–1883) of 50 years prior: that economic motivation determined religious experience and not the other way around. With the industrialization of England as his evidence, Marx posited that human relationships in an industrialized society are defined by their economic dimension. One's economic role determines the way one thinks, perceives, and reasons. In Marx's words, "the modes of production" (1867/1977, p. 929), that is, economic interactions, determine human existence and consciousness. Since workers become alienated from their products through industrialization's division of labor, their social relationships become defined by money and the commodities that money can buy.

In earlier periods where modes of production were agricultural or mercantilist, production was directly of a person's own making and one could identify with the finished product, which gave a sense of pride, accomplishment, and humanity. But in a capitalist system, according to Marx, social relationships are divided into either owners of production or means (labor) of production. Both roles are dehumanized because in neither case can people identify (feel proud of, or give service through) their works. What do assembly line workers in Southeast Asia know about the person wearing or using the shoes they assemble? What does a Wall Street manager know about a family who just received a subprime mortgage? When alienation from one's work occurs, money takes on excessive "fetish" power. As long as the distribution of wealth remains uneven, people will focus on it. Thus, for Marx, industrialization directs human consciousness to economic realms. Although Marx's ideas about communism are unfashionable today, it is ironic how those who have the most antipathy toward Marx still endorse his materialistic view that economics dominate human experience.

Assumption 4: We Must Progress

Even if the Protestant ethic had not provided a religious framework for modern industrial development, the moral imperative of individuals at work for material gain would still be bolstered by the West's allegiance to the notion of progress. To Westerners, time is a linear event and they expect that during its passage, growth will occur. In contrast, many preindustrial cultures see the passage of time in circular terms, bounded by the cycles of nature (and even in some cases, positing the reincarnation of the human being into repeating lifetimes). People in the West are married to the idea of forward progress. They see time not as a circle, but as a line: a sequential series of events revealing continuous development. To return to a previous state is to go backward, to regress, to fail.

Where does the devotion to the idea of progress come from? Some cite Charles Darwin (1809–1882), whose theory of evolution is often misinterpreted as suggesting a continual growth of complexity and adaptation in species, although Darwin specifically argued that there was no goal or purpose to evolution. However, evolutionary theory became a popular tool for conceptualizing progress, thanks in large part to the efforts of the English philosopher, Herbert Spencer (1820–1903). Spencer proposed that societies, like everything else, undergo an evolution from simple to complex:

> Whether it be in the development of the Earth, in the development of life upon its surface, in the development of society, of government, of manufactures, of commerce, of language, literature, science, arts, this same evolution of the simple into the complex, through successive differentiations, holds throughout. From the earliest traceable cosmical changes down to the latest results of civilization, we shall find that the transformation of the homogenous into the heterogeneous, is that in which progress essentially consists. (1891/1969, p. 124)

It was hard to put a price on progress.
Real hard without a calculator.

Thus, like species, societies evolve; for instance, from simple agrarian communities to complex industrialized societies. Formulated in a country busily expanding its wealth through colonialization and industrialization, it is no surprise that Spencer's ideas became widely popular: what better concept with which to condone the imposition of British rule on the "less evolved savages" of Asia, Africa, Australia, and America!" "Throughout the Edwardian period, ordinary people were encouraged to believe that the empire stood for the expansion of civilized values as well as the accumulation of profits" (Bowler, 1989, p. 200). Thus, the progress of society and of economic development were tightly linked in the Victorian mind, which, we are arguing, is still operative in the DSP.

As if to prove Spencer's point, the new country of the United States, as England's offspring, complicated and extended the idea of progress. After all, the New World stretched out in what must have seemed infinite wilderness, and the lure of the West soon pulled settlers whose visions of fortune were matched by visions of religious conversion: "American expansionism and Indian salvation began to become synonymous" (White, 1991, p. 72). Although westward expansion was debated, many saw it as inevitable, at least those who believed in "manifest destiny."

> The American claim is by the right of our manifest destiny to overspread and to possess the whole of the continent which Providence has given us for the development of the great experiment of liberty and federative self-government intrusted to us. It is a right such as that of the tree to the space of air and Earth suitable for the full expansion of its principle and destiny of growth. (White, 1991, p. 73)

Manifest Destiny expressed a moral imperative to use whatever was needed in order for the great experiment of liberty to grow and "possess the whole of the continent." We think it ironic that the metaphor of a tree was chosen to suggest the rights of North Americans to "their full expansion and destiny of growth" since millions of trees were cut for human settlements, and consequently denied their "space of air and Earth." No matter. The spirit of westward expansion was more potent than its logic. Even though the phrase "manifest destiny" was invented by a New York journalist, whose words appear above, it captured the self-righteous and land-hungry spirit of the newly migrating pioneers.

Thus, the particular United States spin on progress was to focus on the freedom of individuals to make life better for themselves, through widespread land ownership. Progress is made when individuals enjoy the right to own and control their own property. Just as Locke argued, progress occurs when individuals apply technology to convert their land to income. Progress through private land is the explicit assumption of U.S. culture, but it is also, we are arguing, the assumption of Western culture in general.

We are not suggesting that land ownership is necessarily a bad idea. In light of the environmental problems of China and East European countries, it may be less destructive than massive state ownership. What we are saying, however, is that private ownership without group responsibility—the sense that this is my land and I can do anything I want with it—is a deeply ingrained legacy of the Western tradition. Consequently land use challenges will threaten deeply held commitments to the "American way of life."

Progress, through land ownership and economic wealth, is the fundamental feature of the Western worldview. The perception that human life is perched in a *linear time* marked by progress toward something better is mirrored by the Greek and Christian view that we are perched in a *linear power order* as well. In the traditional Western view of the cosmos, God reigns over men, who rule over women, children, animals, plants, and inorganic matter, in that order. This ordering makes humans more important than animals, men more important than women, organic matter more important than inorganic matter, mammals more important than insects, plants more important than dirt. Intellectual historian Arthur Lovejoy (1936/1960) termed this idea *The Great Chain of Being* and attributed its origin to the Greeks, especially Aristotle. Aristotle proposed that all beings are arranged in a single continuum, a *natural scala*, according to "their degree of perfection." This perfection is based on the amount of soul or potential realization that differs for each kind of being. The amount of soul determines how close they are to God, who of course, sits at the top. And who is right up there next to God: no surprise, it's man. In addition to legitimating sexism and anthropocentrism (to be discussed further in Chapter 4), this linear view of the universe exhibits hierarchical spatial ordering, so familiar in many other Western institutions: the priestly hierarchy, the divine power of kings, the military with its chain of command, the corporation with its vertical structure of power and status, the taxonomy of biological organisms, and even the reductionistic idea of science that complex wholes are made up of simpler parts.

Yet democratic institutions have gradually undermined the strict idea of hierarchy given by The Great Chain of Being. To allocate one vote to one citizen is to begin to level the power hierarchy (although continued discrimination based on class, race, gender, and ethnicity still helps to maintain it). While modernity has weakened the vertical concept of reality, it has not annihilated it (Manes, 1996). And vertical organization combines with linear progress to saturate the Western viewpoint of reality.

In this way, Western thinking is dominated by a line—of progress, of power, and of consciousness (or closeness to God). The line is a potent basis of modernist visions. It sanctions and promotes the idea of growth, which is good and diminishes the value of sustainability, which is stagnation. The line promotes resource extraction, production, consumption, and waste to the detriment of finding ways to reuse waste as food for the next cycle (we'll say more about this in Chapter 11). Here our point is that people in industrialized societies are deeply wedded to the hope of progress, improvement, growth, ascendance, and enhancement. International development efforts focus on increasing the standard of living, meaning increasing life spans, education, literacy, and technological conveniences of other countries. At the national level, U.S. quarterly reports are saturated with criterion of economic growth. Presidents are elected for their promise of economic growth and measured against the accomplishment of it.

For centuries of Western thought and the implementation of it in the United States and around the globe, progress has seemed not only possible but evident and incontrovertible. Life spans have increased. Water and land have been claimed for human needs. The average person in an industrialized country today lives at a level of material comfort that the richest person of a century ago could hardly imagine. In the last century, progress in terms of material comfort, technological innovation, human population growth, and resource utilization is undeniable.

Yet, in the early years of the twenty-first century, we must question a larger vision of progress, as technological feats have brought on dangerous ecological threats that were unimaginable a few decades ago. Mounting difficulties lead all of us to ask how beneficent our progress is turning out to be. Is it progress to be changing the global climate with greenhouse gasses? To have produced millions of tons of nuclear waste with no known way of insuring its safe storage? To habitually use thousands of chemicals that cause cancer and disrupt brain development? Is it progress to be cutting the last 5% of North America's ancient forests? To be doubling the already problematically sized human population in the next 30 years? To be spending one third of the planet's wealth on military operations?

The linear view has brought us into troubling relationship with the physical world. As Swedish physician and environmental policy maker Karl-Henrik Robert observed:

> For roughly the past hundred years, humans have been disrupting the cyclical processes of nature at an accelerating pace. All human societies are, in varying degrees, now processing natural resources in a *linear* direction. Our resources are being rapidly transformed into useless garbage. With few exceptions, none of this garbage finds its way back into the cycles of society or nature; it is not taken up for repeated use by industry, nor is it put back into the soil. The ultimate consequences of all this are impossible to foretell. (Robert, 1991, p. 11)

We will argue in Chapter 11 that it is long since time to start thinking again in terms of circles instead of lines.

At the start of the twenty-first century, John Locke's assertion "that there is land enough in the world to suffice double the inhabitants" is also no longer true. Perhaps the Western worldview is faltering because there is no more New World, no more inland vacant places in America for us to plant, no more infinite sinks into which we can dump. Perhaps the old notion of progress and linear technology requires empty space, which on an increasingly crowded planet is more of a historical memory than a current reality.

As we question the linear notion of progress, we may begin to question some of the other assumptions that are intimately tied to it: the inherent goodness of material consumption, the sanctity of the individual and of individual freedom to live without responsibility to the larger whole, and a natural world that is primarily dead and inert. A vivid way to examine assumptions is to confront worldviews that make a different set.

THE NATURE OF NONINDUSTRIALIZED THOUGHT

In most traditional (nonindustrialized) societies, people live in small groups of closely knit relationships, deriving a sustained subsistence from the land, either through hunting and gathering, or from hand- or animal-based agriculture (Sabloff, 2001). The events of the natural world have enormous and direct impact on the well-being of people in traditional societies, and people immediately experience the rhythms and changes in weather, water, sun, and wind. For instance, the Inuit (an indigenous population) in the Arctic are already experiencing cultural and mortality impacts as a result of climate change, and are advocating for its consideration as a human rights issue (Spicer, 2007). In most native cultures that anthropologists have studied, the natural world is a key part of cultural and family life. For example,

> Native American teachings describe the relations all around— animals, fish, trees, and rocks—as our brothers, sisters, uncles, and grandpas. Our relations to each other, our prayers whispered across generations to our relatives, are what bind our cultures together. . . . These relations are honored in ceremony, song, story, and life that keep relations close—to buffalo, sturgeon, salmon, turtles, bears, wolves and panthers. These are our older relatives— the ones who came before and taught us how to live. (LaDuke, 1999, p. 2)

In the vast majority of preindustrial societies, nature is seen as a living organism, often as a mother, which is nurturing, beneficent, and ordered, but also at times wild, violent, and chaotic. To personify nature as a female has important ramifications that we will discuss in subsequent chapters, but for now let us consider the effects of seeing nature as an alive being. In Merchant's words:

> The image of the earth as a living organism and nurturing mother had served as a cultural constraint restricting the actions of human beings. One does not readily slay a mother, dig into her entrails for gold or mutilate her body, although commercial mining would soon require that. As long as the earth was considered to be alive and sensitive, it could be considered a breach of human ethical behavior to carry out destructive acts against it. For most traditional cultures, minerals and metals ripened in the uterus of the Earth Mother, mines were compared to her vagina, and metallurgy was the human hastening of the birth of the living metal in the artificial womb of the furnace—an abortion of the metal's natural growth cycle before its time. Miners offered propitiation to the deities of the soil and subterranean world, performed ceremonial sacrifices, and observed strict cleanliness, sexual abstinence, and fasting before violating the sacredness of the living earth by sinking a mine. (1980, pp. 3–4)

If the natural world is alive, people live in kinship with it. Other species are neighbors and family. Human responsibility is to protect and nurture, rather than to use and transform. People listen to and learn from other life-forms as relatives and support them as kin.

> People have the responsibility to help complete their life cycles as part of the universe in the same way they are helping people. Human beings are not above nature or above the rest of the world. Human beings are incomplete without the rest of the world. Every species needs to give to every other species in order to make up a universe. (DeLoria, DeLoria, Foehner, & Scinta, 1999, p. 226)

If people in the West were to experience other species as family members, and the natural world as alive, would they continue to destroy the ecosphere?

We hope that this chapter has convinced you that *the DSP is a product of an intellectual heritage, not that one paradigm is better or worse than another.* While we believe alternative worldviews have something to teach us, we are not arguing that we should dump the Western viewpoint and trade it for a preindustrial one (not that it would even be possible). No one worldview has all the answers to all human existence, least of all to the complicated problems of modern life, including ecological ones that people have hardly even begun to face. While humans in traditional cultures feel a stronger connection to nature, their lives are difficult: Infant mortality rates are high, physical safety and survival is uncertain, and physical comforts are rare. Moreover, social belongingness comes with psychological confinement: identities and roles are determined by birth, rather than by choice. In spite of their more sustainable use of resources, the threats of disease (not to mention their treatment of women) would be unbearable. Nevertheless, traditional cultures have some wisdom for creating sustainability.

All worldviews have both assets and limits. Because this point is so crucial, allow us to describe one last example in some detail: Deborah's visit to Nepal in 1994. Kathmandu, the capital city, was and still is a wonderfully cacophonous place, and walking through its streets means confronting, appreciating, and dodging the best and the worst of many Asian cities: Hindu and Buddhist temples; festivals filled with dignified yet casual participants, incense, flowers, and tinka powder; half paved or dirt roads crammed with deafening, asphyxiating traffic; obnoxious street hawkers, ragamuffin children, and hideously diseased beggars; exquisite crafts and intricately carved wooden buildings; revolting piles of garbage, complete with human excrement and dead dogs floating in the main river that supplies the city water. Even today, after treatment, Kathmandu's water is still sub-standard (NGO Forum, 2008). Add to this list the impossibly gentle expressions of the Nepalese, smiling serenely behind their face masks as they pick their way through the mess (there is so much bacteria carried in the dust of that city that it is possible to get seriously ill by simply breathing the air). To say that the streets of Kathmandu are a culture shock to the Western tourist is a considerable understatement: Kathmandu is also a real physical blow to any immune system accus-tomed to sanitation procedures like sewers and garbage collection. What is even more disturbing about the condition of Kathmandu is that Nepal has received as much foreign aid as any country in the world, and yet still remains one of the world's poorest, both in terms of gross national product, as well as more direct social indices like life expectancy, literacy, infant mortality, and nutritional status. How could Nepal in general, and Kathmandu in particular, have wasted so much financial assistance?

There are many answers to this question: ineffective aid planning, rampant corruption by the Royal Family (which has subsequently brought on a revolution), lack of infrastructure for completing con-struction projects, and runaway population growth. But one of the most oft cited reasons is the Nepali worldview. Nepal has been heavily influ-enced by the Hindu notion of caste. Although the caste system in Nepal is not as rigid as India's, it does lead to a sense of fatalism, so that one's birth into the social structure determines everything. Concomitantly, Nepalese are generally indifferent to ideas of both progress or personal competence. In the words of an important Nepali political scientist, Dor Bahadur Bista,

> The absolute belief in fatalism, that one has no personal control over one's life circumstances, which are determined through a divine or powerful external agency . . . has had a devastating effect on the work ethic and achievement motivation, and through these on the Nepali response to development. It has . . . led to the expec-tation of foreign aid as a divinely instigated redistribution. In the present context aid becomes merely something that is justly due to Nepal and not a resource that is meant to be considered seriously and used productively. (Bista, 1991, pp. 4, 5)

The Nepali worldview is not bad—nor good—although it might seem problematic for industrial development and useful for human equa-nimity in the face of physical suffering. That advantage may become more useful as global systems decline, necessitating more effective psychological mechanisms to deal with traumas caused by extreme weather events and climate change, sudden resource shortages, and population migrations.

Nonetheless people can't replace worldviews. They can, however, tweak them. Like LaFreniere (2008), we believe there is much value in examining how certain features of the Western view of nature came about, so that we might be more able to modify them. Knowing that assumptions that seem like common sense are actually constructed from historical discourse delivers the opportunity to critically reconsider them in a fresh light. As the DSP evolves from holding the the primary goal of human experience to be material growth, to involve a new goal of ecological sustainability, an integrated set of worldviews, institutions, and technologies will also shift (Beddoe et al., 2009).

CONCLUSIONS

The Western worldview (DSP) that sees the natural world as a separate and dead set of resources awaiting conversion into production stands in marked contrast to traditional cultures, which view the universe as filled with living relationships. In terms of human history, industrialized culture is very recent, having evolved during a few hundred years from the political and academic institutions of Europe and the United States. Preindustrial societies are quickly disappearing as capitalism spreads. Growing international markets have quickly replaced traditional cultures and their diversity of languages, their kinship with other species, and their view that the natural world is alive, with the Western view that nature is dead. As your authors, we believe this rapid spread of the Western worldview does not bode well for building sustainable societies.

All worldviews are socially constructed, taught as common sense, and deliver both blind spots and wisdoms. As you consider and question your own worldview, you can better think through the ramifications of it. As you deconstruct some unquestioned assumptions, perhaps it will be easier to rethink and tweak them in order to better fit the present reality of globally faltering ecosystems. Examining the thinkers who shaped the Western worldview highlights the ways in which it was developed over several centuries of intellectual history. Moreover, *understanding that assumptions about nature are constructed leads to awareness that environmental issues are deeply philosophical and psychological ones.*

Without the hard intellectual work of confronting philosophical assumptions, people behave unconsciously, and ultimately, unwisely. Human behavior to date has brought us to the brink of environmental collapse in part because of unexamined habits, values, and practices. No one saw the nefarious impact of unconscious motivations and blind spots on human behavior more vividly than Freud and the psychoanalytic thinkers, to whose work we now turn.

3

PSYCHOANALYTIC PSYCHOLOGY: BECOMING CONSCIOUS OF THE UNCONSCIOUS

How can people know about environmental problems, and yet continue with business as usual? Why do people go on overconsuming and degrading resources, even while realizing that they are doing it? Why does the public so often relegate matters of the environment, which is the basis of human existence and survival, to the periphery, as though the environment is the special interest of a group of folks called "environmentalists" (Nicholsen, 2002)? Somehow, people must split off their awareness so that they understand environmental problems and yet forget them at the same time. Apparently, people do not behave as intelligently and consciously as they think they do. These considerations lead us to consider the enormous contributions of psychoanalytic psychology, and its founder Sigmund Freud, the first and most influential psychologist to theorize about the unconscious.

In this chapter, we examine the main features of psychoanalytic psychology for insights into environmental problems. We begin with Freud's ideas, which laid the foundation for neo-Freudians and the modern analytic tradition that followed. Object relations theory (ORT) in particular goes further than Freud in articulating the basis for impaired relationships between human beings and their environment. Finally, we examine both Freudian and ORT for their utility in changing environmentally relevant behavior. Paradoxically, Freud's emphasis on the unconscious elements of human functioning points to strategies for increasing awareness. The most important contribution of psychoanalytic psychology is the recognition that environmental problems are deeply rooted in unconscious motives. Recognizing this fact begins the crucial project of becoming conscious. As one of Sue's meditation teachers once said, "when you realize you aren't conscious, you become conscious." Awareness can then be utilized for creative solutions.

THE INFLUENCE OF FREUD

Although Freud (1856–1939) is often dismissed or ignored by academic psychologists because they find his work unscientific, we believe his contributions are crucial for understanding environmental problems because his views are so relevant, his ideas so useful, and his impact so enormous. While little of his theory can be empirically tested with controlled experiments, Freud's work has had huge impact on Western culture and also began the practice of clinical psychology. Furthermore, contemporary research in cognitive neuroscience validates many of his concepts (Huprich, 2008; Schore, 1999; Shevrin, Bond, Brakel, Hertel, & Williams, 1996), including his general claim that most of what people do is unconscious (e.g., Bilder & LeFever, 1998; Gazzaniga, 2004); we will discuss this point in more detail below. Ironically, recent and much needed attention to the unconscious reactions elicited by climate change (Maiteny, 2002; Moser, 2007; Stoll-Kleemann, O'Riordan, & Jaeger, 2001) and other environmental problems (Macy & Brown, 1998; Norgaard, 2006; Opotow & Weiss, 2000) does not recognize the intellectual debt owed to Freud.

Freud's ideas are not particularly comfortable or attractive, even though they are widely used. Paradoxically, Freud is only tangentially regarded as a psychologist by most academic psychologists (in fact, he was trained as a physician), and yet he is recognized by the public as one of psychology's most famous figures. Due to Freud's work, popular culture has become "psychologized": his ideas are common household terms, even if they are not well understood (Frosh, 1987). Before Freud, people in the West had no notion of neurosis, the unconscious, defenses, psychotherapy, or clinical psychology. The idea that emotional problems could be treated as a mental illness was not even conceptualized, much less accepted or implemented.

Looking back on Freud's work, we see spectacularly insightful concepts alongside the most misguided. Of course, judgments as to which is which proceed from one's own assumptions about human nature. As you read through this chapter, keep track of the ideas you find reasonable and those that seem outlandish. Regardless of your analysis, in all of psychology's century-and-a-half history, no other psychologist surpasses Freud's productivity, genius, or influence.

One reason that Freud's views are often difficult to accept is that they do not paint an attractive picture of human beings. In Freud's eyes, humans are at core weak, irrational, selfish, and rigidly determined. In the words of one of his most compassionate biographers,

> Freud's estimate of the human animal is far from flattering, and his message is sobering in the extreme. To expose oneself to the full gravity of Freud's thought is therefore risky and unsettling, and many have found it more soothing by far to soak up fragments of that thought through bland popularizations, or to rely on the doubtful wisdom of common discourse. Freud took some pride in disturbing the sleep of mankind [sic], and mankind has responded by trivializing him, watering him down or finding reasons—whether by denouncing his theories or denigrating his character—for disregarding him altogether. (Gay, 1989, pp. xiii–xiv)

But while his ideas are often dismissed, many thinkers, including the immodest Freud himself, have described his contribution equivalent to those of Copernicus and Darwin, because all three systematically dislodged human beings from viewing themselves as the center and pinnacle of the universe (Burtt, 1954; Butterfield, 1960; Koyre, 1968). Copernicus showed that the planets don't revolve around the earth, but instead around the sun; Darwin helped humans realize they aren't categorically different from other animals, but instead share common ancestry; and Freud showed how irrational and biologically determined people are, rather than the logical, intelligent, and god-like beings they assumed they were after the Enlightenment thinkers (see Chapter 2). Tough lessons for the human ego!

Nowhere is human frailty more saliently observed in Freud's work than in his thinking about the human struggle against nature. Theorizing early in the twentieth century, at the peak of industrialization, Freud believed that although humans construct impressive technologies to ward off nature's destructive powers, their efforts are only temporarily successful. Consider his words from *The Future of an Illusion* (1927):

> The principal task of civilization, its actual raison d'être, is to defend us against nature. We all know that in many ways civilization does this fairly well already, and clearly as time goes on it will do it much better. But no one is under the illusion that nature has already been vanquished; and few dare hope that *she* will ever be entirely subjected to *man*. There are the elements which seem to mock at all human control: the earth, which quakes and is torn apart and buries all human life and its works; water, which

deluges and drowns everything in turmoil; storms, which blow everything before them. . . . With these forces nature rises up against us, majestic, cruel and inexorable; *she* brings to our mind once more our weakness and helplessness, which we thought to escape through the work of civilization. (italics added; Freud, 1927, p. 693)

In this passage Freud claims that human beings are weak opponents of nature. (As we saw with other writers in the previous chapter, notice that Freud also brings a gendered understanding of this conflict by his reference to humans as male, and nature as female; we will discuss the implications of this distinction in Chapter 4). For Freud, both the natural world and the inner psychological world of the human being are untamable and unmasterable. The best people can hope for is temporary, fragile, uneasy, anxiety-based truces, and compromises between the competing forces both within and outside the individual psyche. As you read Freud, you may feel belittled and diminished. Understandably, you may have defensive reactions to his views, the same sort of defensive reactions that occur when people read about the seriousness of the ecological plight discussed in Chapter 1. In fact, the notion of defense mechanisms is one of Freud's most important contributions, as you shall see.

The Basis and Basics of Freud's Theory

Since Freud's writing filled 24 volumes produced over a 50-year career (Strachey & Freud, 1964), his work is impossible to thoroughly describe in one chapter. Nonetheless, there are three main principles to Freud's thought that underlie the particular concepts and case studies that make up the bulk of his writing. When you grasp these three principles, you will have a good foundation from which to apply Freudian thought to ecological issues:

1. Much of human behavior is a result of unconscious motivations
2. Conflict is universal, chronic, inevitable, and painful
3. In order to reduce pain, humans unconsciously protect themselves against unwanted thoughts, feelings, and desires, using defense mechanisms to disguise and contain their anxiety.

We will examine each of these principles, explaining what Freud meant by them as well as how he came to believe them. In order to properly comprehend Freud's theory, however, it is important to first understand something about the **Zeitgeist** (the implicit values and beliefs at work in a culture during a particular period of time) that nurtured his ideas.

Freud helped formulate the Western worldview (also called the dominant social paradigm [DSP]; see Chapter 2), ushered in by the Enlightenment. This worldview assumes that both the environment and human behavior are determined by material, physical events. This idea flourished in the latter half of the nineteenth century, when Europe's increasingly materialist culture was supported by an industrial revolution in full gear. Freud learned from his brilliant and world famous mentors, Ernst Brucke and Hermann Helmholtz, that mental life is the result of activity of the central nervous system, and that all psychological events could and should be understood as physical energy that circulates through the brain and nerves. Such a view seems obvious now, but in the late 1900s it was a progressive idea, as it contradicted the then more popular notion that psychological events emanate from some vital force, such as a soul. Instead, Freud was an utter materialist: All of psychological life can be understood as a product of physical forces. To buttress their newfound materialism, Freud and his teachers enthusiastically embraced the newly published work of Charles Darwin. Natural selection replaced God's will as an explanation for human existence. A secular worldview emerged in which the entire universe became a set of physical elements.

The burgeoning materialism fed the industrial revolution as people came to believe that the primary goal of human beings was to convert natural resources to products and profit. As industrialism and capitalism fed each other, the older ecological worldview faded; no longer were humans a small part of a spiritualized world, existing as vulnerable beings who had to respect and cooperate with their natural environments. As Europe was industrialized, people left their agriculturally based lives in rural villages to take industry jobs in urban settings, thereby cutting themselves off from their place of origin, their extended families, and their previous embeddedness in natural (nonbuilt) places. From a psychoanalytic viewpoint, the spaces where humans live profoundly affect their personhood (Bodnar, 2008).

This shift to urban life in support of industrialized capitalism was rapid, and Freud was caught up in the new openness and vitality of enlightenment thinking. But he also worked in a sexually repressive society that forbade his patients, mostly women, opportunities for expressing their sexual desires. Impressed by the bizarre symptoms that he treated in his patients, Freud concluded that psychological functioning is a creative outcome of the interplay between physical, instinctually based drives and the social, cultural, and moral pressures to tame, channel, subdue, or repress them. And because of severe societal taboos on sexual expression, he came to see sexual instincts in particular, which Freud called **Eros**, central to the life force that is fundamental in shaping the personality of the adult. For Freud, Eros included not only sexual desire, but also drives for physical pleasure, such as pleasure from eating, touching, and sensual experience. Freud also proposed an opposite drive, **Thanatos**, the death force that conflicts with Eros, as he watched with horror the unfolding of World War I in Europe, and concluded that the massive killing he witnessed could only be explained by an unconscious, inborn, irrational need for destruction. The fact that three of his sons fought in that war only increased his dismay.

Unconscious Motivations   In Chapter 1 we described ways in which humans are systematically destroying the planet's life support systems. From a psychoanalytic perspective, humans are driven to overconsume and overpopulate by their unconscious libidinal instincts (Eros). Rushing through existence in order to procure more and more appetitive satisfaction, humans instead enjoy less and less. Driven also by Thanatos, they unconsciously destroy their habitat, building weapons of mass destruction that threaten to annihilate people and other species. Both Eros and Thanatos propel environmental destruction.

In spite of human beings' sophisticated attempts to deny and conceal these conflicting drives, they are still ruled by them. Eros (sexual pleasure and reproduction) and Thanatos (aggression, violence, and destruction) determine human behavior, but becoming aware of environmental problems does not mean that humans can easily resist these innate drives and stop ruining their habitat. It wouldn't at all have surprised Freud that people continue to trash their environment, even while becoming conscious of doing it. Since behavior results from deeply buried instinctual drives, it is difficult to change. Were he alive today, Freud might have even said that environmental collapse is inevitable.

Freud believed the human psyche is predominantly unconscious and unobservable, similar to an iceberg that has 80% of its mass below the surface. He posited that if human beings were aware of their unconscious sexual and aggressive motivations, they would be greatly disturbed. But instead, human psyches expend energy to keep impulses below the surface so that people can fool themselves into thinking they behave for rational or moral reasons, when in fact, much behavior is driven by subversive needs, wishes, fears, and impulses that are quite selfish and unacknowledged.

The view that human behavior is primarily unconscious is supported by recent work in cognitive neuroscience (Wilson, 2002). For the most part, people behave and then explain what they did and why they believe they did it (Gazzaniga, 2004, 2005). For example, if you threw something in the trash and someone asked you why you didn't recycle it, you would invent a reason ("Oh, the trash can was more convenient"). Unconscious mechanisms guide most of human behavior, although these mechanisms are far more complicated than the two instincts Freud proposed. People can rarely explain their ability to navigate body movements in space, yet they navigate all the time when executing environmentally relevant behavior. How did you coordinate your arm muscles to throw the can into the recycling container, rather than the trash container? The unconscious, according to neuroscientists, contains sophisticated processes that guide behavior without verbal control.

Conflict   As a materialist who believed that psychological functioning originates in physical actions in the nervous system, Freud's ideas built on other important thinkers, none more important than Sir Isaac Newton. The conservation of energy, one of Newton's key principles, served as a pivotal organizing feature of Freud's theory about the psychological life of human beings. All energy is supplied by the nervous system and must be divided up between three psychological structures: the **id**, consisting of the appetitive desires, seeking pleasure; the **ego**, a reality-oriented mechanism that considers realistic constraints on impulse expression; and the **superego**, the moral principles that are internalized from parents and society. Since there is a limited amount of energy, if it is given to one structure, it must necessarily be reduced in another.

For example, consider the conflict one might experience when buying a fast-food hamburger. The id experiences hunger; the ego considers price, convenience, and nutrition; the superego might ask about the moral implications of contributing to environmental and social damage, as most hamburger is produced in conditions horrific to both cattle and meat packers (Schlosser, 2001), and often from cattle raised on cleared tropical rain forests. Since psychological structures compete for energy, concerns about rainforest habitat might dwindle with intense hunger (the superego might be overpowered by a very strong id); or one might not be hungry enough to wait in a long line (a weak id might be overpowered by a pragmatically oriented ego). Many environmental choices involve conflicts of just this sort. People are able and willing to enact environmentally beneficial behaviors as long as inconvenience, high prices, and strong appetites are not in the way. At the other extreme, superego guilt or shame normally nag when id appetites go unchecked, producing unresolved anxiety. (These insights are supported by empirical research on attitudes and behavior, as discussed in Chapter 4.)

"I assure you the animals didn't suffer.
All of our meat comes from animals who died
naturally of old age while vacationing in Miami."

Thus, environmentally relevant behavior depends on the distribution of physical energy to these competing psychological structures. In Freud's view, conflicts are both intrapersonal and interpersonal: The same conflict over the allocation of physical energy *within* the individual is mirrored in one's relationship to society and to nature. That people compete with others for a finite amount of energy in the physical system is congruent with the problem of planetary carrying capacity, discussed in Chapter 1.

Defenses Psychological conflict is painful. Freud postulated that humans defend themselves from conflict and anxiety by fragmenting their awareness, so they remain essentially unconscious about their instincts without entirely ignoring them. This point is a crucial psychoanalytic principle for understanding environmental problems, as we will see in more detail below. Compromises between needs, thoughts, and shoulds allow humans to behave in ways that express both the instinct and its denial. Here are Freud's own words to describe this process:

Let us suppose, then, that a child's ego is under the sway of a powerful instinctual demand which it is accustomed to satisfying and that it is suddenly frightened by an experience which teaches it that the continuance of this satisfaction will result in an almost intolerable real danger. It must now decide either to recognize the real danger, give way to it and renounce the instinctual satisfaction, or to disavow reality and make itself believe that there is no reason for fear, so that it may be able to retain the satisfaction. Thus there is a conflict between the demand by the instinct and the prohibition by reality. But in fact the child takes neither course, or rather he [*sic*] takes both simultaneously, which comes to the same thing. He replies to the conflict with two contrary reactions, both of which are valid and effective. On the one hand, with the help of certain mechanisms he rejects reality and refuses to accept any prohibition; on the other hand, in the same breath he recognizes the danger of reality, takes over the fear of that danger as a pathological symptom and tries subsequently to divest himself of the fear. It must be confessed that this is a very ingenious solution of the difficulty. Both of the parties to the dispute obtain their share: the instinct is allowed to retain its satisfaction and proper respect is shown to reality. But everything has to be paid for in one way or another, and this success is achieved at the price of a rift in the ego which never heals but which increases as time goes on. The two contrary reactions to the conflict persist as the center-point of a *splitting of the ego*. (Freud, 1938/1964, pp. 275–276; italics added)

This same fragmenting occurs when people are driven by instinctual, appetitive desires in the face of impending ecological disaster.

Here is the planet's collective problem: People seek pleasure— comfortable housing, delicious food, stimulating entertainment, personal mobility, procreation, successful careers. Each of these desires leads to behaviors that contribute to an impending ecological collapse, an event so dire and overwhelming that no one can fully fathom its consequences. Too much anxiety makes this situation unthinkable (Lertzman, 2007; Nicholsen, 2002). Just as the child Freud described, wouldn't splitting the ego (to use Freud's phrase) be an ingenious solution, allowing people to both maintain their behavior and still retain their knowledge of reality? This is precisely the state in which most people find themselves—a split off, fragmented, dissonant state where they continue with their destructive behaviors while paying some, though not full, heed to mounting environmental threats.

How do people manage such ingenious and effective splits? Freud suggested that they construct partitions through a variety of **defense mechanisms**. As we show in the following list of examples, people use defense mechanisms to protect themselves from discomfort, enabling them to believe that they are behaving quite reasonably. Defenses are actually quite irrational: they hide reality, lead to distorted thinking, and eventually create greater problems. But defenses are also functional because they reduce distress in the short run. Very much like the principle of **cognitive dissonance** (a cognitive form of conflict discussed in Chapter 4), defenses demonstrate the illogic and irrationality of human behavior. Every once in a while, however, material slips through the defense structure to produce a **Freudian slip**, as in the case of a skeptical student of Deborah's who once wrote on an exam that "Fraud believed women have penis envy." A wide variety of defense mechanisms get used by people everyday.

Rationalization. One of the most common defense mechanisms, occurs when people create an attractive but untrue explanation for behavior. Most people rationalize frequently. Deborah rationalizes when she tells herself that she bought a new sweater because it was on sale. Given that she really didn't need another sweater, her purchase, however small, contributes to the collapse of ecosystems by enhancing the market for unnecessary goods. Like most middle-class people in the United States, Deborah finds it too uncomfortable to recognize that fact, so she supplies a more attractive explanation for her behavior and claims that she bought it because it was cheap. Unnecessary purchases are never really cheap—they are costly both from an environmental and social perspective, but rationalization keeps her anxiety at bay.

Intellectualization. Similarly, most people intellectualize about environmental problems by failing to recognize their own hand in creating them, or the serious implications for their future. Intellectualization occurs when people distance themselves emotionally by describing something in abstract, intellectual terms, failing to recognize their personal contributions to it. "Top soil loss affects farmers, not me." "Extinction is a problem for other species, not our own." Intellectualizing helps people stay defended by allowing them to superficially understand an issue without experiencing anxiety about its impact. When information is presented as abstract statistics, risks about climate change and other environmental threats do not evoke strong emotional responses (Weber, 2006; see also discussion of **quantitative illiteracy** in Chapter 7). Students and professors are especially likely to use intellectualization and rationalization as they study environmental problems, since academia rewards thinking rather than feeling.

Displacement. A similar kind of distancing is achieved by the defense mechanism called displacement. Freud suggested that displacement occurs when people express feelings toward a less threatening target. For example, instead of yelling at the stranger driving a gas-guzzling car or sport utility vehicle (SUV), Sue yells at her partner for missing a turn and having to drive a few extra blocks out of the way. People often express their environmental concerns through indirect and ineffective, but more comfortable, routes. Consider, for example, buying a T-shirt with a picture of a whale and the phrase, "Save the Whales" on it. The T-shirt does not help the environment, although the imagery and verbiage leads people to think that it does. To use an even more uncomfortable example, recycling gives people the feeling that they are doing something good for the planet, and to some degree, they are. However, recycling is considerably less effective than cutting consumption in the first place. Reducing consumption is more difficult, so recycling is a displacement for anxiety. While recycling is better than nothing, it will not solve environmental problems and people use it as a defense when they think it will.

Suppression. Sometimes people are aware of their anxiety, and actively try to think about something else. Suppression is the conscious attempt to put the anxiety-provoking thoughts out of one's mind. Most people use suppression quite regularly. For instance, when walking past a homeless person, contemplating the effects of driving cars on climate change, or hearing a disturbing newscast about deteriorating ecosystems, people often shift attention away from the bad news—by changing the radio station, their eye contact, or their thoughts to avoid discomfort. Perhaps when you read Chapter 1 you experienced some anxiety, and you intentionally tried to change your awareness to reduce it. Consider the following example, from a recent study conducted in Norway:

> It's terrible to think of, that we live so well while others live in such miserable circumstances. Of course, it's very good to have a comfortable life . . . I enjoy it . . . but I feel so bad about others. I have a guilty conscience, that's why I try not to think about it, keep it at a distance. I still think these are important matters, but it's as if I can't make myself be concerned all the time, not any more. . . . Terribly important these matters, but I don't feel involved in a way, don't want to get involved. (quoted by Norgaard, 2006, pp. 386–387)

Even scientists use suppression, when they avoid contemplating the terrifying ramifications of climate change and instead focus only on reducing emissions, a strategy which may not suffice in preventing catastrophic consequences (Vince, 2009).

Reprinted from © Chris Madden, [http://www.chrismadden.co.uk/]. With permission.

Repression. Whereas suppression is a conscious defense, repression is unconscious. When people use repression, they do not realize they are doing it. They don't try to put the anxiety provoking material out of their mind—it just happens. A good example of repression is Deborah's surprise at "finding out" about the nuclear waste at a nuclear production site (Hanford, Washington) just a few miles from where she once lived. Even though information about Hanford had been in the news on and off for 20 years, and she had driven past the reservation many times, she didn't "discover" the problem for a long time. She unconsciously repressed not only the hazardous waste, but the entire nuclear reservation, somehow not hearing the news stories or seeing them in the newspaper. Although repression occurred naturally without any conscious attempt on her part, the government's placement of nuclear reservations in out-of-the-way locations, and use of tight security to prevent publicity, helped set up an environment in which repression was easy. When a citizens' action group succeeded in getting 19,000 pages of previously classified documents released, Deborah's (and many other people's) repression ended and anxiety replaced it instead.

Denial. Repression is certainly the most effective defense, but it is not easy to maintain, especially when information from the world threatens to lift its protective force.

The facts are coming! The facts are coming!

When that happens, people often use denial, and insist that the anxiety-provoking material doesn't exist, while simultaneously expressing some anxiety. For example, Deborah recently got an earful from a neighbor about her work on sustainability projects in their community. This neighbor expressed anger and irritation at the idea that local people need to work together to insure food security. He then used sarcasm and humor to reject threats of climate change and muttered the phrase "politically correct" (p.c.) to dismiss uncomfortable thoughts about not only the environment, but also racial inequalities and other social injustices. When denial is used as a defense, there is a subtext of frustration or hostility (Rush Limbaugh's tone on A.M. radio is a classic example). Anxiety is leaked alongside the mechanism of repression, which gives denial its own special flavor of emotional strain.

Like all defense mechanisms, denial can be enhanced by collective narratives that are promoted by groups for financial reasons, which is why denial has recently received research attention from sociologists. Conservative think tanks, funded by industry and conservative foundations, have promoted denial about climate change by publishing books urging doubt about well-documented environmental problems (Jacques, Dunlap, & Freeman, 2008). A congressional aid reported that at least one conservative think, long funded by ExxonMobil, offered scientists $10,000 to write articles undercutting claims about climate change. "The denial machine is running at full throttle" (Begley, 2007, p. 7). This strategy was effective in producing public skepticism about the scientific evidence on climate change, as well as maintaining government resistance to regulations such as fuel efficiency standards, emission controls, and pollution caps. Denial about environmental problems includes minimizing their severity, seeing them as irrelevant, and seeing oneself as not responsible (Opotow & Weiss, 2000). Collective narratives support not only government resistance, but also public opinion and emotional defenses, by encouraging "cultural stories" that reduce public anxiety. Consequently "individuals will have to have a different relationship with emotions of powerlessness, fear, and guilt" in order to respond to climate change (Norgaard, 2006, p. 392).

Reaction Formation. Like denial, reaction formation is used to deny a painful feeling, but in this case, *also* gives intense energy to expressing its opposite. For example, the vehemence with which some environmentalists proclaim self-denying, holier-than-thou, judgmental attitudes about yuppies suggests that they haven't thoroughly dropped their own instinctual drives toward creature comforts themselves (Randall, 2005). Likewise the sneering hostility with which Wise Use proselytizer Ronald Arnold described environmentalists as "pathological fools"

(Arnold, 1993, p. 42) who buy into "spiritual crap" (p. 30) makes us wonder about his former role as a Sierra Club official. In these cases, it is not the belief or attitude that is questionable, but the hostility with which it is expressed that suggests underlying emotional conflict.

Projection. Projection occurs when people perceive in others what they fail to notice in themselves; thus, like denial and reaction formation, projection reflects underlying anxiety. Most judgments and criticisms of others involve some degree of projection, especially when criticisms are heated or derisive. After all, it is much easier to recognize weaknesses in others than in oneself. For example, Deborah was very irritated by (the 2008 Republican Vice Presidential candidate) Sarah Palin's view that resource use and development is the essence of Alaska: "From further oil and gas development, to fishing, mining, timber, and tourism, these developments remain the core of our state" (Palin, 2007). This statement entirely disregards native peoples, who rarely profit from developers. How myopic! Yet, it is painful for Deborah to recognize that she, too, often overlooks the interests of native peoples. Building a new home in Hawaii has changed the landscape for local people who have lived there for generations, not to mention helped to raise the tax base, putting stress on people with lower incomes. Seeing herself similar to Sarah Palin in this respect is very uncomfortable. People project when they fail to acknowledge that their own behaviors are like those they are criticizing. For example, consider the Norwegian who claimed:

> The Kyoto agreement is about cutting carbon dioxide emissions by 5 percent. And even that ridiculous[ly slow] pace was too much for the climate-hooligan George W. Bush in the United States. The head of USA's environmental protection department said that "we have no interest in meeting the conditions of the agreement." Well, that may be so, but it is other countries that will be hit the hardest from climate change. (Norgaard, 2006, p. 388)

The interviewer commented:

> Yet despite widespread criticism of the U.S. for taking such a position, this is essentially the same move that the Norwegian government made in dropping national emissions targets, increasing oil development, and shifting the focus from a national to an international agenda (Norgaard, 2006, p. 388)

Apathy. Although not one of Freud's defense mechanisms, we are adding the concept of apathy to our list as an important emotional defense. Environmentalists have lamented the public's apparent apathy (indifference or boredom) concerning environmental problems, as environmental concern peaked in the 1990s, to be later eclipsed by worries about terrorism and the economy (Brechin & Freeman, 2004; Dunlap, 2006). Obviously, people know about environmental problems, but they seem to have lost their ability to care about them. However, from a psychoanalytic perspective, the public is not apathetic about environmental concerns; more likely, apathy serves as a defense mechanism. Since people do not see easy solutions, they eventually stop paying attention if problems seem insurmountable. People often go numb and shut down emotionally in times of trauma (Lifton, 1982). Thus, the problem with the public may not be that they lack caring, but that they are paralyzed by caring so much. Psychotherapy can provide clues on how to deal with people who display apathy:

> Rather than act like a disciplinarian therapist who shouts at a patient for being too slow, neurotic or unable to face the truth, we can learn lessons from how good psychoanalytic practice works: by finding the right ways both to inform and inspire, and stimulate action rather than paralysis. (Lertzman, 2008, para 11; Segal, 1987)

Sublimation. Finally, Freud proposed that the most mature and healthy defense mechanism is sublimation, when people channel unconscious anxiety into socially acceptable projects. Expressing pain through creative music, poetry, or painting, or alleviating anxiety by writing a book (!) are popular forms of sublimation. Joining an environmental organization, working to reduce pollution in your community, and modifying your own consumption habits are all examples of sublimation. By channeling the feelings into a culturally useful creation, the individual is protected while also contributing something of value. Freud, himself a disciplined and arduous worker, continually sublimated his own anxiety through his prolific and brilliant writing.

Freud believed that defense mechanisms are inevitable and necessary; indeed, he argued that civilization depends on the inhibition of basic impulses and thus on the defenses that prevent their direct expression. Without them, people would inappropriately display all sorts of dangerous libidinal or aggressive behavior (like promiscuous sexuality or murderous rage). Defenses allow for the normal functioning of the individual in a society that requires people to behave, conform, cooperate, and adapt in spite of strong biological drives.

But defenses always extract a price. Defenses use emotional and physical energy, that limited physical commodity, for which various psychic structures compete. To the extent that energy is tied up by defense mechanisms, less is available for creativity, spontaneity, or realistic problem solving. The extreme case of a completely defended person is the textbook neurotic who spends so much time warding off unacceptable impulses that little else is possible. Surely you have met a few people like this in your lifetime, people who are afraid of experiencing anything new, and can only rigidly perform familiar behaviors; such rigidity is maintained at the expense of emotional intimacy, creative vitality, or productive service to others. These people are shut off: from others, from the larger world, as well as from their own creative potential. The more completely people defend themselves against emotional discomfort, the more inauthentic is their experience (Cox, 1982; Lertzman, 2007), and the more wasted is their existence (Bodnar, 2008).

Humans need all their creative potential to solve environmental problems. Thus, from a Freudian point of view, people must gradually confront their defenses, loosening them slowly so that they may go beyond them without being overwhelmed by anxiety. To do this, they must be willing to experience gradually increasing states of discomfort; experiencing discomfort is the first step toward solving environmental problems. For example, people cannot begin the difficult problem of environmental cleanup until they allow themselves to feel the anger, disgust, or guilt that confronting hazardous waste sites will elicit. Humans must be willing to feel dismay, sadness, and fear about their ecological predicament in order to free up the psychic energy used by the defenses, so that energy can be redirected to creative problem solving.

Critique of Freud and Psychoanalysis

Much of Freud's theory about sexual drives, symbolic expressions, and therapeutic interventions has been reworked or abandoned by contemporary psychoanalysts. The importance of Freud's contribution has been matched by the vehemence with which his ideas have been attacked. As psychologists who are basically more appreciative than critical of his views, we are often impressed by the hostility with which his ideas are criticized (and wonder about the defense mechanisms that might be at work!). Nevertheless, there are important flaws in Freud's theory to address.

First, Freud's work is criticized most often because there are few empirical studies to support it. Freud claimed to be a scientist, but as he, himself, admitted, he didn't have the means to scientifically test his ideas about how the brain functioned (Bilder & LeFever, 1998). Most of his major principles do not easily translate into measurable observations. A related problem is that quite opposite behaviors are explained by the same mechanism, making it difficult to test whether the mechanism is present or absent. For example, if you violently object to Freud's theory, he might say you are defending against your anxiety: because his theory is so accurate, you find it threatening. Here Freud's theory is untestable because there is no way for it to be contradicted. Whether or not you approve of his theory, his theory is supported. A proposition that cannot be empirically contradicted cannot be empirically supported.

Others criticize Freud for his biased, culturally relative ideas about sexuality and gender roles. In particular, feminists have critiqued his distorted view of women, and his inability to take them seriously. His belief that females have "penis envy" is particularly repugnant, although the fact that females might desire the power given to males in a patriarchal society is less problematic. Feminist psychoanalysts have abandoned some of his concepts, while relying on others. For example, focusing on the unconscious elements of parenting relationships, a psychoanalytic theory of gender development by Nancy Chodorow (1978, 1989) has been widely influential. This theory posits that because the daughter separates from the mother later than the son does, daughters have relatively greater needs than sons for maintaining connected relationships. Boys have relatively greater needs for building and maintaining separation. Thus, girls are socialized to care about relationship and the needs of others, and this psychoanalytic explanation can help explain their relatively greater environmental concern (discussed in more detail in Chapter 4).

In spite of the controversy surrounding Freud's work, it is worth underscoring his extraordinary contributions. Freud launched clinical psychology by addressing, defining, and treating the neurotic patterns in his patients as psychological disorders. His revealing self-analysis helped show that normal people use defenses and display character patterns that are simply more obvious in the neurotic patient, but not qualitatively different from normal functioning. His careful scrutinizing, theorizing, and prodigious writing contributed an insightful theory of the unconscious, illumination into an array of defense mechanisms, and elucidation of the concept of conflict in everyday behavior. Although specifics of his treatment techniques and interpretations have been largely discarded, his theorizing about defenses has withstood the test of time, research, and empirical test (Smith, Nolen-Hoeksema, Fredrickson, & Loftus, 2003). Cognitive dissonance theory (described in Chapter 4), for example, produced a set of empirical demonstrations of rationalization. Thus, in spite of some limitations, Freud's contributions remain profound.

OBJECT RELATIONS THEORY:
REEXPERIENCING THE MOTHER

ORT complements Freudian theory in explaining why some people care so passionately about the condition of ecosystems, the well-being of other species, future generations, and other people in far-off lands, while other people seem oblivious. The central premise of ORT is that *people develop their sense of self from their interactions with others, particularly the person who was their primary caretaker* (a biological or adoptive mother or father, or other caretaker). Interaction with that important first person lays a template upon which human beings organize and interpret later relationships. The self is not a given, but a complicated psychological project that takes several years to be completed.

From an ORT perspective, the phrase Mother Earth makes tremendous sense: People experience their relationship with the planet in terms of their relationship to their mother. The earliest encounter with the first object—the caretaker or mother—becomes a foundation for relationship with all other objects, including the earth. Although there do not seem to be any experimental tests of this claim, it makes conceptual sense that humans would project their earliest relationship on to their understanding of the world. Hence, the phrase Mother Earth is widespread across cultures (Merchant, 1980).

The term *object* in ORT may seem unfortunate in reference to other people, implying that they are to be treated as things rather than human beings. The term clearly comes from Freud who wrote repeatedly about how the child learns to channel biological drives from the target of the mother to other "love-objects". In his words,

> The child's first erotic object is the mother's breast that nourishes it; love has its origin in attachment to the satisfied need for nourishment. There is no doubt that to begin with, the child does not distinguish between the breast and its own body. . . . This first object is later completed into the person of the child's mother, who not only nourishes it, but also looks after it and thus arouses in it a number of other physical sensations, pleasurable and unpleasurable . . . [Herein] lies the root of a mother's importance, unique, without parallel, established unalterably for a whole lifetime as the first and strongest love-object and as the prototype of all later love relations. (Freud, 1940/1964, p. 56)

There are many variations of ORT and longstanding controversies about specifics (Greenberg & Mitchell, 1983). However, all object relations theorists agree that one's sense of self is constructed over time, in interaction with one's earliest caretakers. Empirical research has validated the central view that attachment processes occurring early in life affect later emotional functioning (Bowlby, 1989). More recently it has been argued that the ability to care deeply about the condition of the planet requires secure early attachments (Jordan, 2009).

Margaret Mahler (1972) proposed one widely held view of the developing self that takes place over several years. In her model, as the baby and caretaker learn to read each other's cues, they bond together and experience **symbiotic unity**. Although this unity is illusory, it is crucial for the child in order for it to learn to trust. If the caretaker is unresponsive to the infant's needs, or places too many demands on the infant in return, attachment will be impaired and a host of personality impairments will affect healthy relationships later in life. Gradually, however, the separation/individuation process begins. While learning to separate itself from the caretaker, the child frequently returns quickly for affirmation and comfort. Finally, the child learns constancy of self and object, coming to see itself in relationship to other separate beings. Healthy development makes it possible for people to experience themselves as integrated, multidimensional beings, who, like other people, possess both gifts and faults. Healthy object relations development gives rise to adults who can appreciate and care for themselves, while being able to love, bond, and serve others, without compulsive dependency on the one hand or fear of intimacy on the other.

The ability to experience one's separateness and yet bondedness with others is a complicated developmental task, which can be jeopardized during the critical days as well as years after birth. There are at least two ways in which the self–other relationship can be damaged, which would produce later impairment in relationships with other people and the environment: excessive early demands and attention withdrawn too early.

Excessive Early Demands

If the caretaker puts excessive demands on the baby, failing to read its cues, and inflicting instead the caretaker's needs, the child would learn to build a **false self** in which tending to the requirements of others is mistaken for attending to one's own most authentic needs. In this case, attachment would not involve the infant's genuine self, but instead an expected or attempted self. Such an individual would be incapable of true creativity because life would be lived in a state of exacted conformity.

For example, if the caretaker forces the child to eat when it is not hungry, wakes the child when it would prefer to sleep, or otherwise inflicts environmental pressures on the infant that do not fit its internal needs, an orientation to the external world would be created before the child organized its internal one. A rigid feeding schedule, popular with parents during the 1940s and early 1950s, would produce these too frequent demands, too early in the maturation process. The result would be a child who builds a false self, responding too often to outside pressures without being sufficiently tuned to one's internal bodily sensations. Split off from its own internal truth, the baby would develop into an adult who is focused on satisfying the norms of the social group, without adequate self-insight or direction.

Much of the irrationality of environmentally unsustainable behavior can be attributed to a false self-system. Without a firmly rooted internal organization, people are likely to use external objects to express who they are. Thus, people pursue material pleasures that really function as symbols of the self in relation to others. Automobiles are an example of a material luxury that do much more than move people from one location to the next: they also make a statement to others about who the drivers are. Some people feel personally embarrassed by (or proud of) driving one style of car rather than another. Clothes are another case of the use of material possession to express the externalized self. Clothes are typically chosen for style, and many people feel uncomfortable if they are not properly dressed for a certain occasion or diminished if their clothes do not feel attractive for one reason or another. Thus, most luxury items function to fulfill pleasure as well as status; *people enjoy not only what the object gives them, but also what it says about them.* Overconsumption is driven by a false self-process (Bodnar, 2008; Kanner & Gomes, 1995).

Even if people did not get caught up in conspicuous consumption, the false self-system would drive environmentally destructive behaviors by propelling them to take up careers that do not satisfy their deeper values or commitments. Many, perhaps most, jobs are done because they are available, rather than because people deeply believe that doing them will make the world a better place. No matter what work one does, a person is healthier psychologically if the job is chosen out of a belief that it is significant work, work that needs to be done in order for society to function more effectively. Pride in one's job and a sense of its value are signs of a healthy internal organization. Regardless of one's choice, questions about the right livelihood eventually surface, often in painful ways during midlife or old age, when people are likely to assess their contribution to the world. Less reliance on the false self makes it easier to choose the right livelihood earlier in life.

Attention Withdrawn Too Early

At some point, all caretakers must withdraw attention, but if it is done too early, trust in the outer world will be damaged. Most people are fortunate to have had enough good caretaking to bond with their caretaker and then tolerate well enough the inevitable separation–individuation that ensues (Winnicott, 1986). Yet because initial interaction with the caretaker is so delicate and so primordial, it rarely is perfect. Whatever small inadequacies it delivers, it lays the foundation for the experience of all other objects in the baby's psychological reality: the crib, the toy, the rest of the family, and eventually the group, the work unit, and finally the sense of the world. In short, one's relationship to the caretaker sets the foundation for one's relationship with the environment. Healthy functioning requires that people have faith that their needs will be met in the future; without this confidence, trust in the world is damaged. Damaged trust can lead to at least four neurotic reactions that are likely to impact environmentally relevant behavior: narcissism, compulsion, depression, and paranoia.

Narcissism. If an infant suffers a prolonged state of unmet needs, its orientation can become fixated on need gratification, producing a chronic state of narcissism. The child learns it cannot depend on the world to satisfy its desires. Such a child would have difficulty recognizing or respecting objects and people outside the self who do not offer to alleviate its needs.

From this viewpoint, environmental problems result from collective narcissism, in which people assume that nature exists for their need gratification. Inability to appreciate nature for its own complexity and beauty signals deeply seated narcissism, where people see the natural world only as resources that should be extracted and used for the comfort and convenience of human beings alone. At best, other species are irrelevant; more likely their well-being is threatened by their utility to satisfy humans' narcissistic needs.

In these terms, the anthropocentrism of the Western worldview (see Chapter 2) indicates limited psychological development. Psychological immaturity is expressed by assuming that humans are on top of the biological spectrum. The argument is not that humans should be forbidden to use other species or elements of the ecosphere; all species feed on one another, and life in general would be impossible without the food chain that subjects one species to another's biological needs. However, the Western tendency to regard *all* of the natural world as simply a storehouse of natural resources awaiting human use, misuse, and waste is narcissistic.

Narcissism can also prevent recognition of responsibilities to members of one's own species; for example, living for oneself and trying to suppress fears about the well-being of the next generation. When people focus on the safety of their own family and ignore others in their neighborhood or those in developing countries, psychological damage is maintained. Recognizing and concerning oneself with the needs of others requires going beyond individual need gratification, to widen one's caring for other humans and animals (see also our discussion of **scope of justice** in Chapter 4).

Compulsion. Narcissism can also set up the personality for addiction. Addictive behaviors are maintained by what Freud called **compulsion**, meaning any repetitive action that a person feels driven to make and is unable to resist. Compulsions involve drug or alcohol abuse, overeating, shopping, gambling, overworking, sexual hyperactivity, among other behaviors. As a defense mechanism, compulsions help people manage anxiety, because they organize experience around need satisfaction; the world is simply a place that offers or denies opportunities to satisfy one's addiction. Unfortunately, however, addictive needs and narcissistic impulses are never satisfied, because the target objects cannot feed the deeper unmet psychological need for self-definition (Fish, 2009; this idea of a deeper self is described in more detail in Chapter 10). Like environmentally destructive behaviors, addictions are not easy to manage, but can be, with diligence, patience, and social support (DiClemente, 2006; see also Chapter 5).

Depression. If the baby experiences caretaker withdrawal too suddenly, unmet needs can lead to chronic despair. The child would become vulnerable to depression, suffering a primal loss of confidence in the outside world and its own ability to affect it. A chronic sense of loss, hopelessness, cynicism, or grief would pervade the personality, especially whenever real losses are incurred. The ability to "keep the faith" would be difficult for such people.

Depression is a serious psychological problem that often leads to suicide or suicide attempts. In 2005–2006, more than 1 in 20 people in the United States experienced serious depression; suicide is now the third leading cause of death among persons 10–24 years and the second leading cause of death among 25–34 year olds (Centers for Disease Control and Prevention [CDC], 2008). From an ORT viewpoint, high rates of suicide are understandable in light of the large number of babies who are born to parents who are physically and/or emotionally unavailable to them, either through overwork, divorce, teenage pregnancy, substance abuse, or their own narcissism. Empirical evidence demonstrates that adults who are prone to depression are more likely than average to have lost a parent early in life (Barnes & Prosen, 1985). The psychoanalytic approach to depression underscores its link to unresolved mourning and loss (Leader, 2008).

Adult reactions toward environmental difficulties can easily lead to despair, especially as the complexity and the enormity of the problems become clearer (Macy & Brown, 1998). Understanding environmental problems can shrink one's trust that the world will provide, and in some ways diminished trust seems appropriate. On the other hand, finding active and creative solutions to a deteriorating physical world also requires that people stay hopeful, if not always confident. Ideas about how to maintain emotional fortitude in light of environmental threats are included at the end of this chapter and in Chapters 8 and 11.

Paranoia. Finally, a child could translate lack of trust into chronic paranoia, in which it experiences the world as an antagonistic place where only bad things happen. Such a person lives in a chronic state of fear and suspicion, fearful that at any moment someone may turn against her or him. Full scale paranoia is an unusual pathology, but more subtle versions are quite common. Consider, for example, Freud's view that nature stands in opposition to human existence, and must be tamed by technology so that its nefarious effects are reduced. From an ORT perspective, this view of a separate and threatening universe illustrates a cultural pattern of diminished trust projected onto nature (Miranda, 2007).

By now, you might be thinking that this is a lot of blame to place on early caretakers. Other schools in psychology, such as the behaviorists (who are the focus of Chapter 5), put more attention into investigating present causes of behavior, rather than people's early history. Focusing on the present can make it easier to see what and how to change. However, consider how hard it is to change habitual behaviors! Simply knowing one should change is rarely enough; perhaps you have noticed how difficult it is to change some of your own behaviors, including environmentally relevant ones. Therefore, it seems plausible to us that deeply patterned and unconscious experiences of the self, especially the self in relation to the world, play a crucial role in shaping adult behavior. From the ORT perspective, environmental problems result from early disruptions in psychological development (Plotkin, 2008; Sattmann-Frese & Hill, 2008). The key contribution of ORT is the proposition that the self is developed from many experiences that occur early in life, and lay down character patterns that are often durable and difficult to change.

Difficult, but not impossible. Although becoming conscious of character patterns is not easy, awareness offers the opportunity to make choices outside of those patterns. A paranoid person may become aware of the paranoia, and with the help and experience of more trustworthy relationships, choose to trust instead, even while knowing that trust feels awkward and difficult. Similarly, a compulsive shopper may become aware that shopping is an addiction that directly contributes to overconsumption and pollution, and choose to satisfy needs for connection through some other method, even though the unconscious impulse would still lead the person in the direction of the shopping mall. Choosing to contradict the pattern will not happen until one becomes conscious of it, and the myriad ways in which behavior is unconsciously driven. The important insight is that the sense of self in relationship to the world, as well as the defenses that people use to manage anxieties, are deeply organized patterns of perception, feeling, and behavior. Becoming aware of these patterns and habitual defenses offers the opportunity to see their constraints and begin to act outside of them.

USING FREUD'S IDEAS

One of the most important implications of the psychoanalytic approach is the need for negotiating defense mechanisms. Unfortunately, communications about environmental problems often stimulate defensive reactions by arousing fear and anxiety. Research shows that appeals based on fear rarely work to produce desired behavior change because anxiety motivates people to reject the message, rather than change their behavior (de Hoog, Stroebe, & de Wit, 2005; Janis & Freshbach,

1953; Ruiter, Abraham, & Kok, 2001). On the other hand, messages that include concrete actions that people can take to reduce threats are more effective because they stimulate hope (Groopman, 2004; Morse & Doberneck, 1995), as has been demonstrated with information campaigns about climate change (Rabkin & Gershon, 2007; Watrous & Fraley, 2007). Knowing something about the audience is also important. People who self-identify as environmentalists will act in more environmentally friendly ways after they are given negative feedback about their ecological footprint; but those who don't see themselves as environmentalists won't (Brook, 2005).

The form of psychotherapy Freud developed, called psychoanalysis, helps illuminate how to work with defense mechanisms to make the unconscious conscious. Since defense mechanisms block awareness, psychoanalysis requires that people learn to experience the feelings against which they are defending. Freud believed that emotional material must be allowed to surface and be expressed. He called this expression catharsis, a term borrowed from Aristotle. Catharsis is a spontaneous and powerful emotional expression that slips past the defenses. Freud saw psychic energy analogous to energy in a steam engine; if the energy isn't expressed somewhere, the system will eventually explode. Emotional discharge frees people from their tightly organized system of defenses, releasing energy that was tied up in keeping the unacceptable feelings unconscious.

Although catharsis isn't a popular idea in experimental psychology, it still carries import in psychoanalytic circles where it refers to the expression of emotional energy, though not necessarily explosive expression. People will not be able to creatively develop solutions to environmental problems unless and until they allow themselves to feel and express the painful emotions that environmental problems cause. Thus, the first step in solving environmental problems is to *experience what people don't want to experience: unpleasant feelings*, including anger, sadness, disappointment, despair, shame, fear, perhaps even terror. Some psychoanalytic thinkers have suggested that people resist thinking about environmental problems because to do so elicits their anxiety about death (Mishan, 1996; Nicholsen, 2002). But anxiety, terror, shame, and so forth are legitimate reactions to impending environmental collapse, and attempts to block them only stand in the way of true healing and successful problem solving. Without the direct experience and expression of such feelings, psychic energy must be allocated toward arranging a defense against them, thus robbing people of their full intelligence for finding creative solutions.

But how are people to experience these feelings without being overwhelmed by them? Psychoanalytic theorists (Nicholsen, 2002), and therapists using ORT, known as relational therapists (e.g., Santostefano, 2008), argue that people need to experience them in the safety of **holding environments** that is, the psychological security of a caring relationship. Originally the loving bond was the caretaker, but adults must find trusted allies who can be present with the expression of strong feelings, without themselves being overwhelmed by them. These allies can be therapists, mentors, teachers, and in some cases, close friends or partners.

Some workshops offer opportunities to work within holding environments; one form is called **despair and empowerment** groups (Macy, 1983; Macy & Brown, 1998*). Despair rests just under the surface of the psyche, embedded in feelings of powerlessness and meaninglessness (Lifton, 1982). Expressing despair often leads to concomitant experience of fear and anger. Such catharsis of powerful feelings liberates psychic energy, allowing the person to redirect energy toward adaptive solutions.

> Repression is physically, mentally and emotionally expensive: it drains the body, dulls the mind and muffles emotional responses. When repressed material is brought to the surface and released, energy is released as well; life comes into clearer focus. Art, ritual, and play have ever played a cathartic role in our history—just as, in our time, psychotherapy does too. By this process the cognitive system appropriates elements of its experience, and by integrating them gains a measure of both control and freedom. (Macy, 1983, p. 23)

Thus, from a psychoanalytic perspective, being willing to suffer the recognition of a collapsing ecosystem is *healthy and necessary.* The seriousness of the planetary predicament *should* produce strong feelings of terror, deep sadness, horror, and helplessness. People don't *want* to feel painful feelings, and they use myriad defenses to stay away from them. But once the feeling is fully experienced, the unconscious processes are interrupted and the full power of the person is newly available. Much resistance to full experience is a fear that such powerful feelings will be immobilizing. "If I allow myself to experience sadness, I will be overcome by chronic despair." Yet, just the opposite happens. Once you let

---

* See also Joanna Macy's Web site at http://www.joannamacy.net/

yourself experience the fullest degree of feeling, energy is mobilized and available for redirection. And when people become conscious of their negative feelings, they can learn to avoid them by taking positive actions, including proenvironmental behaviors. A recent field study showed that when people know they will feel badly about not recycling or taking public transportation, they are more likely to do both (Carrus, Passafaro, & Bonnes, 2008).

From a psychoanalytic perspective, deeply set instinctual drives will be difficult to change unless defenses are lifted and consciousness is increased. Adult character is built on an infantile pattern of neediness, and the accoutrements of adult society function as symbolic expressions of those needs. Although people do not really need luxury cars, they DO need validation that such a car (at least temporarily) provides. Thus it will be difficult to give up hard won ego accomplishments (Lertzman, 2008; Searles, 1972, 1979) unless people are willing to deconstruct social meanings of high status luxury items in a consumer culture. But insight into the ways in which behaviors are irrational expressions of underlying needs sets the opportunity for those needs to be satisfied in more direct ways. When people do the necessary emotional work of confronting and experiencing deeper feelings, behavioral changes will be sustained, rather than superficial and fleeting. Old habits can gradually be replaced by more aware and responsible behavior.

The Psychoanalysis of Environmentalists

Since defense mechanisms are inevitable, environmentalists are just as likely to use them as any one else. People who identify as environmentalists must also become conscious of unconscious processes by recognizing the emotional reasons for their behavior, including tracking their defenses and character patterns. For example, moralizing, holier-than-thou attitudes may reflect an unacknowledged repression of desire. Burnout, exhaustion, and internalized guilt are hefty emotional liabilities for environmental activists who remain out of touch with their emotions. The opposite syndrome, the role of eco-warrior, can be a form of narcissistic protection, enabled by the use of reaction formation to distance oneself from feelings of vulnerability (Randall, 2005). Only willingness to suffer uncomfortable feelings will provide the insight, energy, and creativity needed to stay on course to solve complicated environmental problems.

Reprinted from © Joseph Farris, Cartoon Stock [www.CartoonStock.com]. With permission.

In sum, a Freudian perspective suggests that you can begin to create a sustainable world by:

1. Being willing to experience your own despair, anxiety, sadness, or anger over a faltering physical world and the enormity of the global dimensions that drive its environmental crises.
2. Expressing those feelings fully in a safe place so that energy ordinarily used by your defenses can be freed up and redirected to creative solutions.
3. Recognizing your own defenses and gently working with them, seeking out troubling information and noticing how uncomfortable it makes you, noticing your reactions that help you avoid discomfort and patiently choosing alternative behaviors.

4. Recognizing your own unconscious needs to express personal identity through material consumption; finding alternative ways to direct your energy and your needs for self fulfillment.
5. Choosing behaviors that contribute to the creation of a sustainable world (for many examples of where to begin, see the Appendix).
6. Allowing and forgiving your inconsistent, ambivalent, anxious, or inefficient attempts to enact the new behaviors while remembering the huge instinctual forces that drive environmental destruction; being compassionate with yourself and others as you embrace change.

CONCLUSIONS

The psychoanalytic tradition provides a rich set of ideas with which to consider current ecological degradation. Freud formulated important understandings of the role of the unconscious, conflict, and defense mechanisms. ORT extended Freud's work to focus on the unconsciously constructed self and a way of thinking about variations in the self–world experience. In general, the psychoanalytic tradition suggests that changing humans' relationship to nature will not be an easy task. People have deeply rooted reasons to believe they are separate beings, competing for the resources of nature. But the psychoanalytic tradition also encourages reconsideration of these assumptions, by illuminating the unconscious and irrational mechanisms that support them.

Noticing how deeply seated are the impulses for environmentally inappropriate behavior also suggests that people should be compassionate with themselves and with others, realizing that humans are collectively facing a monumental task. Behavior change will not be easy; disappointment and frustration about its slow pace is likely. But over time, in safe emotional relationships, people can free up psychic energy for the crucial task of changing behavior and building a sustainable world. Compassion is crucial for one's self (forgiving one's own errors) as well as for others (especially those who don't agree with one's perspective). One of Sue's students provides a good example of this point. Her father was adamant about his antienvironmental opinions. After taking Sue's class on environmental psychology and reading about defense mechanisms, the student practiced hearing his views, listening with full attention, letting him know that she understood his perspective, and then gently offering alternative viewpoints. Ultimately he shifted some of his environmentally destructive behaviors. When people feel heard, understood, and cared for, it is a lot easier to change longstanding patterns.

Freud himself was more pessimistic. As a determinist, Freud saw little hope for the ability of human beings to survive and transcend the incontrovertible forces of nature that ply against them at every turn. Freud well understood human efforts to fend against nature, and even glimpsed the destructive potential that fighting nature could bring. By suggesting that we "have gained control over the forces of nature to such an extent that [we] would have no difficulty in exterminating one another to the last [hu]man" (Freud, 1930/1964, pp. 39, 92), Freud recognized the destructive power that control of nature elicits, even 20 years before the creation of the atomic bomb. Since it is no easier to control human nature than it is to control physical nature, an illusion of technological control is both dangerous and disturbing. Likewise, one traditional analytic thinker recently argued that "desire is not sustainable at the level of the individual. We are not green" (Roth, 2008), meaning that humans can never find refuge from their instincts and can never escape conflict.

Yet people do not have to adopt either Freud's determinism or his pessimism to use and profit from psychoanalytic approaches. To the extent that you are willing to experience some discomfort, you can begin to examine your own defense structure, and the underlying object relation pattern that it supports. Have you ever noticed that it is the more mature, self-aware and insightful people who are able to note their limitations without being devastated by them? They are even able to laugh at their own errors. When people have enough ego strength to embrace failure, they can pursue difficult challenges (Crocker, Brook, Niiya, & Villacorta, 2006) and even confront death (Vess & Arndt, 2008) without becoming defensive. In the meantime, recognizing the dangers posed by thinking shortcuts, attempts to justify actions and ward off discomfort, and habitual endeavors to soothe vulnerable self-concepts can enable people to become more mature, more compassionate, more conscious, and ultimately more likely to survive.

Although making the unconscious conscious takes hard work, sustaining one's insights and behavior changes is unlikely without social support. Many contemporary ORT thinkers use "relational theory" (Mitchell, 1988), which emphasizes the multiple and fluid ways that other people influence unconscious patterns. From this vantage point, the early caretaker is joined by the family, peer groups, and culture as key players affecting the individual. After all, each individual must learn "how to encounter, support and nourish a true self in a society that has long ago abandoned that mission toward individuals, as well as toward the planet upon which our lives depend" (Bodnar, 2009, personal communication). In other words, supportive human relationships are crucial for creating wise people, especially in a culture that generally encourages behaviors that are destructive to both persons and the environment. This point brings us to the topic of social psychology, which is focused on the pivotal role that others play in environmentally relevant behavior.

4

SOCIAL PSYCHOLOGY: UNDER
THE INFLUENCE OF OTHERS

Imagine that you are at a party with some friends. One of them is talking about the Environmental Issues Club she belongs to and its work on the Endangered Species Act (ESA). The ESA, a federal regulation adopted in 1973, makes it illegal to engage in any practice that threatens the extinction of a species, like the Northern Spotted owl or Chinook salmon. Since its adoption, lawmakers have continuously discussed revising or dropping the ESA because efforts to protect certain species hinder some industries, such as timber and oil. Your friend explains that her group is collecting signatures to send to Congress to urge them *not* to weaken the ESA. You don't know much about the issue one way or another, but you like your friend a lot, so along with the rest of the people standing there, you decide to sign her petition. After all, it does seem reasonable to try to protect species from extinction. Her argument that other species shouldn't perish because of human actions makes sense.

A few days later she calls to thank you for your support, and tells you there is a meeting next week to learn more about the legislation and the grassroots efforts to save the ESA. As she is talking, you start thinking about a letter you read earlier that morning in the newspaper. It was written by a prominent community business man and it argued that the ESA is a threat to freedom and the free market system. He believes that protecting wildlife is a luxury we can't afford in hard economic times. You thought the letter was well written and you see his point about government interference with business opportunities, especially with so many people losing their jobs and homes. Now you feel torn. What do you tell your friend? Will you go to the meeting? Are you more likely to go to the meeting because you previously signed the petition? How does your liking for your friend stack up against your respect for the businessman in influencing your decision? Are you likely to weigh his opinion more because he is male? Does the fact that he is a male affect his attitudes about environmental issues?

In this example we see some important topics of **social psychology**, the scientific study of social influence. *Social influence refers to the impact of other people on one's thoughts, feelings, and behaviors.* Even when you are by yourself, social influence keeps working because you internalize what you learn from others, including beliefs about who you are, how the world works, and how to think about everything, including environmental problems. In the ESA example, even though you go back to your room alone to consider your friend's request, you carry your social world with you. Although people like to think their attitudes and behaviors are based on rational and logical assessment of facts, a glimpse at social psychology reveals the enormous power of social influence, which generally goes unrecognized in daily life. One's attitudes, reasoning, values, and actions are all continually impacted by other people. From a social psychological perspective, then, understanding and actions about environmental issues are largely social phenomena (Clayton & Brook, 2005; Clayton & Myers, 2009).

In this chapter, we examine the social psychology of environmental problems in the context of major topics that have received much research attention: norms, values (especially materialism), attitudes, social identity, and gender. By the end of the chapter, we hope you'll agree that what you do about environmental problems arises from an intriguing composite of powerful social influences.

NORMS

A **norm** is a rule for expected behavior. Norms guide individual actions by suggesting what is normal, expected, or correct. Whether you are aware of it or not, you are constantly "reading" social settings to determine appropriate language, manner, gestures, and other behaviors. For example, if most of your friends sign the ESA petition, that provides a norm and increases the likelihood that you will also sign. People become so dependent upon these kinds of cues that they usually only notice how important they are when it is difficult to decipher them. Social psychologists distinguish between several types of norms, which exert their influence through different mechanisms (see Table 4.1).

Social Norms

Social norms refer to the behavior of others. One type is called **descriptive norms**, which are beliefs about what other people do in a particular situation (Cialdini, Reno, & Kallgren, 1990). Descriptive norms are crucial for promoting environmental behavior. A classic example of how descriptive norms get communicated for littering behavior was conducted in a parking garage (Cialdini, Kallgren, & Reno, 1991). Researchers placed handbills on the windshields of cars. Drivers approaching their cars from the garage elevator experienced one of two conditions: either the garage was littered with handbills, or the garage was clean and litter free. The experimenters observed what the drivers did with the handbill on their windshield. Knowing something about norms and how they are communicated, what would you predict? Drivers were far more likely to throw their handbill on the ground in the already littered garage.

This experiment explains something Deborah could never figure out about the neighborhood where she once lived in South London. The streets were constantly blowing with litter and she often observed Londoners contributing even more to it. As a visitor from the United States, she was revolted by such behavior and thought her neighbors crass and insensitive. A more social psychological explanation

Table 4.1 Norms that Influence Environmental Behavior

Concept		Definition	Example
Norm		Rule for expected behavior	Don't litter
Social		Norms communicated by other people	
	Descriptive	Perception of what others are doing	Litter accumulating in a parking lot
	Injunctive	"Ought to" statements	People shouldn't litter
Personal		Your own moral code	I feel responsible for having a small ecological footprint
	Introjected		I feel guilty if I buy nonorganic milk
	Integrated		I buy organic milk because it makes sense and is habitual

would be that the litter continued by virtue of the descriptive norm it expressed. Analogously, Deborah attended a convention of the American Psychological Association, where she noticed recycling containers placed in some hallways but not others. Notably, there were no containers at the convention registration desk, as there had been at previous conventions, so people weeding out their folders had no place to recycle. Many looked for bins with (what appeared to be) frustration. Previous placement of the containers had communicated a norm for recycling behaviors, but when the containers were no longer available, the norm persisted and produced distress.

Descriptive social norms can either increase or decrease proenvironmental behavior (Cialdini, 2003). Case in point: You may have noticed signs posted in college dorms stating the percentage of college students who have more than four drinks in one evening. These campaigns were intended to discourage binge drinking by presenting descriptive norms. However, they weren't very effective (Wechsler et al., 2003), in part because they inadvertently communicated that abstaining from drinking is deviant! Likewise and more central to our point: Energy consumption can be increased or decreased by descriptive norms depending on whether the norm is above or below one's current energy use. When researchers communicated average neighborhood energy use in one community, people who had been above the norm used less energy, while those who learned they were below the norm subsequently used more! (Schultz, Nolan, Cialdini, Goldstein, & Griskevicius, 2007).

In contrast to descriptive norms, **injunctive norms** are beliefs about social approval or disapproval for particular behaviors (Cialdini et al., 1990). In Deborah's rural community, for example, she sees many home vegetable gardens (a descriptive norm), and the Country Fair gives prizes for the best produce, which communicates publicly that vegetable growing is valued by others (an injunctive norm). Many environmentally relevant behaviors including littering, stealing petrified wood from a national park, and recycling are affected by indications of approval or disapproval from others. Unfortunately, injunctive norms can be subverted by destructive descriptive norms (Cialdini, 2003). If you see others throwing cigarette butts on the ground (descriptive norm), an injunctive norm communicated by a sign saying, "Protect our stream! Please dispose of butts and other trash responsibly" will likely be ignored. On the other hand, injunctive and descriptive norms can operate in parallel. Recent research demonstrated that more guests reused towels in hotel rooms when signs were placed in bathrooms indicating that other guests had requested such conservation measures (injunctive norm), and mentioning the large number of guests who reuse their towels (descriptive norm; Schultz, Khazian, & Zaleski, 2008).

Most people underestimate the degree to which their behavior is affected by social norms. People believe they act because of common sense, or their logical decisions, rather than because of social pressure to conform to others' behavior. Social psychologists call this error the **introspection illusion** (Pronin, Berger, & Molouki, 2007). For instance, we all wear clothes that seem appropriate without questioning where our sense of appropriateness comes from: observing what others are wearing. Introspection illusions are an important factor in promoting proenvironmental behaviors, which are often caused more by norms than one might think. One study showed that intentions to conserve energy correlated more highly with beliefs about how often neighbors conserve than the desire to save money, save the environment, or benefit society in general (Nolan, Schultz, Cialdini, Goldstein, & Griskevicius, 2008). And yet, people in this study reported that their beliefs about neighbors' behavior had less impact than their desire to save money or the environment. Thus, people are not very conscious about social influences on their behavior.

Social norms can be transmitted by subtle features of a situation, or by hearing about what other people are doing. **Social diffusion** occurs when people change their behavior to be in line with what others do. Like a fashion that spreads throughout a group, environmentally appropriate behavior can be induced through interactions with others. You are much more likely to sign the ESA petition if everyone else at the party is signing it because others communicate a norm that is easy to read. Likewise, the personal relationship with your ESA friend and the ESA-relevant attitudes of your other friends are going to be important determinants of your response to her request. One classic study demonstrated that the best predictor of whether or not people purchased solar equipment was the number of acquaintances they had who owned solar equipment (Leonard-Barton, 1981). Similarly, a strong predictor of recycling is having friends and neighbors who recycle (Oskamp et al., 1991). Community energy conservation programs that send information through existing social networks are effective (Darley & Beniger, 1981; Stern, Dietz, & Black, 1986; Weenig, 1993), and people are more likely to switch over to nontoxic cleaners when they have a chance to discuss doing so in groups (Werner, 2003; Werner, Byerly, & Sansone, 2004). People often change behaviors when they see neighbors, family, or friends change theirs (Rogers, 1995).

Reprinted from © Chris Madden [http://www.chrismadden.co.uk/]. With permission.

When people conform to friends and neighbors, they use them as a reference group: A constellation of others who portray standards with which to evaluate one's own attitudes, abilities, or current situation. A reference group consists of people who are liked or respected, and they can have big effects on environmentally relevant behavior through the power of normative influence. For example, Deborah noticed that she is much less likely to order meat when dining out with her vegetarian friends than with her meat eating friends, and is more likely to bring used paper to write on when she goes to Conservation and Recycling Committee meetings than other committee meetings. Other people in our environment serve as models (Bandura & Walters, 1963); their behaviors communicate social norms. Remember the parking lot experiment with handbill littering? Subsequent research showed that when someone was observed picking up handbills from the ground, littering decreased (Kallgren, Reno, & Cialdini, 2000).

Reference groups don't have to be physically present to be powerful. Simply making norms salient is enough to change environmentally relevant behavior:

> The Washington Energy Office enlisted high-profile architects and builders and used highly publicized meetings between the governor, the builders, and the building owners in designing

its Energy Edge program. . . . The Energy Edge program made energy-efficient design prestigious and a status symbol for new buildings. Smaller, lesser-known developers indirectly disseminated the technology by imitating the program's features. (Dennis, Soderstrom, Koncinski, & Cavanaugh, 1990, p. 1115)

Obviously, people do not just pay attention to presented facts. Even if they don't realize it, people attend to a host of other variables, including the social status of the communicator. One of the earliest findings in social psychology is that the **credibility of the source makes a difference.** If two different people present exactly the same information, the one seen with more credibility—typically the one with higher social status—will be more persuasive. Environmentally responsible consumer choices are influenced by high status people who know about and choose environmentally friendly behaviors (Flynn & Goldsmith, 1994). In one classic study, New York City residents cut their electricity use by 7% when asked in a letter with New York State Public Service Commission letterhead (Craig & McCann, 1978). But when the same letter was sent on Con Edison stationary, the plea had no effect. Apparently, people trusted or respected the Public Service Commission more than they did Con Edison. That's why actor Leonardo DiCaprio's documentary *The 11th Hour* (DiCaprio et al., 2007) may be a useful contribution to environmental awareness; certainly Al Gore's *An Inconvenient Truth* (David et al., 2006) did much to stimulate public consciousness about climate change.

The importance of source credibility is the foundation of the Union of Concerned Scientists; a group of over 150,000 scientists "whose *modus operandi* is to bring credible science into public discourse and the policy process in an accessible manner" (Cole & Watrous, 2007, p. 183). On the other hand, social scientists working on climate change also recognize the persuasive influence of "people like us" (Chess & Johnson, 2007). Since climate change is a global issue and the public tends to think its effects will be distant, they do not prioritize it over other issues like the economy, education, and health care (Leiserowitz, 2007). For this reason, messages that emphasize local effects communicated by local figures can be more effective than those made by nationally recognized scientists (Cole & Watrous, 2007; Leiserowitz, 2007). Balancing messages to maximize both scientific credibility and public engagement is an art in matters about climate change (Dilling & Moser, 2007), as it is with all environmental issues.

Some behaviors are difficult to influence via social norms because they are typically not done in public. For example, backyard composting is usually unobservable to neighbors. But when householders were asked to post decals that demonstrated their participation in a composting program, backyard composting in the neighborhood increased (McKenzie-Mohr, 2000b). Likewise, when people were given information about their neighbors' recycling behavior, they increased their own recycling and sustained that increase (Schultz, 1998).

Laws and regulations contribute greatly to social norms by requiring environmentally responsible behavior. The Civil Rights Act of 1964 outlawed racial discrimination and set into motion a tidal change of public rejection of segregation. Likewise, federal laws regulating Corporate Average Fuel Economy (CAFE) standards that reduce oil consumption and emissions can communicate acceptable minimum levels of fuel efficiency and could facilitate public scorn of fuel inefficient travel. Fortunately, President Obama has already increased CAFE standards (Hansen, 2009).

Personal Norms

Personal norms are feelings of obligation to act in a particular way. Personal norms are potent influences on environmental behavior because people try to avoid the guilt and remorse experienced when they are broken. Personal and social norms often function in parallel; for example, you might feel guilty for not showing up to the ESA meeting after learning that most of your other friends did. But personal and social norms can be different. Deborah feels guilty when she forgets to take her reusable stainless steel cup to the coffee shop because of her personal norm about wasting paper cups, though she rarely sees others bringing their own cups, which would communicate a social norm.

Personal and social norms are important for choosing public transportation. You might take the bus instead of driving because you feel morally obligated (personal norm), or because you believe others would disapprove of your driving (injunctive social norm), or you see that everyone else in your neighborhood is taking the bus (descriptive social norm). Recent research in two German cities shows that choosing to use public transportation depends on (a) believing other people think it's important (injunctive social norm), and (b) feeling personally obligated out of moral principles (personal norm; Bamberg, Hunecke, & Blobaum, 2007).

People act on personal norms to avoid guilt, whether or not other people disapprove. For this reason personal norms are considered deeper and more potent than social norms. When people are intrinsically motivated by their own values to act in environmentally friendly ways, they are more consistent and committed, relative to people who act out of extrinsic reasons, such as group pressure, rewards, or convenience (Pelletier, Tuson, Green-Demers, Noels, & Beaton, 1998; Ryan & Deci, 2000).

Recent research has distinguished two types of personal norms: Introjected norms cause guilt if broken, whereas integrated personal norms are deeper and so well internalized into one's behavior that avoiding guilt isn't even an issue (Thogersen, 2006). For example, when Deborah first started taking her own cloth bags to the grocery store, she felt guilty if she didn't; years later she does it because it seems like a sensible thing to do and she doesn't consciously think about it. In this case, the norm is integrated and has become a habit. Various proenvironmental behaviors such as buying organic produce and dairy products, buying energy saving light bulbs, composting kitchen waste, and using public transportation for work and shopping are all under the control of different kinds of personal norms. Buying organic food appears to be more internalized, and use of public transportation, least (Thogersen, 2006).

Identity

When norms become very deeply internalized (integrated) they give rise to identity: a sense of oneself, of who one thinks one is. Identities have both personal and collective features. For example, you may be a straight-A student (personal identity), as well as a member of a soccer team (social identity). In Chapter 10, we will explore more fully the personal dimensions of environmental identity known as ecological identity, when one experiences one's self as an integral part of the natural world. Personal and social identities can overlap. For now, we focus on social identity—identity that is derived from a group. Groups shape important dimensions of one's sense of self, and can thereby powerfully affect environmentally relevant behavior. When Deborah defines herself as an environmentalist, it carries collective meaning. It implies participation in a social movement (Dunlap & McCright, 2008b), and when she goes to meetings of her local environmental group, Sustainable Kohala, she experiences her group identity. Not surprisingly, when people see themselves as environmentalists, they act in more environmentally friendly ways (Dunlap & McCright, 2008b; Kempton & Holland, 2003; Wade-Benzoni, Li, Thompson, & Bazerman, 2007). They also participate in environmental groups and believe the environmental movement is important (Dunlap & McCright, 2008b).

Unfortunately, group membership also inspires stereotypes and prejudice because people quickly make distinctions between the in-group and out-group (Tajfel & Turner, 1986), withholding resources and treating members of the out-group with less concern than those in their in-group (Whitley & Kite, 2006). One study showed that ranchers and environmentalists in conflict over rangeland perceived each other quite negatively, each claiming the moral high ground, and dubbing the other group as hypocritical and undeserving (Opotow & Brook, 2003). Group identities often lock in conflict and prevent constructive solutions to environmental problems. Promoting environmentally responsible behavior can be facilitated by recognizing the risks of we–they thinking and taking steps to reduce it (Winter, 2006), for example, by noticing negative judgments and expressing vulnerability. Likewise, collaborative learning between groups can facilitate solutions by shifting group identities and promoting superordinate goals (Samuelson, Peterson, & Putnam, 2003).

Personal Norms and Environmental Justice

Personal norms (at least of the introjected type) guide one's sense of right and wrong. People feel guilty when they break them, as Deborah does when she fails to bring her cup to the coffee shop. Although stores give small (3¢–10¢) rebates for bringing bags or cups, her guilt is not about financial loss or disapproval from friends, but a sense of responsibility to future generations and betrayal of her caring for the planet. Since the rewards for many proenvironmental behaviors are more personal than social, recycling and other actions have often been considered as moral behavior (Thogersen, 1996). In general, principled moral reasoning, the most advanced of moral development, predicts concern for the environment (Karpiak & Baril, 2008).

A sense of moral responsibility and fairness brings us to the concept of **environmental justice**, which the U.S. Environmental Protection Agency (2009) defines as "fair treatment and meaningful involvement of all people, regardless of race, color, national origin or income, with respect to the development, implementation and enforcement of environmental laws, regulations, and policies." Unfortunately, clear and disturbing patterns of unfair environmental policies place populations of color and lower income at greater risk for exposure to pollution and other environmental hazards (Bullard, 1983, 1990, 1993, 1994, 1996; Bullard & Johnson, 2000). Although it was unjust patterns of pollution in the United States that led to the concept of environmental justice, the same picture is increasingly true globally: Industrialized countries export toxic waste and build hazardous sites in developing nations, putting their citizens at risk (Miller, 2008; Pellow, 2007). Likewise, on a global level, climate change is likely to adversely affect those least responsible for contributing to it (Agyeman, Doppelt, Lynn, & Hatic, 2007; Congressional Black Caucus Foundation, 2004; McNeeley & Huntington, 2007).

You would probably agree that all people should have a voice in environmental decisions regardless of race, color, or income and that environmental problems should be shared. Environmental justice seems an obvious moral guideline. However, the term *environmental justice* is tricky because both self-proclaimed environmentalists and antienvironmentalists use similar moral claims to justify opposing positions. For example, like environmentalists, antienvironmentalists appeal to claims for equal access by different groups, arguing that environmentalists are immoral when they promote banning access to public lands, because those regulations eliminate jobs or harm communities (Clayton, 1994). The film *In Light of Reverence* (2001) details the different worldviews of various groups (tribes, outdoor recreationists, miners, New Age spiritualists) competing for use of sacred places, each claiming that the other is immoral and violating their own right to access.

As defined by the EPA, environmental justice is a form of **distributive justice** as it implies that environmental resources, access, and problems ought to be distributed equally among different groups (Clayton, 2003b). Distributive justice contrasts with **procedural justice**, the fairness with which environmental decisions are made. While environmental and antienvironmental groups differ in their assessment of distributive justice, all groups greatly value procedural justice. Most people would agree that all stakeholders should have a voice and that harmful consequences should be minimized. But harmful consequences to whom? Distributive justice implicates equal distribution for all, including more distant interests, such as future generations and nonhuman species. Do future generations and nonhuman species have moral standing in questions of environmental justice? Or is it enough to concern ourselves with the underprivileged human beings who are currently alive, which is a big number in and of itself? Here our question about the ESA is directly at stake. How wide is your net of moral responsibility and what psychological mechanisms determine to whom you feel responsible?

While not very conscious about it, most humans usually assume their own species is an in-group (Crompton & Kasser, 2009), believing that other species have less right to exist and less moral standing. This view has been called **speciesism** (Singer, 1977/1990), a form of prejudice

Reprinted from © Dave Coverly. With permission.

analogous to racism, ethnocentrism, ageism, and sexism. Speciesism brings us back to the problem of the ESA, as well as animal rights and wildlife preservation. Speciesism depends on the assumption of a clear dividing line between humans and other animals, and so is:

> Challenged by every report of parrots who can count, of whales with globe-spanning languages, of elephant mourning and memory, of gorillas who acquire extensive sign language vocabularies, of cephalopods who solve spatial problems, of cows who escape slaughterhouses with prodigious feats of athleticism and cunning, of lifelong devotional pairings between birds, of ants who form intentional alliances in super colonies that stretch across hundreds of miles, or remarkable feats of dolphin intelligence. (Seager, 2003, p. 952)

Nobody has an infinitely wide **scope of justice** and those who fall outside it are seen as expendable, undeserving, or irrelevant (Opotow 1990, 1994, 2001; Opotow & Weiss, 2000). People avoid responsibility to those who are excluded in at least three ways (Opotow & Weiss, 2000):

- Denying outcome severity, by using double standards or concealing harmful outcomes ("they wouldn't care about water pollution"; "their water quality isn't that bad").
- Denying stakeholder inclusion ("they don't deserve clean water because they don't pay taxes").
- Denying self-involvement ("I'm not poisoning their water supply").

When Deborah smashed the carpenter ant in her kitchen (see Chapter 2), she didn't feel guilty because ants fall outside her scope of justice. Obviously her house and its other inhabitants (namely, her husband, dog, and cat) were inside her scope of justice and the ant, outside.

Why do people draw this arbitrary line? **Deep ecologists** (Devall & Sessions, 1985; Katz, Light, & Rothenberg, 2000; Sessions, 1995; Taylor & Zimmerman, 2005) argue that they shouldn't; other species have just as much right to their place on the planet as human beings. This idea is explored more fully in Chapter 10. For now, our point is that environmental justice can be fragile because it is so difficult to notice threats to the well-being of those who lay outside one's scope of justice. When people cannot hear the moral claims of those who disagree, and refuse to notice the ways in which their own moral judgments rest on denial and moral exclusion, environmental conflicts will endure.

Altruism, Morality, and the Values Beliefs Norms Theory

One way to highlight the moral dimension of environmentally relevant behavior is to conceptualize it as a case of **altruism, the motive to increase another's welfare without conscious regard for one's self-interests** (Myers, 2010). People help others, even if they do not gain personally. According to the **norm activation theory of altruism** (Schwartz, 1977), people help others (people or nonhumans) when situations elicit their feelings of personal obligation that is, introjected norms. The **Values Beliefs Norms (VBN) theory** (Stern, 2000; Stern, Dietz, & Kalof, 1993) builds on this idea and predicts that people will engage in proenvironmental actions when situations activate personal norms. But why doesn't everybody feel morally responsible about the environment? The VBN theory suggests that activation of personal norms depends on one's beliefs about the issues, which in turn depend on one's values (see Figure 4.1).

Values are desirable end states that transcend specific situations (Dietz, Fitzgerald, & Shwom, 2005; Schwartz & Bilsky, 1987). For example, you might go to the ESA meeting because you value wildlife and believe habitats should be preserved. Research demonstrates that people who behave in environmentally responsible ways value self-transcendence, unity with nature, and benevolence, rather than self-enhancement (power, wealth, achievement; Karp, 1996; Schultz & Zelezny, 1998).

The VBN theory underscores the pivotal role of values by positing them as basic in two ways (Dietz, Fitzgerald, & Shwom, 2005). First, values influence other elements in the model, exerting their effects on beliefs, which in turn affect norms, and then predict behaviors. In other words, how people interpret information, what they attend to, what they think humans are responsible for, and what they do about it, all stem from their basic value orientation. Values appear first in the model (on the far left of Figure 4.1) because they have

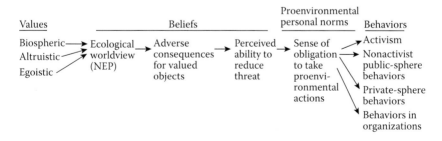

Figure 4.1 "Value-Belief-Norm Theory of Environmentalism." NEP: New Environmental Paradigm (see chapter 2). (Reprinted from Stern, P.C. (2000). *Journal of Social Issues, 412,* 56. With permission.)

the most widespread effects. You might have noticed that it is difficult to reduce someone's reliance on driving if they don't value the environment. Second, values are also basic because they are the most stable determinants of environmental behavior and thus the hardest to change.

A popular version of the VBN theory distinguishes between three categories of values: egoistic, altruistic, and biospheric (Stern et al., 1993). **Egoistic values** lead to concern about the environment because of direct impacts on the individual. The phrase, "**not in my backyard**" reflects an egoistic orientation. Some people only care about environmental issues if they are affected personally, for example, by a waste dump in their neighborhood that could poison their water supply, or the construction of wind farms that might ruin their view.

In contrast, people with **altruistic values** care about the environment because of its relevance for other *humans* including children, community members, future generations, and society in general. People with

© Benita Epstein

Tell the wild animals I have arrived.

www.benitaepstein.com

EGO TOURISM

altruistic values would find air pollution in Mexico City a problem because of its impact on residents' health, even if they personally would never travel there; climate change is a concern because it will lead to food shortages and starvation in many parts of the world, even though they themselves might be dieting to lose weight.

Finally **biospheric values** lead people to find environmental degradation problematic because it impacts ecological systems (the biosphere) including nonhuman animals, plants, oceans, forests, and so forth. Like deep ecologists, people with biospheric values regard ecological systems as important in themselves, beyond what they mean for human survival (altruistic) or personal comforts (egoistic).

In the VBN theory, **beliefs** mediate between values and norms to influence behavior (see Figure 4.1). Beliefs include those measured by the New Ecological Paradigm (NEP scale, discussed in Chapter 2), as well as *awareness of consequences* (driving a car contributes to climate change) and one's *perceived ability to reduce the threat* ("Even though I'm only one person, my driving contributes to pollution and climate change."). These beliefs affect how people perceive what others are doing or should be doing (norms), and the likelihood of acting in an environmentally responsible way.

The VBN theory can help predict whether you'll go to the ESA meeting by considering the fundamental role of values. Someone with an egocentric value system has a hard time understanding why business interests should be mitigated by the well-being of other ("less important") species. If you have biospheric values, you would be more likely to attend the meeting because you value the existence of other species for their own sake, you are more likely to feel responsible for their well-being (personal norm), and more likely to believe that political activism is useful (perceived ability to reduce threat). On the other hand, if your values are egocentric, you probably wouldn't attend, unless you saw that the ESA might impact your personal situation (perhaps your property value would be enhanced by safeguarding an endangered bird species). With egocentric values, you are less likely to experience personal responsibility for preserving biodiversity (i.e., "it's not my problem"), and you'd be less likely to see utility from political activism ("what difference does it make if I show up for the meeting?").

The VBN theory has generated a lot of empirical support (Black, Stern, & Elsworth, 1985; Fuhrer, 1995; Guagnano, 1995; Guagnano, Dietz, & Stern, 1994; Hansla, Gamble, Juliusson, & Gärling, 2008; Kaiser, Hubner, & Bogner, 2005; Karp, 1996; Schultz, 2001; Slimak & Dietz, 2006; Snelgar, 2006; Stern, Dietz, Abel, Guagnano, & Kalof,

1999). Values have been shown to underlie beliefs, which then affect personal norms (Steg, Dreijerink, & Abrahamse, 2005). Furthermore, feelings of personal obligation predict environmental behaviors (Bratt, 1999; Kaiser, Ranney, Hartig, & Bowler, 1999; Widegren, 1998). Proenvironmental behaviors like recycling (Vining & Ebreo, 1992), using public transportation (Hunecke, Blobaum, Matthies, & Hoger, 2001), and energy conservation (Kals, Schumacher, & Montada, 1999) are more likely when people feel morally responsible to undertake them (that is, experience an introjected norm).

Furthermore, both biospheric and altruistic values directly predict environmentally friendly behaviors such as buying organic food, contributing to environmental groups, and recycling (Karp, 1996). The VBN theory has brought the role of values to the fore, and illuminated their importance for framing messages to promote proenvironmental actions. Public messages should take into account the value orientations of the listeners (Schultz & Zelezny, 2003). For instance, the World Wildlife Federation recently discussed the VBN theory in a report urging greater focus on values, in order to accelerate the public's environmentally responsible behavior change (Crompton, 2008).

As one might expect, values differ across cultures. Although altruistic values are most commonly observed around the world, United States and European samples show a priority of egoistic over biospheric concerns, whereas Latin American countries tend to show higher biospheric than egoistic concerns (Schultz, 2002a; Schultz & Zelezny, 2003). In a recent study of six countries, five (Brazil, India, Germany, New Zealand, and the Czech Republic) scored higher on biospheric than egoistic concerns (Schultz et al., 2005). Across cultures, biospheric concerns directly correlate with proenvironmental behavior; egoistic concerns correlate negatively. That is, the more egoistic values people have, the less they are likely to engage in environmentally friendly behaviors.

Both the VBN theory and the concept of environmental justice emphasize the role of moral choices in proenvironmental behaviors. On the other hand, some have argued that appealing to morality is not necessarily the best strategy because doing so may overemphasize the implication of self-sacrifice (Kaplan, 2000). Assuming a moral perspective can communicate to people that they will have to give up their creature comforts, causing them to reject or ignore environmental information. Environmentalists have been accused of promoting feelings of helplessness and futility via "green guilt and ecological overload" (Roszak, 1994). Indeed, proenvironmental messages are more effective when framed in positive rather than negative terms (Lord, 1994); for example, "Ride the bus to help reduce climate changing emissions" rather than "Reduce your driving to reduce emissions." Thus, promoting empowerment and hope is likely to be more effective than moral appeals.

One way to offset helplessness and despair is to put people in problem-solving groups that bolster optimism (Kaplan, 2000). Since group support mitigates isolation, and both problem solving and collaborating with others are effective stress reducers (see Chapter 8), action groups may be a more effective strategy than appeals to morality. In other words, an alternative to the altruism and morality framework is to arrange conditions so that people experience success and social support for proenvironmental behaviors. From a social psychological perspective, groups that supply social norms of hope and positive vision are effective facilitators of environmentally responsible behavior.

A second problem with approaching environmental behavior as a moral issue is the likelihood that it can sponsor attribution problems. People rarely see the social world strictly in terms of overt actions; instead, **attributions** are constantly developed for explaining others' behaviors. He smiles when he's hiking in the wilderness because he's happy (an attribution). She drives her SUV (Sport Utility Vehicle) to work rather than taking public transit because she's selfish (an attribution). Attributions help people make sense of their world, create a sense of order and consistency, and provide convenient shortcuts for interacting with others. But attributions are often distorted by self-serving biases. During conflicts, people usually see their own behavior as honest, well meaning, and fair, and attribute the other's behavior to selfishness, greed, ignorance, or dishonesty (Winter, 2006). Interpreting environmental behavior as moral can contribute to this difficulty, by promoting attributions of others' behavior to immorality, thereby locking in conflict.

Theory of Planned Behavior

Rather than focusing on the values and morality underlying behavioral choices, the Theory of Planned Behavior (TPB) focuses on **intentions** (Ajzen, 1991, 1998). Specifically, TPB predicts that one's intention to act in environmentally responsible ways depends on three psychological elements: attitudes, norms (including both personal and social), and perceived behavioral control (see Figure 4.2).

An **attitude** is an evaluative belief about something (Eagly & Chaiken, 1998), like respect for your friend, skepticism about government regulations, or appreciation of wilderness. In a sense, the link

Table 4.2 Some Key Terms Used in this Chapter

Term	Definition	Example
Social Identity	Sense of who one is with regard to one's group membership	I am an environmentalist; I belong to Sustainable Kohala
Worldview	Generalized beliefs about the world	NEP or DSP (described in Chapter 2)
Values	Desired end points	Healthy ecosystems; wealth and material possessions
Egoistic		"Not in my backyard"
Altruistic		I worry about people in the Arctic Circle who are losing their habitat
Biospheric		I worry about polar bears in the Arctic Circle who are losing their habitat
Beliefs	Understandings about people, objects, and concepts	Species are going extinct; climate change is just liberal propaganda
Intention	Willingness or preference for undertaking a behavior	I plan to ride my bike instead of driving
Attitude	Evaluative belief about a specific object or person	The ESA is important because it protects other species
Behavioral control	Belief about your ability to do an action	I can't take a bus because there isn't one at the time I need it
Role	Set of norms that define how a person should behave	I am an environmentalist, so I buy used clothing

between attitudes and behavior is the central question of this book: Why is it that people seem concerned about environmental problems, and yet behave in environmentally irresponsible ways? The TPB says that behavior is an outcome of intention—but one's intention doesn't just depend on one's attitude. Intentions are also a function of perceived behavioral control and subjective norms. The TPB uses the term **subjective norm** to signify the perceived social pressure to perform an action. According to this theory, pressure can result from either descriptive or personal norms or both.

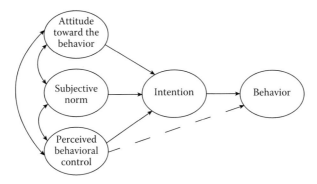

Figure 4.2 The theory of planned behavior predicts that intentions determine proenvironmental behavior, and that attitudes, norms, and control determine intentions. (Reprinted from Ajzen, A., *Organizational Behavior and Human Decision Processes, 50*(179), 182. With permission.)

The TPB also focuses on perceived **behavioral control,** which is believing one has the ability to perform a particular environmentally relevant action, and believing that action will be successful in accomplishing the intention. Behavioral control brings us to the concept of **constraints.** When a behavior is difficult, or you believe your behavior won't have any impact, perceived behavioral control is low and consequently, so is environmentally responsible behavior. For example, you can't recycle #4 plastic if your recycling station doesn't accept it. Thus, the TPB helps illuminate why behaviors often contradict attitudes and personal norms: Even if one wants to be environmentally responsible, it is not always possible to do so because of low levels of control. When constraints are high, they outweigh attitudes and values (Stern, 2005).

One obvious constraint is inconvenience or task difficulty. If the ESA meeting is held 800 miles away or at the same time as your sister's wedding, you won't attend the meeting no matter what your attitude is about the issue. Conversely, if the task is very convenient, the meeting is being held next door just as you pass by and have time to drop in, you'll be more likely to attend. In that case, the strength of your attitude won't predict your behavior very well either. Attitudes predict behavior best when the behaviors are only moderately difficult (Kaiser & Schultz, 2009); consequently, one of the best ways to promote environmentally responsible behavior is to make them easy. In other words, reduce the barriers to behavior change.

In addition to distance or cost, lots of other barriers get in the way of environmentally friendly actions. In an obvious example, regardless of attitudes or awareness about the implications of driving, people who live in areas without mass transport are more likely to drive (Tanner, 1999). Household energy use depends more on income and household size (financial and physical barriers), than attitudes or values (Gatersleben, Steg, & Vlek, 2002). Consequently, an important strategy for promoting proenvironment behavior called **Community Based Social Marketing**[*] (McKenzie-Mohr, 2000a, 2000b) urges community leaders to learn about specific barriers that prevent people from making good choices in any situation, and design interventions that minimize or reduce specific impediments. Focusing attention on reducing barriers will be more effective than trying to change people's moral choices.

In positing that behavior is a logical outcome of intentions, the TPB is "a theory of reasoned action" (Ajzen & Fishbein, 1980). The TPB thus emphasizes the more conscious and reasonable dimensions of environmentally relevant behavior, and it does a good job of predicting behaviors in a variety of domains, such as use of water saving technologies (Lynne, Casey, Hodges, & Rahmani, 1995), household recycling (Boldero, 1995; Taylor & Todd, 1995), choice of travel (Bamberg, Ajzen, & Schmidt, 2003; Bamberg & Schmidt, 2001), as well as general ecological behavior (Kaiser, Wolfing, & Fuhrer, 1999). Along with VBN theory, TPB is powerful and popular.

Recent research on TPB has added components that enhance the link between attitudes and behavior to increase its ability to predict intentions, and thus behavior. For example, knowing people's previous recycling behaviors and habits, as well as their perception about the availability of recycling facilities, increases investigators' ability to predict intentions (Knussen, Yule, MacKenzie, & Wells, 2004). The power of the TPB in predicting recycling behavior is further strengthened by knowing what people think about (their attributions of) the typical nonrecycler (Mannetti, Pierro, & Livi, 2004). When people think negatively about a nonrecycler (lazy, immoral, clueless) they are more likely to recycle, and the predictive ability of the TPB model is strengthened when this information is added (Ohtomo & Hirose, 2007). The TPB is also enhanced by knowing whether people self-identify as environmental activists (Fielding, McDonald, & Louis, 2008). Thus, attitudes predict behavior when other factors that affect intentions are addressed, such as behavioral constraints, norms, social identity, and stereotypes. For these reasons, TPB can help illuminate why it is that although people like to believe that they behave in line with their attitudes, decades of research shows that proenvironmental

[*] See http://cbsm.com/

behaviors are only moderately related to proenvironmental attitudes (Kaiser & Schultz, 2009).

Cognitive Dissonance Theory

Some of the earliest and most important insights into the relationship between attitudes and behavior came from **Cognitive Dissonance Theory** (Festinger, 1956). This theory posits that whenever people experience a discrepancy between two thoughts, cognitive dissonance produces an uncomfortable state of tension that motivates them to take steps to reduce it. People might change a belief *or* a behavior in order to be consistent. Cognitive dissonance theory predicts that your friend's follow-up telephone call would create internal stress because her request to attend the meeting would elicit two contradictory attitudes: On the one hand, you feel allegiance toward your friend, some agreement with her view about the importance of saving the ESA, and an urge to appear consistent with having recently signed her petition. On the other hand, you also value freedom, appreciate the articulate nature of the anti-ESA letter, respect the businessman, and feel concerned about the current economy; thus, you also have some sentiment against the ESA. To resolve the dissonance and corresponding discomfort, cognitive dissonance theory predicts that you will diminish the importance of one viewpoint and elevate the importance of the other. For example, if you do agree to go to the Environmental Club meeting, you will likely find some reason why the businessman is not very convincing (perhaps you'll decide that business people are shortsighted about environmental problems). Alternatively, if you refuse to go to the meeting, the letter will seem more convincing (what else is more important than protecting freedom?). Dissonance theory emphasizes the importance of postdecision shifts in reasoning: Once committed to a decision, people rearrange conflicting attitudes to fit their choices. Thus behavior often determines attitudes, rather than the reverse.

Dissonance theory can be used to promote environmentally friendly behaviors with the **foot-in-the-door** technique. If someone gets you to agree to a small action, you'll be more likely to subsequently undertake a bigger one. The foot-in-the-door strategy would predict that you'll probably go to the ESA meeting (a big action) because you previously signed the petition (a little action). Researchers have successfully used this technique to increase energy conservation actions by getting people to commit to something publicly. For example, one classic study involved families who volunteered to participate in conservation studies, randomly assigning them to two different groups

(Pallak, Cook, & Sullivan, 1980). One group was asked to allow their names to be published in the newspaper (they all agreed to this relatively easy action); the other group was not asked. Even though none of the names were ever published, the group that gave permission (a smaller action) showed a 15% greater reduction of gas use and a 20% greater reduction of electricity use (both larger actions) than the group that was not asked. Apparently, the intent to go public was enough to induce behavior change, because people try to live up to their public image.

The foot-in-the-door technique is powerful, applicable to a variety of environmentally relevant behaviors. People who simply signed a form indicating interest increased their curbside recycling more than people who received a flyer about recycling (Werner et al., 1995). People recycled more grass clippings if researchers asked them to speak to their neighbors about it relative to those who were not asked (Cobern, Porter, Leeming, & Dwyer, 1995). Likewise, requesting people to complete a survey about recycling, or asking them to send a prorecycling postcard to the city council, increased recycling (Arbuthnot et al., 1977).

In another classic study, researchers mailed water-flow restrictors to randomly selected sets of households, together with information about conserving water; another set of households received only information (not the devices). Not surprisingly, the group that received the water restrictors used less water (Hutton, 1982). But in addition, foot-in-the-door effects were also demonstrated by the device group, which, relative to the nondevice group, also turned down their hot water heaters, cleaned their furnaces, and installed automatic thermostats. Since they started conserving one way, they also conserved in other ways. Getting people to adopt a small environmentally responsible behavior can thus lead them to adopt bigger ones, presumably because behaviors are changed to maintain consistency. Making a public commitment can even outweigh financial rewards for increasing recycling behavior (Hornik, Cherian, Madansky, & Narayana, 1995), and decreasing energy use (Katzev & Johnson, 1984). Thus, your friend was smart to get you to sign a petition before asking you to come to an ESA meeting.

Although the foot-in-the-door technique is useful, it doesn't always work for creating sustained change (Burger, 1999). Public commitment like signing a petition can have an effect, but the strength of a person's private commitment is central for long-term behavior change. People who make strong, written (Pardini & Katzev, 1983–1984) or personal commitments (Wang & Katzev, 1990) are more likely to continue recycling than those who make weaker verbal ones or none at all. Moreover, this technique's effect is unlikely to enhance very different environmentally relevant behaviors. Getting people to sign a petition about recycling might increase recycling, but may not do much for bicycle riding or energy conservation. Cognitive dissonance is more likely to exert its effect on different types of environmentally friendly behaviors when people see the connections between them (Thogersen, 2006). The effectiveness of the technique can be increased by (a) enhancing the connections, by overtly labeling the person as helpful, or as a supporter of environmental causes; (b) requiring more than a minimal amount of effort to perform the initial request; and (c) making the target (larger) request essentially a continuation of the initial request (Burger, 1999), thus enhancing the pull of consistency. The motive to look and feel consistent is a powerful form of social control.

Comparison of Models Linking Behavior to Attitudes

Since attitudes are only moderately related to behavior (Kaiser & Schultz, 2009), a tremendous amount of research has focused on understanding why, and under what conditions, the attitude–behavior link can be strengthened. So before we go on, let's review and compare the three theories linking attitudes to behavior. Cognitive dissonance theory is the older theory and holds that environmental behavior isn't necessarily rational (as also posited by psychoanalytic theorists described in Chapter 3), but instead results from attempts to be consistent and reduce the discomfort of dissonance. Since behavior can change attitudes, dissonance theory is useful for creating foot-in-the-door effects. This theory would underscore potentially big payoffs from small behavioral changes, because they can lead to even bigger changes due to the urge to reduce internal dissonance.

In contrast, the two more recent theories, TPB and VBN, see environmental behavior as a logical result of attitudes, beliefs, and norms. VBN theory stresses the role of personal norms and moral obligation stemming from underlying values; TBP highlights intentions and their impact. Both theories seem plausible and have attracted a great deal of attention from social psychologists. In a statistical comparison of the two theories, both were shown to have impressive predictive power. TPB's intentions accounted for a staggering 95% of the variance in environmental behavior, and VBN's personal norms accounted for 64% (Kaiser et al., 2005). Some evidence suggests that the norms measured by VBN theory might also be measured by TPB as attitudes or beliefs. A recent analysis of over 50 studies showed that intentions are a strong predictor of environmental behavior, but that attitudes, behavioral control, problem awareness, and personal moral norms also predict behavior and intentions (Bamberg & Moser, 2007).

We believe that research will continue to merge these two theories by identifying the constraints and intentions addressed by TPB along with the beliefs and values addressed by VBN theory. All three theories are useful in helping strategize ways to increase environmentally responsible behavior, explain why attitudes don't perfectly predict behavior, and why providing information alone won't change it (see also Chapter 5 and Chapter 7).

WHO CARES ABOUT THE ENVIRONMENT?

As you know, some people care more about environmental issues than others. Although there are exceptions, research generally indicates that environmental concern and behaviors are more prevalent among people who are White (Johnson, Bowker, & Cordell, 2004), better educated (Casey & Scott, 2006; Shen & Saijo, 2008; Van Liere & Dunlap, 1980), younger (Corbett, 2005; National Research Council, 2002), politically liberal (Dunlap, Van Liere, Mertig, & Jones, 2000), and female. Of these factors, gender differences have been studied the most.

Gender: Women tend to show greater environmental concern and more proenvironmental behaviors than men (Casey & Scott, 2006; Hunter, Hatch, & Johnson, 2004; Karpiak & Baril, 2008; Snelgar, 2006; Stern et al., 1993; Zelezny, Chua, & Aldrich, 2000). Of all the demographic variables such as age, race, education, and political affiliation, gender is the strongest predictor of concern for protecting wildlife (Kellert & Berry, 1987). Women usually score higher on the New Environmental Paradigm (NEP) scale (see Chapter 2) and are particularly concerned about hazards that impact the local community or health of the family (Mohai, 1992; Stern et al., 1993; Zelezny et al., 2000). These differences hold up across age and across countries (Hunter et al., 2004; Zelezny et al., 2000). Women also litter less (Kallgren et al., 2000) and eat less meat (Gossard & York, 2003). Sometimes gender differences show up in the private rather than public realm; in other words, females are more likely to recycle than men, but men are more likely to attend political meetings (Johnson et al., 2004; McStay & Dunlap, 1983; Zelezny et al., 2000).

Although these differences are reliable, they are generally small. Not all women are more environmentally responsible than all men, and many men feel more environmental responsibility than some women. The distributions of men and women overlap as shown in Figure 4.3.

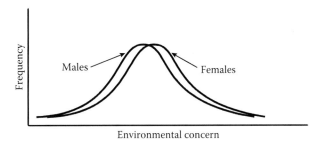

Figure 4.3 Gender differences are small but consistent.

Note that gender differences do not suggest that environmental problems are men's fault. Women clearly play a significant role in contributing to environmental devastation, especially when they participate in overconsumption, overpopulation (reproduction), and pollution. To solve environmental problems will require the best efforts of both men and women alike. However, it is clear that on average, women demonstrate more environmental concern and proenvironmental actions. To put it in terms of our previous discussion, women show a larger scope of justice with respect to the well-being of other people and species. Why would this be so?

One answer is that women are more likely to see the connection between environmental conditions and harm to others (Stern et al., 1993). This analysis draws on the work of Carol Gilligan, who argued that women evaluate social issues using an ethic of care because they are socialized to the role of caretakers. A **role** is a "set of norms that define how a person in a given situation should behave" (Myers, 2008, p. G-6). Across cultures, women are taught to be more nurturing, cooperative, and helpful, whereas males are socialized to be more independent and competitive (Chodorow, 1974; Gilligan, 1982; Keller, 1996). Women demonstrate this role during stress, as they are more likely to "tend-and-befriend" in response to stress, in contrast to men, who more often react with a fight or flight response (Taylor et al., 2000; see also Chapter 8). Women are more accepting than men of messages that link environmental conditions to potential harm to themselves, others, and other species or the biosphere, because they are more likely to see interconnections and think in terms of relationships.

The view that women have a special connection with the environment is called **ecofeminism,** a movement that emerged in the 1970s as the women's and ecology movements developed simultaneously (Diamond & Orenstein, 1990; Spretnak, 1990). Ecofeminists argue that patriarchy oppresses both women and nature by promoting a worldview valuing dominance, hierarchy, dualistic thinking, and relationships based on power. Some ecofeminists go further and posit that women's reproductive systems, their menstrual cycles, and their capacity to give birth, place them closer to the physical world, the lunar cycles, and the rhythms of nature. Others would simply claim that women's roles as family caretakers means they have to be more concerned about, and in touch with, the natural environment, because the health of their families depend on it. Ecofeminists recognize differences of race, class, and culture, but they focus on the common experiences of women around the world: unremunerated housework, volunteer work, and especially their primary responsibility for taking care of others, while being excluded from central roles in policy and decision making.

It seems reasonable to us that women are drawn into environmental concerns because they are often first to notice the damaging effects of polluted water, food, and air on their family's health. Rachel Carson's best selling book *Silent Spring* (1962) catalyzed the environmental movement in the United States and serves as an example of the ways in which women frame environmental problems. Grassroots resistance to male-run environmentally destructive projects are legendary throughout the world: in India, women hugged trees to prevent logging (Mishra & Tripathi, 1978; Shiva, 1994, 1988); in Kenya, women planted trees throughout the Green Belt (Maathai, 2003); in the Philippines, pregnant women, nursing mothers, old women, and children formed a human barricade to prevent tractors from clearing land that was used for community food (Ayupan & Oliveros, 1994); and in New York, Lois Gibbs organized a clearinghouse for hazardous waste through her efforts to uncover the infamous Love Canal toxic waste dump (Gibbs, 1995). Male scientific experts have been quick to characterize the environmental movement as hysteria, and to call these women "hysterical" (a female problem, related to the word *hystero*, or uterus).

Gender differences in environmental concerns have wide ranging implications. Throughout the world, in both developed and developing nations, women are primarily responsible for childcare, housework, food preparation, and family clothing (Bakker, 1994; Dankelman & Davidson, 1988). In rural subsistence economies, women are the main providers of fuel, food, and water, and they depend heavily on community-owned waterways, forests, grasslands, and croplands for accomplishing these chores. When international development efforts convert community resources to privately owned farms, women must go farther and work harder to provide necessities of food, water, and fuel (Shiva, 1988). As a result, resources are more quickly depleted because more people are forced to forage on smaller community spaces. In southern Zimbabwe, for example, forests were cut in order to install mines and mining towns to support a cash economy. This clearance forced women to gather their fuel from leftover forests and severe deforestation resulted (Jacobson, 1992). Women (like men) who are desperate to provide for their families will deplete available resources, but when development efforts pay attention to the crucial roles that women fulfill, they are less likely to cause environmental devastation (Kabeer, 2001). Because of their responsibilities for obtaining family necessities from communally owned resources, women have traditionally been more knowledgeable, experienced, and concerned about sustainable environmental practices than men. To the extent that development efforts ignore and undermine women, they also ignore and undermine sustainability.

Although rarely articulated, development projects that discount women's roles and input stem from a stereotypic belief about men and women: the assumption that men are wage earners and women are dependents (Winter, 2002). This erroneous view of women translates into projects that focus on men and their access to jobs, in spite of data that show the nutrition of children is more closely tied to the status of women than men (International Food Policy Research Institute, 2003; Jacobsen, 1992; United Nations Children's Fund [UNICEF], 2008). In the developing world, poverty, overpopulation, and environmental destruction coincide. Poverty drives overpopulation because there is no other form of social security than children who will take care of their parents in old age; gender bias requires that women continue to have babies until enough sons are born to provide for them and perform sacred funeral rites. For these reasons, development that ignores women increases both environmental destruction and population pressures by increasing poverty. The gender bias of international development demonstrates the important role of psychology in what seem like nonpsychological issues: economics, foreign policy, and agriculture.

Likewise, gendered notions of nature can contribute to environmental destruction. What does it mean to call unexplored land "virgin territory" or the planet "Mother Earth"? Consider the words of an Exxon senior vice president describing the aftermath of the Valdez accident: "water in the [Prince William] Sound replaces itself every 20 days. The Sound flushes itself out every 20 days. Mother Nature cleans up and does quite a cleaning job" (Sitter, 1989, as quoted by Seager, 1993).

Reprinted from © Over the Hedge. With permission from United Feature Syndicate, Inc.

The view that "Mom will pick up after us" seems plausible because it is women who do the vast majority of housework, cleaning, laundry, and tidying. Although the term Mother Earth might elicit feelings of love and devotion, it can also be problematic by reducing human responsibility. One feminist geographer argued that

> There is no warm, nurturing, anthropomorphized earth that will take care of us if only we treat her nicely. The complex, emotion-laden, conflict-laden, quasi-sexualized, quasi-dependent mother relationship . . . is not an effective metaphor for environmental action. . . . It is not an effective political organizing tool: if the earth is really our mother, then we are children, and cannot be held truly accountable for our actions. (Seager, 1993, p. 219).

Noticing the gendered dimensions of environmental thinking can promote awareness of unconscious sexism and its nefarious effects on environmentally relevant behavior, not to mention on women.

THE SOCIAL PSYCHOLOGY OF MATERIALISM

Also unfortunate is the problematic role social psychology has played in promoting **materialism**, observable when people explicitly endorse the accumulation of wealth and possessions as a basic goal in life. Many applied social psychologists have careers in advertising, using their insights about social influence to persuade audiences to buy unnecessary products. Today, the most frequent and explicit messages people receive are sales pitches, which use social norms, reference groups, and appeals to egocentric values to sell products and services to consumers. Commercials have increasingly become a ubiquitous part of daily life.

Yankelovich, a market research firm, estimates that a person living in a city 30 years ago saw up to 2,000 ad messages a day, compared with up to 5,000 today. About half the 4,110 people surveyed last spring by Yankelovich said they thought marketing and advertising today was out of control. (Story, 2007)

Ads are everywhere: They appear as outright pleas in media and increasingly as spam messages, internet pop ups, and product placements in film and television shows.

Not surprisingly, materialistic values have also surged in the last few decades. Data on incoming college students over 30 years show that they increasingly value materialism above other values, including finding personal meaning, helping others in difficulty, becoming an authority in one's field, and raising a family (Myers, 2010; see Figure 4.4). Materialistic values are problematic because people who hold them have larger ecological footprints, that is, they consume more of the earth's resources due to their lifestyle choices regarding food, transportation, and housing (Brown & Kasser, 2005). In the laboratory, they also cooperate less in games involving social dilemmas (conflicts between

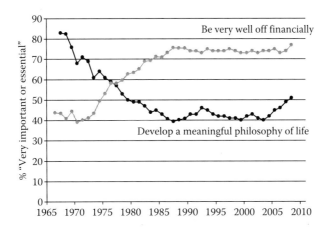

Figure 4.4 In the last 40 years, incoming college students have steadily increased their endorsement of materialism over personal meaning. Data from surveys of more than 200,000 entering U.S. collegians per year, based on The American Freshman surveys, UCLA, 1966 to 2007. (Reprinted from Myers, D.G. (2010) *Social Psychology*, 10th ed., McGraw-Hill, p. 581. With permission.)

personal and group interests), depleting resources faster than less materialistic participants (Sheldon & McGregor, 2000; see further discussion in Chapters 5 and 10). Outside the laboratory, materialists report fewer environmentally friendly behaviors, such as riding a bike, reusing paper, and buying used products from secondhand stores (Brown & Kasser, 2005; Richins & Dawson, 1992). Materialistic values negatively correlate with environmental concern (Abramson & Inglehart, 1995; Schwartz, 1996) and identifying with nature (Reist, 2004; see also Chapter 10).

Materialistic values vary across nations. Wealthier countries, whose citizens value achievement and status, emit more carbon dioxide and have bigger footprints than those where citizens are less materialistic (Kasser, 2008). The result is that people in industrialized countries use far more than their share of global resources. The ecological footprint of the United States surpassed its biocapacity (what the land could produce) in 1969, and the Earth's population now uses one and a third planets' worth of resources (see Figure 4.5). Per capita in 2004, people in the United States used the oil equivalent of 2 Germans, 6 Thais, 15 Kenyans, or 48 Bangladeshis (Nationmaster, 2004). This disproportionate use and abuse of the planet's resources not only pollutes and depletes, but fuels a global trade system that feeds some countries as other countries fall into debt, poverty, and disintegration. Differential wealth also breeds resentment and armed conflict (Christie, Wagner, & Winter, 2001). In these ways, global systems that encourage materialism and overconsumption lead to not only ecological collapse, but also to violence and war (Pilisuk, 2001).

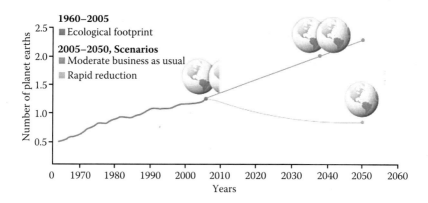

Figure 4.5 Global resource demand and waste absorption uses the equivalent of 1.3 planets. It currently takes the Earth 16 months to regenerate what people use in 12 months. (Reprinted from Global Footprint Network, National Footprint Accounts, 2008 Edition. [www.footprintnetwork.org]. With permission.

What inspires materialistic values? Clearly, one answer is advertising, through its messages that status and pleasure can be obtained with the next purchase. Research has shown a positive correlation between materialism and amount of television watching. This relationship holds across age groups (Kasser & Ryan, 2001; Sirgy, Lee, & Kosenko, 1998), and across countries (Cheung & Chan, 1996; Khanna, 2001; Nairn, Ormrod, & Bottomley, 2007). Advertising that encourages people to see themselves as deprived until a product is purchased, unfulfilled until a new gadget is owned, or hungry until that next burger is consumed is especially effective. As one advertising agency put it 40 years ago, "It's our job to make people unhappy with what they have" (Puckett, as quoted by Berg-Cross, 2000, p. 494). Watching attractive models enjoy luxury goods, exotic vacations, and expensive surroundings leads to what social psychologists have termed **relative deprivation**, the sense that one is less well off than others to whom one compares oneself (Merton & Kitt, 1950), that is, relative to one's reference group. People who are materialistic are more likely to compare themselves with wealthy people (Richins, 1991) and believe their purchases bring approval from others (Schroeder & Dugal, 1995).

Overt advertising is not the only way materialistic values get transmitted. Popular Hollywood movies contribute to the adoration of conspicuous consumption by glorifying luxury lifestyles lived by likable lead characters. Movies can also subtly promote environmentally destructive behaviors, such as *Heights* (2004), in which the lead character gets accosted on a subway (public transport), and is then shown happily hopping into a taxi cab (private transport). In these ways films and television subtly promote wealth and consumption as a positive trait. Just after September 11, 2001, messages from the White House extolling the healing effects of buying during times of national emergency, portrayed consumption as patriotism (Winter, 2004). Perhaps the recent global economic downslide will make conspicuous consumption embarrassing, given so many people who are suffering financially (Roberts, 2008).

An important psychological contribution to materialism is unmet emotional needs. A growing body of research suggests that people become more materialistic in colder emotional climates. One study of materialistic adolescents showed that they had mothers who made more negative comments about them and who provided less interpersonal warmth (Kasser, Ryan, Zax, & Sameroff, 1995). Materialistic children have less communication with their parents (Moschis, 1985), and parents who are less supportive of their needs for autonomy (Williams, Cox, Hedberg, & Deci, 2000). Materialistic young adults are more likely to have parents who divorced (Rindfleisch, Burroughs, & Denton,

1997). Even momentary anxiety can enhance materialism. One study asked participants to write essays about their death, and found they reported higher expectations for spending and salary in their future, and became greedier in a social dilemma game, relative to those who wrote essays about music (Kasser & Sheldon, 2000). People raised in financially stressed times are more materialistic than those raised in more prosperous times (Abramson & Inglehart, 1995). Nations with higher scores on materialism have children who score lower on a variety of measures, including health, education, peer and family relationships, and subjective well-being (Kasser, 2009b).

The Unhappy Results of Materialism

Across cultures, materialistic people are unhappier (Ryan et al., 1999). College graduates with yuppie values, who prefer a high income and occupational success over close friends and happy marriage, report much more unhappiness (Perkins, 1991). Reduced well-being among materialistic people may be due to feelings of insecurity (Kasser & Ryan, 2001); greater self-involvement (Kasser & Ryan, 1996); less developed social skills and lower ability to show empathy (Sheldon & Kasser, 1995; Solberg, Diener, & Robinson, 2004); less feelings of autonomy; and more feelings of guilt or doubt (Srivastava, Locke, & Bartol, 2001).

Concomitantly, consumption does not make people happy. Research shows that above a minimal subsistence level, reports of personal happiness are unrelated to financial income or material possessions. Since 1950, the purchasing power of U.S. citizens has doubled, yet their personal happiness has remained essentially constant (see Figure 4.6). One analysis of 135 nations showed that rates of environmental resource use has no effect on subjective well-being (Dietz, Rosa, & York, 2009). One reason more is not more satisfying may be that "too muchness—too many activities, too many consumer choices, too much to learn," leads to stress, frustration, and depression (Schwartz, 2004a, p. 74; 2004b).

Instead of contributing to happiness, materialism is more likely to detract from it by reducing experiences that lead to personal well-being. Research on happiness over the last few decades has shown that the strongest predictors of personal happiness are:

1. Close and supportive relationships with family and friends.
2. Positive thinking habits: optimism, perceived control, and self-esteem.
3. Social support for one's sense of meaning, often attained from faith and/or service communities (Myers, 2010).

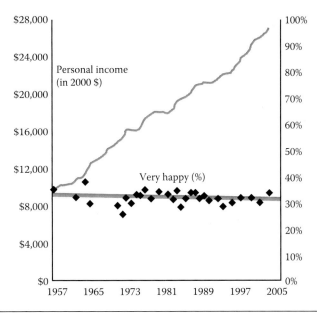

Figure 4.6 Wealth does not buy happiness. Above minimal subsistence levels, self-reported happiness is not related to income. (Reprinted from Myers, D.G. (2010) *Social Psychology,* 10th ed., McGraw-Hill, p. 583. With permission.)

These same factors also enhance immune system function and predict overall health and well-being (see Chapter 8). But in the mad rush to work harder and own more, rewarding social networks, leisure time to pursue meaningful activities, and personal control tend to become scarce.

Consumerism has hoodwinked us into gorging on material things because we suffer from social, psychological, and spiritual hungers . . . Consumption itself has little part in the playful

camaraderie that inspires the young, the bonds of love and friendship that nourish adults, the golden memories that sustain the elderly. The very things that make life worth living, that give depth and bounty to human existence, are infinitely sustainable. (Durning, 1990, p. 169)

Thus, materialism is bad for both the environment and the person.

Materialism and the Economy

Years before the world's economic crisis became evident in late 2008, materialistic values led many people and governments to overspend their earnings. Both national and personal debt has been increasing in the United States for decades. Materialistic values likely contributed to the economic breakdown. When people are excessively focused on having possessions and making money, especially competitive forms of capitalism develop without crucial governmental regulation (Kasser, Cohn, Kanner, & Ryan, 2007; Schwartz, 2007). People are more likely to make risky and unethical decisions when operating from materialistic values (Kasser, Vansteenkiste, & Deckop, 2006). Thus, when a culture is saturated with materialistic values, its citizens, politicians, and financial leaders are likely to promote policies that lead to economic disasters.

Decades ago, the U.S. economy began its tremendous growth based on consumption. As the chairman of President Eisenhower's Council of Economic Advisers once said, the U.S. economy's "ultimate purpose is to produce more consumer goods" (quoted by Suzuki, 2003, para. 4). Not public education, not health care, not national security, not environmental security, but consumer goods. The rupture in economic structures that led to the economic crisis in 2008 gives all of us opportunity to question the purpose of an economy and corresponding assumptions about growth. Growth per se is not sustainable. One way or another, the world will have to transition from oil-based economies that devour limited natural resources to produce cheap consumer products, because the natural resources that have fueled them are disappearing. Instead, an economy that depends on sustainable use of resources and using green technologies is required. Transitions to a green economy are underway in 2009 with the Obama Administration's funding of green jobs. On a global scale, considerable employment potential exists in the arenas of green energy, industry, transportation, buildings, agriculture, and forestry (United Nations Environment Programme, 2008; see further discussion in Chapter 11). As you consider future career possibilities perhaps you will decide to help lead the way.

Meanwhile, making green choices as a consumer is a useful method to build market supports for a sustainable economy. Nearly half of the citizens in the United States say they are willing to reward or punish companies with their purchasing decisions to promote more responsible climate change-related activities, and a majority of those say they already have (Leiserowitz, Maibach, & Roser-Renouf, 2009a). Research shows that people who make green food purchases (buying local, organic food with less packaging) have positive attitudes about environmental protection, feel less time pressure, and shop less often in supermarkets (Tanner & Kast, 2003). "Surprisingly, green purchases are not significantly related to moral thinking, monetary barriers, or the socioeconomic characteristics of the consumers" (Tanner & Kast, 2003, p. 883). These findings suggest that addressing the social context of food choices is crucial for promoting a sustainable food economy. They also add to previous work on happiness to suggest that "time affluence" (Kasser, 2009a) rather than "material affluence," may be a useful guide to both sustainable lifestyles and sustainable economies. Likewise, mindfulness training is a promising antidote to consumer culture and overconsumption (De Wit, 2008; see also Chapter 10).

If environmental health and human happiness are to be seriously considered in the transition to a sustainable economy, alternative economic indexes will need to be developed. The current calculation of Gross Domestic Product not only hides the environmental costs of materialism, it hides many other costs of environmental damage—site clean-up, environmental restoration, medical care of environmentally based diseases, law suits, and so forth. When costs are not subtracted, they contribute to the GDP instead of lowering it (Kasser, 2009a). Better indices would be a Genuine Progress Indicator (Clark & Lawn, 2008), Bhutan's Gross National Happiness Index (Shrotryia, 2006), or other measures that involve direct assessments of subjective well-being (Diener & Seligman, 2002; Layard, 2005). In addition, immediate changes are needed in current tax laws that favor corporate profits at the expense of human and environmental health (Kasser, 2009b).

CONCLUSIONS

From a social psychological perspective, environmentally relevant behavior is a function of social influence. Norms, roles, and reference groups determine choices by influencing what people think of as appropriate behavior. Even though they are usually unaware of it, people imitate and are influenced by others in their reference group, as well as by messages from media. The consistency (or inconsistency) between people's attitudes toward environmental problems and their environmentally responsible behavior depends on their intentions, values, beliefs, and constraints on their behavior. When cognitive consistency, personal norms, and intentions are enhanced, proenvironmental behaviors can be promoted. People care about those inside their scope of justice, and make attribution errors about those they exclude, leading to environmental injustice. Relative to men, women care more about the environment, its impact on others, and the well-being of the biosphere. This gender difference most likely arises out of women's differing roles, and leads to different levels of moral responsibility. Finally, research shows that wealth does not make people happier. Materialism, facilitated by a form of applied social psychology known as advertising, is depleting the planet's resources, as well the psychological well-being of its inhabitants.

The good news is that insights from social psychology can help us redesign and optimize norms, reference groups, and social influence mechanisms that induce environmentally responsible behavior and reduce overconsumption. From a social psychological point of view, you can increase your own environmentally responsible behavior by deliberately avoiding situations with environmentally destructive norms, while simultaneously joining groups, cultivating activities, friendships, and commitments that support sustainability.

If there is any single message from social psychology, it is that changes are much easier to make and keep if we put ourselves in social situations that support them. Our immediate reference groups of friends, relatives, and colleagues are enormously powerful social influence agents. As Kurt Lewin observed at the outset of social psychology,

 It is easier to change individuals formed into a group than to change any of them separately. As long as group values are unchanged the individual will resist changes. . . . If the group standard itself is changed, the resistance which is due to the relation between the individual and the group is eliminated. (1959, p. 228)

Thus, understanding and changing environmentally relevant behavior requires paying attention to the immediate social context. Focusing on the situation in which behavior occurs rather than on deep-seated traits or personality patterns is also a fundamental principle of behavioral psychology, to which we now turn.

5

BEHAVIORAL PSYCHOLOGY: CONTINGENCY MANAGEMENT

Most thoughtful people agree that the world is in serious trouble. . . . That many people have begun to find a recital of [the] dangers tiresome is perhaps an even greater threat. . . . Traditional explanations of why we are doing so little are familiar. It is said that we lack responsibility for those who will follow us, that we do not have a clear perception of the problem, that we are not using our intelligence, that we are suffering from a failure of will, that we lack moral strength, and so on. Unfortunately, explanations of that sort simply replace one question with another. Why are we not more responsible or more intelligent? Why are we suffering from a failure of will? A better strategy is to look at our behavior and at the *environmental conditions* of which it is a function. There we shall find at least some of the reasons why we do as we do. (Skinner, 1991, pp. 19–20; italics added)

Behaviorism, or **behavioral psychology**, focuses on the ways in which behavior is controlled by the environment. In this context, the word *environment* refers to the total physical, social, political, and economic situation in which a person behaves. This is a wider meaning than we have employed up to now in this book; previously, environment referred to the physical dimensions of ecosystems such as resources, nonhuman species, air quality, water, and wilderness.

From a behavioral perspective, the total environment cues certain behaviors, which then are followed by consequences (i.e., rewards or punishers). Accordingly, global threats such as those reviewed in Chapter 1 result from environmental conditions that maintain destructive human behaviors.

If that is true, what does it take to change environmentally harmful actions? You might think first about educating people and changing their attitudes and beliefs so they can make more appropriate choices. However, as we saw in Chapter 4, beliefs and attitudes are only indirectly related to behavior. Behaviorists would not be surprised by our claim in the opening pages of this book that people suffer from knowing *about* environmental problems, but not knowing what to *do* about them. Ironically, research on environmental attitudes has flourished in the last decade while research on behavioral interventions has declined (Lehman & Geller, 2004). Yet behavioral psychologists would posit that trying to change inner events like feelings or attitudes is a waste of precious time; instead let's cut to the chase and target efforts directly on behavior change. Technological solutions might be important and impressive, but without a *behavioral technology* that changes what people actually *do*, sustainability can not be achieved.

Skinner was one of the first psychologists to repeatedly relate the issues of resource depletion, pollution, and overpopulation to psychology. His best-selling novel *Walden Two* (1948) explored the question of utopia from a behavioral perspective, and is a thoughtful and provocative look at how behavioral principles can be used to design a healthier and more sustainable society. A more formal analysis of the behavioral approach to human problems appeared later in Skinner's book, *Beyond Freedom and Dignity* (1971). In both works, Skinner examined the problem of designing a sustainable culture, and argued that humans must redesign environments to shape more appropriate behavior. He proposed that people need a technology of behavior that focuses on maintaining the health of the environment in which behavior occurs.

Although the behavioral approach in psychology is not as popular as it was several decades ago, we believe that its insights significantly enhance understanding of both environmental problems and their solutions. Paradoxically, the influence of behaviorism has been so strong that it may have been too successful for its own good: Important elements of the behavioral viewpoint have been so thoroughly assimilated into mainstream psychology that they are not even discussed anymore. Measuring observable behavior is so common a feature of good research that it is no longer called behaviorism (Boring, 1950/1957).

Behaviorism grew out of the **functionalist** school of psychology. This perspective emphasized the ways that behavior serves an adaptive function within its context, and thus reflected the influence of Darwin's theory of evolution by natural selection. For example, **classical** (also called **Pavlovian** after its founder, Ivan Pavlov) and **operant** (**Skinnerian**) forms of **conditioning** depend on the fact that animals learn to respond to new stimuli (classical), and alter the ways in which they operate on their environment depending on their experiences with consequences (operant). Both of these adaptive mechanisms for learning are useful for understanding environmentally destructive behavior and the contexts in which it occurs. However, we will focus on operant conditioning, as it is the focus of most of the relevant research. Much of this work grew out of Skinner's research, although contemporary applications of behavioral psychology incorporate aspects of social and even cognitive perspectives (Toates, 2009). Thus, some of the following discussion overlaps with issues examined in Chapter 4 and Chapter 7.

OPERANT CONDITIONING

Operant conditioning procedures build on Thorndike's (1898, as cited in Skinner, 1953) **Law of Effect**, which stated that behavior followed by a favorable consequence would be stamped in (**positive reinforcement** in Skinner's terminology), whereas behavior followed by an unfavorable consequence would be stamped out (**punishment**). Reinforcement literally refers to strengthening or increasing the likelihood of behavior. As an example, Oregon and several other states have a "bottle bill" where the purchase price of products in glass bottles and aluminum cans includes a 5¢ deposit, refundable upon return of the bottles and cans. If a customer returns their bottles and gets a refund, the nickel serves as a *positive reinforcer*. In contrast, punishment decreases the probability of a particular behavior. If mom yelled at you for throwing a returnable can in the garbage, that's punishment; presumably that behavior is unlikely to recur (at least not in her presence).

Skinner elaborated by noting that removing a desirable stimulus can also reduce a behavior (termed **negative punishment**; e.g., removing privileges or reducing your allowance after a transgression), and removing some aversive stimuli **negatively reinforces** or increases the associated behavior. For example, recycling is negatively reinforced if it terminates mom's scolding. In both cases, the term *negative* refers to the inverse relationship between the behavior and stimulus (see Table 5.1).

Both positive and negative reinforcement can be used to *increase* proenvironmental behaviors. Correspondingly, both positive and negative punishment can be equally effective for *reducing* environmentally harmful behaviors. Positive punishment might involve yelling at someone for driving an SUV; negative punishment could be imposed by the government in the form of a fine for operating gas-guzzling vehicles (taking money to *reduce* driving). Although all four

Table 5.1 Operant Conditioning: Relationships between Consequences and Behavior.

	Increases Behavior	Decreases Behavior
Stimulus Added	Positive reinforcement (Return bottles, get 5¢)	Positive punishment (Waste water, get yelled at)
Stimulus Taken Away	Negative reinforcement (Turn water off, terminate mom's yelling)	Negative punishment (Dump toxins into river, lose operating license)

behavior-consequence relationships are relevant for thinking about behavioral change, Skinner determined that positive reinforcement is generally more effective because positive punishment often produces undesirable behavioral side effects such as aggression or avoidance of the person implementing the punishment.

These processes can illuminate Sue's behavior concerning water use. She grew up hearing the phrase "waste not, want not" and was taught to use water sparingly while brushing her teeth or washing dishes. As an adult, Sue lived for several years in a home with a well (rather than city water) and took conservation even more seriously out of fear the well would run dry, an outcome that would punish wasteful behavior. For example, she and her partner adopted the strategy "if it's yellow, let it mellow; if it's brown, flush it down" for conserving water in toilets. More recently, it occurred to her that the water with which U.S. toilets are flushed is cleaner than the water many people have to drink. More than one billion people (or one out of every six people on this planet) do not have safe drinking water, and about half of all people in the world do not have sufficient water for basic sanitation and hygiene (Gardner, 2002). For all of these reasons, Sue continues to be conscientious about water use and hates to see waste (e.g., leaky faucets, people's wasteful behaviors such as letting water run while brushing teeth). From her perspective, waste was *positively punished* by getting yelled at as a child, and terminating the anxiety conditioned by being scolded or running out of a scarce resource acts as a *negative reinforcer* for conserving water.

Feelings are important in maintaining many behaviors shaped by operant conditioning. This statement may come as a surprise to readers who think that behaviorists discount feelings and other internal events; a common misconception. Rather, behaviorists argue that internal events like feelings cannot *cause* behavior; the causes of behavior lie in the external environment. According to Skinner, emotions and thoughts resemble other *behaviors* and are thus susceptible to the same **contingencies**; that is, the environmental events that shape and maintain actions, including reinforcers and punishers. Thus, when Sue was punished for wasting water, her behavior changed and she also experienced certain emotions such as shame. Feeling ashamed became associated with waste, and now when Sue has been or is tempted to be wasteful, that same feeling recurs. Escaping feelings of shame or guilt continues to negatively reinforce her conservation behaviors.

Not only does behavior change because of its relationship to consequences, but the **schedule of reinforcement** makes a difference in the strength and durability (persistence) of the behavior. The phrase *schedule of reinforcement* really means *schedule of consequences*, as it refers to both reinforcement and punishment and includes positive and negative (inverse) relationships with the behavior. People's actions tend to change most quickly when consequences are consistently administered (a **continuous** reinforcement schedule). However, if the schedule is **intermittent** rather than continuous, behaviors will last longer when reinforcers are withdrawn; in operant terminology, behavior will **extinguish** more slowly (see Figure 5.1). For example, the Coast Guard inspects industrial wastes from processing plants on inland waterways on a random schedule (Cone & Hayes, 1980). Companies do not know when the inspection will take place, just as drivers do not know when a patrol car will be checking their speed. These random (intermittent) schedules are powerful forms of behavioral control. The industrial chemical company and highways may not be patrolled for months, but since the schedule is intermittent, violations are controlled for a longer time than if people notice the continuous presence of, and then the sudden disappearance of, a patrol boat or police car.

There are different kinds of **intermittent reinforcement schedules**. For instance, most people recycle their bottles on a **variable ratio schedule**, where the number of responses varies for each reinforcer. When Deborah brings a box of bottles to the recycling center and gets the rebate for her effort, many separate behaviors of rinsing and saving bottles have accumulated to result in the monetary reinforcement. Sometimes she brings in 40 bottles, sometimes 42, sometimes 48, depending on the size of the bottles and how long she has put off the task. If Deborah recycled bottles every Saturday, her behavior would be on a **fixed interval schedule** (i.e., a fixed amount of time).

Behaviors developed under optimal reinforcement schedules can become habitual and thus very durable, as illustrated with another example from Deborah's experience. A few decades ago she lived in

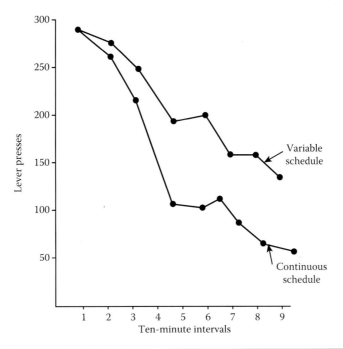

Figure 5.1 Variable reinforcement schedules produce behavior that is more resistant to extinction than continuous reinforcement schedules.

Denmark for seven months, a country in which people usually brought their own cloth shopping bags to the grocery store because the plastic bags at the counter cost almost $1.00 a piece. It was easy for her behavior to change in Denmark because the reinforcement for doing so (saving $1.00) was continuous as well as sizable. When Deborah returned to her home in the Pacific Northwest of the United States, shopping bags were free but deforestation was very visible. Not only were stories about forest issues continually in the news, but driving across the state to return home she was shocked to see huge patches of clear-cuts in what had been a rich forest cover when she left. Even though there were no monetary reinforcers for bringing her own bag, this seemed a more appropriate behavior because so many forests are lost to unnecessary paper production. In fact, through a community volunteer group, Deborah helped set up a cloth bag project, making cloth shopping bags available in local supermarkets, and trying to persuade friends to use them instead of the paper and plastic bags given at the counter (she became known as "the bag lady"!).

Here's where the reinforcement schedule is relevant. After having become known to friends as a person committed to cloth grocery bags, it was embarrassing to meet one of them in a supermarket without having her cloth bags. Deborah never knew when she would see one of her friends, but the chance of meeting one helped maintain the habit of bringing a bag every time she entered the store, or returning to the car to get one if she initially forgot it. After a while, bringing the bag became automatic, and Deborah no longer thinks about whether she will meet a friend or not. The intermittent schedule helped keep the rate of responding so high for such a long time that the behavior became habitual and will be very resistant to extinction. Unfortunately, most other people do not have strong continuous reinforcers to shape their behavior in the first place. Grocers still give free paper and plastic bags and many stores do not offer a rebate for customer's bags. Consequently, use of cloth bags has not been established in the U.S. public. Even though many people bought the bags, they find it difficult to remember to use them: A behaviorist would say that effective reinforcement schedules have not yet been arranged for changing this behavior.

Like other animals, humans **discriminate** between stimuli by learning to respond only to those that signal when reinforcement will follow, and not to respond when behavior is unlikely to be reinforced. For example, humans discriminate between bottles that are marked for rebate (soda and beer bottles stating "5¢ deposit redemption value") and those that are not (juice or wine bottles). The discrimination occurs because bringing in the former will be reinforced, while bringing in the latter will not.

Thus, behavior is also controlled by **discriminative stimuli**, denoted as S^Ds. The environment is filled with S^Ds, including prompts and models, which are discussed more fully below. For now, the point is that behavior is embedded in two different kinds of *contingencies*, those that cue the behavior, called S^Ds, and those that follow the behavior, called S^Rs (reinforcing stimuli) or S^Ps (punishing stimuli). Since of the operation of discriminative stimuli and the consequences of behavior, Skinner said that behavior is under **stimulus control**. Conceptually then, behaviorists look at behavior as a series of responses (R) each with its own discriminative and consequent stimuli. The units of behavior may be indicated by

$$S^D: R \rightarrow S^R \text{ (or } S^P),$$

where a discriminative stimulus (S^D) sets the context in which a particular behavior (R) will be reinforced or punished.

Before examining some of the specific ways in which behaviorists have developed a technology of environmentally appropriate human behaviors, consider a question about how a behaviorist might explain environmental degradation in the first place. How can ecological troubles be due to inappropriate behavior if actions are simply products of stimulus control? That is, behaviorists argue that behavior is a result of environmental contingencies, not of some inner events like attitudes or values. In that case, behavior cannot be right or wrong, it simply reflects what is occurring in the situation. As Skinner once said "the organism is always right" (1977, p. 1007). If that is true, how can human behavior be so destructive?

Behaviorists would argue that maladaptive behaviors result when short- and long-term consequences differ. Behavior is generally under the control of short-term reinforcers even if it brings delayed punishers. Driving may ultimately be bad for health (as people get less exercise) and for the planet (air pollution and climate change). However, the immediate reinforcement is so powerful (getting people to where they want to go quickly and conveniently) they do it anyway. In other words, people are caught in a **contingency trap** (Baum, 1994). Many bad habits, including environmentally destructive actions, are very difficult to change because breaking habitual behavior usually involves a short-term cost. Thus, one way of thinking of environmental degradation is in terms of the difficulty of bringing present (unsustainable) behavior and its associated reinforcers to change in line with consequences that are both distant and remote (Nevin, 2005; Toates, 2009). As a result, people must deliberately change the short-term consequences to be more consistent with long-term outcomes. For instance, Sue refuses to purchase a parking permit at Willamette University where she works so she is not tempted to drive. If Sue succumbs to the short-term convenience of driving, her behavior will result in immediate negative punishment (a parking ticket). She specifically altered the contingencies to control her behavior so it is more in line with her long-term concerns about climate change and pollution.

Culture, a complex conglomeration of reinforcement schedules, also plays an important role in maintaining inappropriate behavior (see also Penn, 2003). For centuries, reproductive behavior was highly rewarded by societies with small populations. Now, however, reproductive behavior is producing dangerous overpopulation. In most societies, the threat of material scarcity encouraged families to accumulate extra resources; now overconsumption pollutes and depletes resources. For several centuries, North Americans were reinforced for settling wilderness and "conquering nature"; now there is very little wilderness left. Thus, cultures or the planet itself will ultimately discontinue the original reinforcers (e.g., parents of large families may not enjoy as much social support as they once did; finite resources like oil will disappear). When a behavior is no longer reinforced it will *eventually* extinguish, but the natural evolution of behavior can take decades if not lifetimes. Given the exponential growth of environmental difficulties, there is not enough time to wait for behavioral evolution to take place.

For these reasons, behaviorists believe that humans can and should facilitate behavior change by redesigning the contexts in which environmentally relevant behaviors take place. **Behavioral engineering** involves altering the contingencies creating or maintaining destructive actions to motivate proenvironmental behaviors (Geller, 1987, 1992). Researchers employ two main strategies: (1) those which focus on the stimuli that signal behavior (S^Ds) called **antecedent strategies**; and (2) those which focus on the consequences of behavior (S^Rs/ S^Ps) termed **consequence strategies**. Reinforcers, punishers, and the schedule of reinforcement are all important variables in consequence strategies.

Antecedent Strategies: Changing the S^Ds

Sustainable behaviors cannot be reinforced before they occur, so environments that signal appropriate behavior must be designed by manipulating antecedent stimuli, the S^Ds. Three types of S^Ds are typically utilized: **prompts**, **information**, and **modeling**, and each can have some effect on environmentally relevant behaviors. **Prompts** signal proper actions (i.e., they communicate norms, see Chapter 4). For example, positioning aluminum recycling bins in areas where canned soft drinks are consumed enables convenient and appropriate disposal (Lehman & Geller, 2004). Prompts are often verbal stimuli providing instructional control. Signs placed over light switches reminding users to turn off the light when they leave a room have reduced energy use. Research suggests that the more specific the prompt, the greater its efficacy. A sign saying "Faculty and students—please turn off lights after 5 p.m." is more effective than one that reads "Conserve Electricity." Polite prompts are more effective than demanding ones (the word please can make a difference), and the closer the prompt to the behavior point the better (a sign over a light switch is more effective than a sign across the room). Thus, polite, specific, and well-placed reminders can significantly change behavior (Geller, Winett, & Everett, 1982; Lehman & Geller, 2004).

Although common sense suggests the need to educate people about environmental problems, education by itself does very little to change behavior (see reviews by Abrahamse, Steg, Vlek, & Rothengatter, 2005; Gardner & Stern, 2002; Lehman & Geller, 2004). Millions of dollars spent on disseminating information resulted in only 2–3% energy conservation (Hirst, Berry, & Soderstrom, 1981). Consequently, delivering general information through slogans, pamphlets, solicitations, or articles is less effective than giving specific prompts or instructions. For instance, providing maintenance garage managers with tailored information about how *their* employees can reduce polluting behaviors at *their* facility resulted in more positive change than general information about oil pollution (Daamen, Staats, Wilke, & Engelen, 2001). Likewise, providing clear and precise information about *how* and *why* to change; i.e., *procedural* and *persuasive information* (Grundy & Osbaldiston, 2006) was successful in reducing use and inspiring proper disposal of household toxins (Werner, 2003).

Information that is especially vivid and focused on outward behavior can be effective as well. In one study, energy conservation practices were shown in a video by a person turning down a thermostat, wearing warmer clothes, and using heavy blankets. With this treatment, viewers reduced their energy use by 28% (Winett et al., 1982). Demonstrating appropriate behavior is called **modeling** (Bandura, 1977), which works better than simply describing desired behaviors.

A wonderful example of the power of modeling was observed by some social psychologists in a men's shower at the University of California–Santa Cruz field house. Although most students at this university would describe themselves as environmentalists, very few conserved water in the shower. Even when the researchers put up a sign asking users to "(1) Wet down, (2) Turn water off, (3) Soap up, (4) Rinse off" only 6% followed these water conserving instructions. However, when the researchers had a confederate demonstrate the appropriate behavior whenever someone entered the shower room, compliance with the instructions rose to 49%. When two confederates were used, 67% imitated the models (Aronson & O'Leary, 1983). Live modeling is a powerful form of stimulus control, much more powerful than mere information or instructions. Sue has frequently experienced this phenomenon during walks with friends: when she bends down to pick up litter during the walk, her friends do so as well.

In general, antecedent stimuli signal the probable reinforcement of particular behaviors. For example, access to recycling facilities indicates the efficacy of individual acts of recycling (Barr, 2007), and neighborhoods that offer summertime farmer's markets provide the chance to purchase locally grown produce (Monroe, 2003). In other words, *opportunity* and *convenience* significantly impact whether or not a given action is performed and consequently reinforced; this finding relates to removing barriers to change, discussed in Chapter 4.

It may be useful to distinguish between different types of proenvironmental or conservation behaviors, because they fall under different kinds of stimulus control; that is, different S^Ds and S^Rs/ S^Ps (Barr, 2007; Monroe, 2003). One investigator identified the following classes of environmental behaviors (Monroe, 2003, p. 115), and we have added some possible antecedent stimuli that could trigger the behaviors. Perhaps you could identify some potential reinforcers (or punishers) of these actions:

- Environmental activism (actively participating in environmental initiatives). The S^D might be a poster or friend publicizing an organizational meeting.
- Nonactivist political behaviors (e.g., signing a petition or writing a check). The S^D might be a Web site with a "Take Action" component (some are included in the Appendix of this book).
- Consumer behaviors (purchasing "green" products, recycling, reducing energy use, and altering consumption habits). The S^Ds would include product labels or secondhand stores.
- Ecosystem behaviors (such as putting up bird boxes, planting sea oats, counting wildlife populations, promoting prescribed fire). One S^D could be information and service projects concerning endangered species in a class lecture.
- Other behaviors that are specific to one's expertise or workplace (e.g., reducing waste in the production process, establishing mortgage criteria for energy efficient houses, suing a polluter, etc.). The S^D would be technical training and knowledge.

Consequence Strategies: Changing the S^Rs

Although manipulating S^Ds can have some effect, many researchers are more interested in **consequence strategies**. If behavior is reinforced, by definition it will increase in frequency. The most important priority for changing behavior, then, is to reward environmentally appropriate behaviors by changing the S^Rs. Unfortunately, most environmentally *in*appropriate behaviors are currently rewarded by convenience, social status, comfort, and pleasure, whereas environmentally appropriate behaviors are not—and they may even be punished. A clear example of negative punishment is the exorbitant cost of public transportation in the United States. From a behavioral perspective, these contingencies must be rearranged.

Rewarding proenvironmental behaviors was a popular research methodology in the 1970s and was shown to be effective for increasing bus ridership (Everett, Hayward, & Meyers, 1974), increasing litter clean-up (Baltes & Hayward, 1976; Casey & Lloyd, 1977; Powers, Osborne, & Anderson, 1973), and reducing energy consumption (reviewed in Abrahamse et al., 2005). This strategy has declined in use, however, as it is difficult and costly to implement, and behavioral changes do not typically last once the rewards are removed; that is, the new behaviors are easily extinguished (e.g., Geller, 2002). Further, people are more likely to act in environmentally responsible ways when reinforcers are **intrinsic**; that is, when the activity is enjoyable or because it is in alignment with the person's values (DeYoung, 2000; Leiserowitz, Maibach, & Roser-Renouf, 2009b; Osbaldiston & Sheldon, 2003). Although values aren't typically sufficient to motivate behavior, the opportunity to reduce **cognitive dissonance**, the disconnect between attitudes and behavior described in Chapter 4, is reinforcing (e.g., Monroe, 2003).

Feedback as $S^R s$ Due to the challenges of implementing reinforcement strategies, it is often more practical and effective to reward the *results* of behavior (e.g., reduced financial or environmental costs) than the behavior itself. Simply giving people **feedback** on progress is usually reinforcing, so there is no need to give them money or raffle tickets as well. Feedback seems to be effective because it has both informational and motivational properties: it tells participants their movement toward a goal. Providing feedback can also be much cheaper than rebates and rewards, especially if its delivery is automatic. Many researchers have investigated the power of giving feedback about proenvironmen-tal behaviors (reviewed in Abrahamse et al., 2005; Gardner & Stern, 2002; Lehman & Geller, 2004). For instance, providing individual or group information about recycling patterns was effective in increas-ing rates of recycling; recall the power of **descriptive norms**, described in Chapter 4. Simply posting the number of aluminum cans retrieved from a recycling container increased the number of cans subsequently recycled by 65% (Larson, Houlihan, & Goernert, 1995). Similarly, giv-ing consumers information about their energy use via more frequent billing and usage information, including graphs that demonstrate energy use over the past year, helps them reduce it. Energy use is an important area for behavioral change as about one third of the typical homeowner's energy purchase is wasted through inefficient appliances and poor insulation (Esswein, 2008).

Free home energy audits are widely available due to the National Energy Conservation Policy Act of 1978. Such audits are becoming more popular as energy costs increase (Badal, 2007), although many people may not actually employ the recommended conservation mea-sures for several reasons (Harrigan, 1994):

- Unfamiliar and intimidating (I've never touched my water heater, let alone adjusted it).
- Confusing, with too many choices (There are 15 kinds of caulk on this shelf, which one should I get for my windows? For my dryer vent?).
- Difficult to do (How do I change my showerhead to a low-flow model?).
- Unpleasant (My water heater is in the basement, and it's dark and dirty down there).
- Done in isolation (My neighbors haven't told me that they turned down their water heater thermostat, so why should I do it?).
- Difficult to evaluate, results virtually invisible (I turned down my water heater thermostat and wrapped the tank, but I can't tell whether doing so made any difference in my bill).
- Easy to ignore (I think I have done everything I can to make my home more energy efficient).
- Expensive (I know I should do something, but I don't have the money to invest in insulation right now).

Expense is the most common explanation for not adopting house-hold energy conservation measures, just ahead of lack of knowledge to implement changes, or the effort or time involved (Leiserowitz et al., 2009b). In other words, performing the behaviors is perceived as *punishing*, thus establishing a powerful barrier to enacting proenvironmental actions. For that reason, an important form of consequence strategies called **Community Based Social Marketing (CBSM)** focuses on interventions that reduce or remove punishing aspects of behavioral change (McKenzie-Mohr 2000a, 2000b;* McKenzie-Mohr & Smith, 1999). The four aspects of CBSM take into account the mechanisms of stimulus control:

- Recognizing the barriers to environmentally appropriate behavior (i.e., identifying the antecedent stimuli (S^Ds) that signal potentially punishing outcomes of performing the behavior)
- Selecting particular behaviors to promote
- Designing programs that effectively address specific barriers (including use of reinforcers and feedback)
- Following-up after the intervention to evaluate its success.

Publicly recognizing individuals (i.e., in the local newspaper) for making positive changes or for committing to change represents positive reinforcement that can mitigate the influence of some of the obstacles listed above. For instance, if someone identifies time and effort as barriers (punishers), the opportunity to receive social reinforcement or avoid social disapproval might provide an incentive, and make the effort seem more worthwhile. Providing individualized and personalized information (antecedent stimuli) can help inspire and guide people's conservation measures, and giving direct feedback about specific progress reinforces their efforts (Harrigan, 1994; McKenzie-Mohr, 2000b). One recent study demonstrated the overall success of an e-mail list-serv social marketing campaign in prompting recipients to adopt energy saving behaviors like checking the efficiency of their refrigerators and vehicle tire pressure as well as installing compact fluorescent lightbulbs (Artz & Cooke, 2007). Not surprisingly, behaviors that are perceived as relatively easy to implement are more likely to be adopted (e.g., Fujii, 2006; see also discussion of barriers and CBSM in Chapter 4).

Prices, Incentives, and Real Costs   In general, attempts to curtail environmentally destructive behavior are likely to extinguish if not consistently prompted (using S^Ds) or reinforced. Consequently, it may

---

* See also http://www.cbsm.com

be more effective to provide incentives (S^Rs) like rebates to motivate one-time actions that produce significant increases in efficiency, such as purchasing a fuel-efficient vehicle and energy-efficient appliances (often identified by an S^D like the Energy Star label), insulating a house, or investing in solar power (Gardner & Stern, 2008; McKenzie-Mohr, 2000a; Stern, 2000). More than half of U.S. residents recently surveyed reported that they made changes to their homes in order to improve energy efficiency, by buying more efficient furnaces and appliances or insulating (Leiserowitz et al., 2009b). Such actions are generally more effective at reducing energy use and are also more appealing to consumers than changing repetitive behaviors such as reducing one's driving or turning off lights and appliances. However, rebound effects can occur, where individuals become lax about conservation efforts once they have acquired a highly efficient appliance (Kurz, 2002): "It's okay for me to drive because my car gets great mileage!"

Changing prices or instituting tax breaks requires government or social control on a much larger scale than that available to a researcher. For the most part, behavior analysts have not brought their principles to discussions of public policies, in part because they are seen, and see themselves, as scientists rather than policy makers (Geller, 1990; 2002). Nonetheless, it is important to examine the ways in which financial incentives often encourage (prompt) environmentally *in*appropriate behavior.

For example, humans continue to deplete resources because the **real costs** of consumption are not yet contingent on actions. When people pay artificially low prices that do not reflect the cost of resource replacement or the pollution clean up involved in production, they are rewarded for inappropriate behavior. Fossil fuel consumption is a classic example. Gasoline prices reflect short-term market availability, not long-term costs incurred from air pollution and climate change. Consequently, people are in a contingency trap as they continue to drive cars even though the long-term impacts are exorbitant (Nevin, 2005).

> The marketplace gives us the wrong information. It tells us that flying across the country on a discount airline ticket is cheap when it is not. It tells us that our food is inexpensive when its method of production destroys aquifers and soil, the viability of ecosystems, and workers' lives. (Hawken, 1993, p. 56)

From a behavioral perspective, an important way to confront the depleting carrying capacity of the planet is to begin calculating, and then charging, the real costs of resource depletion and pollution. The market needs to induce the public to pay as it goes rather than incur ecological debts to be paid by future generations.

The ship of fools and the rocks of
short-term economic planning

Of course, calculating real costs involves a lot of guesswork, but even approximations can help envision how to better control environmentally relevant behaviors. Deforestation represents one example. Overall, more than one half of the forests that once existed on the planet are gone, and many countries including the United States retain *less than 10%* of their original forest cover (Davis, 2007). Many factors contribute to accelerating rates of global deforestation: slash and burn agriculture, urban development, and consumption of wood products (paper, fuel, and construction materials). However, the most powerful factors are economic: People simply do not yet pay the real price for lumber. Worse, many governments subsidize timber industries that weaken protections for forests and exacerbate deforestation (Sizer, 2000).

Currently, only about 7% of the world's forest timber is certified as produced by sustainable procedures (sufficient replanting, selective cutting, and delayed harvesting), making sustainably produced wood difficult to procure (Davis, 2007). (Difficult, but not impossible; The Forest Stewardship Council maintains a Web site where you can determine where to buy wood grown sustainably.*) Current practices make sustainably harvested wood seem expensive even though in the long run it is cheaper than wood extracted unsustainably. Intact forests provide many critical services such as

---

* See http://www.fsc.org/buy-fsc-products.html

Climate regulation, erosion and flood control, habitat and watershed protection, non-wood forest products . . . and other significant economic benefits on an on-going basis. International trade in non-wood forest products alone is worth over $11 billion a year, not counting the even greater local value of these products and the millions of jobs created. (Worldwatch Institute, 2002)

Thus, unsustainably extracted wood is astronomically expensive. Even more than 15 years ago, a mature tree in India was estimated to be worth $50,000. The real cost of a hamburger from cattle raised on cleared rainforest was $200, and a wild Chinook salmon from the Columbia River was estimated to be worth $2,150 to sports and commercial fishers (Durning, 1993).

If calculating real costs is difficult, charging them is even more problematic. No one could price their product in terms of real ecological costs and stay competitive against others who do not, at least not without government intervention. However, recent market-based initiatives such as **cap and trade** and **voluntary carbon dioxide offsets** show some promise for addressing one of the most serious environmental challenges: climate change. Cap and trade systems limit (cap) greenhouse gas emissions to an allowable amount by a region, state, or country. If larger emitters like factories and power plants make improvements that reduce emissions below the caps, they can sell remaining credits to other companies whose emissions are greater than the caps. Essentially, this system "puts a price tag on emissions and creates an economic incentive to reduce them" (Chafe & French, 2008, p. 91). Similarly, voluntary carbon offsets can be purchased by individuals, companies, or groups of people to help alleviate the emissions produced by their actions. For instance, individuals purchasing airline tickets can pay an additional fee that offsets the carbon dioxide that will be released during their flight, or can buy packages to compensate for their regular activities such as driving and using energy in the home.* Such fees go to projects supporting renewable energy, reforestation, and reducing or utilizing emissions created by farms and landfills. In behaviorist terms, this **altruistic** behavior benefiting other humans and ecosystems is self-reinforcing (Toates, 2009).

Manipulating prices or imposing fines and taxes to effect behavior change is based on the **rational economic model**, which states that consumers act rationally to reduce costs while maximizing their purchases. Most economic theory rests on this behavioral view of human

---

* For example, see http://www.carbonfund.org/; http://www.terrapass.com/buy-carbon-offsets/

nature, although there is very little evidence that the rational model of behavior is valid (Kurz, 2002; Thaler, 1999). While behaviorists argue that reinforcers control actions, they recognize that humans are reinforced by many things besides money. Environmentally appropriate behaviors are a product of

> The rich mixture of cultural practices, social interactions, and human feelings that influence the behavior of individuals, social groups, and institutions. . . . Instead of assuming that people invest in energy efficiency if and only if they expect to save money, [we should also] hypothesize that people invest because they have heard from people they trust that the investment will pay or because their friends have already made investments and are satisfied with the results. (Stern, 1992, pp. 1224–1225)

On the other hand, prices can be more important than social reinforcers depending on the relative size of each. Both policy analysts and behaviorists have argued that the United States simply has not yet been subjected to effective price controls (Geller, 1990; Zoumbaris & O'Brien, 1993). For instance, at the end of 2008, steep increases in gas prices (reaching more than $4 per gallon) were credited with significant reductions in driving and market demand for more fuel-efficient vehicles. Any subsequent return to lower prices will likely correlate with a reversal of those changes. And for many U.S. residents, even doubling the price of gas or electricity still makes energy relatively inexpensive in the face of their wealth compared to the rest of the world's people. When gasoline prices are significantly raised through stiff gasoline taxes as in other countries, consumption is reduced. Furthermore, taxes collected on energy production and use could be used to reduce those collected on income or savings, thereby reinforcing nonconsumptive behaviors while discouraging consumptive ones.

The most obvious problem with a price incentive strategy is that it is difficult to change the reinforcement history of those who are responsible for *setting* prices and taxes. In order for political leaders to implement appropriate pricing, they must be willing to lose financial support from industry and special interest groups that lobby to keep artificially low prices in place. Political leaders are on a short reinforcement schedule of 2–6 years, when they face the problem of financing their reelection campaigns. Disappointing their contributors will end the opportunity to continue their careers. However, appropriate pricing requires a commitment to the effects of collective behavior over a much larger time frame, perhaps the next 20–50 years. Thus, from a behavioral viewpoint, pricing mechanisms will not work because the reinforcement schedules of those who could implement them are inappropriate for the task. These considerations lead us and others to suggest that **campaign finance reform** in the United States should be a high priority for solving environmental issues including climate change (Shellenberger & Nordhaus, 2004).

Social Traps as Reinforcement Dilemmas The mismatch between election cycles and appropriate pricing strategies represents another contingency trap. There are both individual and social versions of such traps; the social versions are known as **social dilemmas or social traps.** Hardin's (1968) description of the *tragedy of the commons* is the classic example, based on farmers who graze their cows on a limited piece of common land. If too many animals graze there, overgrazing will ruin the land, as each farmer:

> Will try to keep as many cattle as possible on the commons. . . . The rational herdsman concludes that the only sensible course for him [*sic*] to pursue is to add another animal to his herd. And another; and another. . . . But this is the conclusion reached by each and every rational herdsman sharing the commons. Therein is the tragedy. Each man is locked into a system that compels him to increase his herd without limit—in a world that is limited. . . . Freedom in a commons brings ruin to all. (p. 1244)

This phenomenon illuminates evolutionary mechanisms where any action promoting a relative advantage persists. In the tragedy of the commons, herdsmen are compelled to do whatever is necessary to provide more milk and meat for their offspring in order to ensure the transmission of their genes to future generations (Nevin, 1991). In this particular social dilemma as well as in many other environmentally relevant situations, there is an inherent conflict between an individual's self-interest and the interest of the larger group, and between the relative short- and long-term consequences. Social dilemmas contribute to environmental degradation in several ways (e.g., Gardner & Stern, 2002; Osbaldiston & Sheldon, 2002; Vlek & Steg, 2007):

- First, in the *commons dilemma* described above (Hardin, 1968), individuals take more than their fair allotment of a shared resource, such as by careless or excessive water use (Van Vugt, 2001).
- Second, in *public goods dilemmas*, individuals do not contribute their fair share to a pooled resource (for instance, by voting down a bill that would increase taxes to fund community bus or train services).

- Third, in *risk dilemmas,* acting from self-interest leads to one contributing more than one's share to the hazards suffered by the greater whole. A clear example is commuters' reliance on the convenience of cars, rather than using public transit (Joireman, Van Lange & Van Vugt, 2004a), thereby increasing air pollutants and climate changing gases, as well as traffic problems.
- Fourth, *ecological dilemmas* occur when acting from self-interest upsets the larger balance of things, such as when a landowner fills in a wetland on his property, thereby interfering with waterfowl migration.

In these if not all environmental problems, rewards to the individual are much more immediate and compelling than the delayed costs to the population. The likely result is a damaged biosphere, particularly when adverse consequences of irresponsible behavior are uncertain, and solutions depend upon the actions of large numbers of people (e.g., Staats, 2003).

We are not likely to take the advice we are now being offered [about altering environmentally destructive patterns] because the immediate consequences [of change] are punishing. The old susceptibilities to reinforcement are still with us, and the behavior they strengthen is naturally incompatible with any attempt to suppress it. It takes strong advice to induce most people to stop consuming irreplaceable resources, to moderate the joys of procreation and parenthood, and to destroy weapons that make them feel secure against their enemies. (Skinner, 1991, p. 20)

Thus, humans are often fighting evolution-based patterns in their attempts to behave in environmentally responsible ways, a theme that is explored further in Chapter 7.

Yet, environmentally inappropriate behavior regarding shared resources can be changed by altering the reinforcement contingencies that support it in three ways (Platt, 1973):

1. Reducing the interval between short-term reward and long-term punishment (for example, making the long-term costs more apparent).
2. Adding incentives or reinforcers for environmentally appropriate behavior (e.g., instituting tax breaks for conservation behavior).
3. Adding punishers for inappropriate behavior (such as taxes for polluting emissions).

Follow-up research has shown the merit of Platt's analysis, for instance, in laboratory simulations in which undergraduates play a game with shared resources (Birjulin, Smith, & Bell, 1993). One recent study used an interactive game to simulate climate change, a social dilemma that cannot effectively be addressed without the cooperation of the entire international community (Milinski, Sommerfeld, Krambeck, Reed, & Marotzk, 2008). In the short-term, countries are likely to incur adverse economic impacts as they work to reduce emissions of greenhouse gases, but the long-term consequences of failing to adequately respond will be disastrous to humans and ecosystems, and will deliver horrendous economic costs (reviewed in Chapter 1). In the simulation, participants were given an allotment and then asked to make decisions about how much money to contribute to a group climate account. Contributions were anonymous. If the target amount was reached, each individual would get the remaining portion of his or her allotment; if the goal was not reached, they would lose money. The amount of loss varied between conditions. The target sum was reached most often when the stakes were highest; that is, when failure to personally invest enough money would result in the greatest loss to one's self (Milinski et al., 2008). The authors concluded that people will tend to cooperate with others working toward a common goal (such as reducing global emissions) if they are convinced of the high probability that they would be personally and adversely impacted should the target goals not be reached. In this study, long-term and personal costs were emphasized, stressing the importance of all participants contributing their fair share for the effort to be effective. Such an appeal reminds them of the social reinforcers and punishers in play. Enhanced social reputation or social sanctions are key reinforcers and punishers for action.

Likewise, many studies have shown that people will forego immediate personal reinforcers for longer term group goals, especially if they identify with the group and feel responsible toward it (Dawes, 1980; Gardner & Stern, 2002; Van Vugt, 2002; see also Chapter 10), and if they perceive the long-term benefits of collective action as relevant to them personally as well as to the larger group (Milinski et al., 2008; Ostrom, Burger, Field, Norgaard, & Policansky, 2007). In other words, "cultural practices can oppose the evolutionary susceptibility to immediate reinforcement and the contingencies of individual experience" by making social approval contingent on behaviors that reflect group goals (Nevin, 1991, p. 43).

Behavioral Self-Control

More congruent with a behavioral viewpoint than manipulating economic regulations is to focus on behavioral engineering that takes place at the individual, rather than governmental, level; this strategy can be implemented in three ways: (1) intentionally reinforcing another person's behavior through compliments and appreciation or course credit; (2) changing one's own behavior; and (3) modeling appropriate behaviors so that others can copy them, as in the shower study described above.

When Deborah's father explained his ingenious system for saving water (recycling water from the sink, to tub, to toilet), she expressed genuine admiration and approval to him directly. Such **social reinforcers** are powerful controls on behavior and provide the basis for entire cultural organization. Thus, expressing reactions to others' behavior can help change it. Unfortunately, such expressions can also backfire and cause the recipient to feel manipulated or nagged depending on how the reinforcer is delivered. When Deborah asked a colleague to print memos on both sides of the paper, she received a nasty (one-sided) note telling her to mind her own business!

Perhaps the most effective way to change individual behavior is to start by changing one's own. This approach, called **self-control**, occurs when an individual changes reinforcing and discriminative stimuli in order to change one's own behavior (Skinner, 1953). If you have ever dieted, put yourself on a study schedule, or disciplined yourself in some other way to achieve a goal, then you have implemented a self-control project. Such approaches can be used to change environmentally relevant behaviors.

The following represent the steps of a self-control project so you can see the procedure in enough detail to design your own (adapted from Martin & Pear, 2009).

1. Define the problem
2. Set a goal
3. Make a public commitment
4. Observe baseline behavior
5. Design stimulus control
6. Formulate a contract
7. Check on changed behavior
8. Consider ways of generalizing the change to related behaviors.

Step 1. *Define the problem.* As an illustration, a self-control project could focus on reducing paper waste. In this case, *the problem* is that approximately one quarter of the world's timber harvest is used to produce paper. Perhaps not surprisingly, with less than 5% of the world's population, the United States is responsible for *more than one quarter* (27%) of global wood use (Matthews, 2000). Paper is the largest component (constituting one third) of the municipal solid waste generated in the United States (U.S. Environmental Protection Agency, 2007b). Although a little more than half is recovered for recycling, every stage of paper production and consumption constitutes a significant environmental threat (e.g., Vanasselt, 2001): Most wood extraction procedures lead to deforestation and loss of forest diversity; toxic liquid pollutants are released during pulp- and papermaking; paper products in landfills generate methane, a gas that contributes to climate change; and incineration of paper bleached with chlorine releases dioxin, a highly toxic chemical that is a known carcinogen and **endocrine (hormone) disruptor** (see further discussion in Chapter 6). Thus, even small actions undertaken by many people could significantly reduce the harmful impacts of paper manufacturing, use, and disposal.*

Step 2. *Set a specific behavioral goal* to enable measurement of progress. An intention to reduce consumption or minimize paper waste is too vague; defining the goal specifically in behavioral terms enhances the probability of success. With respect to paper use, your goal might be to reduce paper use by 50%. The goal should represent a significant but realistic change. In behavioral terms, this could involve the following plans:

• Read articles on-line, only printing when absolutely necessary.
• Photocopy on both sides of each page of paper.
• Print drafts of manuscripts and informal notes on the backs of junk paper.
• Reuse envelopes for informal mail.
• Reuse gift wrapping received from others.
• Use scrap paper for lists, notes, and reminders.
• Use cloth towels and napkins instead of paper.
• Go to the public library to read magazines and books instead of purchasing your own.
• Bring a cloth bag to the grocery store rather than taking paper (or plastic) ones.

Step 3. *Make a public commitment* to reduce paper waste by telling someone about the project. Research suggests that people who have made a commitment are considerably more likely to follow through with changing the behavior, particularly if feedback on progress is also given (e.g., Abrahamse et al., 2005; Monroe, 2003; see also Chapter 4).

---

* For other ideas about projects to reduce your **ecological footprint**, take the quiz at http://myfootprint.org/ or see the appendix in the back of this book.

Step 4. *Observe baseline behavior.* In order to track current use and measure progress, assign points to individual paper saving behaviors indicating the relative importance of each, as well as points for wasteful actions. Table 5.2 shows one example of how to set up a point system.

Use the point system to count and graph the relevant behaviors over a period of time, say two weeks *prior to initiating any attempt at change.* This provides a **baseline** measure of behavior as it is occurring with existing contingencies. Given this picture of unaltered behaviors, you can also monitor what situations are likely to accompany them. For example, you may be good at photocopying on two sides of the paper unless you are rushed. Since the photocopy machine is more likely to jam when making double-sided copies, you might avoid doing it when you have limited time. Similarly, it might be easy to use cloth napkins instead of paper when at home, but not when you go out to eat. Analysis of this kind might suggest that paper overuse occurs because of time pressure (an S^D) or convenience (S^R). Figure 5.2 shows what a behavioral record would look like in graph form, both for the baseline period and the period where the contingencies are changed.

Step 5. *Design stimulus control* by changing the S^Ds and S^Rs. Following the analysis in Step 4, contingencies can be altered to reduce paper use. In terms of antecedent stimuli (S^Ds), you might realize that readings must be done at least 48 hours before class to ensure computer time and minimize the need for printing or photocopying. To reduce napkin use, you could keep a cloth napkin in your backpack so you'll have it with you when you go to meals. You might notice that it is easier to reuse envelopes opened with a letter opener than ones that get torn when you open them by hand. Thus, placing a letter opener where you open mail will help with that part of your goal. Designing such antecedent conditions enables more effective management of one's behavior.

Table 5.2 Paper Wasting Behaviors With Assigned Points

Paper Wasting Behaviors	Points
Photocopy on one side of page	1/page
Printing draft on new paper	1/page
Use new envelope for informal mail	1/envelope
Use new wrapping paper for gift wrap	1/gift
Use new paper for list, note	1/note
Use paper instead of cloth towel	1/towel
Buy magazine instead of using library	5/magazine
Use paper bag at grocery instead of cloth	1/bag

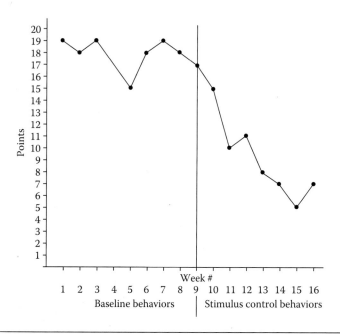

Figure 5.2 Graph of paper wasting behaviors.

Manipulating consequent stimuli (S^Rs) can also be very helpful. If you manage to change your behavior to specified levels, you could reward yourself with a special treat that is environmentally appropriate. Perhaps inviting a friend over for lunch, swimming for an hour, or watching a rented video movie would be reinforcing events. Similarly, you could institute punishers. You could ask a friend to scold you (or scold yourself) when you forget to bring your own bags to the store (positive punishment). By keeping a running account of the cost of paper use, you can experience more directly the adverse impacts of waste (i.e., negative punishers): how much money is spent on gift wrapping, unnecessary photocopy paper, paper towels, and magazines. If this loss of money is not sufficient to create discomfort, you could do something more active about waste: Donating money to an organization listed in the appendix for replanting tree projects or personally planting a certain number of trees for a given amount of paper wasted.

Step 6. *Drawing up a formal contract* increases the potential for behavioral change. For example, "I will reward myself with a rented video if my paper waste points average below 5 for any given week, or if I increase my paper conservation points above 20 in any given week."

Step 7. *Check on changed behavior.* Continue to record and graph the paper use–waste behaviors under the altered antecedent and consequence strategies so you can judge the extent to which the project is successfully changing paper use. Meeting predetermined goals indicates effective behavior change.

Step 8. *Consider generalizing the change.* At some point, the new behaviors should become habitual or at least performed more often than not. Then you might start noticing other ways in which you can **generalize** to include additional behaviors within a category (e.g., Osbaldiston & Sheldon, 2003). For example, the goal of conserving paper might broaden to reducing takeout container waste by bringing Tupperware to restaurants for leftovers, or conserving energy by lowering the thermostat, turning off appliances when not in use, or carpooling and bicycling instead of driving alone.

Self-control projects have an additional payoff besides changing individual behavior: they also provide the opportunity to model environmentally appropriate behavior for others. When you send a note on the second side of a piece of paper, reuse an envelope, wrap a gift in the funnies, or carry a Tupperware container into a restaurant, you demonstrate behavior to others that they may begin to enact as well.

Limitations of the Behavioral Approach

Like all of the perspectives described in this text, the behavioral approach does not guarantee instant success. In fact, research on behavioral engineering has not been widely applied for several important reasons (Geller, 2002; Lehman & Geller, 2004).

- First, the audience of the research is usually limited to psychologists as it is published in professional journals and books. These individuals have "little interest or influence in large scale dissemination and application" or marketing the techniques (Geller, 2002, p. 526).
- Second, the target behaviors selected in the research studies may not be the most important. *Overpopulation and overconsumption constitute the most important obstacles to achieving environmental sustainability* (Howard, 2000; Oskamp, 2000), not litter control and recycling efforts, which are the targets of most behavior-change programs because they are easier to implement locally. Note, however, that modeling (an antecedent strategy) may be effective for addressing significant social problems including overpopulation and consumption (Bandura, 2002).

Reprinted from © Dave Coverly [http://www.speedbump.com/]. With permission.

- Third, organizational and industrial systems are critical for initiating sustainability efforts because of their polluting practices, the extent to which they can make green products available, and their contributions to an infrastructure that encourages or requires unsustainable behaviors (Stern, 2000). Although it can be difficult to design stimulus control strategies for the people who manage and regulate these practices, at least some businesses are starting to take sustainability to heart, and are discovering considerable financial benefits of doing so (e.g., Savitz & Weber, 2006; see also the discussion in Chapter 11).

From a behavioral perspective, the most important obstacle to adopting proenvironmental behaviors may be that environmentally destructive behaviors are strongly habitual. A person's reinforcement history often strengthens inappropriate behaviors to a point where they are difficult to change, and new actions require considerable practice. Short-term reinforcers like convenience maintain inappropriate behaviors and must be countered by stronger reinforcers. If you have ever tried to modify your own behavior, you know that instant and permanent change doesn't happen. Any new behaviors are inconsistent and weak.

A model from the clinical psychology of addiction is applicable here, as many people are addicted to unsustainable consumption patterns. As we saw in the self-control project, behavioral change entails considering triggering stimuli (S^{D}s), and the relative advantages and disadvantages of change (i.e., reinforcers and punishers), designing a plan and committing to it, and checking on progress. Thus, change requires patience and perseverance because most people relapse; that is, the new behaviors extinguish at least temporarily when one falls back on old (previously reinforced) habits (see Figure 5.3).

However, weak behaviors can eventually become very consistent and durable if reinforcement contingencies are appropriately maintained. Remember Deborah's cloth shopping bag example. Even though behavior change doesn't occur overnight, conscientious and consistent practice can enable new habits to be firmly set.

Changing the consequences of one's own and others' actions can be tricky, although waiting for natural forces to do it will be too slow to prevent catastrophe. Either systematically or by necessity, behavior will adapt to changing environmental contingencies as ecosystems are further stressed or collapse. The main question is whether humans can effectively

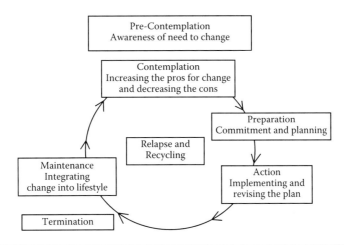

Figure 5.3 The Stages of Change Model. Reprinted from DiClemente, C. (2003). *Addiction and Change: How Addictions Develop and Addicted People Recover*, New York: Guilford, Figure 3, p. 30. With permission.

change the reinforcers controlling destructive behavior in time. And if so, why should anyone forego rewards and conveniences now in order to sustain a planet for future generations? What's in it for them?

Skinner (1971) directly posed this question in his book *Beyond Freedom and Dignity* when he asked "Why should I care whether my [culture or species] survives long after my death?" His answer was "There is no good reason why you should be concerned, but if your culture has not convinced you that there is, so much the worse for your culture" (p. 137). He suggested that evolution selects cultures that *do* get people to care about the next generation. This doesn't indicate *why* people should care, only that they probably do. The question of why poses the perceptual problem of embracing future generations, so a worldview that emphasizes responsibility toward future generations may be required (see also Chapter 2 and Chapter 10). Although world-view is not a typical concern of behaviorists, Geller (1995), who has done extensive work applying behavioral principles to environmental problems over the last few decades, proposed that behavioral interventions should be designed to increase people's "active caring" about ecological issues.

Forgoing Freedom

Despite the limitations of the behavioral approach, this subdiscipline makes many important contributions to promoting a more sustainable world. Behavioral principles help examine particular features of the environment that control behavior including both antecedent (S^Ds) and consequent stimuli (S^Rs and S^Ps). Since human behavior results in environmental degradation, human behavior must change in order to secure future comforts and even survival. Behaviorists delivered a conceptual tool for designing a behavioral technology, even if changing the really powerful stimuli gets into the more complicated realms of interpersonal interaction, social policy, governmental legislation, and economic market analysis.

From a behaviorist's perspective, there is no need to focus on beliefs and attitudes, nor is there a need to speak about human freedom. To posit individual freedom is to draw a separation between the self and the environment, a separation that is arbitrary and false. It is true that people like to *experience* themselves as free, and generally they do *if* their behavior is controlled by positive reinforcement. Under those conditions, people usually experience the freedom to choose their actions. For example, we both believe it is a choice to work on this book in order to communicate our concern and insights about the psychology of environmental problems, an experience that has been reinforcing to us both in the past. On the other hand, imagine if one of us was threatened with losing her job if she did not write this book. In that case, she would not feel free to write it. Her behavior would be controlled by punishers, and she would feel coerced and manipulated. The behavior is controlled either way, but whether or not one *feels* free depends largely on the type of consequence. As people are likely to react or rebel when they feel controlled or manipulated (e.g., DeYoung, 2000), efforts to encourage environmentally responsible behavior should focus on positively reinforcing achievements rather than punishing inappropriate behaviors or using scare tactics. As Skinner himself (1991) noted, unfortunately "the principle modus operandi of [environmental] organizations is to frighten people rather than offer them a world to which they will turn because of the reinforcing consequences of doing so" (p. 28).

The experience of freedom is also affected by knowing about the consequences controlling behavior. Imagine that you are shopping for a new car. If you are completely ignorant about stimulus control, you might feel free to select any model. If you select one advertised as high fuel efficiency (an S^D), you experience your selection as a choice. Yet if you were coerced or threatened to buy a particular car, you would not feel free to choose. In either case, the choice is not really free but people feel free if they either do not know what the contingencies are or are controlled by positive reinforcers. In sum, behavior reflects the environmental contingencies at play, whether or not people develop verbal behaviors to describe them.

Reprinted from © Mark Stivers. With permission.

As you can probably imagine, Skinner had a tough time convincing the U.S. population of his views about individual freedom. Freedom is a central concept in democratic society, and those in the United States experience freedom in many ways: personal mobility (driving cars, traveling, and changing jobs and residences) far greater than citizens of other countries; U.S. cultural heroes like Rocky and President Obama, who demonstrate the quintessential belief that anything is possible through personal effort; and a political heritage that emphasizes "Life, Liberty, and the Pursuit of (individual) happiness." Most people not only think of themselves as free, but feel belittled by the idea that they are not. Behavioral engineering elicits fears of Orwell's *1984* or Huxley's *Brave New World*. Sinister motives are attributed to those who would implement behavioral technology, and Skinner himself has been badly misrepresented and misunderstood as a cold, cruel scientist.

While these reactions might be understandable, they are actually illogical and erroneous. People ask and pay for behavioral engineering when they send their children to school, hire consultants to help solve problems, or read textbooks that improve test taking or paper writing behaviors. In fact, you (or your parents) pay professors to change your behavior. In so doing, you must temporarily acknowledge that you want others to control you. Since it is easy to see some behavior as controlled, is it not consistent to see all behavior as controlled, even during the experience of personal choice? Such a view might challenge the traditional sense of freedom, and it would also challenge the sense of blame and accomplishment as behavior merely reflects the play of environmental contingencies. However, in return, you may come to perceive and think more clearly about the situational determinants of human behavior, and thus be more effective at changing them rather than wasting emotional energy blaming yourself or others.

CONCLUSIONS

Currently, most contingencies are not yet powerful enough to change environmentally destructive behaviors. This is true in part because many people are caught in the social trap of knowing that their behaviors are irresponsible, but still choosing short-term, personal benefits with delayed, long-term costs to themselves and others. Nobody has yet been forced to pay the real costs for products and services because current pricing does not reflect resource depletion, pollution, and poverty produced with these goods. Consequently, it is critical to encourage lawmakers to address this discrepancy. At the same time, cues and feedback are needed to facilitate proenvironmental behaviors, as well as enhanced social connections that foster a sense of collective responsibility.

Institutional changes can be addressed through task forces to examine energy use, conservation measures, recycling procedures, and so forth, and each person can take initiatives to influence schools, workplaces, communities, and municipal agencies. For example, Deborah was successful in getting her professional organization, the American Psychological Association, to adopt a Green Report Card, in which it reported annually on its efforts at reducing resource use. Happily, sustainability efforts on college campuses are flourishing, providing students, professors, and administrators with information and mechanisms for promoting sustainable campuses (see the Association for the Advancement of Sustainability in Higher Education*).

Behavior exists in a feedback loop where actions change the environment, and in turn, the environment changes actions. A sharp distinction between self and environment is arbitrary and artificial. Specifically, as people demand more environmentally friendly products (e.g., those made from recycled, durable, or less toxic materials), industry and organizations will adjust their manufacturing processes accordingly, and as more sustainable products and services become available, costs typically come down and more people take advantage of these offerings. Correspondingly, many environmentally relevant behaviors (e.g., taking public transit) are not just individual actions, but are also a product of the prevailing environmental contingencies. The social infrastructure (e.g., availability, scheduling, and personal access to trains and buses) makes public transportation possible. Yet the more people who take advantage of such offerings when they are available, the more likely services are to increase.

To see this point more clearly, imagine a transportation infrastructure within a sustainable society. All the cues (S^Ds) encouraging driving would be gone. Nobody would be climbing into a car alone, cars would be prohibitively expensive to operate, roads would be less available and inconvenient. People would live within walking or biking distance to their workplace, commute in groups using electric cars, or use accessible and inexpensive public transportation. Electronic commuting would be far more frequent with Internet, fax, conference calls, and electronic mail used to communicate with colleagues. Schools and shops would be located close to residences, allowing people to complete errands without the use of a car. A convenient system of solar-powered vans or trams would supplement in cases of bad weather, heavy packages, or infirmed

---

* See http://www.aashe.org/

persons. Under such conditions, driving a petroleum-based car would be very costly or inconvenient, making more environmentally appropriate commuting behaviors easy to enact and maintain. People would not try to change out of moral responsibility or proenvironment attitudes; they would simply emit environmentally appropriate behaviors because the environment had been designed to support them.

Such communities are being developed; one example is Pringle Creek in Salem, Oregon.* Their system of smart transportation features walking and biking paths, and all houses are in close proximity to the proposed transit center. In addition, residences are rated for net-zero energy consumption for electricity, heating, and air conditioning; all homes are constructed using the best **green building** practices (see Chapter 8); and rainwater is collected and used for gardens and park areas.

Thus, behaviorism offers a glimpse into how to redesign human behavior by redesigning residential, commercial, and industrial environments and situations.

> If human nature means the genetic endowment of the species, we cannot change it. But we have the science needed to design a world that would take that into account and correct many of the miscarriages of evolution. It would be a world in which people treated each other well, not because of sanctions imposed by governments or religions but because of immediate, face-to-face consequences. . . . It would be a world in which the social and commercial practices that promote unnecessary consumption and pollution had been abolished. (Skinner, 1991, pp. 26–27)

Behaviorists offer an opportunity to experience the unity of personal relationships with the environment, to see oneself not as a victim but as an agent, a consumer as well as restorer, a reactor as well as designer. They illuminate the circular relationship between what people do and what is happening as they do it. Much of the present difficulty stems from people considering themselves separate from, or even *above*, the natural environment. Instead, our actions are both a product and cause of the environment in which we behave. It is time to recognize the interdependence of human actions and environmental conditions, and become effective agents of change toward a sustainable world. The abundance of toxic chemicals used in homes, gardens, and various industries represents a good place to start, as we turn our attention to the Neuropsychology of Toxic Exposures.

---

* See http://www.pringlecreek.com/

6

NEUROPSYCHOLOGY OF TOXIC EXPOSURES

Each summer, Sue's neighbor launches a vigorous chemical attack on the weeds that populate his property and the alley separating their homes. What is particularly disturbing is that when his child was a toddler, she rode in a snuggly on his back while he applied the pesticides. Although he is an intelligent and educated man, he seems unaware of the potentially harmful effects of such exposures, particularly for children. Weed killers and other hazardous products are widely available and used, yet much research demonstrates that they can cause serious health problems, including interfering with **neurodevelopment** (i.e., brain development) and function, causing learning, behavioral, and attention disabilities.

Rachel Carson (1962) was the first to focus public attention on the link between environmental pollutants and compromised health. In Carson's words, "we have seen that [toxins] contaminate soil, water, and food, that they have the power to make our streams fishless and our gardens and woodlands silent and birdless. Man [sic], however much he may like to pretend the contrary, is part of nature" (p. 188). Unfortunately, almost 50 years after her book *Silent Spring* (1962) was published, the use of toxic chemicals has greatly increased in homes and industries, even while concern about air and water pollution has grown. As human neurological systems are so sensitive to environmental toxins, people damage themselves and their children when polluting the environment.

In this chapter, we will look at how this happens through the lenses of two subdisciplines: **Physiological psychology** (also known as **biological psychology**, or **biopsychology**), a branch of the neurosciences (brain sciences) that analyzes behavior as a function of physiological processes, often using nonhuman animal models; and the related field of **neuropsychology**, which is similar in its study of physiological effects on cognition and behavior but focuses on the study of humans suffering from **neurological** (nervous system) disease or dysfunction.

We begin this discussion by considering the broad range of substances to which humans are regularly exposed (i.e., lead, mercury, pesticides, and industrial and consumer chemicals), and the physiological, neurological, and psychological effects of some particular exposures including developmental disabilities, psychiatric symptoms, accelerated aging, Parkinson's Disease, and reproductive abnormalities. Since it is difficult, if not impossible, to establish causal connections between a particular type of exposure and a specific outcome in people, we describe some of the methodological complexities associated with research in environmental health. We conclude with a review of some legislative and behavioral approaches that can reduce the toxic burden and its associated health risks.

TOXIC EXPOSURES

The manufacture, use, and disposal of consumer products constitutes "the prime driver of the toxification of Earth" (Ehrlich & Ehrlich, 2008, p. 225) and its inhabitants. Seemingly ordinary substances like weed and flea killers, hair dyes, paint thinner, flame resistant pajamas and bedding, and even plastic bottles and toys, contain chemicals that alone, or in combination, are harmful to the health of humans and ecosystems. Billions of tons of chemicals are released every year and no one can escape exposure.

Many substances act as **persistent bioaccumulative and toxic pollutants** (PBTs; U.S. EPA, 2002a; also known as **persistent organic pollutants (POPs)**; McGinn, 2002). They are *persistent*, meaning they can remain in the environment for long periods of time (years or decades) without breaking down or losing their potency. *Bioaccumulation* means that such substances become more and more concentrated as they move up the food chain, becoming most toxic and potentially fatal later in the consumption cycle. For example, in the 1950s, phytoplankton in Clear Lake, California, absorbed low levels of a **pesticide** (a chemical designed to kill a species that humans consider pests). The chemical became more concentrated in the fish that ate the phytoplankton and reached lethal levels in the birds that ate the fish (Nadakavukaren, 2000). Since humans are at the end of many food chains, 48 of the 50 states have issued advisories, especially to pregnant women, about eating fish that contain high levels of PBTs (U.S. EPA, 2007a). The majority of advisories (88%) concern **mercury** (a heavy metal), Polychlorinated biphenyls (**PCBs)** and **dioxins** (industrial chemicals), chlordane (a pesticide), and DDT (a pesticide that was banned in 1975, thanks to activism stimulated by Carson's *Silent Spring*).

Ingredients of commonly used pesticides for agricultural, home, and garden applications qualify as PBTs, as do various industrial chemicals and emissions, manufacturing by-products, and other hazardous wastes that continually contaminate air, water, and soil. People consume meat and by-products (milk, cheese, and eggs) from tainted animals, and PBTs are found in a variety of products including plastics, computers, other electronics, cosmetics, and personal care products (McGinn, 2002; Muir & Zegarac, 2001). Furniture, mattresses, clothing, electronic appliances, upholstery, and other consumer items are commonly treated with flame retardant chemicals that are also PBTs (Costa & Giordano, 2007). All PBTs are stored in one's body fats and

Reprinted from © Dave Coverly [http://www.speedbump.com/]. With permission.

other tissues and build up with repeated exposures (another way in which they *bioaccumulate*).
PBTs can be harmful to humans in at least four ways:

- They can act as direct **neurotoxins** by destroying or damaging nerve cells in the brain (**neurons**). Damage can occur to parts of the neuron such as the **axon**, the portion of the cell that carries its signal known as an **action potential**; or it can degrade the **myelin sheath**, the fatty insulation on axons. Chemical transmission (**neurotransmission**) between neurons can also be disrupted by PBTs (e.g., Gilbert, 2004; see Figure 6.1 for a diagram of an intact neuron).
- The PBTs that are **endocrine**, or **hormone disruptors**, bind to naturally occurring receptors and block hormones from attaching, thus preventing hormones from doing their job. PBTs can also mimic the effects of hormones, in some cases producing **estrogenic** (feminizing) effects (see Figure 6.2).
- PBTs can suppress the **immune system** (**immunosuppressants**), interfering with the body's defenses against infection and disease.
- Many chemicals also act as **carcinogens**, or cancer-causing agents, for example by causing cellular **mutations**.

We will focus on neurotoxic and endocrine-disruptive effects in this chapter; the last two types of effects are addressed in Chapter 8.

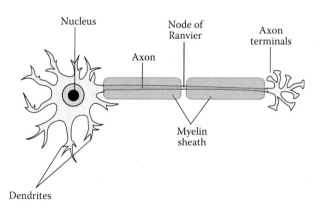

Figure 6.1 Diagram of a neuron.

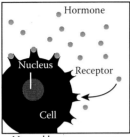
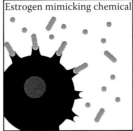
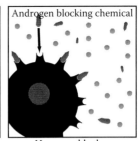

| Normal hormone process | Hormone mimic | Hormone blocker |

Figure 6.2 Hormone disruptors. Hormones are chemical messengers in the endocrine system, regulating brain development, physical growth, and reproductive processes. Various PBTs impact normal hormone functioning, for example, by mimicking or blocking their action. (From graphic design by Darick Dang, Willamette University. With permission.)

Neurodevelopment

The developing nervous system is particularly vulnerable to the effects of chemicals that act as neurotoxins and endocrine disruptors. Nervous system development occurs in a precise sequence of anatomical and chemical events and is very sensitive to chemical interference at virtually all stages of development (i.e., from soon after conception until long after birth). Brain development begins early in the fetus, as neurons divide, migrate to different regions, differentiate into different types of cells, and form **synapses** (connections) with other cells. Neural migration continues through infancy and the second year of life, and the formation of myelin, synapses, and overall brain development persists into adolescence (see Figure 6.3). During the prenatal period, both nutritional substances and toxic chemicals enter the placenta from the maternal bloodstream, affecting fetal growth and brain development (Weiss, 1997). Postnatally, infants consume significant concentrations of PBTs present in the fat of breast milk and other foods. Because of bioaccumulation, breast milk contains levels of toxins that are even greater than in the mother's blood, although experts continue to recommend breast-feeding because of its significant nutritional benefits (Landrigan, Sonawane et al., 2002).

Immune system and detoxification processes are undeveloped in fetuses and infants, increasing their susceptibility to chemical exposures. Young children also encounter higher levels of PBTs than adults because of the **spatial ecology of childhood** (Weiss, 2000). Since young children spend considerable time on floors, they stir up and breathe dust and residues, and their contact with dust may

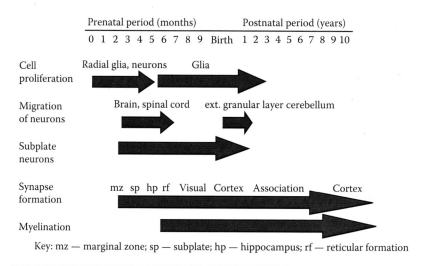

Key: mz — marginal zone; sp — subplate; hp — hippocampus; rf — reticular formation

Figure 6.3 Timelines of developmental processes in humans. During brain development, over one billion nerve cells (neurons) and one trillion glial, or support, cells are produced. Neurons migrate, form synapses, and become myelinated. The peak number of synapses is reached during early childhood. Chemical interference at any stage can cause alterations throughout the cascade. (Graphic from Stein, J., Schettler, T., Wallinga, D., Miller, M., & Valenti, M., *In Harm's Way: Training Program for Health Professionals*, Greater Boston, Physician's for Social Responsibility, 2002; Data adapted from Rice D., & Barone, S. (2000). *Environmental Health Perspectives, 108*(Suppl. 3), 511–533. With permission from Environmental Health Perspectives and Ted Schettler.)

be 10 times greater than that of adults. Children naturally explore their environments by putting potentially contaminated items into their mouths. Perhaps most disturbingly, plastic baby bottles and children's toys contain chemical additives that disrupt the endocrine system, which we'll describe in more detail later in the chapter. The fact that children ingest relatively more juice, fruit, and water than adults gives them increased exposure to residues and contaminants in those substances, and significant levels of pesticide residues continue to be found on popular (and nutritional) foods such as peaches and apples (see Figure 6.4).

Although most parents are aware of the risks of poisoning through accidental ingestion of household chemicals, nearly one million children under the age of six experience such poisonings every year (U.S. EPA, n.d.). Exposures occur because products are not stored properly outside the reach of children, or they are used in and around where children live, play, and go to school. Early signs of acute exposure to pesticides include nervousness, restlessness, and anxiety; not surprisingly,

Environmental Working Group's
SHOPPER'S GUIDE TO
PESTICIDES
in PRODUCE

DIRTY DOZEN   CLEANEST 12
Buy these organic   Lowest in pesticides

Worst	Best
Peaches	Onions
Apples	Avocado
Sweet bell peppers	Sweet corn (Frozen)
Celery	Pineapples
Nectarines	Mango
Strawberries	Sweet peas (Frozen)
Cherries	Asparagus
Lettuce	Kiwi
Grapes (Imported)	Bananas
Pears	Cabbage
Spinach	Broccoli
Potatoes	Eggplant

Don't see your favorites? Get the full results at www.foodnews.org
& support EWG research with an online gift.
ENVIRONMENTAL WORKING GROUP

Figure 6.4 Shopper's guide to pesticides in produce. These produce rankings were developed by analysts at the not-for-profit Environmental Working Group (EWG) based on the results of nearly 51,000 tests for pesticides on produce collected by the U.S. Department of Agriculture and the U.S. Food and Drug Administration between 2000 and 2005. A detailed description of the criteria used in developing the rankings as well as a full list of fresh fruits and vegetables that have been tested is available [www.foodnews.org]. Reprinted with permission.

these symptoms are often improperly diagnosed (Weiss, 1998). More apparent indicators of acute poisoning are headache, weakness, dizziness, and nausea (U.S. EPA, n.d.), but even these reactions are often mistaken for the flu. Some pesticides cause acute symptoms such as severe abdominal pain, vomiting, diarrhea, difficulty breathing, and potentially convulsions, coma, and death (Nadakavukaren, 2000; Weiss, 1997). Chronic impacts include birth defects, organ damage, cancers, asthma, and learning, behavioral, and emotional problems (Sanborn et al., 2007; U.S. EPA, n.d.).

In sum, children are at particular risk for the harmful effects of PBTs because:

- Normal brain development is based on exquisitely choreographed sequences of cellular events that can be disrupted by chemical exposures.
- Toxic chemicals are ubiquitous in air, water, foods, consumer products, as well as home, yard, school, and park environments.
- The spatial ecology of childhood compounds ambient exposures.

Thus, PBTs can contribute to a range of neurodevelopmental and psychiatric disabilities.

NEURODEVELOPMENTAL DISABILITIES

Do you, or does someone you know, suffer from attention deficit disorder or a learning disability? According to the Centers for Disease Control and Prevention (CDC; 2006), approximately 17% of U.S. children (i.e., 12 million individuals) under the age of 18 are affected by one or more developmental disabilities. By themselves, learning disabilities expressed as reading and writing difficulties and other disorders of academic skills affect nearly three million school-age children (i.e., 1 out of every 5); about one third of these children also suffer from attentional problems (National Institutes of Health, 2008).

Although there are many variables that can contribute to the rising prevalence of such disorders including genetics, nutrition, and social influences (see Figure 6.5), toxic exposures are an important *and potentially preventable* risk factor. Roughly 25% of developmental defects are estimated to result from toxic exposures, either singly or in combination with other factors such as maternal lifestyle choices (diet, tobacco, alcohol; Landrigan, Kimmel, Correa, & Eskenazi, 2004).

Considerable research links exposures to various PBTs including heavy metals (mercury and lead), pesticides, and industrial and household chemicals with intellectual and attentional delays or disabilities. Each of these toxic impacts is considered in turn.

Cognitive and Attentional Impairments

Mercury. Mental retardation, IQ reductions, learning disabilities, and attention disorders can result from prenatal or postnatal exposure to mercury (e.g., Bellinger & Adams, 2001; Myers & Davidson, 2000). Mercury acts as a direct neurotoxin, damaging or killing neurons (Myers

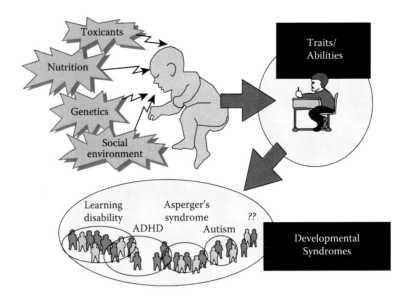

Figure 6.5 Multiple factors interact in complex ways during critical periods of vulnerability to affect neurodevelopment. Several developmental syndromes can result, including some not yet identified (represented by ?? in the figure). These causes include nutritional and chemical exposures during vulnerable periods in early life, genetic factors (which should not be viewed in isolation), and the social environment. Among the multiple causes of disability, chemical exposures deserve special scrutiny because they are preventable causes of harm. (Reproduced graphic from Stein, J. et al. (2002). *In Harm's Way: Training Program for Health Professionals*, Greater Boston, Physician's for Social Responsibility. With permission from Ted Schettler.)

& Davidson, 2000). Eight percent of women in the United States are at risk of bearing children with learning disabilities and other neurological problems because of mercury exposure, primarily from eating contaminated fish and seafood, putting more than 300,000 babies at risk annually (U.S. EPA, 2008c; you can view your own state's advisories online*). While seafood offers nutritional benefits that can support neurodevelopment, there is considerable evidence justifying caution in its consumption, particularly for children and women of childbearing age (Adams & Schantz, 2006).

Coal-fired power plants and waste incineration are the primary sources of mercury-contaminated air pollution, yet these industrial practices continue emitting mercury and other toxins. Mercury in the air can travel considerable distances prior to settling in soil and bodies of water where it contaminates fish stocks (Schettler et al., 2000). Disturbingly, the medical and dental industries use and generate considerably more mercury-containing waste than other sources

* See http://map1.epa.gov/

(Sattler, 2002), waste that is typically incinerated. Further, mercury thermometers continue to be sold in most states. Due to consumer ignorance or carelessness in disposing of thermometers, mercury ends up in landfills where it can leach into water supplies. Even minimal amounts are cause for concern. As little as 1/70th of a teaspoon of mercury can disperse to contaminate a 25 acre lake (McGinn, 2002).

Lead. Harmful effects of lead include deficits in intelligence, language function, learning, memory, attention, and executive function as well as mental retardation at higher exposure levels (Bellinger & Adams, 2001; Needleman, 2004). These effects are generally well known due to intensive public awareness campaigns and governmental interventions in the 1970s to remove lead from gasoline and paint. Yet despite this legislation exposures continue, particularly in urban communities where it persists in dust and the paint of older houses (Haynes, Lanphear, Tohn, Farr, & Wioads, 2002). Most toys (80%) and many other consumer products are imported from China, where lead contamination led to massive recalls of children's toys (Mouawad, 2007*). Tragically, even though the toxicity of lead has been recognized for millennia, it remains an important contributor to decreased intellectual function and failures in school (Lanphear et al., 2005; Needleman & Landrigan, 2004).

© U.S. Environmental Protection Agency. With permission.

---

* You can find information about contaminated toys at http://www.healthytoys.org/

Lead provides a valuable case study, as regulations governing lead exposure were largely based on an understanding of the dangers of acute, high-dose poisonings. Chronic or low-dose exposure was considered benign until Needleman and colleagues' (1979) landmark observation of an association between higher teeth lead levels and difficulty following classroom instruction, unruly behavior, greater distractibility, and reduced auditory and verbal processing, attention, and IQ scores, particularly on verbal components. These results demonstrated that intellectual impairments and problematic behaviors result from lead levels that were considered normal (Rice et al., 1996; see also Lanphear et al., 2005).

Thirty years ago, Needleman (1980) predicted that "the standard for acceptable exposure to lead, given the history of scientific progress, will require further downward revision as new information is gathered and evaluated" (p. 45). He was right: There is no safe level of lead exposure. Lead concentrations falling below levels of concern set by the CDC and World Health Organization (WHO) are inversely correlated with intellectual function (Canfield et al., 2003; Lanphear et al., 2005), and a strong positive correlation exists between childhood lead exposure and **attention deficit hyperactivity disorder** (ADHD; Braun et al., 2006). Thus "current effects of lead exposure on human brain development could be even greater than previously thought" (Grandjean & Landrigan, 2006, p. 2170).

Pesticides. Although they play an important role in food production and the control of diseases carried by mosquitoes, rodents, and other pests, pesticides are toxic by design and are produced and released intentionally into the environment (Colborn, 1995; Weiss et al., 2004). Whether they are meant to kill weeds (*herbicides*), bugs (*insecticides*), rats and mice (*rodenticides*), microbes (*disinfectants*), or any other so-called pest, humans are not impervious to the properties that render them toxic. Many insecticides act as direct neurotoxins as they are designed to disable the nervous systems of insects through mechanisms directly relevant to human physiology (Weiss et al., 2004).

Based on controlled testing of nonhuman animals (e.g., rodents), it is clear that several different classes of pesticides (i.e., organophosphate, organochlorine, pyrethroid, pyrethrin) produce neurodevelopmental toxicity during vulnerable neonatal periods (e.g., day 10 of life; Schettler, Stein, Reich, & Valenti, 2000). Even small exposures during **critical periods** of development permanently affect brain neurotransmitter receptors. Since the parallels in brain development between rodents at postnatal day 10 and humans during the last trimester of pregnancy, potential for similar effects exist in the offspring of women exposed while pregnant. Despite their potential risks, pesticide use (primarily insecticides and herbicides) increased since 1995, and nearly three fourths of all U.S. homes use some type of pesticide (Ashley et al., 2006).

Prenatal exposure to some insecticides interferes significantly with neurological development, resulting in brain atrophy and mental retardation (Bellinger & Adams, 2001). Marked impairments in a population of Mexican children exposed to pesticides have been observed in the Draw a Person task, a nonverbal measure of cognitive ability (Guillette et al., 1998; see Figure 6.6). Children exposed to pesticides also demonstrate reduced memory, creativity, and attention (Grandjean & Landrigan, 2006).

Based on our review of the sensitivity of the developing brain, it is perhaps not surprising that neurotoxic substances (mercury, lead, some pesticides) are associated with serious brain dysfunctions like intellectual and attentional impairments. However, *indirect* effects on brain development and function can result from exposure to various PBTs that interact with neurotransmitters and hormones, the body's internal chemical systems (Colborn, 2004; Weiss, Amler, & Amler, 2004).

Other consumer and industrial PBTs. Research is burgeoning on the cognitive correlates of exposures to *endocrine disruptive chemicals* found in plastics, flame retardants, solvents, sunscreens, and cosmetics, as well as in pesticides and the heavy metals discussed above (lead and mercury; Weiss, 2007). Such exposures are linked to ADHD (vom Saal et al., 2007)

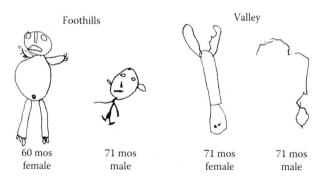

Foothills   Valley

60 mos   71 mos   71 mos   71 mos
female   male   female   male

Figure 6.6 Drawings of a person by 5-year-old Mexican Yaqui Indian children in a study of the effects of pesticide exposure on neurological development. (Reprinted from Guillette, E. A., Meza, M. M., Aquilar, M. G., Soto, A. D., & Garcia, I. E. (1998). *Environmental Health Perspectives, 106*, 351. With permission.)

and mental retardation (Weiss, 2006). Endocrine disruptors can also impact overall intellectual ability. For example, lower IQ scores have been observed in children exposed prenatally to **PCBs** (Jacobson & Jacobson, 1996). PCBs are industrial chemicals used in lubricants, coatings, and insulation in electrical transformers. Although they were banned from production years ago, they continue to contaminate meats and fish, as well as "fatty foods, fast foods, cheeses, ice cream, and even the most rigid vegan diet" (Colborn, 2004, pp. 947–948).

PCBs and other industrial chemicals like **dioxins** (an unintentional by-product of waste incineration, chlorine-based pulp and paper bleaching, and other industrial processes) interfere with thyroid hormones, which are essential for normal brain development. Prenatal or neonatal exposure to thyroid-disrupting chemicals can cause significant neurological abnormalities including impaired neurotransmission. As a result, deficits in overall IQ, learning, memory, attention, verbal skills, and reading comprehension are associated with prenatal exposure to PCBs (Porterfield, 2000).

In addition to the documented effects of various toxins on cognition and attention in children, several other conditions are associated with PBT exposures: autism, disrupted behavior and movement, psychosocial and psychiatric disorders, adult neurological impairments, and reproductive abnormalities. We will discuss the evidence for each in turn.

Autism

Autism is characterized by impaired social and language functions and "unusual, repetitive, or severely limited activities and interests" (National Institute of Neurological Disorders and Stroke, 2008). Hazardous air pollutants such as mercury, lead, and several solvents are associated with autism (Curtis & Patel, 2008; Windham et al., 2006), and autism is connected to maternal residence in regions of agricultural pesticide applications during prenatal neurodevelopment (Roberts et al., 2007). The link between autism and vaccines containing thimerosal, a preservative that includes mercury, has received considerable attention in the popular press, although evidence for this relationship is inconclusive (Curtis & Patel, 2008). Nonetheless, the majority of contemporary cases of autism undoubtedly reflect a significant influence of toxic exposures, which are often compounded by genetic susceptibility (Cone, 2009; Deth et al., 2008).

Behavioral and Motor Problems

Prenatal exposure to some insecticides is associated with slowed reflexes (Young et al., 2005). Young children exposed to agricultural pesticides manifested impaired motor skills and social interaction (Guillette et al., 1998), and long-term psychological impairment is common following pesticide poisonings. Visual-motor integration is impaired in children who initially showed signs of central nervous system effects such as lack of coordination, poor reflexes, "incoherence, loss of consciousness, [and] lethargy" (Bellinger & Adams, 2001, p. 179). In rural populations where pesticides are regularly applied, frequent contact is correlated with deficits in balance, hand-eye coordination, and reaction time (Bellinger & Adams, 2001; Grandjean & Landrigan, 2006).

In addition, mercury exposures can disrupt visual-spatial abilities, producing psychomotor retardation, lack of coordination, and/or seizures, depending on dose (Schettler, 2001). Lead exposure is also correlated with a variety of behavioral impairments in children including deficits in motor coordination at higher doses (Mendola et al., 2002).

Psychosocial and Psychiatric Disorders

Some children exposed to an agricultural insecticide exhibited greater impulsiveness, anger, and other interpersonal problems (Ruckart, Kakolewski, Bove, & Kaye, 2004). Psychosocial symptoms of lead exposures include antisocial, aggressive, and delinquent behavior (Needleman et al., 1996, 2002), violence (Masters, 1997, 2003), and criminality (Nevin, 2000). In general, such behavioral and emotional problems in children and adolescents are classified as **conduct disorder**, characterized by aggressive behavior directed both at people and animals, destruction or theft of property, and other behaviors that demonstrate "difficulty following rules and behaving in a socially acceptable way. [These children] are often viewed as 'bad' or delinquent, rather than mentally ill" (American Academy of Child & Adolescent Psychiatry, 2004, para. 1). Conduct disorder is associated with elevated blood lead levels (Braun et al., 2008).

Recent research shows that childhood lead exposure may also be a risk factor for **schizophrenia** (Opler et al., 2004; Opler & Susser, 2005), a severe mental illness (**psychosis**) marked by delusions, hallucinations, and speech disorganization. Several of the known effects of lead such as reduced academic abilities and psychosocial impairments resemble early antecedents of schizophrenia (Opler & Susser, 2005). Psychotic symptoms such as hallucinations and paranoia are not only observed with lead exposure but also contact with mercury, pesticides, and solvents; similarly, all of these toxins are related to more common mental illnesses such as anxiety, depression, and insomnia (Collaborative on Health and the Environment, 2008; Rhodes, Spiro, Aro, & Hu, 2003).

To summarize, various psychological processes involving cognitive, attentional, behavioral, social, or emotional functions can be adversely impacted by neurotoxic and endocrine disruptive chemicals released intentionally or unintentionally into the environment. It is highly likely that toxins combine with other factors to impact the developing brain (Bellinger & Adams, 2001; Weiss, 2000). Even though a relatively small number of children experience clinical poisoning severe enough to attract medical intervention, a much larger population is affected by subclinical poisoning, detectable by neuropsychological testing. Latent, or "silent" toxicity only emerges with additional risks, such as inter-actions with other toxins or other health issues. The effects may not become evident until the child enters school or faces other intellectually and socially challenging situations (Weiss, 2000, p. 377; see Figure 6.7). In fact, early brain damage (i.e., fetal or neonatal) may not be observable until much later in life when the brain is less adaptable (Weiss, 1998). Thus, adult neurological diseases including schizophrenia, Alzheimer's, and Parkinson's may actually originate in toxic exposures occurring during neurodevelopment.

TOXIC EFFECTS IN ADULTS

As we have seen, the developing pre- and postnatal brain is particu-larly sensitive to chemical exposures; however, adults are not immune to health risks associated with PBTs. Toxins accumulate in body tissues and interact with other stressors (see Chapter 8). Consequently, some effects are not observable until later in life.

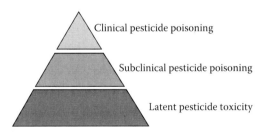

Figure 6.7 The toxicity pyramid for pesticides is designed to show that, although only a small proportion of children will manifest clear signs of excessive exposure, many more will show effects detectable by neurobehavioral testing, and even more will endure latent or silent toxicity that only emerges with additional challenges such as other pesticides, other environmental chemicals or other health problems. (Reprinted from Weiss, B. (2000). *Environmental Health Perspectives, 108*(Suppl. 3), 377. With permission.)

Accelerated Aging

Older adults often joke that they're experiencing a "senior moment" when they have difficulty remembering a word or event or learning a new skill. Most people assume that cognitive decline is associated with normal aging. However, it is likely that the decline is caused or accelerated by neurotoxic exposures (Stein, Schettler, Rohrer, & Valenti, 2008; Weiss, Clarkson, & Simon, 2002; Weiss & Simon, 1975).

For example, workers exposed to lead exhibited accelerated cognitive deterioration (Stewart & Schwartz, 2007) and associated loss in regional brain volumes (Schwartz et al., 2007) as adults and upon aging. Greater exposures to lead are related in adults to decreased verbal learning, memory, manual dexterity, decision making, and executive ability. Most important, these effects were seen long after the exposures occurred (Schwartz et al., 2000).

Various substances that disrupt endocrine functions (e.g., lead, pesticides, chemicals in plastics, flame retardants, cosmetics, PCBs, dioxins, etc.) can adversely impact cognitive performance in adults and the elderly and can enhance the risk of **Alzheimer's Disease** (Stein et al., 2008; Weiss, 2007). Alzheimer's is a progressive and ultimately fatal disorder that deteriorates memory, language, planning, interpersonal skills, and basic life-sustaining processes. There are 2.5 to 4.5 million U.S. residents that suffer from the disease, making it the most frequent cause of **dementia** (cognitive disruption and impairment) in the elderly (National Institute on Aging, 2008).

Parkinson's Disease

Exposure to pesticides likely contributes to the development of **Parkinson's Disease** (Landrigan et al., 2005; LeCouteur et al., 1999; Stein et al., 2008), a degenerative neurological disorder that affects approximately one out of every 100 adults over the age of 65. Symptoms include difficulty initiating movement, tremors, and subtle cognitive deficits, such as difficulty using spatial information to guide movement, memory problems, or changes in mood (Strange, 1992). In the final stages of the disease, about 10–15% of patients experience dementia, reflected by a decline in intellect, memory, and abstract thinking. While Parkinson's Disease is also thought to have a genetic component (a family history increases one's risk for the disease), what may be inherited is a metabolic deficiency. In other words, the enzymes that normally break down and detoxify chemicals like pesticides fail to function properly in susceptible individuals (LeCouteur et al., 1999).

Parkinson's and other neurodegenerative diseases could also result from long-term, low-level exposures to mercury. Initially, the brain may be able to compensate for the loss of nerve cells caused by exposures. Over time, however, cell death from the toxin alone or in combination with losses due to aging likely overwhelms compensatory mechanisms and results in symptom manifestation (Weiss et al., 2002).

Reproductive Abnormalities

In addition to neurological effects, PBTs profoundly impact many species' ability to reproduce, altering fertility rates, egg and sperm production or viability, genital development, and procreative behaviors. Such effects are associated with endocrine disruption, particularly via chemicals that block or mimic the actions of the natural hormones **estrogen** and **androgens** (e.g., *testosterone*; Colborn, Dumanoski, & Myers, 1997). Yet exposures to these substances continue unabated.

Do you drink beverages (including water) from plastic bottles? Eat food from plastic containers? It is virtually impossible to avoid doing so. Unfortunately, additives in plastics, including **phthalates** (pronounced THAL-ates) and **bisphenol A** (BPA) can disrupt functioning of the endocrine system, adversely impacting reproductive systems as well as metabolism and brain development (see Table 6.1 for a list of common products that contain these PBTs). Phthalates are found in toys made for infants and small children, including those that are meant to be chewed, as well as lotions, powders, and shampoos (Sathyanarayana et al., 2008). BPA is a component of many plastics including baby bottles.

Reproductive system abnormalities are associated with phthalate exposure in both human (Swan et al., 2005) and nonhuman animals (McGinn, 2002). Women of childbearing age (between 20 and 40 years

Table 6.1 Endocrine Disruptors: BPA and Phthalates

Bisphenol A (estrogenic)	Phthalates (antiandrogenic)
Baby bottles	Perfumes
Can linings	Hair sprays
Nail polish	Soaps, shampoos
Polycarbonate water bottles	Skin moisturizers
Microwave ovenware	Nail polish
Flame retardants	Food packaging
PVC stabilizers	Plastic wrap
Artificial teeth and tooth sealant	Pesticides ("inert" ingredients)
Adhesives	Detergents
Enamels and varnishes	Adhesives
Returnable containers	Medical tubing

Source: Weiss, B. (2007). *NeuroToxicology, 28*, 945. With permission from Bernard Weiss.

Table 6.2 A Summary of the Potential Effects of Persistent Bioaccumulative Toxins (PBTs)

PBT Effects	Mechanism	Potential Outcome
Neurotoxic	Pre-, postnatal brain development	Neurodevelopmental disabilities: cognitive impairment, mental retardation, learning and memory disabilities, verbal and sensory dysfunction, ADD/ADHD, autism, uncoordinated and slow reflexes, behavioral, interpersonal, and emotional problems, psychiatric disturbances (Schizophrenia, conduct disorder, depression and anxiety).
	Adult brain structure and function	Accelerated aging, Alzheimer's Disease, Parkinson's Disease
Endocrine-disruptive	PBTs bind to, mimic, or block hormone receptors	Reproductive abnormalities, birth defects, neurodevelopmental disabilities, cancer

old) exhibit the highest rates of phthalates in their urine, nine times higher than any other part of the population (Colborn, 2004), perhaps because of their relatively greater use of cosmetics. Researchers believe that BPA and other endocrine disruptors are contributing to genital abnormalities and decreases in the quality and potency of male semen, as well as initiating early puberty in girls (vom Saal et al., 2007). (For a review of the effects of PBTs, see Table 6.2).

ESTABLISHING CAUSE AND EFFECT: A RESEARCH NIGHTMARE

The research reviewed above is compelling and represents the extensive knowledge available on a handful of neurotoxic and endocrine disruptive substances: lead, mercury, some pesticides, and a few industrial and consumer chemicals. However, there are *more than 85,000* commercial use chemicals registered with the EPA, with more than 3000 produced or released in high volumes (see Figure 6.8). Even if manufacturers were required to perform tests for neurotoxicity (they are not, as we will discuss later in this chapter), a number of methodological difficulties stand in the way of conducting experiments on PBTs. As a result, conclusive evidence regarding the causal effects of most toxins, particularly for chronic low-level human exposures, remains disturbingly sparse.

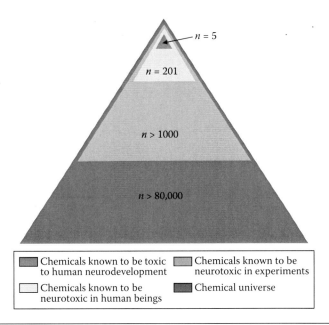

Figure 6.8 Diagram of the extent of knowledge of neurotoxic chemicals. Of the more than 80,000 known chemicals, only a very small fraction have been specifically tested and proven to cause developmental neurotoxicity in humans. Although this evidence does not represent the true potential for industrial chemicals to cause neurodevelopmental disorders, assessments of need for preventive measures nonetheless rely on that information. (Reprinted from Grandjean, P. & Landrigan, P. J. (2006). *Lancet, 368,* 2175. With permission.)

Yet low doses can be even more harmful than larger doses because mechanisms that control vomiting, for example, are not activated; thus, low dose exposures bioaccumulate in body tissues.

At least eight issues account for the difficulty establishing causal relationships between toxic chemical exposure and disabilities in humans, particularly when exposures occur at relatively low doses (see literature reviews in Koger, Schettler, & Weiss, 2005; Schettler et al., 2000).

1. Chemicals with known toxic and neurotoxic or endocrine-disrupting properties bathe the entire planet. Even in the most remote places, people and other animals show measurable levels of PBTs in their tissues. Thus, no good **control group** exists with which to compare exposed populations.
2. Humans are routinely exposed to a "toxic soup" of chemicals, rather than individual substances. Since research is conducted on one or two compounds at a time, cumulative or interactive effects will typically go undetected.

3. Behavioral and cognitive effects from toxins are often subtle and difficult to diagnose; they may thus go unnoticed. In the words of a former director of the National Institute of Environmental Health Sciences, "suppose that thalidomide [a sedative], instead of causing the birth of children with missing limbs, had instead reduced their intellectual potential by 10%. Would we be aware, even today, of its toxic potency?" (Rall, as quoted by Weiss, 1998, p. 37).

4. A related issue is that the majority of research on chemical toxicity is conducted on laboratory animals, and subtle cognitive impairments are often difficult to detect in nonhumans (particularly those involving language skills!). Thus, findings from nonhuman studies can significantly underestimate impacts to human populations.

5. There is typically a long **latency period** between exposure (prenatal or early postnatal) and when effects may be observable or measurable. For instance, most intellectual or attentional deficits are not apparent until a child enters school.

6. The developing brain is particularly vulnerable during **critical periods** of time. Consequently, exposure to a chemical outside that window may appear to have no effect, even if the same exposure would seriously damage brain development during another time period. Thus, the precise timing, nature, and magnitude of the exposures must all be factored into the research design. This information may be difficult, if not impossible, to attain for exposed human populations.

7. **Genetic factors** interact with environmental exposures, as genes regulate the metabolism and excretion of substances, and chemicals may alter gene expression.

8. Finally, the impact of toxins is often compounded by social factors. For example, *environmental racism* (also known as environmental injustice, discussed in Chapter 4) occurs because relative to higher status groups, minority and low-income populations are exposed to more pollution, and environmental and public health laws are often inadequately enforced in their communities (Bullard & Johnson, 2000). Economically disadvantaged and minority groups are more likely to live in regions containing toxic waste sites (Nadakavukaren, 2000), and lower-income families often inhabit older houses where lead paint was used; roughly one third of urban African–American children exhibit elevated levels of lead in their blood (e.g., McGinn, 2002). In addition, toxic effects can be magnified

when people have poor nutrition. For example, lead is absorbed more readily from the gastrointestinal tract when the person's diet is deficient in calcium or iron (Peraza et al., 1998). Thus, certain genotypes or socially disadvantaged individuals represent particularly vulnerable subpopulations that may not be represented in research studies. As a result, disproportionate impacts to those individuals may go unrecognized.

Interactions between physiological, environmental, and social factors thus make it difficult to draw direct causal links between specific toxic exposures and neurological outcomes. However, intellectual development will be more compromised in someone born in a violent neighborhood following poor prenatal care and exposure to pesticides than someone raised in a more privileged environment who is also exposed to toxins (Weiss, 2000). Individual risk factors might not exert obvious influence by themselves, but conjointly they produce damaging impacts on development (Weiss, 2000; see Figure 6.9; see also Evans, 2004).

In sum, because experimental research in neurotoxicology is suffused with challenges, investigators may never be able to precisely determine the extent to which toxic exposures impact neural functioning and produce psychological disabilities in humans. Science is largely based on avoiding false positive statements (stating that an association exists when it truly

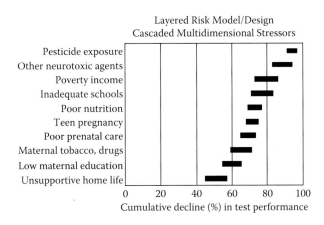

Figure 6.9 Schematic model to show how individual components of a stressful environment might cumulate to reduce performance on IQ and other tests. The individual stressors are shown as overlapping to suggest a lack of independence, and their length is meant to indicate that no single component is overwhelming in isolation. (Reprinted from Weiss, B. (2000). *Environmental Health Perspectives, 108*(Suppl. 3), 379. With permission.)

does not; i.e., **Type I errors**), rather than avoiding false negative conclusions (failing to recognize associations that do exist; i.e., **Type II errors**). Although this statistical strategy is accepted as appropriately conservative in the sciences, it is not the optimal strategy for protecting human health. Given sufficient political and public will, however, the hazards of PBTs are preventable—more so than most other risks to healthy development (Schettler et al., 2000). Unfortunately, prevention is not typically assigned a high priority, particularly when it is the less fortunate members of society who are most at risk (Albee, 1998; Needleman, 1998).

LEGISLATIVE ISSUES

Twenty-five years ago, only a small handful of the chemicals registered with the U.S. EPA received even minimal toxicity evaluation (National Academy of Sciences, 1984); that situation remains largely unchanged today. Although testing for neurotoxic effects of pesticides was established as a priority 10 years ago (U.S. EPA, 1999), there is no mechanism for enforcement (Grandjean & Landrigan, 2006). Tests specifically addressing neurodevelopmental toxicity are not currently required; rather, most of the research focuses on carcinogenicity and neurotoxicity in adult animals (Colborn, 2006; see also Lanphear, Vorhees, & Bellinger, 2005). Perhaps even more troubling is the apparent conflict of interest because the EPA typically relies on data provided by chemical manufacturers, failing to consider much of the environmental health literature (Colborn, 2006).

Reprinted from Clay Bennett © 2002, The Christian Science Monitor [www.CSMonitor.com]. With permission.

The widespread production, use, and disposal of inadequately tested chemicals essentially constitute large-scale human experimentation, yet the ethical guidelines that generally protect human subjects from harm in research or clinical trials (i.e., as implemented by Institutional Review Boards) are not implemented (Weiss, 2001). Regulatory efforts to reduce toxic exposures are reactionary rather than preventive; that is, chemicals are considered "innocent until proven guilty." Although pharmaceutical companies are required to demonstrate evidence of safety *prior* to marketing, other chemical manufacturers are not. Thus, chemical regulations frequently lag behind scientific evidence (Koger et al., 2005).

Following the demonstration of significant levels of flame retardant chemicals in maternal and fetal blood as well as breast milk, combined with knowledge of their endocrine disruptive effects (reviewed in Charboneau & Koger, in press), California was the first U.S. state to institute a ban on certain classes of flame retardants in new products (California Department, 2007). Governor Schwarzenegger signed the most comprehensive legislation in the United States to "evaluate, label, and in some cases, ban industrial chemicals linked to cancer, hormone disruption, and other deadly effects" (Roosevelt, 2008, para. 1). Other states have enacted or are considering relevant legislation, and some major electronics manufacturers including Nokia, Sony-Ericsson, and Samsung have eliminated or are phasing out certain flame retardants from production (Lunder & Jacob, 2008). Concomitantly, legislation to ban some phthalates in children's products was recently passed by the U.S. Congress in an effort to "strengthen the federal Consumer Product Safety Commission, which has been criticized in the past several years for failing to protect children from hazardous substances in toys and other products" (Sissell, 2008, para. 1).

Of course, these legislative actions are occurring after everyone on the planet has been exposed to the PBTs. The required scientific proof of harm puts all current and future generations at considerable risk. The production of persistent toxins should be *prevented*, instead of attempting to regulate their use, release, and disposal (International Joint Commission, 1992, pp. 5, 25).

In contrast to U.S. policy, and for more than 10 years, Sweden has taken a **precautionary approach** to the regulation of chemicals; its decision makers act conservatively to prevent harm to humans and the environment (Environmental Working Group, 2007; Swedish Government Chemicals Policy Committee, 1997; see also Grandjean, 2004, for a discussion of the precautionary principle). For example, the Stockholm Convention on POPs is an international agreement to regulate 12 of the most troublesome PBTs (e.g., pesticides, industrial chemicals, and unintentionally produced pollutants) including reducing their production, use, and release (Europa, 2007). The European Union adopted an implementation plan in 2007; as of this writing, the United States has yet to ratify the agreement or develop an implementation strategy.

To date, residents of the United States have not been able to count on industry or government for protection from hazards associated with PBTs, perhaps because both factions benefit from the production and distribution of these substances (Shabecoff & Shabecoff, 2008). It is worth investigating political campaign contributions from industries that manufacture toxins or contribute to pollution. Happily, President Obama pledged "to protect our children from health hazards and developmental disabilities caused by environmental toxins, such as lead, mercury, particulate matter, and industrial land waste" (Obama–Biden, 2007, p. 6, para. 3).

The Costs of Neurotoxins

Despite the methodological limitations outlined above, knowledge concerning the impacts of various toxic agents is persuasive enough to demand caution. Some industry representatives and legislators argue that it is too costly and impractical to increase regulation, especially if it involves requiring evidence that products are safe *before* allowing them on the consumer market or to be emitted from industrial processes. For example, the REACH proposal (Registration, Evaluation and

"Where there's smoke, there's money."

Authorization of Chemicals) in Europe requires manufacturers to assess the safety of industrial chemicals before marketing; a recent deadline for companies' compliance with the law resulted in more than two million preregistrations of substances (Scott, 2008). The REACH proposal was vigorously opposed in the United States by the George W. Bush administration and the chemical industry.

> The administration said publicly that the proposal would threaten the $20 billion in chemicals that the U.S. exports to Europe each year because the cost of testing would be prohibitive . . . [Then Secretary of State, Colin] Powell warned that $8.8 billion in products were at risk of being banned or severely restricted under Europe's proposed system. (Becker, 2004)

Consequently, improperly evaluated exposures continue in the United States.

This outcome is ironic given the vast amounts of money spent on treatment and services for the disabled and diseased. Between $81.5 and $167 billion is spent each year in the United States on neurodevelopmental deficits, hypothyroidism, and related disorders, depending on costs of special education and whether loss of earning potential is included (Muir & Zegarac, 2001). Conservatively, even if only 10% of the incidence of cerebral palsy, mental retardation, and autism are attributable to exposure to environmental toxins, the cost is $9.2 billion annually (Landrigan, Schechter, Lipton, Fahs, & Schwartz, 2002). A recent study of the annual "costs of environmentally attributable disease and disability" just in the state of Oregon reaches $1.57 to 2 billion; childhood lead exposure alone in Oregon is estimated at $878 million including lost earning potential from the loss of IQ; neurobehavioral disorders reach $187 million each year (Hackenmiller-Paradis, 2008). The costs of caring for people with Alzheimer's Disease are almost $150 billion per year while Parkinson's Disease is estimated to cost between $13 to $28.5 billion per year in the United States (Stein et al., 2008). Slowing the progression of Parkinson's Disease by just 10% would save $327 million per year (Parkinson's Action Network, 2002).

Even if the effects of toxic substances on cognitive ability are subtle, the economic and social effects can be profound. As Weiss (2000) noted, "if environmental contamination diminishes IQ in the U.S. population by an average of 1%, the annual cost would come to $50 billion and the lifetime costs to trillions" (p. 380). This sum is most likely an underestimate because any decrease of average population IQ not only decreases "the number of people with IQs above 130, but concurrently increases the number of those with IQs below 70, thereby increasing demand for remedial education and other services" (p. 380).

To determine the *real costs* (Chapter 5) of exposure to pollution and various toxic chemicals, it is crucial to develop a measure of reduced or lost cognitive and behavioral function. But what is the true value of avoiding or preventing developmental disabilities?

> Surely, the ultimate pollution is the chemical contamination of the brain, mind, and intelligence that form the source of our good fortune. This pollution not only affects the educational attainment, economic performance, and income of the individual, but it also has an impact on the dynamic performance of the economy as a whole. (Muir & Zegarac, 2001, p. 892)

An additional and important economic consideration is that if products and chemicals made in the United States do not conform to international safety regulations, the country will lose money in exports and domestic jobs. Alternatively, prevention of deficits associated with environmental toxicants can pay. One analysis concluded that the reduction in lead exposures since regulations were increased in the 1970s could increase each year's newborns' earning power as much as $110 to $318 billion, relative to that of the previous generation (Grosse, Matte, Schwartz, & Jackson, 2002).

Yet we wonder if monetary cost-benefit analyses are even relevant to the question of ensuring healthy cognitive and behavioral development in children. Can you really put a price on having an autistic or learning disabled child? What exposure levels and associated disabilities is society willing to tolerate?

BUILDING THE PERFECT BEAST: THE IRONY OF PESTICIDES

Health risks are not the only hazards of some PBTs such as pesticides. What most homeowners don't realize is that attempts to eliminate or control pests will inevitable backfire. You are probably familiar with the concept of **resistance**, when bacteria in the human body build up a tolerance to antibiotics. A similar process occurs with pesticide use: Any organisms that are not destroyed by the pesticides will multiply, and the characteristics that enabled the original survivors to escape the destructive effect are transmitted to their offspring. The pesticide is thus rendered ineffective for dealing with the next generation. A compounding effect occurs via the Volterra Principle in which the application of general pesticides kills both pest and predator species. Thus, consumers of pesticides or pesticide-treated products contribute to the development of highly resistant strains of the very organisms they were hoping to destroy, and destroying the ones that would normally keep their populations in check. Eliminating pests with chemical strategies will become increasingly more difficult for future generations.

BEHAVIORAL SOLUTIONS

Many people may not be aware of these principles or of the potential health hazards, and may not realize that there are safe, effective alternatives to many PBTs including pesticides. For instance, people can pull weeds by hand and buy **organic** products whenever possible (including clothing and mattresses made from organic cottons). Perhaps people can learn to be more tolerant of some pest damage and weeds and lobby for Integrated Pest Management techniques, which capitalize on natural controls and minimize environmental disruption (McGinn, 2002; Nadakavukaren, 2000). It is also important to evaluate *social norms* (see Chapter 4) that compel people to have a weed-free lawn and to fear insects. Disregarding such pressure may be difficult, particularly when the proliferation of these chemicals support the social norm of chemical lawn care.

The ability to seek out nontoxic or less toxic options requires knowledge of the risk in the first place as well as resources to purchase what may be more expensive items. Most consumers are disadvantaged by lack of access to information or resources or both, and the public has

Reprinted from © Dave Coverly [http://www.speedbump.com/]. With permission.

little control over the majority of toxins to which they are exposed in the air they breathe, the water they drink, and much of the food they eat. Knowing they lack control can produce considerable anxiety, and many people avoid thinking about it in order to reduce those unpleasant feelings—remember Freud's defense mechanisms? However, ignoring problems will not solve them. Taking even small steps toward improving a situation can create a feeling of empowerment and even greater motivation to work for change (see additional discussion in Chapter 8).

Although there is a strong tendency for both legislators and citizens to react to crises rather than attempt to prevent them, there are alternatives. People do not need to continue supporting industries that are willing to put the health of people and the planet's ecosystems at risk until the chemicals it sells are *proven* dangerous. There are many ways to reduce your own exposure to PBTs and the resulting disruption to physiological systems; some strategies are reviewed in the Appendix.

The topics discussed in this chapter are the focus of much contemporary research and activism. We refer readers to the following organizations for the most current information: Collaborative on Health and the Environment, Institute for Children's Environmental Health, Our Stolen Future, and the Environmental Working Group.*

CONCLUSIONS

The uniquely human ability to significantly alter the physical environment has led to the production and use of compounds that aid convenience but produce devastating consequences. PBTs abound in contemporary environments and are contributing to a range of neurological consequences. The developing brain is particularly vulnerable to chemical disruption, which can impact cognitive function, attention, language, and learning ability in addition to emotional states, sensory and motor function, various behaviors, and physical growth. Toxic exposures are strongly linked to developmental disabilities in children as well as adult disorders such as Alzheimer's and Parkinson's Diseases. In addition, reproductive abnormalities in many species are linked to toxic exposures.

It is both ironic and promising to note that the serious hazards of PBTs are, for the most part, preventable. The use of many toxins

---

* See corresponding Web sites, available at http://www.healthandenvironment.org/; http://iceh.org/; http://www.ourstolenfuture.org/; http://www.ewg.org/

proliferated because of their perceived beneficial applications (e.g., pesticides and fertilizers made the Green Revolution possible, along with the subsequent increase in the global availability of food; plastics have revolutionized the consumer product market). However, myriad detrimental effects lead us to question whether the benefits are worth the costs.

These costs will continue to soar until increasing numbers of us change our lifestyles drastically in ways that are simultaneously self-caring and planet-caring. . . . We humans display blatantly contradictory attitudes and behaviors in our individual health practices and in the ways we treat the environment. . . For example, [every day] Americans jog 27 million miles for their health, but eat 3 billion gallons of ice cream (mainly fat [containing various PBTs] and sugar), and produce one and a half million tons of toxic waste. (Clinebell, 1996, p. 3)

Since the United States is one of the major players in the creation of toxic pollution, it is unfortunate that its regulatory policies are based on "innocent until proven guilty," particularly since proof of direct causation is so difficult to demonstrate in human exposures. Precautionary approaches used in other nations are wise and should be implemented globally as international agreements (i.e., the Stockholm Convention and REACH) are ratified.

The good news is that the human species is also unique in its ability to recognize the consequences of destructive patterns, experience concern and other feelings, and (hopefully) change behavior accordingly. The necessary changes in personal, social, and legislative climates will not be easy, but it appears that awareness is growing about the damage of current practices, for example, increasing availability and consumer markets for organic foods and products.

We are hopeful that you, our readers, will be the generation that recognizes the paradoxes of *driving* (releasing carbon dioxide and particulate matter) to a health club with a case of bottled water (leaching BPA) in the back seat. That someday you'll watch your children play in fields of dandelions while ladybugs dance in the grass because healthy brain development is more important than weed control. And that you'll hold accountable the leadership in Washington, DC for delivering on promises to revitalize protections for clean air, water, and regulations on pollution and toxic chemicals.

7

COGNITIVE PSYCHOLOGY: INFORMATION PROCESSING

The major problems in the world are the result of the difference between the way nature works and the way [people] think.

(Gregory Bateson, 1976*)

Do you recycle paper? Why or why not? Please take a moment to record your response before continuing.

If you answered "yes" to this question, your reasons probably included thoughts about the importance of saving natural resources. You may have mentioned that it takes a lot of energy and processing with toxic chemicals to convert trees to paper. Even if you did not consider these technical facts, you probably contemplated the importance of conserving scarce resources. If you answered "no," perhaps you reasoned that it does not really make that much difference. Or that recycling bins are never available when you need them. Or that recycling is just a fad. These kinds of responses illustrate a basic tenet held by cognitive psychologists: In order to understand behavior, we must understand people's thought processes.

Cognitive psychology is defined as the study of mental processes. From this perspective, understanding the way people think about environmental problems is crucial for understanding their actions. However, cognitive (along with social) psychologists have demonstrated that the relationship between beliefs and behavior is much more

---

* As quoted by Devall and Sessions, 1985, p. 1.

complicated than one might suspect; that people like to think they are more rational and logical than they actually are, and that human perceptual and reasoning processes are limited and can result in faulty judgments. Cognitive and perceptual biases, errors, and shortcuts cause overreactions to some hazards, and underreactions to others. Yet, cognitive and perceptual processes are crucial organizing features of behavior. These mechanisms were shaped by eons of evolution, are modified by personal experiences, and generally function pretty effectively. If they didn't, no one would have survived very long.

In this chapter, we will explore environmental issues from the perspective of cognitive psychology, and consider why it is often so difficult to respond effectively. Our discussion is based on an information processing model that assumes behavior is a function of the quality of available information and how adequately it is processed.

INFORMATION PROCESSING MODELS

Cognitive psychologists use models to describe how information is mentally represented, manipulated, and stored. Information processing models emphasize the adaptive nature of the brain, enabling people to be "cognitive misers" (Fiske & Taylor, 1984): Human perceptual systems only take in as much information as is required to navigate in a particular situation. People simplify reality by creating **mental maps** of situations or experiences. Such maps enable anticipation, reaction, and consideration of possible upcoming events (Kaplan & Kaplan, 1989).

Public reactions to environmental issues are impacted by mental maps. For example, in the mid-1990s, Mitsubishi planned to build a desalination plant in a pristine area of Mexican coastal waters that serves as a birthing and nursery area for grey whales. After international environmental groups and celebrities publicized the development plans, more than one million letters of protests, coupled with public boycotts of Mitsubishi products, were successful in terminating the project in 2000. People's mental maps of the area consist of whale habitat, not industry.

Mental maps thus impact experiences and judgments, and while they speed processing time and efficiency, they can also result in biases or inaccuracies. Many people's misunderstandings about climate change, such as confusing it with weather patterns, thinking it reflects natural variability, or believing it is due to ozone depletion, contribute to their subsequent failures to respond (Bostrom & Lashof, 2007). Likewise, the abundance of conflicting and highly technical information about various environmental issues often fails to resonate with people's mental models, causing confusion, overwhelm, and inaction (Kaplan & Kaplan, 2008).

Mental maps are made possible by **associative networks**, interconnected units of information. The idea of associative networks originated with Hebb's (1949) insight that when events occur close together in time, associations are formed between the neurons that code those events (i.e., **neural networks**; Collins & Loftus, 1975; Kaplan, & Kaplan, 1989). **Learning** occurs via this associative mechanism: Connections between nerve cells are changed by experience in ways that subsequently alter behavior. Throughout infancy and early childhood, a child is taught to associate words with objects, and to group related objects together. For example, the neighbor's furry creature with four legs is a dog, just like Sue's family pet Phoebe is a dog, even though their features are quite different (size, hair length, color, ear appearance, etc.). Similarly, one can learn to associate paper with recycling bins rather than trash cans, or associate certain products (e.g., pesticides and plastics) with toxic impacts (see Chapter 6). When one concept in an associative network is activated during cognitive processing or memory retrieval, activation spreads to related concepts. People create different networks (and mental maps) from their specific experiences, memories, and beliefs, and thus can have very different responses to the same concept. For example, when an environmentalist thinks of the concept "logging," the related thoughts of habitat loss, species extinction, and watershed degradation become activated. Meanwhile, a logger would think of jobs, provide for family, or wood products (see Figure 7.1).

Such differences in associative networks can account for many environmental conflicts. Negotiations between groups often fail because each side assumes the other's goals directly oppose theirs (e.g., Bazerman, 1983).

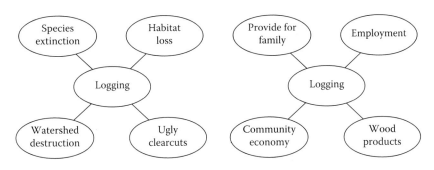

Figure 7.1 Different associative networks, representing an environmentalist's (left) and a logger's (right) cognitive concepts associated with logging.

However, by examining associative networks, areas of overlapping values and agreement can be addressed; focusing on that overlap is an important route to conflict resolution (Lord, Lepper, & Preston, 1984; Mayer, 2000; Moore, 1996). For example, typical forest management practices, such as overharvesting old growth timber and suppressing natural fires, characterize a *contingency trap* (Chapter 5). The short-term economic motivation endangers the health of the forest ecosystem, and will adversely impact all interested parties in the long-term. Loss of timber forests due to unregulated clear-cutting not only affects the timber industry and associated logging communities, but also the various native species that depend on healthy forests for oxygen, habitat, watershed, and reproductive protection. For these reasons, finding common ground between the associative networks of competing groups is the road to sustainability (e.g., Kitzhaber, 2002; see Figure 7.2). All factions benefit from "keeping their eyes on the prize"; that is, focusing on the shared, long-term benefits of sustainable forests, rather than on divisive concepts in their differing associative networks. This process can be facilitated by encouraging all parties to see the other's side of the issue (Fisher & Ury, 1991).

The Computer Revolution

It is probably not overstating things to say that the creation of the computer revolutionized the field of cognitive psychology. Originating in military research, computers quickly emerged as a principal tool for processing information. By 1948, computers were compared to human brains in terms of their apparently similar operations (Hunt, 1993), and

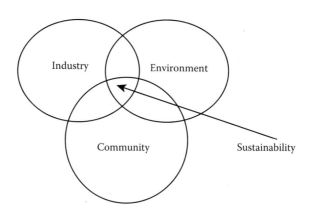

Figure 7.2 Venn diagram, illustrating overlapping interests of industry (economic), community, and environmental interests. The area of intersection represents sustainability.

the metaphor of the brain as a computer had instant appeal. Both seem to depend on digital events: the firing of a neuron and the firing of a bit are on–off occurrences. More importantly, both the brain and the computer process information similarly: data are inputted and then transformed according to some rules or decisions, and, finally, output is generated. Complicated but orderly decision sequences enable both the machine and the brain to behave intelligently.

Despite considerable advances in computer science, the capacity and ability of the human brain continues to amaze and challenge researchers across disciplines. Computer modeling, artificial intelligence, cognitive psychological approaches, and neuroscientific techniques like brain imaging, together with theoretical insights from linguistics and philosophy, have converged to launch the interdisciplinary field of **cognitive science**. This collaborative approach to the study of human information processing is now one of the most dynamic areas of international research and curricular development. Yet even a sophisticated, efficient and intelligent system like the brain does not always work perfectly. Thus, one way to understand environmentally destructive behavior is to see it as a product of imperfect information processing.

The Constraints of GIGO

There is a familiar saying in computer science: garbage in, garbage out (GIGO). No computer can do a good job if incoming data are flawed. Likewise, mental maps, like computer programs, depend on the accuracy of the information on which they are based. If information is inaccurate, limited, or irrelevant, responses will likely be inappropriate. We'll look at these three types of information problems in turn.

Wrong Information   Obviously, GIGO can result from wrong information. Good decision making requires accurate knowledge, but information that seems accurate can later be discovered to be inaccurate. Historically, many people mistakenly believed that small or moderate doses of otherwise toxic substances were not harmful. The adage "the dose makes the poison" suggested that the larger the amount ingested or absorbed, the greater the impact. Concerns about safety were based on obvious and debilitating physical damage (burns, birth defects, cancer, coma, or death; Gilbert, 2004). However, over the last few decades, agencies including the EPA and WHO have continually lowered the reference dose (the level below which harm is suspected to be unlikely) for lead, mercury, and other substances, because research has demonstrated adverse effects on brain development and function at progressively lower exposure levels. Much contemporary research on **toxicology** focuses attention on the toxic impacts for intellectual and attentional functions, rather than on more obvious physical damage. Consequently, it is now commonly believed that there is no safe level of exposure to substances that can impact the developing human brain (Biello, 2009; Koger, Schettler, & Weiss, 2005; Schettler, Stein, Reich, & Valenti, 2000). No information is perfect, but a commitment to improving information and revising decisions accordingly is an important principle of all good public policy.

Limited Information   Information can also be inadequate because it is limited. First of all, there are inherent limitations in the hard wiring of sensory organs. Human visual systems respond to only a tiny range of the entire spectrum of electromagnetic radiation, namely wavelengths between approximately 400 and 700 nanometers, which is called light. Yet the continuum of electromagnetic energy extends from short cosmic rays of four trillionths of a centimeter, to long radio waves, traveling up to several miles. Humans are blind to the vast majority of this information: "Instead of experiencing the world as it is, people experience only about one trillionth of outside events: a small world indeed!" (Ornstein & Ehrlich, 2000, p. 73).

Despite these physical constraints, the vast majority of humans are **visual-dependent**. Sight uses a greater part of the human brain cortex than do the other senses (hearing, smell, touch, or taste), leading people to rely more heavily on visual information than any other kind. Consequently people notice litter or smoke pouring out of factories, but not the carcinogenic or neurotoxic contaminants in air, water, and food. Since greenhouse gases and pesticides are not visible, they are less likely to draw attention, making it difficult for people to respond appropriately to climate change and hazardous chemicals.

Most institutions concerned about public opinion try to apply the principle of visual dependency to their advantage. For example, using the notion of "out of sight, out of mind," the U.S. Forest Service (USFS) has officially sanctioned sets of cosmetic strips: that is, intact forests directly bordering public highways. The USFS calls these strips *viewsheds*, and they are maintained in order to reduce public concern and reactions about logging and clear-cutting practices. In published planning documents for each National Forest, the size and placement of viewsheds are explicitly specified. "Areas (viewsheds) with high visual sensitivity (as seen from selected travel routes, developed use areas, or water bodies), are managed to attain and perpetuate an attractive, natural-appearing landscape" (U.S. Department of Agriculture Forest Service, 1990, p. S-29).

Visual dependency is a powerful principle of human information processing, a principle that has been exploited by all sides of environmental debates. Sometimes, however, the reliance on vision can backfire. Consider the "owl versus jobs" controversy, which symbolized the debate about the forests of the Pacific Northwest during the 1990s. Spotted owls depend on old growth forests; that is, forests that have not been previously cut and replanted. Old growth forests are more complex ecosystems than are replanted forests, so spotted owls serve as an indicator species: Their presence signifies the health of an intricate system of interdependent species and habitat and the ability of other species to survive. The only available legal means for saving the last old growth forest was for environmentalists to argue that the 1972 Endangered Species Act protects the owl from extinction. Any number of other species could have been selected, from the red-backed vole to the mycorrhizal fungi (Maser, 1988), but environmentalists were smart to choose the owl: Owls have a strong visual image and are a lot cuter than a vole or a fungus. An owl has large eyes and a small nose, comprising what physiologists call a **neotenic face**, meaning a face that approaches the proportions of a baby's face. Humans have a built in, genetically hard-wired response to neotenic faces (Ornstein & Ehrlich, 2000): People find them "cute," like them, and feel protective of them.

But the owl's visual appeal has also backfired. When the debate is framed as "owls versus jobs," families whose livelihoods depend on the timber industry quite rightly ask how environmentalists could think that saving some owls would be more important than feeding their children. Due to the owl's visual appeal, it is difficult for the public to remember that the owl signifies an entire forest ecosystem, comprising hundreds, perhaps thousands, of species, upon whose healthy functioning humans are also dependent. An *endangered ecosystem* is really the issue (Novacek, 2008). Some environmental philosophers (Callicott, 1994; Leopold, 1949, 1972) have argued that people must develop a "land aesthetic" that goes beyond naïve visual dominance. An uneducated reliance on vision leads people to value wilderness only when it is attractive. Instead, people must learn to perceive much more complex ecosystems, even if such perception requires seeing beyond prettiness.

In addition to the limitations imposed by visual dominance, three additional principles of human perceptual systems are likely to result in GIGO through limited information: selective attention, sensory adaptation, and proximal cognition.

Selective attention. Even though people perceive an extremely small range of electromagnetic information, if visual systems processed everything in that range, human experience would be chaotic—a "buzzing, blooming confusion" to use William James's (1890, p. 488) well-known phrase. Instead, perception is quite selective. In order to make sense of the world, large portions must be relegated to "ground," while focusing on some "figure." A considerable amount of the information that falls within the parameters of sensory systems' detection capabilities is discarded, because of limits in cognitive architecture— that is, the way people pay attention and decide which stimuli are relevant.

These decisions are made unconsciously all the time. People don't notice the fossil fuel burning in the gas tank while driving, the electricity feeding the computer while writing, or the trees used to build the rooms in people's homes. As cognitive misers, humans delegate attention only to those items that need it, and tune out the rest. The phenomenon of **change blindness** demonstrates that a visual scene can change dramatically without being noticed because of constraints on the ability to process, retain, and compare information from one moment to the next (Simons & Ambinder, 2005). For example, in one study, participants were repeatedly shown a picture (with a large tree in the background), followed by a brief empty display, and then an altered image (same scene without the tree). Participants had difficulty noticing the change (Simons & Ambinder, 2005). As a result, major environmental alterations could occur virtually right before our eyes and most of us wouldn't perceive the change unless we were specifically (selectively) attending to those features.

Sensory adaptation. Human nervous systems are built to signal alterations in the environment rather than constancies. Stimuli that do not change quickly lose their ability to activate neural transmission; consequently, situational features that remain the same fade from awareness while those which change too slowly never reach awareness at all. Although these aspects of cognitive systems are generally adaptive (selective attention and sensory adaptation enable people to ignore what is often less important information), they can have negative consequences. Like the frog who will jump out of a pot of very hot water if suddenly thrown in, but will allow itself to be boiled to death if placed in a very slowly heating pot; humans will endure quite noxious environmental events if they are introduced gradually enough.

IT IS NOT TRUE THAT A FROG WILL IGNORE A GRADUALLY HEATED ENVIRONMENT + WILL BOIL TO DEATH...

...THE VERDICT ISN'T IN ON SOME OTHER SPECIES.

The smog level of Los Angeles, California is a good example of the role of sensory adaptation:

> A visitor to the LA basin, arriving on a smoggy day, is often immediately appalled by the quality of air he or she is expected to breathe. But, as with many other constant phenomena, the locals hardly notice. A few years ago one of us arrived at John Wayne Airport in Orange County [California] in the early evening to give a lecture. Every streetlight was surrounded by a halo of smog, and his eyes immediately began watering profusely. As a visitor from the (relatively) smog-free San Francisco area, he felt obliged to kid his host: "Well, at least we have a nice clear night for the lecture." His host's serious response: "Yeah—you should have been here a couple of weeks ago. We had a lot of smog then." (Ornstein & Ehrlich, 2000, p. 76)

Proximal cognition refers to the tendency to be more motivated by short-term, concentrated benefits, rather than long-term, widespread costs (Bjorkman, 1984), and future benefits are often less compelling than short-term costs. You might recognize this as the *contingency trap* (described in Chapter 5) or from economics, where it is called **subjective discount rates** (Howard, 2000, 2002). For example, it is difficult to expend money now to purchase a new refrigerator or upgrade the insulation in your home, even though these actions would save significant amounts of energy and money in the long run, and would also reduce climate changing emissions (Bazerman, 2006). Thus, proximal cognition can explain why Deborah never replaced her inefficient, double-paned windows (discussed in Chapter 1). Behaviors that lead to increased energy efficiency can result in a return on investment of 30% to 50% per year, much greater than the performance of most stocks, bonds, and money market funds, even in a good economy (Bazerman & Hoffman, 1999). Yet, most people focus on what is affecting them in the present, rather than engaging in behaviors that have future impacts. Due to the ability to conduct large scale, environmental destruction hasn't occurred until very recently in human evolution, the impacts of proximal cognition are historically unprecedented (Vlek, 2000).

These mechanisms—visual dependence, selective attention, sensory adaptation, and proximal cognition—all make sense from an evolutionary point of view (for a thorough discussion of the evolutionary basis of environmental problems, see Penn, 2003; Penn & Mysterud, 2007). Human ancestors were probably well adapted to their environment *precisely because* of these ways of processing information. However, modern life is quite different from that in which the human species evolved. Although they enable greater cognitive efficiency and are thus adaptive in most situations, these mechanisms now serve as "limitations" because they contribute to GIGO. The media reinforce this problem when they use brief headlines that oversimplify issues ("owls vs. jobs" is a classic example), and cater to a public with a limited attention span. Fleeting stories are quickly taken up and then dropped by the press, television, and radio. Due to these information processing mechanisms, the same old bad news about population growth, climate change, and resource depletion do not sell papers or retain viewers. Thus, most people need far more information than they currently receive or actively seek out, so their ability to make sophisticated decisions about complicated issues is jeopardized.

In addition, corporations intentionally limit information by hiding environmental consequences of consumer choices. For instance, governmental agencies require food labeling to inform consumers of the nutritional dimensions: fat content, calories, and chemical additives are listed. No information is yet made available, however, about environmental information: number of gallons of petroleum used to grow and distribute a food product; number of people injured by the use of pesticides; whether or not the food was produced in the United States or on foreign soil where environmental regulations are more lax; whether genetic engineering was used to produce the foods or protect them from pest damage or disease, and so forth. Making informed consumer choices on food and other products is not easy, although reframing food choices in these terms would lead to the obvious conclusion that buying strawberries in January is a less environmentally appropriate action than buying them at a local farmer's market in June. Fortunately, some companies are responding to an emerging market for organically produced foods, and products that bear fewer negative environmental and social impacts (i.e., protecting biodiversity, and farmworker health and safety). In any case, more information about corporate practices can lead to better environmental choices.

Irrelevant Information   Too much information can also produce GIGO if the information is confusing; many reasoning difficulties come from being distracted by or using **irrelevant information**. Irrelevant information abounds in advertising, and at times people actively pursue it via biases and misinterpreting events. Advertisers often employ irrelevant information to increase the desirability of their products. For example, the information printed on a grocer's plastic bag demonstrates this tendency (see Figure 7.3).

Ink regulation and incineration are irrelevant information, as plastic bags are rarely burned at high enough temperatures to be nontoxic. Claiming the product is "recyclable" borders on the fraudulent, since less than 1% of plastic bags are recycled at all, and this company neither recycles nor uses recycled bags. "Reusable" would have been a more appropriate term. Inaccurate and irrelevant information is displayed in an attempt to make this company appear environmentally conscious, a practice termed **greenwashing** by some environmental groups.

However, individuals do not need the efforts of advertising to become confused by irrelevant information. There are two ways in which people *actively pursue* irrelevant information. One is called the **confirmation bias**. When testing hunches against incoming data, most make the mistake of looking for confirming rather than disconfirming information (Wason, 1960). Seeking lots of confirmatory information feels good, and is consistent with the associative network theory: it is more difficult

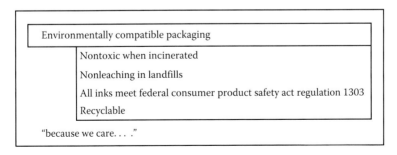

Figure 7.3 Irrelevant information printed on a grocer's plastic bag.

to process and store material that conflicts with cognitive networks. People generally do not like to experience disconfirmations, so they do not seek them. Consequently, environmentalists tend to read material that confirms their views, such as publications of the Sierra Club and Natural Resources Defense Council, rather than *The National Review*.

In addition to using confirmation biases, people will often interpret random events as meaningfully related to some human action out of a need to believe that they have some control over the world. The principle of **regression toward the mean** illustrates this tendency. Chance events fall on a normal curve, with extreme occurrences far less likely than more typical ones. Since extreme events are rare, the next event is likely to be less extreme, simply due to chance alone. For example, extremely hot days are more likely to be followed by cooler ones than by hot ones, simply by chance. But human beings, looking for meaning, are prone to explain occurrences in terms of human actions.

The significance of regression artifacts in environmental science may seem less important than in the allegedly "softer" social sciences, until we recall that environmental remedies are applied precisely because some aspect of the environment is in an extreme state. Regression to the mean predicts, for example, that after a species has been declared endangered it will tend to become more abundant. This is not an effect [of the "endangered" declaration] at all, but a reflection of the fact that the human decision to declare a population in bad trouble is based upon its being *in extremis*. To the extent that that condition is caused by a variety of factors—as is virtually always the case in the natural setting—some of them will fluctuate in the next year, and the fluctuations will on average tend to bring the population up. In the early years of the Columbia Basin program [in the Pacific Northwest of the United States], before any of the rehabilitation measures could be carried out, there was a resurgence of salmon populations from the historic lows of the late 1970s, when the Northwest Power Act was passed. It took a special effort of political will not to take credit for this change, even though there was as yet no cause to which such an effect could be attributed. (Lee, 1993, pp. 71–72)

In other words, because human beings are prone to make up explanations for random events, they easily misinterpret actions as causing something that is happening purely by chance.

If problems are presented simply enough, a person can usually come up with an appropriate answer, but unfortunately, life is usually not very simple. Even when people are not being manipulated by advertisers or actively looking for it, irrelevant information can get in the way. For example, consider the following set of statements (based on a problem Zukier, 1982, presented to laboratory participants):

1. Assuming you have access to sunlight, heating a house with passive solar heat costs 30–40% less over the lifetime of the house than heating with conventional systems, such as electricity, gas, coal, or oil. If you want to save money on heating, which system should you choose?

2. You are planning your dream home, in which you plan to live for the rest of your life. Assuming you have access to sunlight, heating a house with passive solar heat costs 30–40% less over the lifetime of the house than heating with conventional systems, such as electricity, gas, coal, or oil. Passive solar systems add 5–10% more to the construction costs. Some people believe that rooftop solar collectors are ugly and detract from the architectural design of a structure. In order to get the maximum efficiency from your passive system, you have to open and shut windows and shades to regulate heat distribution, although this could be accomplished by an inexpensive computer. Your access to solar energy could be disrupted if someone decided to build an interfering structure, since right now there are no laws to guarantee owner access to sunlight (such legislation has been opposed by builders of high-density developments).

If you want to save money on heating, which system should you choose? The irrelevant information (irrelevant to the question of saving money) contained in the second problem is likely to distract readers from the crucial sentence "heating a house with passive solar heat costs 30% to 40% less over the lifetime of the house than heating with conventional systems" and confuse the issue. Since most environmental questions are complex and involve many different considerations, it is difficult not to get waylaid.

The public's tendency to be distracted by irrelevant information is a concern among policy makers whose job it is to convince the public to reduce energy use. Most energy conservation programs are based on the assumption that the public is primarily interested in saving money and will act rationally to do so. This **rational-economic model** (previously encountered in Chapter 5) rests on the assumption that if a technology will save its owners and operators money over the life of the equipment, it "will be adopted once the owners become aware of the benefits" (Stern, 1992, p. 1224).

off the mark.com   by Mark Parisi

©2005 MARK PARISI DIST. BY UFS INC.

THE WOLLEYS SAVE ON THEIR
ENERGY BILL BY HARNESSING
HAPPY-DOG POWER

Reprinted from © Mark Parisi and Off the Mark. With permission.

However, research shows that instead of using a purely rational economic model for decisions about conservation issues, most people rely on a folk model that looks *irrational* to energy experts.

The "folk model" typically used by individual consumers calculates current dollar savings as compared to pre adoption expenditures and fails to reveal that the initial cost of the investment is paid back faster because of rising fuel prices. Thus, folk calculations based on naive and "irrational" assumptions cause consumers to make fewer energy-saving investments than an expert analysis would recommend. In addition, a variety of non-economic factors (e.g. style, status, performance, safety, comfort, and convenience) influence decision making and contribute to the apparent irrationality of conservation behavior. (Costanzo, Archer, Aronson, & Pettigrew, 1986, p. 525)

These additional dimensions are important to consumers, often more important than price. Thus, the concept of **bounded rationality** may be more useful, as it acknowledges that people do not function in order to fully maximize potentially beneficial outcomes (Gardner & Stern, 2002; Gigerenzer, 2000; Kaplan, & Kaplan, 1989). Rather "bounded rationality . . . necessarily takes shortcuts, simplifies complex problems, uses certain tricks, and shows certain biases . . . which work reasonably well" most of the time (Gardner & Stern, 2002, p. 228).

The concept of irrelevant information provokes the question "irrelevant to whom?" When experts (either policy analysts or cognitive psychologists) define a problem, they typically do it in narrower terms than laypersons do. We will say more about the problem of who defines what is relevant in our discussion of risk assessment (below).

Additional Constraints on Information Processing

Cognitive systems evolved to process information quickly and efficiently, using previous experiences to guide subsequent decision making. Yet sometimes biases and shortcuts get in the way of making good decisions. Thus, GIGO is not the only information processing problem. Even when information is accurate, comprehensive, and relevant, people sometimes overuse preconceptions and expectations. Reasoning shortcuts based on limited information may lead to snap decisions. Quantitative processing, particularly with large numbers, is difficult for most people, presumably because such information was only very recently encountered in human evolutionary history. The way information is framed, or the context in which it is presented, also influences decision making. In this section, we explore these cognitive mechanisms and their relationship to environmental issues.

Learning and experience, with their changed associative networks and mental maps, provide a framework for how to interpret information. Human behavior would be totally chaotic without some **preexisting biases** based on previous experiences. To paraphrase Bloom (1987), too much open-mindedness would make our brains spill out! While preexisting beliefs are necessary, they can also get in the way, potently affecting perception and interpretation of an event. Consider how two different people interpreted the same traffic accident on I-95 in Springfield, Massachusetts involving a tractor-trailer carrying 11,000 pounds of radioactive uranium that overturned and burned:

> A representative of the antinuclear group Nuclear Information and Resource Service [said] that "People should be plenty concerned," since the accident signaled more trouble in the future: "Accidents happen at the same rate to nuclear shipments as for all other shipments—one per every 150,000 miles the truck travels." In contrast, a representative for the U.S. Council for Energy Awareness, which is supported by the nuclear industry, took the accident as a signal of assurance: "The system works," he said. "We had an accident including fire and there was no release of radioactivity." (Cvetkovich & Earle, 1992, p. 8)

Since people use preexisting biases to interpret events, discourse about specific environmental problems can be divided, if not derisive. While acknowledging the opposite viewpoint is not easy, its effects are valuable.

Reasoning Strategies: Heuristics In order to comprehend a complex world, people not only depend on biases but also **heuristics**; reasoning devices that help people think quickly and efficiently, like a shortcut that allows effective functioning because it usually works. However, heuristics can also lead to inappropriate snap judgments. Consider the following problem based on a classic experiment (Tversky & Kahneman, 1983):

> John is a 31-year-old white male, single, outspoken, and very committed to environmental issues. He and his friends have demonstrated in many confrontational protests over logging, mining, and land use operations.

> Which statement is more likely:

> 1. John is a bank teller.
> 2. John is a bank teller and a member of Green Peace.

Most people think statement #2 is more likely because the description fits the stereotype of Green Peace members, or what cognitive psychologists call a **representativeness heuristic**. This heuristic refers to the tendency to judge an event as likely if it represents the typical features of its category (Medin, Ross, & Markman, 2001). Objectively, however, statement #1 is more likely based on probability: the conjunction of two events can never be more likely than either event alone. That is, any one event occurs more frequently alone than it occurs with another event. In this case, using a representativeness heuristic leads to poor reasoning. Such errors often appear in choice of language, for example, the frequency with which conservatives refer to environmentalists as "radical environmentalists." Exclusive use of this phrase suggests that their mental representation of an environmentalist does not include room for moderates or conservatives.

Similarly, the **availability heuristic** refers to a tendency to form a judgment on the basis of what is readily brought to mind, which may explain people's underestimation of some environmental problems. For instance, individuals may have difficulty imagining climate change because of a lack of vivid, personal experiences with melting icecaps and rising sea levels. On the other hand, dramatic environmental hazards, such as oil spills, feature prominently in people's memories and therefore may receive more attention and resources than are warranted relative to other less perceptually vivid, but more insidious, hazards (Gardner & Stern, 2002).

The availability heuristic can be used to encourage environmentally responsible behavior, as was demonstrated when researchers persuaded people to sign up for energy conservation home improvements:

> They trained California home energy auditors to communicate their findings to homeowners in vivid, memorable images. Rather than simply point out small spaces around doors where heat is lost, the auditor would say "if you were to add up all the cracks around and under the doors of your home, you'd have the equivalent of a hole the size of a football in your living room wall." With such remarks, and by eliciting the homeowners' active commitment in helping measure cracks and state their intentions to remedy them, the trained auditors triggered a 50 percent increase in the number of customers applying for energy financing programs. (Myers, 1993, p. 56)

By drawing a vivid image of a "hole the size of a football in your wall" these researchers were much more convincing than when speaking in more abstract, conceptual terms. In both cases, the information is the same, but the vivid example is more persuasive because it creates a more memorable image that is more available to memory.

Some heuristics help people feel good about themselves in spite of their behavior or circumstances. **Comparative optimism** is a cognitive bias that leads individuals to believe they are less vulnerable than other people, even though objectively there would be no reason to think the risks are any greater or lesser for one individual versus another (Pahl, Harris, Todd, & Rutter, 2005). **False consensus** is a heuristic that helps people maintain positive self-esteem by convincing themselves that many others engage in the same undesirable behaviors that they do. For example, a water shortage following a tropical storm prompted a temporary shower ban at Princeton University in 1999, which inspired a 5-day field study during and after the ban (Benoît & Norton, 2003). The researchers found that students who defied the shower ban overestimated the prevalence of this socially irresponsible behavior in others. In addition, those who showered were seen by others as caring very little about the greater good, whereas those who did not shower were seen as caring very much. However, self-report data suggested that the attitudinal positions of these two groups were much closer together than either group realized (i.e., both groups cared about the larger group's welfare). **False polarization** is the tendency to perceive the views of those on the opposing side of a partisan debate as more extreme than they really are. All of these tendencies distort the perception of one's behavior relative to others', while they help maintain feelings of safety (comparative optimism), sense of self-esteem (false consensus), and the view of oneself as more reasonable than those who would disagree (false polarization).

Quantitative Illiteracy   Without specific technical training in a quantitative field, most people have difficulty conceptualizing very large and very small numbers, a limitation termed **quantitative illiteracy**. A billion may as well be a trillion or a gazillion—only specialists deal in these types of numbers often enough to have a well-developed understanding of their differences. Consequently, when environmental problems are described in quantitative terms, the average person loses track of the numbers and reasons poorly. For instance, most people react more strongly to environmental and other threats after reading a story about one, personally salient individual rather than statistics concerning thousands or a million potential victims (Slovic, 2007; Slovic & Slovic, 2004–2005). Consider the following claim: "Scientists predict in 40 years global warming will displace 20 million people from Beijing, 40 million from Shanghai and surrounding areas, and 60 million from Calcutta and Bangladesh." These statistics are too abstract to inspire action because they don't stimulate compassion for any single, real person (Bennett, 2008, p. 2, para. 5).

It is often difficult to make good decisions about environmental issues relative to other societal projects because of the difficulty conceptualizing costs. In Washington state, for example, the Hanford Nuclear Reservation was the primary site of nuclear weapon development during the Cold War, and still represents one of the planet's most polluted sites. Millions of gallons of highly toxic plutonium and radioactive wastes contaminate groundwater and soil and seep into the Columbia River. Clean up costs have already exceeded $35 billion and are expected to cost at least another $50 billion over several decades (Helman, 2005; Stiffler, 2002). How does this number compare to the U.S. national debt? To the annual cost of social security? To federal expenditures on education?* For most people, these numbers are too big to comprehend or relate to each other.

Similarly, proenvironmental behaviors are often undertaken with less than optimal results because their quantitative dimensions get lost. For example, electric lights use about 5% of home electricity. In the 1970s, the energy crisis induced many people to conserve energy by being conscientious about turning off lights. When their behaviors failed to show impact on their electricity bills, people gave up trying to save energy altogether. Unfortunately, they did not realize that home heating and cooling uses 50%–70% of domestic energy, so turning down one's thermostat in the winter and turning it up in the summer by just a few degrees would save far more energy than consistently turning off lights. Here's a key point: *Choosing major appliances that are energy efficient is the single most important behavior for reducing energy use* (Gardner & Stern, 2008; Stern, 2000); refrigerators alone use about 19% of household energy. Likewise, many people are quite careful about recycling, but less aware that *reducing use* is considerably more effective for saving natural resources. For instance, reducing packaging materials by buying products in refillable plastic containers (such as shampoo from local health foods stores) is much more important than recycling plastic bottles, yet far fewer people use refillable bottles than recycle.

---

* In 2008, the answers to these questions were: National debt equaled more than 10.6 trillion (10,656 billion; U.S. Treasury Department, retrieved online [http://www.treasurydirect. gov/NP/BPDLogin?application=np]); Social Security expenditures were $658.4 billion (Social Security Administration, retrieved online [http://www.ssa.gov/finance/2008/ FinPosition.pdf, p. 35]); Amount spent on education in 2006 was $166 billion for total education expenses (representing 6.3% of the federal budget; Retrieved December 15, 2008 [http://www.census.gov/compendia/statab/tables/08s0210.pdf]).

Reprinted from © Mark Parisi and Off the Mark. With permission.

Framing Effects

Finally, people are also susceptible to **framing effects**, which are induced when the same information is structured in different ways. For example, people responding to surveys are more likely to deny harming the environment, than to claim that they help it (Bazerman & Hoffman, 1999), and customers are more likely to invest in a water heater wrap if it was presented as a way to avoid losing money, rather than as a way to save it! (Yates, 1982). Framing various phenomena as *environmental* is politicizing and polarizing, and results in relegating the issues to the concern of environmentalists rather than the public at large (Broder, 2009; Shellenberger & Nordhaus, 2004). An assessment of framing effects revealed that *climate change* is less politicizing than *global warming*, and speaking more specifically about "the air we breathe, [or] the water our children drink" is more widely engaging than the phrase "the environment" (Broder, 2009).

USING COGNITIVE PSYCHOLOGY TO SOLVE ENVIRONMENTAL PROBLEMS

The picture that cognitive psychology paints of human beings is not an especially attractive one. The physical constraints of sensory processes, reasoning biases and errors, and inexperience in quantitative matters can all adversely impact judgments and behavior. Most people like to think of themselves as rational and open-minded, but research shows that rationality is bounded. Add these limitations to the emotional influences of anxieties and defenses (discussed in Chapter 3) that also affect decision making, and it is easy to conclude that only experts should be making environmental decisions. Unfortunately, experts are just as likely to make errors, as we discuss below.

Because all this seems to undermine the point of this book, which is to understand the psychological dimensions of environmental destruction so that people might start doing things differently, let us add a very important point here. Although *everyone* tends to be deceived by these processes, one does not have to be. Rather, people can learn to avoid these errors by understanding how they function (Bazerman, 2006; Tversky & Kahneman, 1974). Everyone can reason more effectively by learning to recognize naïve errors, and by putting forth the necessary effort to overcome these powerful predispositions.

Thus, from a cognitive perspective, people can start changing environmentally inappropriate choices by getting better information about the effects of their actions. All institutions have some vested interest in their own point of view, and may distort information in order to maintain it. This is no less true of environmental groups than it is for businesses, governments, military organizations, or local landowners. In sum, citizens can become more environmentally friendly by doing the following three things:

- *Getting better information and acting on it.* For example, asking difficult questions about environmental issues; pursuing answers, even when they are not forthcoming; learning more about the environmental consequences of various actions, especially consumer choices; and expressing preferences to store managers and legislators. (A number of good guides are available that give information about the environmental impact of consumer goods; some of them are included in the Appendix.)
- *Noticing and correcting reasoning errors.* Specifically, forcing one's self to make a counterargument in order to appreciate other sides of complex issues, being willing to admit that

information and/or reasoning is flawed, and being open to learning more about one's limitations.

- *Taking personal responsibility* by being confident enough to learn more about complicated issues, and refusing to leave environmental solution efforts entirely to experts who may have different priorities.

This last point is most important for effectively addressing environmental destruction. Thus, we use the remainder of the chapter to address it in more detail.

RISK ASSESSMENT: WHOSE QUANTIFICATION PROBLEM IS IT?

Many environmental conditions threaten human and planetary well-being (Chapters 1, 6 and 8). How does one evaluate the risks of these threats? Who is responsible for determining risk to the general public? An important area where cognitive psychology is applied to environmental problems is called **risk assessment**, where human health hazards associated with various substances and activities are evaluated and quantified. Over the last 50 years, public concerns about environmental risks have grown continuously, becoming an important issue in government and industry circles. Regulations developed and overseen by the U.S. EPA are based on identifying hazards, estimating probabilities of damage, reducing risks, and communicating risk to the public.

To get a feel for how risk assessment works, please rank in order the following hazards according to your perception of how much of a health risk each poses. After you have completed your rankings, look at the footnote to see how your answers compare with samples of respondents (lay-persons and experts) in the United States.*

Radiation	Persistent organic pollutants	Pesticides
Global warming†	Hazardous waste sites	Population growth

---

* U.S. respondents rated hazardous waste sites and persistent organic pollutants as posing the highest risks, followed closely by radiation (ranked respectively as #1, #2, and #4 out of 24). Population growth ranked as #6, and global warming and pesticides were perceived as posing moderate risk (rated as #10 and #11, respectively). Professional risk assessors, on the other hand, ranked these hazards as follows: Population growth was seen as the most risky (#1), followed by global warming (#3), and persistent organic pollutants (#5). Pesticides were ranked as moderate risk (#11), with hazardous waste and radiation ranked near the bottom (#19 and #21, respectively; Slimak & Dietz, 2006, p. 1695).

† Although the phrase "climate change" seems to be the preferred phrase among most scientists, this particular study used the term "global warming."

Professionals who assess risk usually define it as the number of deaths caused by a hazard in 12 months (or some other time unit). For example, about 50 deaths worldwide resulted directly from nuclear radiation since World War II, with most of those occurring during the accident at Chernobyl in 1986 (Robertson, 2000), although as many as 9,000 cancer deaths could still occur in the survivors and clean up crew from Chernobyl (World Health Organization, 2006). The worst case scenario of a large scale nuclear accident (such as a successful terrorist attack on a nuclear facility) could result in more than 100,000 deaths (Bunn & Bunn, 2002).

The number of casualties per year is easy to count and thus easy to conceptualize. However, counting fatalities gives the impression that death is the only relevant outcome of a risk, and that everything important can be quantified. These illusions are promoted by the use of complicated formulas that estimate exposure rates, event probabilities, and financial costs. For instance, computer programs can estimate the number of deaths caused every year by a hazard, compared to the price of regulation controls and the economic costs associated with one death. Risk assessment programs require that a number be given for the value of a human life. Social costs are then calculated to be a

sum of the regulation and mortality costs. These approaches rest on the rational economic model (Stern, 1992), described earlier.

Such quantitative efforts have led some people, including former EPA policy analyst Ken Bogen, to call risk assessment a form of "probabilistic cannibalism" (Miller, 1993), which trades lives for dollars. Abstract numbers can hide the effects of environmental hazards; as risks become quantified, their social dimensions get lost. Consider the issue of pesticides, for example. Legal levels of U.S. licensed pesticide residues on food cause between 2000 and 10,000 cancer deaths in real but nameless U.S. citizens each year, who were not given an opportunity to give informed consent (Miller, 2007).

When health risks such as cigarettes, alcohol, and drug abuse cost hundreds of thousands of lives, billions of dollars, and tremendous human suffering, some might argue that trying to eliminate environmental risks is wasteful and unjustified. Yet relative to drugs and alcohol, people who are harmed from pollution, pesticide-contaminated food, and effects of climate change are not informed or presented with a choice. They are also unequally distributed among the population: Environmental risks are incurred much more often by lower income groups, minorities, and children (Bullard & Johnson, 2000; Laituri & Kirby, 1994; Opotow & Clayton, 1994; see also discussion in Chapters 4 and 6). Extreme weather events associated with a changing climate are likely to exacerbate *environmental injustice* via disproportionately impacting racial minorities in poor communities, effects already seen during Hurricane Katrina (Agyeman, Doppelt, Lynn, & Hatic, 2007). These social considerations disappear when risks are quantified and are therefore irrelevant to risk analysts, but they are not irrelevant to the public.

The public and experts use different definitions of risk, and thus evaluate them differently; consequently, laypeople rarely agree with experts about specific risks (Slovic, 2000). Experts tend to focus on probability of event occurrence and the severity of consequences, whereas public perceptions are affected by a number of experiential, emotional, social, and moral factors, in addition to scientific and technological aspects (Hendrickx & Nicolaij, 2004; Leiserowitz, 2005; Slovic, 2000). The public cares more about personal health and safety than about quantifiable data (Miller & Keller, 1991). Most people's perception of risk includes an appraisal of one's abilities to avoid personal harm, to take action to reduce the threat, and a consideration of the response costs (money, time, effort; Grothmann & Patt, 2005).

One study showed that nonexpert groups rated nuclear power as the highest risk among 30 hazards, whereas experts rated it quite low (20th out of 30; Slovic, Fischhoff, & Lichtenstein, 1979). The public feared nuclear power much more than experts, a trend that remained 20 years later (Slovic, Flynn, Mertz, Poumadere, & Mays, 2000). In general, the public expresses greater levels of concern about local, immediate threats like hazardous waste and radiation contamination, compared to experts' focus on global, longer-term issues, such as population growth and climate change (Slimak & Dietz, 2006). Thus, although the scientific community has detailed the clear and devastating risks associated with climate change, the public largely maintains a wait and see attitude, and does not seem to understand the need to drastically and immediately reduce emissions in order to stabilize the climate (Sterman, 2008), although they do report concern about potential human health risks (Sundblad, Biel, & Gärling, 2007).

To illustrate public perception of risk, Slovic and colleagues (1985) proposed a model based on two dimensions: degree of controllability (including fatality, equitability, risk to future generations, voluntariness) and the degree of observability (including knowledge of those exposed, delay of effects, amount of scientific knowledge available; see Figure 7.4).

Yet matters of observability, voluntariness, equitability, and knowledge are much more difficult to quantify than are number of deaths per year. Some critics of risk assessment suggest that hazards can never be adequately quantified, and so risk assessment should not be used to make major policy decisions. Likewise, it may be impossible to compare risks. "How does one compare a case of lung cancer in a retired petrochemical worker to the loss of cognitive function experienced by an urban child with lead poisoning?" (Durenberger, Mott, & Sagoff, 1991, p. 50). Others argue that risk assessment is an inadequate, even dangerous way to make policy decisions because it fools people into thinking that rational, objective decisions can be made based on numerical formulas derived from epidemiological and nonhuman data, which may be flawed or inappropriate.

The Role of Emotions in Judgment of Risk

Emotional associations and responses, also known as **affect**, contribute to the judgment of risk, and may be more powerful than rational assessments (e.g., Hine, Marks, Nachreiner, Gifford, & Heath, 2007). Emotions influence the availability of certain memories; individuals are more likely to recall emotionally charged events than more mundane ones. When a hazard evokes feelings of dread (e.g., cancer, terrorism), it will be perceived as a greater risk than less dreaded events, such as traffic accidents (Slovic, Finucane, Peters, & MacGregor, 2002). Slovic and colleagues refer to this process as the **affect heuristic**, where judgment and decision making are guided by images that accompany

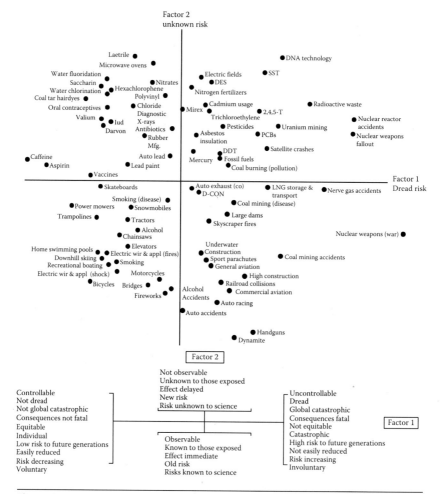

Figure 7.4 Location of 81 hazards on Factor 1 (controllability) and Factor 2 (observability), derived from the interrelationships among 15 risk characteristics. Each factor is made up of a combination of characteristics, as indicated by the lower diagram. (Reprinted from Slovic, P., Fischhoff, B., & Lichtenstein, S. (1985). *Perilous progress: Technology as hazard*, Boulder, CO: Westview. With permission.)

positive and negative feelings. The effect can occur without conscious awareness, accounting for **subliminal** influences. Advertising capitalizes on such effects by showing smiling, healthy people using potentially hazardous substances such as pesticides, or gas-guzzling and climate changing sport-utility vehicles.

The affect heuristic leads people to misjudge potential hazards. If people enjoy an activity, they judge the risks low and the benefits high;

if they dislike the activity, they do the opposite, judging the risk high and the benefits low (Slovic et al., 2002; see Figure 7.5). For example, someone who enjoys eating meat (positive affect) will tend to downplay the health and environmental risks more than someone who doesn't like the taste of meat. Likewise, a recent study demonstrated that people who have positive associations with wood fires underestimate the health risks associated with wood smoke (including serious respiratory, developmental, and immune dysfunction) and are less likely to support regulations on wood burning (Hine et al., 2007). These effects may be due to associative networks. That is, certain feelings or moods enable recollection of any concepts previously connected to that emotion, thereby influencing judgment and decision-making processes (Forgas, 1999; Leiserowitz, 2006).

Clearly, emotional reactions to risks do not necessarily correlate with objective risks or costs, such as number of deaths per year. People may respond with very little fear to automobiles or pesticides, even though these pose dangerous risks (climate change, accidents, neurological impacts, cancer). On the other hand, stimuli such as spiders, snakes, and heights can evoke profound fear reactions, despite awareness that one really has little to fear from these stimuli. This pattern can be explained from an evolutionary perspective (Öhman & Mineka, 2003) as the **mismatch hypothesis** (Gaulin & McBurney, 2001): Evolution has not yet prepared people to respond seriously to modern hazards (e.g., Slovic et al., 2002; see further discussion in Chapter 8). Thus, the discrepancy between ancestral and current environments can account for a variety of cognitive limitations that contribute to ecological problems.

Other heuristics also impact both public and experts' assessment of risk, especially when the experts are outside their area of expertise (Finucane, 2005). For example, fear of hazards are affected by

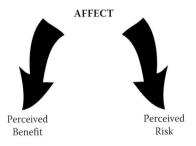

AFFECT

Perceived
Benefit

Perceived
Risk

Figure 7.5. The affective evaluation of a stimulus influences judgments of risk and benefit. (Adapted from Finucane, M.L., Alhakami, A., Slovic, P., & Johnson, S.M. (2000). *Journal of Behavioral Decision Making, 13*, 4. With permission from graphic artist, Darick Dang, Willamette University.)

the availability heuristic, as people tend to overestimate the incidence of infrequent but very salient events (like nuclear accidents or terrorist attacks) and underestimate the incidence of frequent ones (such as toxic exposures). This error is understandable in light of the fact that unusual situations get a lot of press, while more commonplace occurrences are much less publicized. Consequently, the average person may fear less likely hazards more than likely ones (Fischhoff, 1990).

Most environmental threats reflect high levels of uncertainty concerning specific outcomes, and greatly delayed impacts that are expected to occur at distant locations; these characteristics can lead people to discount the danger, or take it less seriously, than "risks with negative outcomes that occur for sure, now, here, and to us" (Gattig & Hendrickx, 2007, p. 22; see also Leiserowitz, 2007).* You might recognize this point as an example of *proximal cognition*, discussed earlier. Furthermore, people underestimate all types of risks to themselves relative to other people, including environmental threats like air and water pollution, or nuclear accidents (Pahl et al., 2005). On the other hand, this *comparative optimism* can act as a defense mechanism (Chapter 3), protecting people from difficult emotions associated with potential harm to their health and safety, and reducing their likelihood to undertake actions to reduce the threat.

Consequently, public concern about risks like climate change will likely increase as its impacts occur more locally and immediately, and thus become more salient; for instance, as severe weather events such as hurricanes become more common and their relationship to climate change is emphasized (Sunstein, 2006). Visceral fear responses (i.e., the **stress response**, described in Chapter 8) mobilize people to respond to threats by escaping, or ideally by changing the external situation (solving the problem). Activating emotional reactions relative to the danger of climate change and other environmental threats will thus be critical for mustering individual and collective responses (Weber, 2006), while providing specific actions people can take to reduce feelings of being overwhelmed (Bennett, 2008).

It is well worth monitoring the ways in which experts think about and document risk assessment because without public input, their judgments (like everyone's) are likely to be distorted by the institutions that

---

* Although the majority of people discount based on delayed consequences, many people (30–50%) do not in the case of environmental threats (Gattig & Hendrickx, 2007; Hendrickx & Nicolaij, 2004).

train, hire, and pay them. Cognitive processes, including perception of risk, are not entirely rational, whether they are made by experts or laypeople. For example, framing effects can influence both physicians' and patients' treatment preferences (e.g., surgery or radiation for cancer); choices changed depending on whether the prognosis was framed as probability of living versus the probability of dying (McNeil, Pauker, Sox, & Tversky, 1982). Risks framed as gains ("air quality is bad, but this vehicular emissions device could help") are accepted more readily by decision makers than when framed as a potential loss ("air quality isn't great but it's okay; this emissions device could help but it might also make things worse"; example adapted from Gattig & Hendrickx, 2007). Thus, risk evaluation by both experts and nonexperts is impacted by the way the risk is framed, and differences in framing can contribute to difficulties resolving disputes concerning environmental issues, such as water regulations, toxic clean-ups, and national park management (Brummans et al., 2008).

Retaining a Voice

"Risk management is, fundamentally, a question of values. In a democratic society, there is no acceptable way to make these choices without involving the citizens who will be affected by them" (Morgan, 1993, p. 32). Thus, effective risk assessment requires that experts work with the public. Public input is critical to risk management because individuals directly affected by regulations have the right to participate in decision making; members of the public possess wisdom and knowledge about local conditions; and public support increases the success of implementing risk decisions (Dietz & Stern, 2008; Finucane, 2005). Responding to climate change offers a current and relevant illustration. The relatively small U.S. population (representing less than 5% of the world's inhabitants) is responsible for a considerable portion of global greenhouse gases (nearly one quarter; Energy Information Administration, 2008a). Consequently, the cooperation of U.S. residents is critical to reducing emissions, in terms of their support for policy changes (treaties, regulations, taxes, and subsidies), as well as their direct consumption of fossil fuels and resulting emissions (Leiserowitz, 2005, 2007).

The danger of most current risk assessment practices is that public participation is not typically sought or respected by experts. Correspondingly, many people assume the experts know what they are doing, even though public trust in industry and government officials is not high (Covello, 1993; Slovic et al., 2000). Leaving important risk decisions to experts while not entirely trusting them is problematic, but usually happens when people assume the questions are too complicated, too enormous, or too overwhelming.

In many arenas, leaving decisions to experts makes sense. For example, automobiles and buildings should be designed by engineers and architects with far more knowledge than the public could ever possess. In a representative democracy, elected and nonelected leaders alike are entrusted to be good stewards of society, to be educated in their areas of influence, and to make responsible decisions. However, engineering problems and risk assessments are fundamentally different domains because the latter involve human values. There is no reason to think that experts can make the crucial judgments about the value of human life any better than laypeople. What authority would an industry official have over a full-time parent in determining how many lives are worth risking for any particular technological advancement?

Despite the fact that risk assessments are not perfect, and tend to differ between laypeople and experts, it is unlikely that society can afford to dispense with the service that risk assessment performs: forcing people to explicate assumptions, empirically measure available data, and consider the diversity of concerns that different groups bring to the problem. Risk assessment should not be abandoned—but rather it should be improved by including more effective public participation in decisions that impact everyone. Hopefully, risk assessment work will continue to advance. When it began, the public was called irrational, and ignored or blamed for not agreeing with experts' assessments of environmental risks. Now scientists are attempting to understand and involve the public. In the future, we look forward to the time when risk assessment evolves to understanding of the larger systems that create victims and risks in the first place (Freudenburg & Pastor, 1992).

CONCLUSIONS

The main contribution of cognitive psychology to approaching environmental problems is the view that inappropriate environmental behaviors can result from inadequate, mistaken, distorted, or missing information about the consequences of human actions, resulting in processing errors. Properties of perceptual and cognitive systems that are otherwise adaptive can sometimes lead to overestimating or underestimating risks, depending on the available information and how it is processed. Unless trained to do otherwise, experts are just as likely to make errors as laypeople. By recognizing that much of human behavior relies more on nonconscious preferences than rational calculations, people can become more effective in their decision making. For example, making environmentally appropriate consumer choices requires thoughtful consideration of what constitutes sustainability and making decisions accordingly. The biases discussed in this chapter can be overcome, *if* one is alert to them, and intentionally and consistently practices methods of subverting them. Everyone must address problems of sustainability with a rigorously attuned "ecological intelligence" (Goleman, 2009), an intelligence that is strengthened, rather than undermined, by learning about cognitive limitations. Yet doing so may be stressful; thus, we turn to a consideration of health and the psychology of environmental stress (Chapter 8).

8

HEALTH AND THE PSYCHOLOGY
OF ENVIRONMENTAL STRESS

To seek human health and sustainability without considering the importance of environmental sustainability is to invite potentially devastating consequences for the health and well-being of whole populations . . . Natural environments are an ideal setting for the integration of environment, society and health . . . Public health has a key role to play in environmental conservation, and environmental administration has a key role to play in human health and well-being.

(Maller, Townsend, Pryor, Brown, & Leger, 2006, pp. 49–50).

Imagine that you walk into a room; immediately your eyes start to water, and you feel an irritation in your nose and throat. You notice you are holding your breath, your heart is beating faster, and your face feels flushed. Then you see a sign that says "Fresh Paint." Your heartbeat quickly returns to normal as you conclude that it's no big deal, and you open a window to air out the room while you go for a short walk. On the other hand, if you are a pregnant woman who has recently read that paint fumes may be toxic to your developing fetus, you will likely feel a much more intense and sustained stress response. This deceptively simple example illustrates the complex interactions between environmental conditions, physiological responses, and psychological processes including cognition, emotion, and behavior in the creation and experience of **stress**. This chapter will demonstrate that contemporary environments and environmental degradation are stressful on many levels, and will discuss ways in which people can mitigate harmful effects to themselves as well as the environment.

STRESS

Poor air quality, noxious odors, toxins, and other physical and psychological demands put pressure (i.e., stress) on physiological systems and are referred to as **stressors.** Some researchers (e.g., Sarafino, 1998; Stein & Spiegel, 2000) distinguish between

- **Environmental stressors,** including air pollution, climate change, traffic, noise, and catastrophic events like Hurricane Katrina or nuclear accidents;
- **Physical stressors,** for example, illness, surgery, aging, infection, or malnutrition
- **Psychological stressors,** such as emotional distress over the loss of a loved one, unemployment, disease diagnosis, time pressures, or hazards such as climate change and toxic waste sites.

However, these categories are not independent of each other. For example, witnessing the terrorist attacks on September 11, 2001 and the devastation wrought by hurricanes or learning of other *environmental stressors* causes thoughts and feelings that, in turn, act as *psychological stressors* and perhaps also *physical stressors* if one develops headaches or insomnia as a result of the event. One rarely encounters stressors individually; rather, multiple stressors interact and produce greater effects than would be expected from simple additive effects (e.g., Wallenius, 2004). There is little difference between stressors in terms of the physiological responses they evoke. Human bodies respond to environmental and physical stressors and to anxiety, fear, and worry in similar ways.

Physiology of the Stress Response

When you encounter an environmental stressor like fresh paint or other potentially threatening event, or even find yourself worrying about some personal or planetary issue, your **stress response** is activated. Regardless of the type of stressor, the stress response consists of physiological and psychological components (Evans & Cohen, 1987), although the boundaries between the physiological and psychological are becoming increasingly blurred as neuroscience illuminates the biochemical and anatomical underpinnings of thoughts, feelings, and actions.

Several pathways in the nervous system process environmental stimuli and function in an integrated manner. All stressors activate the **sympathetic nervous system**, a division of the **autonomic nervous system** (ANS). The ANS regulates respiration, cardiovascular functions, and other life support mechanisms and is a component of the **peripheral nervous system** (PNS). The PNS generally acts as an interface between the outside world and the **central nervous system** (CNS; brain and spinal cord; see Figure 8.1).

Sympathetic nervous system activity is often referred to as the **fight or flight response**, and is responsible for the increase in heart rate and facial flushing when you meet an **acute** (immediate) stressor, such as the paint fumes. Your body is mobilizing its energy stores to respond to the threat. The ANS works in conjunction with the **endocrine system**, a network of glands that release **hormones**, chemical messengers that travel through your bloodstream and affect tissues and organs in various parts of the body (see Figure 8.2). Part of the sympathetic response

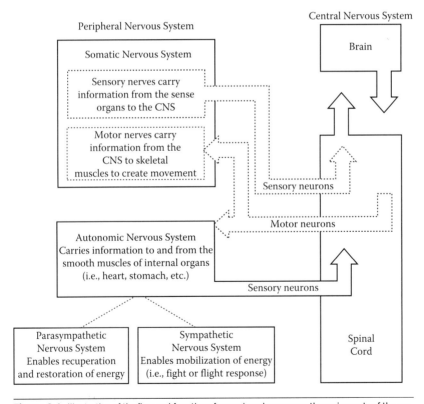

Figure 8.1 Illustration of the flow and function of nerve impulses among the major parts of the nervous system. (Printed from graphic design by Darick Dang, Willamette University. With permission.)

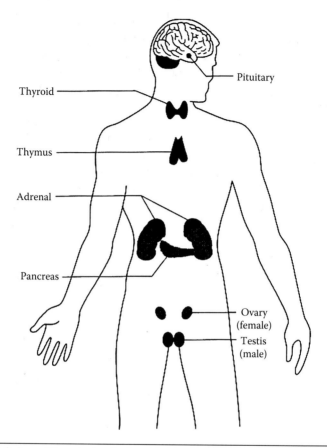

Figure 8.2 Some of the endocrine glands and their locations in the body. (Reprinted from Sarafino, E.P., *Health Psychology: Biopsychosocial Interactions,* p. 42, © John Wiley & Sons, Inc., New York, 1998. With permission.)

includes stimulation of glands near your kidneys; thus, when you smell the noxious odors, you feel a rush of **adrenaline** (also known as **epinephrine**), a hormone released by the adrenal glands (*ad renal* means toward kidney in Latin; *epi nephron* means upon the kidney in Greek; Carlson, 1995, p. 65).

The endocrine component of the stress response is also triggered by **chronic** (long-term) stressors and mimics the direct sympathetic response, except that the additional hormones produce a much longer-lasting effect (Gevirtz, 2000). The overall result is an increase in blood pressure, respiration, and metabolism of **glucose**, which provides energy to cells throughout your body. Endocrine activity also stimulates the release of **cortisol**, a hormone that suppresses **immune system** responses (**immunosuppression**; Parsons & Hartig, 2000), leaving you more vulnerable to infections and colds during times of prolonged stress. You may have experienced this yourself if you ever came down with a cold or the flu during final exams.

The sympathetic and endocrine systems are well suited to dealing with relatively short-lived stressors, such as breathing potentially poisonous odors or being chased by a saber-toothed tiger. When the stressor terminates, the **parasympathetic division** of the ANS becomes active, enabling restoration and conservation of energy. Parasympathetic activity stimulates digestion and relaxation, a combination that accounts for the fatigue many people feel after a large meal.

Through the course of evolution, the stress response evolved to deal with sudden and obvious (acute) threats. According to Darwin's theory, animals that were able to respond in a way that protected them from a threat (i.e., by successfully fighting it off or getting away from it; thus the phrase "fight or flight response") tended to survive and go on to reproduce, passing along the genes that enabled such behaviors. Other animals did not live to pass on their nonadaptive genes. As a whole, animal species became hardwired to deal with threatening stimuli in sudden, intense bursts of energy and nervous system activity. However, because many modern stressors are on-going or chronic (e.g., career and school responsibilities, crowding and air pollution), rather than acute as they were during evolutionary history, the stress response is no longer adapted to the prevailing environment. This distinction between ancestral and current environments has been termed the **mismatch hypothesis** (Gaulin & McBurney, 2001), and may explain why chronic stress and other components of contemporary lifestyles produce such a range of adverse effects, as we will see in subsequent sections (Boaz, 2002).

Research on gender differences in responses to stress reveals that the phrase "fight or flight" fits men better than women (Taylor et al., 2000). Women more often respond to sympathetic arousal with "tend and befriend" behaviors, seeking comfort through connection and relationships rather than aggression or withdrawal. Thus, although men and women have similar physiological responses to stressors, their behavioral reactions may be very different. For this reason, we refer to sympathetic activity as "the stress response" rather than "fight or flight," which distorts understanding about stress by emphasizing male patterns. The important causes and ramifications of different gender patterns are explored in Chapter 4.

Psychological Components of the Stress Response

Cognitive and behavioral factors are critically important in determining the duration and extent of the stress response. Perception of stimuli in the environment, made possible by activity within the brain's cerebral cortex, allows you to interpret and analyze situations. Thus, psychological stress depends upon your assessment of the meaning of environmental events, your actual or perceived control over the stressor, and your evaluation of the resources you have to cope (deal effectively) with the events (Evans & Cohen, 1987; Lazarus, 1966; Lazarus & Folkman, 1984). These conscious, cognitive processes can either exacerbate or mitigate the physiological responses.

In general, coping efforts may help to escape, remove, tolerate, or accept the threat (Sarafino, 1998), and can be emotion-focused or problem-focused (Spedden, 1998). Emotion-focused coping can make a situation seem more manageable by creating distance or hope for future control, like Scarlett O'Hara's approach in *Gone with the Wind* (1936) when she said "I'll think about that tomorrow." This technique was called *suppression* in Chapter 3. You could use emotion-based coping to ignore the paint fumes and stay in the room, telling yourself that you'll get used to the smell and it probably will not hurt you (or the unborn baby). On the other hand, problem-focused strategies include decision making, problem solving, and direct action. Under ideal circumstances, coping involves resolving the issue, for example, using only paints with low VOC content (volatile organic compounds, i.e., toxic gases). Other problem-solving strategies could include opening the window to air out the room, removing yourself from the situation by going for a walk, or putting on a gas mask. Both emotion-focused and problem-focused approaches can serve to reduce or increase distress, and either may be preferable depending on the specific situation, but problem-focused strategies are required for effective, long-term solutions.

In Chapter 7, we described factors influencing people's perceptions of risk. Perhaps not surprisingly, if a situation is perceived to be dangerous (risky), individuals report greater degrees of stress whether or not the event has been proven to have harmful health consequences. For example, people indicated that they felt stressed about the *potential* health risks of a proposed waste incinerator in their neighborhood (Lima, 2004). Much empirical evidence demonstrates that "environmental problems are frequently appraised as threatening or damaging to personal well-being and especially to personal health" (Homburg & Stolberg, 2006, p. 2). Encouragingly, such appraisal can lead to problem solving and specific behaviors that act to reduce the risks

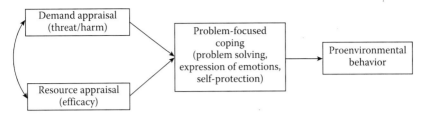

Figure 8.3 A cognitive theory of stress can be used to understand and explain proenvironmental behavior. (Reprinted from Homburg, A. & Stolberg, A., *Journal of Environmental Psychology,* 26, 3, 2006. With permission.)

(see Figure 8.3). One innovation in problem-focused coping is reflected in the **Environmental Health Clinic** at New York University.* Based on other university health clinics, "impatients" (people who are tired of waiting for legislative action) make appointments to discuss environmental health concerns ranging from toxic chemicals and pollution to climate change, and receive "prescriptions" for actions: opportunities to engage in local data collection and projects aimed to improve environmental health. The goal is to "translate the tremendous amount of anxiety and interest in addressing major environmental issues into something concrete that people can do whose effect is measurable and significant" (Schaffer, 2008, para. 5). This would be termed *sublimation* in Freudian parlance (Chapter 3).

Stress-Associated Health Risks

The relationships between environmental factors, stress, and health are complex. The fields of **psychoneuroendocrinology** and **psychoneuroimmunology** study the interdependence of these factors, analyzing psychosocial, nervous system, endocrine, and immune effects on health outcomes. Environmental stressors can produce physical symptoms and directly cause disease; disease itself is a physical stressor; and a serious diagnosis for one's self or a loved one can create a great deal of emotional (psychological) stress (see Figure 8.4). In addition, being aware of living in potentially dangerous circumstances can cause stress, and such psychological stress is also hazardous because it can produce adverse health effects. Emotional or psychological stress activates the same mechanisms that are stimulated by physical and environmental stressors, and chronic activation of these systems can seriously compromise physical as well as mental health. Below we review several of

---

* See http://www.environmentalhealthclinic.net/environmental-health-clinic/

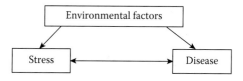

Figure 8.4 The interactions between environmental factors, stress, and disease.

the most common health outcomes of stress, various environmental stressors, and conclude with some strategies for reducing the stress response. The good news is that human health-promoting environments also protect and preserve ecological integrity.

Most readers are probably aware that prolonged stress damages the gastrointestinal system (e.g., causing ulcers, irritable bowel syndrome, or other digestive issues) as well as the **circulatory** and **cardiovascular** systems. Frequent mobilization of the stress response increases blood pressure (i.e., **hypertension**), escalating one's risk for **stroke**, when blood vessels serving the brain are blocked or ruptured, or **heart attack**, a disruption of blood flow to the heart. Strokes usually impair cognitive functions such as speech production, comprehension, and memory or voluntary movement. Many of the patients **neuropsychologists** see have suffered strokes.

Although stress hormones aid in memory consolidation and can account for vivid recollection of traumatic events (i.e., **flashbulb memories**), prolonged stress produces damage in certain parts of the brain and associated deficits in learning and memory (Lupien, Maheu, Tu, Fiocco, & Schramek, 2007). It may also accelerate age-related cognitive decline and risk for **Alzheimer's disease**, particularly in combination with other risk factors (Pardon & Rattray, 2008).

As mentioned above, stress can interfere with normal **immune** functioning, decreasing or increasing immune system activity depending on many factors. The nature of the stress, whether it is acute or chronic, the person's interpretation and behavioral response, and access to resources such as social support, all influence the effect of stress on immunity (Goodkin & Visser, 2000). Recent evidence suggests that stress-related responses such as hostility, anger, and **depression** can increase inflammatory processes within the immune system, increasing the risk for hypertension and heart disease (Boyle, Jackson, & Suarez, 2007).

Symptoms of depression commonly result from stress, and this effect may also be mediated by the immune system. **Cytokines** (proteins that enable communication between cells) released during an immune response may contribute to depression (Maddock & Pariante,

2001). The resulting behaviors include "fatigue, loss of appetite, sleep disturbance, social withdrawal, decreased libido, depressed mood and general malaise" (p. 159), and also accompany infections. Thus, these "sickness behaviors" can produce depression (Maddock & Pariante, 2001; see Figure 8.5).

Research suggests a relationship between stress and **cancer** via several mechanisms:

- First, stress hormones contribute directly to at least some cancers; that is, ovarian, nasopharyngeal, and multiple myeloma (Weinhold, 2008).
- Second, immunosuppression resulting from stress leaves the body more susceptible to viruses and other organisms that can cause cancer (Boaz, 2002; Hardell et al., 1998).
- Third, immunosuppression can promote the growth of existing tumors (Stein & Spiegel, 2000).
- Fourth, cell proliferation repairs tissue damaged while responding to a threat, so if the cells have genetic mutations the result is a potentially cancerous tumor (Nadakavukaren, 2000).
- Fifth, environmental stressors such as air pollution, pesticides, endocrine disruptors, and other toxic chemicals (i.e., PBTs, described in Chapter 6) can directly cause or increase the risk

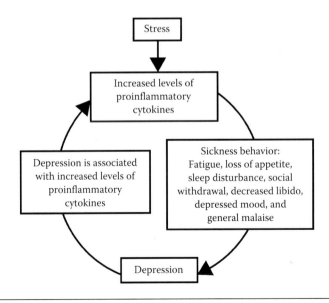

Figure 8.5 The Stress, Cytokine, Depression model. (Reprinted from Maddock, C., & Pariante, C. M. (2001). *Epidemiologia e Psichiatria Sociale, 10*(3), 160. With permission.)

for various cancers: lung, breast, brain, cervical, ovarian, prostate, kidney, as well as leukemia and non-Hodgkin's lymphoma (Bassil et al., 2007; Clapp, Jacobs, & Loechler, 2008; Colborn, Dumanoski, & Myers, 1997; vom Saal et al., 2007).

• Finally, individuals who experience stress are more likely to engage in unhealthy behaviors such as smoking, eating a poor diet, or drinking alcohol excessively. Such behaviors increase the risk of several forms of cancer and other illnesses (Sarafino, 1998).

Among the public as well as the medical establishment, gender differences in environmentally related cancers have been under recognized until recently. This neglect is partially because cancer research has traditionally focused on men (Marcus, 2005), and also because women have traditionally hidden their illness from public view (Seager, 2003). One of the most important early environmental leaders, Rachel Carson, died from breast cancer. Surprisingly few people know this. Carson herself was resolutely unforthcoming about her diagnosis, most likely fearing that disclosure of her cancer would be used to question her integrity as a critic of the chemical industry. But Carson's dual legacy as one of the most prominent whistleblowers on synthetic chemicals and as a casualty of a "women's" disease that was given short shrift by the male medical establishment has sparked a remarkable effort to trace the linkages between chemical assaults and breast cancer (Seager, 2003, pp. 961–962).

Environmental, physical and psychological stressors also interact in diseases like **asthma**. Every year, millions of people suffer asthma attacks, or breathing difficulties, due to inflammation or mucus that obstructs their airways. It is a major cause of illness and hospitalization of children under 15, and kills nearly 4000 people each year (CDC, 2009). Asthma prevalence rates are apparently increasing as a result of climate change and associated increases in pollen quantities (Beggs & Bambrick, 2005). Although asthma is usually caused by irritation from allergens or air pollution (environmental stressors), it can also result from strenuous exercise (physical) or emotional (psychological) responses (Gevirtz, 2000; Sarafino, 1998).

Stress-Associated Behavioral Disorders

Behavioral disorders such as overeating, smoking, and alcohol abuse are reaching epidemic proportions and often are associated with feelings of stress. For example, stress can stimulate eating disorders

(Arnow, Kenardy, & Agras, 1992), and you have probably experienced how your own nutrition suffers when under stress. Such patterns are likely contributing to the epidemic of obesity in the United States and other developed countries. According to the U.S. Department of Health and Human Services (2008), 16.3% of children and adolescents and more than one third (34.3%) of adults were overweight in 2005–2006; 142 million Americans age 20 and older are overweight or obese (American Heart Association, 2008). Most overweight adolescents do not change their habits and remain overweight in adulthood. Obesity is associated with increased risk of cancer, heart disease, stroke, and diabetes. Almost as many deaths each year are related to obesity (365,000) as to smoking (440,000; Flegal, Graubard, Williamson, & Gail, 2005; U.S. Department of Health and Human Services, 2004).

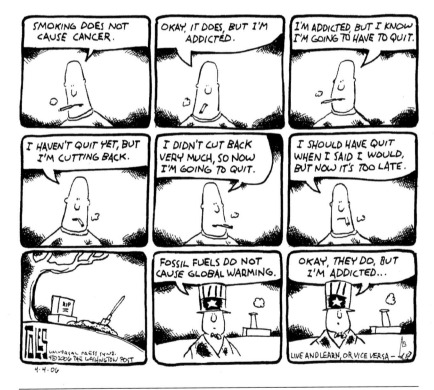

Overeating and other addictive disorders drive environmental problems (Fish, 2007; Riebel, 2001). For example, food is a limited resource that is often taken for granted, similar to water and fossil fuels. Awareness of internal states (like feelings, hunger, or satiety) is numbed when a person is distracted through television, music, and addictions to food, coffee, cigarettes, or shopping. Consequently, nature is disrespected; plants and animals are seen only in terms of their ability to satisfy addictions; impact on other humans such as exploited farmworkers and factory laborers is ignored; and shared responsibility is denied, as addictions are seen as an individual's problem. "We consume the earth to ease our pain. But the success of this strategy is fleeting— the pain comes back, so we do more of the same, demanding more consumption-induced oblivion" (Riebel, 2001, p. 48). Riebel also notes that eating disorders themselves are a direct threat to the environment, since so much food is misused and wasted. This waste exacerbates the problem of overpopulation, necessitating further conversion of land for food production.

Even aside from eating disorders, most North American's choices of food are dangerous to their health. Again, evolution probably played a role (Boaz, 2002): People crave fats and salt, apparently because these substances were rare in ancestors' environments, and people needed to stock up when they encountered them. Similarly, sweetness indicated ripe fruit. With the current abundance of these flavors in grocery stores and fast-food chains, most people get more than they should with serious consequences to their weight and health. What is less widely known is that an appetite for meat, dairy products, and other fatty substances also increases exposure to *persistent bioaccumulative toxins* (PBTs; see Chapter 6). As PBTs accumulate in fatty tissue, eating animal-based products exposes the eater to even greater concentrations of these substances. Current agricultural practices compound this risk, as animals are routinely treated with growth hormones and antibiotics that also adversely impact human health (Motavalli, 2002; Sherman, 2000), and agriculture is a major user of pesticides, another type of PBT.

Not surprisingly, the same food choices that negatively impact health also adversely affect ecosystems. Toxic pesticides and chemical fertilizers accumulate in water, soil, and human bodies. Along with pollution from factory farms, massive environmental costs are incurred from using water, grain, energy, and land to produce meat. Meat production accounts for an incredible amount of water use: In

California, it takes *2464 gallons* of water to produce *one pound* of beef because of low rainfall and irrigation; that is more than you would use showering for an entire year (Robbins, 2001). Hunger is pervasive throughout the world because of the eating behaviors of those in developed nations. The grain that goes into creating one eight ounce steak could alternatively "fill 45 to 50 bowls with cooked cereal grains" (Motavalli, 2002, p. 29). In the United States, reducing meat production by just 10% would free enough grain to feed 60 million people. Animal rights and worker safety are also jeopardized by the meat industry because of the appalling (and very stressful) conditions to which the animals and those who slaughter them are exposed (Schlosser, 2001).

On the other hand, eating a nutritious and balanced diet, and taking the time to notice and enjoy what one is eating, can aid in reducing one's experience of stress (Peurifoy, 1995). The World Health Organization (WHO, 2008b) promotes a healthy diet as one of the three major ways (along with regular exercise and avoiding tobacco) to prevent cardiovascular abnormalities leading to heart disease and strokes. Slowing down can facilitate food choices that are better for individual health as well as that of the planet. A growing **slow-food movement** reflects these values, in a commitment to food that is produced in ways that benefit ecosystems, biodiversity, and human health.*

Just as the experience of stress impacts behavioral choices, many behaviors in turn create stress. People frequently create more stress in their lives to maintain a certain standard of living that seems appealing or is socially valued. Most citizens in industrialized countries strive to earn a salary sufficient to pay a mortgage, make car payments, and buy luxury material goods. United States citizens in particular purchase many more goods than are necessary for basic, comfortable survival and consider it normal to do so.

What is "normal"? Normal is getting dressed in clothes that you buy for work, driving through traffic in a car that you are still paying for in order to get to the job that you need so you can pay for the clothes, car, and the house that you leave empty all day in order to afford to live in it. (Goodman, 2001, p. 1).

---

* For more information, see http://www.slowfoodusa.org/

Ironically, the advent of many devices intended to improve the ease and efficiency of people's lives has instead exacerbated personal and professional stressors and has a correspondingly detrimental impact on the planet. The term **technostress** originally referred to an inability to effectively cope with the burgeoning computer culture (Brod, 1984); more recently the term's meaning has been generalized to include adverse impacts caused directly or indirectly by the plethora of contemporary technological devices (Weil & Rosen, 1997*). Millions of people in the United States show signs of being addicted to technologies including the Internet, MP3 players, cell phones, and other electronic gadgets; 40% of the U.S. population spends more than $100 each month on such items (Americans need their gadgets, 2005) and 83% check their e-mail every day during vacations (Soong, 2008). Our classrooms are now filled with students who can't seem to get through an hour without accessing their laptops, cell phones, or iPods.

The abundance of information readily available via the Internet paradoxically makes it more difficult to stay current because of information overload. You have probably experienced how stressful it can be when a device you've come to depend on malfunctions or becomes unavailable. Built-in obsolescence and associated pressures to continually learn and use new technologies causes professional stress and insecurity, and can significantly *reduce* worker productivity (Wang, Shu, & Tu, 2008). The drive to be more efficient and productive by staying connected leaves little time for a break. Even when people are off-duty they are often still thinking about and actively engaging in work via a mobile device or computer. In the words of one physician, being constantly connected and busy is "as harmful as obesity or cigarette smoking" (Soong, 2008).

---

* Not surprisingly, there's a relevant Web site, http://www.technostress.com/

Cornered

by Mike Baldwin

1-3 © 2008 Mike Baldwin / Dist. by Universal Press Syndicate www.cornered.com
cornered@comic.com

"That article you sent me about how
technology causes a lot of stress crashed
my computer."

People also pay for this technology addiction in their interpersonal relationships. Direct, personal communication is frequently replaced by e-mail and chat rooms, increasing feelings of alienation (Weil & Rosen, 1997). Rather than have a dinner conversation, families often sit around the television. Arguments between friends or family members inspire quick and inflammatory e-mails, reducing the likelihood of calm discussions after a cool-off period. In extreme cases, the emergent phenomenon of cyberbullying, involving text messages or e-mail, has led some children to commit suicide or kill another child (National Crime Prevention Council, 2008). In contrast, social support, especially face-to-face connections with family and friends, is one of the most powerful stress relievers and predictors of health and well-being (Cohen & Wills, 1985).

Meanwhile, huge environmental costs are generated from electronic equipment. Electronic waste, or e-waste, consists of televisions, computers, cell phones, electronic toys, and other devices that largely end up in landfills or incinerators; only about 10% is recycled (Miller, 2007). The United States, with less than 5% of the world's population, is responsible for about *one half* of all the e-waste produced. Such consumption not only depletes resources including plastics (made from oil) and metals, but also generates tremendous amounts of toxic wastes such as lead, mercury, and synthetic endocrine disruptors (see Chapter 6). Most of the e-waste from the United States is transported to developing nations where underpaid workers, including children, dismantle the devices for reusable parts and suffer the effects from exposure to the toxins (Miller, 2007).

Stress-Associated Psychological Disorders

In addition to adverse physical and behavioral effects, stress can generate serious psychological outcomes, such as acute and post-traumatic stress disorders (PTSD). Both conditions are forms of anxiety disorder, and include reexperiencing traumatic events through thoughts or dreams, flashbacks, increased arousal, and attempts to avoid reminders of the triggering experience (American Psychiatric Association, 2000). Acute stress disorders and PTSD are differentiated by the timing of onset and the duration of symptoms: Acute stress disorder develops within one month of exposure to an extreme trauma; the onset of PTSD can be delayed up to several months or even years (American Psychiatric Association, 2000). Other signs of stress disorders include social withdrawal, emotional numbing, depression, anger, sleep disruption, nightmares, and somatic symptoms such as gastrointestinal distress and aches and pains. Symptoms are frequently observed as long as a year or more after the traumatic event (Bell, Greene, Fisher, & Baum, 2001). Personal traumas as well as environmental and social disasters (extreme weather events, earthquakes, nuclear accidents, terrorist attacks, etc.), can produce stress disorders (Davidson & Baum, 1996; Lundberg & Santiago-Rivera, 1998; van Griensven et al., 2006).

Comparable to trauma, many chronic stressors cause stress disorders. For example, living in a community near a hazardous waste site, incinerator, nuclear plant, or lake where fish are inedible can produce considerable mistrust, anxiety, depression, or anger concerning the obvious or invisible health effects (Bell et al., 2001; Lima, 2004; Lundberg, 1998). Mood disorders such as depression and anxiety are associated with environmental stressors including pollution, noise, and crowding (Bell et al., 2001). These disorders can overlap in symptomatology with acute stress disorder and PTSD (Lundberg, 1998). Less severe psychological effects include self-reports of stress and related symptoms, such as nervousness, tension, irritability, distractibility, impaired interpersonal behaviors, and deficits in task performance and concentration (Evans & Cohen, 1987; Weil & Rosen, 1997). These symptoms can be explained, at least in part, by the model of **learned helplessness**: When one is unable to escape or exert control over a stressful situation, people (and other animals) are inclined to give up (Seligman, 1975; see also Evans & Stecker, 2004). When they do, they show signs of depression and reduced motivation, and these characteristics often persist even when environmental conditions change so that their actions would be effective in altering the situation.

You are probably familiar with many of these impacts of stress. When you envision the typical middle-class family in the industrialized world (perhaps even your own family), do you see harried people who often work more than 40 hours per week, and who have little leisure time to relax with their families and friends? Perhaps you personally suffer from symptoms of stress: headaches, tension in your shoulders and back, stomach ulcers or acid reflux, high blood pressure. Perhaps a family member has been diagnosed with hypertension and is at risk for a heart attack or stroke. Do people you know engage in behaviors that further compromise their health, yet help them to *feel* more relaxed: smoking, consuming alcohol, or using illegal drugs? Maybe they simply zone out in front of the television or computer because they are too tired to spend quality time in more meaningful or productive activities. Unfortunately, this picture has become increasingly common and our collective health, along with the health of the planet, is suffering for it.

STRESSFUL ENVIRONMENTS

As we have seen, environmental, physical, and psychological stressors are all detrimental to health and well-being. Yet stressors abound in contemporary society, ranging from crowding to pollution to catastrophic events. Further, stressful environments are increasing in number and intensity, particularly with expanding urban development.

Urban Living

Since the early 1900s, urbanization has increased at a rapid pace. Currently, about one half of the world's population and 80% of North Americans live in an urban area (United Nations, 2005). Although urban development can maximize resource use via high density housing, and may provide alternatives to cars (walking, biking, or public transportation), most people have a preference for settings that are "spacious, green, and quiet" (van den Berg, Hartig, & Staats, 2007, p. 81). Urban settings are generally associated with harmful features including industrial pollution and hazardous waste. Simply living in an urban environment and enduring its noise, pollution, and crowding produces sympathetic nervous system arousal, with adverse effects on mood and cognitive performance (Bell et al., 2001). In addition to these directly negative consequences, signs of **neighborhood disorder** (such as visual pollution, abandoned and rundown buildings, apparent drug and alcohol use, and crime and vandalism) stimulate feelings of powerlessness and mental illness including depression and anxiety (Downey & van Willigen, 2005; Ross, Reynolds, & Geis, 2000; see Figure 8.6). Urban settings are also associated with increased anger, behavioral aggression, and violence (Hartig, Evans, Jamner, Davis, & Gärling, 2003; Kuo & Sullivan, 2001).

While urban environments provide homes and work for individuals across socioeconomic lines, lower socioeconomic status is generally related to greater exposures to hazardous environments, and more limited access to psychological resources to aid coping (see also discussion of *environmental justice* in Chapter 4). Poorer populations also have higher overall levels of illness and premature death (Marmot, Friel, Bell, Houweling, & Taylor, 2008). At one time, it was believed that people who lived below the poverty line preferred to live near environmental hazards, because the factories that caused these hazards also provided jobs and allowed for participation in the American Dream (Downey & van Willigen, 2005). However, like the majority of people in the middle and upper classes, individuals of low social economic status view industrialized regions negatively, and those who live in direct proximity to these areas experience more stress. Industrialization and lax environmental standards are associated with poor mental and physical health, regardless of social class (Bevc, Marshall, & Picou, 2007; Downey & van Willigen, 2005).

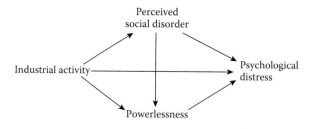

Figure 8.6 Causal model of the relationship between industrial activity, powerlessness, disorder, and depression. (Reprinted from Downey, L. & van Willigen, M. (2005). *Journal of Health and Social Behavior, 46,* 293. With permission.)

Noise Pollution

Urban environments are noisy. In addition to direct physical effects on the ear including partial or complete deafness, ringing, or ear pain, noise is an environmental stressor impacting health and psychological functioning. Like other stressors, noise produces sympathetic nervous system activity: increases in blood pressure and heart rate, as well as rises in blood cholesterol and hormonal secretions (Bronzaft, 1996, 2002) with associated cardiovascular, psychiatric, and psychosocial effects (Babisch, 2005). Not surprisingly, individuals living near airports, highways, and railroads suffer the most adverse effects of noise pollution. People do not adapt but rather are continually disturbed by it. Lack of sleep is a frequent consequence of noise, affecting task performance in children as well as adults. Sleep is particularly important for children because of its role in brain development (Dang-Vu, Desseilles, Peigneux, & Maquet, 2006).

In addition, noise causes several community problems. In noisy environments, people are less likely to help others and more likely to be aggressive toward each other (Bronzaft, 1996). People report more feelings of helplessness and a greater number of neighborhood disruptions, all of which contribute to stress, mental illness, and reductions in motivation and personal efficacy (Downey & van Willigen, 2005; Evans & Stecker, 2004).

Climate Change, Weather and Air Pollution

Urban environments are expected to warm as the climate changes, causing air pollution to worsen and changing weather patterns. Poor weather and air pollution have been linked to increases in emergency room visits related to depression and schizophrenia (Briere, Downes, & Spensley, 1983; Szyszkowicz, 2007). Rising temperatures are also associated with aggression and violence; thus, global warming will likely lead to an increase in violent crime (Anderson, 2001).

Air pollution is directly linked to fatalities. The WHO (2008a) estimates that *two million* premature deaths occur annually from respiratory, cardiac, and lung diseases caused by various sources of air pollution. *Two thirds of U.S. citizens* (200 million people) have an elevated risk for developing cancer due to exposure to toxic emissions released by automobiles and trucks, power plants, and other industrial sources (U.S. EPA, 2002c). Air pollution is also associated with coronary heart disease (Hassing et al., 2009), immune system dysfunction, reduced fertility, and impaired neurodevelopment (U.S. EPA, 2008a). Pollution from vehicle exhaust can affect brain function and lower scores on intelligence tests comparable to the effects of maternal smoking and lead exposures (Suglia, Gryparis, Wright, Schwartz, & Wright, 2008). As we saw with toxic chemicals (Chapter 6), children are particularly vulnerable to the neurotoxic impacts of air pollutants (including lead and mercury), as well as suffering damage during lung development and increased rates of asthma (Committee on Environmental Health, 2004).

In Chapter 1, we saw that global climate change is expected to increase the frequency and intensity of extreme weather events. The myriad hazards predicted to result from climate change (floods, windstorms, droughts, wildfires; i.e., environmental stressors) and increased prevalence of physical illnesses (infectious or insect-born diseases, undernutrition related to food shortages, respiratory illness, heat stroke, etc.; see Table 8.1) will create profound stress due to experiences of loss, disruption, and displacement, and worry about future consequences (Few, 2007; Fritze et al., 2008). A panel of physicians concluded that climate change represents the biggest global health threat of the twenty-first century (Boseley, 2009). As a result, the prevalence and severity of stress disorders will increase, including acute and PTSD and related problems such as grief, depression and suicide attempts, anxiety, and substance abuse (Fritze, Blashki, Burke, & Wiseman, 2008).

Natural disasters often strike the hardest in poor and highly populated areas where people are ill-prepared to cope with such events. For example, mental health services were needed to treat depression, anxiety, and PTSD in approximately 250,000 survivors of Hurricane Katrina in 2005. Yet the storm devastated the infrastructure of Louisiana's Mental Health Office, a system that had only accommodated 40,000 patients prior to the catastrophe (Siegel, 2007). Likewise, the tsunami that hit six southwestern provinces of Thailand on December 26, 2004 killed nearly 5400 individuals, injured more than 8000, and almost 3000 were never found. Survivors showed many symptoms of PTSD including anxiety and depression (van Griensven et al., 2006).

Thus, climate change promises to be a profound source of environmental, physical, and psychological stress, and related adverse health outcomes. The impacts on mental health are both direct (stress-related disorders) and indirect (social, economic, and environmental upheaval). In a clear example of environmental injustice, the harshest and most chronic consequences will be delivered on the most disadvantaged members of international populations (Agyeman, Doppelt, Lynn, & Hatic, 2007; Fritze et al., 2008).

Table 8.1 There are Various Health Impacts Associated with Weather and Climate Change

Health Outcomes	Known Effects of Weather
Heat stress	Deaths from cardiopulmonary disease increase with high and low temperatures Heat-related illness and death increase during heat waves
Air-pollution-related mortality and morbidity	Weather affects air pollutant concentrations Weather affects distribution, seasonality, and production of aeroallergens
Health impacts of weather disasters	Floods, landslides, and windstorms cause direct effects (deaths and injuries) and indirect effects (infectious disease, long-term psychological morbidity) Droughts are associated with increased risk of disease and malnutrition
Mosquito-borne diseases, tick-borne diseases (e.g., malaria, dengue)	Higher temperatures shorten the development time of pathogens in vectors and increase potential transmission to humans Vector species have specific climate conditions (temperature, humidity) necessary to be sufficiently abundant to maintain transmission
Undernutrition	Climate change may decrease food supplies (crop yields, fish stocks) or access to food supplies
Water-/food-borne diseases	Survival of important bacterial pathogens is related to temperature Water-borne diseases are most likely to occur in communities with poor water supply and sanitation Increases in drought conditions may affect water availability Extreme rainfall can affect transport of disease organisms into water supply

Source: Kovats, R.S., Campbell-Lendrum, D., & Matthies, F. (2005). *Risk Analysis, 25,* 1411. With permission.

Environmental Toxins

Toxic chemicals such as those reviewed in Chapter 6 and noxious fumes constitute *physical stressors*, as they can directly impact neural systems; cause symptoms such as hyperventilation, nausea, and vomiting; and in severe poisoning cases, convulsions, unconsciousness, and death (Nadakavukaren, 2000; Weiss, 1997). Pollution, along with industrial and household chemicals, are all considered *environmental stressors* because they are present in environments where people live and work. The phrase, **environmental illness**, describes various allergies, chemical sensitivities, and "sick building syndromes" associated with air pollution (Arnetz, 1998). Environmental illness tends to co occur with psychiatric conditions including mood and anxiety disorders, as well as **somatoform** complaints; that is, physical symptoms with no apparent physical cause, including nausea, dizziness, and pain (Bornschein, Hausteiner, Konrad, Forstl, & Zilker, 2006). Depression is directly associated with exposures to chemicals such as pesticides (Weiss, 1998; Whited, 2008) and indirectly associated with feeling pessimistic or stressed about the quality of the environment and one's ability to affect change (i.e., learned helplessness).

Mercury is a particularly well-studied environmental toxin. In some places, such as the Yatsushiro Sea in Japan, mercury poisoning is disturbingly common due to factory wastewater overflow (Ushijima, Miyake, Kitano, Shono, & Futatsuka, 2004). The majority of the 200,000 people living in this region have been exposed. Mercury contamination poses a severe, chronic stressor, not only via food sources (primarily fish), but also to fishermen's livelihood. One clear impact of exposure is Minimata Disease, a neurological and physical impairment. Typical symptoms of Minimata Disease include hearing loss, tremors, disordered movement (ataxia), and sensory impairment (Ushijima et al., 2004). While medical aspects of mercury exposure are well documented, only recently has attention focused on mental health impacts. In the Yasushiro region, more than 84% of residents report experiencing high levels of stress and symptoms of poor mental health. More individuals ranked themselves as extremely stressed from living in this area than did individuals who were survivors of the atomic bomb (23%) or earthquake refugees (67%; Ushijima et al., 2004).

Fears of potential poisonings such as those that could result from terrorist attacks are significant *psychological stressors*. For example, concerns about anthrax poisonings following the attacks of September 11, 2001, generated 2300 false reports of anthrax exposure in early October 2001. The social, psychological, and economic effects of **mass sociogenic illness** caused by psychological reactions and associated anxiety may be as significant as that which results from an actual attack (Wessely, 2002).

Why Do People Choose Stressful Behaviors and Environments?
The infamous Ted Kaczynski (the Unabomber) "attributed the social and psychological problems of modern society to the fact that *society requires* people to live under conditions radically different from those under which the human race evolved" (quoted by Wright, 1995; italics added). Kaczynski's statement is consistent with the mismatch hypothesis, but it also illustrates a common misconception: that society or culture *produces* stress. The problem with that explanation is that the terms society and culture simply refer to how a group of people tends to behave. For instance, most U.S. citizens consume more than they need; *therefore*, they live in a materialistic, consumptive society. Some abstract society is not *causing* people to be materialistic or consumptive. Thus, the idea that society causes stress is circular: Stress is caused by behaving in ways that produce stress! The implication, however, is profound: If people are behaving in ways that produce stress, presumably they could do otherwise. If that is true, why don't they?

Most people engage in activities that stress bodies, brains, and ecosystems because there is some gain from doing so. Those living in industrialized nations have become dependent on various technologies, lifestyles, consumption patterns, and chemicals that are hard to give up despite their potential for hazard. Habits are hard to change. In addition, there are incentives for many stress-inducing behaviors. For example, Sue has been working for the last 12 hours on revisions to this chapter. When she lets herself think about it, she feels physically stressed, with tension in her shoulders, back, and legs. She also feels emotionally stressed from working under a deadline and is experiencing insomnia as a result. On a broader level, she is stressed about the myriad environmental problems we are addressing in this book, and is aware of the environmental costs of the computer, energy, paper, and other resources that go into this project. Yet she is also excited about the benefits of her work. She loves this book, and believes it is a useful contribution to students and faculty. Since knowledge is power, she believes that books like this can help change destructive patterns. And on a professional level, Willamette University has expectations for faculty scholarship, so publishing this book will enhance her professional record.

As this example illustrates, people are drawn to stressful lifestyles because of personal, professional, or social reinforcers (see also Chapter 5). Does that mean adverse health effects are inevitable? We don't think so. There are many ways people can reduce their reactions to stress, and positively affect the environment, as well.

SOLUTION APPROACHES: STRATEGIES FOR REDUCING STRESS

In general, decreasing stress requires changes in all aspects of the stress response: removing environmental stressors, realistic cognitive appraisal, and behavioral strategies that enable effective problem solving (Homburg & Stolberg, 2006; Ulrich et al., 1991). For example, cognitive interpretation or analysis of a threat can either increase or decrease the intensity of the stress response. Jean-Paul Sartre once said, "What is important is not what happens to us, but how we respond to what happens to us." Fortunately that means people have some control over the extent to which they are adversely affected by stressors. **Cognitive behavior modification** techniques emphasize calming self-talk (Peurifoy, 1995): "This is not a crisis; I don't need to overreact. What do I need to do to solve this problem? Relax, take a deep breath."

Exerting any form of **control** during a stressful situation reduces harmful health effects. If you are anxious about air pollution or climate change, modify your behavior to reduce consumption of fossil fuels by walking or biking whenever possible, buying a more fuel-efficient vehicle, and reducing your home energy use. (Guidelines for designing a behavior modification project are included in Chapter 5; see also the Appendix for ways to increase proenvironmental activities. These behaviors can help you feel empowered, and enhance the activity of your immune system. Participating in community efforts to restore native plants or deal with polluting industries can be both environmentally and personally beneficial, as these behaviors positively impact one's immediate environment, enhance a feeling of community and social connectedness, and increase control over stressors (S. Kaplan, 2000). We can "clean and green" the cities and buildings in which we live, work, play, and worship to heal ourselves as well as the environment (Clinebell, 1996; see also Schaffer, 2008).

In general, psychological well-being, measures of immune function, and physical health are inextricably connected, and all benefit from the following (Feaster et al., 2000):

- Adequate social support and feelings of social connection
- Use of active coping strategies (including planning and problem solving)
- Positive attitudes such as optimism and humor (see also Herzog & Strevey, 2008; Stein & Spiegel, 2000).

Restorative Environments

Just as environmental degradation is detrimental to human health and well-being, experiences in **natural**, or undisturbed, settings can have many beneficial results (Frumkin, 2001; Herzog & Strevey, 2008; Maller et al., 2006; Ulrich, 1981; van den Berg, Hartig, & Staats, 2007). As early as the seventeenth century, people recognized the healing effects of natural landscape elements, including plants, grass, trees, sunlight, and fresh air (Cooper Marcus & Barnes, 1999). The field of **horticulture therapy** utilizes gardening to aid people with various kinds of disabilities to learn skills, rehabilitate from injuries, and enhance cognitive and emotional processing.* Although it has not been subjected to as rigorous a clinical evaluation as medication or surgical procedures, horticulture therapy shows promise for inspiring interdisciplinary research and training for horticulturalists and landscape architects in addressing the health aspects of their work, and for health scientists and practitioners to consider the importance of nature (Frumkin, 2004).

People strongly prefer natural environments containing vegetation or water (lakes, rivers, oceans) and lacking buildings and cars (R. Kaplan, 2001; R. Kaplan, & S. Kaplan, 1989; van den Berg et al., 2007; see Figure 8.7). Natural settings provide restoration and rejuvenation by offering the experiences of:

- "Being away" from the demands of regular life
- "Soft fascination" with sensory dimensions of the setting that are inherently appealing
- "Extent" or "scope" that gives a sense of vastness or connection between the experience and one's knowledge of the world
- "Compatibility" with the person's activity preferences (S. Kaplan, 1995).

---

* See the Web site for the American Horticultural Therapy Association, http://www.ahta.org/

Figure 8.7 The two upper pictures are examples of restorative environments, the two lower pictures are examples of nonrestorative environments. (Reprinted from Berto, R. (2005). *Journal of Environmental Psychology, 25,* 252. With permission.)

Evolutionary processes can explain the power of natural environments (Ulrich, 1983; Ulrich et al., 1991). The **psychoevolutionary theory** posits that natural settings, particularly those containing water or offering the opportunity to see without being seen, historically provided occasions for obtaining food and avoiding predation risks (Appleton, 1975; Kahn, 1997b; S. Kaplan, 1992; Ulrich et al., 1991; White & Heerwagen, 1998). Thus, such environments are naturally stress reducing, and can provide microrestoration from everyday stressors (R. Kaplan, 2001), including those associated with urban living (van den Berg et al., 2007).

As we explained earlier, restoration from the stress response involves activity of the parasympathetic nervous system, providing recovery from sympathetic arousal by reducing blood pressure, heart rate, and other physiological measures of stress. Gardens and nature reserves reduce stress, including "relief from physical symptoms . . . and improvement in overall well-being and hopefulness" (Cooper Marcus & Barnes, 1999, p. 3; see also Hartig et al., 2003; Ulrich, 1999). Viewing natural settings through a window, or even on videos, decreased measures of depression, anger, and tension (van den Berg, Koole, & van der Wulp, 2003) as well as blood pressure (Hartig et al., 2003) and heart rate (Laumann, Gärling, & Stormark, 2003), while increasing overall happiness and concentration (van den Berg et al., 2003). Ninety-five percent of patients surveyed at a children's hospital and psychiatric facilities reported a positive change in mood after spending time outside in gardens or fresh air (Cooper Marcus, 2006). Activities such as gardening, caring for indoor plants, and interacting with nonhuman animals such as pet dogs, can all reduce stress (Frumkin, 2001). Simply being in a room with an indoor plant can improve task performance and mood (Shibata & Suzuki, 2004). People with views of nature from their workspace reported fewer headaches, greater job satisfaction, and less job stress (R. Kaplan, 1993; R. Kaplan, & S. Kaplan, 1989).

Hospitalized patients heal faster and more completely, experience fewer complications, and require less medication if their rooms contain indoor plants, provide open windows for fresh air, or offer views of natural landscapes such as trees (Park & Mattson, 2008; Ulrich, 1984, 1991). Studies have also demonstrated decreased health complaints in prison inmates, reduced blood pressure and anxiety during dental procedures, and improved pain management resulting from contact with nature (reviewed in Frumkin, 2003). Green spaces can also mitigate health inequalities related to income disparities. People in lower socioeconomic classes tend to have higher rates of circulatory disease and mortality; these health outcomes are inversely correlated with access to natural, restorative environments (Mitchell & Popham, 2008).

In addition to stress reduction, nature can also provide recovery from prolonged **directed attention**; that is, focused and continuous mental effort (Berto, 2005; Hartig & Staats, 2006; Staats, Kieviet, & Hartig, 2003; van den Berg et al., 2003). **Attentional** or **mental fatigue** is the worn-out feeling that occurs during long-term cognitive exertion; you've probably experienced this during midterm and final exams. One can suffer from such fatigue even when the work is enjoyable, and consequently experience reduced concentration, productivity, and accuracy along with social insensitivity and irritability. Most people know that mental fatigue and other forms of stress generate a bad mood—tired, short-tempered, anxious. Attentional fatigue often co occurs with symptoms of stress, but natural, restorative environments can mitigate the effects of both (S. Kaplan, 1995; van den Berg et al., 2003). Such findings support the **attention restoration theory** regarding experiences in nature (S. Kaplan, 1995; R. Kaplan & S. Kaplan, 1989, 2008; see further discussion in Chapter 9). Thus, to the extent that nature is restorative, it can also help to enhance interpersonal relations and overall life functioning (Herzog & Strevey, 2008).

Wilderness Therapy

While it is true that wilderness settings can sometimes provoke fear or even terror (Kahn, 1997a; van den Berg & Heijne, 2005), we think that most readers can relate to the point that natural settings frequently offer relaxing and healing experiences. Experiences in wilderness like back-packing and boating are purported to have various therapeutic properties (Greenway, 1995; Harper, 1995; S. Kaplan & Talbot, 1983; White & Heerwagen, 1998; see further discussion in Chapter 9). Although **wilderness therapy** may be a fairly new application of psychology, it has existed in some form for thousands of years. For example, in many cultures, young men go into the wilderness to better understand themselves and prepare for adulthood (Peel & Richards, 2005). Many health benefits, such as increased strength, endurance, and cardiovascular output, result from programs that include intense physical activity (Werhan & Groff, 2005). While wilderness therapy typically uses nature or outdoor settings to encourage personal growth and self-exploration, it can also be used as a recreational tool or meditative setting to reduce stress responses (Peel & Richards, 2005).

In sum, natural restorative settings provide at least four types of benefits: positive emotions such as pleasure, happiness, satisfaction, peace, and tranquility; positive physiology in terms of reduced sympathetic or increased parasympathetic nervous system activity; positive cognition by way of attention restoration; and overall improved health (see also Han, 2003). Restorative experiences in nature can also help to motivate environmentally responsible behavior such as recycling (Hartig, Kaiser, & Bowler, 2001).

Recognizing the value of restorative environments is important, but doing so could also lead to exploitation. Saving natural resources only for the ways in which they benefit humankind is a limited and anthropocentric view. As Greenway (1995) put it

> Perhaps the clearest evidence of our recovery will be that we do not demand that wilderness heal us. We will have learned to let it be. For a wilderness that must heal us is surely a commodity, just as when we can only look at wilderness as a source of endless wealth. (pp. 134–135)

Green Urban Planning

As more and more regions of the globe are urbanized, fewer and fewer people have direct access to natural environments. Consequently, many urban planners are incorporating aspects of nature in their designs. This represents an important strategy to combat the **sprawl** that results from peoples' preferences for natural landscapes (R. Kaplan & Austin, 2004). Ironically, those with higher levels of education and environmental concern often choose to live in areas that are ecologically sensitive, posing a serious problem for conservation of biodiversity (Peterson, Chen, & Liu, 2008).

Studies demonstrate that the overall availability of urban green spaces increases residents' satisfaction (e.g., Bonnes, Uzzell, Carrus, & Kelay, 2007), and increased biodiversity (such as birds, butterflies, plants, etc.) in parks and green spaces results in psychological benefits (University of Sheffield, 2007). Furthermore, increasing urban parks and trees can also help mitigate the effects of climate change. A recent report indicated that a minimal 10% increase in urban green spaces could reduce surface temperatures as much as 4 °C (University of Manchester, 2007).

Thus, urban development that is considered sustainable not only emphasizes conserving energy and other resources (e.g., building materials), reducing sprawl, and minimizing emissions of greenhouse gases and toxic wastes, but also includes access to natural elements like trees, lawns, and parks (Beatley, 2000; Maller et al., 2006; van den Berg et al., 2007). "Natural spaces and public-owned parks not only preserve and protect the environment; they also encourage and enable people to relate to the natural world" (Maller et al., 2006, p. 52). We'll say more about the importance of this in Chapters 9 and 10.

Like other forms of contact with nature, taking a walk in a natural preserve is restorative, reducing blood pressure, anger, and aggression, while improving positive affect and attentional capacity relative to a walk in an urban setting (Hartig et al., 2003). You have probably heard about the overall health benefits of **exercise**, including its role in reducing stress. The mechanism probably relates to the evolution of the stress response. Human anatomy and physiology are adapted to an active life, and the sympathetic nervous system prepares people for physical exertion, as indicated by the phrase "fight or flight" (Boaz, 2002). By channeling energy into physical activity like exercise, the system is used in ways in which it evolved, and consequently enables the parasympathetic system to provide more complete recovery. Interestingly, physical exercise can also aid in detoxification from hazardous chemicals, by mobilizing fatty tissues that store toxins to speed excretion (Sherman, 2000).

Despite these benefits, however, fewer than one third of U.S. residents meet the federal recommendations of at least 30 minutes of moderate physical activity, five days a week; 37% of adults engage in no physical activity at all (U.S. Department of Health and Human Services, 2008). Unfortunately, urban environments typically *discourage* physical exercise by emphasizing roads for vehicular travel rather than walking and bicycle paths. Thus, land use planning and public policy decisions guiding the design of built environments have important implications for environmental impacts on health (Frank & Engelke, 2001; Frumkin, 2003; Lawrence, 2002). With good urban planning, communities can

- Reduce environmentally harmful behaviors (e.g., burning fossil fuels from automobiles) and subsequent exposure to the associated pollutants
- Decrease stress such as that associated with traffic congestion and vehicular noise
- Enhance public health through encouraging exercise, which is beneficial both directly and via reducing the impact of stress.

"You gotta think green. I used to be driven to distraction—now I walk."

Chicago is a U.S. leader in this area, implementing strategies for sustainable development created by students and faculty in urban planning, architecture and landscape at the University of Illinois. Narrowed roadways, an elevated bikeway, and filtration gardens are a few of the features of their "Green Schemes" (University of Illinois at Chicago, 2008).

Green Buildings

Like sustainable urban planning, implementation of sustainable architecture is growing dramatically (e.g., American Institute of Architects, 2008). Businesses and homeowners are increasingly recognizing the importance of reducing energy use and associated costs, as well as the health and productivity benefits of living and working in "greener" environments (Gies, 2008; Noiseux & Hostetler, 2008). For example, indoor air quality is a significant predictor of health in the short-term, and designs that reduce air pollutants and greenhouse gases are health promoting in the long-term (Frumkin, 2003).

The construction of green buildings includes choosing recycled or sustainably harvested materials that do not off-gas toxic chemicals; installing rainwater catchment systems; and minimizing energy costs with passive solar and wind technology (Gies, 2008; Hart & Hart, 2008). **Greenroofs** (also known as *living-* or *eco-roofs*) are planted gardens on top of buildings such as homes, offices, and hotels. Green roofs not only provide habitat for nonhumans and restorative settings for people, but also reduce storm water runoff, blacktop and associated heat generation, and provide insulation from energy loss (Holtcamp, 2001; Michaels, 2008*).

Washington was the first state in the United States to enact green building legislation. All major public agency facilities, including state-funded school buildings, are required to meet or exceed LEED (Leadership in Energy and Environmental Design) standards in construction or renovation (U.S. Green Building Council, 2008). LEED is a project of the U.S. Green Building Council, which makes available national standards for green buildings and helps guide green construction. Since 2005, the Washington project has annually saved 20% in energy and water costs, 38% in wastewater production, and 22% in construction waste. The United States is not the only country that has been working on green construction. Australia, Canada, Germany, India, Israel, Malaysia, Mexico, South Africa, and New Zealand are also establishing their own rating systems (many of which are much more rigorous

---

* See also http://www.greenroofs.com/

than those of the United States), and passing legislation to encourage and enforce green building. In fact, more than 39 countries have some form of green building program (Rainwater & Martin, 2006).

The small liberal arts college where Sue works, Willamette University in Oregon, uses LEED guidelines in every new building, which will cut energy consumption in half by 2020 (Willamette University, 2008). Willamette's newest residence hall is certified as LEED "gold" because it uses solar power and collects rainwater for sewer and wastewater use (Dempsey Foundation Funds, 2007). The food service provider buys locally and uses in-season produce, and the campus grounds are fertilized with compost tea rather than chemical fertilizers.

As emphasized throughout this chapter (and text), the consumptive lifestyles of U.S. residents are particularly hazardous to the planet as well as to human health. One obvious example is the "McMansions" that have sprung up all over the country and the associated urban sprawl. Thus, one of the most important things a potential homeowner can do to minimize her/his **ecological footprint** is to think small. Realizing that a large home is not required for comfortable living is a giant step in the direction of green building. It is also likely to make life simpler, less expensive, and less stressful! Sustainable home building and renovations of existing residences focus on renewable energy sources, conserving water, using local and natural materials, reducing reliance on forested products, using recycled materials, and building to last (Hart & Hart, 2008*).

Finally, **biophilic architecture** uses natural objects and shapes to design buildings. Biophilic buildings are designed to resemble the nonhuman animal and plant worlds, because nature-based forms and organizations in architecture can aid in human emotional and cognitive functioning (Joye, 2007, see Figure 8.8). Once again, evolutionary processes can explain the preference for, and comfort with, buildings and other objects that reflect natural characteristics (Gaulin & McBurney, 2001).

CONCLUSIONS

The human species evolved under environmental conditions radically different from those in which people live today, but biological evolution proceeds at a snail's pace—especially relative to cultural evolution. As a result, human physiology is having a hard time making sense of and coping with current environments despite the fact that humans created

---

* See http://www.greenhomebuilding.com

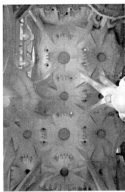

Figure 8.8 The interior of Gaudi's Sagrada Familia contains schematic interpretations of natural contents. (Left) columns as treelike structures. (Right) flowerlike canopies. (Reprinted from Joye, Y. (2007). *Review of General Psychology, 11,* 315. With permission.)

them! People are experiencing unprecedented levels of chronic stress, damaging both human and planetary health.

Whereas the sympathetic nervous system's stress response is elegantly suited to confronting immediate, short-term threats, the stressors with which people currently grapple are profound and on-going. Particularly during the last two centuries, marked technological progress and urbanization have led to widespread destruction of other species and natural landscapes that feed one's spirit and mind, and have reduced opportunities for quiet contemplation and community. People have created noisy, built environments that pollute the air and water on which all lives depend. These choices are changing the global climate and creating devastating weather patterns. It is clearly an understatement to say that such conditions are stressful and adversely impact health. Although "modern 'westernization' has doubled our life expectancy, it has also created disparities between ancient and present ways of living that may have paved the way for the emergence of new serious diseases" (Maller et al., 2006, p. 45). Disorders including depression, anxiety, hypertension, heart attacks, strokes, and cancers are epidemic. Cardiovascular and mental illnesses such as those resulting from stress are expected to be the primary disease outcomes worldwide by 2020.

Fortunately, developing solutions to environmental problems not only reduces personal experiences of stress but also mitigates destructive patterns of human behavior. Cognitive appraisal of human-caused environmental threats such as pollution, climate change, and resource depletion "can activate problem-focused coping, which in turn leads to pro-environmental behavior" (Homburg & Stolberg, 2006, p. 1) such as activism, resource conservation, purchasing recycled materials, and working to design more sustainable products (see also Gardner & Stern, 2002; Schaffer, 2008). People can choose whether to purchase products and support technologies that stress their bodies, brains, and biosphere.

To do this, all of us must become better informed as consumers, citizens, and voters. People can exercise more and eat in more healthful and planet-friendly ways. There are clear economic benefits to such choices, either directly (spending less money on gas while walking or biking more) or indirectly (reduced health care costs). Choices based on environmental implications rather than monetary cost must be made. "In the long-run, what is more humane and cost-effective than to prevent [health risks]?" (Sherman, 2000, p. 233). Such efforts in turn feed a sense of empowerment and optimism, provide opportunities for social connections, and thereby reduce the intensity of the stress response and its harmful impacts.

Healthy, nondegraded natural settings are enjoyed and preferred relative to built environments; thus, humans should be intrinsically motivated to protect and preserve them. The research reviewed in this chapter reveals many positive health outcomes resulting from contact with nature, including reduced stress. "Green" urban spaces such as parks and nature reserves constitute important public health resources and are a crucial part of environmentally sustainable urban planning. Improving quality of life for people via establishing opportunities for greater harmony with nature can correspondingly improve the quality of nature. And as we will see in the next chapter, interactions with healthy nature are particularly important for promoting the health and well-being of children.

9

DEVELOPMENTAL PSYCHOLOGY: GROWING HEALTHY CHILDREN IN NATURE

The ultimate test of a moral society is the kind of world that it leaves to its children.

(Dietrich Bonhoeffer*)

We initiate our children into an economic order based on exploitation of the natural life systems of the planet. To achieve this attitude we must first make our children unfeeling in their relation with the natural world …. For children to live only in contact with concrete and steel and wires and wheels and machines and computers and plastics, to seldom experience any primordial reality or even to see the stars at night, is a soul deprivation that diminishes the deepest of their human experiences.

(Thomas Berry, 1999, pp. 15, 82)

How did you spend your free time when you were a child? Can you remember times in your childhood when you were particularly happy? Many adults asked to name their fondest childhood memories describe outdoor experiences (e.g., Chawla, 1990; Thomashow, 1995). For example, Deborah instantly thinks of hiking in the rolling hills where she grew up in southern California, making forts from tall grasses, playing hide-and-seek with her pals. When she thinks about it now, she can almost smell the

---

* Quoted by Environmental Resources 4 Sustainable Development. Available at http://olc. spsd.sk.ca/de/resources/conservation08/resources.html

dry weeds and feel the warm sun as she remembers her joy in finding new hiding places, making little shelters, and exploring new trails. Childhood and adolescent recreational activities have changed dramatically over the last 50 years. For many children, particularly those living in urban settings, riding a bike and climbing trees have largely given way to watching television or playing video games. In fact, relative to the early 1980s, children today spend considerably more time indoors rather than playing outside and experiencing nature (Hofferth & Curtin, 2005; White, 2004). Yet as we will see later in this chapter, experiences in natural environments contribute importantly to healthy child development. Like adults, children benefit in many ways from being in nature, findings that received a lot of public attention following the description of **Nature Deficit Disorder** in the bestselling book, *Last Child in the Woods* (Louv, 2005, 2008).

In this chapter, we review the growing phenomenon of "indoor children," and describe how it is linked to detrimental health, societal, and environmental impacts. We then discuss the developmental benefits of experiences in natural settings, showing how they can promote the intellectual, moral, emotional, social, mental, and physical health of children. We then describe how early outdoor experiences foster both adult **environmental ethics** and **proenvironmental behaviors**, and analyze features of effective environmental education (EE). We conclude that as more regions are urbanized, efforts to give children experiences in the natural world are increasingly important.

INDOOR CHILDREN

Many parents do not want their children to play outside, citing **stranger danger** as their reason (Clements, 2004; Pyle, 2002; White, 2004). Increased media coverage of criminal activities leads parents to fear that if their children are left alone, they will be harmed (Louv, 2008; Pyle, 2002; White, 2004). A clear majority (82%) of U.S. mothers with children aged 3–12 say they do not allow unsupervised outdoor play because of worries about crime (Clements, 2004). In addition to stranger danger, many parents are afraid of insect-borne illnesses, ultraviolet rays, and pollution (White, 2004). This **culture of fear** reflects the anxiety many people have about their surroundings, and these fears are cultivated in younger generations (Louv, 2005). Consequently, fearful parents may discourage backyard play. Yet if the backyard is the only nature available to children, preventing them access significantly decreases outdoor engagement.

Less time outside is contributing to the burgeoning use of technology by young people. The average child in the United States spends more than six hours a day in front of a TV or other media source such as a computer or video game (Strasburger, 2007); some estimates are as high as nine hours per day (Roberts, Foehr, & Rideout, 2005). Even very young children are becoming dependent on technology. Fifty-nine percent of children in the United States *under the age of two* watch 2 + hours of TV or videos per day, and 43% of children *under age one* watch TV everyday (Kanner, 2007). Many products are marketed specifically to this demographic. Sue recalls a friend's purchase of *Baby Einstein* videos, "created from a baby's point-of-view [that] incorporate a unique combination of real world objects, music, art, language, poetry, and *nature* ... providing an opportunity to introduce your baby to the world around them in playful and enriching ways" (Baby Einstein, n.d., para. 2, italics added). Paradoxically, the recordings are purported to enhance parent–child interaction and the child's natural curiosity. Yet current levels of media viewing are in direct opposition to the American Academy of Pediatrics (n.d.) recommendations of *zero* hours/day for those under age two, and *no more than two* hours per day of screen time for older children. As their literature states "media exposure at a young age ... often substitutes for important parent/caregiver/child activities that encourage early brain development, such as playing, singing, and reading" (p. 2, para. 3).

Increased time with gadgets means less quality time interacting with siblings, parents, and peers, less time spent doing homework (as much as an 18% reduction), and less creative play (Vandewater, Bickham, & Lee, 2006), including outdoors. Even small amounts of online activity are correlated with reduced social interactions, a loss of self-confidence, and difficulties interacting with others due to shyness (Henderson,

Zimbardo, & Graham, 2001), as well as increased loneliness and depression (Kraut et al., 1998). In general, greater levels of television watching and less socializing are associated with reduced feelings of happiness, although the direction of causality is not clear (Rabin, 2008).

Furthermore, children who watch a lot of television or engage in other sedentary activities often snack on unhealthy foods (Christakis, 2006; Dietz & Gortmaker, 1985; Gortmaker et al., 1996). Correspondingly, since 1980, the rate of obese children (ages 2–5) has more than doubled and the number of overweight adolescents has more than tripled; by 2006, 17% of children aged six through 19 were overweight (Centers for Disease Control and Prevention [CDC], 2008a). As in adults, childhood obesity is associated with hypertension, type two diabetes, respiratory problems, orthopedic ailments, anxiety, and depression (American Academy of Pediatrics, Committee on Nutrition, 2003). Food misuse and overuse also contribute to environmental degradation (Riebel, 2001; see additional discussion in Chapter 8).

Perhaps it is not surprising that time spent watching television is negatively correlated with academic achievement, particularly reading comprehension, mathematics, applied problem solving, and written expression (Comstock, 1995; Hofferth & Curtin, 2005); television is also associated with attentional problems (Christakis, Zimmerman, DiGiuseppe, & McCarty, 2004). Television viewing prior to age three is especially harmful to later cognitive abilities, although it is unclear whether that is due to the specific content, the pace at which information is presented, or because children are engaging less in other behaviors such as creative play (Zimmerman & Christakis, 2005).

Much of the programming oriented toward children is fashion-oriented, sexualized, or violent in content (Kanner, 2007; Linn, 2008). Violent television and video games are clearly linked to childhood and adolescent aggression and diminished prosocial behaviors (e.g., Anderson & Bushman, 2001). But even more nefarious for the health of the planet is the fact that increased time interacting with media exposes children to an astonishing amount of marketing. The average child sees over 40,000 advertisements on television each year (Linn, 2004). Marketing to children is a $7 billion per year industry, representing an extraordinary increase from 1983 expenditures of roughly $100 million per year. Contemporary advertisers utilize television, the Internet, computer games, cellular telephones, MP3 players, DVDs, virtual world Web sites, as well as books and school advertisements (Linn, 2008). In addition to negatively impacting a child's development, this commercialization of childhood constitutes the foundation of the highly destructive consumer culture that depletes resources and degrades the environment (Kasser, 2002; Linn, 2008; see also the discussions of consumption in Chapters 1 and 4). The Campaign for a Commercial-Free Childhood* is an advocacy group that works to educate citizens on the effects of commercialism on children, and to reduce or eliminate some of the more egregious marketing campaigns.

Materialism, which prioritizes consumption and defines self-worth in terms of possessions, is increasing in the United States (see also Chapter 4). Children who score high on measures of materialism have greater incidence of conduct problems, difficulties in social interactions, and mental health issues such as anxiety, depression, discontent, and substance abuse (Bee-Gates, 2007; Kasser, 2005). Materialistic values increase with age from fifth to eighth grade, demonstrating effective indoctrination into the consumer culture (Kasser, 2005). Over time, excessive materialism diminishes emotional development by encouraging superficiality and loss of emotional connection to self, others, and the natural world (Orr, 2002). Thus, consumerism is associated with self-centeredness and reduced concern about others' welfare, including the well-being of their communities or the earth and its other inhabitants (Bee-Gates, 2007; Kasser, 2006; Orr, 2002). Perhaps not surprisingly, materialistic values are related to bigger *ecological footprints* (see Chapter 1) because of the environmental costs of excessive resource use (Brown & Kasser, 2005). Children and adolescents with high scores on a materialism scale failed to perform even small proenvironmental behaviors like turning off lights, reusing materials (paper, plastic bags, and aluminum foil), conserving water while brushing teeth or bathing, and walking or biking instead of driving (Kasser, 2005).

In addition, teens in higher social classes, with correspondingly greater material wealth, show less joy, happiness, cooperation, and engagement (Csikszentmihalyi, 2004). These children often live in homes where both parents work, thereby raising the material standards of the family, but leaving the children largely to themselves. A failure to experience socially acceptable challenges and opportunities for interpersonal cooperation may lead to delinquent behaviors. Thus, making proenvironmental behavior, social justice, and cooperation into challenging, enjoyable activities rather than "letting children fall into mindless activities" is a critical component of creating a sustainable society (Csikszentmihalyi, 2004, p. 365).

---

* See http://commercialexploitation.com/

Reprinted from Dave Coverly © [http://www.speedbump.com/]. With permission.

Television viewing is also associated with lower levels of concern about the environment and less environmental activism. This relationship is attributed to a dearth of programming about nature and environmental issues, as well as the materialistic and consumerist values promoted by most programs and advertisements (Good, 2007). Media can also inspire fear and negative views of natural things, that is, **ecophobia**, in children (Zaradic & Pergams, 2007). Many forms of media depict nature as evil and dangerous, or as something for humans to manipulate or conquer (Roth, 2005). For instance, in the popular Disney movie, *Snow White and the Seven Dwarfs,* and the more recent *Harry Potter* books and films, the forest is portrayed as a terrifying, evil place.

On the other hand, not all media exposures are harmful. As they are so accessible and influential, various forms of entertainment can also be valuable educational venues. Some of Sue's students recall being intensely affected by reading Dr. Seuss's (1971) book, *The Lorax,* as children. The story is a poignant characterization of personal greed leading to the loss of trees and habitat for various species, as well as pollution. The Discovery Channel's series, *Planet Earth,* is a popular depiction of nature's beauty and the importance of human stewardship and care (Novacek, 2008); nature videos and books foster ecological and moral attitudes in children (Eagles & Demare, 1999); and "virtual experiences" in nature correlate with increased environmental awareness (Levi & Kocher, 1999). For those who do not have direct access to nature, the Internet can offer vicarious experiences to otherwise inaccessible areas. Technology can also help create electronic social networks for children who would otherwise feel isolated (Heerwagen & Orians, 2002). However, children may also be lured away from nearby nature and interpersonal interactions by these high-tech renditions (Zaradic & Pergams, 2007). In sum, although there are some benefits to vicarious encounters (e.g., television, movies, computers, books, pictures, etc.) as well as indirect experiences (visits to zoos, museums, and nature centers), effects may be smaller and more transitory than those gleaned from direct outdoor experiences (Kellert, 2002).

BENEFITS OF NATURE

As we have shown, the rising emphasis on technology and consumption during development is generally associated with values and behaviors that diminish both personal health and well-being, and contribute to environmental degradation. (Note that similar points were made in Chapters 4 and 8.) In contrast, experiences in natural settings during

childhood can play a significant, perhaps irreplaceable, role in cognitive, moral, emotional, and social development, and promote more environmentally responsible behavior (Clayton & Opotow, 2003; Kahn, 1997b, 1999; Kahn & Kellert, 2002; Kellert, 1993, 1997, 2002). Although there is a dearth of well-controlled, experimental studies (Faber Taylor & Kuo, 2006), the existing literature points to the conclusion that childhood experiences in nature support important developmental processes by providing mental and sensory stimulation, as well as opportunities for creative play, exploration, and divergent thinking (Cobb, 1977; Faber Taylor, Kuo, & Sullivan, 2001). Playing outside also cultivates motor skills and physical fitness (Fjørtoft, 2001; Pellegrini, 2005).

Definitions of nature vary widely. Some researchers refer to nature as the "non-human world" (Vining, 2003, p. 96), contrasting with civilization, or the built environment (Haluza-Delay, 2001). Others distinguish between experiences with "wild nature" (hiking, playing in the woods, camping, hunting, or fishing) and "domesticated nature" (picking flowers or vegetables from a garden, planting or caring for trees and plants (Wells & Lekies, 2006).

> For children, nature comes in many forms. A newborn calf; a pet that lives and dies; a worn path through the woods; a fort nested in stinging nettles; a damp, mysterious edge of a vacant lot— whatever shape nature takes, it offers each child an older, larger world separate from parents. (Louv, 2008, p. 7)

In this chapter, we define nature as green spaces of any kind that include other living species, including landscaped areas (such as backyards, parks and gardens) as well as wilderness settings. Trees, plants, open spaces, sunshine, and fresh air are psychologically important dimensions of nature (Kahn, 2003), which can be present in various degrees.

Regardless of cultural background, most people name natural settings as their favorite places (e.g., Newell, 1997; Thomashow, 1995). Characteristics that enhance the appeal of such settings include rustic and relatively pristine environments, natural beauty, quiet, serenity, and remoteness (Schroeder, 2002). Feeling free seems to be a critical feature of positive experiences in nature. Most children appreciate opportunities for spontaneous play or activity in areas that are generally outside human intervention and control (Chawla, 1990; Kellert, 2002; Pyle, 1993). "We all need spots near home where we can wander off a trail, lift a stone, poke about, and merely wonder: places where no interpretive signs intrude their message to rob our spontaneous response" (Pyle, 1993, p. 148). Although solitude is frequently an aspect of such spaces, autonomy, or an escape from adult supervision, may be more important to children (Mergen, 2003). Opportunities for independent adventure, risk taking, and exploration likely contribute to a sense of mastery, self-sufficiency, and confidence in young people (Derr, 2006).

Children are inherently attracted to settings that offer refuge and corresponding feelings of safety in both natural and built environments (Kirkby, 1989). Many children can play happily for hours in a tree house, fort, or cave carved into the side of a mountain, as Deborah did in the California hillsides. Researchers believe this proclivity has its basis in evolutionary processes, as those who gravitated toward environments where they could see without being seen, and where they were protected from the elements, would have held a selective advantage (Appleton, 1975; Ulrich, 1993). Due to the environmental conditions in which the human species evolved, E. O. Wilson (1984) proposed the **biophilia hypothesis**, which postulates that humans possess an innate (genetically based) need to affiliate with nature and other living organisms (see also Kahn, 1997b; Kellert, 1997; Kellert & Wilson, 1993). The affinity for natural environments is universal and unlearned. Empirical evidence demonstrates that most people strongly prefer them over built environments, and nature enables restoration from stress and cognitive demands (Kaplan & Kaplan, 1989; Ulrich, 1993), as we saw in Chapter 8. Nature supports and fulfills various psychological and spiritual needs; many people report profound spiritual connections while in nature (Berry, 1999; Davis, 1998; Frumkin, 2001; Maller, Townsend, Pryor, Brown, & St. Leger, 2006; van den Berg, Hartig, & Staats, 2007; Wilson, 1984; see also the discussion in Chapter 10). On the other hand, **biophobia** underlies the avoidance of certain stimuli that posed a threat during human evolution. Most people and other primates share an aversion or overt phobic response to potentially dangerous natural stimuli, such as spiders and snakes (Ulrich, 1993).

You are probably familiar with the **nature–nurture** debate concerning child development: Historically, researchers have attempted to separate the relative influences of genetic predisposition and environmental–experiential factors underlying intelligence, language, personality, social attachments, and other characteristics. Since development of the brain structures underlying these capacities is extraordinarily complex, advances in neuroscience are revealing intricate and dynamic interactions among both inherited and experienced factors as humans mature (Stiles, 2008). One perspective suggests that genetic factors *prepare* infants for certain kinds of experiences, enabling more rapid learning and retention of particular associations and responses; especially those that would have promoted survival in earlier humans (Seligman, 1970, 1971; Ulrich, 1993). Consequently, it is likely that an innate (genetically predisposed) attraction to nature (biophilia), coupled with positive early experiences, results in a stronger proclivity for natural settings than either influence acting alone. This evolutionary analysis helps explain preferences for experiences in nature, and why they would be beneficial for the cognitive, moral, emotional, and social development of children.

Cognitive Development and Reasoning Skills

A significant part of a child's intellectual development involves learning to discriminate, categorize, and name different objects. Due to the wide range of things, features, and behaviors observable within nature, experiences therein provide extensive opportunities for children to acquire these abilities (Kellert, 1997, 2002). Observing natural phenomena such as weather patterns and nonhuman animal habitats facilitate children's comprehension of relationships; snow falls and ice forms only when temperatures are in a certain range; ducks are seen near water, and so forth (Kellert, 2002). Symbolic imagery from nature (i.e., pictures of animals such as bears and lions) regularly appear in children's books, movies, and cartoons. How many readers enjoyed the book *Where the Wild Things Are* (Sendak, 1963) as children? In addition to the apparent entertainment value, such images aid language acquisition and cognitive skills like counting and naming (Kellert, 1997).

The foundation of these learning processes is an intuitive understanding and reasoning capacity about the world (Carey, 1985; Coley, 2000). Humans possess an innate tendency to perceive, categorize, and think about properties of living versus nonliving things. **Folkbiology theory** posits that these processes do not need to be taught in formal biology lessons. For example, 4-year-olds readily understand that both plants and animals can grow (Hickling & Gelman, 1995) and heal when injured (Backscheider, Shatz, & Gelman, 1993), although inanimate objects cannot. These findings not only demonstrate implicit understanding of biological fundamentals (growth and healing) but also that children apply these principles across species and categories (e.g., plants and animals; Coley, Solomon, & Shafto, 2002).

Research suggests that the amount and quality of contact with nonhumans and plants impact the development of these folkbiological (intuitive biological) cognitive processes (Ross, Medin, Coley, & Atran, 2003), suggesting an interaction between genetic and experiential factors. For instance, in one study, children were told that humans (or wolves or bees) have something called *hema* inside them, and then shown pictures of other animals or objects (trout, worms, rocks, bicycles). Children were then asked whether these other animals or objects also contained the substance ("Do trout have hema inside, like humans do?"). **Anthropocentric** (human-centered) thinking was demonstrated when children made projections of similarity from humans to other animals ("If humans have it, wolves would have it too"), but not the reverse ("Wolves have it, but people don't"). **Biocentric** (nature-centered) thinking was shown when projections were bidirectional (from humans to other animals, and vice versa).

Relative to nonnative children in this study, Native American children made more bidirectional (biocentric) projections. Nonnative children raised in rural settings were more biocentric than those raised in urban settings. Since Native American and rural children have more opportunities to explore nature and come into contact with intact ecosystems, they are exposed to a wider variety of animals, witness how these animals interact and rely on each other, and thus become more biocentric in their thinking patterns (Ross et al., 2003).

Likewise, children are able to assign animals into appropriate **taxonomic categories** by the age of six (e.g., mammal, bird, insect, tree, and plant). However, understanding particular animals' **ecological or habitat categories** (i.e., the environmental conditions and regions in which the animals live) is better developed in rural than urban children (Coley, Freeman, & Blaszczyk, 2003). Thus, it appears that anthropocentrism can result from fewer experiences and less knowledge about the environment. The converse is also true: greater understanding of biological resemblances and relationships among species increases biocentrism (Ross et al., 2003; see also Chapter 10).

Moral Development

Like thinking and reasoning patterns, value-based judgments and morality can vary between anthropocentrism and biocentrism. Although psychologists once believed that children did not make moral judgments based on the importance of nature for its own sake (i.e., biocentrism), research has shown that children consider both human- and nature-oriented impacts of environmental disasters (Kahn, 1997a). For example, the Exxon Valdez oil spill in Alaska in 1989 dumped nearly 11 million gallons of oil into Prince William Sound, killing thousands of marine animals and birds, and destroying beaches and shorelines. A majority of children interviewed shortly thereafter perceived the pollution as a moral violation, primarily because of the resulting harm to animals in the wild, but also because of the effects on humans, including the fishermen and recreational users in the Sound (Kahn, 1997a). They thus demonstrated biocentric beliefs in their intrinsic valuing of other species, even while realizing that what was harmful to the natural world was also bad for people (an anthropocentric value).

In several cross-cultural studies, children showed strong moral prohibitions against pollution and associated damage to other species for both anthropocentric and biocentric reasons (reviewed in Kahn, 2003). Anthropocentric justifications center on (a) personal concerns (i.e., pets and animals to play with); (b) aesthetics (appearance and physical beauty); and (c) human health and welfare. In contrast, a biocentric perspective sees natural systems and communities as having inherent value, deserving respect comparable to humans (Kahn, 2003). As illustrated by one child's comments: "if nature made birds, nature does not want to see birds die.... [the birds] need the same respect we [humans] need" (Kahn, 2003, pp. 116–117).

It is common for children to perceive species ranging from squirrels to trees as similar to humans in various ways, such as being alive and able to feel pain (Gebhard, Nevers, & Billmann-Mahecha, 2003). Reasoning that involves similarities between one's self and natural species can "evoke feelings of empathy for [an] object that permit it to be regarded as something worthy of moral consideration" (Gebhard et al., 2003, p. 92). Although young children's moral concern for both humans and nonhumans apparently spring from the same source, direct interactions with animals, including pets, can foster concerns about justice and fair treatment of others, and caring for their needs while preventing harm (Myers, 2007).

When children recognize themselves to be part of nature, and understand that protecting nature is key to their own survival and well-being, they develop an ecological self, a concept that is explored further in Chapter 10. A child's self-concept is significantly shaped by experiences of kinship and connection with the nonhuman world, and the greater the sense of relationship with nature and other species, the more likely the child is to try to protect it (Gebhard et al., 2003; Kals & Ittner, 2003; Myers, 2007; Searles, 1960).

However, the degraded conditions that an increasing number of children encounter today make identification with nature more difficult (Kals & Ittner, 2003), and may thus be contributing to a reduced sense of moral responsibility toward other species and nature as a whole. Since adequate opportunities for direct environmental interactions are quickly eroding, children are experiencing an extinction of experience; a sense of alienation from nature, and a loss of the intimacy that would motivate concern and conservation (Pyle, 1993, 2002; see also Kellert, 2002). "The extinction of experience is thus a cycle whereby [environmental] impoverishment begets greater impoverishment" (Pyle, 2002, p. 312).

Sadly, environmentally degraded conditions can come to seem normal. For instance, two thirds of children interviewed in Houston, Texas revealed that, despite knowledge of the general issue of pollution, they did not believe their air or water was a problem. To them, current levels of pollution were normal (Kahn, 2007). The phrase **environmental generational amnesia** describes the phenomenon of using current environmental conditions as a baseline for what is natural or normal in order to evaluate future degradation (Kahn, 2002, 2007):

> We all take the natural environment we encounter during childhood as the norm against which we measure environmental degradation later in our lives. With each ensuing generation, the amount of environmental degradation increases, but each generation in its youth takes that degraded condition as the non-degraded condition—as the normal experience. (Kahn, 2002, p. 106)

Sue can relate to this phenomenon. Growing up in New Jersey, she remembers going to the Jersey shore and not even thinking about the litter on the beach and the poor water quality (green and murky) until she had the opportunity to go to a beach in Massachusetts one summer. Standing in the water up to her knees, she could actually see her toes and the little rocks scattered along the sea bed. The beach itself was free of cigarette butts, plastic wrappers, and soda cans. It finally occurred to her that ocean water *should* be relatively translucent, and that the Jersey coast was *polluted*, not normal!

Emotional and Social Development Outdoor settings in nature are uniquely capable of captivating both children's and adults' fascination, thereby providing restoration from cognitive effort and stress (R. Kaplan & S. Kaplan, 1989; S. Kaplan, 1995; see also discussion in Chapter 8). A breadth of experiences in natural settings provides many opportunities for joyful interactions and emotional involvement, which foster exploratory and creative tendencies, and underlie affective (emotional) maturation (Kellert, 2002):

> Variations in vegetation, wind, sun, smell and physical scale—the small bug to the large tree—contribute to nature's fascinating qualities. Nature's variety serves as a springboard for creative stories, while textural and malleable materials such as sand, water, and snow can immerse children in an imaginative world of play. (Trancik & Evans, 1995, p. 315)

People seem to have an innate desire to interact and identify with nature, as suggested by the biophilia hypothesis. Many adults, including well-known writers and environmental activists, can describe in passionate detail natural places that were particularly important and emotionally evocative for them as children (Chawla, 1988, 1990, 1994, 1998b; Mergen, 2003; Pyle, 1993; Thomashow, 1995). Natural spaces that provide a cultural context or connection with family and community promote place attachment (Derr, 2006) and create a sense of home. The phrase *ecstatic places* refers to the wonder and delight common in environmental memories that provide meaning and metaphor, serenity, sense of self, and creative inspiration (Chawla, 1990; see also Cobb, 1977). It is possible that adults romanticize their childhood experiences (Derr, 2006), and it is difficult to establish causal relationships between childhood experiences in nature and creative abilities in adults (Mergen, 2003; see also Chawla, 1998a, 2001). However, examining the emotional dimensions of experiences in nature can aid in understanding its role in development (along with the role of other types of experiences; Chawla, 1998a, 1998b, 2001), and provide clues about how to design EE curricula, as we'll see in that section, below.

A child that is able to recognize others' feelings, demonstrate compassion, and form emotional connections is socially intelligent and more successful in social settings (Goleman, 1995). Successful interpersonal functioning, or **emotional intelligence**, includes five key aspects (e.g., Goleman, 1995; Zeidner, Matthews, Roberts, & MacCann, 2003):

- Self-awareness (i.e., identification of one's own feelings)
- Self-regulation (appropriate expression of emotions)
- Motivation (appropriate use of the information and inspiration provided by emotions)
- Empathy (understanding others' emotions) and
- Social skills (ability to utilize understanding of self and others in communicating and interacting).

Social–emotional (as well as cognitive) development is heavily influenced by children's play (Piaget, 1962; Rubin, Fein, & Vandenberg, 1983). By playing with others, children learn important skills including cooperation, concern for other people, altruistic behaviors, social roles, self-control, conflict management, and emotional regulation, as well as language and problem-solving skills (Faber Taylor, Wiley, Kuo, & Sullivan, 1998, Howes, 1988; Howes & Matheson, 1992).

Children play more creatively and with greater frequency in areas with more vegetation than in less-vegetated areas (Faber Taylor et al., 1998). These findings were not attributable to a simple preference for green settings, although landscaping designs that contain trees and other foliage tend to attract larger groups of people, including both adolescents and adults (Coley, Kuo, & Sullivan, 1997). Green spaces increase the potential for social interactions, and thus social–emotional development.

Mental Health

Mental health also benefits from experiences in nature. Children living in rural communities with more nearby nature have less psychological distress, including anxiety, depression, and conduct disorders such as bullying (Wells & Evans, 2003). Contacts with nature are associated with a reduction of the adverse effects of childhood trauma and grief, as well as strengthened self-worth. Studies have also demonstrated that symptoms of **attention deficit hyperactivity disorders (ADD/ADHD)** can be ameliorated by "green activities" such as camping, fishing, soccer, or a simple "walk in the park" (Faber Taylor et al., 2001; Faber Taylor & Kuo, 2009). Even passive time spent in green settings while relaxing or reading a book outside is negatively correlated with ADD symptoms (Faber Taylor et al., 2001; see also Kuo & Faber Taylor, 2004). Further, having a view of nature from one's residence can improve children's attentional capacity (Wells, 2000).

While methodological issues may limit some causal inferences (Canu & Gordon, 2005; Kuo & Faber Taylor, 2005), these studies suggest promising research directions for the growing problem of ADD/ADHD. Children who suffer from ADD/ADHD are typically treated with stimulants such as Ritalin, Adderall, or Strattera, and use of such prescriptions is increasing dramatically (National Institute of Mental Health, 2007). While these medications reduce ADD/ADHD symptoms for most individuals, improvements are often temporary and do not necessarily change the long-term social and academic success of the children. The medications also have side effects including appetite suppression and sleep disruption. Thus, to the extent that experiences

Reprinted from Calvin and Hobbes © 1995 Watterson. With permission from Universal Press Syndicate. All rights reserved.

in nature can improve concentration and other symptoms, they offer an attractive alternative or supplement to medication (Faber Taylor et al., 2001; Faber Taylor & Kuo, 2009; Kuo & Faber Taylor, 2004, 2005). Nature experiences may also serve preventive functions: simply having views of natural features (trees and grass) can increase self-discipline, at least in girls, by enhancing concentration, inhibiting impulsive behaviors, and promoting delay of gratification (Faber Taylor, Kuo, & Sullivan, 2002).

One explanation of the beneficial effects of outdoor experiences is *attention restoration* (Kaplan, 1995; see also Chapter 8). Ability to concentrate increases after resting in natural environments due to relief from **directed** (deliberate and sustained) **attention, such as that** required by school work. Nature offers an opportunity for **involuntary attention** (not directed at an activity or forced; S. Kaplan, 1995). After experiencing such a rest, ability for directed attention increases (Faber Taylor et al., 2001; Faber Taylor & Kuo, 2009). For this reason, breaks from mental effort are crucial. An opportunity for unstructured play and exploration outdoors during recess in elementary school provides a respite from effortful cognition, with subsequent benefits to attentional capacity (Pellegrini, 2005).

Experiences in nature aid children's rehabilitation from various forms of physical and mental stress, including temporary disability due to an accident or operation or psychological trauma (Moore, 1999). Children with chronic physical and mental conditions (formerly termed "handicapped") also benefit from gardens located in the treatment facility. For these reasons, **healing gardens**, where patients can spend restful time, are once again becoming common features of health care facilities, such as hospitals, residential and day care programs, or rehabilitation centers (Hartig & Cooper Marcus, 2006).

Wilderness therapy (also known as *outdoor behavioral health care*) integrates individual and group counseling techniques with adventure recreation in outdoor wilderness areas (Russell, 2001, 2005; see also Chapter 8). Participants are guided in developing both personal and interpersonal skills while learning relevant techniques (rock climbing, rafting, or simply preparing food and shelter), most of which require effective teamwork (Wilson & Lipsey, 2000). Wild settings provide "solace, spiritual contact, and healing" by allowing many people to connect with their ancestral history and their "natural state of being" (Cooley, 1998, p. 18).

Children are the most frequent participants in wilderness therapy programs, with more than 10,000 between the ages of 12 and 17 participating each year (Cooley, 1998; Werhan & Groff, 2005). This popularity may be due to rising adolescent mental health problems (Werhan & Groff, 2005). At least 10% of U.S. children and adolescents experience impairment due to some mental health issue each year (National Institute of Mental Health, 2009). Wilderness therapy is an increasingly common intervention for children having behavior problems, such as defiance, impulsivity, and anger management issues (Harper, Russell, Cooley, & Cupples, 2007); that is, children commonly considered delinquent or antisocial (Clark, Marmol, Cooley, & Gathercoal, 2004; Wilson & Lipsey, 2000). Wilderness therapy may also be effective for treating substance abuse, anxiety, and depression often seen in adolescents (Clark et al., 2004), as well as avoidant personality disorder, which is marked by social inhibition and feelings of inadequacy (Eikenaes, Gude, & Hoffart, 2006). The range of positive outcomes includes improved physical health, social skills, and academic adjustment, as well as increased self-control and self-esteem, and decreased antisocial behaviors (Werhan & Groff, 2005).

Do you know any children who spend most of their time playing on computers? Perhaps they seem shy and withdrawn, uncomfortable interacting with peers, and anxious when their parents insist they go outdoors. What would these children need to overcome their fears of people and natural settings? One approach to working with such children is called relational therapy and uses a psychoanalytic framework (Santostefano, 2004, 2008; see Chapter 3). In this technique, a therapist takes a child client outdoors to play games, explore, and enjoy each others' presence. Gradually, the child learns to relax and feel safe in natural environments. This approach assumes that it is not outdoor experiences per se that are important, but outdoor experiences enjoyed in relationship to other human beings, which build attachments to natural settings as well as to other people (Derr, 2006).

Research on significant life experiences reveals that many children and adolescents first become concerned about the environment because of nature experiences, along with the influence of significant role models (e.g., Chawla, 1988, 1998b; Monroe, 2003; Tanner, 1980). These experiences must be repeated; rarely do children learn to enjoy being outdoors from singular events. But recurring experiences are powerful teaching moments in which children learn to feel connected with the larger world. Concomitantly, children learn to trust another human being, a central feature of emotional development and mental health (Santostefano, 2008). Likewise, wilderness therapy and other therapeutic interventions that involve the family unit are especially effective (Harper et al., 2007).

Children and Animals

Did you have a pet as a child? Do you now? Most children are intrinsically attracted to and fascinated by nonhuman animals (Myers, 2007), and pets are often important family members from a child's (as well as many adults') perspective. Developmental psychologists have largely neglected the study of children's relationship with animals, even though animals are a primary focus in children's lives in a variety of forms: as live, stuffed, or imaginary companions; as captive or wild specimens; as zoo attractions; as targets of cruelty; as characters in books and on television; and as roles the children themselves assume. Recently, however, a few developmental psychologists have proposed that in order to fully understand the development of children's perceptual systems, their love relationships and empathy, their play patterns, their fears, and their sense of self, researchers must extend the list of important influences on children to include non-human animals—perhaps even putting animals at the top of the list (Melson, 2001, 2003; Myers, 2007; Myers & Saunders, 2002).

Emotional bonds with animals are deep and reflect a variety of processes (Vining, 2003, p. 94), including:

- Comfort, companionship, and social support and facilitation
- Reinforcement of self-worth via unconditional love
- Provision of a sense of self and self-presentation (see also Myers, 2007)
- Aid in healing both psychologically and physiologically
- Connection with nature and
- A sense of awe and wonder.

Investigators have shown that animal contacts increased communication skills in children (Beck & Katcher, 2003). Even autistic children demonstrated improved attention, social interactions, and positive emotions following time with animals (Katcher & Wilkins, 1993). Similarly, children with ADHD showed increased interest in animals, ability to sustain attention, and better impulse control after zoo visits (Katcher & Wilkins, 1993). Interactions with animals reduce stress in children, an effect that can also be achieved via stuffed animals (Louv, 2005). Teddy bears can calm children of nearly any age and help lower their stress. In fact, police often carry teddy bears in their safety kit to use when they encounter a child who has been hurt or is afraid (Beck & Katcher, 2003).

From a very young age, most children possess the desire to protect and help weaker beings, including both people and nonhuman animals (Beck & Katcher, 2003; Myers & Saunders, 2002; White, 2004).

Due to biophilia, evolutionary theorists suggest that animals and small children elicit love, affection, and caretaking in similar ways. Young creatures of all species share many **neotonous** (baby-like) features (Gaulin & McBurney, 2001), including proportionately large eyes and head, high forehead, and small nose and mouth; these features are commonly perceived as cute. Animals can thus help children develop feelings of empathy and learn about the care and nurturing of others (Ascione, 2005; Derr, 2006; Myers, 2007). Although some children (particularly boys) are intentionally cruel to other species of animals, cruelty is generally a symptom of an unusual psychological disturbance such as conduct disorder (Ascione, 2005; Dadds et al., 2004).

Giving children instruction and opportunities to pet and care for animals sponsors compassion and responsibility for others, crucial for later adult functioning in healthy families and communities. Experiences at petting farms and zoos can foster concern that generalizes to caring about and protecting animals' habitats (Myers & Saunders, 2002). Thus, positive experiences with nonhuman animals may be the simplest way to increase children's awareness about environmental issues.

FOSTERING PROENVIRONMENTAL BEHAVIORS IN CHILDREN

As children care about animals, framing climate change and other forms of environmental degradation in terms of risks to polar bears, penguins, or other species may inspire them to develop more proenvironmental behaviors; certainly, environmental organizations utilize engaging animal imagery to advance their agendas (Myers, Saunders, & Garrett, 2004). Sue recalls that as a child, she was profoundly affected by images of baby harp seals being brutally clubbed to death for their fur, and she suspects that her passion for environmental conservation and animal protection resulted from her sense of empathy and indignation at such inhumane treatment. On the other hand, engaging children too early in the realities of environmental crises can cause *ecophobia*, a fear of the natural world and its problems, and subsequent emotional distancing and apathy (Sobel, 1996, 1999). We'll say more about this in the section below concerning EE.

In general, however, experiences in nature, interactions with nonhumans, and associated emotional responses (i.e., love of nature) are important ingredients for fostering a proenvironmental ethic and behaviors (e.g., Chawla, 1988, 1998a, 1998b; Kals & Ittner, 2003; Kals, Schumacher, & Montada, 1999; Kellert, 1993, 2002; Myers & Saunders, 2002). Some investigators have argued that love of nature and concern about its protection is *only* developed with regular, consistent contact, and play outside (Chawla, 1988; Pyle, 2002; Sobel, 1990; Wilson, R.A. 1993). Activists and ecologists often attribute their environmental concern to early personal experiences in wild or semi-wild places; to family members who modeled appreciation and respect for nature; or to distress over the destruction of a favorite natural place (Chawla, 1988, 1998b; Chawla & Cushing, 2007; Thomashow, 1995). Such experiences can create profound emotional connections and concern about environmental protection.

Emotional affinity formed during previous (childhood) as well as current experiences in nature involves positive feelings of love, happiness, and joy, as well as anger when natural areas are insufficiently protected or irresponsibly managed. Affiliation with nature is related to a willingness to engage in conservation behaviors and sign environmentally related petitions as adults (Kals et al., 1999). Recent studies demonstrate that positive childhood play experiences in wild places are correlated with many adult behaviors and values, including proenvironmental attitudes, concern about biodiversity, choice of occupation, voting for candidates based on their environmental views, recycling, and other nature-protective behaviors (Bixler, Floyd, & Hammitt, 2002; Kals & Ittner, 2003; Wells & Lekies, 2006). As predicted by the **social learning theory** (Bandura, 1977), children's attitudes are greatly influenced by their parents' and teachers' environmentally relevant activities (Kals & Ittner, 2003; see also Chawla, 1998b). Children learn from observing models who practice behaviors like recycling or organic gardening, as well as by directly participating (Musser & Diamond, 1999).

off the mark.com   by Mark Parisi

Just as parents and other significant adults in a child's life can foster love and concern for nature, adults can reinforce negative associations by discouraging outdoor play or more importantly, encouraging behaviors that are environmentally harmful. In general, socialization that leads children to experience themselves as separate from nature allows them to view the environment as merely a resource for personal gain, and can result in misuse, exploitation, and domination. Lack of experience in nature can lead to ecophobia, with outcomes ranging from feelings of discomfort outdoors, to outright contempt for anything that is not human-created or controlled (Orr, 1993). Although some anxieties are normal and predicted by biophobia (the innate desire to avoid potentially hazardous stimuli such as snakes, spiders, and heights), greater time outdoors and positive role models diminish the influence of such fears. Hence, those who are apprehensive about spending time in nature, particularly in wilderness, typically did not have outdoor experiences as children. In one study of urban adolescents, negative views of nature, including fear of danger or discomfort (i.e., due to bee stings, snake bites, getting lost) were inversely correlated with interest in outdoor recreational activities (e.g., hiking, camping, canoeing), utilization of walking paths, and choice of environmentally oriented work and study atmospheres (Bixler & Floyd, 1997). Consequently, failure to experience the natural world can result in apathy and disregard for environmental protection; that is, extinction of experience.

Environmental Education

Due to the average child in the United States today spends less than 30 minutes per week engaged in outdoor activities (Hofferth & Curtin, 2005; Hofferth & Sandberg, 2001), EE is increasingly important for teaching children about the biophysical environment, the problems created by human activity, and strategies for addressing those problems (e.g., Coyle, 2005; Fisman, 2005; Orr, 2004). "EE is not only education *about* and *in* the environment, but … perhaps foremost, [EE is] education *for* the environment … it is inevitably education for change" (Wals, 1994, p. 19). The goal of EE is to directly engage participants in solving environmental issues and promoting sustainability (Global Development Research Center, n.d.; Vincent & Focht, 2009) to provide "a varied, beautiful, and resource-rich planet for future generations" (Tanner, 1980, p. 20).

EE fosters **ecological literacy**, an interdisciplinary understanding gleaned from the natural and social sciences about what it takes to create a sustainable society (Orr, 2004), and the attitudes, abilities, and actions that reflect competence and responsibility concerning one's environmentally relevant behavior (Chawla & Cushing, 2007; Coyle, 2005; Disinger, 2001; Disinger & Roth, 1992; Gotch & Hall, 2004; Hungerford & Volk, 1990; Monroe, 2003). Successful approaches to EE enhance children's interest and concern about nature and other species, their knowledge about environmental problems and potential consequences, and relevant skills for a valid sense of empowerment (Chawla & Cushing, 2007; Hungerford & Volk, 1990). An ecologically literate person is considerably more likely to act in proenvironmental ways than someone uneducated about environmental issues (Coyle, 2005).

Curriculum development resources for teachers and EE program developers are burgeoning for K–12 as well as higher education (e.g., Facing the Future, The Environmental Literacy Council, and the Association for the Advancement of Sustainability in Higher Education).* One survey revealed that more than 60% of K–12 teachers in the United States included environmental topics in their classes (Survey Research Center, 2000). However, a mere 10% of teachers were specifically trained in EE, and only 25% had environmental science or related courses, suggesting that teacher training is insufficient for effectively addressing EE (Coyle, 2005).

Historically, EE was based on exploratory field trips; children were put on buses and sent to nature reserves. However, this approach does not teach children about the nature within their own neighborhoods (Fisman, 2005), nor does it offer the sustained contact that is so critical to forming a connection (Kahn, 2007; Pyle, 1993; Santostefano, 2008; Sobel, 1990). Access to local green spaces is particularly important for urban children of lower income families who may not have many opportunities to visit nature reserves and national parks (Fisman, 2005). Experiencing natural settings in a contrived way, such as on a school field trip, can produce a sense of detachment from nature. If encounters only occur in pristine, distant environments, children will not understand their own connection to nature, and will not relate their behaviors to conservation and protection efforts (Haluza-Delay, 2001).

Traditional approaches to EE are also ineffective if they assume that information alone is sufficient for promoting proenvironmental behavior, as we have discussed throughout this text (see also Chawla,

---

* For information concerning K–12 environmental education curricula, see http://facingthefuture.org/ (also see http://eelink.net/pages/EE-Link+Introduction and http://www.enviroliteracy.org/teachers-index.php). Resources concerning higher education efforts in sustainability are available (http://www.secondnature.org/ and http://www.aashe.org/) and support for integrating environmental issues into psychology classes in particular is available (http://www.teachgreenpsych.com/).

1998a; Chawla & Cushing, 2007; Hungerford & Volk, 1990). Worse, EE programs that include global issues like species extinctions, deforestation, climate change, or acid rain can cause dissociation, anxiety, and ecophobia because such abstract problems are beyond the child's direct understanding and control (Sobel, 1996, 1999). As with adults, issues that appear too distant fail to garner attention (recall the discussion of risk and proximal cognition in Chapter 7) and lack of personal control leads to feelings of helplessness and depression (Chapter 8).

The well-known ecologist and conservation advocate, Aldo Leopold, wrote that EE will remain ineffective so long as it fails to help people develop a "love, respect, and admiration for land, and a high regard for its value" separate from its economic worth (1966, p. 239; see also Kahn, 2003). Thus, children should be encouraged to care about nature before they are taught specific information and responsibility (e.g., Sobel, 1996; White, 2004; Wilson, 1997), because their emotional systems mature before their ability to process abstractly and rationally (Kellert, 2002). "If we want children to flourish, to become truly empowered, then let us allow them to love the earth before we ask them to save it" (Sobel, 1996, p. 39).

Successful EE must also take into account the innate tendencies for both attraction and revulsion toward certain aspects of nature that were relevant to the survival of human ancestors (i.e., biophilia and biophobia). Specifically, EE can capitalize on the fact that children are inherently attracted to nonhuman animals and understand some of their characteristics at very young ages (i.e., three months of age); these cognitive foundations enable empathy for other creatures that can ultimately promote proenvironmental behaviors (Kahn, 2003; Myers, 2007; Myers & Saunders, 2002). As we saw earlier, enhancing knowledge and experience in nature can help children become more biocentric by demonstrating connections between humans, animals, plants, and all other aspects of the natural world. EE can also assist children in reframing their apprehensions or aversions, leading to the appreciation of the intrinsic value of nature, and the importance of its protection (Bixler & Floyd, 1997). Rather than romanticizing nature, effective EE should address reasonable concerns about dangers in nature (snake bites, bee stings, etc.), and common reactions such as disgust at the dirtiness and unappealing qualities of some plants and animals (e.g., slugs and snails that are soft and slimy).

In general, EE is effective when it considers children's unique perspective, curiosity, and need for direct exploration (Sobel, 1996; White, 2004). Environmental educators should focus on problems that are within "the geographical and conceptual scope" of children, particularly prior to fourth grade (Sobel, 1996, p. 27; see also Hart, 1997).

Place-based education (also known as **community problem solving;** Wals, 1994) addresses these concerns by developing interdisciplinary, experiential curricula in local environments, fostering student learning as well as the health of the surrounding community (e.g., Theobald, 1997; Woodhouse & Knapp, 2000).* Nearly half (46%) of the place-based educational programs recently surveyed demonstrated measurable improvements in air quality (Duffin, Murphy, & Johnson, 2008). Examples of the initiatives include a **no-idling** policy, including posting signs, at a high school in New Hampshire; and Washington state middle school students who measured CO_2, mold, odors, airflow, and air particulate levels before and after administrative and maintenance interventions. All indicators reflected improvements in the postassessment. Effective local action fosters the understanding that *all* ecological issues are "informed and influenced by global patterns and processes," enabling a sense of interconnection and interdependence (Thomashow, 2002, p. 7). Such learning opportunities contribute to the formation of an **ecological identity**, an awareness of one's self as embedded in the environment (Clayton & Opotow, 2003; see also Chapter 10).

One conceptual model of developmentally appropriate EE emphasizes processes relevant to different phases of early and middle childhood and early adolescence (Sobel, 1996). Young children (ages 4–7) require opportunities to *empathize* with creatures in the natural world through play activities where they are encouraged to mimic or "become" a non human animal. Middle childhood (ages 8–11) is a time for *exploration.* These children need to investigate their local neighborhoods, beginning with the areas surrounding their houses and school, and expanding to nearby forests and streams. Activities include caring for animals, making forts, and learning about natural resources. Finally, *social action* is key to early adolescence (ages 12–15), so educational activities for them occur in groups that take responsibility for particular projects (such as energy conservation or recycling programs; Sobel, 1996; see also Hart, 1997). Thus, EE should be custom designed for students, targeted to their interests, abilities, and knowledge.

A friend of Sue's who teaches elementary school once heard a pupil exclaim, "Worms are gross!" Sue's friend replied that worms help break things down; then she set up a compost bin to demonstrate how the students' orange peels and apple cores quickly become dirt the class could use to fertilize the school garden. The teacher discussed these and related concepts in terms of behaviors that are (or are not) "good

---

* For more information and resources, see http://www.promiseofplace.org/ and http://www.placebasededucation.org/home/index.php

for the earth." The children responded enthusiastically, and parents reported back that their children chastised them for throwing out food waste that could be composted, as well as littering or failing to recycle. Some have argued that recycling became common in the United States because elementary teachers educated their students about it; the students then went home and nagged their parents (Quick, 2007).

When young people engage in service projects that integrate knowledge about ecological issues with practical ways of addressing them, they feel empowered, which helps sustain their involvement (Booth, 1998; Coyle, 2005); you'll recognize this as problem-focused coping (Chapter 8). The most effective programs for establishing behavior change last over extended periods of time and involve achievable goals based on specific actions, such as "writing letters to advocate wildlife protection, making nesting boxes for birds, carrying out energy conservation activities, or initiating community projects" (Chawla & Cushing, 2007, p. 441). Such action-oriented educational programs targeted at youth involve at least five types of activities (adapted from Schusler, Krasny, Peters, & Decker, 2009, p. 113):

- Improving physical environments (e.g., restoring habitat)
- Educating other community members (i.e., festivals and information fairs, distributing newsletters, brochures, or videos)
- Gathering information via community assessments or surveys, environmental monitoring, or conducting experiments to inform or evaluate action
- Researching, analyzing, and advocating for policy change (e.g., concerning impacts of wastewater treatment regulations) and
- Developing products or services contributing to the community (e.g., growing food sustainably for sale at farmers' markets or local cooperative markets).

The potential for EE-motivated behavioral change is estimated to be worth at least *$75 billion a year* in measurable environmental benefits (Coyle, 2005).

Participating in action-oriented EE can contribute to the development of confidence and self-esteem, critical thinking, problem-solving skills, and a work ethic, in addition to fostering enthusiasm for continued engagement in environmental issues (Monroe, 2003; Schusler et al., 2009). The interaction between youth and their communities thus creates a positive feedback cycle: Constructive action that betters the ecological and social climate fosters participants' personal growth and sense of efficacy, and greater feelings of empowerment lead to more environmental and social change (Schusler et al., 2009, see Figure 9.1).

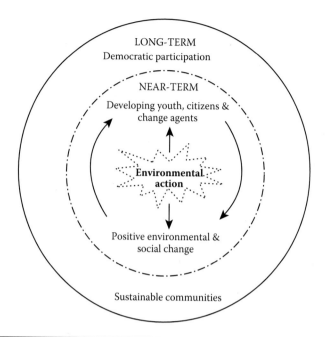

Figure 9.1 There is a positive feedback loop between youth participation in environmental action and both individual and community development. (Reprinted from Schusler, T.M., Krasny, M.E., Peters, S.J., & Decker, D.J. (2009). *Environmental Education Research, 15,* 122. With permission from © Taylor and Francis Publishers.)

Children have a vested interest in a sustainable future, and can provide a unique and critical contribution to that endeavor (Heft & Chawla, 2006). Fostering children's perspective and voice on environmental and other issues is key to democratic societies (Hart, 1997), and children who experience clear standards and have the opportunity to express themselves are more likely to become socially responsible (Baumrind, 1971; Chawla & Cushing, 2007). Enabling students to engage in the political process is a critical component of EE (e.g., Hart, 1997; Schusler et al., 2009) because environmental destruction is "structurally anchored in society and our ways of living" (Jensen & Schnack, 1997, p. 164).

In sum, effective EE emphasizes both individual and collective action, enabling engagement with democratic processes, and manifesting change at both local and global levels. Such experiences not only promote healthy children, they also facilitate the environmental awareness, concern, and behaviors needed by adults to build a sustainable world.

Back to Nature   Fortunately, because recent media interest in the importance of nature for children has increased, so has relevant legislation. For instance, in 2006, Washington Governor Gregoire signed the *Leave No Child Inside Initiative*, providing $1.5 million annually for programs encouraging underprivileged children to spend more time outside. In 2007, the U.S. Forest Service created the *More Kids in the Woods* program, which funds programs that support children's outdoor experiences (Charles, Louv, Bodner, & Guns, 2008). Other initiatives include *Take A Child Outside* and the National Wildlife Federation's recommendation of a daily *Green Hour.** Many traditional organizations continue to sponsor outdoor creative play, such as 4-H, Scouts, Camp Fire USA, as well as local nature centers and preserves. These programs also promote parental and community participation (Charles et al., 2008). As noted in Chapter 8, urban planners are increasingly incorporating parks, gardens, and green spaces in their designs to provide greater community access to nature. Such opportunities for outdoor experiences are crucial for counteracting the rising rates of indoor children playing videogames, watching commercials on television, eating junk food, and suffering resulting, physical, cognitive, and emotional–social problems.

CONCLUSIONS

For many people, the concept of nature evokes thoughts about habitats for other animals. However, the research reviewed in this chapter demonstrates that the young human animal needs nature too. Experiences with healthy, natural settings, and interactions with nonhuman animals make important contributions to healthy child development. Children residing in areas containing natural elements have access to more explorative and restorative experiences, and thus enjoy multiple benefits: improved cognitive and attentional functions, enhanced emotional and social skills, better motor coordination, and improved mental health.

Sadly, contemporary culture, particularly in the United States, promotes destructive practices that damage children's growth (Mergen, 2003; Orr, 2002). In Chapter 6, we described many substances found in built environments that are directly toxic to children's brain development and function. In addition, the loss and degradation of natural spaces, along with a rising emphasis on technology, reduce children's

---

* Resources on various beneficial outdoor activities for children are available at http://www.takeachildoutside.org/ and http://www.greenhour.org/

opportunities to engage with nature. A variety of adverse health outcomes may result: obesity, depression, anxiety, learning impairments, and ADHD are increasing, as well as violence and other sociocultural ailments. These symptoms are also associated with materialistic values that promote resource overconsumption and environmental destruction (Brown & Kasser, 2005; Kasser, 2006; Orr, 2002).

In contrast, sustainable cultures allow children to play and explore outdoors in healthy environments, because everyone needs nature to thrive. Given the many benefits conferred by experiences in nature to child development, mental health, and overall functioning, urban planning and landscaping efforts should consider children's particular needs such as those imposed by their limited mobility, and ensure adequate opportunities for safe access and play (Berg & Medrich, 1980; Spencer & Woolley, 2000). Optimal designs of children's facilities (schools, day care centers, hospital units, etc.) include natural, restorative features (e.g., Moore, 1999; Trancik & Evans, 1995). These characteristics help children form connections with others, the larger community, and nature as a whole. Such places provide special meaning for children as well as adults by virtue of the available activities, and promotion of social connections with friends and family (Derr, 2002). Consequently, places in nature often play a critical role in the creation of an ecological identity (e.g., Kals & Ittner, 2003; Sobel, 1990; Thomashow, 1995), a sense of being part of a larger whole. We discuss this point in detail in Chapter 10.

10

HOLISTIC APPROACHES: GESTALT
AND ECOPSYCHOLOGY

What would you call the following?

. . . . . .
.
.
.
.

If you answered "T," you are responding to the relationship between these dots, rather than to the dots themselves. Instead of answering "10 dots," you perceived a meaningful configuration based on the way they are organized.

Your response illustrates the central theme of this chapter: the relationship between parts can be more important than the parts themselves. If we presented the same configuration of small x's, you would still respond with "T," even though all of the separate elements changed. Both of the psychological perspectives we will talk about in this chapter emphasize this principle of **holism**: the whole is more than the sum of its parts. From this perspective, environmental problems are best approached by considering the system in which they are created. Just as you could not understand the answer "T" if you insisted on reducing the study of this configuration to the study of 10 separate dots, environmental problems cannot be adequately addressed by focusing exclusively on people as isolated actors, separate from the ecosystems of which they are part.

From a holistic approach, environmental degradation is caused by humans failing to see the whole. But since holistic approaches do not tend to separate causes from effects, it would also be true that environmental problems themselves distract people from seeing the whole. Cause and effect work both ways from this standpoint. The modern worldview, which emphasizes individualism (see Chapter 2) and contemporary psychology, which is conducted as a science, are both **reductionistic**. In other words, assuming that experience can be partitioned (reduced) into smaller elements and that individuals can be separated from each other, as well as from their communities, culture, and the rest of the natural world is distorted, inaccurate, and dangerous (Kidner, 2001). Seeing the world as consisting of separate elements leads to one-way causal thinking, in which specific causes are assumed to impact specific outcomes. Instead, holistic approaches stress an interconnected existence within a complex system. When a butterfly flaps its wings, the whole universe is changed, and the whole universe determines how that butterfly's wings flap.

As holistic approaches contradict the dominant social paradigm (see Chapter 2), it should be no surprise that these approaches are marginalized in mainstream psychology. However, we do not believe they should be dismissed; rather, their marginalization expresses their potential contribution. Clearly, dominant viewpoints have led civilization down a very destructive and unsustainable path. Other perspectives, including those with something important to say about a more holistic way of seeing, will be required for a change in course.

In this chapter, we lay out some fundamental principles of holistic psychology and see how they can be applied to understanding and solving environmental problems. We begin by articulating the roots of Gestalt psychology, and discuss empirical support for some of its implications in social dilemma games. We then go on to look at Gestalt therapy and how that approach leads directly to the concept of the ecological self. With these insights, we then examine ecopsychology, noting its contributions and challenges. We conclude by addressing insights of ecopsychology for the psychology of place and sacred places.

GESTALT PSYCHOLOGY

Gestalt is a German word that does not have an easy equivalent in English, but we can roughly define it as form, whole, structure, or meaning. The "T" you saw in the dot formation above is a Gestalt—a form or whole. The term *Gestalt* was first used by von Ehrenfels (Boring, 1950/1957), who illustrated the idea with melodies. If you transpose a tune from the key of C to the key of D, every note would change, but the melody would still be recognizable. Thus, the melody is defined by the *relationship between* the notes, rather than the notes themselves. The whole is more than the sum of its parts; the melody forms a Gestalt, independent of its individual notes. From this perspective, environmental problems result from the inability to accurately perceive relationships within larger ecosystems. We humans tend to behave in destructive ways because we see ourselves separate from other species and the natural world as a whole. Thus, change will require recognizing and remembering interconnections and interdependency within ecosystems.

The work of Gestalt psychologist Wolfgang Kohler (1947/1975), who described learning as perceptual reorganization, can help us here. In his famous studies, he put bananas out of range of hungry apes and chimpanzees. In order to reach the fruit, they had to stand on boxes or ladders and use sticks as tools to knock the bananas down. Kohler noticed that the animals learned how to solve these problems quite suddenly. Instead of a gradual change, they roamed around for a while and then suddenly placed the objects in the correct position to reach the bananas. Moreover, once they had solved the problem, they could quickly solve it again. Kohler argued that the animals showed **insight learning**: a sudden perceptual reorganization of the field so that a box was no longer seen as just a box, but as a stepping stool. With these demonstrations, Kohler asserted that learning is not a consequence of associated responses built up over time, as behaviorists had argued. Instead, learning depends on perception; it is a consequence of perceptual reorganization, suddenly seeing relationship and connection between so-called isolated elements.

Such insight learning could be crucial for solving environmental problems. For example, when Deborah's niece Danielle was nine years old, she visited one summer. While they were hanging up towels on the clothesline outside, Danielle asked why they didn't just put them in the electric dryer. Deborah explained that people should always let the sun do whatever work it can, because electricity use creates problems. For example, in the Pacific Northwest, electricity largely comes from hydroelectric dams, and those dams are destroying salmon populations. So using a dryer without needing to unnecessarily kills fish. Danielle's response was "Oh no, we don't want to kill those fish," and she enthusiastically helped hang up the towels. Kohler would say that she experienced a sudden perceptual reorganization that allowed her to see her behavior connected to the well-being of another species. Her response was an enthusiastic embrace of more environmentally responsible behavior. This sudden perceptual shift can be experienced in Figure 10.1.

Figure 10.1 The sudden perceptual shift emphasized by Gestalt psychology can be experienced by staring at this figure and noticing how it shifts from two faces to a vase and back again.

Laboratory Confirmation: Group Effects in Social Dilemma Games

If Gestalt principles apply to environmentally relevant behaviors, people ought to behave in more appropriate ways when they are reminded of their group membership. Individuals who act from pure self-interest would be more likely to deplete a resource than those who realize their behavior affects the well-being of the larger group of which they are a part; you may recall from Chapter 5 that this conflict between personal and group interests is known as a **social dilemma** (also known as a **social trap**).

In general, laboratory research has validated Garret Hardin's (1968) notion of "the tragedy of the commons." When research psychologists ask participants to simulate management of common resources, people usually behave quite individualistically, grabbing as much as they can quickly, and exhausting the commons so its resources are quickly depleted. Thus, dilemma game players will overharvest their trees (Bell, Petersen, & Hautaluoma, 1989), forfeit long-range and bigger payoffs (Dawes, 1980), or overspend their credit cards, in order to procure smaller but more immediate individual rewards. Globally, fish stocks have been depleted because of the tragedy of the commons (Hirsh, 2009; Revkin, 2008).

Resource depletion can be driven by fear that others will use it first (Lynn, 1992). Deborah experienced this kind of hoarding when she served as a camp cook for her husband's geology field camp one summer. Although she did her best to estimate group uses of various foods, within a week in the wilderness area, she realized they were running low on hot chocolate. She hoped that as scarcity became apparent to other camp members, its value would go up and they would be more careful about using it, rationing it till the end. Instead, as soon as scarcity became apparent, the remainder of the hot chocolate disappeared quickly, much faster than it was used before scarcity was obvious. Apparently, camp members wanted to be sure they got their share before it completely ran out. Being somewhat of a hoarder herself, Deborah wanted to put the chocolate away and use it only on special occasions, so that it would last. Simply perceiving a commodity as scarce will increase the demand for it. Restaurant servers use this principle when they strategically hint to their customers that they should preorder the chocolate truffle cake because there aren't many left and then sell a record breaking number of the dessert.

Thus, scarcity and individualism can drive competitive behavior that is ultimately self-defeating; emphasizing the long-term costs to the individual or increasing short-term costs (e.g., for overusing a resource) can be effective for countering social trap behaviors as we saw in Chapter 5. As one would predict from a holistic perspective, cooperation should eclipse competition when people see themselves to be part of a group. There are at least three ways to make group membership more obvious: limit and clarify the size of the group, reduce social distance, and appeal to norms (described in Chapter 4). We will briefly examine empirical evidence for each of these claims.

Limit and Clarify Group Size   At least in laboratory social dilemma games, the smaller the group, the more cooperatively players behave. Two person groups are more cooperative than three person groups, and groups of three are more cooperative than six (Dawes, 1980). Researchers have concluded that in the smaller group, people feel more identified with each other and with the group's success. Smaller groups give people an **illusion of efficacy** (Kerr, 1989), a feeling they can control outcomes. When group size is clear, players tend to harvest with equal distribution among players, but when it is unclear, cooperation decreases (deKwaadsteniet, van Dijk, Wit, & DeCremer, 2008).

Reduce Social Distance   Anything that helps people feel more connected to their group increases their cooperation. One of the most well-documented findings in social dilemma games is that when players have a chance to communicate with each other, their cooperation is enhanced (Bicchieri, 2002; Bicchieri & Lev-On, 2007; Biele, Rieskamp, & Czienskowski, 2008; Dawes, 1980; Dawes, van de Kragt, & Orbell, 1990). Being able to talk to each other during the game is best (Sally, 1995), but even partial communication is helpful. Meeting face-to-face in a brief meeting before playing increases cooperation (Boone, Declerck, & Suetens, 2008), as does social identification with the group (De Cremer & Van Vugt, 1999). When players' choices are made public to other players, their behavior is more cooperative than when they are allowed to behave competitively in private (Fox & Guyer, 1978; Jerdee & Rosen, 1974). Feelings of attachment to one's community increases self-restraint and decreases self-interested behavior (Van Vugt, 2001). Cooperation also increases when players are given information about their group's unequal access to resources (Smith, Jackson, & Sparks, 2003), which is good news for promoting environmental justice, because it indicates that people behave more considerately when they become aware of inequality (see Chapter 4). Communication appears to increase cooperation through several processes: players humanize other players, they understand the social dilemma better, they commit to cooperative policies, and they convey social norms.

Establish Social Norms A *norm* is a belief about what is appropriate (Chapter 4). *Descriptive norms* develop when players are led to believe that other players are cooperating; consequently cooperation increases. Even bogus feedback that leads players to believe that others are cooperating increases cooperation (Cress & Kimmerle, 2007).

Although Hardin argued that we can't solve our common problems by appealing to altruistic norms, research on laboratory dilemmas (as well as VBN theory, see Chapter 4) suggests he was wrong. While it is true that dilemma game players often get trapped into what they know is group-defeating and ultimately self-defeating behavior, when moral appeals are given prior to group play, cooperative behavior can be dramatically increased. In fact, people make sacrifices all the time: parents sacrifice for their children, soldiers for their country, and donors for their charity.

Thus, the literature on group effects on dilemma games leads us to predict that small communities that have good communication channels, stable populations, and clear norms, are effective in sustainable management of resources. Research supports this claim (Gardner & Stern, 2002; Ostrom, 1990). When people are accountable to their neighbors, believe others are cooperating, and can discuss rules and policies about the use of common resources, especially face-to-face, their ability to create successful management operations increases markedly.

From a holistic perspective, ecological problems are exacerbated by living anonymously in large urban populations, and mistakenly assuming people are separate individuals whose behavior has little effect on other humans, much less on the other biological and physical dimensions of the planet (Cahalan, 1995). For two centuries, people in the industrialized world have assumed that what human beings did would have no impact on the ecosphere. The idea that humans could actually change the climate seemed absurd even 50 years ago; now it is clear that the human-made build-up of carbon emissions is a dangerous reality. Shifting perception to see human behavior embedded in larger systems is required before people will be able to adopt more environmentally appropriate behavior.

Gestalt Therapy

Why don't humans see the interconnections and embedded relationships with fellow human beings and the ecosystem more consistently? One answer comes from **Gestalt therapy**, a form of group and individual psychotherapy that became popular in the 1970s, and is still widely practiced in the United States and Britain today. Gestalt therapy was developed by husband and wife team Laura (1905–1990) and Fritz Perls (1893–1970). The Perls (1969, 1971, 1978) synthesized Gestalt and Freudian theories, and as neo-Freudians, they agreed with Freud that much of what people do is based on unconscious motives (Chapter 3). According to the Perls, defensiveness results from a fragmentation of various parts of the psyche. Awareness brings about an integration of these dissociated parts, so that people can experience their full range of feelings without blocking off parts of their consciousness (Perls, 1942).

So far, the emphasis on defenses and transcending them is not very different from Freud's approach. But the Perls departed from Freud by stressing the senses and their function in the present moment. According to them, in order to become conscious, people must more effectively examine the *present*, rather than erecting entertaining but irrelevant explanations from the *past*. Full integrity actually exists in the present, but people are unaware of it because they block out so much of what is actually happening right now. People stay unaware by refusing what the Perls called **contact**. Contact refers to sensual registering—seeing, hearing, smelling, touching, and moving with awareness—in the present. By shutting down one's contact, people become numb to their connection with their surroundings. And they also become victims to their intellectual abstractions, which cannot communicate the unity of being. Instead, overintellectualizing and underexperiencing the present moment leads to fragmented understandings and neuroses.

Reprinted from MUTTS © Patrick McDonnell, King Features Syndicate. With permission.

Several thinkers have used Gestalt principles to approach ecological problems (Abram, 1987; Cahalan, 1995; Cohen, 1997; Swanson, 1995, 2001). Others use these principles without necessarily identifying themselves as Gestalt theorists. One good example is Laura Sewell (1995, 1999), a perceptual ecopsychologist, who argued that sensory experiences of taste, smell, sight, touch, and hearing are the primary means of deep connection with the world. However, because their senses have been deadened by modern life, people do not fully experience their deeply embedded existence in physical ecosystems. Instead, they live in the past and future rather than the present. To reconnect with the world, people must learn how to attend to present experience more fully, quietly, and deeply; to see, hear, taste, and feel more clearly.

This perspective converges with the spiritual practices of Buddhism, and its teachings about the importance of mindfulness in generating **Right Action**, human responsibility to other people, other species, and the rest of the world (e.g., Nhat Hanh, 1991). Sewell (1995) wrote that practicing mindful attention will bring people to a more accurate and richer picture of who they are within a global framework, and will help them discover the beauty of it. In Sewell's words:

> The earth calls continually. She [sic] calls us with beauty, sometimes truly breathtaking, sometimes heart wrenching, and always provocative and visceral. We are embedded in a multidimensional web of beauty. It is where we are, now.... . The moment calls for the reperceiving of our Earth, for perceiving the myriad and magical relations that may inform an ecological ethic. If we are receptive to the ways in which the landscape speaks to us, or the ways in which perception serves as a channel for communication, we may reawaken and preserve a sense of human integrity within the family of all relations. (1995, p. 215)

This argument reminds Deborah of one of her favorite poems by Mary Oliver:

> You do not have to be good.
> You do not have to walk on your knees
> for a hundred miles through the desert, repenting.
> You only have to let the soft animal of your body love what it loves.
> Tell me about despair, yours, and I will tell you mine.
> Meanwhile the world goes on.
> Meanwhile the sun and the clear pebbles of the rain
> are moving across the landscapes,
> over the prairies and deep trees,
> the mountains and the rivers.
> Meanwhile the wild geese, high in the clean blue air
> are heading home again.
> Whoever you are, no matter how lonely,
> the world offers itself to your imagination,
> calls to you like the wild geese, harsh and exciting—
> over and over announcing your place in the family of things.

(Oliver, 2004, p. 19)

Mindfulness

Experiencing full sensory contact and engagement requires quieting the intellect, the part of the mind that provides continual commentary, analysis, judgment, or chatter about one's experiences (Kabat-Zinn, 1994; Kornfield, 1993). To become mindful is to reduce this internal chatter and raise awareness of present experience (Langer, 1989, 1997). Mindfulness plays a central role in Buddhism, which teaches people ways to develop their attention through meditation practice (Nhat Hanh, 1991). In the West, meditation techniques have been taught without the religious dimensions of Buddhism to reduce stress, promote healing, and relieve depression (Kabat-Zinn, 1990, 1994; Ludwig & Kabat-Zinn, 2008; Williams, Teasdale, Segal, & Kabat-Zinn, 2007).

Mindful practices in natural settings enhance people's experience of the present moment, and thereby, their felt connection with surrounding ecosystems (Cahalan, 1995; Macy & Brown, 1998; Swanson, 2001). For example, silently experiencing the sounds of a forest can bring a sense of deep identity with it. Focusing on breathing helps quiet the intellect and illuminate a deep connection with the universe. As one Gestalt therapist puts it

I invite clients to know that they, I, and all the rest of the animal kingdom are now taking in oxygen produced by the plant kingdom, and are releasing carbon dioxide back to the plants . . . that energy came to [us] from the sun through [our] food, and is being released in [us] with each breath of oxygen and beat of [our] heart. (Cahalan, 1995, p. 219).

With mindful practice, the trivial objects of human worry, planning, and regretting are replaced by a silent sense of connection to the sensual world.

As we mentioned in Chapter 4, mindful practice is a good way to reduce the impact of consumer culture on overconsumption (De Wet, 2008; Goleman, 2009), as well as reduce materialistic values, increase ecologically friendly behaviors (Amel, Manning, & Scott, 2009), and lower ecological footprints (Brown & Kasser, 2005). "On a political level, mindfulness can help in our work against consumerism, sexism, militarism, and many other isms that undermine the integrity of life" (Sivaraksa, 2009, p. 83). For these reasons mindfulness training might be more effective than information campaigns about environmental problems, which so often raise anxiety about environmental issues, but do little to promote proenvironmental behavior (Crompton & Kasser, 2009).

TRY THIS MINDFULNESS PRACTICE

1. With one or more companions, go to a natural or seminatural area—a park, riverside, forest, field, or whatever is available.
2. Read these instructions together and discuss them so there is shared understanding.
3. Go out individually and silently into the natural area, agreeing to meet again in about 20 minutes.
4. As you walk along, sense your natural attractions. When you are attracted to a plant or tree, ask for permission to visit it. If you feel permission is denied, move on.
5. If you feel you have permission, sit with the plant and explore it with all your senses.
6. Breathe with the plant, exchanging gases. Imagine how the plant is providing you with oxygen and you are providing the plant with carbon dioxide. Both of you need each other.

7. When your time is up, express your gratitude to the plant and the natural area.
8. When you gather together again, take turns describing what happened and how it felt. There is no need to interpret, explain, or compare experiences. Just share them without judgment.
9. Thank each other for doing this activity together.
10. When you are finished, ask yourself how you feel. If it is a good feeling and one you would like to repeat, explore ecopsychology more deeply through an online course, book, workshop, therapist, or group (Scull, 2001).

THE ECOLOGICAL SELF: THE SELF BEYOND THE SELF

To experience one's place in the world provides an expanded sense of self. The holistic approach to environmental problems suggests that ordinary perceptions of one's self as an isolated being encapsulated in a separate skin is misleading and dangerous. As we discussed in Chapter 2, the Western notion of a separate self arose during the Enlightenment period that paralleled industrialization (Baumeister, 1987). People in the West mistakenly learned to see themselves as primarily autonomous. Yet to successfully address environmental problems requires recognition of one's **ecological self**, the part of one's identity that is continuous with the natural world. The phrase *ecological self* was first coined by Naess (1985) who argued that changing environmentally relevant behavior will require people to experience themselves as larger and more connected selves (see also Bragg, 1996; Cohen, 1993; Conn, 1995; Hillman & Ventura, 1992; Keepin, 1992; Kidner, 2001; Roszak, 1992; Shepard, 1998). An ecological self gives rise to the biospheric values discussed in Chapter 4.

The ecological self represents integration of two selves: the separate physical self, which one normally experiences as a person in the Western world, *as well as* a larger self that identifies with the ecosphere. One cannot trade a small separate self for a larger spiritual self; instead, the larger self is integrated with the smaller. This concept builds on insights originally outlined by object-relations theorists (discussed in Chapter 3), where people construct a sense of self from relationships with others. Yet, the holistic framework goes further. From this perspective, the ecological self is a natural part of the developmental process, and embracing it is required for addressing environmental problems. Consequently, the typical sense of self as a separate, autonomous being seriously jeopardizes the ability to live harmoniously within larger human and nonhuman contexts.

How could people possibly become so identified with nature that they protect it as they would protect themselves? One answer lies with **empathy** (Fox, 1990), the cognitive and emotional understanding of another's perspective. Small children learn to empathize with others as they observe others' happiness, disappointment, anger, or joy, and as they interact with animals (Myers, 2007). Similarly, adults empathize with the natural world when they experience commonality with it. People usually find it easy to empathize with their pets—Deborah has no trouble believing her dog Sophie has emotional reactions of happiness or shame. But it is more difficult to empathize with a slug that crawls into Sophie's food dish.

Difficult but not impossible. A few years ago Deborah attended several meditation retreats over the course of a summer. The days and evenings were filled with sessions of sitting meditation, silent walking, silent meals, or silent gardening of the flower gardens. Sitting in the meditation hall one of those afternoons, she grew very quiet and heard many sounds that she would not normally hear: the creek babbling nearby, a bird's wings flapping, a dog snoring across the yard. Someone walked by on the lawn and Deborah was filled with tenderness as she felt the blades of grass being crushed. It wasn't that she felt those boots crushing her, but she could feel them crushing the grass. She felt the vulnerability and the fragility of the natural world—a feeling she is ordinarily not in touch with. In Fox's words, she identified with the grass. She knew that she was Deborah, sitting in the meditation hall, and that the grass was outside being crushed. But she felt an enormous commonality with that grass, as if she could feel what happened to it, as if she could feel it happening to someone whom she deeply loved.

Can people increase the strength of their ecological self by increasing empathy? Laboratory research suggests the answer is yes. When participants are shown photos and asked to take the perspective of animals being harmed by environmental conditions, they increase their biospheric concern (Schultz, 2000) because their empathy increases (Sevillano, Aragones, & Schultz, 2006). In addition, willingness to allocate funds for protection of other species, environmental education, and conservation of wild spaces is increased as well (Berenguer, 2007). Thus, concern about the ecosphere can be increased, and *scope of justice* enlarged (as discussed in Chapter 4) by intentionally taking on the point of view of those normally outside one's scope.

Teaching people to take the perspective of nonhuman beings also takes place in Council of All Beings Workshops (Macy & Brown, 1998;

Seed, Macy, Fleming, & Naess, 1988). In this guided group experience, participants role-play different creatures or elements in the ecosphere by expressing their reactions to human impact. Through fantasy, ritual, and dialogue, participants develop a deeper identification with their animal, plant, or element, whose reactions are ordinarily not heard or recognized. Most people who complete this workshop find it deeply powerful for shifting their identification with the smaller separate self, to a larger, ecological self. Empirical research shows that people answer the question "Who am I" with more ecological statements (I am water, I am hawk) after the workshop than before it (Bragg, 1996). These experiences of the ecological self are also associated with a greater sense of well-being (Reist, 2004).

People get in touch with their ecological selves when they feel connection with other people, other life-forms, ecosystems, and the planet. They experience it when they sense a deep resonance with other species and a quality of belonging and connection to the larger ecological whole. As you might imagine, people frequently experience their ecological self in wilderness settings (Coburn, 2006; Williams & Harvey, 2001). Ecological self-hood is also associated with mystical experiences from using psychedelic drugs (Jagel, 2008).

This is not to say you have to take wilderness trips or drugs to experience your ecological self. Artists and writers also deliver this awareness through evoking connection with the natural world. The large literature from the lyric poets such as Walt Whitman, Tennyson, Keats, as well as more modern poets and writers such as Gary Snyder, Annie Dillard, Mary Oliver, Wendell Berry, and Barry Lopez, powerfully communicate the experience of ecological self-hood. Whether you find this consciousness through literature or in wilderness, the key is a sense of reverence and respect for the natural world, "a profound courtesy, an unalloyed honesty" to use Barry Lopez's (1990, p. 49) words. This respect means seeing nature less as a commodity and more as a teacher, less as property and more as a shrine. Whether people develop their ecological self through sensitive reading of the lyric poets, or gardening, or meditating in a temple, or hiking to the peak of a mountain, they are changed in several ways:

1. Cognition: A heightened sensitivity toward information about the well-being of other people, species, and ecosystems.
2. Emotion: Feelings of sympathy, caring, empathy, and belonging toward other people, species, and ecosystems.
3. Motivation: A willingness to act on behalf of the well-being of other people, species, and ecosystems (Bragg, 1996).

Most importantly for the planetary predicament, development of one's ecological self leads to environmentally appropriate behaviors, not out of a sense of self-sacrifice or self-denial, but out of a sense of love and common identity. In Naess' words:

> We need environmental ethics, but when people feel they unselfishly give up, even sacrifice, their interest in order to show love for nature, this is probably in the long run a treacherous basis for conservation. Through identification they may come to see their own interest served by conservation, through genuine self-love, love of a widened and deepened self. (Naess, 1988, p. 43)

(The same point about the possible ineffectiveness of altruistic appeals was discussed earlier in Chapter 4).

ECOPSYCHOLOGY

The ecological self is a key focus of an emerging field called **ecopsychology**, the study of synergistic relations between planetary and personal well-being. The term *ecopsychology* was first coined by Theodore Roszak (1992), who argued that alienation from nature and from other people flourishes in cities. Modern psychiatry has contributed to this alienation by ignoring the most primal part of the psyche: the **ecological unconscious**—"the living records of cosmic evolution, tracing back to distant initial conditions in the history of time" (Roszak, 1992, p. 320). This emphasis on the early, prehuman memories in the unconscious gives an "inherent sense of environmental reciprocity" so that "when the Earth hurts, we hurt with it" (Roszak, 1992, p. 308). Roszak, a historian and social critic, also popularized the term *counterculture* (1969), which shares elements of ecopsychology by emphasizing human spirituality and reconnection with nature. A central feature of ecopsychology is that one must recover the child's enchanted sense of the world, the deeply rooted sense of ethical responsibility to the planet and to other people. In this way, ecopsychology resembles the **deep ecology** movement in philosophy, which emphasized the inherent value of other beings and nature as a whole (Naess, 1985, 1990).

For many ecopsychologists and deep ecologists, the cosmos is a single organism, with feeling, intelligence, and soul. Human beings are born knowing this, but in Western civilization, children are taught otherwise. To Piaget and other developmental psychologists who followed, animism represents an immature and confused stage of cognitive development. To many ecopsychologists on the other hand, animism represents an earlier and wiser stage of cognitive development that should be cultivated, rather than dismissed (Gebhard, Nevers, & Billman-Mahecha, 2003).

The view of a living cosmos reflects the thinking of astrophysicist James Lovelock and biologist Lynn Margulis (Lovelock, 1979). Their **Gaia** (pronounced Guy-ya) **hypothesis** proposed that the Earth is a living system:

The atmosphere, the oceans, the climate, and the crust of the Earth are regulated at a state comfortable for life because of the behavior of living organisms. Specifically, the Gaia hypothesis says that the temperature, oxidation state, acidity, and certain aspects of the rocks and waters are at any time kept constant, and that this homeostasis is maintained by active feedback processes operated automatically and unconsciously by the biota. Solar energy sustains comfortable conditions for life. The conditions are only constant in the short term and evolve in synchrony with the changing needs of the biota as it evolves. Life and its environment are so closely coupled that evolution concerns Gaia, not the organisms or the environment taken separately. (Lovelock, 1990, p. 19)

In other words, the system of living organisms (the biota) is so intricately tied to inorganic systems through feedback loops and homeostasis that the earth's entire organic–inorganic system can be considered a living being. Lovelock and Margulis named this living system "Gaia" after the Greek goddess of the Earth. Their subsequent discussions with other scientists led them to emphasize the changing features of Gaia, noting that the evolution of life forms has undergone large periods of homeostasis, sprinkled by quantum leaps of change, so that homeostasis is a relative, not an absolute principle. The central feature of Gaia, however, still holds: that "there is no clear distinction anywhere on the Earth's surface between living and non-living matter" (Lovelock, 1990, p. 40). Lovelock advocated for a discipline called geophysiology that would study the earth's systems as a single living organism. From this perspective, environmental problems are symptoms of Gaia's disease: the "carbon dioxide fever" of global warming; "the acid indigestion" of pollution; "the dermatologists' dilemma" of ozone depletion.

Seeing the earth as a living being helps people identify with its well-being. However, Lovelock also states that:

It is the health of the planet that matters, not that of some individual species of organisms. This is where Gaia and the environmental movements, which are concerned first with the health of people, part company. [Environmental problems] are real and potentially serious hazards but mainly to the people and ecosystems of the First World—from a Gaian perspective, a region that is clearly expendable. It was buried beneath glaciers, or was icy tundra, only 10,000 years ago. (Lovelock, 1990, p. xvi)

Thus, Gaia will go on. If "her" systems take a sudden turn for the worse (worse to humans that is), other species will evolve to fill available niches, whether or not humans survive. Human existence is thoroughly dependent upon the current balance of Gaia's regulatory systems; human survival is certainly not assured.

Ecopsychology's claim that humans are born with a sense of unity with the ecological world is paralleled by E. O. Wilson's **biophilia hypothesis** (1984; Kellert & Wilson, 1993), "the innate tendency to focus on life and lifelike processes" (p. 1); see also Chapter 9). Wilson and other scientists have argued that human survival on the planet will require that people recognize this affinity for life that is so deeply a part of all of us. Ecopsychologists urge people to recognize Gaia and biophilia and thereby realize their ecological self.

In sum, some of the key tenets of ecopsychology are:

1. The core of the human mind is the ecological unconscious, repression of which causes a collusive madness; to heal, people must become aware of their fundamental, primal connection to their ecological home by recovering the repressed ecological unconscious (Glendinning, 1994; Shepard, 1998).
2. The ecological unconscious contains a record of cosmic evolution, connecting people to all other life-forms.
3. There is a reciprocal relationship between planetary and personal well-being, such that as one is healed, so is the other. In this healing, people will find ways to design small scale social institutions and personal empowerment that nurture ecological selves, and withdraw people from the "gargantuan urban-industrial culture" that destroys the ecosystem along with the psyche (Roszak, 1992).
4. Disconnection from the ecological self leads to overconsumption, a form of narcissism in which people overidentify with the small personal self that tries to meet unmet spiritual and intrinsic needs with extrinsic material goods (Kanner & Gomes, 1995; Kasser, 2009b).
5. Through ecologically based transcendent experience, people can learn to reclaim their ecological selves. Transcendent experiences of ecological connections are induced through a variety of techniques, including shamanic rituals (Gray, 1995), perceptual practice (Sewell, 1995), horticultural therapy (Clinebell,

1996), community restoration (Shapiro, 1995), structured group process (Macy & Brown, 1998), mindful contact with nature (Chard, 1994; Cohen, 1997; Swanson, 1995, 2001) and wilderness trips (Harper, 1995).

Thus, from the perspective of ecopsychology, environmental problems are not so much a crisis of technology as they are a crisis of insight (Fisher, 2002). When people mistake social or bureaucratic identity for their core sense of self, they quite naturally abuse the environment with which they feel no identification, connection, or empathy. However, through a deeper inquiry into their true interdependence with other people and other species, people may come to a more intelligent, deeper relationship to the ecosphere, which gives a sense of common identification. When people act from the ecological self, they do not have to **try** to make environmentally responsible choices. Instead, choices are naturally less intrusive, more sensitive, and less toxic because people appreciate the larger context, and they care about those whose well-being their behavior affects. Recent empirical evidence supports this claim: When people construe themselves as interdependent, rather than independent, they show more ecological concern, more cooperation over resources, and report more environmentally friendly behaviors (Arnocky, Stroink, & DeCicco, 2007).

Evaluating Ecopsychology: The Measurement Problem

Ecopsychologists tend to be clinicians, therapists, and philosophers, rather than scientists, in part because ecopsychology looks at aspects of human experience that are difficult to measure. This measurement problem is notable because academic psychologists define psychology as the scientific study of behavior and mental life (see Chapter 1). Scientific methodology enables hypothesis testing under controlled conditions with empirical observations, observations that are typically quantified (Banaji & Crowder, 1989). Consequently, ecopsychology is often ignored by mainstream psychologists and even treated with contempt by some (Beringer, 2003).

This division between ecopsychologists and other psychologists working on environmental problems is another version of the scientist–practitioner split that often fuels debates in psychology. Although psychology is taught in higher education as a science, the majority of psychologists are working on applied problems, rather than gathering data and testing hypothesis. Unfortunately, the scientist–practitioner split draws attention away from ecopsychology, so that it is not well represented in most discussions of the psychology of environmental problems. For example, one academic psychologist argued that:

There are many psychologists working in the environmental arena who have serious reservations about ... ecopsychology ... which draws from, in part, very mixed popular culture, new age, anti-psychiatry, and analytic and psychoanalytic roots, and which increasingly has a strong clinical, counseling, and often spiritual emphasis and application. (Reser, 2003, p. 170)

While we certainly do not agree that drawing on clinical and qualitative work with a spiritual emphasis should diminish the value of ecopsychology, we are glad to see new empirical research measuring the ecological self. Research may empirically validate some of the claims of ecopsychologists, and thus put it in more direct view of the research scientists (namely *conservation psychologists*; see Chapter 1). Although measurement has benefits and drawbacks, we believe that the psychology of environmental problems will progress as measurement tools are developed for what was previously believed to be unmeasurable. On the other hand, as trained experimental psychologists, we know the limits of measurement, and believe it important to remember that whenever something gets measured, something else gets missed. When something is quantified, scientists often assume it is understood, and thereby fall into what ecopsychologists have labeled the reductionist trap: missing deeper understandings because a concept has been reduced to a number. With this caveat, we find the following measures potentially valuable for exploring some of the claims of ecopsychology.

Verbal measures consist of a series of statements with which respondents indicate degree of agreement:

1. Environmental Identity scale (EID; Clayton, 2003a), a self-report survey of 24 items that measures "a sense of connection to some part of the non-human natural environment, based on history, emotional attachment and/or similarity" (p. 45). The EID scores correlate with values of self-transcendence, collectivism, moral obligation toward the environment, and reported environmental behavior.
2. Connectedness to Nature scale (CNS; Mayer & Frantz, 2004, 2005), a 14-item, self-report survey that measures emotional connections to the natural world. CNS scores correlate with New Environmental Paradigm (NEP) scores (see Chapter 2), identity as an environmentalist, ecological behavior, and

subjective well-being. CNS scores decrease when people are put in a laboratory situation with a mirror that draws attention to the personal self (Frantz, Mayer, Norton, & Rock, 2005) and increase after experiences in natural settings (Mayer, Frantz, Bruehlman-Senecal, & Dolliver, 2008).

3. The Nature Relatedness scale (NR; Nisbet, Zelenski, & Murphy, 2008), a 21-item, self-report scale that measures thoughts, feelings, and experiences people have with nature. NR scores correlate with proenvironmental behavior, NEP scores, and time spent in nature.

4. The Nature Inclusiveness Measure (NIM; St. John & MacDonald, 2007), a 30-item, self-report scale that measures experiences of being unified with nature and concern about its protection. NIM scores correlate with an expanded sense of self, identification as an environmentalist, and mental and spiritual well-being.

Nonverbal measures: Recall that ecopsychologists claim that the ecological self is unconscious, a deep understanding that is forgotten as people are socialized to industrialized modern life. The unconscious ecological self may be called a "primitive belief" (Dunlap, Van Liere, Mertig, & Jones, 2000) because people are not often asked to articulate it, so they find it difficult to explicitly respond to questions about it. For this reason, nonverbal measures may be more useful for tapping the ecological self. Two measures have been developed to quantify the concept using noverbal means:

1. The Inclusion of Nature in Self (INS) scale, shown in Figure 10.2, measures how connected people feel with nature.

Please circle the picture below that best describes your relationship with the natural environment. How interconnected are you with nature?

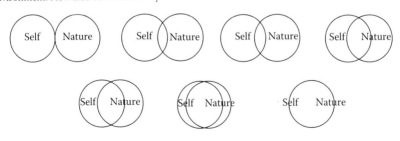

Figure 10.2 Nature and self: Pick the pair that best describes your relationship with nature. (Reprinted from Schultz, P.W. (2002). *The Psychology of Sustainable Development*, Kluwer, New York. With permission.)

This measure correlates with NEP scores, biocentrism, and self-reported environmental behaviors (Schultz, 2000, 2002b).

2. The Implicit Association Test (IAT; Schultz, Shriver, Tabanico, & Khazian, 2004; Schultz & Tabanico, 2007). To measure the implicit quality of the ecological self, participants are presented with a word such as "car" or "animal," and asked to decide whether these words are more like "nature" or "built," and more like "me" or "not me." Reaction times to each question are recorded. By comparing response rates on a long series of these types of questions, participants' implicit connection with nature is measured. The speed with which people associated "me" and "nature" positively correlates with biospheric concerns and negatively correlates with egoistic concerns.

All of these measures offer empirical support for the ecopsychologists' claim that environmentally responsible behavior comes from, or at least with, a sense of connection and concern for the well-being of the natural world. Work has also demonstrated that the ecological self isn't necessarily very conscious, a point that the ecopsychologists made with the term *ecological unconscious*.

In spite of ambivalent receptions from environmental psychologists (e.g., Reser, 1995, 2003), ecopsychology is a flourishing field with an online, peer-reviewed journal,* as well as ongoing newsletters and information resources;† graduate programs (Naropa University, Project NatureConnect); methods for developing the ecological self (Cohen, 1993, 1997; Kahn, 1999; Swanson, 2001; Thomashow, 1995); presentations at professional conferences, and a growing number of practitioners.‡ We believe ecopsychology will continue to flourish because it speaks to deeply felt experiences that people have in relationship to the natural world. Ecopsychology offers therapeutic insights into wilderness experiences, which often draws young people who experience benefits from outdoor recreation (see discussion of wilderness therapy in Chapter 9). Ecopsychology makes an important contribution to clinical psychology by expanding the practice of psychotherapy to places outside offices and hospitals into gardens and wilderness settings (see also Chapter 8), and **ecotherapy** is garnering increased professional attention (Buzzell & Chalquist, 2009).

---

* See http://www.liebertpub.com/eco
† For example, http://www.ecopsychology.org/journal/ezine/gatherings.html (also see http://www.ecopsychology.net/ and http://www.thoughtoffering.blogs.com/ecotherapy/)
‡ See http://www.ecopsychology.org/people.html

Furthermore, ecopsychology's claims have been endorsed by mainstream psychologists, even if they do not know about or trust some of ecopsychology's techniques. For instance, with regard to the point that human beings are distressed when ecosystems are distressed, clinical psychologists are urged to take clients' anxiety about ecological problems seriously, rather than assuming that it is displaced anxiety (White, 1998). Ecotherapists are conceptualizing new ways of "waking up to nature" in the counseling session (Milton, 2009). And as we have seen elsewhere in this text (Chapters 8 and 9), evidence is accumulating for the therapeutic effects of mindful contact with nature (Frumkin, 2001; Irvine & Warber, 2002; Mind Week Report, 2007). Contact with nature also correlates with a sense of humor and psychological well-being (Herzog & Strevey, 2008).

As ecopsychology continues to grow, it will likely develop a more critical perspective, examining its contradictions and limitations (Fisher, 2002). For example, one thorny theoretical issue is that it is sometimes easier to empathize with nonhuman species and ecosystems than with other people. Consider the ecopsychological aim to help people "think like mountains" (Seed et al., 1988). It is worth asking whether people should first think about oppressed humans:

> There is a blind spot in ecopsychology because the field is limited by its Eurocentric perspective, in the same way that the environmental movement as a whole has been blind to environmental racism.... Why is it so easy for ... people to think like mountains and not be able to think like people of color? (Anthony, 1995, pp. 264, 273)

We depart from some ecopsychologists' skepticism about the value of empirical research: "The challenge for ecopsychology is ... to give up psychology's attachment to the various forms of objectivism" (Fisher, 2002, p. 32). In contrast, as trained experimental psychologists, we believe that looking at empirical evidence is one useful way of evaluating a set of ideas, although certainly not the only way. We value not only scientific data, but also experiential data (Davis, 1996). We believe both are crucial for understanding how to build a stronger ecopsychological perspective and thus a sustainable world.

Biodiversity from an Ecopsychological Perspective

In 2008, debate over the Endangered Species Act (ESA) erupted when the George W. Bush Administration enacted a "midnight rule" that

Reprinted from Rhymes with Orange © Hilary B. Price, King Features Syndicate. With permission.

significantly weakened the law by ruling that federal agencies do not have to consult with Fish and Wildlife biologists on actions that could endanger species (Protections in peril, 2008). The ESA is one of the world's toughest set of environmental regulations, making it illegal for U.S. citizens to engage in any practices that endanger a species, such as buying, selling, hunting, killing, collecting, or injuring them (see also Chapter 4). Species listed as threatened or endangered by the Fish and Wildlife Service or the National Marine Fisheries Service are thereby legally protected. Moreover, the law also makes it illegal to engage in habitat destruction, which is why the listing of the Northern Spotted Owl in 1990 and wild salmon in 1992 by the Fish and Wildlife Service infuriated countless loggers and fishermen. Consequently, extractive industries continue to lobby Congress to amend the ESA to take economic considerations into account in the classification of endangered species.

The 2008 ruling would have allowed each federal agency to determine for itself if its projects (such as building highways, dams, or other constructions) would pose a threat to species, rather than being required to get clearance from the Fish and Wildlife biologists who frequently recommend modification. The state of California immediately filed suit, joining the Center for Biological Diversity, Greenpeace, and Defenders of Wildlife, claiming that the new rules threatened endangered wildlife and are illegal because they gut the ESA. Observers believe the rule change was motivated by oil drilling Alaska, where the polar bear is threatened by melting ice caps caused by climate change (Protections in peril, 2008; Cart, 2008). Fortunately, the Obama Administration reversed the ruling early in 2009.

Reprinted from © John Deering, Creators Syndicate. With permission.

Debate over changing the ESA bring us to the heart of ecopsychology. Should species be protected for their economic and utilitarian features, or simply because they have an inherent right to exist, as deep ecologists argued (Naess, 1990)? From an ecopsychological perspective, the planet's diverse species are precious in their own right, and saving them from extinction is crucial. As discussed in Chapter 1, however, the planet is losing species at a rate that experts call mind-boggling. Humans are watching the greatest episode of extinction ever to occur since they have been on the planet (Wilson, 2006). Current estimates range from 13 to 40 per day. At this rate, half of the worlds species will vanish by the end of this century, and one-fifth will vanish by 2030 (Miller, 2007). Scientists have only catalogued about 1.4 million species; estimates of how many species exist vary from 10 million to 80 million. Since no one knows how many species exist before they are destroyed, the losses are literally incalculable.

Why should anybody care about the end of a species that people don't even know about? With 80 million (or even 10 million) you might conclude there are plenty to spare. Variations in answers to this question reveal the particular vantage point of the ecopsychological perspective. Most frequently, lawmakers and scientists give answers in economic, and thus, anthropocentric terms (see the discussion of *real costs* in Chapter 5). Even back in the early 1990s, financial estimates were staggering:

Forests provide the following economic services: gene pools (including wild plants exported for $24 billion in 1991); water regulation and flood control (estimated in India alone to be worth $72 billion); watersheds which reduce soil erosion (worth $6 billion a year in lost hydropower due to siltation of reservoirs); fish (the Pacific Northwest salmon industry alone is worth $1 billion); climate control, through mitigation of greenhouse gases and carbon storage (worth $3.7 trillion a year) and recreation (estimated in the U.S. to be worth more than timber, grazing, mining and other commodities). Wood, then, which is extracted with unsustainable procedures, is astronomically expensive. A mature forest tree in India, for example, is estimated to be worth $50,000. The real cost of a hamburger from cattle raised on cleared rainforest is $200. And a wild Chinook salmon from the Columbia River is estimated to be worth $2150 to future sports and commercial fishers. (Durning, 1993, p. 21.)

Even if biodiversity is not translated into monetary terms, most tropical forest advocates argue that species should be saved because of their as yet unknown utility to humans and for their potential contributions to meeting future human needs. For example, tropical forests are essential as sources of new foods, pharmaceutical medicines, and energy products such as green gasoline, as well as important regulators of climate and producers of the global oxygen supply (Miller, 2007).

Ecopsychologists would give a different answer, one that is based on their shared perspective with deep ecologists:

All things in the biosphere have an equal right to live and blossom and to reach their own individual forms of unfolding and self-realization within the larger Self-realization. This basic intuition is that all organisms and entities in the ecosphere, as parts of the interrelated whole, are equal in intrinsic worth. (Devall & Sessions, 1985, p. 67)

Species are important to save, not by virtue of what they can do for humans, but because they are part of an intricate ecosystem to which humans belong but do not own. And that ecosystem represents the larger ecological self. For example, trees don't just have ecological functions, they are spiritually significant (Sommer, 2003). People worship trees in myth, song, poetry, and religion because they identify with them and love them from a deeper place than their immediate physical functions of providing shade, oxygen, or commodities. In this way, ecopsychologists join deep ecologists in arguing that ecological health is not just about saving human civilization, but more profoundly about expanding human consciousness to remember its deep identity with the whole of the natural world.

Emotional Dimensions of Ecopsychology

As two conservation psychologists noted in the introduction to their volume on environmental identity, passions run strong around environmental issues:

> Because we live far apart, we meet to exchange new ideas and enjoy the camaraderie of collaboration. One evening, over dinner at a vegetarian restaurant in Ann Arbor, Michigan, we discussed the powerful way that fairness and identity interact in environmental conflict. After dinner we saw our ideas crystallized with bracing directness in a graffiti exchange on the wall of the women's restroom. The first comment admonished: "eat organic—no poison food. Love Earth—don't poison your home." A crude response jeered; "Eat shit you tree hugging faggot." People are impassioned about environmental issues, their environmental beliefs can affect other aspects of who they are, and environmental positions perceived as different than one's own can elicit a violent reaction. (Clayton & Opotow, 2003, p. 1)

The ardor that human beings feel toward wildlife issues has even been mentioned in an environmental law textbook. Introducing a discussion of the Endangered Species Act, the author notes that peoples' relationship to

> wildlife taps the deepest wellsprings of human emotion and behavior... . It is a source of inspiration and art, recorded from the Paleolithic cave works to the contemporary cartoons of Gary Larson. It is the font and fodder of religion, as no one would doubt who has seen images of the spotted owl nailed to the cross in the heart of logging country in Forks, Washington. It is the crucible that forges the best thinking about human ethics and morality.

It is the subject of a worldwide network in trade that is staggering in its scope, avariciousness, and destructiveness. And it is the arena in which some of the most passionate performances of contemporary environmental conflict are played out, in the dangerous and violent confrontations to protect marine mammals at sea, in the no-holds-barred sabotage and other "monkeywrenching" activities on land, and in the courageous and lonely undercover work necessary to beat the poachers at their own game. (Rodgers, 1994, pp. 993–995)

In other words, connection with wildlife draws energy from the deepest core of human feeling. The religious and spiritual dimensions of protecting biodiversity are not only recognized by ecopsychologists, but by experts in law and forestry. Those spiritual dimensions lead people to safeguard the Grand Canyon, the Acropolis in Athens, even Central Park in New York City, which would otherwise be seen as "economic wastes of top-value real estate" (Myers, 1984, p. 352).

Spiritual passions feed people on both sides of the issue. Members of the Earth Liberation Front, who chain themselves to trees and risk bodily harm to themselves and others, express their deepest conviction about the importance of saving wilderness, just as those who nail a spotted owl to a cross communicate their similarly intense, though opposite, convictions. Ecopsychologists focus on the spiritual dimensions of environmentalism, but like religion, strong passion can also grow into rigid, unbending zealousness, as this description of "wildernism" from an antienvironmentalist suggests:

Wildernism provides most if not all the characteristics of a standard religion as recognized by scholars of the subject: a sense of distinctiveness and community, of awe and cosmic unity, standards of morality and irreproachable beliefs, rituals, tests of faith and grounds for expulsion, a central dogma that must be protected and so on. The adherents of wildernism are convinced of their moral and ethical superiority, are blind to reason on the questions of dogma, and feel that they have an exclusive hold on the truth. It all adds up to religious behavior, and one does not expect objective rationality from religious behavior, one expects devotion, and at the extreme, zealotry. (Arnold, 1993, p. 44)

Unfortunately, loving and identifying with nature doesn't always lead to responsible environmental actions. You probably know people who fly long distances to take wilderness vacations, for example. What is required is not emotional passion, but emotional intelligence: humility as well as passion, listening as well as speaking, negotiating as well as lobbying, silence as well as speaking out.

On the other hand, empirical evidence does show that emotional affinity can be a powerful predictor of proenvironmental behavior (Vining & Ebreo, 2002), as is indignation about insufficient protection (Kals, Schumacher, & Montada, 1999). Emotional affinity results from positive experiences in wilderness settings, especially in the company of friends and close relations (see also Chapter 9). People's willingness to engage with the natural world is related to their emotional connection with nature and their environmental identity (as measured by EID scores, see above; Hinds & Sparks, 2008). When emotional connection to nature combines with righteous anger concerning insufficient protection and guilt over one's own inadequate efforts, people are more likely to vow to protect the environment (Kals & Maes, 2002).

Direct encounters with nature are often required for deeper emotional responses and spiritual understandings. In fact, a large majority of people report having had intense, spiritual experiences, known as **peak experiences**, in response to the beauty of nature; these occurrences are marked by feelings of contact with the sacred, universal harmony, or feelings of being deeply moved (Davis, 1998). People usually cannot feel the full depth of their ecological being, nor their accompanying feelings, from information on paper, unless the writing is particularly gifted. For an example of both the importance of direct experience *and* the power of great writing, consider the words of Terry Tempest Williams, as she testified before the U.S. Congress, urging them to protect the Pacific yew tree:

I am asking you as members of this subcommittee, as my lawmakers, my guardians of justice, for one favor. Will you please go visit the trees? See them for yourself—these beautiful healing trees growing wildly, mysteriously, in the draws of our ancient forests, and then go visit the adjacent forests, and then go visit the adjacent clear-cuts, walk among the wreckage, the slash piles, forage through the debris, and look again for the Pacific yew. Think about health. Think about the women you love—our bodies, the land—and think about what was once rich and dense and green with standing. Think about how our sacred texts may be found in the forest as well as in the Psalms, and then, my dear lawmakers, we ask you to make your decision with your heart, what you felt in the forest in the presence of a forgotten language. And if you cannot make a decision from this place of heart, from this place of compassionate intelligence, we may have to face as a people the horror of this nation, that our government and its leaders are heartless. (Williams, 1994, pp. 130–131)

From this perspective, ecological damage stems from limited experiences of the complexity, beauty, magic, and awesome power of the natural world. When human hearts and spirits are closed down because a culture emphasizes separation and autonomy, consumption and fashion, convenience and efficiency, the environment will suffer. Housed in separate homes, often not even knowing their neighbors, much less the natural physical world that surrounds them, people maintain psychological separation from each other and from the ecosystem of which they are an integral part. Decisions about how much timber should be harvested out of ancient forests in the Pacific Northwest are made in Federal offices, located in concrete cities thousands of miles away, based on abstract logic and knowledge from video screens, rather than direct experience. But humans will need more than severed intellects, no matter how information-rich they are, to make wise decisions about the sustainability of the planet. Decisions must also be based on a deeper identification with the natural world, a sense of the interconnectedness of all people and species, and a sense of awe for the exquisite beauty of creation. These sensitivities just can't be produced in an office, with symbolic information as our only experience. (Of course, the same can be argued about decisions promoting regulations or protections.)

To assume that logic and rationality are the only bases for intelligent decisions is to continue what one leading neurologist (Damasio, 1994a, 1994b) has called, in the title of his book, *Descartes' Error*. Without essential anatomical knowledge, Descartes believed that the body and mind were separated into two dichotomous realms, the body housing the emotions and the mind housing rational intellect. Yet modern research shows the complex interconnections between emotional and cognitive centers in the brain, making intelligent decision making dependent upon emotion and passion. To not have access to feelings is least as pernicious for rationality as excessive affect (Slovic, Finucane, Peters, & MacGregor, 2004). "Cognition would be rudderless without the accompaniment of emotion, just as emotion would be primitive without the participation of cognition" (Davidson, 2000, p. 91). Without emotions, people do not feel deeply connected to anything, including their place. The importance of feelings about the local environment brings us to consider the ecopsychology of place.

The Ecopsychology of Place

Have you ever felt a deep sense of belonging, love, and perfection in a particular place? Ecopsychologists underscore the power of place attachment (Roberts, 1998; Thomashow, 1998). Human beings experience the world in terms of different places, an observation that has given rise to **place theory** (Altman & Low, 1992; Porteous, 1990; Proshansky, Fabian, & Kaminoff, 1993; Relph, 1976; Seamon, 1979, 1984; Tuan, 1974). Some places provide deep meaning and emotional bonding. People develop attachment when they interact with the particulars of a place, its features, people, and landscape, which leads to a sense of identity with it (Bott, Cantrill, & Myers, 2003; Hill, 2003; Roberts, 1998). Place attachment is accompanied by feelings of stability and security (Brown & Perkins, 1992), a sense of mystery and connection (Frederickson & Anderson, 1999), and anger or grief when the place is threatened (Rogen, O'Connor, & Horwitz, 2005). Even dangerous places, for example Gaza, elicit strong attachment to home and place because of the religious and community meanings they provide (Billig, 2006).

Places are not only landscapes and built environments, they are also social networks (Relph, 1976). Place attachment and community are reciprocal processes. For example, on the Hawaiian island of Moloka'i, "people create places of belonging for themselves from their experiences on site and the social networks that they form. A community emerges when individuals attempt to sustain meaningful places" (Yazawa, 2008, p. 146). In other words, places are not only locations, they are people with stories and meaningful history together. Conversely, natural disasters exert their psychological damage by disrupting both place and social communities. Survivors must rebuild not only their neighborhoods, but also their social networks. Emergency foreign aid often hampers community recovery, if local leaders are disempowered by foreign experts, who quickly appear with material resources, but do not promote repair of social networks (Diaz & Dayal, 2008).

Sacred Places Spiritual experiences in special places often occur in wilderness settings, where people feel a sense of perfection, meaning, and connection with something larger than themselves (Frederickson & Anderson, 1999). "Sacred spaces evoke strong emotional ties of commitment and connectedness, a sense of history, belonging, and rootedness" (Mazumdar & Mazumdar, 1993, p. 237). When places are the site of rituals, use of artifacts, storytelling, and frequent visits, people experience them as sacred (Mazumdar & Mazumdar, 2004). Sacred places need harmonious group dynamics, that is, a feeling of

318 • The Psychology of Environmental Problems: Psychology for Sustainability

trust and belonging to others who share that space (Frederickson & Anderson, 1999).

A recent application of Gestalt theory to the psychology of place argues that places become meaningful when they promote Gestalts: a perception of balance, fit, coherence, and order (Schroeder, 2007). People choose to be in these types of places, and become emotionally attached to them, because the Gestalt experience of fit elicits the perception of beauty and perfection. These places give rise to moral responsibility (Tuan, 1993). Thus emotional attachment to place brings with it caring and moral obligation. For these reasons, place attachment can predict environmental concern better than demographic variables such as age, gender, and occupation (Vorkinn & Riese, 2001).

Psychological damage is caused by loss of place attachment in modern urban and corporate life. When people relocate every few years, or rush through their vacation travel without experiencing silence, rootedness, ritual, and belonging, or experience regular life trapped in the daily rush of commuting to work and back, how is it possible to experience belonging to one's place? Living as a tourist makes it difficult to develop concern and responsibility for one's environment (Gustafson, 2001). That is why one feature of sustainability will be immersion in the particulars of a place. When people participate fully in the geography and community of a particular place, they are more likely to feel accountable for its health and find ways to protect it (Driver, Dustin, Baltic, Elsner, & Peterson, 1996; Kelly & Hosking, 2008).

CONCLUSIONS

The basic principle to be drawn from both historical Gestalt theory and contemporary ecopsychology is that ordinary experiences of people as separate autonomous beings is inaccurate and destructive. Recognizing embeddedness in the larger ecosphere requires a perceptual shift (emphasized by Gestalt psychology) and deeper experience (emphasized by ecopsychology) as a bigger, more connected, more inclusive self. This shift is more than a cognitive event—it is also a profoundly emotional and/or spiritual event. One feels identified with the planet and with other species and peoples on an experiential, rather than simply an informational, level. This shift is more powerful, and also more ineffable than simply taking in new knowledge. It is less about information and more about identification. Less of a decision and more of a dropping into a fuller experience of oneself. Less about behaving, and more about being. Less about knowing and more about appreciating.

Thus the ecological self is an expanded, more gracious, more spacious sense of self, realized through direct experience.

An important element of direct experience is silence, either through solitude or as shared silence. Silence is often scarce in our modern world, which is filled with entertainment, information, and the noise of urban environments, not to mention the busy brains of contemporary people. Fritz Perls would have endorsed the importance of silence, as he frequently noted the ways in which head "chatter" blocks fuller experience of wholeness. As this experience rarely occurs while people are chatting, people are more likely to "fall into it" when they become very quiet, as in Deborah's experience in the meditation hall described earlier. When quiet, senses open, perceptions grow richer, acuity sharpens, and people recognize the subtleties and richness of the natural world, subtleties missed when thinking or talking. Rituals can enhance the experience of nature, for example, singing or chanting to celebrate the rising of the full moon, gatherings to mark the changing of the seasons (such as equinox and solstice); or simply taking time to go outside to appreciate a summer rain, a snowfall, a sunset, or a sunrise.

It is not difficult to imagine that most people enjoy—even crave—these kinds of experiences, yet find them difficult to schedule into increasingly busy lives. As the field of horticultural therapy demonstrates, growing gardens is a healing activity (Clinebell, 1996).* Going for a walk, relating to a landscape or a nonhuman being is inherently restorative (see Chapter 8). Ecopsychologists would simply remind people to expand these activities into experiences in which to learn about and appreciate the biotic world (without trying to manipulate or change it) and other animals (without owning them).

As the larger ecological self claims more of one's existence, the environmentally depleting, smaller self claims less. People will want to commit themselves to more environmentally appropriate actions and activism, not from a sense of guilt or moral reasoning, but out of a sense of love and devotion. As people identify themselves with a larger unity, environmental activism becomes a natural extension of the self (Nisbet et al., 2008; Thomashow, 1995).

From the holistic vantage point, the consumer culture is a sign of spiritual affliction; it arises from and feeds on small, segmented selves, impoverished and hungry for something to fill the void (Kanner & Gomes, 1995; Kasser, 2009a; see also Chapter 4). Our driven, materialistic society runs on a core experience of emptiness, and people use

---

* See http://www.ahta.org/

consumer products to try to satiate that inner vacuum. Thus, over-consumption is caused by greed, craving, and lack of understanding of truer selves. When people experience their ecological selves, how-ever, they are filled with a sense of perfection and completion. They stop craving, wanting, scheming, worrying. They rejoice in the incred-ible beauty of the world and their shared identity. They don't have to be *trained* to stop overconsuming because experiencing the ecological self replaces that inner craving with a deeply satisfying sense of whole-ness and abundance. From this perspective, the way out of the shopping mall is back into an earlier connection with the natural world, through silence, ritual, art, or simply spending more time outside in biotically rich settings. As all spiritual traditions of the world teach, fulfillment comes with simplicity and quiet awareness, not with material wealth.

This kind of spiritual awakening will also lead to dissatisfaction with the status quo, however, because seeing the larger picture illuminates social injustice, environmental racism, and the suffering of other beings. Feeling connected to the whole means feeling empathy with others who are oppressed by unhealthy environments. Freed from the compulsion of satisfying cravings, people will naturally focus more energy on solv-ing bigger problems, and be naturally drawn to environmental projects that heal both the planet and its various inhabitants. Thus environ-mental identity leads to many forms of community and political action (Kempton & Holland, 2003). Ecotherapists (e.g., Conn, 1995) encour-age their clients to become active in local, regional, national, or global environmental issues, working from a sense of devotion and caring, as well as playfulness and lightness. Since humans are connected to the whole, they are also part of that which appears as "the enemy"—the unconscious guzzling consumer, the advertising executive, the "wise use" advocate, the antienvironmentalist, the slash and burn farmer, or the toxin producer. Social action not only helps solve pressing environ-mental problems, but helps people heal their erroneous separation from each other. As people come into contact with others who do not share their views, remembering their underlying connection, the human bond with each other and with the ecosystem on which all species depend, gives rise to gentle but focused political action. Thus, social engagement is a way to practice basic spiritual values. Holistic psychology illumi-nates a path to both environmental responsibility and compassion for oneself and for the world.

11

PUTTING IT TOGETHER: USING PSYCHOLOGY TO BUILD A SUSTAINABLE WORLD

One day fairly soon we will all go belly up like guppies in a neglected fishbowl. I suggest an epitaph for the whole planet: "We could have saved it, but we were too darn cheap and lazy."

(Kurt Vonnegut, 1990)

If I knew the world would end tomorrow, I would still plant an apple tree today.

(Martin Luther, quoted by Lindberg, 2000, p. 276)

Throughout this book, we have looked at the planet's serious environmental problems and argued that they are really *behavioral problems*, caused by the collective actions of human beings and their underlying thoughts, feelings, and values; thus, the field of psychology is critical for developing and implementing solutions. It seems paradoxical that phenomena such as resource depletion and climate change are considered *environmental* whereas poverty and war are not; such framing helps people distance themselves from environmental problems, as well as from their responsibility for them (Shellenberger & Nordhaus, 2004). Instead, viewing climate change and other environmental challenges as *psychological* leads to insights and solutions not offered via technological or political frames (Mayer & Frantz, 2008). Bringing the behavioral dimension to attention is crucial for solving environmental problems. By applying the psychological principles reviewed in this text, we believe people *can* change in order to address the quickly deteriorating ability of the planet to support human and other life forms. "Yes, we can,"* although it's not clear that we will. Vonnegut may be right.

As we write these words, the unsustainable structures of the world's economic system—markets-based on fossil fuels, unregulated speculation, and conspicuous consumption—are in free fall. In Chapter 1, we discussed how the United States is a major culprit in these trends, particularly because of its massive ecological footprint relative to its population: less than 5% of the world's population consumes more than *one quarter* of the world's fossil fuel resources (Worldwatch Institute, 2008), and generates over 20% of the global greenhouse gases contributing to climate change (Energy information Administration, 2008a). The people and governments of the United States have created a much larger national security issue than international terrorists ever could: climate change and toxic chemicals are much more significant causes of death and suffering, for far greater numbers of citizens, than terrorist attacks (Steffen, 2006). The social, economic and military effects of climate change alone—agricultural and water shortages, migration of refugees, pandemics, and associated extremist uprisings—pose extraordinary national security challenges (CNA, 2007).

Fortunately, or unfortunately, the global economic collapse is providing an unprecedented opportunity and impetus to transition to green industries and economies. Though this transition is producing much hardship and anxiety, cultural (and personal) change doesn't often occur without a crisis to motivate that change (Beddoe et al., 2009). So, we are hopeful. And even after detailing looming ecological catastrophes, we write this concluding chapter at a historical moment of national optimism. After eight distressing years of ravaging environmental regulations by the George W. Bush Administration (Kennedy, 2004), we are excited about the election of President Obama, and grateful for his early legislative efforts. For instance, by signing The American Recovery and Reinvestment Act,† President Obama committed to a radically different economic policy based on "developing clean fuels, modernizing rail transit, pursuing energy efficiency, developing high-mileage electric vehicles, and scaling up electrical generating stations powered by the wind, sun, and heat of the earth" (Schneider, 2009, para. 1, 4). The stimulus package reflects collaborative efforts among environmental, labor, industry, and social organizations known as the Apollo Alliance, "working to catalyze a clean energy revolution that

---

* The campaign slogan for *Barack Obama for President*, 2008.
† Detailed information about the bill and its progress is available at http://www.recovery .gov/

will put millions of [U.S.] Americans to work in a new generation of high-quality, green-collar jobs."*

We are also pleased that psychologists are expanding their research contributions to help solve these issues. *Conservation Psychology* is emerging as an important interdisciplinary investigation into behaviors that promote or detract from environmental health (Clayton & Brook, 2005; Clayton & Myers, 2009; Saunders, 2003). Because human behavior is rooted in institutional structures, scholarship is quickly exploding to illuminate how humans can alter political, economic, social, as well as individual systems to sustain existence on the planet (e.g., Clayton & Myers, 2009; Gifford, 2007; R. Kaplan & S. Kaplan, 2008; Mayer & Frantz, 2008; Moser & Dilling, 2007; Schmuck & Schultz, 2002; Vlek & Steg, 2007). Interdisciplinary collaborations are critical for changing the larger organizations that reinforce and maintain destructive behaviors (Smith, Positano, Stocks, & Shearman, 2009).

It is certainly the case that if future generations are to have a chance at their own potential existence, let alone experience the diverse wonders of the natural world, people will need a robust psychology to help make crucial changes in their behaviors, thoughts, feelings, and values. How to sustain the planet and its myriad life-forms could become psychology's core question, offering an intellectual coherence to a discipline increasingly fragmented by diverse concerns. And just as recognizing the interconnectedness of humans and other species is necessary for creating a sustainable future, understanding the connections between different areas of psychology will enhance its full contribution.

COMPARING THE APPROACHES: PSYCHOLOGICAL INSIGHTS

Each of the psychological perspectives we have discussed provides some understanding of the basis of environmentally destructive behavior, and offers important insights to the project of building a sustainable world. The following summary details some commonalities and general conclusions from the different approaches reviewed in this text.

Contemporary ecological crises can be attributed at least in part to the *Western worldview*, which emphasizes individual human beings' pursuit of private wealth and happiness, and encourages the unrestricted use of natural resources to achieve material gain (Chapter 2). The *Dominant Social Paradigm* (DSP), which has operated for centuries

---

* Quoted from the Apollo Alliance Web site, available at http://apolloalliance.org/about/mission/

324 • The Psychology of Environmental Problems: Psychology for Sustainability

in the West, assumes that nature is robust and regenerative relative to human impact; that humans are the only important species in the biosphere; and that hard work and materialist motives enable people to solve any problems that may arise. Like the *Boomsters* described in Chapter 1, Western views place an implicit trust in the power of human ingenuity and technology to solve environmental problems. Unfortunately, these beliefs and associated behaviors have not only encouraged resource depletion and pollution, but also a set of interlocking difficulties: poverty, homelessness, undernourishment, and warfare (Schmuck & Schultz, 2002).

When people confront the serious dangers of environmental problems, they use *defense mechanisms* to relegate anxiety and other difficult feelings to the *unconscious* (Chapter 3). Let's face it: openly acknowledging the probable collapse of the planet's ecosystems *should* trigger powerful negative feelings, including terror, despair, bewilderment, grief, anger, and so on. As one bumper sticker puts it, "If you're not outraged, you're not paying attention!" Emotional defenses explain how people can know about environmental problems and yet not change their relevant behaviors. People make excuses, fail to notice or take responsibility for what they are doing, and seem apathetic toward their fellow human beings, other species, and the future. Furthermore, personal and corporate levels of denial feed upon each other. Feelings of helplessness can lead to depression and reduced motivation to change (Evans & Stecker, 2004; see also Chapter 8). However, knowing more about one's personal patterns of defenses allows one to be less habitual using them.

Concomitantly, *evolutionary pressures* have created largely *unconscious perceptual* and *cognitive mechanisms* that are adaptive in many circumstances, but can produce faulty information processing that interferes with people's registering and responding to environmental threats (Chapter 7). A dependence on *vision,* coupled with *selective attention* and *sensory adaptation* leads many to ignore invisible or gradually developing conditions such as increasingly polluted environments and a changing climate. Cognitive psychology underscores the tendency of humans to take cognitive and perceptual shortcuts, leading to errors of *oversimplification* and *overgeneralization.* Thus, reasoning processes often disempower citizens in the face of experts, who conceptualize environmental problems and risks differently than the public does. Like psychoanalytic theory, cognitive psychology underscores the importance of staying open to new information, being skeptical about one's assumptions, and being curious about new ways to think about environmental problems. Although people are prone to making cognitive errors in the interest of efficient and rapid processing, when they are alerted to potential errors, they make better judgments about complex situations.

However, because people know much more than they seem willing to act on, information cannot be the only problem. In fact, one of the biggest challenges people have regarding environmental issues is information overload and confusion. Thus, approaches that spotlight behavior change are critical. Behaviorism's focus on behavior in the present, rather than deeper meaning and underlying motivations, is therefore valuable (Chapter 5). Skinner concentrated on immediate situations in which behavior occurs, and extended this principle by arguing that what people do is largely shaped by the previous consequences of their behavior. The behaviorists' emphasis on specification, measurement, and *stimulus control* helps illuminate the *reinforcement contingencies* that signal and maintain environmentally irresponsible behavior.

Yet, because behavior is also rooted in institutional structures, humans must also work toward changing larger organizations that reinforce destructive actions. In contrast to rats in Skinner boxes, people do not behave alone, separated from others. Rather, they behave in families, schools, corporations, neighborhoods, and countries that all have environmentally relevant policies that greatly impact individual behavior. Consequently, social psychologists' focus on the various group influences that affect human behavior in the present is a critical contribution (Chapter 4). Situations subtly or explicitly provide *norms*, communicating what is appropriate or normal in particular settings. Social psychologists would also echo Freud in that unconscious motivations to conform to group behaviors (social norms) or to behave congruently with one's values and beliefs (personal norms) underlie much environmentally relevant behavior. Norms, *roles*, and *reference groups* exert potent influences on what people mistakenly assume to be private, personal views, and conscious choices. Situation-specific constraints can make it difficult (or costly, inconvenient, or awkward) for people to act on their proenvironmental values; thus, it is crucial for psychologists to apply their knowledge and skills for effecting change at institutional and legislative levels, as well as the level of the individual.

In addition to emphasizing behavior in the present, both behavioral and social psychologists highlight the discrepancies between short- and long-term costs–benefits, and relative costs–benefits to one's self versus the interests of the larger group (i.e., *contingency traps* and *social dilemmas*), a critical problem for creating sustainable societies (Gardner & Stern, 2002; Osbaldiston & Sheldon, 2002; Vlek & Steg, 2007). Pressing environmental threats such as climate change represent social dilemmas on multiple levels: They involve decisions about whether or not to profit now at the expense of others, or at the expense of one's self at some future time; they reflect inequities between "haves" and "have nots"; and many individual actions have the greatest impact at distant, less salient locations (Oskamp, 2002). Fortunately, growing evidence about the factors that induce cooperation in social dilemmas (Chapter 10) suggests that when people are aware of the implications of their actions on their cohorts in the dilemma, they behave more cooperatively. Although *proximal cognition* (Chapter 7), leads most people to focus on clear, present, and personal dangers, people can learn to enlarge their *scope of justice* (Chapter 4); that is, to understand and develop concern for others, and assume moral responsibility for other people, species, and ecosystems, both in the present and future (i.e., intergenerational justice; Schmuck & Schultz, 2002).

Although attitudes and values are not strong predictors of behavior, they do have some effect. People with *biocentric values* express concern for the inherent rights and protection of other species (Chapters 4, 9 and 10), and are more likely to engage in proenvironmental behaviors. People who hold biocentric values cooperate more with others, share resources, and take actions to protect other species, landscapes, and natural resources. In contrast, egocentric and materialistic values emphasize personal wealth and status, and are not only associated with less environmental and social concern, but also less happiness and self confidence (Kasser & Ryan, 2001; Ryan et al., 1999).

There is reason to believe that biocentric values are a product of human evolutionary history, as posited by the *biophilia hypothesis* (Wilson, 1984; Chapters 9 and 10). Most people prefer natural over built landscapes (R. Kaplan & S. Kaplan, 1989), and feel an emotional affinity for other species and nature as a whole (Kals, Schumacher, & Montada, 1999). However, one's early experiences with caretakers also impacts both sense of self and experienced interconnection with nature, other species, and the biosphere. *Object Relations theory* (ORT; Chapter 3) helps explain why people might experience that connection differently. Experiences in nature contribute greatly to emotional, physical, cognitive, and social aspects of children's development (Chapter 9), as well as to physical and mental health in both children and adults (Chapter 8). The formation of an *ecological self* (Chapter 10) and the adoption of the *New Environmental Paradigm* (NEP; Chapter 2) often depend on experiences in nature, especially during childhood. The NEP stresses the fragility and limits of the natural world in the face of human activity, and the responsibility of human beings to act more carefully to protect and preserve it. Sustainability requires greater levels and mechanisms of cooperation, both between humans and other species, as well as among human beings themselves.

Human health and well-being are inextricably connected to planetary health (Chapters 6, 8, and 9). Anthropocentric values that emphasize consumption and convenience have led to industrial, agricultural, and social practices that pollute environments and stress human physiological systems to the point of malfunction and disease. Chemical pollutants are especially hazardous to young children, who are not only exposed to greater concentrations of substances, but whose developing biological systems are particularly vulnerable. As a result, *learning disabilities* impacting cognition, emotion, attention, and behavior, as well as *Parkinson's Disease, Alzheimer's Disease*, accelerated aging, and reproductive abnormalities are all increasing in prevalence. Concomitantly, modern urban environments enclose increasing numbers of people in metal and cement structures, with noise, crowding, and pollution replacing fresh air and quiet green spaces. The result is deteriorating human health on physical, mental, and social levels, as well as degradation of the planet. The chronic nature of *environmental stressors* leads to a variety of disorders with adverse outcomes, costly treatments, and great losses in human creativity and well-being. Fortunately, the same environments that are restorative to humans also promote ecological health.

Furthermore, *problem-focused* actions that reduce adverse environmental impacts can mitigate one's experience of stress (Chapter 8). Freud suggested a similar point with his concept of *sublimation* (Chapter 3). Psychoanalytic approaches delineate *emotionally focused strategies* (defenses), and suggest ways for moving beyond defenses. For example, when people allow themselves to experience their feelings, the intensity of those feelings subsides and gives rise to increased energy and creativity for solving environmental problems.

Small changes in environmentally responsible behavior can inspire larger changes through *foot-in-the-door* effects (Chapter 4), or *generalization* (Chapter 5) to other classes of behavior that impact the environment. These perspectives underscore the importance of creating behavior changes that lead to feelings of empowerment. And engaging in proenvironmental behaviors serves as a *model* to other people that can change social norms, thus inspiring change on a broader level (Chapter 4).

The inherent interconnections between human beings and the natural world suggest that environmental problems result from the mistaken belief that humans are separate from each other and from larger ecological systems (Chapter 10). *Gestalt psychology* and *Ecopsychology* acknowledge human embeddedness in the world. By highlighting relationship and wholeness, psychologists working with these models offer a rich set of methods for enhancing human experience of connection with nature and other species, methods that are increasingly being used in *ecotherapy* (Buzzell & Chalquist, 2009). The basic insight they deliver—that people are part of nature, rather than outside it—is a fundamental theme of this book.

Thus, central to our entire discussion of the psychology of environmental problems is the recurring principle of *interconnection*. Just as ecosystem health is based on interactive relationships, so too is sustainable human behavior. Living creatures depend on each other and on the ambient environment; social systems and various institutions (e.g., government, industry, religious, community, educational) interact and are interdependent; and important aspects of human existence reflect values of interconnection (family life, intellectual stimulation and growth, creative expression, and moral and spiritual engagement; Savitz & Weber, 2006).

Because of these overlapping insights, we don't find questions about which psychological approach is best to be particularly helpful. Human behavior is enormously complex and no one subdiscipline can capture everything. It may be easier to immediately focus on information, or emotions, or social settings, or hormones, and each of these explanatory devices is useful at different times. Environmental behavior is multiply determined. For example, when people are asked about their reasons for adopting environmentally relevant household behaviors, they cite a wide variety of reasons, including past experience, role models, altruism, convenience, feelings, values, and rewards (Bamberg, Hunecke, & Blobaum, 2007; Barr, 2007; Dolnicar & Grun, 2008; Hallin, 1995). In this text, we emphasize each perspective's relevance to environmental problems by concentrating on their contributions and utility. We have organized our discussions around theoretical perspectives to make sensible the enormous explosion of recent research. But ecosystems do not care if we spend time debating the relative merits of social or behavioral or cognitive theory, nor which theory wins the most followers. Only *changing individual and collective behaviors* will make any difference to the outcome. Thus, we suggest getting on with using psychology; it matters less what theory you use to act, than that you *choose to act*.

We believe the following six operating principles can help to shift behavior toward *sustainability*; that is, meeting the requirements of current and future generations, while respecting the interconnectedness of environmental, economic, and social factors (e.g., Schmuck & Schultz, 2002). As you will see, these principles are grounded in psychology and connect to theories and research described in previous chapters:

- Visualize healthy ecosystems
- Work with small steps and big ideas
- Think circle instead of line
- Consider ways in which less is more
- Practice conscious consumption
- Act on personal and political levels, especially local community participation

VISUALIZE AN ECOLOGICALLY HEALTHY WORLD

Any serious look at current environmental conditions presents a troubling future. No matter how it is accomplished, sustaining life on the planet will require huge changes in the way human societies are organized and conducted, changes that may not be easy or pleasant (Korten, 2006). For example, whether or not people successfully design and implement sustainable technologies using renewable energy sources, global dependence on fossil fuels will soon end because supply is quickly dwindling. There simply is not enough oil on the planet to forever run the number of automobiles currently produced, much less a car for every Chinese household. The goal of a car in every garage in China would require 80 million barrels of oil a day, much more than what the world produces or will ever produce, since global oil production will peak in the next 10–20 years (Flavin, 2008). Humans will reduce dependence on fossil fuel one way or another, whether by intelligently designing alternative technologies, or fighting over the last remaining reserves with armed conflict. The U.S. militarization of the Middle East is just one of the huge and ugly costs of oil dependency. Modern warfare parallels ecological collapse for its destructive capacity and both bring tremendous suffering.

Do you ever wonder why more people aren't concerned about these issues? Does it seem odd that most people you know appear curiously oblivious about the dangerous path that civilization is on? That they still drive their SUVs with little thought about how doing so supports both international war and climate change? Perhaps you yourself think, "if other people aren't changing their behavior, why should I?" A big part of the public's problem in confronting these issues is "green guilt and ecological overload" (Roszak, 1994). Environmentalists have traditionally disregarded the fear, anxiety, and denial caused by their messages, leading one writer to suggest they should do a "Psychological Impact Statement" whenever they discuss disturbing information (Roszak,

1994, p. 537). Instead of trading on fear, guilt, and despair, ways of tapping into empowerment, joy, and nobility must be found. One model, called **positive psychology**, shifts attention from psychology's historical focus on pathology—what goes wrong with people—toward "human behavior that includes courage, hope, optimism, and creativity, [to] see how these can be fostered and supported" (Csikszentmihalyi, 2004, p. 361; see also Seligman & Csikszentmihalyi, 2000).

We agree that it is critically important to build motivation from a positive, rather than a negative, source. Consider the civil rights movement: "Martin Luther King Jr.'s 'I have a dream' speech is famous because it put forward an inspiring, positive vision that carried a critique of the current moment within it. Imagine how history would have turned out had King given an 'I have a nightmare' speech instead!" (Shellenberger & Nordhaus, 2004, p. 31). Positive images of a healthy environmental future are desperately needed to spur both one's own and others' commitment to solving environmental problems. Consequently, when Deborah found the following passage, she was deeply grateful:

Imagine for a moment a world where cities have become peaceful and serene because cars and buses are whisper quiet, vehicles exhaust only water vapor, and parks and greenways have replaced unneeded urban freeways. OPEC has ceased to function because the price of oil has fallen to five dollars a barrel, but there are few buyers for it because cheaper and better ways now exist to get the services people once turned to oil to provide. Living standards for all people have dramatically improved, particularly for the poor and those in developing countries. Involuntary unemployment no longer exists, and income taxes have largely been eliminated. Houses, even low-income housing units, can pay part of their mortgage costs by the energy they *produce*; there are few if any active landfills; worldwide forest cover is increasing; dams are being dismantled; atmospheric CO2 levels are decreasing for the first time in two hundred years; and effluent water leaving factories is cleaner than the water coming into them. Industrialized countries have reduced resource use by 80% while improving the quality of life. Among these technological changes, there are important social changes. The frayed social nets of Western countries have been repaired. With the explosion of family wage jobs, welfare demand has fallen. The progressive and active union movement has taken the lead to work with business, environmentalists, and government to create "just transitions" for workers as society phases out coal, nuclear energy, and oil. In communities and towns, churches, corporations, and labor groups promote a new living-wage social contract as the least expensive way to ensure the growth and preservation of valuable social capital. (Hawken, Lovins, & Lovins, 1999, pp. 1–2)

When Deborah read this paragraph she thought, now that's worth working for! And she wondered how it might be possible. In their book, *Natural Capitalism*, Hawken and colleagues (1999) detailed myriad examples of how corporations, communities, and individuals were already (more than 10 years ago) accomplishing specific changes in this direction. Their conclusion was that this vision of an ecologically healthy human society is not a futile utopian dream, but a doable possibility, given modern trends in technology: cars that run on fuel cells; factories that restore water while making sturdy, nontoxic products; materials designed for durability rather than mass production; food that is grown organically; and new, nontoxic materials that are stronger than steel and lighter than plastic.

A global network of communities working toward these visions called Transition Towns* provides citizens with tools and strategies for making their communities more sustainable (Hopkins, 2008). Using the principle of positive visioning, Transition Towns enlist community members to act on their imaginings. For example, participants write newspaper articles from the vantage point of the future, highlighting sustainable practices their community will have achieved. One town (Lewes, England) created the *Ecotopian Grapevine Gazette,* which contained "imaginary news stories about events or innovations that had not happened yet . . . written as if they had happened. At the end of each article, [was] the name of someone readers could call and participate in making that story a reality" (Hopkins, 2008, p. 98). Transition Towns use positive experiences and techniques to build community networks, community resilience, and link existing local political structures to move communities off of oil dependence and into healthier ecosystems. As of this writing, there are over 130 towns in 14 countries officially designated Transition Towns, and many more considering how to become one.

We propose that an important psychological approach to building a sustainable society is to keep positive visions of the future in focus, and to work diligently on making them happen. The importance of providing positive images flows directly from psychoanalytic psychology. With positive images of the future, people can direct more energy toward changing behaviors that enable accomplishments, and use less

---

* See http://www.transitiontowns.org/

Reprinted from Kris Rieck. With permission.

of it defending against negative feelings such as anxiety. Thus, any psychologically sophisticated approach to environmental problems must include ways of protecting people from overload and despair. Hope is a crucial psychological commodity for building a sustainable future, as it is for emotional intelligence in general (Goleman, 1995; Seligman, 1975).

But perhaps just as important as hope is the realization that everyone is capable of making a positive difference in their community and in the larger world. And *with ability comes responsibility*.

When we realize the degree of agency we actually do have, we no longer have to "hope" at all. We simply do the work. We make sure salmon survive. We make sure prairie dogs survive. We make sure grizzlies survive. We do whatever it takes. (Jensen, 2006, para. 14, 19).

All of us can join with family members, neighbors, and other community members in the transition to a sustainable world. In fact, there is an international social movement in the making, which is historically unprecedented in its size and scope (Hawken, 2007).*

---

* See also the associated networking site at http://www.wiserearth.org/

The Internet makes it possible for most everyone to participate. Joining with others to work on big problems reduces despair, while enhancing interconnection and potency.

WORK WITH BIG IDEAS AND SMALL STEPS

Nurturing the development of a sustainable society will require diligent perseverance. Unfortunately, when faced with huge challenges, psychologists, like most people, are liable to resort to small problems and ideas because they reduce anxiety. Everyone feels more comfortable when distracted from troubling realities. Yet this book has presented some big ideas for some big problems that may feel overwhelming and discouraging, especially since new ideas often elicit vigorous resistance from others.

Instead of distracting ourselves with small problems, however, we suggest using small steps to work on big problems, using the big theories of psychology to help design a sustainable world (Winter, 2000). Weick (1984) made the same suggestion decades ago, noting that people can't solve problems if they are emotionally overwhelmed by them. He used the **Yerkes-Dodson Law** of arousal (Broadhurst, 1959; Yerkes & Dodson, 1908) to argue that people perform optimally when experiencing moderate levels of arousal or stress. When arousal is too high, people tend to respond with more primitive coping mechanisms, which means that more highly refined and contextually valid responses are the first to go. On the other hand, arousal that is too low also hurts problem solving. When problems are depersonalized, distant, or abstract, people become inactive and apathetic (Gattig & Hendrickx, 2007). To keep arousal in the optimal, moderate range, Weick suggested defining problems in terms of small wins. Small wins have immediacy, tangibility, and controllability that reverse powerlessness and apathy. For example, Alcoholics Anonymous is successful helping alcoholics because it doesn't insist on complete abstinence for the rest of one's life. Instead, the goal is to stay sober "one day at a time."

If your small steps seem trivial, consider the fact that producing one pound of meat causes the emissions equivalent of roughly 16.5 pounds of carbon dioxide. That means you can significantly help curb climate change by eating less meat, as well as riding a bike, and being a frugal shopper (Pachauri, 2008). Such small changes, one day at a time, reflects a small win, but eventually (and collectively) make a huge contribution. Many successful reforms are adopted because of their size, specificity, and visibility (Weick, 1984); these are hallmarks of the behavioral approach, which breaks down large behaviors into smaller, measurable ones (Chapter 5). The self-control project outlined in Chapter 5 is a good example of the psychology of small wins. Small wins facilitate feelings of success, thus fostering momentum and motivation for further change. Recall also the defense mechanism of *sublimation* (Chapter 3), the *foot-in-the-door strategy* (Chapter 4), and the fact that implementing *problem-solving coping* strategies reduces stress (Chapter 8).

THINK CIRCLE INSTEAD OF LINE

One of the most optimistic glimpses of a positive future based on sustainable innovation is depicted in the video *The Next Industrial Revolution* (2001; see also Krupp & Horn, 2008; McDonough & Braungart, 2002). These visionaries offer an idea of the future "where humanity works with nature, where technical enterprises are continually reinvented as safe and ever renewing natural processes."* The first industrial revolution brought unparalleled prosperity, productivity, and profits to large numbers of people, along with physical comforts, extended life spans, and increased personal mobility. But the same industrial revolution is also changing planetary climate patterns, and putting billions of pounds of toxic waste into the air, water, and soil every year, some so dangerous that they will require constant vigilance by many future generations (ironic, given the reduced attention and intellectual capacity resulting from such exposures!). Industrialization has depleted natural capital (fresh air and clean water, intact forests, healthy fish stocks, and coral reefs), destroyed huge amounts of habitat for the majority of species, and required thousands of complex regulations to keep people from poisoning each other too quickly (McDonough & Braungart, 1998).

Industrialization rests on the "common sense" that supports it. One belief that gave rise to the first industrial revolution was the assumption that natural resources are inexhaustible. This idea seemed accurate during the seventeeth to twentieth centuries, when Europeans and North Americans were busy expanding their populations and colonizing other lands. But this view is clearly out of date in the twenty-first century. "What we thought was boundless has limits . . . and we are beginning to hit them" (Robert Shapiro, CEO of Monsanto, as quoted by McDonough & Braungart, 1998, p. 82).

An important principle of the *Next Industrial Revolution* is that of **closed systems**, where nothing is added or taken away. Nature has a lot of closed systems: the hydrological, carbon, and nitrogen cycles

---

* Quoted from the Web site, http://www.thenextindustrialrevolution.org/context.html, para. 1; see also information about sustainable designs at http://www.mbdc.com/overview.htm

are a few examples. For instance, as a global system, water is never produced or depleted, but constantly transformed as rain, fog, clouds, rivers, and snow through evaporation and precipitation. Water can be polluted beyond healthy use (and far too often it is) or cleaned by purification methods, but it operates in a closed cycle. In contrast, human-made systems usually function as linear structures, eating up inputs (resources), and exuding wastes. Even though there is really no "away" to throw things, people act as if there is by filling dump sites, oceans, skies, and water sources with the wastes from industrial activities.*

Instead of using the linear model, where disappearing inputs are manufactured to produce intolerable wastes, it is time to design human activities that follow natural laws of circular exchange. In this model, "wastes" must become food, just as they are in natural cycles where organic wastes serve as fertilizers for the next generation of growth. Given that humans belong to closed systems, the design and use of material products must be changed. In other words, we'll need **cradle to cradle**, rather than "cradle to grave" manufacturing designs (Hawken et al., 1999; McDonough & Braungart, 2002). Most companies have traditionally operated to maximize their bottom line: profitability. But this singular focus has brought horrendous environmental and social problems. A sustainable future requires a focus on the **triple bottom line**, addressing social (people) and environmental (planet), as well as economic (profit) factors (Savitz & Weber, 2006; see Figure 11.1). The United States was recently ranked 66th on the **Sustainable Society Index**, a measure developed to evaluate 151 countries' performance in terms of *personal development* (health conditions, education, gender equality), *environmental health* (air, water, land quality), *societal balance* (governance, employment, income distribution), *resource use* (waste recycling, renewable energy, and water sources), and overall *sustainable world* measures (forest area, biodiversity, greenhouse gas emissions, ecological footprint, and international cooperation; van de Kerk & Manuel, 2009).

Thus, **sustainable performance** requires industry assessments of the following criteria (Talberth, 2008, pp. 27–28):

- Establishing **certification processes** to identify products that are humanely and sustainably produced

---

* An engaging 20 minute explanation of the problems encountered by using linear thinking in production is available in the online video, *The Story of Stuff*, available at http://www.storyofstuff.com/

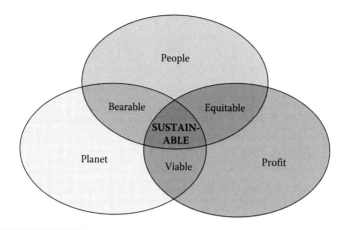

Figure 11.1 The triple bottom line (profit, planet, and people) must be maximized for sustainable business practice. (Adapted from Greeninnovation [http://www.greeninnovation.com.au/aboutGreenInnovation_sustainability.html]. With permission.)

- Producing **zero-waste**, via increasing recycling rates and product longevity and reducing emissions
- Enhancing **eco-efficiency** by expanding use of recycled materials, while simultaneously reducing the energy, water, and materials used in production
- Improving **workplace well-being** in terms of job satisfaction and reduced turnover
- Promoting **community vitality** based on obtaining goods and services from local providers, enhancing the local economy and charitable donations, and establishing a **living wage**, that is, salaries that are sufficient to meet the local costs of living.

Sound too good to be true? This vision is already being realized. One of the largest technology companies, 3M, is implementing zero-waste practices, monitoring and reducing their waste stream to achieve an overall reduction of more than *2.2 billion pounds* of pollutants, and saving $1 billion in reduced pollution mitigation (Talberth, 2008). Many manufacturers, such as those that produce photocopy machines, are renting their products rather than selling them for eventual disposal. When items are rented and returned to the manufacturer, incentives are created for making durable and reusable parts. Designers are making floor coverings with the same goal. When you rent a carpet and pay for the service of having your floor covered, you do not have to throw it away when you want to replace it. Instead you return it to the manufacturer who has produced it for its recycleability.

Legislation in 29 countries requires manufacturers to **take back** their products or packaging for remanufacture or reuse; 15 countries legislate similar requirements for batteries (Cole, 2000). The European Union recently instituted restrictions of lead, mercury, and some flame retardants, among other toxins based on consideration of the "whole life impacts" of electronic equipment (i.e., supply, production, as well as material recovery); they also require manufacturers to develop greener chemical alternatives (Aspen Publishers, 2007, p. 1). Over the last several years, more than one third of U.S. states have implemented regulations on *e-waste* (Verespej, 2008), surprisingly with the support of two major companies, Hewlett Packard and RadioShack (Ecocycle, n.d.). Electronics take-back legislation is particularly important for compelling manufacturers to assume responsibility for reducing the careless disposal, incineration, and international export of computers and other electronics that release toxins such as those discussed in Chapter 6.

Industrial communities based on sharing resources, maximizing efficiency, and utilizing each other's waste materials are spreading. Currently, there are more than 20 operational **eco-industrial parks** (including several in the United States), and many more are being developed (Gibbs & Deutz, 2007). The complexes are modeled on the original site in Kalundborg, Denmark, where a fish farm, a power plant, a manufacturer of gypsum wallboard, a pharmaceutical company, a cement factory, local farmers, and an oil refinery each use by-products of another's production. In this way, waste becomes food. Other benefits include reduced costs for energy use, waste mitigation, and material acquisition (Tudor, Adam, & Bates, 2007).

In each of the above examples, natural resources do not end up in sewers and landfills, but are used in new production cycles, thus mimicking how natural systems operate. This technique, called **biomimicry**, inspired Toyota Motor Corporation to add solar panels to its production plants and to paint outside walls and other surfaces with a special coating that breaks down climate changing gases. These changes will be as effective in cleaning the air as planting 2000 poplar trees in the area (Lovins, 2008).

Harnessing **renewable energy** sources is another example of the circle design. Both British Petroleum (BP) and Shell started investing in renewable energy over a decade ago because of their greater likelihood for future markets; BP has committed to moving "beyond petroleum" (Savitz & Weber, 2006) by attempting to remake itself as an "energy company rather than an oil company" (Gardner & Prugh, 2008, p. 16). Investment in renewable energy has increased dramatically since 2000: wind turbine and solar cell production grew by 17 and 46%, respectively, *each year*; yet demand continues to outpace supply, providing escalating profits (Flavin, 2008). The state of Hawaii recently required all new homes be built with solar hot water heaters. Solar water heaters could eventually supply one half of the world's hot water; solar panels mounted on only half of all appropriate rooftops could provide 25% of U.S. electricity. Likewise, wind power generated in just three U.S. states (Kansas, North Dakota, and Texas) could *fully* meet the nation's electricity demand, while simultaneously protecting environmentally sensitive areas (Flavin, 2008, pp. 82–83).

Reprinted from © Chris Madden. With permission.

Manufacturers are exploring sustainable technologies for powering automobiles with solar, wind, or renewable biofuels (Flavin, 2008). But even smarter are the strategies being implemented by Volkswagen and Toyota to transform themselves into *service providers*, rather than product manufacturers. Using the idea of the increasingly popular **Zipcar** (a.k.a., **Flexcar**), companies provide access to vehicles without drivers having to own them (Savitz & Weber, 2006). Because even hybrid, renewable energy, or fuel-cell cars are resource intensive, one Zipcar replaces seven to 10 private vehicles; Zipcars also aid in reducing traffic and overall emissions.

The first industrial revolution rested on the assumption that human beings are separate from nature, and meant to transform it to satisfy human needs. But, as we emphasized in Chapters 6 and 8, when industrial processes produce pollution, pesticides, and other toxins, as well as the associated stress of noise, traffic, and visual disorder, they harm neurodevelopment and overall human and planetary health. Because humans are physiological beings, wastes from agriculture and manufacturing lodge as poisons in their bodies. Thus, when people realize they are linked at the chemical level to industrial processes, the importance of promoting benign technologies becomes more obvious. From the vantage point of ecopsychology, this awareness means consciousness of one's larger *ecological identity* (Chapter 10).

LESS IS MORE

A big problem in getting people to think about the future is that many assume sustainability means hardship and sacrifice. But instead of presupposing that a sustainable future will be spartan and severe, consider the principle that with increased human attention, *less can be more*. This rule is grounded in physics and ecology, as well as psychology.

Physics. At the physical level, *less is more* means enhanced efficiency. Engineers around the world are working for **Factor 10** or even **Factor 20**, involving 10- to 20-fold increases in efficiency of energy and materials use (Lovins, 2008). If this goal sounds impossible, consider the hideous inefficiency of the automobile. Eighty percent of the energy from the gasoline it burns is used to run and cool the engine and deal with its exhausts. Only 5% of the remaining 20% is used to move the person; the rest is used to move the car. Thus, only 1% of the total energy in gasoline goes to moving the driver—the rest is wasted (Hawken et al., 1999). Even worse, a lot of that energy is spit out as exhaust, contaminating air and contributing to climate change. As gasoline and other fossil fuels become more expensive and/or become subject to taxes, the *real costs* (Chapter 5) of such unsustainable inefficiencies will become more and more apparent.

Ecology. At the environmental level, fewer emissions not only mean greater efficiency but also better overall system health. Climate change is currently at the front of business and political leaders' concerns. A growing number of corporations have publicly committed to reduce their carbon emissions, and taken significant steps to do so, because they see the market benefits (Arroyo & Preston, 2007). Many cities and states are developing local responses,* and communities are initiating household campaigns to combat climate change, which can provide a model for other regions. For example, Portland, Oregon developed a Low-Carb Diet to reduce household carbon dioxide by 5000 pounds in 30 days (Rabkin & Gershon, 2007). Several influential parties are developing important emission controls, including the following (adapted from Scott, 2007; see also Krupp & Horn, 2008):

- The European Union instituted an emission trading scheme similar to the *cap and trade* systems described in Chapter 5. This represents the largest effort to date involving multiple countries and industries worldwide.
- General Electric launched its "Ecoimagination" program, doubling their investment in research and development in "cleaner technologies," reducing greenhouse gas emissions and water use.
- An oil and gas company in Norway has stored carbon dioxide for more than a decade in response to the country's goal to reduce carbon emissions and become carbon neutral by 2050.
- The largest sugar and ethanol producer in Brazil is preparing to respond to the expected acceleration in demand for biofuels.
- Renewable energy suppliers are expanding efforts to harness wind, solar, and ocean waves.
- Major food companies (including Whole Foods, with locations in the United States) are focusing on locally acquired foods to reduce transportation, packaging, and energy impacts while composting wastes.

---

* For example, see https://www.gcgtools.com/connect/public/GCG/GGCS2009/

"I know I'm just a kid, but isn't it counterintuitive
to package organic produce in cellophane
and styrofoam?"

In sum, new technologies are being designed to combat climate change in virtually every sector: energy sources, power generation, retail, transportation, engineering, buildings and construction, as well as household goods, financial services, and electronics. These efforts demonstrate corporate leaders' realization that businesses can profit financially, while delivering environmentally friendlier products and services (Arroyo & Preston, 2007; Savitz & Weber, 2006; Scott, 2007).

Psychology. On the psychological level, *less is more* when it comes to what makes people happy, as we saw in Chapter 4. More wealth does not bring more happiness. Instead, people report more fulfillment when they have close relationships, a sense of belonging to a community, and some faith in larger meanings. These activities do not require material wealth, and in fact, can be interrupted by the harried pursuit of more money and possessions, as discussed in Chapter 8. "*Affluenza*, [the] unhappy condition of overload, debt, anxiety, and waste resulting from the dogged pursuit of more" is hazardous to physical, mental, and planetary health (Walljasper, 1997, p. 19; see also de Graaf, Wann, & Naylor, 2005). From this perspective, less (consumption) is more (pleasure and well-being).

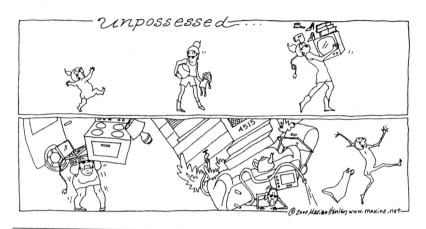

Reprinted from © Marian Henley. With permission.

The **voluntary simplicity** movement makes many of the same points (Cairns, 1998; Elgin, 1981, 1993, 2000).* Voluntary simplicity (VS) is a social movement spreading through Europe and North America in which people choose to downscale their material possessions in order to live "consciously, deliberately, while not being distracted by consumer culture . . . taking charge of a life that is too busy, too stressed, and too fragmented, [while] consciously tasting life in its unadorned richness" (Elgin, 2000). Using principles of Buddhism and other contemplative practices, VS addresses both the stressed spirit and the stressed planet through methods that increase attention to present abundance. Voluntary simplicity teaches methods similar to those used by ecopsychologists (see Chapter 10), so that people learn to appreciate and experience more from less. And research shows that VS is a good route to enhancing proenvironmental habits; VS correlates with environmentally responsible behaviors, such as resisting impulse buying, conserving energy, and buying natural food (Iwata, 1999, 2006).

There's a catchy, old New England maxim that reflects some of these ideas: "Use it up, wear it out, make it do, or do without." One global systems analyst offered another way of approaching the less is more principle, using the ideas of Gandhi:

As a child in the middle-class Midwest, I lived out of a subconscious sense of *abundance*. That sense permits security, innovation, generosity, and joy. But it can also harbor insensitivity, greed, and waste.

---

* Resources are available on the web for supporting readers interested in learning more about VS (http://www.simpleliving.net or see the Center for a New American Dream, http://www.newdream.org).

After returning from India, I lived out of a sense of *scarcity*. That is fine when it fosters stewardship, simplicity, and frugality, but not when it leads to grimness, intolerance, and separation from one's fellows. Now I try to base my life on the idea of *sufficiency*—there is just enough of everything for everyone and not one bit more. There is enough for generosity but not waste, enough for security but not hoarding. Or as Gandhi said, enough for everyone's need, but not for everyone's greed. (Meadows, 1991, p. 17, italics hers)

PRACTICE CONSCIOUS CONSUMPTION

Voluntary simplicity implies the principle of **conscious consumption;** that is, not only reducing *how much* one buys and consumes, but choosing environmentally friendly products whenever possible for necessary purchases, particularly items that are gently used, long-lasting, minimally packaged or refillable, and produced locally. Recall the *unshopping card* illustrated in Chapter 1 (Figure 1.4). As we saw in Chapter 4, people who have proenvironmental attitudes practice ecologically conscious consumer behavior (Roberts & Bacon, 1997; Tanner & Kast, 2003). Specifically, those who agree that "The balance of nature is very delicate and easily upset" and "There are limits to growth beyond which industrialized society cannot expand" are more likely to buy recycled or recyclable products, and avoid excessive packaging or polluting materials.

People make conscious consumer decisions for different reasons: out of concern about conservation of natural resources; and concern about

the wider impact on natural systems, for example, by avoiding pesticides, chemical cleaners, and other toxins, or items subjected to animal testing (Ebreo, Hershey, & Vining, 1999). In general, people show most concern about the toxicity of products and least concern about the suffering of nonhumans when it comes to purchasing consumer products. Whether this is because information about animal testing and suffering isn't salient enough (we think it isn't), or people do not extend their *scope of justice* (Chapter 4) to include nonhumans is not yet known.

In any case, conscious consumption is one of the public's most powerful political and economic tools. Consumer actions have promoted or delayed advancements toward sustainability, particularly when the efforts involved messages that are relatively simple and emotionally evocative, and recruited major media coverage, such as the "Save the dolphins (from the nets of tuna fishermen)" campaign (Friedman, 2002, p. 288). The fast-food chain, McDonald's, ceased using Styrofoam containers for their hamburgers after significant public pressure. Likewise, in 1988, consumers boycotted Burger King because they imported cheap beef from tropical rainforest countries, causing major destruction of precious ecosystems. Burger Kings' sales dropped 12% and shortly thereafter, they cancelled $35 million worth of contracts from Central America, announcing they would no longer import rainforest beef.* Many other examples of successful boycotts exist, along with instances of effective pressure in changing corporate practices. When Deborah wrote the first edition of this book in 1994, she called Starbucks headquarters to inquire about their efforts to purchase fair-trade coffee (grown on smaller, family owned farms that provide farmers with a living wage). She was told that no one cares about that. In the fall of 2000, after years of public pressure, Starbucks began buying fair-trade coffee; by 2008, they boasted of being the "largest purchaser, roaster and distributor of Fair-Trade Certified coffee in North America," (Starbucks Coffee Company, 2008).

Every shopping choice supports something, whether sustainable or not. Responsible shopping is getting easier with the aid of resources that deliver crucial information not yet provided in the aisles of stores, nor on the labels of products. For example, Web sites provide keyword searches by brand, product, or category to find out how companies compare on pollution, recycling, animal testing, and labor practices.† Co-op America's (2008) *National Green Pages* lists goods and services that promote sustainability; *The Better World Shopping Guide* (Jones, 2008) is a handy pocket-sized volume that you can take with you to

---

* See http://rainforestweb.org
† For example, http://www.coopamerica.org/programs/responsibleshopper/

the grocery store, to compare products on environmental and social practices; the Union of Concerned Scientists published the *Consumer's Guide to Effective Environmental Choices* (Brower & Leon, 1999), and several Web sites listed in the Appendix give clear, up-to-date information on responsible consumerism.

At the collective level, corporate shareholders have enormous power to effect change, through resolutions promoting responsible company practices. For example, CVS, Longs, and Safeway agreed to end production and distribution of mercury thermometers because of shareholder pressure (Borkowski, 2004). The nonprofit watchdog, Environmental Working Group, reported that despite insisting that flame retardants are safe, some major electronics manufacturers including Nokia, Sony-Ericsson, and Samsung have eliminated or are phasing out certain classes of endocrine-disrupting fire retardant chemicals in their electronic products (Lunder & Jacob, 2008; see also Chapter 6).

Personal actions that can make the most impact toward sustainable society fall into two main categories: transportation and agriculture; fortunately, these are also relatively easy to change! Driving private cars accounts for a striking 38.6% of individual-household energy use in the United States; thus, utilizing alternate forms of transportation, reducing gas consumption (combining trips, getting frequent tune-ups, avoiding rapid acceleration), carpooling, bicycling, or purchasing a more efficient vehicle can all significantly reduce one's footprint (Gardner & Stern, 2008).

Most people do not realize that their dietary choices can be just as important. While carbon dioxide emissions are the target of many emission-reduction efforts, **methane**, primarily from animal agriculture, causes the release of almost half of the climate changing gasses (Mohr, 2005), even more than those released by cars, buses and airplanes! (Rosenthal, 2008). As global consumption of meat has risen, methane release has grown to more than 100 million tons per year; thus, shifting to a vegetarian or vegan diet can make a dramatic and rapid impact in reducing climate changing emissions (Mohr, 2005). This change would also improve health via reduced exposure to PBTs (see Chapter 6), as well as reduce the appalling treatment of animals raised to be food.

When better information leads to more responsible choices, cognitive psychology (Chapter 7) is at work. Many people currently lack the essential information to make responsible purchasing choices, or do not take the time to do the relevant research. Imagine, for example, how your choices might be affected if you knew whether a product's manufacturing process produces dangerous pollution, whether it is horrifically inefficient, or dangerous for the workers who produce it. Because most people would avoid hurting others or the planet if they could, responsible consumer information is crucial. Behavioral psychology (Chapter 5) is also at work with conscious consumerism, because when a person chooses environmentally responsible products and services, financial reinforcers operate on providers to promote more sustainable business practices.

ACT ON PERSONAL AND POLITICAL LEVELS, ESPECIALLY LOCAL COMMUNITY PARTICIPATION

Deborah didn't personally change Starbucks' practices, but years of political activism by many people did. Environmental devastation is driven by behaviors at both personal *and* political levels. While psychology tends to focus on individual behavior, political advocacy for the larger public good is equally crucial because even when people know about and would like to choose responsible behaviors, it is not always possible to do so. Here's an example: Although we both drive hybrid cars that get around 50 mpg, our vehicles use fossil fuels. We both know that gasoline plays a huge role in current environmental and political events; driving contributes to both climate change and international wars. We are both outraged by the way U.S. dependency on oil has led to militarizing the Middle East, and treating it as if it's a cheap gas station. A small portion of what the world pays for militarization could solve many environmental and social problems.* However, our environmentally irresponsible behavior has structural dimensions beyond our immediate control. For example, the post office, grocery store, and office are 10 miles from where Deborah lives and there is no mass transit system. The road is narrow and curvy, making bike riding dangerous to herself and other drivers. Driving a car is safer—and possible—because roads are built and maintained by tax dollars that she didn't allocate, with designs she didn't choose.

For reasons like these, political approaches to environmental problems are paramount. In order for psychology to make a viable contribution to building a sustainable world, it must also be practiced in collective contexts to change the structural (economic, legal, and political) dimensions of environmental decline. A large-scale **social movement** paralleling the civil rights movement, involving extensive public communication and political mobilization, is required (Meyer, 2007; see also Hawken, 2007). That means using one's citizenship to participate in public decision making. It means taking responsibility for one's own behavior while working to change the norms, rules, and laws that

---

* See the Web site: What the world wants and how to pay for it using military expenditures, available at http://www.unesco.org/education/tlsf/TLSF/theme_a/mod02/www.worldgame.org/wwwproject/index.shtml

shape the behavior of many others. It means tracking and speaking out about local, national, and international legislation. A good way to begin this process is to participate in political activism via Web sites such as those listed in the Appendix.

You've probably heard the dictum "Think Globally, Act Locally." We believe it's an indispensable strategy, but one that isn't enacted frequently enough. Research demonstrates that people are most likely to engage in activism when the issue appears urgent, potential solutions are available, and they believe that their efforts can make a difference (Meyer, 2007). But a disturbing gap exists between how people think about global versus local environmental problems: most people are more concerned about global than local issues, but feel less personally responsible for them (e.g., Uzzell, 2000). This disconnect contributes to a widespread sense of powerlessness about increasingly worrisome global trends. Because it is most difficult to effect change on a global level, local action is imperative (Thomashow, 2002). But people are unlikely to act locally if they do not even know about environmental issues in their local settings.

There are several psychological reasons why people fail to recognize local problems. Many people work in a different location from their residence, and because of busy commuting schedules, they do not see their neighbors or feel a connection with them. Their sense of place is diminished, along with their felt responsibility (Chapter 10). In addition, several psychological mechanisms discussed in this book are at play:

- From a psychoanalytic perspective, people use denial and other defenses to reduce fear and anxiety, and even more so as the risks are closer (Chapter 3). For example, when confronted by the risks of pesticides and other toxins, people sometimes joke, "Well, something's gonna kill me" and "Everything causes cancer."
- Environmental education that focuses only on global issues is too abstract (Chapter 9), leading people to conclude that the problems aren't theirs to help solve, or that their own individual action is irrelevant (Coyle, 2005; Sobel, 1996; Uzzell, 2000). Thus, effective environmental education requires *action* components, whether it be individual behavioral change, community projects, or direct political activism (Coyle, 2005; Meyer, 2007; Thomashow, 2002).
- From a behavioral perspective, local effects of environmentally relevant behavior are not readily noticeable, so rewards and costs are not directly experienced. Sue's advocacy experiences with local legislation and community education about the harmful effects of pesticides provides an illustration. Despite her city's adoption of **integrated pest management** strategies

that reduce pesticide use in parks and other city properties, it is impossible to determine whether or not pesticide exposures are actually decreasing. Furthermore, toxic impacts are often subtle and not directly observable, particularly given the typically long delay between exposure and health outcomes (Koger, Schettler, & Weiss, 2005; Chapter 6).

- Since dramatic, rare causes of death are overestimated (like nuclear accidents), whereas more mundane, common deaths are underestimated (e.g., from respiratory illness or cancer associated with automobile emissions), people are less likely to pay attention to local risks that are present every day (Chapter 7).

- Finally, from an ecopsychology perspective, it may be easier for some people to connect with an abstract notion like Gaia (Chapter 10) than to hold active membership in their local communities where disagreements with neighbors and friends over environmental questions may be upsetting. Working face-to-face with fellow citizens who do not all agree requires well-developed social and emotional skills. Some of these skills are now being taught in public schools under the rubric of conflict resolution and mediation training, but most adults do not have any such systematic training.

Fortunately, environmental psychologists have articulated principles for helping citizens work on local sustainability issues (Koger, Merrick, Kraybill-Greggo, & Kraybill-Greggo, 2006; MacNair, 2006; McKenzie-Mohr & Smith, 1999), and **place-based environmental education** is growing in popularity (Chapter 9). A recent assessment demonstrated that place-based education can effectively address local environmental problems, including air quality (Duffin, Murphy, & Johnson, 2008). Community participation is critical for formulating and making decisions about regional environmental resources and land uses (Wiesenfeld & Sanchez, 2002). Participants in various projects, such as waste incineration and organic agriculture, report that community work helps them think in new ways about how to solve problems. When citizens are involved in community decisions, they are empowered by their responsibility, by ties among members, and by feelings of belonging to place (Chapter 10). Correspondingly, they remain involved because they experience common risks and benefits to the community's water, air, or land use (Clinebell, 1996; S. Kaplan, 2000; Thomashow, 1998).

Strategies for engaging in community-based environmental work has been effectively developed and made widely accessible by McKenzie-Mohr through his framework called **Community Based Social**

Marketing (CBSM; McKenzie-Mohr, 2000a, 2000b; McKenzie-Mohr & Smith, 1999).* CBSM uses principles of social and behavioral psychology, promoting behavior change at the community level via direct contact between residents of a region. Based on the finding that information campaigns have limited effects, CBSM strategies address barriers, design incentives, and deliver information, using commitment, feedback, framing, modeling, norms, prompts, and social diffusion (Chapters 4 and 5). CBSM is used by community groups to change behaviors that are most environmentally impactful: *agricultural practices, transportation, home energy use, water use, overall resource consumption and waste*, and *toxic chemical production and use* (Gardner & Stern, 2008; Miller, 2007). Key steps toward walking more lightly on the earth in these areas are outlined in the Appendix.

Another useful online tool helps citizens map their local communities for green sites, such as hiking trails, wildlife reserves, cultural sites, green businesses, environmental hot spots, and public transportation options.† **Greenmaps** are a good method for citizens to access better information (Chapter 7) about what is available in their communities, put pressure on local businesses to participate in environmentally responsible practices, and monitor progress toward a sustainable world.

One of the most effective tools for enhancing the health of the environment, the health of the local economy, and the health of your body is to purchase locally grown, organic food from neighborhood farmer's markets; these are becoming more available in many areas. Local food is more nutritious and flavorful because it isn't shipped while still ripening; it cuts one's ecological footprint by reducing fossil fuels in transport; and it enhances the local community and its economy by directly supporting the people who grow the food, instead of multinational companies who grow, buy, ship, and increasingly, own patents on genetically modified seeds that produce it. Growing and eating local food (becoming a **locavore**) is part of the *Slow Food Movement*,‡ which embraces the enhanced pleasure and environmental health of eating local food. Even if you do not cook your own food, you can lobby those who do to buy from local farmers; indeed many cafeterias are finding it cheaper, healthier, and more sustainable to do so.

Table 11.1 links the six operating principles to relevant psychological concepts and the chapters where those concepts are discussed.

---

* Available online at http://www.cbsm.com/
† See http://www.greenmap.org/
‡ See http://www.slowfood.com/

Table 11.1 Psychological Support for the Six Operating Principles, and Relevant Chapters

New Operating Principle	Reduce	Related Chapters	Enhance	Related Chapters
Visualize an ecologically healthy world	Despair, overwhelm, defense mechanisms, stress	3: Psychoanalytic 8: Health	Social support	4: Social 8: Health 9: Developmental 10: Holistic
Work with big ideas and small steps	Overwhelm, defense mechanisms, stress, *ecophobia*	3: Psychoanalytic 8: Health 9: Developmental	Specificity and visibility Foot-in-the-door, generalization Problem-solving coping strategies Environmental Education	5: Behavioral 9: Developmental 4: Social 5: Behavioral 8: Health
Think circle instead of line	Assuming nature is infinite and ever-regenerative Assuming nature is separate from humans	2: Nature of Western thought 6: Neuropsychology 2: Nature of Western thought	Nontoxic or less-toxic practices Experiences in nature Ecological identity	9: Developmental 6: Neuropsychology 8: Health 8: Health 9: Developmental 10: Holistic
Less is more	Materialism, overconsumption (affluenza)	4: Social 8: Health 9: Developmental	Awareness of real costs, cap and trade economics Mindful consumption Voluntary simplicity	5: Behavioral 10: Holistic

Action	Barrier	Approach	Strategy	Approach
Practice conscious consumption			Proenvironmental attitudes	4: Social
			Scope of justice	4: Social / 10: Holistic
			Information to the consumer	7: Cognitive
			Economic pressure on producers	5: Behavioral
			Personal and social norms for sustainability	4: Social
Act on personal and political levels	Fear and denial about local issues	3: Psychoanalytic	Personal and social norms	4: Social
	Ignorance about local problems	7: Cognitive	Feedback on local efforts	5: Behavioral
	Abstract, distant environmental education	9: Developmental	Service learning	9: Developmental
	Errors of risk assessment	7: Cognitive	Sense of place	9: Developmental / 10: Holistic
			Place-based education	9: Developmental
			Conflict resolution skills, compassion	10: Holistic

CONCLUSIONS

Using psychology to address and solve environmental degradation means balancing knowledge about the complexity of the problems with a commitment to working diligently on them, especially in personal and local contexts. It means rethinking one's own consumption in light of the billions of people who now live in destitution, disentangling one's behavior from the consumer culture, and promoting self-reliance and cultural integrity. Meeting current challenges will require a serious and difficult look at the planet's distribution of wealth, power, and environmentally damaging patterns, and a personal commitment to changing one's own behaviors as well as the larger structures that propel them.

Moving toward a sustainable society means big changes at both the personal (behavioral, emotional, cognitive, spiritual) and structural (political, economic, legal) levels, and will require extensive interdisciplinary collaborations (Smith et al., 2009). Some key components of a sustainability agenda include maintaining natural resources, safeguarding the health of all species, preserving natural areas and wildlife habitats, and fostering a sense of harmony between humans and the rest of nature. These goals require massive transformations in various sectors including energy production, transportation, agriculture, and consumerism (Vlek & Steg, 2007).

Human behavior is not easy to change but it does change. Consider how quickly your own behavior changes in different settings, or how much human behavior has changed in the last 100 years. The transition to sustainability will need to happen in the next decade or two, and this time pressure may make it difficult to appreciate the pace of your own and others' transition, especially since people are more comfortable with the familiar than they are with the new. Thus, any psychologically sophisticated approach to massive behavior change must consider the crucial roles of resistance and relapse. Whenever situations offer people the ability to make choices, behavior change will be uneven, and fortitude will be required. Change begins by learning about why it's needed, and hopefully this book has promoted this step. Change also requires consideration of the advantages and disadvantages (i.e., reinforcers and punishers), preparation and commitment, action and maintenance (Chapter 5). Most importantly, change requires patience and perseverance, because it inevitably includes setbacks as people fall back to old habits. That is why social support, emotional fortitude, and gentle perseverance are so critical to building a sustainable world.

The Cost of Inaction

As we have seen, one of the ways people contribute to environmental decline is by knowing a lot, but not acting on that knowledge. Higher education is traditionally complicit with inaction. Political action and activism are not typically included as key features of college classrooms, out of fear they will create ideological robots out of students; alternatively, advocating particular political agendas can cause resistance and rebellion. Yet people learn more about an idea from experiencing how it works, especially when remaining diligently open to feedback from experience. Recently developed programs using **service learning** and other forms of place-based learning in higher education addresses this insight about how people learn by integrating experiential learning with traditional classroom formats. President Obama recognized the importance of service learning for enhancing both educational and community programs by signing the Edward M. Kennedy, Serve America Act, funding programs to increase volunteerism in all age groups, and expanding AmeriCorps (Milligan, 2009). At Willamette University in Oregon where Sue teaches, the importance of community involvement as part of college classes is acknowledged by the school's motto "Not unto ourselves alone are we born."

Inaction will insure that business proceeds as usual, yet business as usual is already leading societies to environmental, social, and economic collapse (e.g., Diamond, 2005; Intergovernmental Panel on Climate Change, 2007; Kunstler, 2005; Smith, Shearman, & Positano, 2007; Stern, 2007). Alternatively, undertaking action will change us all, as well as the world around us. In concert with the other sciences, psychology is critical for effective social organizing and policy making; for building coalitions of experts, activists, and citizens; for promoting specific actions that are broadly accessible; and for initiating and supporting political reforms (Meyer, 2007).

The Appendix lists some valuable resources for designing your own responses, joining others in groups or agencies, reconsidering your consumer choices, and helping solve specific resource or pollution problems. No matter what actions you decide to take, becoming aware of your behavior, thoughts, and feelings will significantly facilitate your effectiveness. *But you cannot do anything for sustainability or for yourself until you begin.*

As you select your actions, you will likely experience many of the defenses and cognitive limitations we discussed in this book. You may feel overwhelmed; that is a constant, recurring liability in this

You are one of the forces of nature.
- Jules Michelet

EARTH
DAYS

muttscomics.com

Reprinted from MUTTS © Patrick McDonnell. King Features Syndicate. With permission.

work because as one learns more, it becomes more evident how inter-connected and colossal are the structures that are driving ecological destruction. Focusing on specific behaviors can help mitigate the experience of feeling overwhelmed, even though those feelings are likely to recur. Yet allowing one's self to slip into despair or helplessness is the *most* destructive path; destructive because it undermines personal growth and maturity, and destructive because it insures a planetary outcome that justifies despair. Just as feelings of overwhelm are best confronted with action, so too is despondency:

> If we become the prisoners of our own minds, if we think our-selves into despair, we can step onto wounded ground with a shovel and begin to plant trees. They will grow. They will hold the soil, provide shelter for birds, warm someone's home after we are gone. If we lose faith in ourselves, we can in those moments forget ourselves and dwell on the future of the larger community, on the blessing of neighbors. (Lopez, 1990)

And so it is essential to proceed gently, with conviction, patience, per-severance, and most of all, with trust, trust in yourself, as well as in the interconnected wholeness that embraces you. "If you take one step with all the knowledge you have, there is usually just enough light shining to show you the next step" (M. Murie, as quoted by Williams, 1994).

May your steps be steady, graceful, revealing, and rewarding, and may you know them as part of the greater ecological dance.

REFERENCES

Abrahamse, W., Steg, L., Vlek, C., & Rothengatter, T. (2005). A review of intervention studies aimed at household energy conservation. *Journal of Environmental Psychology, 25*, 273–291.

Abram, D. (1987). The perceptual implications of Gaia. *Revision, 9*(2), 7–15.

Abramson, P.R., & Inglehart, R. (1995). *Value change in global perspective.* Ann Arbor, MI: University of Michigan Press.

Adams, J., & Schantz, S.L. (2006). Editors' note: Methylmercury. *NeuroToxicology and Teratology, 28*, 527–528.

Agyeman, J., Doppelt, B., Lynn, K., & Hatic, H. (2007). The climate-justice link: Communicating risk with low-income and minority audiences. In S.C. Moser & L. Dilling (Eds.), *Creating a climate for change: Communicating climate change and facilitating social change* (pp. 119–138). New York, NY: Cambridge University Press.

Ajzen, I. (1991). The theory of planned behavior. *Organizational Behavior and Human Decision Processes, 50*(2), 179–211.

Ajzen, I. (1998). Models of human social behavior and their application to health psychology. *Psychology & Health, 13*(4), 735–739.

Ajzen, I., & Fishbein, M. (Eds.). (1980). *Understanding attitudes and predicting social behavior.* Englewood Cliffs, NJ: Prentice-Hall.

Albee, G.W. (1998). The politics of primary prevention. *The Journal of Primary Prevention, 19*(2), 117–127.

Altman, I., & Low, S.M. (Eds.). (1992). *Place attachment* (pp. 279–304). New York, NY: Plenum.

Amel, E.L., Manning, C.M., & Scott, B.A. (2009). Mindfulness and sustainable behavior: Pondering attention and awareness as means for increasing green behavior. *Ecopsychology, 1*, 14–25.

American Academy of Child & Adolescent Psychiatry. (2004). *Facts for Families: Conduct disorder.* Retrieved from http://www.aacap.org/cs/root/facts_for_families/conduct_disorder.

American Academy of Pediatrics. (n.d.). *Media matters: Media education in the practice setting. An overview of media and the pediatrician's role.* Retrieved from http://www.aap.org/advocacy/mmguide.pdf

American Academy of Pediatrics, Committee on Nutrition. (2003). Policy statement: Prevention of pediatric overweight and obesity. *Pediatrics, 112,* 424–430.

American Geophysical Union (2007). AGU Position Statement: Human impacts on climate. Retrieved from http://www.agu.org/outreach/science_policy/positions/climate_change2008.shtml

American Heart Association. (2008). *Overweight and obesity statistics.* Retrieved from http://www.americanheart.org/downloadable/heart/1197994908531FS16OVR08.pdf

American Institute of Architects. (2008). *Counties with green building programs have increased almost 500% since 2003.* Retrieved from http://www.aia.org/press/releases/AIAS077048?dvid=&recspec=AIAS077048

American Psychiatric Association. (2000). *Diagnostic and statistical manual of mental disorders* (DSM-IV-TR), Washington, DC: Author.

American Psychological Association. (2010). *Publication manual* (6th ed.). Washington, DC: Author.

Americans 'need' their gadgets. (2005, December 21). *Associated press.* Retrieved from http://www.wired.com/science/discoveries/news/2005/12/69896

Anderson, C.A. (2001). Heat and violence. *Current Directions in Psychological Science, 10,* 33–38.

Anderson, C.A., & Bushman, B.J. (2001). Effects of violent video games on aggressive behavior, aggressive cognition, aggressive affect, physiological arousal, and prosocial behavior: A meta-analytic review of the scientific literature. *Psychological Science, 12,* 353–359.

Anthony, C. (1995). Eco-psychology and the deconstruction of whitemenss. In T. Roszak, M.E. Gomes, & A.D. Kanner (Eds.), *Eco-psychology: Restoring the earth, healing the mind* (pp. 263–278). San Francisco, CA: Sierra Club.

Appleton, J. (1975). *The experience of landscape.* New York, NY: Wiley.

Appuzzo, M. (2008, October 19). Palin hometown a window into her environmentalism. *Associated Press.* Retrieved from http://abcnews.go.com/Politics/wireStory?id=6067083

Arbuthnot, J., Tedeschi, R., Wayner, M., Turner, J., Kressel, S., & Rush, R. (1977). The induction of sustained recycling behavior through foot-in-the-door technique. *Journal of Environmental Systems, 6,* 353–366.

Arnetz, B.B. (1998). Environmental illness: Multiple chemical sensitivity, sick building syndrome, electric and magnetic field disease. In A. Lundberg (Ed.), *The environment and mental health: A guide for clinicians* (pp. 115–146). Mahwah, NJ: Erlbaum.

Arnocky, S., Stroink, M., & DeCicco, T. (2007). Self-construal predicts environmental concern, cooperation, and conservation. *Journal of Environmental Psychology, 27,* 255–264.

Arnold, R. (1993). *Ecology wars: Environmentalism as if people mattered.* Bellevue, WA: Meril Press.

Arnow, B., Kenardy, J., & Agras, W.S. (1992). Binge eating among the obese. *Journal of Behavioral Medicine, 15,* 155–170.

Aronson, E., & O'Leary, M. (1983). The relative effectiveness of models and prompts on energy conservation: A field experiment in a shower room. *Journal of Environmental Systems, 12,* 219–224.

Arroyo, V., & Preston, B. (2007). Change in the marketplace: Business leadership and communication. In S.C. Moser & L. Dilling (Eds.), *Creating a climate for change: Communicating climate change and facilitating social change* (pp. 319–338). Oxford, UK: Cambridge University Press.

Artz, N., & Cooke, P. (2007). Using e-mail listservs to promote environmentally sustainable behaviors. *Journal of Marketing Communications, 13,* 257–276.

Ascione, F.R. (2005). *Children and animals: Exploring the roots of kindness and cruelty.* West Lafayette, IN: Purdue University Press.

Ashley, P., Nishioka, M., Wooton, M.A., Zewatsky, J., Gaitens, J., & Anderson, J. (2006). *Healthy homes issues: Pesticides in the home—Use, hazards, and integrated pest management.* U.S. Department of Housing and Urban Development (HUD). Retrieved from http://www.hud.gov/offices/lead/library/hhi/Pesticide_Final_Revised_04-26-06.pdf

Aspen Publishers. (2007). EU regulations have global reach. *Business and the Environment, 18*(9), 1–3.

Association for the Advancement of Sustainability in Higher Education (n.d). Retrieved from http://www.aashe.org/

Associated Press. (2008, June 24). NASA climate scientist says "We're Toast." CBS News, Science/Technology. Retrieved from http://www.cbsnews.com/stories/2008/06/24/tech/main4204994.shtml?source=mostpop_story

Ayupan, L.B., & Oliveros, T.G. (1994). Filipino peasant women in defence of life. In V. Shiva (Ed.), *Close to home: Women reconnect ecology, health, and development* (pp. 113–120). London, UK: Earthscan.

Babisch, W. (2005). Noise and health. *Environmental health perspectives, 113,* A14–A15.

Baby Einstein Company LLC. (n.d.). 'About Baby Einstein.' Retrieved from http://www.babyeinstein.com/en/our_story/about_us

Backscheider, A.G., Shatz, M., & Gelman, S.A. (1993). Preschoolers' ability to distinguish living kinds as a function of regrowth. *Child Development, 64,* 1242–1257.

Bacon, F. (1620/1939). Preface to the great instauration. In E.A. Burtt (Ed.), *The English philosophers from Bacon to Mill* (p. 23). New York, NY: The Modern Library.

Bacon, F. (1620/1955). Preface of the great instauration. From H.G. Dick (Ed.), *Selected writings of Francis Bacon* (p. 437). New York, NY: The Modern Library.

Badal, J. (2007, October 29). House Calls. *Wall Street Journal—Eastern Edition, 250*(101), pR6.

Bailey, R. (1993). *Eco-scam: The false prophets of ecological apocalypse.* New York, NY: St. Martin's Press.

Bailey, R. (2002). *Global warming and other eco-myths: How the environmental movement uses false science to scare us to death.* New York: Prima.

Bakker, D.J. (1994). Dyslexia and the ecological brain. *Journal of Clinical and Experimental Neuropsychology. 16*(5), 734–743.

Baltes, M.M., & Hayward, S.C. (1976). Application and evaluation of strategies to reduce pollution: Behavior control of littering in a football stadium. *Journal of applied psychology, 61,* 501–506.

Bamberg, S., Ajzen, I., & Schmidt, P. (2003). Choice of travel mode in the theory of planned behavior: The roles of past behavior, habit, and reasoned action. *Basic and Applied Social Psychology, 25*(3), 175–187.

Bamberg, S., Hunecke, M., & Blobaum, A. (2007). Social context, personal norms, and the use of public transportation: Two field studies. *Journal of Environmental Psychology, 27,* 190–203.

Bamberg, S., & Moser, G. (2007). Twenty years after Hines, Hungerford, and Tomera: A new meta-analysis of psycho-social determinants of pro-environmental behaviour. *Journal of Environmental Psychology, 27*(1), 14–25.

Bamberg, S., & Schmidt, P. (2001). Theory-driven subgroup-specific evaluation of an intervention to reduce private car use. *Journal of Applied Social Psychology, 31*(6), 1300–1329.

Banaji, M.R., & Crowder, R.G. (1989). The bankruptcy of everyday memory. *American Psychologist, 44,* 1185–1193.

Bandura, A. (1977). *Social learning theory.* Englewood Cliffs, NJ: Prentice-Hall.

Bandura, A. (2002). Environmental sustainability by sociocognitive deceleration of population growth. In P. Schmuck & W.P. Schultz (Eds.), *Psychology of sustainable development* (pp. 209–238). Boston, MA: Kluwer Academic.

Bandura, A., & Walters, R.H. (1963). *Social learning and personality development.* New York, NY: Holt, Rinehart and Winston.

Barnes, G.E., & Prosen, H. (1985). Parental death and depression. *Journal of Abnormal Psychology, 94,* 64–69.

Barr, S. (2007). Factors influencing environmental attitudes and behaviors. *Environment and Behavior, 39,* 435–473.

Bassil, K.L., Vakil, C., Sanborn, M., Cole, D.C., Kaur, J.S., & Kerr, K.J. (2007). Cancer health effects of pesticides: Systematic review. *Canadian Family Physician, 53,* 1704–1711.

Baum, W.M. (1994). *Understanding behaviorism: Science, behavior, and culture.* New York, NY: HarperCollins.

Baumeister, R.F. (1987). How the self became a problem: A psychological review of historical research. *Journal of Personality and Social Psychology, 52,* 163–176.

Baumrind, D. (1971). Current patterns of parental authority. *Developmental Psychology Monographs, 4,* 1–103.

Bazerman, M.H. (1983). Negotiator judgment: A critical look at the rationality assumption. *American Behavioral Scientist, 27*(2), 211–228.

Bazerman, M.H. (2006). Climate change as a predictable surprise. *Climatic Change, 77,* 179–193.

Bazerman, M.H., & Hoffman, A.J. (1999). Sources of environmentally destructive behavior: Individual, organizational, and institutional perspectives. *Research in Organizational Behavior, 2,* 39–79.

Beatley, T. (2000). *Green urbanism: Learning from European cities.* Washington, DC: Island Press.

Beck, A.M., & Katcher, A.H. (2003). Future directions in human-animal bond research. *American Behavioral Scientist, 47,* 79–93.

Becker, E. (2004, April 2). White House undermined chemical tests, report says. *New York Times,* C2.

Beddoe, R., Costanza, R., Farley, J.U., Garza, E., Kent, J., Kubiszewski, I., . . . Woodward, J. (2009). Overcoming systematic roadblocks to sustainability: The evolutionary redesign of worldviews, institutions, and technologies. *Proceedings from the National Academy of Science (PNAS), 106,* 2483–2489.

Bee-Gates, D. (2007). *I want it now!: Navigating childhood in a materialistic world.* New York, NY: Palgrave MacMillan.

Beggs, P.J., & Bambrick, H.J. (2005). Is the global rise of asthma an early impact of anthropogenic climate change? *Environmental health perspectives, 113,* 915–919.

Begley, S. (2007). The truth about denial. *Newsweek* (U.S. edition), *150*(7), 20–29.

Bell, P.A., Greene, T.C., Fisher, J.D., & Baum, A. (2001). *Environmental psychology* (5th ed.). Fort Worth, TX: Harcourt College.

Bell, P.A., Petersen, T.R., & Hautaluoma, J.E. (1989). The effect of punishment probability on overconsumption and stealing in a simulated commons. *Journal of Applied Social Psychology, 19,* 1483–1495.

Bellinger, D.C., & Adams, H.F. (2001). Environmental pollutant exposures and children's cognitive abilities. In R. J. Sternberg & E.L. Grigorenko (Eds.), *Environmental effects on cognitive abilities* (pp. 157–188). Mahway, NJ: Erlbaum.

Bennett, L. (2008, November 14). Are human beings hard-wired to ignore the threat of catastrophic climate change? From *Greater Good, V*(2), 40–43. Retrieved from http://www.alternet.org/story/106982/?page=entire

Benoît, M., & Norton, M.I., (2003). Perceptions of a fluid consensus: Uniqueness bias, false consensus, false polarization, and pluralistic ignorance in a water conservation crisis. *Personality and Social Psychology Bulletin, 29,* 559–567.

Berenguer, J. (2007). The effect of empathy on pro-environmental attitudes and behaviors. *Environment and Behavior, 39,* 269–283.

Berg-Cross, L. (2000). *Basic concepts in family therapy: An introductory text* (2nd ed.). New York, NY: Hayworth Press.

Berg, M., & Medrich, E.A. (1980). Children in four neighborhoods: The physical environment and its effect on play and play patterns. *Environment and Behavior, 12,* 320–348.

Beringer, A. (2003). A conservation psychology with heart. *Human Ecology Review, 10,* 150–153.

Berry, T.M. (1999). *The great work.* New York, NY: Bell Tower.

Berto, R. (2005). Exposure to restorative environments helps restore attentional capacity. *Journal of Environmental Psychology, 25,* 249–259.

Bevc, C.A., Marshall, B.K., & Picou, J.S. (2007). Environmental justice and toxic exposure: Toward a spatial model of physical health and psychological well-being. *Social Science Research, 36,* 48–67.

Bicchieri, C. (2002). Covenants without swords: Group identity, norms, and communication in social dilemmas. *Rationality and Society, 14,* 192. doi: 10.1177/1043446310201400 2003

Bicchieri, C., & Lev-On, A. (2007). Computer-mediated communication and cooperation in social dilemmas: An experimental analysis. *Politics, Philosophy, & Economics, 6,* 139–168.

Biele, G., Rieskamp, J., & Czienskowski, U. (2008). Explaining cooperation in groups: Testing models of reciprocity and learning. *Organizational Behavior and Human Decision Processes, 106,* 89–105.

Biello, D. (2009, April 3). Are some chemicals more dangerous at low doses? *Scientific American: 60 Second Science.* Retrieved from http://www.sciam. com/blog/60-second-science/post.cfm?id=are-some-chemicals-more-dangerous-a-2009-04-03

Bilder, R.M., & LeFever, F.F. (Eds.). (1998). Neuroscience of the mind on the centennial of Freud's project for a scientific psychology (1895). *Annals of NY Academy of Sciences* (Vol. 843). New York, NY: New York Academy of Sciences.

Billig, M. (2006). Is my home my castle? Place attachment, risk perception, and religious faith. *Environment and Behavior, 38,* 248–265.

Birjulin, A.A., Smith, J.M., & Bell, P.A. (1993). Monetary reward, verbal reinforcement, and harvest strategy of others in the commons dilemma. *Journal of Social Psychology, 133*(2), 207–214.

Bista, D.B. (1991). *Fatalism and development: Nepal's struggle for modernization.* Calcutta, India: Orient Longman.

Bixler, R.D., & Floyd, M.F. (1997). Nature is scary, disgusting, and uncomfortable. *Environment and Behavior, 29,* 443–467.

Bixler, R.D., Floyd, M.F., & Hammitt, W.E. (2002.) Environmental socialization: Quantitative tests of the childhood play hypothesis. *Environment and Behavior, 34,* 795–818.

Björkman, M. (1984). Decision making, risk taking and psychological time: Review of empirical findings and psychological theory. *Scandinavian Journal of Psychology, 25,* 31–49.

Black, J.S., Stern, P.C., & Elsworth, J.T. (1985). Personal and contextual influences on household energy adaptations. *Journal of Applied Psychology, 70,* 3–21.

Block, B. (2008, September 23). Report reveals flawed U.S. e-waste policies. *Worldwatch Institute.* Retrieved from http://us.oneworld.net/article/357583-us-e-waste-policies-need-reform

Bloom, A. (1987). *The closing of the American mind: How higher education has failed democracy and impoverished the souls of today's students.* New York, NY: Simon and Schuster.

Boaz, N.T. (2002). *Evolving health: The origins of illness and how the modern world is making us sick.* New York, NY: John Wiley and Sons.

Bodnar, S. (2008). Wasted and bombed: Clinical enactments of a changing relationship to the Earth. *Psychoanalytic Dialogues, 18,* 484–512.

Boldero, J. (1995). The prediction of household recycling of newspapers: The role of attitudes, intentions, and situational factors. *Journal of Applied Social Psychology, 25*(5), 440–462.

Bonnes, M., Uzzell, D., Carrus, G., & Kelay, T. (2007). Inhabitants' and experts' assessments of environmental quality for urban sustainability. *Journal of Social Issues, 63,* 59–78.

Boone, C., Declerck, C.H., & Suetens, S. (2008). Subtle social cues, explicit incentives and cooperation in social dilemmas. *Evolution and Human Behavior, 29,* 179–188.

Booth, A.L. (1998). Caring for nature 101, or alternative perspectives on educating natural resource managers and ecologically conscious citizens. *Journal of Environmental Education, 29*(3), 4–10.

Boring, E.G. (1950/1957). *A history of experimental psychology.* New York, NY: Appleton-Centry-Crofts.

Borkowski, L. (2004, spring). Shareholders in action: Tackling corporate toxins. *Co-Op America Quarterly, 62,* 14–15. Retrieved from http://www.greenamericatoday.org/PDF/CAQ62.pdf

Bornschein, S., Hausteiner, C., Konrad, F., Forstl, H., & Zilker, T. (2006). Psychiatric morbidity and toxic burden in patients with environmental illness: A controlled study. *Psychosomatic Medicine, 68,*104–109.

Boseley, S. (2009). Climate change biggest threat to health, doctors say. *Guardian* [online edition]. Retrieved from http://www.guardian.co.uk/environment/2009/may/13/climate-change-health-impact

Bostrom, A., & Lashof, D. (2007). Weather it's climate change? In S. C. Moser & L. Dilling (Eds.), *Creating a climate for change: Communicating climate change and facilitating social change* (pp. 31–43). New York, NY: Cambridge University Press.

Bott, S., Cantrill, J.G., & Myers, O.E. (2003). Place and the promise of conservation psychology. *Human Ecology Review, 10,* 100–112.

Bowlby, J. (1989). The role of attachment in personality development and psychopathology. In S.I. Greenspan & G.H. Pollock (Eds.), *The course of life,* (Vol. 1: *Infancy,* pp. 229–270). Madison, CT: International Universities Press

Bowler, P.J. (1989). *The invention of progress: The Victorians and the past* (p. 200). Cambridge, MA: Basil Blackwell.

Boyce, T.E., & Geller, E.S. (2001). Encouraging college students to support pro-environment behavior: Effects of direct versus indirect rewards. *Environment and Behavior, 33,* 107–125.

Boyle, S.H., Jackson, W.G., & Suarez, E.C. (2007). Hostility, anger, and depression predict increases in C3 over a 10-year period. *Brain, Behavior, and Immunity, 21,* 826–823.

Bragg, E.A. (1996). Towards ecological self: Deep ecology meets constructionist self-theory. *Journal of Environmental Psychology, 16,* 93–108.

Bratt, C. (1999). The impact of norms and assumed consequences on recycling behavior. *Environment and Behavior, 31*(5), 630–656.

Bratton, S.P. (1984). Christian ecotheology and the old testament. *Environmental Ethics, 6,* 195–209.

Braun, J.M., Froehlich, T.E., Daniels, J.L., Dietrich, K.N., Hornung, R., Auinger, P., et al. (2008). Association of environmental toxicants and conduct disorder in U.S. children: NHANES 2001–2004. *Environmental Health Perspectives, 116,* 956–962.

Braun, J.M., Kahn, R.S., Froehlich, T., Auinger, P., & Lanphear, B.P. (2006). Exposures to environmental toxicants and attention deficit hyperactivity disorder in U.S. children. *Environmental Health Perspectives, 114,* 1904–1909.

Brechin, S.R., & Freeman, D.A. (2004). Public support for both the environment and an anti-environmental president: Possible explanations for the George W. Bush anomaly. *The Forum: A Journal of Applied Research in Contemporary Politics, 2*(1). Retrieved from http://www.bepress.com/forum/vol2/iss1/art6

Briere, J., Downes, A., & Spensley, J. (1983). Summer in the city: Urban weather conditions and psychiatric emergency room visits. *Journal of Abnormal Psychology, 92,* 77–80.

Broadhurst, P.L. (1959). The interaction of task difficulty and motivation: The Yerkes-Dodson law revived. *Acta Psychologica, 16,* 321–338.

Brod, C. (1984). *Technostress: The human cost of the computer revolution.* Reading, MA: Addison-Wesley.

Broder, J.M. (2009, May 1). Seeking to save the planet, with a thesaurus. *New York Times.* http://www.nytimes.com/2009/05/02/us/politics/02enviro.html

Bronzaft, A. (1996). The increase in noise pollution: What are the health effects? The harmful effects of noise. *Nutrition Health Review* [online edition]. Retrieved from http://findarticles.com/p/articles/mi_m0876/is_n78/ai_20375099/pg_1?tag=artBody;col1

Bronzaft, A.L. (2002). Noise pollution: A hazard to physical and mental well-being. In R.B. Bechtel & A. Churchman (Eds.), *Handbook of environmental psychology* (pp. 499–510). New York, NY: John Wiley & Sons.

Brook, A. (2005). *Effects of contingencies of self-worth on self-regulation of behavior.* Unpublished doctoral dissertation, University of Michigan, Ann Arbor.

Brower, M., & Leon, W. (1999). *The consumer's guide to effective environmental choices.* Cambridge, MA: Three Rivers Press.

Brown, B.B., & Perkins, D. (1992). Disruption in place attachment. In I. Altman, & S.M. Low (Eds.), *Place attachment* (pp. 279–304). New York, NY: Plenum.

Brown, K.W., & Kasser, T. (2005). Are psychological and ecological well-being compatible? The role of values, mindfulness, and lifestyle. *Social Indicators Research, 74*, 349–368.

Brown, R. (1965). *Social psychology* (p. 451). New York, NY: Basic Books.

Brummans, B.H. J.M., Putman, L.L., Gray, B., Hanke, R., Lewicki, R.J., & Wiethoff, C. (2008). Making sense of intractable multiparty conflict: A study of framing in four environmental disputes. *Communication Monographs, 75*, 25–51.

Bullard, R.D. (1983, Spring). Solid waste sites and the Black Houston community. *Sociological inquiry, 53*, 273–288.

Bullard, R.D. (1990, Winter). Ecological inequities and the New South: Black communities under siege. *Journal of Ethnic Studies, 17*, 101–115.

Bullard, R.D. (1993). *Confronting environmental racism: Voices from the grass-roots*. Boston, MA: South End Press.

Bullard, R.D. (1994). *Dumping in Dixie: Race, class and environmental quality*. Boulder, CO: Westview Press.

Bullard, R.D. (1996). *Unequal protection: Environmental justice and communities of color*. San Francisco, CA: Sierra Club.

Bullard, R.D., & Johnson, G.S. (2000). Environmental justice: Grassroots activism and its impact on public policy decision making. *Journal of Social Issues, 56*, 555–578.

Bunn, M., & Bunn, G. (2002). Reducing the threat of nuclear theft and sabotage. *International Atomic Energy Agency*. Retrieved from http://www.iaea.org/NewsCenter/Features/Nuclear_Terrorism/bunn02.pdf

Burger, J.M. (1999). The foot-in-the-door compliance procedure: A multiple-process analysis and review. *Personality and Social Psychology Review, 3*(4), 303–325.

Burke, J. (1985). *The day the universe changed*. Boston, MA: Little, Brown and Co.

Burtt, E.A. (1939). *The English philosophers from Bacon to Mill* (pp. 433–441). New York, NY: The Modern Library.

Burtt, E.A. (1954). *The metaphysical foundations of modern science*. Garden City, NY: Doubleday.

Butterfield, H. (1960). *The origins of modern science, 1300–1800*. New York, NY: Macmillan.

Buzzell, L. & Chalquist, C. (2009). *Ecotherapy: Healing with nature in mind*. San Francisco: Sierra Club Books.

Cahalan, W. (1995). Ecological groundedness in Gestalt therapy. In T. Roszak, M.E. Gomes, & A.D. Kanner (Eds.), *Ecopsychology: Restoring the earth, healing, the mind* (pp. 216–223). San Francisco, CA: Sierra Club.

Cairns, J. (1998). The Zen of sustainable use of the planet: Steps on the path to enlightenment. *Population and Environment, 20*(2), 109–123.

California Department of Toxic Substances Control. (2007). Emerging chemicals of concern. *State of California*. Retrieved from http://www.dtsc.ca.gov/AssessingRisk/EmergingContaminants.cfm

Callicott, J.B. (1994). The land aesthetic. In K.C. Chapple & M.E. Tucker (Eds.), *Ecological prospects: Scientific, religious, and aesthetic perspectives*. Albany, NY: State University of New York Press.

Canfield, R.L., Henderson, C.R., Cory-Slechta, D.A., Cox, C., Jusko, T.A., Lanphear, B.P. (2003). *New England Journal of Medicine, 348*(16), 1517–1526.

Canu, W., & Gordon, M. (2005). Mother nature as treatment for ADHD: Overstating the benefits of green. *American Journal of Public Health, 95,* 371.

Capsi, A., Taylor, A., Moffitt, T., & Plomin, R. (2000). Neighborhood deprivation affects children's mental health: Environmental risks identified in a genetic design. *Psychological Science, 11,* 338–342.

Carey, S. (1985). *Conceptual change in childhood*. Cambridge, MA: Massachusetts Institute of Technology Press.

Carlson, N. (1995). *Foundations of physiological psychology* (3rd ed.). Needham Heights, MA: Allyn & Bacon.

Carrus, G., Passafaro, P., & Bonnes, M. (2008). Emotions, habits, and rational choices in ecological behaviours: The case of recycling and use of public transportation. *Journal of Environmental Psychology, 28,* 51–62.

Carson, R. (1962). *Silent spring*. New York, NY: Houghton Mifflin.

Cart, J. (2008, August 30). Gov. Sarah Palin has put drilling above environment. *Los Angeles Times*. Retrieved from http://www.latimes.com/news/science/environment/la-na-mccainveepenviro30-2008aug30,0,3506869.story

Cart, J. (2008, December 12). Endangered Species Act is modified; Bush administration changes could speed up projects and allow drilling in Alaska's polar bear habitat. *Los Angeles Times*. Retrieved from http://theguzzler.blogspot.com/2008/12/endangered-species-act-is-modified.html

Casey, L., & Lloyd, M. (1977). Cost and effectiveness of litter removal procedures in an amusement park. *Environment and behavior, 9,* 535–546.

Casey, P.J., & Scott, K. (2006). Environmental concern and behaviour in an Australian sample within an ecocentric-anthropocentric framework. *Australian Journal of Psychology, 58*(2), 57–67.

Catholic Coalition on Climate Change. (2008, August 6). *Meeting of the Holy Father Benedict XVI with the clergy of the diocese of Balzano-Bressanone*. Retrieved from http://www.catholicsandclimatechange.org/pdf/Pope_Aug_6_08.pdf

Catton, W.R. (1993). Carrying capacity and the death of a culture: A tale of two autopsies. *Sociological Inquiry, 63,* 202–222.

Centers for Disease Control and Prevention. (2006). *Developmental Disabilities*. Atlanta, GA. Retrieved from http://www.cdc.gov/ncbddd/dd/ddsurv.htm

Centers for Disease Control and Prevention. (2007). *Community-based interventions to reduce motor vehicle-related injuries: Evidence of effectiveness from systematic reviews*. Atlanta, GA. Retrieved from http://www.cdc.gov/ncipc/duip/mvsafety.htm

Centers for Disease Control and Prevention. (2008a). *Overweight and obesity: Childhood overweight and Obesity*. Atlanta, GA. Retrieved from http://www.cdc.gov/obesity/childhood/index.html

Centers for Disease Control and Prevention. (2008b). *Smoking and tobacco use: Health effects of cigarette smoking.* Atlanta, GA. Retrieved from http://www.cdc.gov/tobacco/data_statistics/fact _sheets/health_effects/effects_cig_smoking/index.htm

Centers for Disease Control and Prevention. (2008c). *Suicide: Facts at a glance.* Atlanta, GA. Retrieved from http://www.cdc.gov/ncipc/dvp/Suicide/suicide_data_sheet.pdf.

Centers for Disease Control and Prevention. (2009). *Healthy youth: Health topics: Asthma.* Atlanta, GA. Retrieved from http://www.cdc.gov/HealthyYouth/asthma/index.htm

Chafe, Z., & French, H. (2008). Improving carbon markets. In G. Gardner & T. Prugh (Eds.), *2008 state of the world: Innovations for a sustainable economy. A worldwatch institute report on progress toward a sustainable society* (pp. 91–106). New York, NY: W.W. Norton & Co.

Charboneau, J.P., & Koger, S.M. (in press). Flame retardants and developmental disabilities: A cause for concern. In Paulo B. Merlani (Ed.), *Flame retardants: Functions, properties and safety.* Hauppauge, NY: Nova Science.

Chard, P. (1994). *The healing earth: Nature's medicine for the troubled soul.* Minnetonka, MN: NorthWord Press.

Charles, C., Louv, R., Bodner, L., & Guns, B. (2008). *Children and nature 2008: A report on the movement to reconnect children to the natural world.* Santa Fe, NM: Children and Nature Network. Retrieved from http://www.naturalplaygrounds.ca/files/Children_and_Nature_Network_~The_movement_to_reconnect_children_with_nature.pdf

Chawla, L. (1988). Children's concern for the natural environment. *Children's Environments Quarterly, 5*(3), 13–20.

Chawla, L. (1990). Ecstatic places. *Children's Environments Quarterly, 7*(4), 18–23.

Chawla, L. (1994). *In the first country of places: Nature, poetry, and childhood memory.* Albany, NY: State University of New York Press.

Chawla, L. (1998a). Research methods to investigate significant life experiences: Review and recommendations. *Environmental Education Research, 4,* 383–398.

Chawla, L. (1998b). Significant life experiences revisited: A review of research on sources of environmental sensitivity. *Environmental Education Research, 4,* 369–382.

Chawla, L. (2001). Significant life experiences revisited once again: Response to Vol. 5(4) 'Five critical commentaries on significant life experience research in environmental education. *Environmental Education Research, 7,* 451–461.

Chawla, L., & Cushing, D.F. (2007). Education for strategic environmental behavior. *Environmental Education Research, 13,* 437–452.

Chess, C., & Johnson, B.B. (2007). Information is not enough. In S.C. Moser & L. Dilling (Eds.), *Creating a climate for change: Communicating climate change and facilitating social change* (pp. 223–236). Cambridge, UK: Cambridge University Press.

Cheung, C., & Chan, C. (1996). Television viewing and mean world value in Hong Kong's adolescents. *Social Behavior and Personality, 24*, 351–364.

Chodorow, N. (1974). Family structure and feminine personality. In M.X. Rosaldo & L. Lamphere (Eds.), *Woman, culture, and society* (pp. 43–66). Stanford, CA: Stanford University Press.

Chodorow, N. (1978). *The reproduction of mothering: Psychoanalysis and the sociology of gender.* Berkeley, CA: University of California Press.

Chodorow, N. (1989). *Feminism and psychoanalytic theory.* New Haven, CT: Yale University Press.

Christakis, D.A. (2006). The hidden and potent effects of television advertising. *Journal of the American Medical Association, 295*, 1698–1699.

Christakis, D.A., Zimmerman, F.J., DiGiuseppe, D.L., & McCarty, C.A. (2004). Early television exposure and subsequent attentional problems in children. *Pediatrics, 113*, 708–713.

Christie, D.J., Wagner, R.V., & Winter, D.D. N. (Eds.). (2001). *Peace, conflict, and violence: Peace psychology for the 21st century.* Upper Saddle River, NJ: Prentice Hall/Pearson Education.

Cialdini, R.B. (2003). Crafting normative messages to protect the environment. *Current Directions in Psychological Science, 12*(4), 105–109.

Cialdini, R.B., Kallgren, C.A., & Reno, R.R. (1991). A focus theory of normative conduct: A theoretical refinement and reevaluation of the role of norms in human behavior. *Advances in Experimental Social Psychology, 24*, 201–234.

Cialdini, R.B., Reno, R.R., & Kallgren, C.A. (1990). A focus theory of normative conduct: Recycling the concept of norms to reduce littering in public places. *Journal of Personality and Social Psychology, 58*, 1015–1026.

Clapp, R.W., Jacobs, M.M., & Loechler, E.L. (2008). Environmental and occupational causes of cancer: New evidence, 2005–2007. *Reviews on Environmental Health, 23*, 1–37.

Clark, J.P., Marmol, L.M., Cooley, R., & Gathercoal, K. (2004). The effects of wilderness therapy on the clinical concerns (axes I, II, and IV) of troubled adolescents. *Journal of Experiential Education, 27*, 213–232.

Clark, M.E. (1989). *Ariadne's thread: The search for new modes of thinking.* New York, NY: St. Martin's Press.

Clark, M., & Lawn, P. (2008). A policy analysis of Victoria's genuine progress indictor. *The Journal of Socio-Economics, 37*, 864–879.

Clayton, S. (1994). Appeals to justice in the environmental debate. *Journal of Social Issues, 50*(3), 13–27.

Clayton, S. (2003a). Environmental identity: A conceptual and an operational definition. In S. Clayton & S. Opotow (Eds.), *Identity and the natural environment: The psychological significance of nature* (pp. 45–66). Cambridge, MA: Massachusetts Institute of Technology Press.

Clayton, S. (2003b). Justice and identity: Changing perspectives on what is fair. *Personality and Social Psychology Review, 7*, 298–310.

Clayton, S., & Brook, A. (2005). Can psychology help save the world? A model for conservation psychology. *Analyses of Social Issues and Public Policy, 5*, 87–102.

Clayton, S. & Myers, G. (2009). *Conservation psychology: Understanding and promoting human care for nature.* Oxford, UK: Wiley-Blackwell.

Clayton S., & Opotow, S. (2003). *Identity and the natural environment: The psychological significance of nature.* Cambridge, MA: Massachusetts Institute of Technology Press.

Clements, R. (2004). An investigation of the status of outdoor play. *Contemporary Issues in Early Childhood, 5,* 68–80.

Climate change poses serious threat to U.S. National Security. (2007, April 17). *Science Daily.* Retrieved from http://www.sciencedaily.com/releases/2007/04/070417092232.htm

Clinebell, H. (1996). *Ecotherapy: Healing ourselves, healing the earth.* New York: Haworth.

CNA. (2007). *National security and the threat of climate change.* Retrieved from http://www.cna.org/nationalsecurity/climate/

Cobb, E. (1977). *The ecology of imagination in childhood.* New York, NY: Columbia University Press.

Cobern, M.K., Porter, B.E., Leeming, F.C., & Dwyer, W.W. (1995). The effect of commitment on adoption and diffusion of grass recycling. *Environment and Behavior, 27,* 213–232.

Coburn, M. (2006). Walking home: Women's transformative experiences in the wilderness of the Appalachian Trail. *Dissertation Abstracts International: Section B. The Sciences and Engineering, 67,* 2857.

Cohen, M. (1997). *Reconnecting with nature.* Corvallis, OR: Ecopress.

Cohen, M.J. (1993). Integrated ecology: The process of counseling with nature. *Humanistic Psychologist, 21*(3), 277–295.

Cohen, S., & Wills, T.A. (1985). Stress, social support, and the buffering hypothesis. *Psychological Bulletin, 98,* 310–357.

Colborn, T. (1995). Pesticides: How research has succeeded and failed to translate science into policy: Endocrinological effects on wildlife. *Environmental Health Perspectives, 106*(Suppl. 6), 81–85.

Colborn, T. (2004). Neurodevelopment and endocrine disruption. *Environmental Health Perspectives, 112,* 944–949.

Colborn, T. (2006). A case for revisiting the safety of pesticides: A closer look at neurodevelopment. *Environmental Health Perspectives, 114,* 10–17.

Colborn, T., Dumanoski, D., & Myers J.P. (1997). *Our stolen future: Are we threatening our fertility, intelligence, and survival? A scientific detective story.* New York, NY: Plume.

Cole, N., & Watrous, S. (2007). Across the great divide: Supporting scientists as effective messengers in the public sphere. In S.C. Moser & L. Dilling (Eds.), *Creating a climate for change: Communicating climate change and facilitating social change* (pp. 180–198). Cambridge, United Kingdom: Cambridge University Press.

Cole, S. (2000). Zero-waste-on the move around the world: US Communities, retailers and other countries begin to implement producer responsibility. *Ecocycle Times: Conserving Resources in a Finite World.* Retrieved from http://www.ecocycle.org/TimesFall2000/ZeroWasteonTheMove.cfm

Coley, J.D. (2000). On the importance of comparative research: The case of folkbiology. *Child Development, 71*, 82–90.

Coley, J.D., Freeman, A.C., & Blaszczyk, K. (2003). *Taxonomic and ecological relations in urban and rural children's folk biology.* Retrieved from http://www.psych.neu.edu/faculty/j.coley/pub/CFB2003.pdf

Coley, J.D., Solomon, G.E.A., & Shafto, P. (2002). The development of folkbiology: A cognitive science perspective on children's understanding of the biological world. In P.H. Kahn Jr. & S.R. Kellert (Eds.), *Children and nature: Psychological, sociocultural, and evolutionary investigations* (pp. 65–91). Cambridge, MA: Massachusetts Institute of Technology Press.

Coley, R.L., Kuo, F.E., & Sullivan, W.C. (1997). Where does community grow?: The social context created by nature in urban public housing. *Environment and Behavior, 29*, 468–494.

Collaborative on Health and the Environment. (2008). *Mental health and environmental exposures.* From the Learning and Developmental Disabilities Initiative. Retrieved from http://www.iceh.org/pdfs/LDDI/MentalHealthFactSheet.pdf

Collins, A.M., & Loftus, E.F. (1975). A spreading-activation theory of semantic processing. *Psychological Review, 82*(6), 407–428.

Committee on Environmental Health. (2004). Ambient air pollution: Health hazards to children. *Pediatrics, 114*, 1699–1707.

Comstock, G. (1995). Television and the American child. In C.N. Hedley, P. Antonacci, & M. Rabinowitz (Eds.), *Thinking and literacy: The mind at work* (pp. 101–123). Hillsdale, NJ: Lawrence Erlbaum.

Cone, J.D., & Hayes, S.C. (1980). *Environmental problems/behavioral solutions.* Monterey, CA: Brooks/Cole.

Cone, M. (2009, March 31). Scientists find 'baffling' link between autism and vinyl flooring. *Environmental Health News; Environmental Health Sciences.* Retrieved from http://www.environmentalhealthnews.org/ehs/news/autism-and-vinyl-flooring

Congressional Black Caucus Foundation. (2004). *African Americans and climate change: An unequal burden.* Oakland, CA: Redefining Progress.

Conn, S. (1995). When the earth hurts, who responds? In T. Roszak, M.E. Gomes, & A.D. Kanner (Eds.), *Eco-psychology: Restoring the earth, healing the mind* (pp. 156–171). San Francisco, CA: Sierra Club.

Cooley, R. (1998). Wilderness therapy can help troubled adolescents. *International Journal of Wilderness, 4*(3), 18–20.

Co-op America. (2008). *National green pages: A directory of products and services for people and the planet.* Washington, DC: Author.

Cooperman, A. (2007). Evangelical angers peers with call for action on global warming. *The Washington Post*, Saturday, March 3. Retrieved from http://www.washingtonpost.com/wp-dyn/content/article/2007/03/02/AR2007030201442.html

Cooper Marcus, C. (2006). Healing gardens in hospitals. In C. Wagenaar (Ed.), *The architecture of hospitals* (pp. 314–329). Rotterdam, The Netherlands: NAi.

Cooper Marcus, C., & Barnes, M. (1999). Introduction: Historical and cultural perspective on healing gardens. In C. Cooper Marcus & M. Barnes (Eds.). *Healing gardens: Therapeutic benefits and design recommendations* (pp. 1–26). New York, NY: John Wiley & Sons.

Corbett, J.B. (2005). Altruism, self-interest, and the reasonable person model of environmentally responsible behavior. *Science Communication, 26,* 368–389.

Costa, L.G., & Giordano, G. (2007). Developmental neurotoxicity of polybrominated diphenyl ether (PBDE) flame retardants. *NeuroToxicology, 28,* 1047–1067.

Costanzo, M., Archer, D., Aronson, E., & Pettigrew, T. (1986). Energy conservation behavior: The difficult path from information to action. *American Psychologist, 41*(5), 521–528.

Covello, V.T. (1993). Public confidence in industry and government: A crisis in environmental risk communication. In G.T. Miller (Ed.), *Living in the environment: An introduction to environmental science* (7th ed.). Belmont, CA: Wadsworth.

Cox, J.R. (1982). The die is cast: Topical and ontological dimensions of the locus of the irreparable. *Quarterly Journal of Speech, 68,* 227–239.

Coyle, K. (2005). *Environmental literacy in America: What ten years of NEETF/ Roper research and related studies say about environmental literacy in the U.S.* Washington, DC: The National Environmental Education & Training Foundation. Retrieved from http://www.csu.edu/cerc/documents/ EnvironmentalLiteracyInAmerica2005.pdf

Craig, C.S., & McCann, J.M. (1978). Assessing communication effects on energy conservation. *Journal of Consumer Research, 5,* 82–88.

Cress, U., & Kimmerle, J. (2007). Guidelines and feedback in information exchange: The impact of behavioral anchors and descriptive norms in a social dilemma. *Group Dynamics: Theory, Research, and Practice, 11,* 42–53.

Crocker, J., Brook, A.T., Niiya, Y., & Villacorta, M. (2006). The pursuit of self-esteem: Contingencies of self-worth and self regulation. *Journal of Personality, 74,* 1749–1771.

Crompton, T. (2008). *Weathercocks & signposts: The environment movement at a crossroads.* World Wildlife Fund-United Kingdom Strategies for Change Project. Retrieved from http://www.wwf.org.uk/research_centre/ research_centre_results.cfm?uNewsID=2224

Crompton, T., & Kasser, T. (2009). *Identity campaigning: Bringing the person into the environmental movement.* Godalming, UK: World Wildlife.

Csikszentmihalyi, M. (1990). *Flow: The psychology of optimal experience.* New York, NY: Harper & Row.

Csikszentmihalyi, M. (2004). What we must accomplish in the coming decades. *Zygon, 39,* 359–366.

Curtis, L.T., & Patel, K. (2008). Nutritional and environmental approaches to preventing and treating autism and attention deficit hyperactivity disorder (ADHD): A review. *Journal of Alternative and Complementary Medicine, 14,* 79–85.

Cvetkovich, G., & Earle, T. (1992). Environmental hazards and the public. *Journal of Social Issues, 48*(4), 1–20.

Daamen, D.D.L., Staats, H., Wilke, H.A.M., & Engelen, M. (2001). Improving environmental behavior in companies: The effectiveness of tailored versus nontailored interventions. *Environment and Behavior, 33*, 229–248.

Dadds, M.R., Whiting, C., Bunn, P., Fraser, J.A., Charlson, J.H., & Pirola-Merlo, A. (2004). Measurement of cruelty in children: The cruelty to animals inventory. *Journal of Abnormal Child Psychology, 32*, 321–334.

Damasio, A.R. (1994a). Descartes' error and the future of human life. *Scientific American, 271*(4), 144.

Damasio, A.R. (1994b). *Descartes' error: Emotion, reason, and the human brain.* New York, NY: Grosset/Putnam.

Dang-Vu, T.T., Desseilles, M., Peigneux, P., & Maquet, P. (2006). A role for sleep in brain plasticity. *Pediatric Rehabilitation, 9*, 98–118.

Dankelman, I., & Davidson, J. (1988). *Women and environment in the third world: Alliance for the future.* London, UK: Earthscan.

Darley, J.M., & Beniger, J.R. (1981). Diffusion of energy-conserving innovations. *Journal of Social Issues, 37*(2), 150–171.

David, L., Bender, L., Burns, S.Z., & Chilcott, L. (Producers), & Guggenheim, D. (Director). (2006). *An Inconvenient Truth* (Motion picture). US: Paramount.

Davidson, L.M., & Baum, A. (1996). Chronic stress and posttraumatic stress disorder. *Journal of Consulting and Clinical Psychology, 54*, 303–308.

Davidson, R.J. (2000). Cognitive neuroscience needs affective neuroscience (and vice versa). *Brain and Cognition, 42*, 89–32.

Davis, C. (2007). *January 2007 Monthly Update: Forest Certification and the Path to Sustainable Forest Management.* World Resources Institute. Retrieved from http://earthtrends.wri.org/updates/node/156

Davis, J. (1996). An integrated approach to the scientific study of the human spirit. In B. Driver, D. Dustin, T. Baltic, G. Elsner, & G. Peterson (Eds.), *Nature and the human spirit* (pp. 417–429). Radnor, PA: Venture.

Davis, J. (1998). The transpersonal dimensions of ecopsychology: Nature, non-duality, and spiritual practice. *The Humanistic Psychologist, 26*, 69–100.

Dawes, R.M. (1980). Social dilemmas. *Annual Review of Psychology, 31*, 169–193.

Dawes, R., van de Kragt, A., & Orbell, J. (1990). Cooperation for the benefit of us, not me, or my conscience. In J. Mansbridge (Ed.), *Beyond self-interest.* Chicago, IL: University of Chicago Press.

De Cremer, D., & Van Vugt, M. (1999). Social identification effects in social dilemmas: A transformation of motives. *European Journal of Social Psychology, 29*, 871–893.

De Graaf, J., Wann, D., & Naylor, T.H. (2005). *Affluenza: The all-consuming epidemic.* San Francisco, CA: Berrett-Koehler Publishers.

De Hoog, N., Stroebe, W., & de Wit, J.B. (2005). The impact of fear appeals on processing and acceptance of action recommendations. *Personality and Social Psychology Bulletin, 31*, 24–33.

DeKwaadsteniet, E.W., van Dijk, E., Wit, A., & De Cremer, D. (2008). How many of us are there? Group size uncertainty and social value orientations in common resource dilemmas. *Group Processes & Intergroup Relations, 11*, 387–399.

DeLoria, V., DeLoria, B., Foehner, K., & Scinta, S. (Eds.). (1999). *Spirit and reason: The Vine DeLoria, Jr. Reader*. Golden, CO: Fulcrum.

Dempsey Foundation Funds Environmental Chair at Willamette. (2008). Retrieved from http://blog.willamette.edu/news/archives/2007/05/dempsey_foundat.php

Dennis, M.L., Soderstrom, E.J., Koncinski, W.S., & Cavanaugh, B. (1990). Effective dissemination of energy-related information: Applying social psychology and evaluation research. *American Psychologist, 45*, 1109–1117.

Derr, T. (2006). Sometimes birds sound like fish: Perspectives on children's place experiences. In C. Spencer & M. Blades (Eds.), *Children and their environments: Learning, using and designing spaces.* (pp. 108–123). New York, NY: Cambridge University Press.

Derr, V. (2002). Children's sense of place in northern New Mexico. *Journal of Environmental Psychology, 22*, 125–137.

Descartes, R. (1627/1958). Discourse on method, part 4. In N.K. Smith, (Selected & Trans.), *Descartes' philosophical writings* (p. 119). New York, NY: The Modern Library.

Deth, R., Muratore, C., Benzecry, J., Power-Charnitsky, V.A., & Waly, M. (2008). How environmental and genetic factors combine to cause autism: A redox/methylation hypothesis. *NeuroToxicology, 29*, 190–201.

Deutsch, A. (2007). Indonesian flooding death toll at 36. *Washington Post.* Retrieved from http://www.washingtonpost.com/wp-dyn/content/article/2007/02/05/AR2007020500159.html

Devall, B., & Sessions, G. (1985). *Deep ecology: Living as if nature mattered*. Salt Lake City, UT: Peregrine Smith Books.

De Wet, M.J. (2008). An exploration of modern consumer society and a guide towards mindful consuming. *Dissertation Abstracts International, 69*(3-B), 1948.

DeYoung, R. (2000). Expanding and evaluating motives for environmentally responsible behavior. *Journal of Social Issues, 56*, 509–526.

Diamond, I., & Orenstein, G.F. (1990). Introduction. In I. Diamond & G. F. Orenstein, (Eds.), *Reweaving the world: The emergence of ecofeminism* (pp. ix–xv). San Francisco, CA: Sierra Club.

Diamond, J. (1988). The golden age that never was. *Discover, 9*, 71–79.

Diamond, J. (1992). *The third chimpanzee: The evolution and future of the human animal.* New York, NY: HarperPerennial.

Diamond, J. (2005). *Collapse: How societies choose to fail or survive*. London, UK: Allen Lane.

Diaz, J.O., & Dayal, A. (2008). Sense of place: A model for community based psychosocial support programs. *Australasian Journal of Disaster and Trauma Studies.*

Dick, H.G. (1955). *Introduction: Selected writings of Francis Bacon* (p. ix). New York, NY: The Modern Library.

DiCaprio, L., Conners Petersen, L., Castleberry, C., & Gerber, B. (Producers), & Conners Petersen, L. & Conners, N. (Directors). (2007). *The 11th Hour* [Motion picture. US: Warner Independent Pictures.

DiClemente, C. (2003). *Addiction and change: How addictions develop and addicted people recover.* New York, NY: Guilford.

Diener, E., & Seligman, M.E.P. (2002). Very happy people. *Psychological Science, 13,* 81–84.

Dietz, T.M., Fitzgerald, A., & Shwom, R. (2005). Environmental values. *Annual Review of Environment & Resources, 30,* 1–38.

Dietz, T.M., Rosa, E.A., & York, R. (2009). Efficient well-being: Rethinking sustainability as the relationship between human well-being and environmental impacts. *Human Ecology Review, 16,* 114–123.

Dietz, T., & Stern, P.C. (2008). *Public participation in environmental assessment and decision making.* Washington, DC: The National Academies Press. Retrieved from http://www.nap.edu/catalog.php?record_id=12434

Dietz, W., & Gortmaker, S. (1985). Do we fatten our children at the television set?: Obesity and television viewing in children and adolescents. *Pediatrics, 75,* 807–812.

Dilling, L., & Moser, S.C. (2007). Introduction. In S.C. Moser & L. Dilling (Eds.), *Creating a climate for change: Communicating climate change and facilitating social change* (pp. 1–27). Cambridge, UK: Cambridge University Press.

Dineen, S. (2005). The throwaway generation: 25 billion styrofoam cups a year. *E/The Environmental Magazine.* Retrieved from http://www.emagazine.com/view/?2933

Disinger, J.F. (2001). K-12 Education and the environment: Perspectives, expectations, and practice. *Journal of Environmental Education, 33,* 4–11.

Disinger, J.F., & Roth, C.E. (1992). *Environmental literacy.* Educational Resources Information Center; Clearinghouse for Science, Mathematics, and Environmental Education 351201. Retrieved from http://www.eric.ed.gov/ERICDocs/data/ericdocs2sql/content_storage_01/0000019b/80/12/f4/a7.pdf

Dolnicar, S., & Grun, B. (2008). Environmentally friendly behavior: Can heterogeneity among individuals and contexts/environments be harvested for improved sustainable management? *Environment and Behavior,* Retrieved from http://eab.sagepub.com doi: 10.1177/0013916508319448

Downey, L., & van Willigen, M. (2005). Environmental stressors: The mental health impacts of living near industrial activity. *Journal of Health and Social Behavior, 46,* 289–305.

Dr. Seuss. (1971). *The Lorax.* New York, NY: Random House.

Driver, B.L., Dustin, D., Baltic, T., Elsner, G., & Peterson, G. (1996). *Nature and the human spirit.* State College, PA: Venture.

Duffin, M., Murphy, M., & Johnson, B. (2008). *Quantifying a relationship between place-based learning and environmental quality: Final report.* Woodstock, VT: NPS Conservation Study Institute in cooperation with the Environmental Protection Agency and Shelburne Farms. Retrieved from http://www.peecworks.org/PEEC/PEEC_Research/S03CB4BC4-03CB558E

Duncan, R.C., & Youngquist, W. (1999). *Encircling the peak of world oil production.* Retrieved from http://www.mnforsustain.org/oil_duncan_and_youngquist_encircling_oil.htm

Dunlap, R.E. (2006, November). Show us the data? An examination of the death of environmentalisms' ambiguous empirical foundations. *Organization & Environment, 35,* 7–15, 33–39.

Dunlap, R.E., & McCright, A.M. (2008a). A widening gap: Views on climate change. *Environment: Science and Policy for Sustainable Development, 50*(5), 26–35.

Dunlap, R.E., & McCright, A.M. (2008b). Social movement identity: Validating a measure of identification with the environmental movement. *Social Science Quarterly, 89,* 1045–1065.

Dunlap. R.E., & Van Liere, K.D. (1978). The "New Environmental Paradigm": A proposed measuring instrument and preliminary results. *Journal of Environmental Education, 9*(4), 10–19.

Dunlap, R.E., & Van Liere, K.D. (1984). Commitment to the dominant social paradigm and concern for environmental quality. *Social Science Quarterly, 65*(4), 1013–1028.

Dunlap, R.E., Van Liere, K., Mertig, A., & Jones, R.E. (2000). Measuring endorsement of the new ecological paradigm: A revised NEP scale. *Journal of Social Issues, 56,* 425–442.

Durbin, D. (2008, May 22). Ford cuts N. American production, cuts profit goal. *The Associated Press.*

Durenberger, D., Mott, L., & Sagoff, M. (1991, March/April). A dissenting voice. *EPA Journal, 17*(2), 49–52.

Durning, A.B. (1990). Ending poverty. In Brown, L.R. (Ed.), *State of the world 1990: A worldwatch institute on progress toward a sustainable society* (pp. 123–169). New York, NY: W.W. Norton & Co.

Durning, A.T. (1992). *How much is enough? The consumer society and the future of the earth.* New York, NY: W.W. Norton & Co.

Durning, A.T. (1993). *Saving the forests: What will it take?* (Worldwatch Paper no. 117). Washington, DC: Worldwatch Institute.

Eagles, P.F.J., & Demare, R. (1999). Factors influencing children's environmental attitudes. *Journal of Environmental Education, 30*(4), 33–37.

Eagly, A.H., & Chaiken, S. (1998). *The psychology of attitudes.* Fort Worth, TX: Harcourt Brace.

Ebreo, A., Hershey, J., & Vining, J. (1999). Reducing solid waste: Linking recycling to environmentally responsible consumerism. *Environment and Behavior, 31,* 107–135.

Ecocycle. (n.d.). *Zero waste around the world.* Retrieved from http://ecocycle.org/zero/world.cfm

Ehrlich, P.R., & Ehrlich, A.H. (1991). *Healing the planet: Strategies for resolving the environmental crisis* (pp. 7–10). Reading, MA: Addison-Wesley.

Ehrlich, P.R., & Ehrlich, A.H. (2008). *The dominant animal: Human evolution and the environment.* Washington, DC: Island Press.

Ehrlich, P.A., & Holdren, J. (1971). The impact of population growth. *Science, 171,* 1212–1217.

Eikenaes, I., Gude, T., & Hoffart, A. (2006). Integrated wilderness therapy for avoidant personality disorder. *Nordic Journal of Psychiatry, 60,* 275–281.

Elgin, D. (1981). *Voluntary simplicity: Toward a way of life that is outwardly simple, inwardly rich.* New York, NY: Morrow Quill Paperbacks.

Elgin, D. (1993). *Voluntary simplicity: Toward a way of life that is outwardly simple, inwardly rich* (Rev. ed.). New York, NY: Quill.

Elgin, D. (2000). *The garden of simplicity.* Retrieved from http://www.simpleliving.net/webofsimplicity/the_garden_of _simplicity.asp

Energy Information Administration. (2006). *Renewable Energy Trends, 2006 Edition.* Retrieved from http://www.eia.doe.gov/cneaf/solar.renewables/page/trends/rentrends.html

Energy Information Administration. (2007). *International Energy Annual 2005: World Energy Consumption in Standard U.S. Physical Units,* Table 1.2. Retrieved from http://www.eia.doe.gov/iea/wec.html

Energy Information Administration. (2008a). *Emissions of Greenhouse Gases Report,* Report #: DOE/EIA-0573 (2007). Retrieved from http://www.eia.doe.gov/oiaf/1605/ggrpt/index.html

Energy Information Administration. (2008b). *Greenhouse Gases, Climate Change, and Energy.* Retrieved from http://www.eia.doe.gov/bookshelf/brochures/greenhouse/Chapter1.htm

Engelman, R., Halweil, B., & Nierenberg, D. (2002). Rethinking population, improving lives. In C. Flavin, H. French, & G. Gardner (Eds.), *State of the world 2002: A worldwatch institute report on progress toward a sustainable society* (p. 127). New York, NY: W.W. Norton & Co.

Environmental Working Group. (2007). *Fire retardants in toddlers and their mothers: Gov't and industry actions to phase out PBDEs.* Retrieved from http://www.ewg.org/node/26976

Esswein, P.M. (2008). Plug Your Home's Costly Leaks. *Kiplinger's Personal Finance, 62*(11), 69–70.

Europa. (2007). *POPs—Persistent organic pollutants. European Commission: Environment.* Retrieved from http://ec.europa.eu/environment/pops/index_en.htm

Evans, G.W. (2004). The environment of childhood poverty. *American Psychologist, 59,* 77–92.

Evans, G.W., & Cohen, S. (1987). Environmental Stress. In D. Stokols & I. Altman (Eds.), *Handbook of environmental psychology* (pp. 571–610). New York, NY: John Wiley and Sons.

Evans, G.W., & Stecker, R. (2004). Motivational consequences of environmental stress. *Journal of Environmental Psychology, 24,* 143–165.

Everett, P.B., Hayward, S.C., & Meyers, A.W. (1974). The effects of a token reinforcement procedure on bus ridership. *Journal of Applied Behavior Analysis, 7,* 1–9.

Faber Taylor, A., & Kuo, F.E. (2006). Is contact with nature important for healthy child development? State of the evidence. In C. Spencer & M. Blades (Eds.), *Children and their environments: Learning, using and designing spaces* (pp. 124–140). New York, NY: Cambridge University Press.

Faber Taylor, A., & Kuo, F.E. (2009). Children with attention deficits concentrate better after walk in the park. *Journal of Attention Disorders, 12,* 402–409.

Faber Taylor, A., Kuo, F.E., & Sullivan, W.C. (2001). Coping with ADD: The surprising connection to green play settings. *Environment and Behavior, 33,* 54–77.

Faber Taylor, A., Kuo, F.E., & Sullivan, W.C. (2002). Views of nature and self-discipline: Evidence from inner city children. *Journal of Environmental Psychology, 22*(1–2), 49–63.

Faber Taylor, A., Wiley, A., Kuo, F.E., & Sullivan, W.C. (1998). Growing up in the inner city: Green spaces as places to grow. *Environment and Behavior, 30,* 3–27.

Feaster, D.J., Goodkin, K., Blaney, N.T., Baldewicz, T. T.,Tuttle, R.S., Woodward, C., Szapocznik, J., Eisdorfer, C., Baum, M.K., & Fletcher, M.A. (2000). Longitudinal psychoneuroimmunologic relationships in the natural history of HIV-1 infection: The stressor-support-coping model. In K. Goodkin & A.P. Visser (Eds.), *Psychoneuroimmunology: Stress, mental disorders, and health* (pp. 153–193). Washington, DC: American Psychiatric Press.

Festinger, L. (1956). *When prophecy fails.* Minneapolis, MN: University of Minnesota Press.

Few, R. (2007). Health and climatic hazards: Framing Social Research on vulnerability, Response and adaptation. *Global Environmental Change, 17,* 281–295.

Fielding, K.S., McDonald, R., & Louis, W. (2008). Theory of planned behavior, identity and intentions to engage in environmental activism. *Journal of Environmental Psychology, 28*(4), 318–326.

Finucane, M.L. (2005). The psychology of risk judgments and decisions. In N. Cromar, S. Cameron, & H. Fallowfield (Eds.), *Environmental health in Australia and New Zealand* (pp. 142–155). New York, NY: Oxford University Press.

Finucane, M.L., Alhakami, A., Slovic, P., & Johnson, S.M. (2000). The affect heuristic in judgments of risks and benefits. *Journal of Behavioral Decision Making, 13,* 1–17.

Fischhoff, B. (1990). Psychology and public policy: Tool or toolmaker? *American Psychologist, 45*(5), 647–653.

Fish, L. (2009). *Nature, culture, and abnormal appetites: An ecopsychological analysis of addiction.* Saarbrucken, Germany: Verlag-FDM.

Fish, L.M. (2007). Nature, culture, and abnormal appetites: An ecopsychological analysis of addiction. *Dissertation Abstracts International: Section B. The Sciences and Engineering, 67*(9-B), 5399.

Fisher, A. (2002). *Radical eco-psychology: Psychology in the service of life*. Albany, NY: State University of New York Press.

Fisher, R., & Ury, W. (1991). *Getting to yes: Negotiating agreement without giving in*. New York, NY: Penguin.

Fiske, S.T., & Taylor, S.E. (1984). *Social cognition*. Reading, MA: Addison-Wesley.

Fisman, L. (2005). The effects of local learning on environmental awareness in children: An empirical investigation. *The Journal of Environmental Education, 36*(3), 39–50.

Fjørtoft, I. (2001). The natural environment as a playground for children: The impact of outdoor play activities in pre-primary school children. *Early Childhood Education Journal, 29*, 111–117.

Flavin, C. (2008). Building a low-carbon economy. In L. Starke (Ed.), *2008 state of the world: Innovations for a sustainable economy* (pp. 75–90). New York, NY: W.W. Norton & Co.

Flegal, K., Graubard, B., Williamson, D., & Gail, M. (2005). Excess deaths associated with underweight, overweight, and obesity. *Journal of the American Medical Association, 293*, 1861–1867.

Flynn, L.R., & Goldsmith, E. (1994). Opinion leadership in green consumption: An exploratory study. *Journal of Social Behavior and Personality, 9*, 543–553.

Food and Agriculture Organization (2009). *Women and Food Security*. Retrieved from http://www.fao.org/FOCUS/E/Women/Sustin-e.htm

Forgas, J.P. (1999). Network theories and beyond. In T. Dalgleish & M.J. Power (Eds.), Handbook of cognition and emotion (pp. 591–611). New York: Wiley.

Fox, J., & Guyer, M. (1978). "Public" choice and cooperation in n-person prisoner's dilemma. *Journal of Conflict Resolution, 22*, 468–481.

Fox, W. (1990). *Toward a transpersonal ecology: Developing new foundations for environmentalism*. Boston, MA: Shambala.

Frank, L.D., & Engelke, P.O. (2001). The built environment and human activity patterns: Exploring the impact of urban form on public health. *Journal of Planning Literature, 16*(2), 202–218.

Frantz, C., Mayer, F.S., Norton, C., & Rock, M. (2005). There is no "I" in nature: The influence of self-awareness on connectedness to nature. *Journal of Environmental Psychology, 25*, 427–436.

Frederickson, L.M., & Anderson, D.H. (1999). A qualitative exploration of the wilderness experience as a source of spiritual inspiration. *Journal of Environmental Psychology, 19*, 21–39.

Freud, S. (1927). The future of an illusion. In P. Gray (Ed.), *The Freud reader* (p. 693). New York, NY: W. W. Norton & Co.

Freud, S. (1940/1964). An outline of psycho-analysis. In J. Strachey (Ed. & Trans.), *The standard edition of the complete psychological works of Sigmund Freud*. (Vol. 23, pp. 141–207). London, United Kingdom: Hogarth Press.

Freud, S. (1938/1964). Splitting of the ego in the process of defense. In J. Strachey (Ed. & Trans.), *The standard edition of the complete psychological works of Sigmund Freud* (Vol 23, pp. 275–276). London, United Kingdom: Hogarth Press.

Freudenburg, W.R., & Pastor, S.K. (1992). NIMBYs and LULUs: Stalking the syndromes. *Journal of Social Issues, 48*(4), 39–61.

Friedman, M. (2002). Using organized consumer action to foster sustainability. In P. Schmuck & P.W. Schultz (Eds.), *Psychology of sustainable development* (pp. 277–297). Boston, MA: Kluwer Academic.

Fritze, J.G., Blashki, G.A., Burke, S., & Wiseman, J. (2008). Hope, despair and transformation: Climate change and the promotion of mental health and wellbeing. *International Journal of Mental Health Systems, 2.* Retrieved from http://ijmhs.com/content/2/1/13

Frosh, S. (1987). *The politics of psychoanalysis.* New Haven, CT and London, UK: Yale University Press.

Frumkin, H. (2001). Beyond toxicity: Human health and the natural environment. *American Journal of Preventive Medicine, 20*, 234–240.

Frumkin, H. (2003). Healthy places: Exploring the evidence. *American Journal of Public Health, 93*, 1451–1456.

Frumkin, H. (2004). White coats, green plants: Clinical epidemiology meets horticulture. *Acta horticulturae, 639*, 15–26.

Fuhrer, U. (1995). A social psychology-based theoretical framework for research on environmental concern. *Psychologische Rundschau, 46*(2), 93–103.

Fujii, S. (2006). Environmental concern, attitude toward frugality, and ease of behavior as determinants of pro-environmental behavior intentions. *Journal of Environmental Psychology, 26*, 262–268.

Gardner, G. (2002). The challenge for Johannesburg: Creating a more secure world. In C. Flavin, H. French, & G. Gardner (Eds.), *State of the world 2002: A worldwatch institute report on progress toward a sustainable society* (pp. 3–23). New York, NY: W. W. Norton & Co.

Gardner, G., & Prugh, T. (2008). Seeding the sustainable economy. In L. Starke (Ed.), *2008 state of the world: Innovations for a sustainable economy* (pp. 3–17). New York, NY: W. W. Norton & Co.

Gardner, G.T., & Stern, P.C. (2002). *Environmental problems and human behavior* (2nd ed.). Boston, MA: Pearson Custom.

Gardner, G.T., & Stern, P.C. (2008). The short list: The most effective actions U.S. households can take to curb climate change. *Environment, 50*(5), 12–24.

Gastil, J. (1990).Generic pronouns and sexist language: The oxymoronic character of masculine generics. *Sex Roles, 23*(11/12), 629–642.

Gatersleben, B., Steg, L., & Vlek, C. (2002). Measurement and determinants of environmentally significant consumer behavior. *Environment and Behavior, 34*(3), 335–362.

Gattig, A., & Hendrickx, L. (2007). Judgmental discounting and environmental risk perception: Dimensional similarities, domain differences, and implications for sustainability. *Journal of Social Issues, 63*, 21–39.

Gaulin, S.J. C., & McBurney, D.H. (2001). *Psychology: An evolutionary approach.* Upper Saddle River, NJ: Prentice Hall.

Gay, P. (1989). Introduction. In P. Gay (Ed.), *The Freud reader* (pp. xiii–xiv). New York, NY: W. W. Norton & Co.

Gazzaniga, M.S. (2004). My brain made me do it. In W. Glannon (Ed.), *Defining right and wrong in brain science: Essential readings in neuroethics* (pp. 183–194). Washington, DC: Dana Press.

Gazzaniga, M.S. (2005). *The ethical brain.* Washington, DC: Dana Press.

Gebhard, U., Nevers, P., & Billmann-Mahecha, E. (2003). Moralizing trees: Anthropomorphism and identity in children's relationships to nature. In S. Clayton & S. Opotow (Eds.), *Identity and the natural environment: The psychological significance of nature* (pp. 91–111). Cambridge, MA: Massachusetts Institute of Technology Press.

Gelbspan, R. (2001 May/June). A modest proposal to stop global warming. *Sierra Magazine,* 62–67.

Gelbspan, R. (2004). *Boiling point: How politicians, big oil and coal, journalists, and activists are fueling the climate crisis—and what we can do to avert disaster.* New York, NY: Basic Books.

Geller, E.S. (1987). Applied behavior analysis and environmental psychology: From strange bedfellows to a productive marriage. In D.S. Stokols & I. Altman (Eds.), *Handbook of environmental psychology* (Vol. 1, pp. 361–387). New York, NY: John Wiley & Sons.

Geller, E.S. (1990). Behavior analysis and environmental protection: Where have all the flowers gone? *Journal of Applied Behavior Analysis, 23*, 269–273.

Geller, E.S. (1992). It takes more than information to save energy. *American Psychologist, 47*, 814–815.

Geller, E.S. (2002). The challenge of increasing proenvironmental behavior. In R.B. Bechtel & A. Churchman (Eds.), Handbook of environmental psychology (pp. 525–540), New York: Wiley.

Geller, E.S., Winett, R.A., & Everett, P.B. (1982). *Environmental preservation: New strategies for behavior change.* New York, NY: Pergamon Press.

Genesis, Chapter 1, verses 26–28, *King James' Bible, Authorized Version of 1611.*

Gevirtz, R. (2000). The physiology of stress. In D.T. Kenny , J.G. Carlson, E.F. McGuigan, & J.L. Sheppard (Eds.), *Stress and health: Research and clinical applications.* The Netherlands: Harwood Academic.

Gibbs, D., & Deutz, P. (2007). Reflections on implementing industrial ecology through eco-industrial park development. *Journal of Cleaner Production, 15*, 1683–1695.

Gibbs, L. (1995). *Dying from dioxin: A citizen's guide to reclaiming our health and rebuilding democracy.* (Arlington, VA: Citizen's Clearinghouse for Hazardous Wastes.) Boston MA: South End Press.

Gies, E. (2008). Green building goes mainstream. *World Watch, 21*(4), 12–19.

Gifford, R. (2007). Environmental psychology and sustainable development: Expansion, maturation, and challenges. *Journal of Social Issues, 63,* 199–212.

Gigerenzer, G. (2000). *Adaptive thinking: Rationality in the real world.* New York, NY: Oxford University Press.

Gilbert, S.G. (2004). *A small dose of toxicology: The health effects of common chemicals.* Boca Raton, FL: CRC Press.

Gillham, C. (2008, October 1). Nine ways to avoid household toxins. *Newsweek.* Retrieved from http://www.newsweek.com/id/161841

Gilligan, C. (1982). *In a different voice: Psychological theory and women's development.* Cambridge, MA: Harvard University Press.

Glendinning, C. (1994). *My name is Chellis & I'm in recovery from western civilization.* Boston, MA: Shambhala.

Global Development Research Center (n.d.). *Environmental Education: Creating an environment to educate about the environment. EE Objectives.* Retrieved from http://www.gdrc.org/uem/ee/2-1.html

Global Footprint Network. (2008). *National footprint accounts, 2008 edition.* Available at http://www.footprintnetwork.org.

Goleman, D. (1995/1998). *Emotional intelligence: Why it can matter more than IQ.* New York, NY: Bantam.

Goleman, D. (2009). *Ecological intelligence: How knowing the hidden impacts of what we buy can change everything.* New York, NY: Doubleday.

Good, J. (2007). Shop 'til we drop? Television, materialism and attitudes about the natural environment. *Mass Communication and Society, 10,* 365–383.

Goodkin, K., & Visser, A.P. (2000). *Psychoneuroimmunology: Stress, mental disorders, and health.* Washington, DC: American Psychiatric Press.

Goodman, E. (2001, October). Quoted in *Sustainable Living,* a publication of the Oregon State University Extension Service, Corvallis, OR.

Gordon, P. (2006). Sustainability planning: First, do no harm. *Property Management, 24,* 132–143.

Gore, A. (1992). *Earth in the balance: Ecology and the human spirit* (p. 243). New York, NY: Plume.

Gortmaker, S.L., Must, A., Sobol, A.M., Peterson, K., Colditz, G.A. & Dietz, W. H. (1996). Television viewing as a cause of increasing obesity among children in the United States, 1986–1990. *Archives of Pediatric and Adolescent Medicine, 150,* 356–362.

Gossard, M.H., & York, R. (2003). Social structural influences on meat consumption. *Human Ecology Review, 10,* 1–9.

Gotch, C., & Hall, T. (2004). Understanding nature-related behaviors among children through a theory of reasoned action approach. *Environmental Education Research, 10,* 157–177.

Grandjean, P. (2004). Implications of the precautionary principle for primary prevention and research. *Annual Review of Public Health, 25,* 199–223.

Grandjean, P., & Landrigan, P.J. (2006). Developmental neurotoxicity of industrial chemicals. *Lancet, 368,* 2167–2178.

Gray, L. (1995). Shamanic counseling and eco-psychology. In T. Roszak, M.E. Gomes, & A.D. Kanner (Eds.), *Eco-psychology: Restoring the earth, healing the mind* (pp. 172–182). San Francisco, CA: Sierra Club Books.

Greenberg, J.R., & Mitchell, S.A. (1983). *Object relations in psychoanalytic theory.* Cambridge, MA: Harvard University Press.

Greenway, R. (1995). The wilderness effect and ecopsychology. In T. Roszak, M.E. Gomes, & A.D. Kanner (Eds.), *Eco-psychology: Restoring the earth, healing the mind* (pp. 122–135). San Francisco, CA: Sierra Club Books.

Groopman, J. (2004). *The anatomy of hope: How people prevail in the face of illness.* New York, NY: Random House.

Grosse, S.D., Matte, T.D., Schwartz, J., & Jackson, R.J. (2002). Economic gains resulting from the reduction in children's exposure to lead in the United States. *Environmental Health Perspectives, 110*(6), 563–369.

Grothmann, T., & Patt, A. (2005). Adaptive capacity and human cognition: The process of individual adaptation to climate change. *Global Environmental Change, 15,* 199–213.

Grundy, C.S., & Osbaldiston, R. (2006). Techniques of behavior change. In R.M. MacNair(Ed.), *Working for peace: A handbook of practical psychology and other tools* (pp. 255-262). Atascadero, CA: Impact.

Guagnano, G.A. (1995). Locus of control, altruism and agentic disposition. *Population and Environment: A Journal of Interdisciplinary Studies, 17*(1), 63–77.

Guagnano, G.A., Dietz, T., & Stern, P.C. (1994). Willingness to pay for public goods: A test of the contribution model. *Psychological Science, 5*(6), 411–415.

Guillette, E.A., Meza, M.M., Aquilar, M.G., Soto, A.D., & Garcia, I.E. (1998). An anthropological approach to the evaluation of preschool children exposed to pesticides in Mexico. *Environmental Health Perspectives, 106,* 347–353.

Gustafson, P. (2001). Routes and routes: Exploring the relationship between place attachment and mobility. *Environment and Behavior, 33,* 667–686.

Hackenmiller-Paradis, R. (2008). *The price of pollution: Cost estimates of environmentally-related disease in Oregon.* Oregon Environmental Council, Collaborative for Health and Environment, Oregon Chapter. Retrieved from http://www.oeconline.org/resources/publications/reportsandstudies/pop

Haegele, G. (2008). Creation care, a growing movement. *Business and Politics (News).* Retrieved from http://www.treehugger.com/files/2008/07/creation-care-faith-action.php

Hallin, P.O. (1995). Environmental concern and environmental behavior in Foley, a small town in Minnesota. *Environment and Behavior, 27*(4), 558–578.

Haluza-Delay, R. (2001). Nothing here to care about: Participant constructions of nature following a 12-day wilderness program. *Journal of Environmental Education, 32*(4), 43–48.

Halweil, B. (2002). Farming in the public interest. In C. Flavin, H. French, & G. Gardner (Eds.), *State of the world 2002: A worldwatch institute report on progress toward a sustainable society* (pp. 51–74). New York, NY: W.W. Norton & Co.

Han, K.T. (2003). A reliable and valid self-rating measure of the restorative quality of natural environments. *Landscape and Urban Planning, 64,* 209–232.

Hansen, B. (2009, May 19). US to unveil CAFE standard plans for 35 mpg by 2016. *Platts Oilgram News, 87*(97), 10.

Hansla, A., Gamble, A., Juliusson, A., & Gärling, T. (2008). The relationships between awareness of consequences, environmental concern, and value orientations. *Journal of Environmental Psychology, 28*(1), 1–9.

Hardell, L., Lindstrom, G., van Bavel, B., Fredrikson, M., Liljegren, G., Becher, H., et al. (1998). Some aspects of the etiology of non-Hodgkin's lymphoma. *Environmental Health Perspectives, 106*(2), 679–681.

Hardin, G. (1968, December). The tragedy of the commons. *Science, 162,* 1243–1248.

Hardin, G. (2002). Moral implications of cultural carrying capacity. In G.T. Miller, *Living in the environment: Principles, connections, and solutions* (12th ed., pp. 252–253). Belmont, CA: Wadsworth.

Harper, N., Russell, K., Cooley, R., & Cupples, J. (2007). Catherine Freer wilderness therapy expeditions: An exploratory case study of adolescent wilderness therapy, family functioning and maintenance of change. *Child Youth Care Forum, 36,* 111–129.

Harper, S. (1995). The way of wilderness. In. T. Roszak, M.E. Gomes, & A.D. Kanner (Eds.), *Ecopsychology: Restoring the earth, healing the mind* (pp. 183–200). San Francisco, CA: Sierra Club Books.

Harper, C. L. (2008). *Environment and society (4th edition).* Upper Saddle River, NJ: Pearson/ Prentice Hall.

Harrigan, M. (1994, January/February). Can we transform the market without transforming the customer? *Home Energy Magazine Online.* Retrieved from http://homeenergy.org/archive/hem.dis.anl.gov/eehem/94/940109.html

Hart, K., & Hart, R. (2008). *Green home building.* Retrieved from http://www.greenhomebuilding.com/

Hart, R.A. (1997). *Children's participation: The theory and practice of involving young citizens in community development and environmental care.* New York, NY: UNICEF.

Hartig, T., & Cooper Marcus, C. (2006). Essay: Healing gardens—places for nature in health care. *Lancet, 368,* S36–S37.

Hartig, T., Evans, G.W., Jamner, L.D., Davis, D.S., & Gärling, T. (2003). Tracking restoration in natural and urban field settings. *Journal of Environmental Psychology, 23,* 109–123.

Hartig, T., Kaiser, F.G., & Bowler, P.A. (2001). Psychological restoration in nature as a positive motivation for ecological behavior. *Environment and Behavior, 33*(4), 590–607.

Hartig, T., & Staats, H. (2006). The need for psychological restoration as a determinant of environmental preferences. *Journal of Environmental Psychology, 26,* 215–226.

Haslam, G. (1983). Hawk's flight: An American fable. In S. Ortiz (Ed.), *Earth power coming.* Tsaile, AZ: Navajo Community College. (Quoted from *My name is Chellis and I'm in recovery from Western civilization,* (p. 88), by C. Glendinning, 1994, Boston, MA: Shambala.)

Hassing, C., Twickler, M., Brunekreef, B., Cassee, F., Doevendans, P., Kastelein, J., & Cramer, M. (2009). Particulate air pollution, coronary heart disease and individual risk assessment: A general overview. *European Journal of Cardiovascular Prevention and Rehabilitation, 16,* 10–15.

Hawken, P. (1993, September/October). A declaration of sustainability: 12 steps society can take to save the whole enchilada. *Utne Reader,* (59), 54–61.

Hawken, P. (2007). *Blessed unrest: How the largest movement in the world came into being, and why no one saw it coming.* New York, NY: Viking Press.

Hawken, P., Lovins, A., & Lovins, L.H. (1999). *Natural capitalism: Creating the next industrial revolution.* Boston, MA: Little Brown.

Haynes, E., Lanphear, B.P., Tohn, E., Farr, N., & Wioads, G.G. (2002). The effect of interior lead hazard controls on children's blood lead concentrations: A systematic evaluation. *Environmental Health Perspectives, 110,* 103–107.

Heath, Y., & Gifford, R. (2006). Free-market ideology and environmental degradation: The case of beliefs in global climate change. *Environment & Behavior, 38,* 48–71.

Hebb, D.O. (1949). *The organization of behavior.* New York, NY: Wiley-Interscience.

Heerwagen, J.H., & Orians, G.H. (2002). The ecological world of children. In P.H. Kahn Jr. & S.R. Kellert (Eds.), *Children and nature: Psychological, sociocultural, and evolutionary investigations* (pp. 29–63). Cambridge MA: Massachusetts Institute of Technology Press.

Heft, H., & Chawla, L. (2006). Children as agents in sustainable development: The ecology of competence. In C. Spencer & M. Blades (Eds.), *Children and their environments: Learning, using and designing spaces* (pp. 199–216). New York, NY: Cambridge University Press.

Helman, C. (2005, August 15). Waste Mismanagement. *Forbes, 176*(3), 35–36.

Henderson, L., Zimbardo, P., Graham, J. (2001). *Social fitness and technology use: Adolescent interview study.* Stanford, CA: Stanford Institute and the Shyness Institute. Retrieved from http://www.shyness.com/documents/2002/2000PalyInterviewStudy.pdf

Hendrickx, L., & Nicolaij, S. (2004). Temporal discounting and environmental risks: The role of ethical and loss-related concerns. *Journal of Environmental Psychology, 24,* 409–422.

Herzog, T.R., & Strevey, S.J. (2008). Contact with nature, sense of humor, and psychological well-being. *Environment and Behavior, 40,* 747–776.

Hickling, A.K., & Gelman, S.A. (1995). How does your garden grow?: Early conceptualization of seeds and their place in the plant growth cycle. *Child Development, 66,* 856–876.

Hill, S.B. (2003). Autonomy, mutualistic relationships, sense of place, and conscious caring: A hopeful view of the present and future. In J.I. Cameron (Ed.), *Changing places: Reimagining Australia* (pp. 180–196). Sydney, New South Wales: Longueville.

Hillman, J., & Ventura, M. (1992). *We've had a hundred years of psychotherapy and the world's getting worse.* New York, NY: HarperCollins.

Hinds, J., & Sparks, P. (2008). Engaging with the natural environment: The role of affective connection and identity. *Journal of Environmental Psychology 28,* 109–120.

Hine, D.W., Marks, A.D.G., Nachreiner, M., Gifford, R., & Heath, Y. (2007). Keeping the home fires burning: The affect heuristic and wood smoke pollution. *Journal of Environmental Psychology, 27,* 26–32.

Hirsh, A.E. (2009, February 3). Guest column: Fish shares and sharing fish. *The New York Times, The Wild Side.* Retrieved from http://judson.blogs.nytimes.com/2009/02/03/guest-column-fish-shares-and-sharing-fish/

Hirst, E., Berry, L., & Soderstrom, J. (1981). Review of utility home energy audit programs. *Energy, 6,* 621–630.

Hobbes, T. (1651/1962). *Leviathan: Or the matter, forme, and power of commonwealth ecclesiastical and civil.* New York, NY: Collier.

Hodgkinson, S.P., & Innes, M. (2000). The prediction of ecological and environmental belief systems: The differential contributions of social conservatism and beliefs about money. *Journal of Environmental Psychology, 20,* 285–294.

Hofferth, S.L., & Curtin, S.C. (2005). Leisure time activities in middle childhood. In K.A. Moore & L.H. Lippman (Eds.), *What do children need to flourish? Conceptualizing and measuring indicators of positive development* (pp. 95–110). New York: Springer Publishing.

Hofferth, S.L., & Sandberg, J.F. (2001). Changes in American children's time, 1981–1997. In S. Hofferth & T. Owens (Eds.), *Children at the millennium: Where have we come from, where are we going?* (pp. 193–229). New York, NY: Elsevier Science.

Holtcamp, W. (2001, May–June). A grass-roofs effort: Secret gardens conserve energy and cool the air. *Sierra,* 24–27.

Homburg, A., & Stolberg, A. (2006). Explaining pro-environmental behavior with a cognitive theory of stress. *Journal of Environmental Psychology, 26,* 1–14.

Hopkins, R. (2008). *The transition handbook: From oil dependency to local resilience.* White River Junction, VT: Chelsea Green Publishing.

Hornik, J., Cherian, J., Madansky, M., & Narayana, C. (1995). Determinants of recycling behavior: A synthesis of research results. *Journal of Socio-Economics, 24,* 105–127.

Howard, G.S. (2000). Adapting human lifestyles for the 21st Century. *American Psychologist, 55*(5), 509–515.

Howard, G.S. (2002). *How should I live my life: Psychology, environmental science, and moral traditions.* New York, NY: Rowman & Littlefield.

Howes, C. (1988). Peer interaction of young children. *Monographs of the society for research in child development, 53*(Serial No. 217), i, iii, v, 1–92.

Howes, C., & Matheson, C.C. (1992). Sequences in the development of competent play with peers: Social and social pretend play. *Developmental Psychology, 28*, 961–974.

Hunecke, M., Blobaum, A., Matthies, E., & Hoger, R. (2001). Responsibility and environment: Ecological norm orientation and external factors in the domain of travel mode choice behavior. *Environment and Behavior, 33*(6), 830–852.

Hungerford, H.R., & Volk, T.L. (1990). Changing learner behavior through environmental education. *Journal of Environmental Education, 21*(3), 8–21.

Hunter, L.M., Hatch, A., & Johnson, A. (2004). Cross-national gender variation in environmental behaviors. *Social Science Quarterly, 85*(3), 677–694.

Huprich, S.K. (2008). Psychodynamic therapy: Conceptual and empirical foundations. London, UK: Routledge.

Hutton, R.R. (1982). Advertising and the department of energy campaign for energy conservation. *Journal of Advertising, 11*(2), 27–39.

Intergovernmental Panel on Climate Change (IPCC). (2007). *Climate Change 2007: Synthesis Report.* Retrieved from http://www.ipcc.ch/pdf/assessment-report/ar4/syr/ar4_syr.pdf

International Food Policy Research Institute. (2003). *The importance of women's status for child nutrition in developing countries.* Research Report Abstract #131, Washington, DC: Consultative Group on International Agricultural Research.

International Joint Commission. (1992). (Fulton, E.D., Durnil, G.K., Welch, R.S.K., Cleveland, H.P., Lanthier, C., Goodwin, R.F., commissioners) *Sixth biennial report on great lakes water quality.* Windsor, ON: author.

Irvine, K.N., & Warber, S. (2002). Green healthcare: Practicing as if the natural environment really mattered. *Alternative Therapies, 8*, 76–83.

Iwata, O. (1999). Perceptual and behavioral correlates of voluntary simplicity lifestyles. *Social Behavior and Personality, 27*(4), 379–386.

Iwata, O. (2006). An evaluation of consumerism and lifestyle as correlates of a voluntary simplicity lifestyle. *Social Behavior and Personality, 34*, 557–568.

Jacobsen, J.L. (1992). *Gender bias: Roadblock to sustainable development.* Worldwatch Paper no. 110. Washington, DC: Worldwatch Institute.

Jacobson, J.L., & Jacobson, S.W. (1996). Intellectual impairment in children exposed to polychlorinated biphenyls in utero. *New England Journal of Medicine, 335*, 783–789.

Jacques, P.J., Dunlap, R.E., & Freeman, M. (2008). The organisation of denial: Conservative think tanks and environmental skepticism. *Environmental Politics, 17*, 349–385.

Jagel, J. (2008). Entheogens and ecopsychology: Comparing mystical experiences and ecological orientation. *Dissertation Abstracts International: Section B. The Sciences and Engineering, 68*(11-B), 1649.

James, W.T. (1890). *The principles of psychology.* New York, NY: Holt, Rinehart & Winston.

James, W. (1929). *The varieties of religious experience.* New York, NY: Modern Library.

Janis, I.L., & Feshbach, S. (1953). Effects of fear-arousing communications. *Journal of Abnormal and Social Psychology, 49,* 78–92.

Jensen, B.B., & Schnack, K. (1997). The action competence approach in environmental education. *Environmental Education Research, 3,* 163–178.

Jensen, D. (2006, May/June). Beyond hope. *Orion Magazine,* Retrieved from http://www.orionmagazine.org/index.php/articles/article/170/

Jerdee, T.H., & Rosen, B. (1974). Effects of opportunity to communicate and visibility of individual decisions on behavior in the common interest. *Journal of Applied Psychology, 59,* 712–716.

Johnson, C.Y., Bowker, J.M., & Cordell, K.H. (2004). Ethnic variation in environmental belief and behavior: An examination of the new ecological paradigm in a social psychological context. *Environment and Behavior, 36*(2), 157–186.

Joireman, J.A., Van Lange, P.A., & Van Vugt, M. (2004a). Who cares about the environmental impact of cars? Those with an eye toward the future. *Environment and Behavior, 36,* 187–206.

Joireman, J.A., Van Lange, P.A. M., Van Vugt, M., Wood, A., Vander Leest, T., & Lambert, C. (2004b). Structural solutions to social dilemmas: A field study on commuters' willingness to fund improvements to public transit. *Journal of Applied Social Psychology, 31,* 504–526.

Jones, E. (2008). *The better world shopping guide.* Gabriola Island, BC: New Society Publishers.

Jones, J.M. (2008). In the U.S., 28% report major changes to live "green." Retrieved from http://www.gallup.com/poll/106624/US-28-Report-Major-Changes-Live-Green.aspx

Jordan, M. (2009). Nature and self—an ambivalent attachment.*Ecopsychology, 1,* 26–31.

Joye, Y. (2007). Architectural lessons from environmental psychology: The case of biophilic architecture. *Review of General Psychology, 11,* 305–328.

Kabat-Zinn, J. (1990). *Full catastrophe living: Using the wisdom of your body and mind to face stress, pain and illness.* New York, NY: Delacorte Press.

Kabat-Zinn, J. (1994). *Wherever you go, there you are: Mindfulness meditation in everyday life.* New York, NY: Hyperion.

Kabeer, N. (2001). *Reversed realities: Gender hierarchies in development thought.* New York, NY: Verso.

Kahn, Jr. P.H. (1997a). Children's moral and ecological reasoning about the Prince William Sound oil spill. *Developmental Psychology, 33,* 1091–1096

Kahn, Jr. P.H. (1997b). Developmental psychology and the biophilia hypothesis: Children's affiliation with nature. *Developmental Review, 17,* 1–61.

Kahn, Jr. P.H. (1999). *The human relationship with nature: Development and culture*. Cambridge, MA: Massachusetts Institute of Technology Press.

Kahn, Jr. P.H. (2002). Children's affiliations with nature: Structure, development, and the problem of environmental generational amnesia. In P.H. Kahn, Jr. & S.R. Kellert (Eds.), *Children and nature: Psychological, sociocultural, and evolutionary investigations* (pp. 93–116). Cambridge, MA: Massachusetts Institute of Technology Press.

Kahn, Jr. P.H. (2003). The development of environmental moral identity. In S. Clayton & S. Opotow (Eds.), *Identity and the natural environment: The psychological significance of nature* (pp. 113–134). Cambridge, MA: Massachusetts Institute of Technology Press.

Kahn, Jr. P.H. (2007). The child's environmental amnesia: It's ours. *Children, Youth and Environments 17*, 199–207.

Kahn, Jr. P.H. & Kellert, S.R. (2002). *Children and nature: Psychological, sociocultural, and evolutionary investigations.*Cambridge, MA: Massachusetts Institute of Technology Press.

Kaiser, F.G., Hubner, G., & Bogner, F.X. (2005). Contrasting the theory of planned behavior with the value-belief-norm model in explaining conservation behavior. *Journal of Applied Social Psychology. 35*(10), 2150–2170.

Kaiser, F.G., Ranney, M., Hartig, T., & Bowler, P. (1999). Ecological behavior, environmental attitude, and feelings of responsibility for the environment. *European Psychologist, 4*(2), 59–74.

Kaiser, F.G., & Schultz, P.W. (2009). The attitude-behavior relationship: A test of three models of the moderating role of behavioral difficulty. *Journal of Applied Social Psychology, 39*, 186–207.

Kaiser, F.G. Wolfing, S., & Fuhrer, U. (1999). Environmental attitude and ecological behaviour. *Journal of Environmental Psychology, 19*(1), 1–19.

Kallgren, C.A., Reno, R.R., & Cialdini, R.B. (2000). A focus theory of normative conduct: When norms do and do not affect behavior. *Personality and Social Psychology Bulletin, 26*(8), 1002–1012.

Kals, E., & Ittner, H. (2003). Children's environmental identity: Indicators and behavioral impacts. In S. Clayton & S. Opotow (Eds.), *Identity and the natural environment: The psychological significance of nature* (pp. 135–157). Cambridge, MA: Massachusetts Institute of Technology Press.

Kals, E., & Maes, J. (2002). Sustainable development and emotions. In P. Schmuck & W.P. Schultz (2002). *Psychology of sustainable development* (pp. 97–122). Boston, MA: Kluwer Academic Publishers.

Kals, E., Schumacher, D., & Montada, L. (1999). Emotional affinity towards nature as a motivational basis to protect nature. *Environment and Behavior, 31*, 178–202.

Kanner, A.D. (2007, June 9). The corporatized child. Delivered at the *Psychology-Ecology-Sustainability Conference* at Lewis & Clark College, Portland, Oregon. Retrieved from http://www.earthleaders.org/projects/psf/pes/Kanner.pdf

Kanner, A.D., & Gomes, M.E. (1995). The all-consuming self. In T. Roszak, M.E. Gomes, & A.D. Kanner (Eds.), *Eco-psychology: Restoring the earth, healing the mind* (pp. 77–91). San Francisco, CA: Sierra Club.

Kaplan, R. (1993). The role of nature in the context of the workplace. *Landscape and Urban Planning, 26,* 193–201.

Kaplan, R. (2001). The nature of the view from home: Psychological benefits. *Environment and Behavior, 33*(4), 507–542.

Kaplan, R., & Austin, M.E. (2004). Out in the country: Sprawl and the quest for nature nearby. *Landscape and Urban Planning, 69,* 235–243.

Kaplan, R., & Kaplan, S. (1989). *The experience of nature.* Cambridge, MA: Cambridge University Press.

Kaplan, R., & Kaplan, S. (2008). Bringing out the best in people: A psychological perspective. *Conservation Biology, 22,* 826–829.

Kaplan, S. (1992). Environmental preference in a knowledge-seeking, knowledge-using organism. In J.H. Barkow, L. Cosmides, & J. Tooby (Eds.), *The adapted mind: Evolutionary psychology and the generation of culture.* New York, NY: Oxford University Press.

Kaplan, S. (1995). The restorative benefits of nature: Toward an integrative framework. *Journal of Environmental Psychology, 15,* 169–182.

Kaplan, S. (2000). Human nature and environmentally responsible behavior. *Journal of Social Issues, 56,* 491–508.

Kaplan, S., & Kaplan, R. (1989). *Cognition and environment: Functioning in an uncertain world.* Ann Arbor, MI: Ulrich's Bookstore.

Kaplan, S., & Talbot, J.F. (1983). Psychological benefits of a wilderness experience. In I. Altman & J.F. Wohlwill (Eds.), *Behavior and the natural environment* (pp. 163–203). New York, NY: Plenum Press.

Karp, D.G. (1996). Values and their effect on pro-environmental behavior. *Environment and Behavior, 28*(1), 111–133.

Karpiak, C.P., & Baril, G.L. (2008). Moral reasoning and concern for the environment. *Journal of Environmental Psychology, 28*(3), 203–208.

Kasser, T. (2002). *The high price of materialism.* Cambridge, MA: MIT Press.

Kasser, T. (2005). Frugality, generosity, and materialism in children and adolescents. In K.A. Moore & L.H. Lippman (Eds.), *What do children need to flourish? Conceptualizing and measuring indicators of positive development* (pp. 357–373). New York: Springer Publishing.

Kasser, T. (2006). Materialism and its alternatives. In M. Csikszentmihalyi & I.S. Csikszentmihalyi (Eds.), *A life worth living. Contributions to positive psychology* (pp. 200–214). New York: Oxford University Press.

Kasser, T. (2009a). *Into a warming world: Interlude for state of the world 2009.* Washington, DC: Worldwatch Institute.

Kasser, T. (2009b). Shifting values in response to climate change. In R. Engleman, M. Renner, & J. Sawan (Eds.), *2009 state of the world: Into a warming world* (pp. 122–125). New York, NY: W. W. Norton & Co.

Kasser, T. (2008). Values and ecological sustainability: Recent research and policy possibilities. In J.G. Speth & S. Kellert (Eds.), The coming transformation: Values to sustain human and natural communities. New Haven, CT: Yale School of Forestry & Environmental Studies.

Kasser, T., Cohn, S., Kanner, A.D., & Ryan, R.M. (2007). Some costs of American corporate capitalism: A psychological exploration of value and goal conflicts. *Psychological Inquiry, 18,* 1–22.

Kasser, T., & Ryan, R.M. (1996). Further examining the American dream: Differential correlates of intrinsic and extrinsic goals. *Personality and Social Psychology Bulletin, 22,* 280–287.

Kasser, T., & Ryan, R.M. (2001). Be careful what you wish for: Optimal functioning and the relative attainment of intrinsic and extrinsic goals. In P. Schmuck & K.M. Sheldon (Eds.), *Life goals and well-being: Towards a positive psychology of human striving* (pp. 116–131). Goettingen, Germany: Hogrefe & Huber Publishers.

Kasser, T., Ryan, R.M., Zax, M., & Sameroff, A.J. (1995). The relations of maternal and social environments to late adolescents' materialistic and prosocial values. *Developmental Psychology, 31,* 907–914.

Kasser, T., & Sheldon, K.M. (2000). Of wealth and death: Materialism, mortality salience, and consumption behavior. *Psychological Science, 11,* 352–355.

Kasser, T., Vansteenkiste, M., & Deckop, J.R. (2006). The ethical problems of a materialistic value orientation for businesses (and some suggestions for alternatives). In J.R. Deckop (Ed.), *Human resource management ethics* (pp. 283–306). Greenwich, CT: Information Age Publishing, Inc.

Katcher, A., & Wilkins, G. (1993). Dialogue with animals: Its nature and culture. In S.R. Kellert & E.O. Wilson (Eds.), *The biophilia hypothesis* (pp. 173–197). Washington, DC: Island Press.

Kates, R.W. (1994). Sustaining life on the earth. *Scientific American, 174*(4), 114–122.

Katz, E., Light, A., & Rothenberg, D. (2000). *Beneath the surface: Critical essays in the philosophy of deep ecology.* Cambridge, MA:Massachusetts Institute of Technology Press.

Katzev R., & Johnson, T. (1984). A social-psychological analysis of residential electricity consumption: The impact of minimal justification techniques. *Journal of Economic Psychology, 3,* 267–284.

Kaufman, L. (2009, February 25). Mr. Whipple left it out: Soft is rough on forests. *New York Times, Science: Environment.* Retrieved from http://www.nytimes.com/2009/02/26/science/earth/26charmin.html?_r=1&th&emc=th

Keepin, W. (1992). Toward an ecological psychology. *ReVision, 14,* 90–99.

Keller, E.F. (1996). *Reflections on gender and science.* New Haven, CT: Yale University Press.

Kellert, S.R. (1993). The biological basis for human values of nature. In S.R. Kellert & E.O. Wilson (Eds.), *The biophilia hypothesis* (pp. 42–69). Washington, DC: Island Press.

Kellert, S.R. (1997). *Kinship to mastery: Biophilia in human evolution and development.* Washington, DC: Island Press.

Kellert, S.R. (2002). Experiencing nature: Affective, cognitive, and evaluative development in children. In P.H. Kahn, Jr. & S.R. Kellert (Eds.), *Children and nature: Psychological, sociocultural, and evolutionary investigations* (pp. 117–151). Cambridge, MA: Massachusetts Institute of Technology Press.

Kellert, S., & Berry, J. (1987). Attitudes, knowledge, and behaviors toward wildlife as affected by gender. *Wildlife Society Bulletin, 15*, 363–371.

Kellert, S.T., & Wilson, E.O. (Eds.). (1993). *The biophilia hypothesis.* Washington, DC: Island Press.

Kelly, G., & Hosking, K. (2008). Nonpermanent residents, place attachment, and "sea change" communities. *Environment and Behavior, 40*, 575–594.

Kempton, W., & Holland, D. (2003). Identity and sustained environmental practice. In S. Clayton & S. Opotow (Eds.), *Identity and the natural environment: The psychological significance of nature* (pp. 317–341). Cambridge, MA: Massachusetts Institute of Technology Press.

Kennedy, R.F. (2004). *Crimes against nature: How George W. Bush and his corporate pals are plundering the country and high-jacking our democracy.* New York, NY: HarperCollins.

Kerr, N.L. (1989). Norms in social dilemmas. In D. Shroeder (Ed.), *Social dilemmas: Psychological perspectives* (pp. 287–313). New York, NY: Praeger.

Khanna, S. (2001). *Corrosive messages and capitalist ideology: Well-being, objectification, and alienation from a cross-cultural perspective.* Unpublished Honors Thesis, Knox College, Galesburg, IL.

Kidner, D.W. (2001). *Nature and psyche: Radical environmentalism and the politics of subjectivity.* Albany, NY: State University of New York Press.

Kilbourne, W.E., Beckmann, S.C., & Thelen, E. (2002). The role of the dominant social paradigm in environmental attitudes: A multinational examination. *Journal of Business Research, 55*, 193–204.

Kilbourne, W.E., & Polonsky, M.J. (2005). Environmental attitudes and their relations to the dominant social paradigm among university students in New Zealand and Australia. *Australasian Marketing Journal, 13*, 37–48.

Kirkby, M. (1989). Nature as refuge in children's environments. *Children's Environments Quarterly, 6*, 7–12.

Kitzes, J., Wackernagel, M., Loh, J., Peller, A., Goldfinger, S., Cheng, D., & Tea, K. (2008). Shrink and share: Humanity's present and future ecological footprint. *Philosophical Transactions of the Royal Society of London, Series B, Biological Sciences, 363*, 467–475.

Kitzhaber, J. (2002, September 25). *Keynote address at the forest futures conference.* Salem OR: Willamette University.

Klare, M.T. (2001). Resource wars: The new landscape of global conflict. New York, NY: Henry Holt.

Knussen, C., Yule, F., MacKenzie, J., & Wells, M. (2004). An analysis of intentions to recycle household waste: The roles of past behaviour, perceived habit, and perceived lack of facilities. *Journal of Environmental Psychology, 24*, 237–246.

Koger, S. M., Merrick, C. J., Kraybill-Greggo, J. W., & Kraybill-Greggo, M. J. (2006). Three examples of successful social action groups. In R. M. MacNair (Ed.) and Psychologists for Social Responsibility, *Working for peace: A handbook of practical psychology and other tools* (pp. 121–134). Atascadero, CA: Impact Publishers.

Koger, S.M., Schettler, T., & Weiss, B. (2005). Environmental toxicants and developmental disabilities: A challenge for psychologists. *American Psychologist, 60,* 243–255.

Koger, S.M., & Scott, B.A. (2007). Psychology and environmental sustainability: A call for integration. *Teaching of Psychology, 34,* 10–18.

Kohler, W. (1947/1975). *Gestalt psychology: An introduction to new concepts in modern psychology.* New York: New American Library.

Kornfield, J. (1993). *A path with heart.* New York, NY: Bantam

Korten, D.C. (2006). *The great turning: From empire to earth community.* Bloomfield, CT: Kumarian Press, Inc.

Kovats, R.S., Campbell-Lendrum, D., & Matthies, F. (2005). Climate change and human health: Estimating avoidable deaths and disease. *Risk Analysis, 25,* 1409–1418.

Koyre, A. (1968). *From the closed world to the open universe.* Baltimore, MD: Johns Hopkins.

Kraut, R., Patterson, M., Lundmark, V., Kiesler, S., Mukophadhyay, T., & Scherlis, W. (1998). Internet paradox: A social technology that reduces social involvement and psychological well-being? *American Psychologist, 53,* 1017–1031.

Kristof, N. D. (2007, August 16). The big melt. *New York Times, Opinion.* Retrieved from http://select.nytimes.com/2007/08/16/opinion/16kristof.html?_r=1

Krupp, F., & Horn, M. (2008). *Earth, the sequel: The race to reinvent energy and stop global warming.* New York, NY: W. W. Norton & Co.

Kunstler, J.H. (2005). *The long emergency: Surviving the end of oil, climate change, and other converging catastrophes of the twenty-first century.* New York, NY: Grove Press.

Kuo, F.E., & Faber Taylor, A. (2004). A potential natural treatment for attention-deficit/hyperactivity disorder: Evidence from a national study. *American Journal of Public Health, 94,* 1580–1586.

Kuo, F.E., & Faber Taylor, A. (2005). Mother nature as treatment for ADHD: Overstating the benefits of green. Kuo and Faber Taylor respond. *American Journal of Public Health, 95,* 371–372.

Kuo, F.E., & Sullivan, W.C. (2001). Aggression and violence in the inner city: Effects of environment via mental fatigue. *Environment and Behavior, 33*(4), 543–571.

Kurz, T. (2002). The psychology of environmentally sustainable behavior: Fitting together pieces of the puzzle. *Analyses of Social Issues and Public Policy, 2,* 257–278.

LaDuke, W. (1999). *All my relations.* Cambridge, MA: South End Press.

LaFreniere, G.F. (2008). *The decline of nature: Environmental history and the western worldview.* Palo Alto, CA: Academia Press.

Laituri, M., & Kirby, A. (1994). Finding fairness in America's cities? The search for environmental equity in everyday life. *Journal of Social Issues, 50,* 121–140.

Landrigan, P.J., Kimmel, C.A., Correa, A., & Eskenazi, B. (2004). Children's health and the environment: Public health issues and challenges for risk assessment. *Environmental Health Perspectives, 112(2),* 257–265.

Landrigan, P.J., Schechter, C.B., Lipton, J.M., Fahs, M.C., & Schwartz, J. (2002). Environmental pollutants and disease in American children: Estimates of morbidity, mortality, and costs for lead poisoning, asthma, cancer, and developmental disabilities. *Environmental Health Perspectives, 110(7),* 721–728.

Landrigan, P.J., Sonawane, B., Butler, R.N., Trasande, L., Callan, R., & Droller, D. (2005). Early environmental origins of neurodegenerative disease in later life. *Environmental Health Perspectives, 113,* 1230–1233.

Landrigan, P.J., Sonawane, B., Mattison, D., McCally, M., & Garg, A. (2002). Chemical contaminants in breast milk and their impacts on children's health: An overview. *Environmental Health Perspectives, 110,* A313–A315.

Langer, E. (1989). *Mindfulness.* Reading, MA: Addison-Wesley.

Langer, E. (1997). Mindful learning. *Current Directions in Psychological Science, 9,* 220–223.

Lanphear, B.P., Homung, R., Khoury, J., Yolton, K., Baghurst, P., Bellinger, D.C., . . . Roberts, R. (2005). Low-level environmental lead exposure and children's intellectual function: An international pooled analysis. *Environmental Health Perspectives, 113,* 894–899.

Lanphear, B.P., Vorhees, C.V., & Bellinger, D.C. (2005). Protecting children from environmental toxins: Toxicity testing of pesticides and industrial chemicals is a crucial step. *PLoS Medicine, 2,* 203–208.

Larson, M.E., Houlihan, D., & Goernert, P.N. (1995). Effects of informational feedback on aluminum can recycling. *Behavioral Interventions, 10,* 111–117.

Laumann, K., Gärling, T., & Stormark, K.M. (2003). Selective attention and heart rate responses to natural and urban environments. *Journal of Environmental Psychology, 23,* 125–134.

Lawrence, R.J. (2002). Healthy residential environments. In R.B. Bechtel & A. Churchman (Eds.), *Handbook of Environmental Psychology* (pp. 394–412). New York, NY: John Wiley & Sons, Inc.

Layard, R. (2005). *Happiness: Lessons from a new science.* New York, NY: Penguin.

Lazarus, R.S. (1966). *Psychological stress and the coping process.* New York, NY: McGraw Hill.

Lazarus, R.S., & Folkman, S. (1984). *Stress, appraisal and coping.* New York, NY: Springer Publishing.

Leader, D. (2008). *The new black: Mourning, melancholia and depression*. London, UK: Hamish Hamilton.

LeCouteur, D.G., McLean, A.J., Taylor, M.C., Woodham, B.L., & Board, P.G. (1999). Pesticides and Parkinson's disease. *Biomedicine and Pharmacotherapy, 53*, 122–130.

Lee, K.N. (1993). *Compass and gyroscope: Integrating science and politics for the environment*. Washington, DC: Island Press.

Lee, M. (2008, October 25). Drought, beetles killing forests: More than 10,000 oaks in S.D. County affected. *San Diego Union-Tribune*.

Lehman, P.K., & Geller, E.S. (2004). Behavior analysis and environmental protection: Accomplishments and potential for more. *Behavior and Social Issues, 13*, 13–32.

Leiserowitz, A. (2005). American risk perceptions: Is climate change dangerous? *Risk Analysis, 25*, 1433–1442.

Leiserowitz, A. (2006). Climate change risk perception and policy preferences: The role of affect, imagery, and values. *Climatic Change, 77*, 45–72.

Leiserowitz, A. (2007). Communicating the risks of global warming: American risk perceptions, affective images, and interpretive communities. In S.C. Moser & L. Dilling (Eds.), *Creating a climate for change: Communicating climate change and facilitating social change* (pp. 44–63). New York, NY: Cambridge University Press.

Leiserowitz, A., Maibach, E., & Roser-Renouf, C. (2009a). *Climate change in the American mind: American's climate change beliefs, attitudes, policy preferences, and actions. Yale Project on Climate Change*. George Mason University, Center for Climate Change Communication, Fairfax County, VA. Retrieved from http://envirocenter.research.yale.edu/uploads/climate change-report2.pdf

Leiserowitz, A., Maibach, E., & Roser-Renouf, C. (2009b). *Saving energy at home and on the road: A survey of Americans' energy saving behaviors, intentions, motivations, and barriers*. Yale Project on Climate Change. George Mason University, Center for Climate Change Communication, Fairfax County, VA. Retrieved from http://environment.yale.edu/uploads/SavingEnergy.pdf

Leonard-Barton, D. (1981). The diffusion of active-residential solar energy equipment in California. In A. Shama (Ed.), *Marketing solar energy innovations* (pp. 243–257). New York, NY: Praeger.

Leopold, A. (1949). *A Sand County almanac: And sketches here and there*. New York, NY: Oxford University Press.

Leopold, A. (1966). *A Sand County almanac, with other essays on conservation from Round River*. New York, NY: Oxford University Press.

Leopold, A. (1972). *Round River: From the journals of Aldo Leopold*. New York, NY: Oxford University Press.

Lertzman, R. (2007, June 22–25). *Exploring anxious dimensions of the irreparable: Considerations from psychoanalysis*. Presented at the 9th Biennial Conference on Communication and the Environment, DePaul University, Chicago, IL.

Lertzman, R. (2008). The myth of apathy. *Ecologist.* Retrieved from http://www.theecologist.org/blogs_and_comments/commentators/other_comments/269433/the_myth_of_apathy.html

Levi, D., & Kocher, S. (1999). Virtual nature: The future effects of information technology on our relationship to nature. *Environment and Behavior, 31,* 203–226.

Lewin, K. (1959). *Field theory in social science.* New York, NY: Harper and Bros.

Lifton, R.J. (1982). Beyond psychic numbing: A call to awareness. *American Journal of Orthopsychiatry, 54*(4), 619–629.

Lima, M.L. (2004). On the influence of risk perception on mental health: Living near an incinerator. *Journal of Environmental Psychology, 24,* 71–84.

Lindberg, C. (2000). Eschatology and fanaticism in the reformation era: Luther and the Anabaptists. *Concordia Theological Quarterly, 64,* 259–278.

Linn, S. (2004). *Consuming kids: The hostile takeover of childhood.* New York, NY & London, UK: New Press.

Linn, S. (2008). Commercializing childhood: The corporate takeover of kids' lives (interview by the *Multinational Monitor*). Retrieved from http://towardfreedom.com/home/content/view/1389/1/

Locke, J. (1690/1939). An essay concerning the true original extent and end of civil government. Reproduced in E.A. Burtt (Ed.), *The English philosophers from Bacon to Mill* (pp. 403–503). New York: The Modern Library.

Lomborg, B. (2001). *The skeptical environmentalist: Measuring the real state of the world.* Cambridge, NY: Cambridge University Press.

Lopez, B. (1990). *The rediscovery of North America.* New York, NY: Vintage Books (Random House).

Lord, C.G., Lepper, M.R., & Preston, E. (1984). Considering the opposite: A corrective strategy for social judgment. *Journal of Personality and Social Psychology, 47,* 1231–1243.

Lord, K.R. (1994). Motivating recycling behavior: A Quasi-experimental investigation of message and source strategies. *Psychology and Marketing, 11,* 341–358.

Louv, R. (2005/2008). *Last child in the woods: Saving our children from nature-deficit disorder.* Chapel Hill, NC: Algonquin Books of Chapel Hill.

Lovejoy, A.O. (1936/1960). *The great chain of being: A study of the history of an idea.* New York, NY: Harper & Brothers.

Lovelock, J. (1979). *Gaia: A new look at life on earth.* New York, NY: Oxford University Press.

Lovelock, J. (1990). *The ages of Gaia: A biography of our living earth* (p. 19). New York, NY: Bantam.

Lovins, A.B. (2002). Technology is the answer (but what was the question?) In G.T. Miller (Ed.), *Living in the environment: Principles, connections, and solutions,* (12th ed., pp. 361–362). Belmont, CA: Wadsworth/Thomson Learning.

Lovins, A.B., & Lovins, L.H. (2001, July/August). Fool's gold in Alaska. *Foreign affairs* [Electronic version]. Retrieved from http://www.rmi.org/images/PDFs/Energy/E01-03_FoolsGoldOrig.pdf

Lovins, L.H. (2008). Rethinking production. In L. Starke (Ed.), *2008 state of the world: Innovations for a sustainable economy* (pp. 32–44). New York, NY: W. W. Norton & Co.

Ludwig, D.S., & Kabat-Zinn, J. (2008). Mindfulness in medicine. *Journal of the American Medical Association, 300*, 1350–1352.

Lundberg, A. (1998). Environmental change and human health. In A. Lundberg (Ed.), *The environment and mental health: A guide for clinicians* (pp. 5–23). Mahwah, NJ: Erlbaum.

Lundberg, A., & Santiago-Rivera, A.L. (1998). Psychiatric aspects of technological disasters. In A. Lundberg (Ed.), *The environment and mental health: A guide for clinicians* (pp. 57–66). Mahwah, NJ: Erlbaum.

Lunder, S., & Jacob, A. (2008). *Fire retardants in toddlers and their mothers: Levels three times higher in toddlers than moms.* Environmental Working Group. Retrieved from http://www.ewg.org/reports/pbdesintoddlers

Lupien, S.J., Maheu, F., Tu, M., Fiocco, A., & Schramek, T.E. (2007). The effects of stress and stress hormones on human cognition: Implications for the field of brain and cognition. *Brain and Cognition, 65*, 209–237.

Lynn, M. (1992). Scarcity's enhancement of desirability: The role of naive economic theories. *Basic and Applied Social Psychology, 13*, 67–78.

Lynne, G.D., Casey, C.F., Hodges, A., & Rahmani, M. (1995). Conservation technology adoption and the theory of planned behavior. *Journal of Economic Psychology, 16*, 581–598.

Maathia, W. (2003). *The Greenbelt Movement: Sharing the approach and the experience.* Brooklyn, NY: Lantern Books.

MacNair, R.M. (Ed.). (2006). *Working for peace: A handbook of practical psychology and other tools.* Atascadero, CA: Impact Publishers.

MacPherson, D.B. (1962). *The political theory of possessive individualism: Hobbes to Locke.* Oxford, UK: Clarendon Press.

Macy, J., & Brown, M.Y. (1998). *Coming back to life: Practices to reconnect our lives, our world.* Gabriola Island, BC: New Society Publishers.

Macy, J.R. (1983). *Despair and personal power in the nuclear age.* Philadelphia: New Society Publishers.

Maddock, C., & Pariante, C.M. (2001). How does stress affect you? An overview of stress, immunity, depression and disease. *Epidemiologia e Psichiatria Sociale, 10*(3), 153–162.

Mahler, M.S. (1972). On the first three subphases of the separation-individual process. *International Journal of Psycho-Analysis, 53*, 333–338. (Reprinted in *Essential papers on object relation*, P. Buckley, 1986, New York, NY: New York University Press.)

Maiteny, P.T. (2002). Mind in the gap: Summary of research exploring "inner" influences on pro-sustainability learning and behavior. *Environmental Education Research, 8*, 299–306.

Maller, C., Townsend, M., Pryor, A., Brown, P., & St. Leger, L. (2006). Healthy nature healthy people: 'Contact with nature' as an upstream health promotion intervention for populations. *Health Promotion International, 21*, 45–54.

Manes, C. (1996). Nature and silence. In C. Glotfelty & H. Fromm (Eds.), *The ecocriticism reader* (pp. 15–29). Athens, GA and London, UK: The University of Georgia Press.

Mannetti, L., Pierro, A., & Livi, S. (2004). Recycling: Planned and self-expressive behaviour. *Journal of Environmental Psychology, 24*, 227–236.

Marcus, A.D. (2005, December 6). Researchers probe links between gender and cancer. The Wall Street Journal, D1. Retrieved from http://www.lungcancerealliance.org/news/documents/ResearchersProbeLinkBetweenGenderandCancer-WSJ12-6-05.pdf

Marmot, M., Friel, S., Bell, R., Houweling, T.A.J., & Taylor, S. (2008). Closing the gap in a generation: Health equity through action on the social determinants of health. *Lancet, 372*, 1661–1669.

Martin, G., & Pear, J. (2009). *Behavior modification: What it is and how to do it* (8th ed.). Englewood Cliffs, NJ: Prentice-Hall.

Marx, K. (1867/1977). *Capital, I* (Ben Fowkes Ed., p. 929). New York, NY: Vintage Books.

Maser, C. (1988). *The redesigned forest*. San Pedro, CA: R.E. Miles.

Masters, R.D. (1997). Environmental pollution and crime. *Vermont Law Review, 22*, 359–382.

Masters, R.D. (2003). The social implications of evolutionary psychology: Linking brain biochemistry, toxins, and violent crime. In R.W. Bloom and N.K. Dess (Eds.), *Evolutionary psychology and violence: A primer for policymakers and public policy advocates* (pp. 23–56). Westport, CT: Praeger.

Matthews, E. (2000). From forests to floorboards: Trends in industrial roundwood production and consumption. *World Resources Institute: Earth Trends.* Available from http://earthtrends.wri.org/features/view_feature.php?theme=9&fid=6

Mayer, B. (2000). *The dynamics of conflict resolution*. San Francisco, CA: Jossey-Bass

Mayer, F.S., & Frantz, C.M. (2004). The connectedness to nature scale: A measure of individuals' feeling in community with nature. *Journal of Environmental Psychology 24*, 503–515.

Mayer, F.S., & Frantz, C.M. (2008). Framing the question of survival: Psychological insights and limitations. *Conservation Biology, 22*, 823–825.

Mayer, F.S., Frantz, C.M., Bruehlman-Senecal, E., & Dolliver, K. (2008). Why is nature beneficial? The role of connectedness to nature. *Environment and Behavior*. doi: 10.1177/0013916508319475 Retrieved from http://eab.sagepub.com hosted at http://online.sagepub.com

Mazumdar, S., & Mazumdar, S. (1993). Sacred space and place attachment. *Journal of Environmental Psychology, 13*, 231–242.

Mazumdar, S., & Mazumdar, S. (2004). Religion and place attachment: A study of sacred places. *Journal of Environmental Psychology, 24*, 385–397.

McDaniel, J.B. (1994). Emerging options in ecological Christianity: The new story, the biblical story, and pantheism. In C.K. Chapple (Ed.), *Ecological prospects: Scientific, religious, and aesthetic perspectives*. Albany, NY: State University of New York Press.

McDonough, W., & Braungart, M. (1998). The NEXT industrial revolution. *Atlantic Monthly*, digital edition Available from http://www.theatlantic.com/issues/98oct/industry.htm

McDonough, W., & Braungart, M. (2002). *Cradle to cradle*. New York: North Point Press.

McGinn, A.P. (2002). Reducing our toxic burden. In C. Flavin, H. French, & G. Gardner (Eds.), *State of the world, 2002: A worldwatch institute report on progress toward a sustainable society* (pp. 75–100). New York: W. W. Norton & Co.

McKenzie-Mohr, D. (2000a). Fostering sustainable behavior through community-based social marketing. *American Psychologist, 55*(5), 531–537.

McKenzie-Mohr, D. (2000b). Promoting sustainable behavior: An introduction to community-based social marketing. *Journal of Social Issues, 56*(3), 543–555.

McKenzie-Mohr, D., & Smith, W. (1999). *Fostering sustainable behavior: An introduction to community-based social marketing*. Gabriola Island, BC: New Society Publishers.

McNeeley, S., & Huntington, O. (2007). Postcards from the (not so) frozen North: Talking about climate change in Alaska. In S.C. Moser & L. Dilling (Eds.). *Creating a climate for change: Communicating climate change and facilitating social change* (pp. 139–152). Cambridge, UK: Cambridge University Press.

McNeil, B.J., Pauker, S.G., Sox, H.C., & Tversky, A. (1982). On the elicitation of preferences for alternative therapies. *New England Journal of Medicine, 306*(21), 1259–1262.

McPherson, G.R., & Weltzin, J.F. (2008). Implications of peak oil for industrialized societies. *Bulletin of Science, Technology & Society, 28*, 187–191.

McStay, J.R., & Dunlap, R.E. (1983). Male-female differences in concern for environmental quality. *International Journal of Women's Studies, 6*, 291–301.

Meadows, D.H. (1991). *The global citizen* (p. 17). Washington, DC: Island Press.

Medin, D.L., Ross, B.H., & Markman, A.B. (2001). *Cognitive psychology* (3rd ed., p. 540). Fort Worth, TX: Harcourt College Publishers.

Mehra, R., & Rojas, M.H. (2008). *A significant shift: Women, food security, and agriculture in a global marketplace*. Washington, DC: International Center for Research on Women (ICRW).

Melson, G.F. (2001). *Why the wild things are: Animals in the lives of children*. Cambridge, MA: Harvard University Press.

Melson, G.F. (2003). Child development and the human-companion animal bond. *American Behavioral Scientist, 47*, 31–39.

Mendola, P., Selevan, S.G., Gutter, S., & Rice, D. (2002). Environmental factors associated with a spectrum of neurodevelopmental deficits. *Mental Retardation and Developmental Disabilities Research Reviews, 8*, 188–197.

Merchant, C. (1980). *The death of nature: Women, ecology and the scientific revolution.* San Francisco, CA: Harper.

Mergen, B. (2003). Review essay: Children and nature in history. *Environmental History, 8*(4). Retrieved from http://www.historycooperative.org/journals/eh/8.4/mergen.html

Merton, R.K., & Kitt, A.S. (1950). Contributions to the theory of reference group behavior. In R.K. Merton & P.F. Lazarsfeld (Eds.), *Continuities in social research: Studies in the scope and method of the American soldier.* Glencoe, IL: Free Press.

Meyer, D.S. (2007). Building social movements. In S.C. Moser & L. Dilling (Eds.), *Creating a climate for change: Communicating climate change and facilitating social change* (pp. 451–461). Cambridge, UK: Cambridge University Press.

Michaels, S. (2008, October 10). Hotels taking "going green" to new tops with green roofs. *The Huffington Post.* Retrieved from http://www.huffingtonpost.com/stefanie-michaels/hotels-taking-going-green_b_133748.html

Milinski, M., Sommerfeld, R.D., Krambeck, H.J., Reed, F.A., & Marotzke, J. (2008). The collective-risk social dilemma and the prevention of simulated dangerous climate change. *Proceedings of the National Academy of Sciences, 105,* 2291–2294.

Miller, G.T. (1993). *Living in the environment: An introduction to environmental science* (7th ed.). Belmont, CA: Wadsworth Publishing Co.

Miller, G.T. (2002). *Living in the environment: Principles, connections and solutions* (12th ed.). Belmont, CA: Wadsworth/Thompson Learning.

Miller, G.T. (2007). *Living in the environment: Principles, connections and solutions* (14th ed.). Belmont, CA: Wadsworth/Thompson Learning.

Miller, G.T. (2008). *Environmental Science* (12th ed.). Belmont, CA: Thomson, Brooks Cole.

Miller, T.A., & Keller, E.B. (1991). What the public thinks. *EPA Journal, 17*(2), 40–43.

Milligan, S. (2009, April 22). President signs $5.7 billion measure to boost volunteerism; Edward M. Kennedy Serve America Act expands 16-year-old AmeriCorps. *The Boston Globe, National News,* p. 6.

Milton, M. (2009).Waking up to nature:Exploring a new direction for psychological practice. *Ecopsychology, 1,* 8–13.

Mind Week Report. (2007, May). *Executive summary: Ecotherapy: The green agenda for mental health.* Retrieved from http://www.mind.org.uk

Miranda, R. (2007). From instinct to domination to boundless creativity: An integrative model of human motivation from the perspective of ecopsychology and attachment theory. *Dissertation Abstracts International, 68*(40B), 2688.

Mishan, J. (1996). Psychoanalysis and environmentalism: First thoughts. *Psychoanalytic Psychotherapy, 10*(1), 59–70.

Mishra, A., & Tripathi, S. (1978). *The chipko movement.* New Delhi, India: People's Action/Gandhi Peace Foundation.

Mitchell, R., & Popham, F. (2008). Effect of exposure to natural environment on health inequalities: An observational population study. *Lancet, 372,* 1655–1660.

Mitchell, S.A. (1988). *Relational concepts in psychoanalysis: An integration.* Cambridge, MA: Harvard University Press.

Mohai, P. (1992). Men, women, and the environment: An examination of the gender gap in environmental concern and activism. *Society and Natural Resources, 5,* 1–19.

Mohr, N. (2005). *A new global warming strategy: How environmentalists are overlooking vegetarianism as the most effective tool against climate change in our lifetimes.* New York: EarthSave International. Retrieved from http://www.earthsave.org/news/earthsave_global_warming_report.pdf

Monroe, M.C. (2003). Two avenues for encouraging conservation behaviors. *Human Ecology Review, 10,* 113–125.

Mooney, C. (2007). An inconvenient assessment. *Bulletin of the Atomic Scientists, 63*(6), 40–47.

Moore, C. (1996). *The mediation process: Practical strategies for resolving conflict.* San Francisco, CA: Jossey-Bass.

Moore, R.C. (1999). Healing gardens for children. In C. Cooper Marcus & M. Barnes (Eds.), *Healing gardens: Therapeutic benefits and design recommendations* (pp. 323–384). New York, NY: John Wiley.

Morgan, M.G. (1993, July). Risk analysis and management. *Scientific American,* 32–41.

Morse, J.M., & Doberneck, B. (1995). Delineating the concept of hope. *Image— Journal of Nursing Scholarship, 27,* 277–285.

Moschis, G.P. (1985). The role of family communication in consumer socialization of children and adolescents. *Journal of Consumer Research, 11,* 898–913.

Moser, S.C. (2007). More bad news: The risk of neglecting emotional responses to climate change information. In S.C. Moser & L. Dilling (Eds.), *Creating a climate for change: Communicating climate change and facilitating social change* (pp. 64–80). Cambridge, UK: Cambridge University Press.

Moser, S.C., & Dilling, L. (2007). *Creating a climate for change: Communicating climate change and facilitating social change.* New York, NY: Cambridge University Press.

Motavalli, J. (2002). The case against meat. *The Environmental Magazine, 8*(1), 26–32.

Mouawad, J. (2007, September 27). 550,000 more Chinese toys recalled for lead. *The New York Times,* C-2.

Muir, T., & Zegarac, M. (2001). Societal costs of exposure to toxic substances: Economic and health costs of four case studies that are candidates for environmental causation. *Environmental Health Perspectives, 109*(Suppl. 6), 885–903.

Musser, L.M., & Diamond, K.E. (1999). The children's attitudes towards the environment scale for preschool children. *Journal of Environmental Education, 30*(2), 23–31.

Myers, D. (1993). *Social psychology* (4th ed.). New York, NY: McGraw-Hill.

Myers, D.G. (2008). *Social psychology* (7th ed.) New York: McGraw-Hill.

Myers, D. (2010). *Social psychology* (10th ed.). New York, NY: McGraw-Hill.

Myers, G. (2007). *The significance of children and animals: Social development and our connections to other species.* West Lafayette, IN: Purdue University Press.

Myers, G.J., & Davidson, P.W. (2000). Does methylmercury have a role in causing developmental disabilities in children? *Environmental Health Perspectives, 108*(3), 413–420.

Myers, N. (1984). *The primary source:Tropical forests and our future.* New York:Norton.

Myers, O.E., & Saunders, C.D. (2002). Animals as links toward developing caring relationships with the natural world. In P.H. Kahn, Jr. & S.R. Kellert (Eds.), *Children and nature: Psychological, sociocultural, and evolutionary investigations* (pp. 153–178). Cambridge, MA: Massachusetts Institute of Technology Press.

Myers, O.E., Saunders, C.D., & Garrett, E. (2004). What do children think animals need? Developmental trends. *Environmental Education Research, 10,* 545–562.

Nadakavukaren, A. (2000). *Our global environment: A health perspective* (5th ed.). Prospect Heights, IL: Waveland Press, Inc.

Naess, A. (1985). Identification as a source of deep ecological attitudes. In M. Tobias, (Ed.), *Deep ecology* (pp. 256–270). San Diego, CA: Avant Books.

Naess, A. (1988, March 12). *Self realization: An ecological approach to being in the world.* Murchock University. (As quoted from *Simple in means, rich in ends: Practicing deep ecology,* p. 43, by B. Devall, Ed., 1988, Salt Lake City, UT: Peregrine Smith Books.)

Naess, A. (1990). *Ecology, community, and lifestyle: Outline of an ecosophy/Arne Naess.* In David Rothenberg, Trans. & Rev. Cambridge, NY: Cambridge University Press.

Nairn, A., Ormrod, J., & Bottomley, P. (2007). *Watching, wanting and well-being: Exploring the links.* London, UK: National Consumer Council.

National Academy of Sciences. (1984). *Toxicity testing: Needs and priorities.* Washington, DC: National Academy Press.

National Crime Prevention Council. (2008). *Delete cyber-bullying.* Retrieved from http://www.ncpc.org/cyberbullying

National Institute of Mental Health, U.S. Department of Health and Human Services. (2007). *Global use of ADHD medications rises dramatically.* Retrieved from http://www.nimh.nih.gov/science-news/2007/global-use-of-adhd-medications-rises-dramatically.shtml

National Institute of Mental Health. (2009). *Treatment of children with mental disorders.* Retrieved from http://www.nimh.nih.gov/health/publications/treatment-of-children-with-mental-disorders/index.shtml

National Institute of Neurological Disorders and Stroke. (2008). *Autism fact sheet.* Retrieved from http://www.ninds.nih.gov/disorders/autism/detail_autism.htm

National Institute on Aging, U.S. National Institutes of Health. (2008). *Alzheimer's Disease Fact Sheet.* Retrieved from http://www.nia.nih.gov/Alzheimers/Publications/adfact.htm

National Institutes of Health. (2008). *Learning Disorders.* Retrieved from http://www.nlm.nih.gov/medlineplus/learningdisorders.html

National Research Council. (2002). *New tools for environmental protection: Education, information, and voluntary measures.* Committee on the Human Dimensions of Global Change, T. Dietz & P.C. Stern (Eds.), Division of Behavioral and Social Sciences and Education. Washington, DC: National Academy Press.

Nationmaster. (2004). *Energy statistics: use of oil equivalent (per capita) (most recent) by country.* Retrieved from http://www.nationmaster.com/graph/ene_use_kt_of_oil_equ_percap-kt-oil-equivalent-per-capita

Needleman, H.L. (1980). Lead exposure and human health: Recent data on an ancient problem. *Technology Review, 82*(5), 39–45.

Needleman, H.L. (1998). Childhood lead poisoning: The promise and abandonment of primary prevention. *American Journal of Public Health, 88,* 1871–1877.

Needleman, H.L. (2004). Lead poisoning. *Annual Review of Medicine, 55*(1), 209–222.

Needleman, H.L., Gunnoe, C., Leviton, A., Reed, R., Peresie, H., Maher, C., & Barrett, P. (1979). Deficits in psychologic and classroom performance of children with elevated dentine lead levels. *New England Journal of Medicine, 300,* 689–695.

Needleman, H.L., & Landrigan, P.J. (2004). What level of lead in blood is toxic for a child? *American Journal of Public Health, 94,* 8.

Needleman, H.L., McFarland, C., Ness, R.B., Fienberg, S.E., & Tobin, M.J. (2002). Bone lead levels in adjudicated delinquents: A case control study. *NeuroToxicology and Teratology, 24*(6), 711–717.

Needleman, H.L., Riess, J.A., Tobin, M.J., Biesecker, G.E., & Greenhouse, J.B. (1996). Bone lead levels and delinquent behavior. *Journal of the American Medical Association 275*(5), 363–369.

Nevin, J.A. (1991). Behavior analysis and global survival. In W. Ishaq (Ed.), *Human behavior in today's world* (pp. 39–49). New York, NY: Praeger Publishers.

Nevin, J.A. (2005). The inertia of affluence. *Behavior and Social Issues, 14,* 7–20.

Nevin, R. (2000). How lead exposure relates to temporal changes in IQ, violent crime, and unwed pregnancy. *Environmental Research, 83*(1), 1–22.

Newell, P.B. (1997). A cross-cultural examination of favorite places. *Environment and Behavior, 29,* 495–514.

Newton, I. (1687). *Principea.* Retrieved from http://www.archive.org/details/newtonspmathema00newtrich

NGO Forum. (2008). *Capital's drinking water quality substandard.* Retrieved from http://www.ngoforum.net/index.php?option=com_content&task=view&id=3055&Itemid = 6

Nhat Hanh, T. (1991). *The miracle of mindfulness.* London, UK: Rider Books.

Nicholsen, S.W. (2002). *The love of nature and the end of the world: The unspoken dimensions of environmental concern.* Cambridge, MA: Massachusetts Institute of Technology Press.

Nisbet, E.K., Zelenski, J.M., & Murphy, S.A. (2008). The nature relatedness scale: Linking individuals' connection with nature to environmental concern and behavior. *Environment and Behavior.* doi: 1.1177/0013916508318748 Retrieved from http://eab.sagepub.com hosted at http://online.sagepub.com

Noiseux, K., & Hostetler, M.E. (2008, December 3). Do homebuyers want green features in their communities? *Environment and Behavior OnlineFirst.* doi: 10.1177/0013916508326470

Nolan, J.M., Schultz, P.W., Cialdini, R.B., Goldstein, N.J., & Griskevicius, V. (2008). Normative social influence in underdetected. *Personality and Social Psychology Bulletin, 34,* 913–923.

Norgaard, K.M. (2006). "People want to protect themselves a little bit": Emotions, denial, and social movement nonparticipation. *Sociological Inquiry, 76*(3), 372–396.

Novacek, M.J. (2008). Engaging the public in biodiversity issues. *Proceedings of the National Academy of Sciences, 105*(Suppl. 1), 11571–11578

Obama for America. (2007). *Barack Obama and Joe Biden: Promoting a healthy environment.* Retrieved from http://www.barackobama.com/pdf/issues/EnvironmentFactSheet.pdf

Öhman, A., & Mineka, S. (2003). The malicious serpent: Snakes as a prototypical stimulus for an evolved module of fear. *Current Directions in Psychological Science, 12,* 5–9.

Ohtomo, S., & Hirose, Y. (2007). The dual-process of reactive and intentional decision-making involved in eco-friendly behavior. *Journal of Environmental Psychology, 27,* 117–125.

Oliver, M. (2004). *Wild Geese.* Newcastle, UK: Bloodaxe World Poets.

Opler, M.G.A., Brown, A.S., Graziano, J., Desai, M., Zheng, W., Schaefer, C., . . . Susser, E.S. (2004). Prenatal lead exposure, delta-aminolevulinic acid, and schizophrenia. *Environmental Health Perspectives, 112*(5), 548–552.

Opler, M.G.A., & Susser, E.S. (2005). Fetal environment and schizophrenia. *Environmental Health Perspectives, 113,* 1239–1242.

Opotow, S. (1990). Moral exclusion and injustice: An introduction. *Journal of Social Issues, 46*(1), 1–20.

Opotow, S. (1994). Predicting protection: Scope of justice and the natural world. *Journal of Social Issues, 50*(3), 49–63.

Opotow, S. (2001). Social injustice. In D. Christie, R. Wagner, & D. Winter (Eds.), *Peace, conflict and violence: Peace psychology for the 21st century.* Upper Saddle River, NJ: Prentice Hall.

Opotow, S., & Brook, A. (2003). Identity and exclusion in rangeland conflict. In S. Clayton & S. Opotow (Eds.), *Identity and the natural environment: The psychological significance of nature* (pp. 249–272). Cambridge, MA: Massachusetts Institute of Technology Press.

Opotow, S., & Clayton, S. (1994). Green justice: Conceptions of fairness and the natural world. *Journal of Social Issues, 50*, 1–12.

Opotow, S., & Weiss, L. (2000). Denial and the process of moral exclusion in environmental conflict. *Journal of Social Issues, 56*, 475–490.

Ornstein, R., & Ehrlich, P. (2000). *New world, new mind: Moving toward conscious evolution.* Cambridge, MA: Malor Books, ISHK.

Orr, D.W. (1993). Love it or lose it: The coming biophilia revolution. In S.R. Kellert & E.O. Wilson (Eds.), *The biophilia hypothesis* (pp. 415–440). Washington, DC: Island Press.

Orr, D.W. (2002). Political economy and the ecology of childhood. In P.H. Kahn, Jr. & S.R. Kellert (Eds.), *Children and nature: Psychological, sociocultural, and evolutionary investigations* (pp. 279–303). Cambridge MA: Massachusetts Institute of Technology Press.

Orr, D.W. (2004). *Earth in mind: On education, environment and the human prospect (10th anniversary edition).* Washington, DC: Island Press.

Orr, D.W. (2008). The psychology of survival. *Conservation Biology, 22*, 819–822.

Osbaldiston, R., & Sheldon, K.M. (2002). Social dilemmas and sustainability: Promoting people's motivation to "cooperate with the future." In P. Schmuck & P.W. Schultz (Eds.), *Psychology of sustainable development* (pp. 37–57). Boston, MA: Kluwer Academic Publishers.

Osbaldiston, R., & Sheldon, K.M. (2003). Promoting internalized motivation for environmentally responsible behavior: A prospective study of environmental goals. *Journal of Environmental Psychology, 23*, 349–357.

Oskamp, S. (2000). A sustainable future for humanity? How can psychology help? *American Psychologist, 55*(5), 496–508.

Oskamp, S. (2002). Summarizing sustainability issues and research approaches. In P. Schmuck & P.W. Schultz (Eds.), *Psychology of sustainable development* (pp. 301–324). Boston, MA: Kluwer Academic Publishers.

Oskamp, S., Harrington, M.J., Edwards, T.C., Sherwood, D.L., Okuda, S.M., & Swason, D.C. (1991). Factors influencing household recycling behavior. *Environment and Behavior, 23*, 494–519.

Ostrom, E. (1990). *Governing the commons: The evolution of institutions for collective action.* Cambridge, UK: Cambridge University Press.

Ostrom, E., Burger, J., Field, C.B., Norgaard, R.B., & Policansky, D. (2007). Revisiting the commons: Local lessons, global challenges. In D.J. Penn & I. Mysterud (Eds.), *Evolutionary perspectives on environmental problems* (pp. 129–140). New Brunswick, NJ: Transaction Publishers.

Oxford Company, The (2005). Ancient (and not so ancient) Wisdom: Offering a weekly positive perspective. Retrieved from http://www.oxfordco.com/newsletters/ancient_wisdom/ancient_Nx_130.shtml

Pachauri, R. (2008, January 15). *Lifestyle changes can curb climate change: IPCC chief.* Retrieved from http://newsinfo.inquirer.net/breakingnews/world/view/20080116-112681/IPCC-chief-Lifestyle-changes-can-curb-climate-change

Pahl, S., Harris, P.R., Todd, H.A., & Rutter, D.R. (2005). Comparative optimism for environmental risks. *Journal of Environmental Psychology, 25,* 1–11.

Paine, T. (1791–1792/1953). The rights of man. In N.F. Adkins (Ed.), *Common sense and other political writings of Thomas Paine.* Indianapolis, IN: Bobbs-Merrill Co.

Palin, S. (2007). Sarah Palin on environment. *On the Issues.* Retrieved from http://www.ontheissues.org/2008/Sarah_Palin_Environment.htm

Pallak, M.S., Cook, D.A., & Sullivan, J.J. (1980). Commitment and energy conservation. In L. Bickman (Ed.), *Applied social psychology annual* (Vol. 1, pp. 235–254). Beverly Hills, CA: Sage.

Pardini, A.U., & Katzev, R.D. (1983–1984). The effects of strength of commitment on newspaper recycling. *Journal of Environmental Systems, 13,* 245–254.

Pardon, M.C., & Rattray, I. (2008). What do we know about the long-term consequences of stress on ageing and the progression of age-related neurodegenerative disorders? *Neuroscience and Biobehavioral Reviews, 32,* 1103–1120.

Park, S.H., & Mattson, R.H. (2008). Effect of flowering and foliage plants in hospital rooms on patients recovering from abdominal surgery. *HortTechnology, 18,* 563–568.

Parkinson's Action Network. (2002). *The cost of Parkinson's disease.* Retrieved from http://www.parkinsonsaction.org/oldsite/cost.html

Parsons, R., & Hartig, T. (2000). Environmental psychophysiology. In J.T. Cacioppo, L.G. Tassinary, & G.G. Berntson (Eds.), *Handbook of psychophysiology* (2nd ed.). Cambridge, UK: Cambridge University Press.

Patel, N. (2007, November 22). Warming could spark global warring, warn H.K. scientists. *The Standard.*

Peel, J., & Richards, K. (2005, December). Outdoor cure. An overview and adventure therapy *Therapy Today, 16*(10), 4–8.

Pellegrini, A.D. (2005). *Recess: Its role in education and development.* Mahwah, NJ: Lawrence Erlbaum Associates.

Pelletier, L.G., Tuson, K.M., Green-Demers, I., Noels, K., & Beaton, A.M. (1998). Why are you doing things for the environment? The motivation toward the environment scale (MTES). *Journal of Applied Social Psychology, 28,* 437–468.

Pellow, D.N. (2007). *Resisting global toxics: Transnational movements for environmental justice.* Cambridge, MA: Massachusetts Institute of Technology Press.

Penn, D.J. (2003). The evolutionary roots of our environmental problems: Toward a Darwinian Ecology. *The Quarterly Review of Biology, 78,* 275–301.

Penn, D.J., & Mysterud, I. (2007). *Evolutionary perspectives on environmental problems.* New Brunswick, NJ: Transaction Publishers.

Peraza, M.A., Ayala-Fierro, F., Barber, D.S., Casarez, E., & Rael, L.T. (1998). Effects of micronutrients on metal toxicity. *Environmental Health Perspectives, 106*(Suppl. 1), 203–216.

Perkins, H.W. (1991). Religious commitment, Yuppies values, and well-being in post-collegiate life. *Review of Religious Research, 32,* 244–251.

Perls, F.S. (1942). *Ego, hunger and aggression; a revision of Freud's theory and method.* Oxford, UK: Knox Publishing Company.

Perls, F. (1969). Ego, hunger, and aggression: The beginning of gestalt therapy. New York:Random House.

Perls, F. (1971). *Gestalt therapy verbatim.* New York: Bantam.

Perls, F. (1978). *The gestalt approach: An eyewitness to therapy.* New York: Bantam.

Peterson, M.N., Chen, X., & Liu, J. (2008). Household location choices: Implications for biodiversity. *Conservation Biology, 22,* 912–921.

Peurifoy, R.Z. (1995). *Anxiety, phobias and panic: A step-by-step program for regaining control of your life.* New York, NY: Warner Books.

Pew Research Center. (2007, June 27). *Rising environmental concern in 47-nation survey: Global uneasiness with major world powers.* Retrieved from http://pewglobal.org/

Piaget, J. (1962). *Play, dreams, and imitation in children* (C. Gattegno & F.M. Hodgson, Trans.). New York, NY: W. W. Norton & Co.

Piel, G. (1994, March 21). Defusing the 'population bomb.' *The Nation, 258*(11), 376–380.

Pierce, J.C., Dalton, R.J., & Zaitsev, A. (1999). Public perceptions of environmental conditions. In R.J. Dalton, P. Garb, N.P. Lovrich, J.C. Pierce, & J.M. Whitely (Eds.), *Critical masses: Citizens, nuclear weapons production, and environmental destruction in the United States and Russia* (pp. 97–129). Cambridge, MA: Massachusetts Institute of Technology Press.

Pilisuk, M. (2001). Globalization and structural violence. In D.J. Christie, R.V. Wagner, & D.D. Winter (Eds.), *Peace, conflict, and violence: Peace psychology for the 21st century* (pp. 149–157). Upper Saddle River, NJ: Prentice Hall.

Pirages, D.C., & Ehrlich, P.R. (1974). *Ark II: Social response to environmental imperatives.* San Francisco, CA: W. H. Freeman.

Platt, J.R. (1973). Social traps. *American Psychologist, 28,* 641–651.

Plotkin, B. (2008). *Nature and the human soul: Cultivating wholeness and community in a fragmented world.* Novato, CA: New World Library.

Ponting, C. (1991). *A green history of the world: The environment and collapse of great civilizations.* New York: St. Martin's Press.

Porteous, J.D. (1990). *Landscapes of the mind: Worlds of sense and metaphor.* Toronto, Canada: University of Toronto Press.

Porterfield, S. (2000). Thyroidal dysfunction and environmental chemicals: Potential impact on brain development. *Environmental Health Perspectives, 108*(3), 433–438.

Powers, R.B., Osborne, J.G., & Anderson, E.G. (1973). Positive reinforcement of litter removal in the natural environment. *Journal of Applied Behavior Analysis, 6,* 579–586.

Pronin, E., Berger, J., & Molouki, S. (2007). Alone in a crowd of sheep: Asymmetric perceptions of conformity and their roots in an introspection illusion. *Journal of Personality and Social Psychology, 92,* 585–595.

Proshansky, H.M., Fabian, A.K., & Kaminoff, R. (1993). Place identity, physical world socialization of the self. *Journal of Environmental Psychology, 3,* 57–83.

Protections in peril: A midnight attack on the endangered species act, courtesy of the Interior Department. (2008, December 28). *Washington Post,* p. B6.

Pyle, R.M. (1993). *The thunder tree: Lessons from an urban wildland.* Boston, MA: Houghton Mifflin.

Pyle, R.M. (2002). Eden in a vacant lot: Special places, species and kids in the neighborhood of life. In P.H. Kahn, Jr. & S.R. Kellert (Eds.), *Children and nature: Psychological, sociocultural, and evolutionary investigations* (pp. 305–327). Cambridge, MA: Massachusetts Institute of Technology Press.

Quick, D. (2007, May 17). Children teach their parents well. *The Post and Courier.* Retrieved from http://www.charleston.net/news/2007/may/17/ children_teach_their_parents_well/

Rabin, R.C. (2008, November 19). What happy people don't do. *The New York Times, Research Section.* Retrieved from http://www.nytimes. com/2008/11/20/health/research/20happy.html?em

Rabkin, S., & Gershon, D. (2007). Changing the world one household at a time: Portland's 30-day program to lose 5,000 pounds. In S.C. Moser & L. Dilling (Eds.), *Creating a climate for change: Communicating climate change and facilitating social change* (pp. 292–302). Cambridge, UK: Cambridge University Press.

Rainwater, B., & Martin, C. (2006). *Local leaders in sustainability.* Retrieved from http://www.aia.org/practicing/groups/kc/AIAS077433

Ramstack, T. (2008, April 23). New mileage rules to boost car costs; White House eyes 25% improved efficiency. *The Washington Times,* C-08.

Randall, R. (2005). A new climate for psychotherapy? *Psychotherapy and Politics International, 3*(3), 165–179.

Redman, C.L. (1999). *Human impact on ancient environments.* Tucson, AZ: University of Arizona Press.

Reist, D.M. (2004). Materialism vs. an ecological identity: Towards an integrative framework for a psychology of sustainable living. *Dissertation Abstracts International: Section A. Humanities and Social Sciences. 65,* 1665.

Relph, E. (1976). *Place and placelessness.* London, UK: Pion Limited.

Reser, J. (1995). Whither environmental psychology? The transpersonal ecopsychology crossroads. *Journal of Environmental Psychology, 15,* 235–257.

Reser, J. (2003). Thinking through "conservation psychology": Prospects and challenges. *Human Ecology Review, 10,* 167–174.

Revkin, A.C. (2003, January 8). Environment and science: Danes rebuke a 'skeptic.' *The New York Times,* p. A7.

Revkin, A.C. (2008, November 26). The (tuna) tragedy of the commons. *Dot Earth* Retrieved from http://dotearth.blogs.nytimes.com/2008/11/26/ the-tuna-tragedy-of-the-commons/

Rhodes, D., Spiro, A., Aro, A., & Hu, H. (2003). Relationship of bone and blood lead levels to psychiatric symptoms: The normative aging study. *Journal of Occupational and Environmental Medicine, 45*, 1144–1151.

Rice, D., & Barone, S. (2000). Critical periods of vulnerability for the developing nervous system: Evidence from humans and animal models. *Environmental Health Perspectives, 108*(Suppl. 3), 511–533.

Rice, D., Evangelista de Duffard, A., Duffard, R., Iregren, A., Satoh, H., & Watanabe, C. (1996). Lessons for neurotoxicology from selected model compounds. SGOMSEC joint report. *Environmental Health Perspectives, 104*(Suppl.2), 205–215.

Richins, M.L. (1991). Social comparison and the idealized images of advertising. *Journal of Consumer Research, 18*, 71–83.

Richins, M.L., & Dawson, S. (1992). A consumer values orientation for materialism and its measurement: Scale development and validation. *Journal of Consumer Research, 19*, 303–319.

Riebel, L. (2001). Consuming the earth: Eating disorders and ecopsychology. *Journal of Humanistic Psychology, 41*(2), 38–58.

Rindfleisch, A., Burroughs, J.E., & Denton, F. (1997). Family structure, materialism, and compulsive consumption. *Journal of Consumer Research, 23*, 312–325.

Robbins, J. (2001). *The food revolution: How your diet can help save your life and our world.* Berkeley, CA: Conari Press.

Robert, K. (1991, Spring). Educating a nation: The Natural Step. *In Context, 28*, 11.

Roberts, D.F., Foehr, U.G., & Rideout, V. (2005). *Generation M: Media in the lives of 8-18 year olds* (Publication No. 7251). Menlo Park, CA: Henry J. Kaiser Family Foundation. Retrieved from http://www.kff.org/entmedia/upload/Generation-M-Media-in-the-Lives-of-8-18-Year-olds-Report.pdf

Roberts, E. (1998). Place and the human spirit. *The Humanistic Psychologist, 26*, 5–34.

Roberts, E.M., English, P.B., Grether, J.K., Windham, G.C., Somberg, L., & Wolff, C. (2007). Maternal residence near agricultural pesticide applications and autism spectrum disorders among children in the California central valley. *Environmental Health Perspectives, 115*, 1482–1489.

Roberts, J.A., & Bacon, D.R. (1997). Exploring the subtle relationships between environmental concern and ecologically conscious consumer behavior. *Journal of Business Research, 40*, 79–89.

Robertson, J.A.L. (2000). *Decide the nuclear issues for yourself: Nuclear need not be unclear.* Retrieved from http://www.magma.ca/~jalrober/Decide.htm

Roberts, J.L. (2008, December 8). Luxury shame: Why even the very rich are cutting back on conspicuous consumption. *Newsweek*, Retrieved from http://www.newsweek.com/id/171246

Rodgers, W.H. (1994). *Environmental law* (2nd ed.). St. Paul, MN: West Publishing Co.

Rogen, R., O'Conner, M., & Horwitz, P. (2005). Nowhere to hide: Awareness and perception of environmental change, and their influence on relationships with place. *Journal of Environmental Psychology, 25*, 147–158.

Rogers, E.M. (1995). *Diffusion and innovations* (4th ed.). New York, NY: Free Press.

Roosevelt, M. (2008, September 30). California launches broad effort to control hazardous chemicals. *Los Angeles Times, Local Section.* Retrieved from http://articles.latimes.com/2008/sep/30/local/me-chemicals30

Rosenthal, E. (2008, December 3). As more eat meat, a bid to cut emissions. *New York Times.* Retrieved from http://www.nytimes.com/2008/12/04/science/earth/04meat.html?_r=2&ref=world

Ross, C., Reynolds, J., & Geis, K. (2000). The contingent meaning of neighborhood stability for residents' psychological well-being. *American Sociological Review, 65*, 581–597.

Ross, N., Medin, D., Coley, J.D., & Atran, S. (2003). Cultural and experiential differences in the development of folkbiological induction. *Cognitive Development, 18*, 25–47.

Roszak, T. (1969). *The making of a counter culture: Reflections on the technocratic society and its youthful opposition.* Garden City, NY: Doubleday.

Roszak, T. (1992). *The voice of the earth: An exploration of eco-psychology.* New York, NY: Simon & Schuster.

Roszak, T. (1994). Green guilt and ecological overload. In M. Walker (Ed.), *Reading the environment.* New York, NY: W. W. Norton & Co.

Roth, M. (2005). Man is in the forest: Humans and nature in Bambi and The Lion King. *Invisible culture: An Electronic Journal for Visual Culture, 9.* Retrieved from http://www.rochester.edu/in_visible_culture/Issue_9/issue9_roth.pdf

Roth, M.S. (2008). Psychoanalysis and nature: Commentary on papers by Bodnar and Santostefano. *Psychoanalytic Dialogues, 18*, 536–540.

Rubin, K.H., Fein, G.G., & Vandenberg, B. (1983). Play. In E.M. Hetherington (Ed.), *Handbook of child psychology: Socialization, personality, and social development* (4th ed., Vol. 4, pp. 693–774). New York, NY: John Wiley & Sons.

Ruckart, P.Z., Kakolewski, K., Bove, F.J., & Kaye, W.E. (2004). Long-term neurobehavioral health effects of methyl parathion exposure in children in Mississippi and Ohio. *Environmental Health Perspectives, 112*, 46–51.

Ruether, R.R. (1992). *Gaia & God: An ecofeminist theory of Earth healing.* San Francisco, CA: Harper.

Ruiter, R.A. C., Abraham, C., & Kok, G. (2001). Scary warnings and rational precautions: A review of the psychology of fear appeals. *Psychology and Health, 16*, 613–630.

Russell, K.C. (2001). What is wilderness therapy? *The Journal of Experiential Education, 24*, 70–79.

Russell, K.C. (2005). Two years later: a qualitative assessment of youth well-being and the role of aftercare in outdoor behavioral healthcare treatment. *Child and Youth Care Forum, 34*, 209–239.

Ryan, R.M., Chirkov, V.I., Little, T.D., Sheldon, K.M., Timoshina, E., & Deci, E.L. (1999). The American dream in Russia: Extrinsic aspirations and well-being in two cultures. *Personality and Social Psychology Bulletin, 25,* 1509–1524.

Ryan, R.M., & Deci, E.L. (2000). Self determination theory and the facilitation of intrinsic motivation, social development, and well-being. *American Psychologist, 55,* 68–78.

Saad, L. (2007). *Environmental concern holds firm during past year.* Retrieved from http://www.gallup.com/poll/26971/Environmental-Concern-Holds-Firm-During-Past-Year.aspx

Sabloff, A. (2001). *Reordering the natural world: Human and animals in the city.* Toronto, Canada: University of Toronto Press.

Sachs, J. D. (2006). Ecology and political upheaval. *Scientific American, 295*(1), 37.

Sally, D. (1995). Conversation and cooperation in social dilemmas. *Rationality and Society, 7,* 58–92.

Samuelson, C.D., Peterson, T.R., & Putnam, L.L. (2003). Group identity and stakeholder conflict in water resource management. In S. Clayton & S. Opotow (Eds.), *Identity and the natural environment: The psychological significance of nature* (pp. 273–296). Cambridge, MA: Massachusetts Institute of Technology Press.

Sanborn, M., Kerr, K.J., Sanin, L.H., Cole, D.C., Bassil, K.L., & Vakil, C. (2007). Non-cancer health effects of pesticides: Systematic review and implications for family doctors. *Canadian Family Physician, 53,* 1712–1720.

Santostefano, S. (2004). *Child therapy in the great outdoors: A relational view.* Hillsdale, NJ: The Analytic Press.

Santostefano, S. (2008). The sense of self inside and environments outside: How the two grow together and become one in healthy psychological development. *Psychoanalytic Dialogues, 18,* 513–535.

Sarafino, E.P. (1998). *Health psychology: Biopsychosocial interactions.* New York, NY: John Wiley & Sons, Inc.

Sathyanarayana, S., Karr, C.J., Lozano, P., Brown, E., Calafat, A.M., Liu, F., et al. (2008). Baby care products: Possible sources of infant phthalate exposure. *Pediatrics, 121,* 260–268. Retrieved from http://pediatrics.aappublications.org/cgi/content/full/121/2/e260

Sattler, B. (2002). Environmental health in the health care setting. *American Nurse, 34*(2), 25–38.

Sattmann-Frese, W.J., & Hill, S.B. (2008). *Learning for sustainable living: Psychology of ecological transformation.* Morrisville, NC: Lulu Enterprises.

Saunders, C.D. (2003). The emerging field of conservation psychology. *Human Ecology Review, 10,* 137–149.

Savitz, A.W., & Weber, K. (2006). *The triple bottom line: How today's best-run companies are achieving economic, social, and environmental success—and how you can too.* San Francisco, CA: Jossey-Bass.

Schaffer, A. (2008, August 11). Prescriptions for health, the environmental kind. *The New York Times, Health section.* Retrieved from http://www.nytimes.com/2008/08/12/health/12clin.html?_r=1&scp=1&sq=environmental%20health%20clinic&st=cse

Schettler, T. (2001). Toxic threats to neurologic development of children. *Environmental Health Perspectives, 109*(Suppl. 6), 813–816.

Schettler, T., Stein, J., Reich, F., & Valenti, M. (2000). *In harm's way: Toxic threats to child development.* Cambridge, MA: Greater Boston Physicians for Social Responsibility.

Schlosser, E. (2001). *Fast food nation: The dark side of the all-American meal.* Boston, MA: Houghton Mifflin.

Schmuck, P., & Schultz, P.W. (2002). Sustainable development as a challenge for psychology. In. P. Schmuck & W.P. Schultz (Eds.), *Psychology of sustainable development* (pp. 3–17). Boston, MA: Kluwer Academic Publishers.

Schneider, K. (2009, February 17). Recovery bill is breakthrough on clean energy, good jobs. *Apollo Alliance.* Retrieved from http://apolloalliance.org/new-apollo-program/signature-stories-new-apollo-program/at-last-federal-government-signs-up-for-clean-energy-economy/

Schmuck, P., & Schultz, P.W. (2002). Sustainable development as a challenge for psychology. In P. Schmuck & P.W. Schultz (Eds.), *Psychology of sustainable development* (pp. 3–17). Boston, MA: Kluwer Academic Publishers.

Schore, A. (1999). *Affect regulation and the origin of the self: The neurobiology of emotional development.* Hillsdale, NJ: Erlbaum.

Schroeder, H.W. (2002). Experiencing nature in special places: Surveys in the north-central region. *Journal of Forestry, 100*(5), 8–14.

Schroeder, H.W. (2007). Place experience, gestalt, and the human-nature relationship. *Journal of Environmental Psychology, 27,* 293–309.

Schroeder, J.E., & Dugal, S.S. (1995). Psychological correlates of the materialism construct. *Journal of Social Behavior and Personality, 10,* 243–253.

Schultz, P.W. (1998). Changing behavior with normative feedback interventions: A field experiment on curbside recycling. *Basic and Applied Social Psychology 2,* 25–36.

Schultz, P.W. (2000). Empathizing with nature: The effects of perspective taking on concern for environmental issues. *Journal of Social Issues, 56,* 391–406.

Schultz, P.W. (2001). The structure of environmental concern: Concern for self, other people, and the biosphere. *Journal of Environmental Psychology, 21,* 327–339.

Schultz, P.W. (2002a). Environmental attitudes and behaviors across cultures. In W.J. Lonner, D.L. Dinnel, S.A. Hayes, & D.N. Sattler (Eds.), *OnLine readings in psychology and culture.* Bellingham, WA: Western Washington University, Department of Psychology, Center for Cross-Cultural Research. Retrieved from http://www.wwu.edu/~culture

Schultz, P.W. (2002b). Inclusion with nature: Understanding the psychology of human-nature interactions. In P. Schmuck & P.W. Schultz (Eds.), *The psychology of sustainable development* (pp. 61–78). New York, NY: Kluwer.

Schultz, P.W., Gouveia, V., Cameron, L., Tankha, G., Schmuck, P., & Franek, M. (2005). Values and their relationship to environmental concern and conservation behavior. *Journal of Cross-Cultural Psychology, 36,* 457–475.

Schultz, P.W., Khazian, A., & Zaleski, A. (2008). Using normative social influence to promote conservation among hotel guests. *Social Influence, 3,* 4–23.

Schultz, P.W., Nolan, J., Cialdini, R., Goldstein, N., & Griskevicius, V. (2007). The constructive, destructive, and reconstructive power of social norms. *Psychological Science, 18,* 429–434.

Schultz, P.W., Shriver, C., Tabanico, J., & Khazian, A. (2004). Implicit connections with nature. *Journal of Environmental Psychology, 24,* 31–42.

Schultz, P.W., & Tabanico, J. (2007). Self, identity, and the natural environment: Exploring implicit connections with nature. *Journal of Applied Social Psychology, 37,* 1219–1247.

Schultz, P.W., Unipan, J.B., & Gamba, R.J. (2000). Acculturation and ecological worldview among Latino-Americans. *Journal of Environmental Education, 31,* 22–27.

Schultz, P.W., & Zelezny, L. (1998). Values and pro-environmental behavior: A five-country survey. *Journal of Cross-Cultural Psychology, 29,* 540–558.

Schultz, P.W., Zelezny, L. (2003). Reframing environmental messages to be congruent with American values. *Human Ecology Review, 10,* 126–136.

Schultz, P.W., & Zelezny, L.C., & Dalrymple, N. (2000). A multi-national perspective on the relationship between Judeo-Christian religious beliefs and attitudes of environmental concern. *Environment and Behavior, 32,* 560–575.

Schusler, T.M., Krasny, M.E., Peters, S.J., & Decker, D.J. (2009). Developing citizens and communities through youth environmental action. *Environmental Education Research, 15,* 111–127.

Schwartz, B. (2004a). *The paradox of choice: Why more is less.* New York, NY: Eco/HarperCollins.

Schwartz, B. (2004b, April). The tyranny of choice. *Scientific American.* 290(4), 70–75.

Schwartz, B.S., Chen, S., Caffo, B., Stewart, W.F., Bolla, K.I., Yousem, D., & Davatzikos, C. (2007). Relations of brain volumes with cognitive function in males 45 years and older with past lead exposure. *NeuroImage, 37,* 633–641.

Schwartz, B.S., Stewart, W.F., Bolla, K.I., Simon, P.D., Bandeen-Roche, K., Gordon, P.B., . . . Todd, A.C. (2000). Past adult lead exposure is associated with longitudinal decline in cognitive function. *Neurology, 55,* 1144–1150.

Schwartz, S.H. (1977). Normative influences on altruism. In L. Berkowitz (Ed.), *Advances in experimental social psychology* (Vol. 19, pp. 221–279). New York, NY: Academic Press.

Schwartz, S.H. (1996). Value priorities and behavior: Applying a theory of integrated value systems. In C. Seligman, J.M. Olson, & M.P. Zanna (Eds.), *The psychology of values* (pp. 1–24). Mahwah, NJ: Erlbaum Associates.

Schwartz, S.H. (2007). Cultural and individual value correlates of capitalism: A comparative analysis. *Psychological Inquiry, 18*, 52–57.

Schwartz, S.H., & Bilsky, W. (1987). Toward a universal psychological structure of human values. *Journal of Personality and Social Psychology, 53*, 550–562.

Scott, A. (2008, December 1–8). Industry declares reach pre-registration a success. *Chemical Week, 170*, (37), p. 13.

Scott, M. (2007, July 26). Top 20 companies: Climate change leaders show the way. *ClimateChangeCorp. Climate news for business.* Retrieved from http://www.climatechangecorp.com/content.asp?ContentID=4877

Scull, J. (2001, May–June). Health notes: Harmonizing human health with planetary health. *Encompass, 5.* Retrieved from http://www.encompass.org

Seager, J. (1993). *Earth follies: Coming to feminist terms with the global environmental crisis.* New York, NY: Routledge.

Seager, J. (2003). Rachel Carson died of breast cancer: The coming of age of feminist environmentalism. *Signs, 28*(3), 945–972.

Seamon, D. (1979). *A geography of the lifeworld: Movement, rest and encounter.* New York, NY: St. Martin's Press.

Seamon, D. (1984). Emotional experience of the environment. *American Behavioral Scientist, 27*, 757–770.

Searles, H.F. (1960). *The nonhuman environment in normal development and schizophrenia.* New York, NY: International Universities Press.

Searles, H.F. (1972). Unconscious processes in relation to the environmental crisis. *Psychoanalytic Review, 59*(3), 361–374.

Searles, H.F. (1979). The self in the countertransference. *Issues in Ego Psychology, 2*(2), 49–56.

Seed, J., Macy, J., Fleming, P., & Naess, A. (1988). *Thinking like a mountain: Towards a council of all beings.* Philadelphia, PA: New Society Publishers.

Segal, H. (1987). Silence is the real crime. *International Review of Psychoanalysis, 14*, 3–12.

Seligman, M.E. P. (1970). On the generality of the laws of learning. *Psychological Review, 77*, 406–418.

Seligman, M.E. P. (1971). Phobias and preparedness. *Behavior Therapy, 2*, 307–320.

Seligman, M.E.P. (1975). *Helplessness: On depression, development and death.* San Francisco, CA: Freeman.

Seligman, M.E. P., & Csikszentmihalyi, M. (2000). Positive psychology: An introduction. *American Psychologist, 55*, 5–15.

Sendak, M. (1963). *Where the wild things are.* New York, NY: HarperTrophy.

Sessions, G. (Ed.). (1995). *Deep ecology for the twenty-first century.* Boston, MA: Shambhala.

Sevillano, V., Aragones, J.I., Schultz, P.W. (2006). Perspective taking, environmental concern, and the moderating role of dispositional empathy. *Environment and Behavior.* doi: 10.1177/0013916506292334 Retrieved from http://eab.sagepub.com hosted at http://online.sagepub.com

Sewell, L. (1995). The skill of ecological perception. In T. Roszak, M.E. Gomes, & A.D. Kanner (Eds.), *Eco-psychology: Restoring the earth, healing the mind* (pp. 201–215). San Francisco, CA: Sierra Club.

Sewell, L. (1999). *Sight and sensibility: The eco-psychology of perception.* New York, NY: Tarcher/Putnam.

Shabecoff, P., & Shabecoff, A. (2008). *Poisoned profits: The toxic assault on our children.* New York, NY: Random House.

Shapiro, E. (1995). Restoring habitats, communities and souls. In T. Roszak, M.E. Gomes, & A.D. Kanner (Eds.), *Eco-psychology: Restoring the earth, healing the mind* (pp. 224–239). San Francisco, CA: Sierra Club.

Shekat, D.E., & Ellison, C.G. (2007). Structuring the religion-environmental connection: Identifying religious influences on environmental concern and activism. *Journal for the Scientific Study of Religion, 46,* 71–85.

Sheldon, K.M., & Kasser, T. (1995). Coherence and congruence: Two aspects of personality integration. *Journal of Personality and Social Psychology, 68,* 531–543.

Sheldon, K.M., & McGregor, H. (2000). Extrinsic value orientation and the "tragedy of the commons." *Journal of Personality, 68,* 383–411.

Shellenberger, M., & Nordhaus, T. (2004). *The death of environmentalism: Global warming politics in a post-environmental world.* Retrieved from http://the-breakthrough.org/images/Death_of_Environmentalism.pdf

Shen, J., & Saijo, T. (2008). Re-examining the relations between socio-demographic characteristics and individual environmental concern: Evidence from Shanghai data. *Journal of Environmental Psychology, 28,* 42–50.

Shepard, P. (1998). *Nature and madness.* Athens, GA: University of Georgia Press.

Sherman, J. (2000). *Life's delicate balance: A guide to causes and prevention of breast cancer.* New York, NY: Taylor & Francis.

Shermer, M. (2006, June). The political brain. *Scientific American.* Retrieved from http://www.sciam.com/article.cfm?id=the-political-brain

Shevrin, H., Bond, J.A., Brakel, L.A., Hertel, R., & Williams, W.J. (1996). *Conscious and unconscious processes: Psychodynamic, cognitive and neurophysiological convergences.* New York, NY: Guildford Press.

Shibata, S., & Suzuki, N. (2004). Effects of an indoor plant on creative task performance and mood. *Scandinavian Journal of Psychology, 45,* 373–381.

Shiva, V. (1988). *Staying alive: Women, ecology and survival in India.* New Delhi, India: Zed Press.

Shiva, V. (1994). *Close to home: Women reconnect ecology, health and development worldwide.* London, UK: Earthscan.

Shrotryia, V.K. (2006). Happiness and development: Public policy initiatives in the ingdom of Bhutan. In Y. Ng & L.S. Ho (Eds.), *Happiness and public policy: Theory, case studies and implication* (Chap. 9). London, UK: Macmillan.

Siegel, M. (2007, August 28). New Orleans still facing a psychiatric emergency. *The Globe and Mail (Canada)*, A17.

Simon, J.L. (1981). *The ultimate resource.* Princeton, NJ: Princeton University Press.

Simon, J.L., & Kahn, H. (1984). *The resourceful earth: A response to global 2000.* New York, NY: Basil Blackwell.

Simons, D.J., & Ambinder, M.S. (2005). Change blindness: Theory and consequences. *Current Directions in Psychological Science, 14,* 44–48.

Singer, P. (1977/1990). *Animal liberation.* New York, NY: Avon Books.

Sirgy, M.J., Lee, D., & Kosenko, R. (1998). Does television viewership play a role in the perception of quality of life? *Journal of Advertising, 27,* 125–142.

Sissell, K. (2008, August 4). U.S. lawmakers ban phthalates in some products. *Chemical Week,* 6.

Sitter, S. (1989, May 19). Interview on National Public Radio "All Things Considered," (Quoted from *Earth follies: Coming to feminist terms with the global environmental crisis,* p. 221, by J. Seager, 1993, New York, NY: Routledge.)

Sivaraksa, S. (2009). *The wisdom of sustainability: Buddhist economics for the 21st century.* Kihei, HI: Koa Books.

Sizer, N. (2000). *Perverse habits: The G8 and subsidies that harm forests and economies.* World Resources Institute. Available from http://www.wri.org/publication/perverse-habits-g8-and-subsidies-harm-forests-and-economies

Skinner, B.F. (1948). *Walden two.* New York, NY: Macmillan.

Skinner, B.F. (1953). *Science and human behavior.* New York, NY: The Free Press, Macmillan Publishing Co., Inc.

Skinner, B.F. (1971). *Beyond freedom and dignity* (p. 137). New York, NY: Alfred A. Knopf, Inc.

Skinner, B. F. (1977). Herrnstein and the evolution of Behaviorism. *American Psychologist, 32,* 1006–1012.

Skinner, B.F. (1991). Why we are not acting to save the world. In W. Ishaq (Ed.), *Human behavior in today's world* (pp. 19–29). New York, NY: Praeger.

Slimak, M.W., & Dietz, T. (2006). Personal values, beliefs, and ecological risk perception. *Risk Analysis, 26,* 1689–1705.

Slovic, P. (2000). *The perception of risk.* London, UK: Earthscan.

Slovic, P. (2007). "If I look at the mass I will never act": Psychic numbing and genocide. *Judgment and Decision Making, 2,* 79–97.

Slovic, P., Finucane, M., Peters, E., & MacGregor, D.G. (2002). The affect heuristic. In T. Gilovich, D. Griffin, & D. Kahneman (Eds.), *Heuristics and biases: The psychology of intuitive judgment* (pp. 397–420). New York, NY: Cambridge Univ. Press.

Slovic, P., Finucane, M.L., Peters, E., & MacGregor, D. (2004). Risk as analysis and risk as feelings: Some thoughts about affect, reason, risk and rationality. *Risk Analysis, 24,* 311–322.

Slovic, P., Fischhoff, B., & Lichtenstein, S. (1979). Rating the risks. *Environment, 21,* 14–20, 36–39.

Slovic, P., Fischhoff, B., & Lichtenstein, S. (1985). Characterizing perceived risk. In R.W. Kates, C. Hohenemser, & J.X. Kasperson (Eds.), *Perilous progress: Technology as hazard* (pp. 91–123). Boulder, CO: Westview.

Slovic, P., Flynn, J., Mertz, C.K., Poumadere, M., & Mays, C. (2000). Nuclear power and the public: A comparative study of risk perception in France and the United States. In O. Renn & B. Rohrmann (Eds.), *Cross-cultural risk perception: A survey of empirical studies* (pp. 55–102). Dordrecht, The Netherlands: Kluwer Academic.

Slovic, S., & Slovic, P. (2004–2005). Numbers and nerves: Toward an affective apprehension of environmental risk. *Whole Terrain, 13,* 14–18.

Smith, E.E., Nolen-Hoeksema, S., Fredrickson, B., & Loftus G.R. (2003). *Atkinson & Hilgard's introduction to psychology* (14th Ed.). Belmont, CA: Wadsworth.

Smith, E.R., Jackson, J.W., & Sparks, C.W. (2003). Effects of inequality and reasons for inequality on group identification and cooperation in social dilemmas. *Group Processes & Intergroup Relations, 6,* 201–220.

Smith, J.W., Positano, S., Stocks, N., & Shearman, D. (2009). *A new way of thinking about our climate crisis: The rational-comprehensive approach.* Lewiston, NY: Edwin Mellen Press.

Smith, J.W., Shearman, D., & Positano, S. (2007). Climate change as a crisis in world civilization: Why we must totally transform how we live. Lewiston, NY: Edwin Mellen Press.

Snelgar, R. (2006). Egoistic, altruistic, and biospheric environmental concerns: Measurement and structure. *Journal of Environmental Psychology, 26,* 87–99.

Sobel, D. (1996). *Beyond ecophobia: Reclaiming the heart in nature education.* Great Barrington, MA: Orion Society.

Sobel, D. (1999). Beyond ecophobia. *Yes!* Retrieved from http://www.yesmagazine.org/article.asp?ID=803

Sobel, D.A. (1990). A place in the world: Adults' memories of childhood's special places. *Children's Environments Quarterly, 7*(4), 5–12. Retrieved from http://www.colorado.edu/journals/cye/7_4/CEQ_Vol7(4)_Adults MemoriesOfSpecialPlaces.pdf

Solberg, E.G., Diener, E., & Robinson, M.D. (2004). Why are materialists less satisfied? In T. Kasser & A.D. Kanner (Eds.), *Psychology and consumer culture: The struggle for a good life in a materialistic world* (pp. 29–48). Washington, DC: American Psychological Association.

Sommer, R. (2003). Trees and human identity. In S. Clayton & S. Opotow (Eds.), *Identity and the natural environment: The psychological significance of nature* (pp. 179–204). Cambridge, MA: Massachusetts Institute of Technology Press.

Soong, J. (2008). When technology addiction takes over your life. *WebMD*. Retrieved from http://www.webmd.com/mental-health/features/when-technology-addiction-takes-over-your-life

Spedden, S.E. (1998). Risk perception and coping. In A. Lundberg (Ed.), *The environment and mental health: A guide for clinicians* (pp. 103–114). Mahwah, NJ: Erlbaum.

Spencer, C., & Woolley, H. (2000). Children and the city: A summary of recent environmental psychology research. *Child: Care, Health, and Development, 26,* 181–198.

Spencer, H. (1891/1969). *Essays scientific, political, and speculative* (p. 10). New York, NY: D. Appleton and Company. (As cited from *Social change and history: Aspects of the western theory of development,* p. 10, by R.A. Nisbet, 1969, New York: Oxford University Press.)

Speth, G. (1993). The global environmental challenge. In G.T. Miller (Ed.), *Living in the environment: An introduction to environmental science* (7th ed.). Belmont, CA: Wadsworth.

Speth, J. G. (2008). *The bridge at the end of the world: Capitalism, the environment, and crossing from crisis to sustainability.* New Haven, CT: Yale University Press

Spicer, J. (2007, February 21). Hearing to probe climate change and Inuit rights. *Reuters.* Retrieved from http://www.unep.org/indigenous/pdfs/Climatechange-and-Inuit-rights.pdf

Spretnak, C. (1990). Ecofeminism: Our roots and flowering. In I. Diamond & G.F. Orenstein (Eds.), *Reweaving the world: The emergence of ecofeminism* (pp. 3–14). San Francisco, CA: Sierra Club.

Srivastava, A., Locke, E.A., & Bartol, K.M. (2001). Money and subjective well-being: It's not the money, it's the motives. *Journal of Personality and Social Psychology, 80,* 959–971.

St. John, D., & MacDonald, D.A. (2007). A development and initial validation of a measure of ecopsychological self. *Journal of Transpersonal Psychology, 39,* 48–67.

Staats, H. (2003). Understanding proenvironmental attitudes and behavior: An analysis and review of research based on the theory or planned behavior. In M. Bonnes, T. Lee, M. Bonaiuto (Eds.), *Psychological theories for environmental issues* (pp. 171–201). Aldershot, Hants, UK: Ashgate.

Staats, H., Kieviet, A., & Hartig, T. (2003). Where to recover from attentional fatigue: An expectancy-value analysis of environmental preference. *Journal of Environmental Psychology, 24,* 147–157.

Starbucks Coffee Company. (2008). *Starbucks Corporation: Corporate social responsibility fiscal 2007 annual report: Our commitment to ethical coffee sourcing.* Retrieved from http://www.starbucks.com/aboutus/csrreport/Coffee_Report_PDF_FY07.pdf

Steffen, A. (2006). Why sustainability, not terrorism, should be our real security focus. *WorldChanging.* Retrieved from http://www.worldchanging.com/archives/004799.html

Steg, L., Dreijerink. L., & Abrahamse, W. (2005). Factors influencing the acceptability of energy policies: A test of VBN theory. *Journal of Environmental Psychology, 25*, 415–425.

Stein, J., Schettler, T., Rohrer, B., & Valenti, M. (2008). Environmental threats to healthy aging. *Greater Boston Physician's for Social Responsibility and Science and Environmental Health Network.* Retrieved from http://www.psr.org/site/DocServer/GBPSRSEHN_HealthyAging1017.pdf?docID=5930

Stein, J., Schettler, T., Wallinga, D., Miller, M., & Valenti, M. (2002). *In harm's way: Training program for health professionals. Greater Boston Physician's for Social Responsibility.* Power point presentation retrieved from http://www.psr.org/site/PageServer?pagename=boston_ihwmat#ihwPPtPres

Stein, S., & Spiegel, D. (2000). Psychoneuroimmune and endocrine effects on cancer progression. In K. Goodkin & A.P. Visser (Eds.), *Psychoneuroimmunology: Stress, mental disorders, and health* (pp. 105–151). Washington, DC: American Psychiatric Press.

Sterman, J.D. (2008). Risk communication on climate: Mental models and mass balance. *Science, 322*, 532–533.

Stern, N. (2007). *The economics of climate change: The Stern review.* Cambridge, UK: Cambridge University Press.

Stern, P.C. (1992). What psychology knows about energy conservation. *American Psychologist, 47*(10), 1224–1232.

Stern, P.C. (2000). Psychology and the science of human-environment interactions. *American Psychologist, 55*, 523–530.

Stern, P.C. (2005). Understanding individuals' environmentally significant behavior. *Environmental Law Reporter: News and Analysis, 35*, 10785–10790.

Stern, P.C., Dietz, T., Abel, T., Guagnano, G.A., & Kalof, L. (1999). A value-belief-norm theory of support for social movements: The case of environmentalism. *Human Ecology Review, 6*, 81–97.

Stern, P.C., Dietz, T., & Black, J.S. (1986). Support for environmental protection: The role of moral norms. *Population and Environment, 8*, 204–222.

Stern, P.C., Dietz, T., & Kalof, L. (1993). Value orientations, gender, and environmental concern. *Environment and behavior, 25*, 322–348.

Stewart, W.F., & Schwartz, B.S. (2007). Effects of lead on the adult brain: A 15-year exploration. *American Journal of Industrial Medicine, 50*, 729–739.

Stiffler, L. (2002, April 18). Hanford's unfinished business after countless delays and billions of dollars, the tide may be turning in cleanup of huge nuclear waste site. *Seattle Post-Intelligencer,* A1.

Stiles, J. (2008). *The fundamentals of brain development: Integrating nature and nurture.* Cambridge, MA: Harvard University Press.

Stoll-Kleemann, S., O'Riordan, T., & Jaeger, C.C. (2001). The psychology of denial concerning climate mitigation measures: Evidence from Swiss focus groups. *Global Environmental Change, 11*, 107–117.

Story, L. (2007, January 15). Anywhere the eye can see, it's likely to see an ad. *The New York Times,* Section A., Column 1. p. 1. Retrieved from http://www.nytimes.com/2007/01/15/business/media/15everywhere.html?_r=1

Strachey, J., & Freud, A. (Eds.). (1964). *The standard edition of the complete psychological works of Sigmund Freud.* London, UK: Hogarth Press.

Strange, P.G. (1992). *Brain biochemistry and brain disorders.* New York, NY: Oxford University Press.

Strasburger, V.C. (2007). First do no harm: Why have parents and pediatricians missed the boat on children and media? *Journal of Pediatrics, 151,* 334–336.

Suglia, S.F., Gryparis, A., Wright, R.O., Schwartz, J., & Wright, R.J. (2008). Association of black carbon with cognition among children in a prospective birth cohort study. *American Journal of Epidemiology, 167,* 280–286.

Sundblad, E.L., Biel, A., & Gärling, T. (2007). Cognitive and affective risk judgements related to climate change. *Journal of Environmental Psychology, 27,* 97–106.

Sunstein, C.R. (2006). The availability heuristic, intuitive cost-benefit analysis, and climate change. *Climatic Change, 77,* 195–210.

Survey Research Center. (2000). *Environmental studies in the K-12 classroom: A teacher's view.* Prepared for the North American Association for Environmental Education and the Environmental Literacy Council. Retrieved from http://www.enviroliteracy.org/pdf/survey2001.pdf

Suzuki, D. (2003). *Consumer culture no accident.* Retrieved from http://www.davidsuzuki.org/about_us/Dr_David_Suzuki/Article_Archives/weekly03070301.asp

Swan, S.H., Main, K.M., Liu, F., Stewart, S.L., Druse, R.L., Calafat, A.M., . . . Study for Future Families Research Team. (2005). Decrease in anogenital distance among male infants with prenatal phthalate exposure. *Environmental Health Perspectives 113,* 1056–1061.

Swanson, J. (2001). *Communing with nature.* Corvallis, OR: Illahee Press.

Swanson, J.L. (1995). The call for Gestalt's contribution to ecopsychology: Figuring in the environmental field. *Gestalt Journal, 18,* 47–85.

Swedish Government Chemicals Policy Committee. (1997). Towards a sustainable chemicals policy. Government Official Reports, Ministry of the Environment. Stockholm, Sweden: Omslag: Marschall Annonsbyrå AB.

Szyszkowicz, M. (2007). Air pollution and emergency department visits for depression in Edmonton, Canada. *International Journal of Occupational Medicine and Environmental Health, 20*(3), 241–245.

Tajfel, H., & Turner, J.C. (1986). The social identity theory of intergroup behavior. In W.G. Austin & S. Worchel (Eds.), *Psychology of intergroup relations* (2nd ed., pp. 7–27). Chicago, IL: Nelson-Hall.

Talberth, J. (2008). A new bottom line for progress. In L. Starke (Ed.), *2008 state of the world: Innovations for a sustainable economy* (pp. 18–31). New York, NY: W. W. Norton & Co.

Tanner, C. (1999). Constraints on environmental behaviour. *Journal of Environmental Psychology, 19*, 145–157.

Tanner, C., & Kast, S.W. (2003). Promoting sustainable consumption: Determinants of green purchases by Swiss consumers. *Psychology & Marketing, 20*, 883–902.

Tanner, T. (1980). Significant life experiences: A new research area in environmental education. *Journal of Environmental Education, 11*(4), 20–24.

Taylor, B., & Zimmerman, M. (2005). Deep ecology. In B. Taylor (Ed.), *Encyclopedia of religion and nature* (Vol. 1., pp. 456–460). London, UK: Continuum International.

Taylor, S. E., Cousino-Klein, L., Lewis, B. P., Gruenewald, T. L., Gurung, R. A., & Updegraff, J. A. (2000). Biobehavioral responses to stress in females: Tend and befriend, not fight or flight. *Psychological Review, 107*, 411–429.

Taylor, S., & Todd, P. (1995). An integrated model of waste management behavior: A test of household recycling and composting intentions. *Environment and Behavior, 27*, 603–630.

Thaler, R. (1999). Rethinking thinking. *The Economist, 353*(8150), 63–65.

Theobald, P. (1997). Teaching the commons: Place, pride, and the renewal of community. Boulder, CO: Westview Press.

Thogersen, J. (1996). Recycling and morality: A critical review of the literature. *Environment and Behavior, 28*, 536–558.

Thogersen, J. (2006). Norms for environmentally responsible behaviour: An extended taxonomy. *Journal of Environmental Psychology, 26*, 247–261.

Thomashow, M. (1995). *Ecological identity: Becoming a reflective environmentalist*. Cambridge, MA: Massachusetts Institute of Technology Press.

Thomashow, M. (1998). The ecopsychology of global environmental change. *The Humanistic Psychologist, 26*, 275–300.

Thomashow, M. (2002). *Bringing the biosphere home: Learning to perceive global environmental change*. Cambridge, MA: Massachusetts Institute of Technology Press.

Thompson, R. (2008, February 29). Pele turns up the heat: Flowing lava isolates Big Island homes. Honolulu Star Bulletin, v. 13, Issue 60. Retrieved from http://archives.starbulletin.com/2008/02/29/news/story01.html

Toates, F. (2009). *Burrhus F. Skinner*. Basingstoke, UK: Macmillan Palgrave.

Trancik, A.M., & Evans, G.W. (1995). Spaces fit for children: Competency in the design of daycare center environments. *Children's Environments, 12*, 311–319.

Tuan, Y.F. (1974). *Topophilia: A study of environmental perception, attitudes, and values*. Englewood Cliffs, NJ: Prentice-Hall.

Tuan, Y.F. (1993). *Passing strange and wonderful: Aesthetics, nature and culture*. Washington, DC: Island Press for Shearwater Books.

Tudor, T., Adam, E., & Bates, M. (2007). Drivers and limitations for the successful development and functioning of EIPs (eco-industrial parks): A literature review. *Ecological Economics, 61,* 199–207.

Tversky, A., & Kahneman, D. (1974). Judgment under uncertainty: Heuristics and biases. *Science, 185,* 1124–1131.

Tversky, A., & Kahneman, D. (1983). Extensional versus intuitive reasoning: The conjunction fallacy in probability judgment. *Psychological Review, 90,* 293–315.

Ulrich, R.S. (1981). Natural versus urban scenes: Some psychophysiological effects. *Environment and Behavior, 13*(5), 523–556.

Ulrich, R.S. (1983). Aesthetic and affective response to natural environment. *Human Behavior & Environment: Advances in Theory & Research, 6,* 85–125.

Ulrich, R.S. (1984). View through a window may influence recovery from surgery. *Science, 224,* 420–421.

Ulrich, R.S. (1993). Biophilia, biophobia and natural landscapes. In S.R. Kellert & E.O. Wilson (Eds.), *The biophilia hypothesis* (pp. 73–137). Washington, DC: Island Press.

Ulrich, R.S. (1999). Effects of gardens on health outcomes: Theory and research. In C. Cooper Marcus & M. Barnes (Eds.), *Healing gardens: Therapeutic benefits and design recommendations* (pp. 27–86). New York, NY: John Wiley & Sons.

Ulrich, R.S., Simons, R.F., Losito, B.D., Fiorito, E., Miles, M.A., & Zelson, M. (1991). Stress recovery during exposure to natural and urban environments. *Journal of Environmental Psychology, 11,* 201–230.

Union of Concerned Scientists. (1992). *World scientists' warning to humanity.* Statement available from the Union of Concerned Scientists, 26 Church St., Cambridge, MA 02238.

Union of Concerned Scientists. (2002, October 22). *UCS examines the skeptical environmentalist by Bjørn Lomborg.* Retrieved from http://www.ucsusa. org/global_environment/global_warming/page.cfm?pageID= 533

United Nations. (n.d.). United Nations NGO Sustainability: Brundtland definition: Three-dimension concept. Retrieved from http://www.unngosustainability.org/CSD_Definitions%20SD.htm

United Nations. (2005). *World Urbanization Prospects: The 2005 Revision.* United Nations Department of Economic and Social Affairs Population Division. Retrieved from http://www.un.org/esa/population/publications/WUP2005/2005wup.htm

United Nations. (2007a). *The millennium development goals report 2007.* Retrieved from http://mdgs.un.org/unsd/mdg/Resources/Static/Products/Progress2007/UNSD_MDG_Report_2007e.pdf

United Nations. (2007b). *World population prospects: The 2006 revision, highlights.* United Nations Department of Economic and Social Affairs, Population Division. Working Paper No. ESA/P/WP.202. New York, NY: United Nations. Retrieved from http://www.un.org/esa/population/publications/wpp2006/WPP2006_Highlights_rev.pdf

United Nations Children's Fund (UNICEF). (2008). *The state of the world's children, 2008.* New York, NY: Author.

United Nations Environment Programme. (2008). *Global green new deal.* Retrieved from http://www.unep.org/greeneconomy/index2.asp?id=gnd

United Nations Millennium Declaration. (2000). *Millennium development goals indicators: The official United Nations site for the MDG Indicators.* Retrieved from http://mdgs.un.org/unsd/mdg/Host.aspx?Content=Indicators/About

University of Illinois at Chicago. (2008, March 28). Designing environmentally friendly communities. *ScienceDaily.* Retrieved from http://www.sciencedaily.com/releases/2008/03/080326195000.htm

University of Sheffield. (2007, May 17). There's much more to a walk in the park. *ScienceDaily.* Retrieved from http://www.sciencedaily.com/releases/2007/05/070516095212.htm

U.S. Census Bureau. (2008). *Income, poverty, and health insurance coverage in the United States: 2007.* Current Population Reports, P60-235, Washington, DC: U.S. Government Printing Office. Retrieved from http://www.census.gov/prod/2008pubs/p60-235.pdf

U.S. Conference of Catholic Bishops. (2001, June 15). *Global climate change: A plea for dialogue, prudence, and the common good.* Issued by NCCBAUSCC. Retrieved from http://www.usccb.org/sdwp/international/globalclimate.shtml

U.S. Department of Agriculture Forest Service. (1990). *Summary: Final environmental impact statement, Umatilla National Forest, S-29.*

U.S. Department of Health and Human Services. (2004). *New surgeon general's report expands list of diseases caused by smoking.* Retrieved from http://www.hhs.gov/news/press/2004pres/20040527a.html

U.S. Department of Health and Human Services, Centers for Disease Control and Prevention. (2008a). *Overweight and obesity.* Retrieved from http://www.cdc.gov/nccdphp/dnpa/obesity/

U.S. Department of Health and Human Services. (2008b). *Physical activity facts. The President's Council on Physical Fitness and Sports.* Retrieved from http://www.fitness.gov/resources/facts/index.html

U.S. Environmental Protection Agency Pesticides. (n.d.). *Pesticides and their impact on children: Key facts and talking points.* Retrieved from http://www.epa.gov/oppfead1/Publications/pest-impact-hsstaff.pdf

U.S. Environmental Protection Agency. (1999). *New data will help ensure protection of children. Pesticides: Topical & chemical fact sheets.* Retrieved from http://www.epa.gov/pesticides/factsheets/neurotoxicdata.htm

U.S. Environmental Protection Agency. (2002a, July 23). *Persistant bioaccumulative and toxic chemical program.* Retrieved from http://www.epa.gov/pbt/

U.S. Environmental Protection Agency. (2002b). *Protecting children from pesticides.* Retrieved from http://www.epa.gov/pesticides/factsheets/kidpesticide.htm

U.S. Environmental Protection Agency. (2002c). *Technology transfer network: National air toxics assessment, estimated risk: Summary of results.* Retrieved from http://www.epa.gov/ttn/atw/nata/risksum.html

U.S. Environmental Protection Agency. (2007a, July). *National listing of fish advisories technical fact sheet: 2005/06 National Listing Fact Sheet*; EPA-823-F-07-003. Retrieved from http://www.epa.gov/waterscience/fish/advisories/2006/tech.html#chlordane

U.S. Environmental Protection Agency. (2007b). *Municipal solid waste in the United States: 2007 Facts and figures.* Available from http://www.epa.gov/epawaste/nonhaz/municipal/pubs/msw07-rpt.pdf

U.S. Environmental Protection Agency. (2008a). *About air toxics: Technology transfer network air toxics web site.* Retrieved from http://www.epa.gov/ttn/atw/allabout.html

U.S. Environmental Protection Agency. (2008b). *Executive Order 12898 of Feb 11, 1994.* Federal actions to address environmental justice in minority populations and low-income populations. Retrieved from http://www.epa.gov/fedrgstr/eo/eo12898.htm

U.S. Environmental Protection Agency. (2008c). *Mercury.* Retrieved from http://www.epa.gov/mercury/exposure.htm

U.S. Environmental Protection Agency. (2009). *Environmental justice.* Retrieved from http://www.epa.gov/oecaerth/environmentaljustice/

U.S. Geological Survey (USGS). (2008, May 8). *Pele's cooking more than vog: "Precious" jewels also stirring in her cauldron.* Retrieved from http://hvo.wr.usgs.gov/volcanowatch/2008/08_05_15.html

U.S. Green Building Council. (2008). What LEED is. Retrieved from http://www.usgbc.org/DisplayPage.aspx?CMSPageID=1988

University of Manchester. (2007, May 14). Build parks to climate proof our cities. *ScienceDaily.* Retrieved from http://www.sciencedaily.com/releases/2007/05/070514101534.htm

Ushijima, K., Miyake, Y., Kitano, T., Shono, M., & Futatsuka, M. (2004). Relationship between health status and psychological distress among the inhabitants in a methyl mercury-polluted area in Japan. *Archives of Environmental Health, 59,* 725–731.

Uzzell, D.L. (2000). The psycho-spatial dimensions of global environmental problems. *Journal of Environmental Psychology, 20,* 307–318.

Vanasselt, W. (2001). *No end to paperwork.* Washington, DC: World Resources Institute: Earth Trends. Available from http://earthtrends.wri.org/features/view_feature.php?theme=6&fid=19

Van de Kerk, G., & Manuel, A.R. (2009). *Sustainable society index. The encyclopedia of earth.* Retrieved from http://www.eoearth.org/article/Sustainable_Society_Index

Van den Berg, A.E., Hartig, T., Staats, H. (2007). Preference for nature in urbanized societies: Stress, restoration, and the pursuit of sustainability. *Journal of Social Issues, 63,* 79–96.

Van den Berg, A.E., & Heijne, M.T. (2005). Fear versus fascination: An exploration of emotional responses to natural threats. *Journal of Environmental Psychology, 25,* 261–272.

Van den Berg, A.E., Koole, S.L., & van der Wulp, N.Y. (2003). Environmental preference and restoration: (How) are they related? *Journal of Environmental Psychology, 23,* 135–146.

Vandewater, E.A., Bickham, D.S., & Lee, J.H. (2006). Time well spent? Relating television use to children's free-time activities. *Pediatrics, 117,* 181-191.

Van Griensven, F., Chakkraband, M.L.S., Thienkrua, W., Pengjuntr, W., Cardozo, B.L., Tantipiwatanaskul, P., . . . Tappero, J.W. (2006). Mental health problems among adults in tsunami-affected areas in southern Thailand. *Journal of the American Medical Association, 296,* 537–548.

Van Liere, K.D., & Dunlap, R.E. (1980). The social bases of environmental concern: A review of the hypotheses, explanations, and empirical evidence. *Public Opinion Quarterly, 44,* 181–197.

Van Vugt, M. (2001). Community identification moderating the impact of financial incentives in a natural social dilemma: Water conservation. *Personality and Social Psychology Bulletin, 27,* 1440–1449.

Van Vugt, M. (2002). Central, individual, or collective control? Social dilemma strategies for natural resource management. *American Behavioral Scientist, 45*(5), 783–800.

Verespej, M. (2008). E-waste responsibility laws taking country state by state. *Plastics News, 20*(33), 9–11.

Vess, M., & Arndt, J. (2008). The nature of death and the death of nature: The impact of mortality salience on environmental concern. *Journal of Research in Personality, 42,* 1376–1380.

Vikan, A., Camino, A., Biaggio, A., & Nordvik, H. (2007). Endorsement of the New Ecological Paradigm: A comparison of two Brazilian samples and one Norwegian sample. *Environment and Behavior, 39,* 217–228.

Vince, G. (2009, February 25). How to survive the coming century. *The New Scientist,* Issue 2697. Retrieved from http://www.climateark.org/shared/reader/welcome.aspx?linkid=119681

Vincent, S., & Focht, W. (2009). US higher education environmental program managers' perspectives on curriculum design and core competencies: Implications for sustainability as a guiding framework. *International Journal of Sustainability in Higher Education, 10,* 164–183.

Vining, J. (2003). The connection to other animals and caring for nature. *Research in Human Ecology, 10,* 87–99.

Vining, J., & Ebreo, A. (1992). Predicting recycling behavior from global and specific environmental attitudes and changes in recycling opportunities. *Journal of Applied Social Psychology, 22,* 1580–1607.

Vining, J., & Ebreo, A. (2002). Emerging theoretical and methodological perspectives on conservation behavior. In B. Bechtel & A. Churchman (Eds.), *Handbook of environmental psychology* (pp. 541–558). New York, NY: John Wiley

Vlek, C. (2000). Essential psychology for environmental policy making. *International Journal of Psychology, 35*(2), 153–167.

Vlek, C., & Steg, L. (2007). Human behavior and environmental sustainability: Problems, driving forces, and research topics. *Journal of Social Issues, 63,* 1–19.

vom Saal, F.S., Belcher, S.M., Guillette, L.J., Hauser, R., Myers, J.P., Prins, G. S., . . . Zoeller, R.T. (2007). Chapel Hill bisphenol A expert panel consensus statement: Integration of mechanisms, effects in animals and potential to impact human health at current levels of exposure. *Reproductive Toxicology, 24,* 131–138.

Vonnegut, K. (1990, April 11). Notes from my bed of gloom: Or, why the joking had to stop. *New York Times Book Review,* 14. (In J. Mack *Inventing a psychology of our relationship to the Earth.* In S. Staub & P. Green (Eds.), *Psychology and social responsibility: Facing global challenges* (pp. 237–247). New York, NY: New York University Press.)

Vorkinn, M., & Riese, H. (2001). Environmental concern in a local context: The significance of place attachment. *Environment and Behavior, 33,* 249–263.

Wade-Benzoni, K.A., Li, M., Thompson, L.L., & Bazerman, M.H. (2007). The malleability of environmentalism. *Analysis of Social Issues and Public Policy, 7,* 163–189.

Wallenius, M.A. (2004). The interaction of noise stress and personal project stress on subjective health. *Journal of Environmental Psychology, 24,* 167–177.

Walljasper, J. (1997, September–October). Affluenza warning: Materialism may be hazardous to your health. *Utne Reader.*

Wals, A.E.J. (1994). *Pollution stinks! Young adolescents' perceptions of nature and environmental issues with implications for education in urban settings.* De Lier, The Netherlands: Academic Book Center.

Wang, K., Shu, Q., & Tu, Q. (2008). Technostress under different organizational environments: An empirical investigation. *Computers in Human Behavior, 24,* 3002–3013.

Wang, T.H., & Katzev, R.D. (1990). Group commitment and resource conservation: Two field experiments on promoting recycling. *Journal of Applied Social Psychology, 20,* 265–275.

Wason, P.C. (1960). On the failure to eliminate hypotheses in a conceptual task. *Quarterly Journal of Experimental Psychology, 12,* 129–140.

Watrous, S. & Fraley, N. (2007). Ending the piecemeal approach: Santa Monica's comprehensive plan for sustainability. In S.C. Moser & L. Dilling (Eds.), *Creating a climate for change: Communicating climate change and facilitating social change* (pp. 399–415). Cambridge, UK: Cambridge University Press.

Weber, E.U. (2006). Experience-based and description-based perceptions of long-term risk: Why global warming does not scare us (yet). *Climatic Change, 77,* 103–120.

Weber, M. (1904/1930). *The Protestant ethic and the spirit of capitalism* (1st ed., T. Parson, Trans.). New York, NY: Scribner.

Wechsler, H., Nelson, T., Lee, J.E., Seiberg, M., Lewis, C., & Keeling, R. (2003). Perception and reality: A national evaluation of social norms marketing interventions to reduce college students' heavy alcohol use. *Quarterly Journal of Studies on Alcohol, 64,* 484–494.

Weenig, M.W.H. (1993). The strength of weak and strong communication ties in a communication information program. *Journal of Applied Social Psychology, 23,* 1712–1731.

Weick, K.E. (1984). Small wins: Redefining the scale of social problems. *American Psychologist, 39*(1), 40–49.

Weil, M., & Rosen, R. (1997). *Technostress: Coping with technology @ work @ home @ play.* New York, NY: John Wiley & Sons, Inc.

Weinhold, B. (2008). *Cancer: Stress link redefined.* Retrieved from http://www.ehponline.org/docs/2008/116-2/forum.html

Weiss, B. (1997). Pesticides as a source of developmental disabilities. *Mental Retardation and Developmental Disabilities Research Reviews, 3,* 246–256.

Weiss, B. (1998). Behavioral neurotoxicity. In A. Lundberg (Ed.), *The environment and mental health: A guide for clinicians* (pp. 25–41). Mahwah, NJ: Erlbaum.

Weiss, B. (2000). Vulnerability of children and the developing brain to neurotoxic hazards. *Environmental Health Perspectives, 108*(3), 375–381.

Weiss, B. (2001). Ethics assessment as an adjunct to risk assessment in the evaluation of developmental neurotoxicants. *Environmental Health Perspectives, 109*(Suppl. 6), 905–908.

Weiss, B. (2006). Endocrine disruptors as a factor in mental retardation. In P.W. Davidson, G.J. Myers, & B. Weiss (Eds.), *Neurotoxicity and Developmental Disabilities. A volume in international review of research in mental retardation* (pp. 195–223). San Diego, CA: Elsevier Academic Press.

Weiss, B. (2007). Can endocrine disruptors influence neuroplasticity in the aging brain? *NeuroToxicology, 28,* 938–950.

Weiss, B., Amler, S., & Amler, R.W. (2004). Pesticides. *Pediatrics, 113(4),* 1030–1036.

Weiss, B., Clarkson, T.W., & Simon, W. (2002). Silent latency periods in methylmercury poisoning and in neurodegenerative disease. *Environmental Health Perspectives, 110*(Suppl. 5), 851–854.

Weiss, B., & Simon, W. (1975). Quantitative perspectives on the long term toxicity of methylmercury and similar poisons. In B. Weiss & V.G. Laties (Eds.), *Behavioral Toxicology* (pp. 429–438). New York, NY: Plenum Press.

Weiten, W. (2011). *Psychology: Themes and variation (8th edition).* Belmont, CA: Wadswork.

Wells, N.M. (2000). At home with nature: Effects of "greenness" on children's cognitive functioning. *Environment and Behavior, 32,* 775–795.

Wells, N.M., & Evans, G.W. (2003). Nearby nature: A buffer of life stress among rural children. *Environment and Behavior, 35,* 311–330.

Wells, N.M., & Lekies, K.S. (2006). Nature and the life course: Pathways from childhood nature experiences to adult environmentalism. *Children, Youth and Environments, 16,* 1–25. Retrieved from http://www.colorado.edu/journals/cye/16_1/16_1_01_NatureAndLifeCourse.pdf

Werhan, P.O., & Groff, D.G. (2005, November). Research Update: The wilderness therapy trail. *Parks and Recreation,* 24–29 [online edition]. Retrieved from http://findarticles.com/p/articles/mi_m1145/is_11_40/ai_n15966766/pg_1?tag=artBody;col1

Werner, C.M. (2003). Changing homeowners' use of toxic household products: A transactional approach. *Journal of Environmental Psychology, 23,* 33–45.

Werner, C.M., Byerly, S., & Sansone, C. (2004). Changing intentions to use toxic household products through guided group discussion. *Special Issue 18th International Applied Psychology Conference,* Vienna, Austria, 147–156.

Werner, C.M., Turner, J., Shipman, K., Twitchell, F., Dickson, B., Bruschke, G., & vonBismarck, W. (1995). Commitment, behavior, and attitude change: An analysis of voluntary recycling. *Journal of Environmental Psychology, 15,* 197–208.

Wessely, S. (2002). Protean nature of mass sociogenic illness: From possessed nuns to chemical and biological terrorism fears. *The British Journal of Psychiatry, 180*(4), 300–306.

White, L. (1967). The historical roots of our ecological crises. *Science, 155,* 1203–1207, 1205.

White, R. (1991). *"It's your misfortune and none of my own": A history of the American West.* Norman, OK: University of Oklahoma Press.

White, R. (1998). Psychiatry and eco-psychology. In A. Lundberg (Ed.), *The environment and mental health: A guide for clinicians* (pp. 205–212). Mahwah, NJ: Erlbaum.

White, R. (2004). Young children's relationship with nature: Its importance to children's development and the earth's future. *White Hutchinson Leisure and Learning Group.* Retrieved from http://www.whitehutchinson.com/children/articles/childrennature.shtml

White, R., & Heerwagen, J. (1998). Nature and mental health: Biophilia and biophobia. In A. Lundberg (Ed.), *The environment and mental health: A guide for clinicians* (pp. 175–192). Mahwah, NJ: Erlbaum.

Whited, S. (2008). Pesticides make farmers literally depressed. *Environmental Working Group: NaturalNews.* Retrieved from http://www.ewg.org/node/27306

Whitley, B.E., & Kite, M.E. (2006). *The psychology of prejudice and discrimination.* Belmont, CA: Wadsworth.

Widegren, O. (1998). The new environmental paradigm and personal norms. *Environment and Behavior, 30,* 75–100.

Wiesenfeld, E., & Sanchez, E. (2002). Sustained participation: A community based approach to addressing environmental problems. In B. Bechtel (Ed.). *Handbook of environmental psychology* (p. 629–643). New York: John Wiley.

Willamette University. (2008). *Creating a smaller ecological footprint*. Retrieved from http://www.willamette.edu/about/sustainability/environment/

Williams, C.G., Cox, E.M., Hedberg, V.A., & Deci, I.E. (2000). Extrinsic life goals and health risk behaviors in adolescents. *Journal of Applied Social Psychology, 30*, 1756–1771.

Williams, K., & Harvey, D. (2001). Transcendent experience in forest environments. *Journal of Environmental Psychology, 21*, 249–260.

Williams, M., Teasdale, J., Segal, Z., & Kabat-Zinn, J. (2007). *The mindful way through depression: Freeing yourself from chronic unhappiness*. New York, NY: Guilford.

Williams, T.T. (1994). *An unspoken hunger: Stories from the field*. New York, NY: Pantheon Books.

Wilson, E., & Ng., S.H. (1988). Sex bias in visual images evoked by generics: A New Zealand study. *Sex Roles, 18*, 159–168.

Wilson, E.O. (1984). *Biophilia: The human bond with other species*. Cambridge, MA: Harvard University Press.

Wilson, E.O. (1993). Biophilia and the conservation ethic. In S.R. Kellert & E.O. Wilson (Eds.), *The biophilia hypothesis* (pp. 31–41). Washington, DC: Island Press.

Wilson, E.O. (2006). *The creation: An appeal to save life on earth*. New York, NY: W. W. Norton & Co.

Wilson, E.O. (2007). Foreword. In D.J. Penn & I. Mysterud (Eds.), *Evolutionary perspectives on environmental problems* (pp. xiii–xiv). New Brunswick, NJ: Transaction Publishers.

Wilson, R.A. (1993). *Fostering a sense of wonder during the early childhood years*. Columbus, OH: Greyden Press. Retrieved from http://eric.ed.gov/ERICDocs/data/ericdocs2sql/content_storage_01/0000019b/80/16/d6/d6.pdf

Wilson, R.A. (1997). The wonders of nature: Honoring children's ways of knowing. *Early Childhood News*. Retrieved from http://www.earlychildhoodnews.com/earlychildhood/article_view.aspx?ArticleID=70

Wilson, S.J., & Lipsey, M.W. (2000). Wilderness challenge programs for delinquent youth: A meta-analysis of outcome evaluations. *Evaluation and Program Planning, 23*, 1–12.

Wilson, T.D. (2002). *Strangers to ourselves: Discovering the adaptive unconscious*. Cambridge, MA: Belknap Press/Harvard University Press.

Windham, G.C., Zhang, L., Gunier, R., Croen, L.A., & Grether, J.K. (2006). Autism spectrum disorders in relation to distribution of hazardous air pollutants in the San Francisco Bay Area. *Environmental Health Perspectives, 114*, 1438–1444.

Winett, R.A., Hatcher, J.W., Fort, T.R., Leckliter, I.N., Love, S.Q., Riley, A.W., & Fishback, J.F. (1982). The effects of videotape modeling and daily feedback on residential electricity conservation, home temperature and humidity, perceived comfort, and clothing worn: Winter and summer. *Journal of Applied Behavior Analysis, 15*, 381–402.

Winnicott, D.W. (1986). The theory of the parent-infant relationships. In P. Buckley (Ed.), *Essential papers on object relations* (pp. 233–253). New York, NY: New York University Press.

Winter, D.D. (1996). *Ecological psychology: Healing the split between planet and self.* New York: HarperCollins Text.

Winter, D.D. (2000). Some big ideas for some big problems. *American Psychologist, 55*(5), 516–522.

Winter, D.D. (2002). (En)Gendering sustainable development. In P. Schmuck & W.P. Schultz (Eds.), *Psychology of Sustainable Development* (pp. 79–95).

Winter, D.D. (2004). Shopping for sustainability: Psychological solutions to overconsumption. In T. Kasser & A.D. Kanner (Eds.), *Psychology and consumer culture: The struggle for a good life in a materialistic world* (pp. 69–88). Washington, DC: American Psychological Association.

Winter, D.D. (2006). Moving from the clenched fist to shaking hands: Working with negative emotions provoked by conflict. In R. MacNair (Ed.), *Working for peace: A handbook of practical psychology and other tools* (pp. 170–173). Atarscadero, CA: Impact Publishers.

Winter, D.D., & Cava, M.M. (2006). The psycho-ecology of armed conflict. *Journal of Social Issues, 62,* 19–40.

Woodhouse, J.L., & Knapp, C.E. (2000). *Place-based curriculum and instruction: Outdoor and environmental education approaches.* ERIC Clearinghouse on Rural Education and Small Schools, Charleston, WV. Retrieved from http://www.ericdigests.org/2001-3/place.htm

World Health Organization. (2006). *World Health Organization report explains the health impacts of the world's worst-ever civil nuclear accident.* Retrieved from http://www.who.int/mediacentre/news/releases/2006/pr20/en/

World Health Organization. (2008a). *Air quality and health.* Retrieved from http://www.who.int/mediacentre/factsheets/fs313/en/

World Health Organization. (2008b). *Ten facts on the global burden of disease.* Retrieved from http://www.who.int/features/factfiles/global_burden/en/index.html

World Resources Institute. (2001). *Facts and figures: Environmental data tables, energy and resource use.* Table ERC.5: Resource Consumption [Data file]. Retrieved from http://www.wri.org/trends/index.html

World Resources Institute. (2008). *World resources 2008: Roots of resilience— Growing the wealth of the poor.* World Resources Institute in collaboration with United Nations Development Programme, United Nations Environment Programme, and World Bank. Washington, DC: WRI. Retrieved from http://pdf.wri.org/world_resources_2008_roots_of_resilience_front.pdf

Worldwatch Institute. (2002). *Report calls for rapid scaling up of efforts to preserve health of forests and provide economic benefits.* Retrieved from http://www.worldwatch.org/alerts/pr980402.html

Worldwatch Institute. (2008). *The state of consumption today.* Retrieved from http://www.worldwatch.org/node/810

Wright, R. (1995, August 28). The evolution of despair. *Time, 146*(9), 50.

Yates, S. (1982). *Using prospect theory to create persuasive communications about solar water heaters and insulation* (Unpublished doctoral dissertation). University of California, Santa Cruz, CA.

Yazawa, J. (2008). A sense of place: Change and persistence on Moloka'i, Hawai'i. *Dissertation Abstracts International: 2008-99130-257. International Section A: Humanities and Social Sciences, 69*(1-A), 146.

Yerkes, R.M., & Dodson, J.D. (1908). The relation of strength of stimulus to rapidity of habit-formation. *Journal of Comparative Neurology and Psychology, 18,* 459–482.

Young, J.G., Eskenazi, B., Gladstone, E.A., Bradman, A., Pedersen, L., Johnson, C., ... Holland, N.T. (2005). Association between in utero organophosphate pesticide exposure and abnormal reflexes in neonates. *NeuroToxicology and Teratology, 26,* 199–209.

Zaradic, P.A., & Pergams, O.R.W. (2007). Videophilia: Implications for childhood development and conservation. *Journal of Developmental Processes, 2,* 130–147.

Zeidner, M., Matthews, G., Roberts, R.D., & MacCann, C. (2003). Development of emotional intelligence: Towards a multi-level investment model. *Human Development, 46, 69–96.*

Zelezny, L.D., Chua, P.P., & Aldrich, C. (2000). Elaborating on gender differences in environmentalism. *Journal of Social Issues, 56,* 443–458.

Zimmerman, F.J., & Christakis, D.A. (2005). Children's television viewing and cognitive outcomes: A longitudinal analysis of national data. *Archives of Pediatric & Adolescent Medicine, 159,* 619–625.

Zoumbaris, S.J., & O'Brien, T.P. (1993). Consumption behaviors hinge on financial self-interest. *American Psychologist, 48,* 1091–1092.

Zukier, H. (1982). The dilution effect: The role of the correlation and the dispersion of predictor variables in the use of nondiagnostic information. *Journal of Personality and Social Psychology, 43,* 1163–1174.

APPENDIX: HOW TO DO IT

I am only one. But still I am one.
I cannot do everything, but still I can do something;
And because I cannot do everything,
I will not refuse to do the something that I can do.

Edward Everett Hale (1822–1909)*

There are many excellent guides available for how to become more environmentally responsible. In addition to the various ideas presented throughout this book, the following sections outline more specific and detailed help for improving individual behavior, local communities, and environmental policy. You can start by taking the online quiz at http://www.myfootprint.org/ to determine your own **ecological footprint** (Chapter 1), and consider ways to alter your daily life based on your results.

There are seven aspects of personal lifestyles that most significantly and adversely impact the environment (Gardner & Stern, 2008; Miller, 2007): *agriculture, transportation, resource consumption, waste, home energy and water use, and toxic chemicals*. We recommend that you study these categories, and choose behaviors that will reduce your footprint. If you live in a residence hall, join or create a campus committee to help make changes throughout your campus.

We recommend that you start by selecting at least one behavior in each category. Pick items that are feasible (remember small steps; Chapter 11), behaviors that fit your situation, and behaviors that will

---

* As quoted by the Oxford Company, 2005.

make a difference to your footprint. Create a self-control project using the model outlined in Chapter 5, and graph your baseline behavior and your progress. Get together with a friend (or group) and support each other's efforts with a weekly check-in. After practicing each behavior so that it becomes a habit, choose another in that category to add to your project. In this way, you will make steady progress toward living a more responsible, conscious, and sustainable life, and you will model your valuable behavior changes for others.

AGRICULTURE

- Gradually reduce your meat consumption by eating *no meat* 1 day per week, then increase to two days, and so forth. This helps to preserve biodiversity by reducing the impact of meat production on wildlife habitats. It also helps curb climate change by reducing methane emissions, as well as carbon dioxide from transporting the meat products.
- Buy fresh, locally grown, organic vegetables, instead of processed foods. In the United States, food travels an average of 1300 miles from farm to plate, making a significant environmental impact.
- Plant your own vegetable garden. Even gardening in pots can make a huge contribution to your food supply, and gardening is a great way to reduce stress (Chapter 8).
- Join or create a community garden where you can grow organic food with neighbors and friends.
- Join a Community Supported Agriculture (CSA) program in which you buy a subscription for a box of organic produce from a local farmer each week. Find CSAs in your area at http://www.localharvest.org/
- Inform and assist local schools, food banks, hospitals, restaurants, and so forth in using local organic food.

TRANSPORTATION

- Walk, bike, carpool, or take mass transit as much as you can.
- If possible, work at home or live near your work or school.
- When you have to drive, note that fuel efficiency can be dramatically increased by:
  - reducing your speed
  - avoiding sudden stops and rapid acceleration
  - shutting off the engine rather than idling

- keeping tires properly inflated
- getting regular tune-ups
- turning off your air conditioner.
- Remove unnecessary articles from your car. Each 100 lbs. of weight decreases fuel efficiency by 1%.
- When you buy a new car, choose a small, fuel efficient model (> 35 mpg).
- Write to automobile manufacturers to let them know that you intend to buy the most fuel efficient car on the road.
- Urge local governments to enact restrictions on automobile use in congested areas of town and to initiate **no-idle zones** (i.e., near schools, parks, malls, etc.).
- Work with city planners to create bike lanes, walking paths, mass transport, and ride share programs.

RESOURCE CONSUMPTION

- Refuse, Reduce, and Reuse: use the Unshopping Card (Figure 1.4). Refusing and reusing will save you money, as well as reducing your environmental impact.
- Maintain and repair the items you own.
- Rent or borrow items you don't use often.
- When you have to, buy products that last, and buy used items whenever possible. Become an expert on where to get used items in your community (church and yard sales, thrift stores, etc.)
- Reuse everything you can: coffee cups, refrigerator storage containers for leftovers, plastic bags for multiple uses.
- Bring your own Tupperware containers to restaurants for leftovers and to buy foods in bulk.
- Help your community set up a Free Cycle station where people can donate unwanted items.
- Learn about simpler, less resource-intensive lifestyles, such as voluntary simplicity (Chapter 11).
- Enjoy sports and recreational activities that use your muscles rather than gasoline, electricity, and natural resources.

WASTE

- Start by buying less! (See tips in previous category.)
- Bring your own canvas bags to the grocery store.

- Reuse envelopes, jars, paper bags, plastic bags and containers, scrap paper, and so on.
- Use recycled products, especially printer and toilet paper.
- Eliminate your use of "disposable" items like paper napkins, tissues, and towels, and use cloth versions that you can wash.
- Encourage your government, schools, and businesses to buy recycled paper.
- Learn how to recycle all household goods, from clothing to motor oil to appliances (see http://earth911.com).
- Compost food wastes for your community organic garden.
- Encourage local recycling centers or program to accept items they don't currently accept; work with your city council to improve recycling operations of roadside pickup and hazardous wastes.
- Encourage friends, neighbors, businesses, and local organizations to recycle and sponsor recycling efforts.
- Urge restaurants to use recyclable materials for to-go containers.
- Avoid using items made from, or packaged in, plastics whenever possible.
- Help create community programs to make art from trash, such as a local art or fashion show featuring outfits and objects made of materials that would have been thrown away.
- Junk mail generates an astonishing amount of waste, utilizes an incredible amount of natural resources, and contributes to climate change. Let organizations know that you don't want to receive their newsletters, catalogs, and solicitations, and be sure to recycle mailings you can't refuse. See http://www.41pounds.org/ for assistance in reducing the amount that you receive.

HOME ENERGY USE

- Wear warm clothing and turn down winter heat.
- Close off unused areas in your home from heat and air conditioning.
- Turn off computers, lights, and appliances when not in use.
- Switch to low-wattage fluorescent light bulbs. When they burn out be sure to dispose of them properly, at designated **household hazardous waste** sites.
- Use cold water instead of hot whenever possible.
- Opt for small oven or stove top cooking when preparing small meals.

- Run dishwashers and clothes washers only when full, but do not overload them.
- Hang your laundry to dry whenever possible, and clean the lint screen in dryers.
- Instead of ironing, hang clothes in the bathroom while showering.
- Decrease your energy waste by caulking leaks, adding insulation, and using energy-efficient lights, appliances (EnergyStar), and heating/cooling systems.
- Install solar panels and/or wind turbines for generating power.
- Set refrigerators to 38 °F, freezers to 5 °F, no colder.
- Plant deciduous shade trees that protect windows from summer sun but allow the sun in during the winter.
- Instead of TV and stereo, spend time reading, writing, drawing, telling stories, making music.

WATER USE

- Always turn off the water while brushing your teeth, and consider turning off the water while soaping up, shampooing, or shaving.
- Take quick showers instead of baths.
- Use the flushing rule: If it's yellow, let it mellow, if it's brown, flush it down (urine is sterile).
- Install water-efficient showerheads and sink-faucet aerators.
- Collect rainwater and gray water for gardening.
- Landscape with native plants (xeriscape) that thrive with the water available in the climate where you live. This also encourages biodiversity in yards and gardens.
- Use moderate amounts of biodegradable detergent.
- Install an air-assisted or composting toilet.
- Work with city and community groups to protect local watershed areas.
- Pave as little as possible. Rip up excess concrete.
- Encourage sewage plants to compost sludge.

TOXIC CHEMICAL USE

- Avoid all pesticides in your home and garden (insecticides, herbicides, rodenticides, etc.), and don't allow children or pets to play on pesticide-treated lawns. For information about specific pesticides, their risks, and safer alternatives, see the Web site developed by the Northwest Coalition for Alternatives to Pesticides, available at http://www.pesticide.org

- Avoid chemical cleansers; white vinegar and baking soda are versatile nontoxic alternatives to many cleaning products; vinegar is also an effective herbicide (weed killer). For more nontoxic ideas, see http://www.watoxics.org/files/cleaningproducts.pdf.
- Limit consumption of meats and dairy products, and heed state-issued fish advisories.
- Buy organic products whenever available, and always wash fruits and vegetables thoroughly to remove any pesticide residues.
- Avoid buying bottled water, and reduce your use of plastic by bringing your own refillable containers, buying in bulk, buying things with minimal packaging.
- Purchase food, beverages, and other items in nonplastic containers whenever possible. Bisphenol A in plastics can leach, particularly when the container is scratched or worn and when heated.
- Don't reheat or microwave food in plastic containers or covered with plastic wrap. Many plastics leach toxins when heated. For

Reprinted from Kris Rieck. With permission.

more information on the health risks of plastics, see "Pots, pans, and plastics: A shopper's guide to food safety" (available at http://www.ewg.org/node/27706).

- Limit consumption of canned food. Most canning processes use a resin lining derived from BPA.
- Buy colored fabrics and do not use bleach.
- Use natural fiber and organic clothing, bedding, and towels.
- Think before you buy. Is it really a *necessary* purchase? Check the ingredient list. If you can't pronounce it, it's probably best to avoid it.
- Know what's in your grooming products. Cosmetics and personal care items (e.g., shampoos, lotions, and makeup) often contain endocrine disrupting chemicals such as phthalates (listed as dibutyl and diethylhexyl or just "fragrance") and parabens (often used as a suffix, as in methylparaben). If there is not an ingredients list, log on to http://cosmeticsdatabase.com/ for lists of toxic ingredients in thousands of personal-care products.
- Organize a demonstration at a plant that produces or releases toxic chemicals.
- Dispose of household toxic products properly. Many items—paints, pesticides, batteries, and even energy-efficient compact fluorescent light bulbs—contain toxic ingredients. Be sure to dispose of these items properly, by dropping them off at your local *household hazardous waste* site.
- Perhaps most important, lobby your local and state representatives for health protective legislation, and vote for candidates that support stronger regulations on chemical production and use and pollution control.

In general, you can adopt the following strategies for healing the planet at personal and political levels.

PERSONAL

- Invest your money in environmentally and socially conscious businesses.
- Avoid rainforest products and inform the supplier or manufacturer of your concerns.
- Read and support publications that educate about sustainability (like this one!).
- Live outside and within your local climate as much as possible, instead of isolating yourself from it.

- Establish good communication with neighbors, friends, and family using conflict resolution skills.
- Spend time seeing, hearing, and rejoicing in the beauty of the Earth.
- Think often about the kind of Earth you would like to see for your grandchildren's grandchildren.
- While doing small things, think big. Think about redesigning cities, restructuring the economy, reconceiving humanity's role on Earth.
- Stay informed; stay hopeful; gather people around you who encourage, model, and teach you how to live more sustainably.

POLITICAL

- Start a global climate change study group.
- Educate children about sustainable living practices.
- Join a local environmental organization and plan local environmental projects.
- Join a national or global environmental organization and help support their issues.
- Support zero population growth.
- Support work to alleviate poverty. Poverty compounds deforestation and other environmental problems.
- Write letters to the editor expressing your concern about climate change and other environmental issues.
- Support local, state, and federal legislative candidates who run on environmental platforms.
- Run for local office on an environmental platform.
- Attend city council meetings and speak out for action on climate change, toxins, and other sustainability issues.
- Write your local, state, and national elected officials for action on climate change, children's health, and other issues.
- Donate money to environmental organizations.
- Support disarmament and the redirection of military funds to environmental restoration.
- PDF this list and e-mail it to your family and friends.

MOST OF ALL

- Pray, visualize, hope, meditate, and dream.

ADDITIONAL WEB RESOURCES

Over the last several years, the Internet has become the premier resource for up-to-date information about environmental issues and sustainable living. Particularly useful are the many sites that include "Take Action," routes for you to express your concern to lawmakers and public officials, organize citizens in your community, and implement other forms of activism. Below are some of our favorites, loosely organized by topic (please note that there is considerable overlap between the topics).

Campus Leadership–Higher Education

Association for the Advancement of Sustainability in Higher Education
http://www.aashe.org/
An association of colleges and universities working to create a sustainable future, providing resources, workshops, trainings, and discussion boards.

Focus the Nation
http://www.focusthenation.org/
"Empowering a generation to power a nation." Provides resources and organizational tools to initiate campus events and teach-ins concerning climate change.

Second Nature: Education for Sustainability
http://www.secondnature.org/
Dedicated to transforming higher education by assisting colleges and universities integrate sustainability as a core component of education.

Children

The Campaign for Commercial-Free Children
http://commercialexploitation.com/
A coalition of health care providers, educators, activists, and parents dedicated to reducing the adverse impacts of commercialism on children.

Children & Nature Network
http://www.childrenandnature.org/
News and research that encourages and supports people and institutions "working to reconnect children with nature."

Institute for Children's Environmental Health
http://iceh.org/
Provides resources concerning toxins and impacts on children's health.

Christian

The Catholic Coalition on Climate Change
http://www.catholicsandclimatechange.org/
What are the moral implications of climate change? Who is most impacted? What should the Catholic community do? The Catholic Coalition on Climate Change was launched in 2006 to help the U.S. Conference of Catholic Bishops (USCCB) and the Catholic community address these issues.

United States Conference of Catholic Bishops
http://www.usccb.org/sdwp/ejp/case/index.shtml
An organization dedicated to caring for "God's gift of creation," including protecting the most vulnerable: the poor and children. Provides resources and public policy information concerning environmental justice and children's environmental health.

Climate Change

ClimateArk
http://www.climateark.org/
Provides up-to-date information on the science of climate change, and opportunities to send e-mails on critical issues to key decision makers.

David Suzuki Foundation
http://www.davidsuzuki.org/
A nonprofit organization using science and education to conserve nature and help achieve sustainability, including addressing climate change, clean energy, and sustainability. The site includes various ways to "take action."

Union of Concerned Scientists
http://www.ucsusa.org/index.html
Provides a collective voice on policies regarding climate change, automobiles, energy, security, and other environmental issues. Offers readable public policy statements that are widely circulated and highly regarded.

Conservation

Action Bioscience
http://actionbioscience.org
An educational site providing peer-reviewed articles and links concerning issues such as biodiversity, environment, and biotechnology.

Audubon Society
http://www.audubon.org/
A national network of community-based chapters dedicated to protecting birds and other wildlife and their habitat. Promotes environmental education programs and advocacy.

Defenders of Wildlife
http://www.defenders.org/
Works to protect native wild animals and plants in their natural communities through new approaches to habitat conservation and leadership on endangered species issues.

Forest Protection Portal
http://forests.org/
Provides science-based information and action alerts concerning forest preservation and conservation.

League of Conservation Voters
http://www.lcv.org/
Devoted to shaping a proenvironmental Congress. Through their *National Environmental Scorecard*, LCV holds Congress accountable for environmental decisions. They also run regional offices to build coalitions, promote grassroots power, and train the next generation of environmental leaders.

National Wildlife Federation
http://www.nwf.org/
Educates and assists individuals and organizations of diverse cultures to conserve wildlife and other natural resources.

The Nature Conservancy
http://nature.org/
Works to preserve plants, animals, and natural communities, promoting biodiversity and protection of habitat. This organization also offers the opportunity to purchase carbon dioxide offsets; see http://www.nature.org/initiatives/climatechange/activities/art23932.html

The Rainforest Site
http://www.therainforestsite.com/clickToGive/home.faces?siteId=4
Click daily and sponsors make contributions for habitat protection. Also offers e-cards and shopping that support fair trade.

World Wildlife Fund
http://www.worldwildlife.org/
The largest, privately supported international conservation organization in the world, WWF is dedicated to protecting the world's wildlife and wildlands.

Consumer Culture and Power

Center for a New American Dream
http://www.newdream.org/
Works with individuals, institutions, and communities to counter commercialization, promote responsible consumption, and conserve and protect natural resources.

Co-op America
http://www.coopamerica.org
Gives practical steps for using consumer and investor power to promote environmental responsibility and social justice. Includes Green Pages, information about boycotts, investments, sweatshops, and sustainable products.

Story of Stuff
http://www.storyofstuff.com/
This 20-minute video is an engaging and humorous, "fact-filled look at the underside of our production and consumption patterns . . . [that] exposes the connections between a huge number of environmental and social issues."

Transfair USA
http://www.transfairusa.org/
Maintains an up-to-date list on merchants who sell fair-trade coffee (coffee grown sustainably and sold at a fair price).

Environmental Justice

Basel Action Network
http://www.ban.org/
Seeks environmental justice by working to prevent toxic trade (toxic waste, toxic products, and toxic technology).

Credo Action (formerly known as Working for Change)
http://www.credoaction.com/
A mobile and long-distance phone service that also provides various resources and action opportunities for promoting social and environmental justice.

Environmental Research Foundation
http://www.rachel.org/home_eng.htm
Provides understandable scientific information about environmental
health and justice.

Food

Center for Science in the Public Interest
http://www.cspinet.org/EatingGreen/index.html
Provides information on "eating green" by reducing meat consumption.

Vegsource
http://www.vegsource.com
Provides discussion boards and useful information on environmental
impacts of meat, vegetarian lifestyles, and recipes.

Green Economy

Conservation Economy
http://www.conservationeconomy.net
Outlines what a sustainable society looks like by with information about
57 qualities for a conservation economy (including renewable energy,
community planning, sustainable agriculture, etc.); comprehensively
integrates Social, Natural, and Economic Capital to demonstrate that a
sustainable society is both desirable and achievable.

Growth is Madness!
http://growthmadness.org/
A compendium of articles confronting the "irrational push for unending
growth on a finite earth," leading toward "ecological collapse." Critical
topics include population and economic growth and their relationships
to consumption and energy.

Health and Toxic Chemicals

Collaborative on Health and the Environment
http://healthandenvironment.org/
An international network of 2900 individual and organizational partners working collectively to advance knowledge and effective action to
address growing concerns about the links between human health and
environmental factors.

Environmental Health Coalition
http://www.environmentalhealth.org/About_EHC/index.html
Strives to reduce toxic pollution to protect public health and promote
environmental justice.

Environmental Working Group
http://www.ewg.org/
Information on health, toxins, natural resources, and other environmental issues including ways you can take action.

Northwest Coalition for Alternatives to Pesticides
http://www.pesticide.org/
Works to protect people and the planet by advancing healthier solutions to pest problems.

Washington Toxics Coalition
http://www.watoxics.org/
Works on behalf of public health and the environment by eliminating toxic pollution. The WTC promotes alternatives, advocates policies, empowers communities, and educates people to create a healthy environment.

Legal–Legislative Action

Friends of the Earth
http://www.foe.org/
International grassroots organization with local chapters working on high-profile (often legal) efforts to create a more healthy, just world.

Natural Resources Defense Council
http://www.nrdc.org/
The NRDC advocates for environmentally responsible policies, using law and lobbying to preserve and protect wildlife and wild places and combat environmental threats.

Sierra Club
http://www.sierraclub.org/
Organizes a wide range of action issues to promote environmental responsibility. Maintains an updated log of legislative actions and ways to express your opinions.

Local Communities

Community-Based Social Marketing
http://www.cbsm.com
A valuable resource for people designing strategies (based in psychology) for community interventions regarding composting, energy efficiency, waste, recycling, reuse, transportation, waste reduction, and water efficiency.

Nonviolent Direct Action

Greenpeace USA, Inc.
http://www.greenpeaceusa.org/
Uses nonviolent direct action to expose global environmental problems and promote solutions.

Population

Population Connection
http://www.populationconnection.org/
Formerly known as Zero Population Growth (ZPG), Population Connection works to slow population growth and achieve a sustainable balance between the Earth's people and its resources.

Psychology

Conservation Psychology
http://www.conservationpsychology.org/
Uses scientific study of the reciprocal relationships between humans and the rest of nature to encourage conservation of the natural world.

European Ecopsychology
http://www.ecopsychology.net
Hosts conferences and networking for promoting connections between nature and psyches.

International Community for Ecopsychology
http://www.ecopsychology.org/
A public forum for diverse experiences of the human-nature relationship, in order to provide a bridge towards harmony with the planet.

Psychologists for Social Responsibility
http://www.psysr.org
Uses psychological knowledge and skills to promote peace with social justice; the Environmental Protection and Justice Action Committee works on sustainability issues and their intersection with peace.

Sustainability

The Commons Open Society Sustainability Initiative
http://www.ecoplan.org/
An introduction to world sustainability issues, views and developments from a critical perspective for concerned citizens, researchers, students, policy makers, entrepreneurs, investors, or social activists.

Genuine Progress Index (GPI)
http://www.gpiatlantic.org/
GPI*Atlantic* is an independent, non-profit research and education organization committed to the development of the **Genuine Progress Index** (GPI) – a new measure of sustainability, well-being and quality of life.

Global Footprint Network
http://www.footprintnetwork.org/index.php
The Global Footprint Network enables the measurement of human impact on the earth so people can make more informed choices. The goal is to create a sustainable future where all people have the opportunity to live satisfying lives within the means of one planet.

New Economics Foundation
http://www.neweconomics.org/node
NEF is an independent think-and-do tank that inspires and demonstrates real economic well-being, and promotes innovative solutions that challenge mainstream thinking on economic, environment and social issues.

Redefining Progress
http://www.redefiningprogress.org/
Redefining Progress is a leading public policy think tank dedicated to smart economics, promoting a sustainable and equitable world for future generations.

General

50 Simple Things
http://www.50simplethings.com/
A review of 50 critical issues including ways *you* can help both in terms of individual behavior change and advocacy.

Action Network
http://actionnetwork.org/
Gives information on a variety of problems and provides e-mail alerts and free faxes.

Earth Island Institute
http://www.earthisland.org/
Posts selected articles from its widely read *Earth Island Journal*, and provides action opportunities on a wide range of environmental issues.

EcoEarth.Info
http://www.ecoearth.info/
This is an Internet search engine, the largest one providing direct access
to environmental sustainability news, and original analysis and action
opportunities.

Ecological Footprint Quiz
http://www.MyFootprint.org
How many acres does it take to support your lifestyle? How does your
footprint compare with that of most Americans? Take the quiz online
and find out.

EnviroLink
http://www.envirolink.org/
Provides access to thousands of online environmental resources.

Green Thing
http://www.dothegreenthing.com/
Go green, and have fun doing it! Includes tips, videos, and stories from
individuals trying to make a difference.

Grist Magazine
http://www.gristmagazine.com/
"Gloom and doom with a sense of humor!" Online environmental magazine that doesn't pull punches or accept advertising.

Save Our Environment Action Center
http://www.saveourenvironment.org/
A collaborative Web site of advocacy organizations, organized to
increase public awareness and electronic activism.

Union of Concerned Scientists
http://www.ucsusa.org/index.html
Provides a collective voice on policies regarding climate change,
automobiles, energy, security, and other environmental issues. Offers
readable public policy statements that are widely circulated and highly
regarded.

WiserEarth
http://www.wiserearth.org/
"Connecting you to communities of action." This site provides information and opportunities for networking with thousands of organizations,

people, groups, and employers in the areas of agriculture and farming, biodiversity, coastal and marine ecosystems, community development, and energy.

World Watch Institute
http://www.worldwatch.org/
Offers access to interdisciplinary research with a global focus about building a sustainable world.

AUTHOR INDEX

A

Abel, T., 109
Abraham, C., 88
Abrahamse, W., 110, 141, 143, 144, 154
Abram, D., 296
Abramson, P. R., 124, 126
Adam, E., 337
Agras, W. S., 237
Agyeman, J., 104, 218, 246
Ajzen, I., 111, 114
Albee, G. W., 186
Aldrich, C., 118
Ambinder, M. S., 202
Amel, E. L., 298
American Academy of Child &
        Adolescent Psychiatry, 178
American Psychological
        Association, 98, 163
Anderson, C. A., 143, 245, 264
Appleton, J., 252, 269
Arbuthnot, J., 116
Archer, D., 209
Arndt, J., 93
Arnetz, B. B., 248
Arnold, R., 76, 77
Arnow, B., 237
Aronson, E., 141, 209
Arroyo, V., 340, 341
Artz, N., 145
Ascione, F. R., 279

Association for Advancement of
        Sustainability in Higher
        Education, 163, 437
Atran, S., 270, 271
Austin, M. E., 255
Ayupan, L. B., 120

B

Babisch, W., 245
Backscheider, A. G., 270
Bacon, F., 42–44, 343
Badal, J., 144
Bailey, R., 20, 21
Bakker, D. J., 120
Baldewicz, T. T., 251
Baldwin, M., 256
Baltes, M. M., 143
Bamberg, S., 102, 114, 118, 328
Bambrick, H. J., 236
Bandura, A., 100, 141, 157, 280
Baril, G. L., 104, 118
Barnes, G. E., 86
Barnes, M., 251, 252
Barr, S., 141, 142, 328
Bartol, K. M., 126
Bassil, K. L., 236
Bates, M., 337
Baum, A., 139, 242, 244
Baum, M. K., 251

447

Ellison, C. G., 46
Elsworth, J. T., 109
Energy Information Administration, 24
Engelen, M., 141
Engelke, P. O., 256
Engelman, R., 9, 11
Environmental Research
   Foundation, 441
Esswein, P. M., 144
Evans, G. W., 185, 228, 232, 243,
   244, 245, 252, 253, 255,
   273, 275, 288, 324
Everett, P. B., 140, 143

F

Faber Taylor, A., 268, 274, 275, 276
Fahs, M. C., 189
Feaster, D. J., 251
Fein, G. G., 274
Feshbach, S., 87
Festinger, L., 115
Few, R., 246
Field, C. B., 152
Fielding, K. S., 114
Finucane, M. L., 219, 221, 223
Fiocco, A., 234
Fiorito, E., 250, 252
Fischhoff, B., 218, 222
Fish, L., 85
Fish, L. M., 85, 238
Fishbein, M., 114
Fisher, A., 198
Fisher, A. R., 198
Fisher, J. D., 198, 242, 244
Fiske, S. T., 196
Fisman, L., 281, 282
Fitzgerald, A., 107
Fjørtoft, I., 268
Flavin, C., 12, 16, 329, 338
Flavin, H., 338, 339
Flegal, K., 237
Fletcher, M. A., 251
Floyd, M. F., 280, 281, 283
Flynn, J., 219
Flynn, L. R., 101
Focht, W., 281
Foehner, K., 59
Foehr, U. G., 263
Folkman, S., 232

Food and Agriculture Organization, 47
Forest Stewardship Council, 147
Forgas, J. P., 221
Forstl, H., 248
Fox, J., 294
Fox, W., 300
Fraley, N., 88
Frank, L. D., 256
Frantz, C., 306
Frantz, C. M., 4, 307, 321, 323
Fraser, J. A., 279
Fredrickson, B., 80
Fredrikson, M., 235
Freeman, A. C., 271
Freeman, D. A., 78
Freeman, H., 271
Freeman, M., 21, 76
French, H., 148
Freud, S., 62, 63, 64, 65, 66, 67, 68, 69,
   70, 71, 72, 73, 78, 79, 80, 81,
   85, 88, 92, 93, 295, 325, 327
Freudenburg, W. R., 224
Friedman, F., 344
Friel, S., 244
Fritze, J. G., 246
Frosh, S., 64
Frumkin, H., 251, 253, 256,
   257, 269, 309
Fuhrer, U., 109, 114
Fujii, S., 145
Futatsuka, M., 248

G

Gail, M., 237
Gamba, R. J., 33
Gamble, A., 109
Gardner, G., 13, 15, 16, 17, 26, 29,
   46, 135, 141, 144, 146, 150,
   152, 209, 211, 213, 260,
   294, 325, 337, 345, 349, 429
Gardner, G. T., 260, 294, 325, 345, 349
Gärling, T., 109, 219, 244, 252,
   253, 255
Garrett, E., 279
Gastil, J., 40
Gatersleben, B., 114
Gathercoal, K., 277
Gattig, A., 222, 223
Gaulin, S. J. C., 221, 231, 258, 279

SUBJECT INDEX

A

Action-oriented educational programs for EE, 285
Active caring about ecological issues, 160
Activism, 142
Acute stress disorder, 242
Addictive behaviors, 85
ADHD, *see* Attention deficit hyperactivity disorder (ADHD)
Adolescents, behavioral and emotional problems in, 178
Adults, toxic effects in, 179
   accelerated aging, 180
   Alzheimer's disease, 180
   dementia, 180
   endocrine functions, 180
   Parkinson's disease, 180–181
   reproductive abnormalities, 181
Advertising, 122–123, 125, 130, 205, 220, 264, 266
Affect heuristic, 219–220
Affluenza, 25; *see also* Consumerism; Materialism
African–American children, levels of lead in blood, 184–185
Agrarian communities evolution, 54
Agriculture, 430
   system, salinization and siltation, 7

Air pollution, 18–19, 245–246
Altruism, 107; *see also* Social psychology
Alzheimer's disease, 180
The American Recovery and Reinvestment Act, 322
Anger, 178
Animals
   children and, 278–279
   empathy, 300
   grazing, 150
   rights and wildlife preservation, speciesism, 105–106
Antecedent strategies, 140–142; *see also* Discriminative stimuli
   opportunity and convenience, 141–142
   proenvironmental/conservation behaviors, 142
Anthrax poisonings, 248
Anthropocentrism of Western worldview, 85
Anxiety, 178
Apathy, 77–78
Apollo Alliance, 322–323
Arctic, indigenous population in, 57–58
Aristotle, idea of single continuum, 55
Art from trash, 432
Artificial agricultural system, 7

Despair and empowerment groups, 89
Dioxins, toxic exposures, 167, 177
Discriminative stimuli, 138,
    140–142, 145–146, 155,
    159, 161, 163 ; see also
    Antecedent strategies
Dishwashers and clothes washers,
    use, 433
Disinfectants, 175
Displacement, 73
Disposable items use, 432
Dissonance theory, 115;
    see also Cognitive
    dissonance theory
Distributive justice, 105
Dominant Social Paradigm (DSP), 59,
    323–324
    belief in, 32
    human decisions about
      environment, 36
    intellectual heritage and, 59
    intellectual roots of, 33–38
    Locke's legacy on, 49
    scores and environmental
      problems, 33
    Western worldview, 61
Dominion, 44–45
Doomster responses, 20–23
DSP, *see* Dominant Social
    Paradigm (DSP)

E

Earth
    beauty protection, 436
    development, 53
Easter Island, archaeological evidence
    from, 7
East European countries
    environmental problems of, 55
Eating disorders, 236–238
Ecofeminism, 119–120
Eco-industrial parks, 337
Ecological dilemmas, 151
Ecological footprint, 23, 88, 123–124,
    154, 258, 265, 298, 322,
    349, 429
Ecological identity, 103, 284
Ecological issues and Freud
    theory, 66

Ecological literacy, 281–282
Ecological self, 272, 299–302; *see also*
    Ecopsychology
    awareness of, 301
    changes by development of,
      301–302
    concept of, 299
    empathy and, 300
Ecological unconscious, 302,
    304, 308
Ecophobia, 266, 279
Ecopsychology
    biodiversity from perspective of,
      309–313
    concepts, 302–304
    definition of, 302
    emotional dimensions, 313–316
    and environmental problems, 305
    evaluation of, 305, 309
      nonverbal measures, 307–308
      verbal measures, 306–307
    of place attachment, 317–318
    tenets, 304–305
Ecosystems
    behaviors, 142
    and climate change, 14
    collapsing, healthy and
      necessary, 89
Ecotherapy, 308, 328
Ecotopian Grapevine Gazette, 331
Ecstatic places, 274
Egocentric value system, 109
Egoistic values, 108
Ego, reality-oriented mechanism, 69
EID, *see* Environmental Identity
    scale (EID)
Electronics
    manufacturers, flame retardants
      from production, 187
    take-back legislation, 337
    waste, 241–242
The 11th Hour, 101
Emission control techniques, 340
Endangered Species Act (ESA), 95, 201,
    309–310
    relevant attitudes, 99
Endocrine system, 229–231
    endocrine/hormone disruptors, 168,
      176–177
      BPA and phthalates, 181

programs for, 287
wilderness therapy and, 276–277
human control of, 42–47
Bacon's views, 42
Christianity and, 45
Judeo-Christian God and "His"
creation of universe, 44
relationship to other species, 46
role of women, 47
and scientific heritages, 46–47
of nonindustrialized thought, 57
private economic gain, 47
material wealth, 48
progress, 52
Western view of, 38
Nature Inclusiveness Measure
(NIM), 307
Nature Relatedness scale (NR), 307
Neighborhood disorder, 244
Neotenic face, 201
NEP, *see* New Environmental
Paradigm (NEP)
Nepal, 59–60
Nervous System
Autonomic, 229
Parasympathetic, 231, 252, 254
Sympathetic, 229, 231, 244–245,
252, 254–255, 259
Central, 229
Neural networks, 197
Neurodevelopment
brain, 169
multiple factors interaction and, 173
neural migration, 169
neurotoxic chemicals and, 182
disabilities in humans, 183
synapses, 169
Neurodevelopmental disabilities
cognitive and attentional
impairments
endocrine disruptive chemicals,
176–177
lead, 174–175
mercury, 172–174
pesticides, 175–176
Neuron structure, 168
Neuropsychology of toxic
exposures, 165
Neurotoxins, 168
cost of, 188–190

New Ecological Paradigm scale
statements, 31–32
New Environmental
Paradigm (NEP), 32,
107, 306–307, 326
scale for women, 118–119
Nielsen ratings and healthy advertising
budgets, 20
NIM, *see* Nature Inclusiveness Measure
(NIM)
No-idling policy, 284
No-idle zones, 431
Nonactivist political behaviors, 142
Nonhuman species loss, 18; *see also*
Extinction
Nonrenewable energy, 12
Norms; *see also* Social psychology
credibility of source, 101
diffusion, 99
and environmental behavior, 97
injunctive, 98
integrated, 103
introjected, 103
introspection illusion, 99
laws and regulations, 102
norm activation theory of
altruism, 107
personal, 102
reference group, 100
North America
environmental conditions, 1
North American Free Trade
Agreement, 26
Northwest Power Act, 206
Norway, anxiety study in, 74

O

Obesity, 237
Object relations theory (ORT), 63, 80 326
attention withdrawn too early
compulsion, 85
depression, 85–86
narcissism, 84–85
paranoia, 86–87
contribution of, 87
controversies about, 81
excessive early demands, 82–84
"Mother Earth," and, 81
"object," 81

Stressors
definition of, 228
environmental, 228, 233, 235–236,
242–243
air pollution, 245–246
climate and weather change,
245–247
environmental toxins, 247–248
noise pollution, 245
urban living, 243–244
types of, 228
Stress response, 222, 228
and evolution, 231, 238, 252, 255,
258–259
gender differences and, 231
physiology of, 228
endocrine activity, 230–231
sympathetic nervous system
activity, 229–230
psychological components of
duration and extent, 232
emotion-focused coping, 232
problem-focused coping,
232–233
Subclinical poisoning, 179
Subdue, 44
Subjective discount rates, 203
Sublimation, 78–79
Subliminal influences, 220
Sumerians of Mesopotamia, 7
Superego, 69
Suppression, 73–74
Sustainability, 198
operating principles, 328–329,
350–351
conscious consumption,
343–346
ecologically healthy world,
visualization of, 329–333
less is more, 339–343
personal and political levels, act
on, 346–349
think circle instead of line,
334–339
work with small steps and big
ideas, 333–334
publications, 435
sustainable performance, criteria
for, 335–336
U.S. Government and, 6

Sustainable society/world, 3
creation of, 265, 281, 333, 352–354
Sustainable Society Index, 335
SUV, see Sport utility vehicle (SUV)
Symbiotic unity, 82; see also Object
relations theory (ORT)
Sympathetic nervous system,
229, 231, 244–245, 252,
254–255, 259

T

Target behaviors in research
studies, 157
Tax/taxes, 146, 148–149, 151
Technostress, 240
Television, 125, 263–264
Terrorism, 16, 78, 322
Thanatos, 68
Theory of planned behavior (TPB)
attitude, 111–112
behavioral control, 113
environmentally relevant
behavior, 114
intention, 111
research on, 114
subjective norm, 112
Third World development, 47
Timber industries subsidizing, 147
Toxins
behavioral and cognitive effects
from, 184
chemical regulations, 187
critical periods of time, 184
cumulative/interactive effects, 183
environmental racism and, 184
ethical guidelines for research/
clinical trials, 187
experimental research on, 185
genetic factors, 184
impact of, 184
latency period, 184
real costs of exposure, 190
related issue, 184
toxic chemical use, 433–435
toxic effects in adults, 179
accelerated aging, 180
Alzheimer's disease, 180
dementia, 180
endocrine functions, 180